Home Production
of
Quality Meats and Sausages

Stanley Marianski, Adam Marianski

Bookmagic, LLC.
Largo, Florida

Home Production of Quality Meats and Sausages
Stanley Marianski, Adam Marianski

ISBN: 978-0-9824267-3-9
Library of Congress Control Number: 2010904863

Bookmagic, LLC.
http://www.bookmagic.com

Printed in the United States of America.

Contents

Introduction

Books about making sausages can be divided into two groups. Books that are written by professional sausage makers and books that are written by cooking enthusiasts or restaurant chefs. The second group deals mainly with fresh sausages which are embarrassingly simple to make. They are loaded with recipes but do not explain the rules for making successful products. Those are basically cookbooks where a sausage becomes an ingredient of the meal.

There are just a few books that cover not only the subject of making fresh sausages, but add information on making smoked products, blood sausages, head cheeses, liver sausages and even fermented sausages. Not surprisingly, these books are written by the professional sausage makers or advanced hobbyists who possess a vast amount of knowledge not only about making sausages, but about meat science as well.

The purpose of this work is to build the bridge between meat science and a typical hobbyist. To make those technical terms simple and easy to follow and to build a solid foundation for making different meat products. Many traditional recipes are listed but we want the reader to think of them as educational material to study.

Although recipes play an important role in these products, it is the process that ultimately affects the sausage quality. Not knowing the basic rules for making liver sausages makes the reader totally dependent on a particular recipe which in many cases is of unknown value. This leaves him with little understanding of the underlying process and in most cases he will be afraid to experiment and improvise making sausages by introducing his own ideas. He should also realize that as long as he follows a few basic rules he can come up with dozens of his own recipes and his sausages will be not only professionally made, but also custom tailored to his own preferences. Information in the book is based on American standards for making safe products and they are cited where applicable.

There is a collection of 172 recipes from all over the world which were chosen for their originality and historical value. They carry an enormous value as a study material and as a valuable resource on making meat products and sausages. It should be stressed here that we don't want the reader to copy the recipes only. *We want him to understand the sausage making process and we want him to create his own recipes. We want him to be the sausage maker.*

Stanley Marianski

Chapter 1

Principles of Meat Science

Meat is composed of:
- water - 75%
- protein - 20%
- fat (varies greatly) - 3%
- sugar (glycogen, glucose) - 1%
- vitamins and minerals - 1%

Different animals or even meat cuts from the same animal exhibit *different proportions of above components* and this depends on the animal's physical activity and type of diet. Those factors not only affect animal meat's components, but the color of the meat as well.

Meat contains about 75% of water but fat contains only 10-15%. This implies that a fatty meat will lose moisture faster as it has less moisture to begin with, the fact which is important when making air dried or slow fermented products. As the animal matures, it usually increases in fatness, which causes a proportional loss of water.

Meat Aging

When an animal dies, the oxygen stops flowing and many reactions take place inside. For a few hours the meat remains relaxed and may still be processed or cooked. Then muscles contract and the meat *stiffens* which is known as the *"rigor mortis" stage.* During that stage, which lasts differently for different animals, the meat should not be processed or cooked as *the resulting product will be tough.* Meat stock prepared from meats still in the rigor mortis stage is cloudy and has poor flavor. When this stage ends, the meat enters rigor stage and is kept in a cooler. In time it becomes tender again and is ready for processing. It is widely accepted that this happens due to the changes in the protein structure. The length of rigor mortis or rigor stage directly depends on temperature. The higher the temperature, the shorter the stages and vice versa. Make note that aging meat at high temperature will help bacteria to grow and will adversely affect meat's shelf keeping qualities.

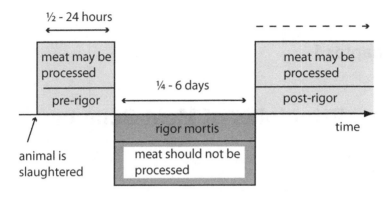

Fig. 1.1. Effect of *rigor mortis.*

Times for onset and resolution of rigor		
	Time to onset of rigor	Time for resolution of rigor
Cattle	12 - 24 hours	2 - 10 days
Pigs	6 - 12 hours	1 - 2 days
Lamb	7 - 8 hours	1 day
Turkey	1/2 - 2 hours	6 - 24 hours
Chicken	1/2 - 1 hour	4 - 6 hours
Rabbit	12-20 hours	2-7 days
Venison	24 - 36 hours	6 - 14 days

Looking at the above data, it becomes conclusive that the aging process is more important for animals which are older at the slaughter time (cattle, venison). Warm meat of a freshly slaughtered animal exhibits the highest quality and juiciness. Unfortunately there is a very narrow window of opportunity for processing it. The slaughter house and the meat plant must be located within the same building to be effective. Meat that we buy in a supermarket has already been aged by a packing house. If an animal carcass is cooled too rapidly (below 50° F, 10° C) before the onset of the rigor (within 10 hours), the muscles may contract which results in tough meat when cooked. This is known as "cold shortening." To prevent this the carcass is kept at room temperature for some hours to accelerate rigor and then aged at between 30-41° F, (-1 - 5° C).

pH of the meat

When an animal is alive the pH (acidity) value of its meat is around 7.0 (neutral point). After the slaughter and bleeding, the oxygen supply is interrupted and enzymes start converting glycogen (meat sugar) into lactic acid. This lowers the pH (increases acidity) of the meat and the process is known as glycolysis. This drop is as follows:

- Beef - pH of 5.4 to 5.7 at 18-24 hours after slaughter.
- Pork - pH of 5.4 to 5.8 at 6-10 hours after slaughter.

The concept of pH is also covered in Chapter 20 - Fermented Sausages. Understanding pH of meat is quite important as it allows us to classify meats by the pH and to predict how much water a particular type can hold. If you drink lemon juice or vinegar you know the acidic taste of it. Gentle foods such as milk will be found on the opposite end of the scale.

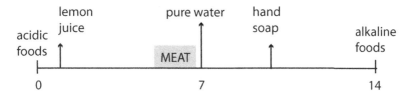

Fig. 1.2 General pH scale.

How fast and low pH drops depends on the conditions that the animal was submitted to during transport and before slaughter. The factors that affect meat pH are genetics, pre-slaughter stress and post-slaughter handling.

Meat	pH	Description
Live animal	7.2	
Normal	5.8 (24 hours after slaughter)	typical red color, good water binding
PSE (Pale, Soft, Exudative)	5.5 (60 minutes after slaughter)	pale color, very soft, poor water binding
DFD (Dark, Firm, Dry)	6.2 (24 hours after slaughter)	dark red color, very good water binding

Water holding capacity is related to the pH of the meat. As the pH decreases so does the water holding capacity of the meat. At the isoelectric point (pH around 5.3), meat has the minimum strength to hold water and the drying is fastest. This relationship is of great advantage when choosing meats for making dry products as their safety depends on water removal. On the other hand when making a boiled ham, we want it to be juicy and meat with a higher pH will be chosen. The meat with a higher pH binds water very well and inhibits drying. This can affect the safety of a drying product as more moisture creates better conditions for the growth of bacteria.

Proteins. Proteins are very important molecules to all forms of life. They are one of four of life's basic building blocks; the other three are carbohydrates (sugars), lipids (fats), and nucleic acids (DNA and RNA). Proteins make up about 15% of your body weight, and serve all types of functions. They are large molecules made up of hundreds of atoms of carbon, hydrogen, oxygen, and nitrogen. A scientist can separate those proteins from one another. Then he can break them down into smaller parts and finally arrive into what is defined as amino acids. By studying those amino acids and the rules that govern their behavior we learn about proteins. There are many proteins and they don't look alike or taste alike. Meat proteins coagulate when heated to 135-155° F (58-131° C). They can be divided into:

- Sarcoplasmic (plasma) - water soluble.
- Myofibrillar (contractile) - or salt soluble.
- Stromal (connective) - relatively insoluble.

Sarcoplasmic proteins are commonly extracted with curing solutions and help to emulsify fat, the factor which is crucial when making emulsified sausages. They are already soluble in the muscle cells, hence called water soluble proteins. The fluid (meat juice) that drips from thawed meat contains these proteins. They also help convert glycogen (meat sugar) into lactic acid which contributes to stronger fermentation when making fermented products. *Myoglobin* which gives meat its color belongs to this group.

Myofibrillar proteins are responsible for the contraction ability of living muscle. They are soluble in high salt solutions what allows them to retain water and encapsulate fats, thus preventing separation during cooking. The most important proteins in this group are *myosin* and *actin*; they contribute to the water holding and emulsifying capacity of meat with ***myosin*** being the most important. By needle pumping meat with curing solution (salt, water, nitrite, phosphates, erythorbate) and applying mechanical action (cutting, tumbling) we can extract these proteins. The resulting solution is the "exudate" which acts as a glue and holds individual meat particles together, the important property when making formed hams. This extraction becomes much stronger when meat is cut in a bowl cutter in the presence of salt and water. As a result an emulsified meat paste is obtained which may be added into the sausage mass or be frozen for later use. The leanest and the most expensive meats generally contain the highest level of these proteins.

Connective tissue proteins function as a supporting structure for the body of an animal. They transmit the movement generated by contraction of the myofibrillar proteins to the skeleton of the body. The most important proteins in this group are *collagen* and *elastin*.

The Structure of Meat

There are three types of animal muscles:

1. Plain or smooth muscles - viscera, especially those of the respiratory and digestive tracts, and the blood vessels.
2. Cardiac muscle - heart.
3. Skeletal, also known as striated or voluntary muscle - striated muscle is attached to bone and produces all the movements of body parts in relation to each other. It is under voluntary control unlike smooth muscle or cardiac muscle.

The most common of the three types of muscle is the striated muscle. Its fibres are long and thin and are crossed with a regular pattern of fine red and white lines, giving the muscle its distinctive appearance and name. Skeletal muscles are usually attached to bone by tendons composed of connective tissue. This connective tissue envelops the entire muscle and is called *epimysium*. This type of muscle is composed of numerous cylindrically shaped bundles of cells (muscle fibres), called *fascicles* and each is surrounded by connective tissue (*perimysium*). Each muscle fiber ensheathed by connective tissue called *endomysium* contains several hundred to several thousand tightly packed strands called *myofibrils* that consist of alternating filaments of the protein substances *actin* (thin filament) and *myosin* (thick filament). The protein complex composed of *actin* and *myosin* is sometimes referred to as *actomyosin*.

In striated muscle, the *actin* and *myosin* filaments each have a specific and constant length on the order of a few micrometers, far less than the length of the elongated muscle cell (a few millimeters in the case of human skeletal muscle cells). The filaments are organized into repeated subunits along the length of the *myofibril*. These subunits are called *sarcomeres*. In the presence of salt, the mechanical action (cutting, grinding, tumbling) extracts myosin and actin proteins from meat filaments and forms sticky solution called "exudate." The exudate acts like glue and holds individual chunks of meat (formed ham) or minced sausage, together. This action is greatly magnified when phosphates are added during meat comminution.

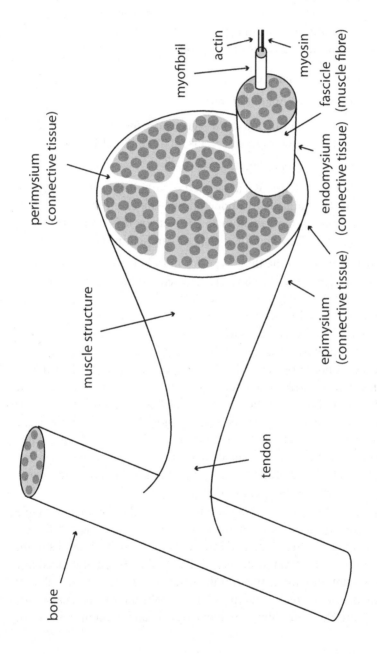

Fig. 1.3 Structure of meat.

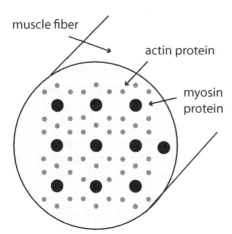

There are six actin proteins (thin filament) to one myosin protein (thick filament). They are surrounded with water, sarcoplasmic (water soluble) proteins, myoglobin, vitamins, minerals, salts etc.

Fig. 1.4 Cross section of a single myofibrillar fibre.

The cell membrane of a muscle cell is called the sarcolemma, and this membrane transfers nerve signals to the individual muscle fibers. *Myosin* receives the signal, attaches itself to *actin* and contracts/ expands the muscle.

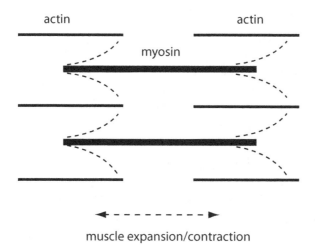

muscle expansion/contraction

Fig. 1.5 Single sarcomere. The *actin - myosin* system. Myofibril consists of many sarcomeres running parallel to each other on the long axis of the cell.

This is the simplified mode of operation of the skeletal muscle. *Myosin* and *actin* proteins made it possible and they play a significant role in processing meat products.

Myosin and *actin* are not straight filaments but rather coiled strands of molecules which resemble a string of beads. They form *actomyosin* matrix and can hold some water. *When meats are cured or marinated, salt penetrates meat's structure and reacts with this matrix.* As a result proteins swell and unravel to some degree. This tenderizes meat and allows the matrix to trap more water making products juicier.

When phosphates are added with salt, this action becomes stronger and the effects are greatly magnified. The protein coils unravel, the matrix opens up and meat cells can trap and hold a lot of water. Not just in curing but during cooking as well. This results in higher yields and profits as there is less cooking loss.

Emulsions. Understanding emulsions is important for making emulsified products such as hot dogs, frankfurters, bologna or liver sausages. During the comminution process fat cells become ruptured and the free fat is released. Fat does not dissolve in water or mix with it well. *The purpose of emulsion is to bond free fat, meat and water together so they will not become separated.* When fat comes out of emulsion it will be lost during cooking which amounts to a higher cooking loss. Emulsions can be of different types:

1. Natural meat emulsion. This is a natural emulsion where meat must form a matrix to hold the fat. *The leaner the meat the stronger matrix* will be created. This matrix will hold water as well and will give a sausage its proper texture. Meat proteins are needed not only for their nutritional value but for their contribution towards emulsification and binding of meat products. Lean meat contains *myofibrillar* and *sarcoploasmic* proteins which are of high quality. Its emulsification value and binding properties are excellent.

- Pork rind emulsion. Pork skins are precooked for about 1.5 hours in hot simmering water and then chopped in a bowl cutter or food processor *when still warm*. About 1/3 of water, 1/3 pork skins and 1/3 back fat are combined to create emulsion. Such emulsion must be used quickly or cooled down and frozen for later use.

- Liver emulsion. Liver contains the natural emulsifying agent and around 30% of liver is added to liver sausages.

2. Caseinate (type of milk protein) and soy-based emulsion. A typical caseinate based emulsion: 5 parts water : 5 parts fat : 1 part caseinate. A typical soy isolate based emulsion: 5 parts water : 5 parts fat : 1 part soy isolate. When less than lean meats are used, the binding will still take place providing enough exudate has formed. It may be further enhanced by lightly sprinkling meat surfaces with powdered gelatin. In addition a variety of materials may be used to enhance binding:

- Soy protein isolate.
- Soy protein concentrate.
- Non fat milk powder.
- Caseinate.
- Carrageenan - comes from algae or seaweed.
- Egg white.

Exudate - *the glue that holds sausages or reformed meats together.* Exudate is the solution of meat proteins with salt. Protein extraction during mincing/cutting or by mechanical action of massaging and tumbling is the main factor that determines the binding strength of the sausage emulsions or restructured meats. *On heating, exudate becomes a solid gel* helping to bind meat parts together. Extracted proteins form more cohesive bonds between the protein matrix and the meat surface. Many sausage recipes include the following sentence: mix all ground meat with spices until the mixture becomes sticky (gluey). After a few minutes of mixing and kneading by hand, the loosely held meat mass starts to stick together and becomes one solid mass. This is due to the binding properties of exudate. Meat proteins were extracted during cutting and combined with salt to form exudate. As mentioned earlier, the leaner the meats used, the more exudate is extracted. This is a logical statement as exudate is a solution of meat proteins with salt and less noble cuts such as connective tissue and fats contain less protein.

Exudate forms on surfaces which are cut. If the connective tissue on the meat surface is intact, the surface should be cut or scored to facilitate exudate extraction and subsequent binding. One of the purposes of massaging and tumbling is to solubilize and extract *myofibrillar* proteins to produce exudate on the surface of the meat.

Sources of Meat

The main sources of manufacturing meats are:

- Cattle - beef, veal.
- Pig.
- Sheep.
- Poultry - chicken, turkey, goose and duck.

In many areas goat and horse are consumed too. In addition hunting enthusiasts bring meats such as deer, wild boar, bear, small game and wild birds to the dinner table. To a large extent the quality of meat relates to the type of feed the animal consumes. Cattle eat grass, hay and grains and their digestive system breaks down those feeds into amino acids and proteins that create a characteristic texture and flavor. Such foods do not contain much fat and consequently beef fat is concentrated in muscles.

Pigs, in contrast, eat a variety of foods and their diet contains more fat. They eat a lot of corn which produces a softer meat. English producers feed their hogs with barley instead as this produces harder bacon which is preferred by the local consumer. In the Eastern part of the USA, hogs were often fed peanuts which resulted in a soft meat and fat that will melt at lower than usual temperatures. Famous Spanish Serrano dry hams are made from hogs that graze freely in oak forests and consume a lot of oak corns. This diet imparts a characteristic texture and flavor to the meat. Polish Kabanosy were originally made from young fat pigs that were fed mainly potatoes. The type of animal diet is very instrumental in producing meat that displays an original flavor and character. Pigs of today are fed commercially prepared foods enriched with antibiotics. They spend their entire life in movement restricted pens that affect the texture of the meat. To satisfy the low fat expectations of a consumer, the fat content of pork meat is much lower than before. The animals are much smaller today compared to the giants that freely walked only 100 years ago.

Meat Cuts

Short of being a farmer, a person living in a large city has little choice but to purchase meats in a local supermarket. Individuals who keep on winning whole hog barbecue contests purchase their pigs from selected farmers. From a manufacturing point of view available meat cuts can be divided into two groups:

- Noble cuts.
- Less noble cuts.

Noble cuts are those cuts which are highly regarded by chefs as:

- They consist almost entirely of desirable lean meat.
- Are easy to prepare as they contain small amounts of bone.
- Contain outside fat which is easy to remove.

- Include little connective tissue.
- Are simple to cook.

They are highly regarded by a consumer as:

- They can be cooked using simple methods.
- Are tender when cooked.
- Taste good.

Noble cuts come from the parts of the animal that exercise less frequently such as beef round, rump, sirloin, loin or pork ham, loin and belly. Less noble cuts exhibit opposite characteristics and come from the parts of the animal that exercise frequently such as beef neck, chuck, shoulder, shin or pork shoulder, picnic and hocks. Such cuts contain many bones, smaller muscles and more connective tissue. As there is a finite number of noble parts the animal carries, the less noble and smaller parts are used for making sausages. This includes cuts and trimmings removed from the more noble cuts and parts such as liver, kidney, heart, tongue, jowls and skin. The only instance when noble meat cuts will be used for making sausages is the shortage of less noble cuts or a recipe such as, for example, ham sausage that calls specifically for chunks of lean leg.

There is a unique meat classification system in the USA:

1. Acceptable grade - the only fresh pork sold in supermarkets.
2. Utility grade - used in processed products and not available in supermarkets for purchase.

Pork meat is divided into five prime areas:

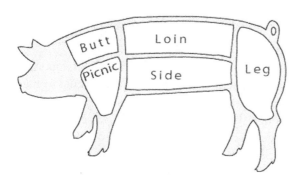

1. Shoulder butt (Boston butt).
2. Shoulder picnic.
3. Loin.
4. Ham.
5. Side (bacon, spare ribs).

Photo 1.1 Pork prime cuts.

Those main cuts are further broken down to additional parts. They all have unique names and numbers and they are listed in a trade catalog. These five primary cuts are the meat that a home sausage maker will be able to purchase in a supermarket. There are many meat products and known sausages that require meats from other parts of the hog's body than those five primary cuts mentioned above. To make liver sausages you need liver, fat, and meat which may come from heads, brains, kidneys, hearts, back fat, lungs, tripes, etc. To make head cheese you need head meat, shank (hocks) and skins as these parts are rich in collagen and will form a gelatin which will hold meat ingredients together. Blood, which is a good binder, is of course needed for blood sausages. Meat processors dealing with slaughter houses have access to those meats and they do use them to manufacture different sausages. A person living on a farm can obtain a hog without much difficulty, however, a person in a large city might find it harder, but can make substitutions.

The factors that are of special interest to us when processing meats are:

- **Moisture.** Meat contains about 75% water but more water can be added during the manufacturing process. This water should be retained by the meat which is especially important for commercial producers as it amount to higher yields and profits.
- **Fat.** Fat contains about 10-15% water. Proper fat selection is important when making fermented sausages.
- **Connective tissue.** Selective meat rich in connective tissue is important when making head cheeses.
- **Cohesion.** Allows binding meat pieces together, for example when making hams.

Moisture. The ability of meat to absorb and hold water is an important factor when making meat products, especially when producing formed hams or emulsified sausages such as frankfurters or bologna. The leaner the meat, the stronger binding capacity it possesses. The finer comminution of the particles, the higher degree of protein extraction and the stronger water binding capacity of the meat. Meat coming from different animals exhibits different water binding properties. For example, beef binds water much better than pork.

1. Adding water. When a piece of meat is cooked it will lose some of the water, fat and juices. Adding water to meat helps offset some of this loss. Meat will lose some of this water anyhow, but because it contained more water when the cooking started, the cooked product will lose less of its original weight as some of the added water would be retained.

2. Adding water and salt. Adding salt into meat extracts meat proteins which form a solution with salt and water inside. This solution acts like glue holding individual pieces of meat and water together. This further improves the meat's water binding properties and results in a smaller cooking loss.

3. Adding water, salt and phosphates. When phosphates are used alone they are less effective, but when applied with salt they force meat to bind water in a formidable way. They accelerate the salt effects allowing the same results to occur sooner.

In other words the combined action of salt and phosphates is greater than applying salt and phosphates individually. Around 0.3% phosphate is a typical dose. The maximum allowed is 0.5% but note that they are quite bitter and adding more than 0.3% may affect the product's flavor. Phosphates commonly used in making meat products are: pyrophosphates $P_2O_7^{4-}$ and tripolyphosphates $P_3O_{10}^{5-}$ An important function of phosphates is their ability to accelerate the extractability of meat proteins. This leads to a uniform, interwoven matrix which entraps water and fat during comminution and holds it together during heat treatment. To increase and accelerate the distribution of a salt and phosphates solution within meat the physical action is employed. This is accomplished by massaging or tumbling machines designed for this purpose.

Fat influences flavor, juiciness and texture of the product; it is commonly said that "fat carries the flavor." It also impacts shelf life and profits. Melting of fat begins at 35-40° C (95-104° F) depending on the type of fat. The type of food a particular animal eats will influence the texture and the melting point of its fat. The molten fat is able to escape from the damaged fat cells. Once the temperature falls into the range of 40-80° C (104-176° F), the fat cells start to break down rapidly. For those reasons fatty products such as sausages should not be smoked or cooked at high temperatures for longer periods of time as the fats will melt affecting the texture of the sausage.

Melting and solidifying temperature of some fats		
Meat	Melting	Solidifying
Pork	82 - 104° F (28 - 40° C)	71 - 90° F (22-32° C)
Beef	104 - 122° F (40 - 50° C)	86 - 100° F (30 - 38° C)
Lamb	110 - 130° F (44 - 55° C)	93 - 113° F (34 - 45° C)
Chicken	~75° F (24° C)	< 50° F (10° C)

An interesting relationship exists between the texture of the fat and its distance from the center of the animal. The internal body fats are hardest, for example kidney fat. By the same token, *the outer layer of back fat is softer than the inside layer*, a fact that should be noted when choosing the hardest fat for making salami.

The color of fat depends on the type of animal and to a smaller degree its age and diet. For example, in colder climates in the summer when animals graze on grass, the fat is more yellow than when the animals are fed a prepared diet in the winter.

Generally the color of fat among animals follows these guidelines:

- Goat - white.
- Pig - white.
- Cattle - light yellow.
- Sheep - white to creamy.
- Horse - yellow.
- Buffalo - yellow.

Pork fat is the best for making sausages as it is white and tastes the best. It exhibits different degrees of hardness depending from which part it comes from. Back fat, jowl fat or butt fat (surface area) have a very hard texture and higher melting point. They are the best choice for making products in which we expect to see the individual specks of fat in a finished product such as dry salami. Soft fat such as belly fat is fine for making fermented spreadable sausages such as mettwurst or teewurst. *For most sausages any fat pork trimmings are fine* providing they were partially frozen when submitted to the grinding process. This prevents fat smearing when temperature increases due to the mechanical action of knives and rotating worm on fat particles.

Beef fat has a higher melting temperature than pork, but has a less desirable flavor. It is yellowish in color which affects the appearance of the product where discrete particles of fat should be visible.

Connective Tissue

The connective tissue consists mainly from fibres of collagen and to a smaller extent from fibres of elastin. *Collagen* is much more prevalent and is found in bone, ligaments, skin, tendon, jowls and other connective tissues. It accounts for about 20% of the total protein. It is a framework that holds the individual muscles fibres and the bundles of muscles together. This function requires connective tissue to be tough and strong. *Collagen* is characterized by inter and intramolecular cross-links, whose number increases with the animal's age. *Collagen* water holding power is weaker than that of protein solution extracted from lean meat, and some of the water is returned during heating. *Collagen* is a tough tissue but becomes a tender meat when cooked for a few hours on low heat. *Collagen* is insoluble in water, but upon heating turns into liquid gelatin, which forms a gel upon cooling. On heating to 148° F (65° C) *collagen* fibers start to shrink and if the heat continues they form a gelatin. Fat that comes from part of the animal not supported by skeleton framework such as belly, must have some connective tissue in order to support the weight above. It can be generalized that the softer the fat, the more *connective* tissue present.

In air dried products such as country ham or prosciutto, collagen becomes tender in time due to natural reactions taking place inside the meat.

Elastin is found in ligaments of the vertebrae and in the walls of large arteries. It has a yellow color and is of minor importance for making sausages.

Meat Binding

Understanding cohesion forces which are responsible for binding meats is important when making formed meats that consist of smaller meat cuts. Those pieces whether stuffed in a large casing or placed in a form, must bind together otherwise the slice of the finished product will not hold together and little holes will form inside. The best example is formed boiled ham which is made of smaller cuts. Such cuts must be carefully selected not only by the size and fat content, but by the meat color as well. And they must bind together so that the fully cooked product will look as if made from one solid chunk of meat. *The binding is improved if pressure is applied to meat pieces.* The binding will also be stronger if *exudate* has formed on the meat surface and the meats are heated to 149° F (65° C) or higher.

A classical example is formed boiled ham where meat cuts are enclosed in a form and pressure is applied. Then the form is immersed in hot water and the ham is cooked. *Collagen* like myosin is extracted by the salt that was added to meat either by needle pumping followed by mechanical action or by the salt added to meat in the bowl cutter. At home conditions it can be extracted by adding salt to the sausage mass and thorough mixing. An egg white is often used as a binding aid to bind different meats together, for example, in Bockwurst sausage.

Water Holding Capacity

Different meats exhibit different capacity for binding water. Under-standing this concept is important for making sausages where we can decide which meats will be used to produce a sausage. This decision will influence the juiciness of the final product and will also contribute to a higher yield and profits.

Water binding quality of different meats	
Excellent	**Beef**: Hot bull meat, chilled bull meat, beef shank meat, beef chucks, boneless cow meat
Good	**Beef:** head meat, cheeks, **Veal:** boneless veal, calf head meat **Pork:** trimmings-extra lean, trimmings-lean,head meat, cheeks (jowls)
Poor	**Beef**: hearts, weasand meat, giblets, tongue trimmings, **Pork:** regular trimmings, hearts, jowls, ham fat **Sheep:** cheeks, hearts
Very poor	Ox lips, beef tripe, pork tripe, hearts, pork snouts, pork lips. These cuts although nutritious, exhibit little water binding properties and are mainly used as filler meat. Pork tripe, snouts and lips should be limited to 25% of the meat total
Hot bull meat: meat from a freshly slaughtered animal.	
The above data adapted from: *Sausage and Ready to Eat Meats, Institute of Meat packing, The University of Chicago.*	

The best quality emulsified sausages always incorporate beef as it easily binds water that has formed from the ice that was added during the cutting process.

There are other factors that influence the water holding capacity of meat but they are difficult to control. These factors are:

- The age - the older the animal, or the longer it has been stored, the poorer its water binding qualities.

- Acidity of meat (pH) - higher acidity, the poorer its water binding qualities.

- Freezing meat - the texture if frozen meat is not as good as in fresh meat, since the muscle fibres are broken by ice crystals.

Meat Color

The color of *fresh meat* is determined largely by the amount of *myoglobin* a particular animal carries. The more *myoglobin* the darker the meat, it is that simple. Going from top to bottom, meats that contain more *myoglobin* are: horse, beef, lamb, veal, pork, dark poultry and light poultry. The amount of *myoglobin* present in meat increases with the age of the animal.

Meat Color	Dark red	Red	Light red	Pink	Light pink	Pale pink
Bull	x					
Cow			x			
Young cow				x		
Veal					x	
Old Sheep	x					
Adult sheep			x			
Young sheep				x		
Old goat	x					
Adult goat		x				
Young goat			x			
Pig				x		
Young pig						x
Buffalo		x				
Rabbit	x					x
Horse	x					

Different parts of the same animal, take the turkey for example, will display a different color of meat. Muscles that are exercised frequently such as legs need more oxygen. *As a result they develop a darker color* unlike the breast which is white due to little exercise. This color is pretty much fixed and there is not much we can do about it unless we mix different meats together.

The color of *cooked* (uncured) meat varies from greyish brown for beef and grey-white for pork and is due to denaturation (cooking) of *myoglobin*. The red color usually disappears in poultry at 152° F (67° C), in pork at 158° F (70° C) and in beef at 167° F (75° C). The color of *cured* meat is pink and is due to the reaction between nitrite and *myoglobin*. The color can vary from light pink to light red and depends on the amount of *myoglobin* a particular meat cut contains and the amount of nitrite added to the cure. Curing and nitrates are covered in details in the chapter on curing.

Meat Tenderness

Tenderness of meat depends on the age of the animal, methods of chilling and meat acidity. The way the meat is cooked is another important factor that must be considered and here the cook decides the tenderness of the final product.

Meat Flavor

Meat flavor increases with the age of the animal. The characteristic flavors of a particular animal are concentrated more in the fat than in the lean of the meat. Low fat meats exhibit weaker flavors. Freezing and thawing has little effect on meat flavor, however, prolonged frozen storage can effect meat's flavor due to rancidity of fat. Rancidity is created by meat's reaction with oxygen which is accelerated by exposure of meat to light.

Chapter 2

Curing And Nitrates

Salting - Brining - Marinating – Sweet Pickle - Curing - What's the difference?

All tenderizing methods such as salting, curing, pickling and marinating rely on breaking down meat protein (denaturing them) to make meat more juicy and tender. The ingredients that break down those proteins are: *salt, vinegar, wine, and lemon juice,* which is why most marinades include them in their formulas. Salt is the strongest curing agent. Some definitions overlap each other and for example when we add salt and nitrites to water, we normally say we are preparing a brine or a pickle although technically speaking it is a curing solution.

Salting is the simplest form of curing and its objective is to tenderize and preserve meat. Water inside the meat spells trouble, it spoils everything and eliminating it by salting and drying allows meat to be stored for longer periods of time. A classical example will be an all American favorite beef jerky. A thousand years ago there was no refrigeration but the merchants were moving barrel-packed salted fish from place to place. To preserve fish that way it had to be heavily salted. Before consumption fish were soaked in water to remove the excess salt and only then were ready to be cooked. In highly developed countries refrigeration is taken for granted, but in many areas of the world even today the meat or fish has to be salted for preservation.

Brining is immersing meat in brine (salt and water) to improve the juiciness and flavor. Brined meats taste better and all cooks know it. When we cook any type of meat, there is an unavoidable loss of moisture, up to 30%. But if we soak the same meat in a brine first, the loss can be limited to as little as 15% because the meat absorbed some of the brine and it was more juicy at the start of the cooking. Another benefit we get from brining is that a salt solution dissolves some of the proteins in the meat, turning them from solid to liquid which in turn increases the juiciness of the meat. A typical brine contains very few ingredients: salt, water, sugar and sometimes spices.

Pickle is another definition of the brine. When sugar is added to a brine solution it is often called sweet pickle and it often contains vinegar. Most brines contain sugar anyhow and both terms describe the same method. If you place chicken in a brine overnight you will most likely roast it at a high temperature the next day and no nitrites are necessary. If you place chicken in a curing solution (salt, water, sugar, sodium nitrite) it can be safely smoked for many hours at low temperatures. It will have a different color, texture, taste and flavor.

Marinade plays an important part in the barbecuing and grilling processes but it does not belong in the real world of curing as it does not call for nitrates. It is a relatively short procedure where the purpose is to soak the meat in marinade which will tenderize it and add a particular flavor. Meat becomes tender and is able to hold more water which makes it juicier. A typical marinade contains ingredients which are known to tenderize meat by swelling meat proteins. There are no fixed rules for the length of the marinating time but about 2-3 hours for 1" meat diameter sounds about right. A larger 6" chunk of meat should be marinating in a refrigerator overnight. Like in any other method a longer processing time will impart a stronger flavor on the marinated item. The composition of a marinade is much richer than that of a curing solution.

What is Curing?

In its simplest form the word 'curing' means 'saving' or 'preserving' and the definition covers preservation processes such as: drying, salting and smoking. When applied to home made meat products, the term 'curing' usually means *'preserved with salt and nitrite.'* When this term is applied to products made commercially it will mean that meats are prepared with salt, nitrite, phosphate, ascorbates, erythorbates and dozens more chemicals that are pumped into the meat. Meat cured only with salt, will have a better flavor but will also develop an objectionable dark color. Factors that influence curing:

- The size of the meat - the larger meat the longer curing time.
- Temperature - higher temperature, faster curing.
- Moisture content of the meat.
- Salt concentration of dry mixture or wet curing solution- higher salt concentration, faster curing.

- Amount of fat-more fat in meat, slower curing.
- pH - a measure of the acid or alkaline level of the meat. (Lower pH-faster curing).
- The amount of Nitrate and reducing bacteria present in the meat.

Curing Temperatures

The curing temperature should be between 36-40° F (3-5° C) which falls within the range of a common refrigerator. Lower than 36° F (3° C) temperature may slow down the curing process or even halt it. Commercial producers can cure at lower temperatures because they add chemicals for that purpose. There is a temperature that can not be crossed when curing and this is when meat freezes at about 28° F (- 4° C). Higher than normal temperatures speed up the curing process but increase the possibility of spoilage. This is a balancing act where we walk a line between the cure and the bacteria that want to spoil meat. The temperature of 40° F (5° C) is the point that separates two forces: below that temperature we keep bacteria in check, above 40° F (5° C) bacteria start spoiling the meat.

Meats were traditionally cured with Nitrates. Before Nitrate can release nitrite (the real curing agent) it has to react with bacteria that have to be present in the meat. Holding Nitrate solution below 40° F (5° C) will inhibit the development of bacteria and they may not be able to react with Nitrate. On the other hand sodium nitrite does not depend on bacteria and works well at refrigerator temperatures. When used with Nitrates/nitrites, salt is an incredibly effective preserving combination. There has not been even one documented incident of food poisoning of a meat cured with salt and Nitrates.

People in the Far East, Africa, South America and even Europe are still curing meats at higher than normal temperatures without getting sick. That does not mean that we recommend it, but if someone in Canada shoots a 1600 lb (726 kg) Moose or a 1700 lb (780 kg) Kodiak Bear he has to do something with all this meat. He is not going to spend 5,000 dollars on a walk-in cooler, is he? These are exceptional cases when curing can be performed at higher temperatures. After the Second World War, ended most people in Europe neither had refrigerators nor meat thermometers and were curing meats at temperatures higher than those recommended today, but any growth of *C. botulinum* bacteria was prevented by the use of salt and Nitrates.

They also predominantly used potassium Nitrate which works best at temperatures of 46-50° F (8-10° C) and those were the temperatures of basement cellars.   delete Salt and nitrite will stop *Cl. botulinum* spores from developing into toxins, even at those higher curing temperatures. Due to increased bacteria growth at those higher curing temperatures the shelf life of a product would be decreased, however, that was of a little concern as the product was consumed as fast as it was made. Remember when handling meats, the lower the temperatures the slower the growth of bacteria and the longer life of the product. Extending the shelf life of the product is crucial for commercial meat plants as the product can stay on the shelf longer and has better chances of being sold.

Curing is a more complicated process than salting. In addition to physical reactions like diffusion and water binding, we have additional complex chemical and biochemical reactions that influence the flavor and color of the meat.

Methods of Curing

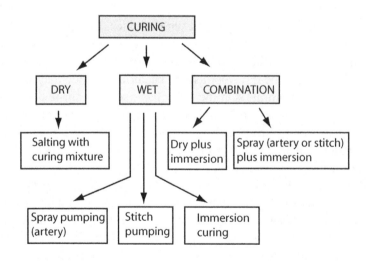

Fig. 2.1 Curing methods.

Salt Curing

Meat and salt are like two hands of the same body, they always work together and we cannot even imagine processing or eating meat without salt. When added to meat it provides us with the following benefits:

- Adds flavor (feels pleasant when applied between 2-3%).
- Prevents microbial growth.
- Increases water retention, and meat and fat binding.

Salt does not kill bacteria, it simply prevents or slows down their development. To be effective the salt concentration has to be 10% or higher. Salt concentration of 6% prevents *Clostridium botulinum* spores from becoming toxins though they may become active when smoking at low temperatures. Adding sodium nitrite (Cure #1) eliminates that danger. The two physical reactions that take place during salting are diffusion and water binding, but no chemical reactions take place. Salting is the fastest method of curing as it rapidly removes free water from inside of the meat. The water travels to the outside surface of the meat and simply leaks out. This gives us a double benefit:

- Less water in meat for the growth of bacteria

- Proportionally more salt in meat inhibits the growth of bacteria

Today the products that will be salted only are pork back fat and some long cured Italian and Spanish hams.

Dry Curing

Dry curing has been performed the same way since the 13th century. Before smoking, the salt with Nitrates had to be rubbed into hams or other meat cuts which was a tough job because it could only be done by hand. Then pork pieces were tightly packed in tubs, covered with more salt, and left there up to 6 weeks. The salt was dehydrating the meat and drawing the moisture out of it. The dry cure method can be used under wider temperature variations than other curing methods.

The dry curing method is best used for all types of sausages, bacon, and hams that will be air-dried. In most cases after curing, meats go for smoking, then for air drying and there is no cooking involved. In addition to salt and Nitrates, the ingredients such as sugar, coriander, thyme, and juniper are often added to the dry mix.

Basic rules for applying dry cure:

When curing times are short, up to 14 days, use Cure #1 according to the standard limit of: 1 oz. cure for 25 lb of meat. For longer times use Cure #2 that contains Nitrate which will keep on releasing nitrite for a long time. The amount of dry mix needed to cure 25 lb of meat by the dry cure method when making dry (fermented) sausages is:

> 2 oz. Cure #2
>
> 12 oz. canning salt
>
> 6 oz. dextrose or brown sugar
>
> seasonings

Dry Curing Times

The length of curing depends very much on the size of the meat and its composition. *Fatty tissues and skin create a significant barrier to a curing solution.* When curing a large meat piece, for example a ham, a curing solution will start penetrating on the lean side of the meat and then will progress deeper forward towards the bone and the skin side. There will be very little penetration on the fatty skin side. It seems logical that removing the fat layer of the skin will speed up curing. It definitely will, but it is not such a good idea. The fat acts as a barrier not only to curing but to smoking and removal of moisture as well. After smoking the ham might be baked or poached in hot water. Here the fat acting as a barrier will prevent a loss of dissolved protein and meat juices that will try to migrate into the water. For more uniform curing, meats should be overhauled (re-arranged) on the third and tenth days of the cure. The curing time will depend on the size of the meat piece and your own preference for a strong or lightly salted product.

A basic rule is 2 days per pound for the small cuts and 3 days per pound for hams and shoulders. For example, a six pound bacon would require about 12 days in cure, while a 12 pound ham would need 36 days. Another formula calls for 7 days of curing per inch of thickness. A ham weighing 12-14 lb and 5 inches thick through the thickest part will be cured 5 x 7 = 35 days. Smaller pieces should end up on top so they can be taken out first allowing larger pieces to continue curing. Otherwise they may taste too salty. Smaller meat cuts like bacon, butt, and loins can be cured with a dry mixture based on the following formula for 100 lb of meat: 4 lbs. salt, 1.5 lb sugar, 2 oz. Saltpeter (1 lb. Cure #2). Divide the mixture into three equal parts. Apply the first one-third and leave the meat to cure. After three days overhaul and rub in the second part. After three more days apply the last third of the mixture and allow to cure for about 12 days. Generally, the addition of spices occurs after the last re-salting has been completed.

Wet Curing

The wet curing method, sometimes called brine (salt and water), sweet pickle (sugar added), or immersion curing has been traditionally used for larger cuts of meat like butts or hams that were smoked. It is accomplished by placing meats in a wet curing solution (water, salt, nitrites, sometimes sugar). Sugar is added only when curing at refrigerator temperatures, otherwise it may begin fermentation and start to spoil the meat.

The wet curing is a traditional, time consuming method, going out of fashion as the large hams had to be submerged for up to 6 weeks and turned over on a regular basis. With such a long curing time there is a danger of meat spoiling from within the center where the bone is located. During that time we have to scoop up the foam and any slime that might gather on the surface, as that might be a source of contamination. Most smaller meat cuts require about 3-14 days of curing time at 40° F (4° C). It is still a fine curing method for smaller cuts of meat that will have a shorter curing time.

The meats have to be turned over on a daily basis and prevented from swimming up to the surface. After curing is complete, the meat pieces must be rinsed in fresh water and placed on wire mesh for draining. We do achieve certain weight gain when curing meats, even without chemicals, but this is not the reason why a home sausage maker cures meats. Meats are cured to produce a top quality product. The weight gain is as follows:

- Canadian bacon   3-4%
- Bacon   3%
- Ham   4%

Wet cure-spray pumping method

There are two methods of spray pumping:

1. The artery pumping - a wet cure method where a long needle, connected with a hose to a pump, will inject a brine solution into the ham's artery. It is a very efficient way of distributing the curing solution quickly and uniformly through the meat. The arterial blood system of the animal becomes a pipeline for the brine distribution throughout the ham. A leg will have to be carefully and professionally butchered so the artery will remain intact. There is of course no possibility of bone removal prior to pumping. It requires people with great processing skills to cut meat without disturbing arteries. In addition the artery had to be left a few inches longer than the meat itself. Then the pump operator had to find the artery, insert the needle and pump the solution at the correct pressure. Multiple arteries were pumped in order to cure ham well.

Artery pumping, though fast, did not thoroughly cure meats and more time was needed to develop a strong curing color and flavor. The meat was subsequently immersed in a solution of equal strength or rubbed in with the salt on the outside. This method was still too slow for commercial applications and was replaced by stitch pumping.

2. The stitch pumping is a wet cure method where the curing solution is applied under pressure to the surface of a ham, bacon, or butt with a bank of needles connected to a pump. This permits to distribute the curing solution rapidly and uniformly.

Photo 2.1 Needle injector.
Photo courtesy UltraSource/Koch Equipment, Kansas City, MO.

A home sausage maker can use a manual meat syringe to perform the same function though on a somewhat limited scale. The syringe holds

4 oz. of brine and has a 5 3/8" long needle with 12 tiny holes around its surface. Smaller syringes for general kitchen use can be found in every major appliances store. They are used for pumping meats with marinade.

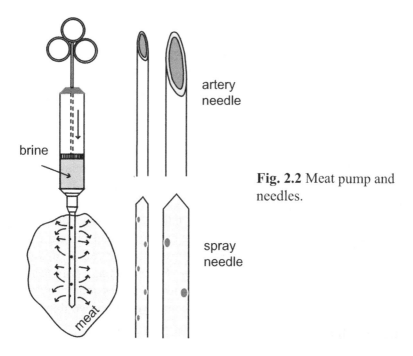

artery
needle

Fig. 2.2 Meat pump and needles.

spray
needle

Combination Curing

Combining the *dry cure* method with *spray pumping*. A ham is spray pumped with a curing solution and the outside is rubbed with dry mix (salt and nitrite). That will allow the inside curing solution to penetrate the meat more evenly while the outside dry mix solution will be moving towards the inside. Combining the *wet cure* method with *spray pumping* (artery or stitch) shortens curing time. A meat cut is spray pumped with a curing solution and then immersed in a container. The meat pieces should be completely covered and weighed down to prevent pieces from rising to the surface. They must also be turned over at least once every day for the duration of curing. The higher salt percentage in a curing solution the faster the curing process. When 26% of salt is added to water, the solution becomes saturated and more salt will not be absorbed by the water. The salt will settle on the bottom of the container. When forcefully rubbing salt into the meat we are introducing 100% of salt. This means that the dry curing method is much faster as it introduces more salt. Another benefit is that no moisture is added into the meat, on the contrary, salt will draw water out of meat creating less favorable conditions for bacteria to grow. For these reasons traditionally made hams relied on the dry cure method.

Making Brine - Use Tables And Brine Testers

There isn't a universal brine and every book and recipe provides customized instructions. Salt of different density and weight (table salt, Morton® Kosher, Diamond® Kosher) is measured with different instruments such as spoons, cups, ounces, pounds, kilograms - water measured by cups, quarts, gallons, liters… a total mess and chaos. We aim to explain the process in simpler terms using some common sense and logic. The main advantage of making your own brine is that you have total control over it and there is no guessing involved.

Firstly, it makes no sense at all to talk about curing time if we don't specify the strength of a brine. We can mix ¾ cup salt with one gallon of water or we can add 5 cups of salt into one gallon of water and it is obvious that *curing times will be different though both brines will do the job.* To prepare your own brine in a professional way and not to depend blindly on thousands of recipes you need two things:

1. Buy a brine tester. They are so cheap that there is no excuse for not having one. The salinometer also known as salometer consists of a float with a stem attached, marked in degrees. The instrument will float at its highest level in a saturated brine, and will read 100° (26.4 % salt solution). This is known as a fully saturated brine measured at 60° F (15° C).

Photo 2.2 Brine tester.

Photo 2.3 Pork loin is injected with curing solution.

Photo 2.4 The scale determines the amount of pick up.

In weaker brines the stem will float at lower levels and the reading will be lower. With no salt present the reading will be 0°. To make brine pour water into a suitable container, add some salt, insert a brine tester and read the scale. Want a stronger solution: add more salt. Need weaker brine: add more water, it is that simple. Keep in mind that a salinometer's scale measures the density of a solution containing salt and water. Once you add other ingredients the salinometer will measure the density of a solution and not the salinity of the brine.

2. Use brine tables (see Appendix A). The advantages of using tables are many: you can calculate the brine strength of any recipe, you can find out how much salt to add to 1 gallon of water to create a particular brine strength, and you don't have to worry whether you use table salt, Morton® kosher salt or Diamond® kosher salt. Brine Tables are especially useful when making a large volume of brine.

Curing With Nitrates/nitrites

Meat cured only with salt, will have a better flavor but will also develop an objectionable dark color. Adding nitrites to meat will improve flavor, prevent food poisoning, tenderize the meat, and develop the pink color widely known and associated with smoked meats. In the past we used potassium Nitrate exclusively because its derivative, sodium nitrite was not discovered yet. *Sodium Nitrate ($NaNO_3$) does not cure meat directly* and initially not much happens when it is added to meat. After a while *micrococci* and *lactobacilli* bacteria which are present in meat, start to react with Nitrate and create *sodium nitrite ($NaNO_2$) that will start the curing process.* If those bacteria are not present in sufficient numbers the curing process may be inhibited.

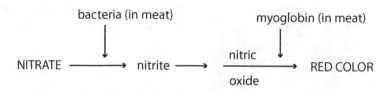

Fig. 2.3 Curing with Nitrate.

The reactions that occur are the following:

KNO_3 potassium Nitrate → KNO_2 nitrite (action of bacteria)
KNO_2 → HNO_2 nitrous acid (in acid medium, pH 5.2 - 5.7)
HNO_2 →   NO nitric oxide
NO   →   myoglobin → nitrosomyoglobin (pink color)

Potassium Nitrate worked wonderfully at 4-8°C (40-46°F) which was fine as refrigeration was not very common yet. If the temperatures dropped below 4°C (40°F) the bacteria that was needed to force Nitrate into releasing nitrite would become lethargic and the curing would stop. Potassium Nitrate was a slow working agent and the meat for sausages had to be cured for 72-96 hours.

The use of Nitrate is going out of fashion because it is difficult to control the curing process. By adding sodium nitrite directly to meat, we eliminate the risk of having an insufficient number of bacteria and we can cure meats faster and at lower temperatures. *Sodium nitrite does not depend on bacteria,* it works immediately and at refrigerator temperatures 2-4° C (35-40°F). At higher temperatures it will work even faster. About 15% of sodium nitrite reacts with *myoglobin* (color) and about 50% reacts with proteins and fats (flavor).

Curing Accelerators

The time required to develop a cured color may be shortened with the use of cure accelerators. Ascorbic acid (vitamin C), erythorbic acid, or their derivatives, sodium ascorbate and sodium erythorbate *speed up the chemical conversion of nitrite to nitric oxide* which reacts with meat *myoglobin* and creates *nitrosomyoglobin* (pink color). They also deplete levels of meat oxygen which prevents the fading color of the cured meat in the presence of light and oxygen.

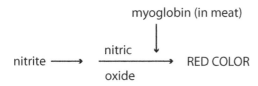

Fig. 2.4 Curing with nitrite.

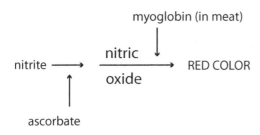

Fig. 2.5 Curing with accelerators.

Cured Meat Color

This color is pretty much fixed and there is not much we can do about it unless we mix different meats together. Cured meats develop a particular pink-reddish color due to the reaction that takes place between meat *myoglobin* and nitrite. If an insufficient amount of Nitrate/nitrite is added to the meat the cured color will suffer. This may be less noticeable in sausages where the meat is ground and stuffed, but if we slice a larger piece like a ham, the poorly developed color will be easily noticeable. Some sections may be gray, some may be pink and the meat will not look appetizing. To check your cured meats, take a sample, cut across it and look for uniform color. About 50 ppm (*parts per million*) of nitrite is needed for any meaningful curing. Some of it will react with *myoglobin* and will fix the color, some of it will go into other complex biochemical reactions with meat that develop a characteristic cured meat flavor. If we stay within Food and Drug Administration guidelines (1 oz. Cure #1 per 25 lb of meat - about 1 level teaspoon of Cure #1 for 5 lb of meat) we are applying 156 ppm of nitrite *which is enough and safe* at the same time. Cured meat will develop its true cured color only after submitted to cooking (boiling, steaming, baking) at 140-160° F (60-71° C). The best color is attained at 161° F (72° C).

More About Nitrates

Rock salts were mined in different areas of the world and exhibited different properties which depended mainly on impurities contained within. Take for example Himalayan salt that is sold on the Internet for cooking - it is pink. In the past when we used salt with a higher potassium Nitrate content, we discovered that the meat had a different taste and color. Potassium Nitrate was the main ingredient for making gun powder and it's commercial name was saltpeter, still used today. Potassium Nitrate (KNO_3-Bengal saltpetre) or sodium Nitrate ($NaNO_3$-Chile saltpetre) were even added to water causing the temperature to drop and that method was used to cool wine in the XVI century.

Nitrates and nitrites are powerful poisons and that is why the Food and Drug Administration established limits for their use. *So why do we use them?* The simple answer is that after testing and experiments, our modern science has not come up with a better solution to cure meats and prevent food poisoning. Only in the XIX century a German fellow Justinus Kemer linked food poisoning to contaminated sausages. It took another 80 years to discover botulinum bacteria by Emile Pierre van Ermengem, Professor of bacteriology at the University of Ghent in 1895. The first scientific papers that explained the behavior of Nitrates were published only in the XX century so why had we been using Nitrates so much? Not to prevent botulism of which we had never even heard of before.

We had been and still are using Nitrates because:
- Nitrates can preserve meat's natural color. The same piece of ham when roasted will have a light brown color and is known as roasted leg of pork. Add some nitrates to it, cook it and it becomes ham with its characteristic flavor and pink color.
- Nitrates impart a characteristic cured flavor to meat.
- Nitrates prevent the transformation of botulinum spores into toxins thus eliminating the possibility of food poisoning.
- Nitrates prevent rancidity of fats.

What's Better, Nitrate or Nitrite?

Both Nitrates and nitrites are permitted to be used in curing meat and poultry with the exception of bacon, where Nitrate use is prohibited. Sodium nitrite is commonly used in the USA (Cure #1) and everywhere else in the world, but many commonly available cures contain both nitrite and Nitrate.

Cure Agent	Nitrate	Nitrite
Cure #1	No	Yes
Cure #2	Yes	Yes
Morton ® Tender Quick	Yes	Yes
Morton ® Sugar Cure	Yes	Yes
Morton ® Smoke Flavored Sugar Cure	Yes	No

Many commercial meat plants prepare their own cures where both nitrite and Nitrate are used. All original European sausage recipes include Nitrate and now have to be converted to nitrite. So what is the big difference? Almost no difference at all. Whether we use Nitrate or nitrite, the final result is basically the same. The difference between Nitrate and nitrite is as big as the difference between wheat flour and the bread that was baked from it. The Nitrate is the Mother that gives birth to the Baby (nitrite). Pure sodium nitrite is an even more powerful poison than Nitrate as you need only about ⅓ of a tea-spoon to put your life in danger, where in a case of Nitrate you may need 1 teaspoon or more. So all these explanations that nitrite is safer for you make absolutely no sense at all. Replacing Nitrate with nitrite eliminates questions like: do I have enough nitrite to cure the meat? In other words, it is more predictable and *it is easier to control the dosage.* Another good reason for using nitrite is that *it is effective at low temperatures* 36-40° F, (2-4° C), where Nitrate likes temperatures a bit higher 46-50° F, (8-10° C). By curing meats at lower temperatures we slow down the growth of bacteria and *we extend the shelf life* of a product.

When Nitrates were used alone, *salt penetration was usually ahead of color development.* As a result large pieces of meat were too salty when fully colored and had to be soaked in water. This problem has been eliminated when using nitrite. Nitrite works much faster and the *color is fixed well before salt can fully penetrate the meat.* Estimating the required amount of Nitrate is harder as it is dependent on:

- Temperature (with higher temperature more nitrite is released from Nitrate).
- Amount of bacteria present in meat that is needed for Nitrate to produce nitrite and here we do not have any control. The more bacteria present, the more nitrite released. Adding sugar may be beneficial as it provides food for bacteria to grow faster.

In the 1920's, the government allowed the addition of 10 lb of Nitrate to 100 gallons of water (7 lb allowed today). The problem was that only about one quarter of the meat plants adhered to those limits and many plants added much more, even between 70 and 90 pounds. There was no control and as a result the customer was eating a lot of Nitrates.

Nitrate Safety Concerns

There has been much concern over the consumption of Nitrates by the general public. Studies have shown that when nitrites combine with by-products of protein (amines in the stomach), that leads to the formation of nitrosamines which are carcinogenic (cancer causing) in laboratory animals. There was also a link that when Nitrates were used to cure bacon and the latter one was fried until crispy, it helped to create nitrosamines. In order to accomplish that, the required temperatures had to be in the 600° F (315° C) range. Most meats are smoked and cooked well below 200° F (93° C) so they are not affected. Those findings started a lot of unnecessary panic in the 1970's about the harmful effects of nitrates on our health. Millions of dollars were spent, a lot of research was done, many researchers had spent long sleepless nights seeking fame and glory, but no evidence was found that when Nitrates are used within the established limits they can pose any danger to our health.

A review of all scientific literature on nitrite by the National Research Council of the National Academy of Sciences indicates that nitrite does not directly harm us in any way. All this talk about the danger of nitrite in our meats pales in comparison with the amounts of Nitrates that are found in vegetables that we consume every day. The Nitrates get to them from the fertilizers which are used in agriculture. Don't blame sausages for the Nitrates you consume, blame the farmer. It is more dangerous to one's health to eat vegetables on a regular basis than a sausage.

Nitrates in Vegetables

The following information about Nitrates in vegetables was published by MAFF, Department of Health and the Scottish Executive before April 1st 2000 when the Food Standards Agency was established. Number 158, September 1998. MAFF UK - NITRATE IN VEGETABLES: Vegetables contain higher concentrations of Nitrate than other foods and make a major contribution to dietary intake.

A survey of vegetables for sale in supermarkets was carried out in 1997 and 1998 to provide up-to-date information on Nitrate concentrations, to assess the health implications for UK consumers and also to inform negotiations on a review of the European Commission Regulation (EC) No. 194/97 (which sets maximum levels for Nitrate in lettuce and spinach).

A study on the effects of cooking on Nitrate concentrations in vegetables was also carried out to provide further refinements for estimating dietary exposure. The vegetables were tested and the mean Nitrate concentrations found were as listed in the table on the right. For comparison the permissible amount of Nitrate in comminuted meat products (sausages) is 1718 mg/kg. If one ate 1/4 lb smoked sausage, the ingoing Nitrate would be 430 ppm. That would probably account for less Nitrates than a dinner served with potatoes and spinach.

Vegetable	Nitrate mg/kg
spinach	1631
beetroot	1211
lettuces	1051
cabbages	338
potatoes	155
swedes	118
carrots	97
cauliflowers	86
brussel sprouts	59
onions	48
tomatoes	17

Ten years later in 2008 another British study concluded: "Our research suggests that drinking beetroot juice, or consuming other Nitrate-rich vegetables, might be a simple way to maintain a healthy cardiovascular system, and might also be an additional approach that one could take in the modern-day battle against rising blood pressure," says Amrita Ahluwalia, PhD, one of the study's researchers. Ahluwalia is a professor at the William Harvey Research Institute at Barts and The London School of Medicine.

Cooking by boiling reduced Nitrate concentrations in most of the vegetables tested by up to 75 percent. Frying and baking did not affect Nitrate concentrations in potatoes but frying caused increases in levels in onions. Dietary intakes of mean and upper range (97.5 percentile) consumers of these vegetables are 104 mg/day and 151 mg/day, respectively. These are below the Acceptable Daily Intake (ADI) for nitrate of 219 mg/day for a 60 kg adult set by the European Commission's Scientific Committee for Food (SCF). *There are therefore no health concerns for consumers.*

How Much Nitrite is Dangerous

According to the report prepared in 1972 for the U.S. Food and Drug Administration (FDA) by Battele-Columbus Laboratories and Department of Commerce, Springfield, VA 22151 – the fatal dose of potassium Nitrate for humans is in the range of 30 to 35 grams (about two tablespoons) consumed as a single dose; the fatal dose of sodium nitrite is in the range of 22 to 23 milligrams per kilogram of body weight. A 156 lb adult (71 kg) would have to consume 14.3 pounds (6.5 kg) of cured meat containing 200 ppm of sodium nitrite at one time. Taking into consideration that nitrite is rapidly converted to nitric oxide during the curing process, the 14.3 lb amount will have to be doubled or even tripled. The equivalent amount of *pure* sodium nitrite consumed will be 1.3 g. *One gram (1 ppm) of pure sodium nitrite is generally accepted as a life threatening dose.*

As nitrite is mixed with large amounts of salt, it would be impossible to swallow it at least from a culinary point of view. Besides, our cures are pink and it would be very hard to mistake them for common salt.

Nitrates And The Law

Maximum in-going Nitrite and Nitrate Limits in PPM (parts per million) for Meat and Poultry Products as required by the U.S. Food Safety and Inspection Service are:

Curing Agent	Curing Method			
	Immersion Cured	Massaged or Pumped	Comminuted *(Sausages)*	Dry Cured
Sodium Nitrite	200	200	156	625
Potassium Nitrite	200	200	156	625
Sodium Nitrate	700	700	1718	2187
Potassium Nitrate	700	700	1718	2187

The European Directive 95/2/CE (1995) allows 150 ppm of nitrite (if alone) or 300 ppm when combined (nitrite plus Nitrate), and the residual values should be less than 50 ppm (if alone) or 250 ppm (if combined). There are more stringent limits for curing agents in bacon to reduce the formation of nitrosamines.

Take note that *nitrosamines can only be formed when products are heated above 266° F (130° C)*. This can only happen when cured bacon is fried or cured sausage is grilled. The majority of cured and smoked meats never reach such high temperatures, but crispy fried bacon will. For this reason, *Nitrate is no longer permitted in any bacon* as it is not easy to calculate. Sodium nitrite, however, can still be used for curing bacon, albeit at lower limits: dry cured (200 ppm), immersion cured (120 ppm), pumped and/or massaged (120 ppm).

As a matter of policy, the Agency requires a minimum of 120 ppm of ingoing nitrite in all cured "Keep Refrigerated" products, unless the establishment can demonstrate that safety is assured by some other preservation process, such as thermal processing, pH or moisture control. This 120 ppm policy for in going nitrite is based on safety data reviewed when the bacon standard was developed. *There is no regulatory minimum in-going nitrite level* for cured products that have been processed to ensure their shelf stability (such as having undergone a complete thermal process, or having been subjected to adequate pH controls, and/or moisture controls in combination with appropriate packaging). *However, 40-50 ppm nitrite is useful in that it has some preservative effect.* This amount has also been shown to be sufficient for color-fixing purposes and to achieve
the expected cured meat or poultry appearance. Some thermally processed shelf-stable (canned) products have a minimum in-going nitrite level that must be monitored because it is specified as a critical factor in the product's process schedule. By the time meats are consumed, they contain less then 50 parts per million of nitrite. It is said that commercially prepared meats in the USA contain about 10 ppm of nitrite when bought in a supermarket. Nitrite and Nitrate are not permitted in baby, junior or toddler foods.

Note: how to calculate Nitrates is presented in Appendix A

Cure #1 (also known as Instacure #1, Prague Powder #1 or Pink Cure #1). For any aspiring sausage maker it is a necessity to understand and know how to apply Cure #1 and Cure #2, as those two cures are used worldwide though under different names and with different proportions of nitrates and salt. Cure #1 is a mixture of 1 oz of sodium nitrite (6.25%) to 1 lb of salt. It must be used to cure all meats that will require smoking at low temperatures. It may be used to cure meats for fresh sausages (optional).

Cure #2 (also known as Instacure #2, Prague Powder #2 or Pink Cure #2). Cure #2 is a mixture of 1 oz of sodium nitrite (6.25%) along with 0.64 oz of sodium Nitrate (4%) to 1 lb of salt. It can be compared to the time-releasing capsules used for treating colds. It must be used with any products that do not require cooking, smoking or refrigeration and is mainly used for products that will be air cured for a long time like country ham, salami, pepperoni, and other dry sausages. Both Cure #1 and Cure #2 contain a small amount of FDA approved red coloring agent that gives them a slight pink color thus eliminating any possible confusion with common salt and that is why they are sometimes called "pink" curing salts. Cure #1 is not interchangeable with Cure #2 and vice versa.

Morton™ Salt Cures

In addition to making common table salt the Morton® Salt Company also produces a number of cures such as Sugar Cure® mix, Smoke Flavored Sugar Cure® mix, Tender Quick® mix, and Sausage and Meat Loaf® seasoning mix. To use them properly one has to follow instructions that accompany every mix.

European Cures

There are different cures in European countries, for example in Poland a commonly used cure goes by the name "Peklosól" and contains 0.6% of Sodium Nitrite to salt. No coloring agent is added and it is white in color. In European cures such a low nitrite percentage in salt is self-regulating and it is almost impossible to apply too much nitrite to meat, as the latter will taste too salty. Following a recipe you could replace salt with peklosól altogether and the established nitrite limits will be preserved. This isn't the case with American Cure #1, that contains much more nitrite in it (6.25%) and we have to color it pink to avoid the danger of mistakes and poisoning.

Country	Cure	% of nitrite in salt
USA	Cure #1	6.25
Poland	Peklosól	0.6
Germany	Pökelsalz	0.6
France	Sel nitrité	0.6
Sweden	Colorazo	0.6
England	Nitrited salt	various
Australia	Kuritkwik	various

How to Apply Cures

Well, there are two approaches:

- Like an amateur - collecting hundreds of recipes and relying blindly on each of them. You lose a recipe and you don't know what to do. And how do you know the recipe is correct the?

- Like a professional - taking matters in your own hands and applying cures according to the USA Government requirements.

In case you want to be the professional, we are enclosing some useful data which is based on the U.S. standards.

Comminuted products - small meat pieces, meat for sausages, ground meat, poultry etc. Cure #1 was developed in such a way that if we add 4 ounces of Cure #1 to 100 pounds of meat, the quantity of nitrite added to meat will comfort to the legal limits (156 ppm) permitted by the Meat Division of the United States Department of Agriculture. That corresponds to 1 oz. (28.35 g) of Cure #1 for each 25 lb (11.33 kg) of meat or 0.2 oz. (5.66 g) per 5 lb (2.26 kg) of meat.

Comminuted Meat (Sausages)	Cure #1 in ounces	Cure #1 in grams	Cure #1 in teaspoons
25 lbs.	1	28.35	5
5 lbs.	0.2	5.66	1
1 lb.	0.04	1.1	1/5
1 kg	0.08	2.5	1/2

Cured dry products - country ham, country style pork shoulder, prosciutto, etc. These products are prepared from a single piece of meat and the curing ingredients are rubbed into the surface of the meat several times during the curing period. If you look at the FSIS nitrite limits you will see that the maximum nitrite limit for Dry Cured Products (625 ppm) is four times higher than for Comminuted Products (156 ppm). The reason that there are much higher allowable nitrite limits for dry cured products is that *nitrite dissipates rapidly in time.* The dry cured products are *air dried for a long time.* When the product is ready for consumption it hardly contains any nitrite left. Those higher limits guarantee a steady supply of nitrite in time. That positively contributes to the safety of the product and its color. To cure meat for sausages and to stay within 156 ppm nitrite limit we must apply no more than 1 oz of Cure #1 for each 25 lb of meat.

To *dry cure* 25 lb of pork butts and to stay within 625 nitrite limits we can apply 4 times more of Cure #1, in our case 4 ounces. Keep in mind that when you add Cure #1 (there is 93.75% salt in it) you are adding extra salt to your meat and you may re-adjust your recipe.

Meat for Dry Curing	Cure #1 in ounces	Cure #1 in grams	Cure #1 in teaspoons
25 lb	4	113.4	20
5 lb	0.8	22.64	4
1 lb	0.16	4.4	3/4
1 kg	0.35	10.0	1.5

Immersed, Pumped and Massaged Products such as hams, poultry breasts, corned beef. Here, it is much harder to come up with a universal formula as there are so many variables that have to be determined first. The main factor is to determine % pump when injecting the meat with a syringe or % pick-up when immersing meat in a curing solution. We will calculate the formula for 1 gallon of water, Cure #1 and 10% pick-up gain. Then the formula can be multiplied or divided to accommodate different amounts of meat. 10% pump or 10% pick-up mean that the cured meat should absorb 10% of the brine in relation to its original weight. For immersion, pumped or massaged products, the maximum in-going nitrite limit is 200 ppm and that corresponds to adding 4.2 oz of Cure #1 to 1 gallon of water.

1 gallon (8.33 lb) of water	Cure #1 in ounces	Cure #1 in grams	Cure #1 in teaspoons
	4.2	120	20 tsp (6 Tbs)

This is a very small amount of brine and if you want to cure a large turkey you will need to increase the volume. Just multiply it by a factor of 4 and you will have 4 gallons of water and 1.08 lb of Cure #1. The following is the safe formula for immersed products and very easy to measure: 5 gallons of water, 1 lb. of Cure #1. In the above formula at 10% pick-up the nitrite limit is 150 ppm which is plenty. Keep in mind that adding 1 lb. of Cure #1 to 5 gallons of water will give you 4.2% salt by weight and that corresponds to *only 16 degrees brine (slightly higher than sea water)*. If we add an additional 2 lb of salt we will get: 5 gallons of water, 1 lb. of Cure #1, 2 lb of salt and that will give us a 25 degree solution which is great for poultry.

What Will Happen if Too Little or Too Much Cure is Added?

With not enough cure, the color might suffer with some loss of cured flavor too. FSIS regulations dictate the *maximum allowed nitrite limits* and *there are no limits for the lower levels*. It has been accepted that a minimum of 40-50 ppm of nitrite is needed for any meaningful curing. Too much cure will not be absorbed by the meat and will be eaten by a consumer. Adding an excessive amount may make you sick, or even put you in danger.

What Will Happen if Curing Time is Shorter or Longer?

If the curing time is too short, some areas of meat (inside or under heavy layers of fat) will exhibit an uneven color which might be noticeable when slicing a large piece of meat. It will not show in sausages which are filled with ground meat, although the color may be weaker. If curing time is longer by a few days, nothing will happen providing the cured meat is held under refrigeration. You don't want to cure bone-in meats longer than 30-45 days as they may develop bone sour even when kept at low temperatures. *Taste your meats at the end of curing. You can always cure them longer in a heavier brine (to increase salt content) or soak them in cold water (to lower salt content).*

Commercial Curing Methods

Meat plants can not afford the luxury of the traditional wet curing as it requires storage space and extra time. The process they employed consists of pumping meats with needle injectors with specially formulated and often patented formulas, then bouncing the meats in tumblers to distribute the curing solution more evenly. Needle injectors pump the meat under pressure with a prepared solution that contains everything that is allowed by law to make the process the shortest and most economical. Some methods allow pumping meat with a curing solution and microscopic parts of meat of any kind.

Meat plants don't use these machines to improve quality, they use them to work faster and save money. A pork butt left for 10 days in a brine solution will be perfectly cured in every area, something a needle injector and tumbler will not do. There is a limit to how many holes can be made in meat with needles as they damage the texture of the meat. These machines are only effective if used with chemicals that will help to cure meat faster. By injecting the curing solution directly into the meat we speed up the process.

The tumbler helps to distribute the solution evenly inside but nitrite needs time to create a pink color. Salt also needs time to cure meat but there is no easy way to notice how well salt did its job. If curing time is too short, some areas of the large piece of meat will turn grey, some lightly pink and some will be red-pink. That is why we use *cure accelerators* so they can cure and color meat at a much faster rate. Using high production stitch pumping machines and a tumbler a ham can be ready for the smoker in 24 hours.

Wiltshire Curing

Wiltshire curing was an English method of curing whole hog sides in brine. Curing bacterial flora was carefully maintained in the same tank for many years. This of course required laboratory testing. More salt and Nitrate was added when needed and the bacteria living in brine kept reacting with Nitrate. The reaction produced nitrite which kept on curing meat.

Curing with Celery Powder

Saying "no nitrates or nitrites added, other than those which naturally occur in celery powder" is just a different way of packaging nitrite. In order to expand sales, producers came up with variety of "natural" and "organic" processed meats employing the catchy slogan such as "no synthetic preservatives" or "no nitrites added." It is hard to blame an average consumer for believing that if the label says no nitrate/nitrite added, the product is healthier. However, *there is another sentence on the label* marked with asterisk * which should be read as well: *"no nitrites or nitrates added": *except for those naturally occurring nitrates and nitrites in celery powder.*

Why celery? Vegetables which contain most nitrite is spinach, beetroot, lettuces, celery, then in smaller amounts cabbages, potatoes, carrots. After careful studies and trials, it has been determined that celery juice was most suitable for meat products as it did not alter much the finished product flavor or appearance.

How much celery juice powder to add to meat is difficult to evaluate. Adding too little will not cure meat properly and may even create a safety hazard for example when making fermented sausages. It has been generally accepted that adding 0.2% - 0.4% celery juice powder to meat will deliver satisfactory results.

Chapter 3

Comminution Process

The purpose of the comminution process is to cut meat down to the required particle size. The typical machines are:

Dicer - meat is cut into uniform size cubes that may be used in many dishes or specialized sausages. For example Polish Krakowska sausage is done with visible chunks of meat. It is very unlikely that a hobbyist will need such a machine as he can perform the same function with a sharp knife.

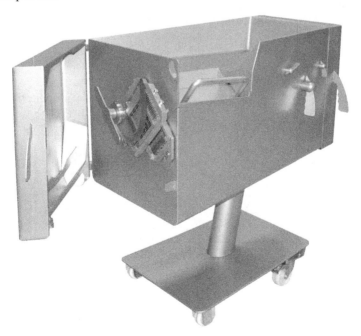

Photo 3.1 Koch SR-1 Turbo Dicer.
Photo courtesy UltraSource/Koch Equipment, Kansas City, MO.

Photo 3.2 Diced ham.   **Photo 3.3** Diced cheese.

Grinder - is the most popular machine that has been around for a long time. There are many commercial brands on the market and some units can grind and mix at the same time which saves time and space. They differ mainly in their output capacity. Grinder as the definition implies, grinds meat and pushes it through the plate, *it does not produce a perfectly clean cut*. There is a large amount of pressure on meat in the feed chamber. This leads to tearing between the auger and the walls of the chamber. As a result the meat is not cut as good as with a bowl cutter. This will be more pronounced when the knife is blunt.

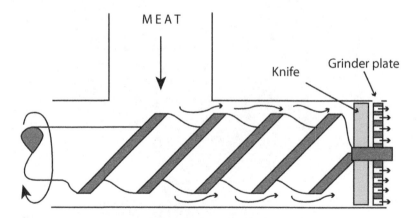

Fig.3.1 Grinder.

It is much easier to grind cold meat taken directly out of the refrigerator. Ideally, meat should always be chilled between 32-35° F (0-2° C) for a clean cut. The fat should be partially frozen or a smeared paste will be produced. When a recipe calls for a second grind, refreeze the first grind and then grind it again. When making emulsified sausages, this operation may be repeated 2-3 times.

Photo 3.4 Thompson 900 Mixer/Grinder is suitable for small to medium processors or supermarkets. Grinder is capable of mincing 4,000 lb of meat per hour.
Photo courtesy UltraSource/Koch Equipment, Kansas City, MO.

At home the manual grinder is the machine of choice. The knife must be sharp, otherwise the meat will smear. The process will come to a stop as the connective tissues will wrap around the knife preventing further cutting. The locking ring on a grinder head should be tight. After a while the meat will lubricate the grinder and the crank will begin to turn with ease. Bear in mind that the grinder, whether electric or manual, generates heat and if it were washed in hot water, it should be cooled off before use.

Home grinders come in the following sizes: 8, 10, 22, 32, number 10 being most popular. It is a fine general purpose grinder for making smaller amounts of sausage. If you think about mincing 20 lbs. of meat or more get #32. It has a bigger throat, bigger knife and bigger plate diameter.

Photo 3.5, above, # 10 grinder.

Fig. 3.2, right, # 22 & 32 grinder.

What grinder to buy?

Although an electrical machine looks impressive, the question to ask is how much meat are we going to process? Manual grinders are wonderfully designed and *very efficient* machines which are very inexpensive. On the other hand, small home type electrical models cost more and work twice as fast at best. The only difference is that you don't have to exercise your hand for 5 minutes. To get any significant output (50 - 100 lb per minute) you have to buy a big industrial model which is heavy and expensive. It is our personal opinion that it is wiser to invest extra money on a quality piston stuffer and grind meats manually. These are general estimates for the output capacity of different grinders:

Manual		Electric (Home Quality)	
Type	Capacity in lb per min.	Type	Capacity in lb per min.
# 10	2-3	# 10	5
# 22	3-4	# 22	9
# 32	4-5	# 32	12

The majority of recipes on the Internet ask for between two and five pounds of meat. This means that most people use less than one pork butt (around 6 lb) of meat. Number 32 manual grinder will perform this task in 1½ minute. Number 10 grinder will do it in 2 minutes. An electrical model will be faster but what's the hurry? If you plan making 50 pounds of sausage, yes, your hand will get tired and the electrical model is a logical choice.

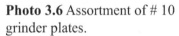

Photo 3.6 Assortment of # 10 grinder plates.

Photo 3.7 Knives for # 10 grinder.

Common grinder plate sizes							
mm	2	3	4	6	10	12	16	19
inch	1/16	1/8	3/16	1/4	3/8	1/2	5/8	3/4

If the recipe calls for a large grinder plate like ¾" and you don't own it, dice meat with a knife, this is how we made sausages in the past.

Bowl cutter - also known as buffalo chopper or silent cutter, can cut meat very finely and is a must have machine for commercial production of emulsified products such as bologna or hot dog.

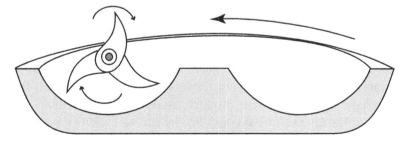

Fig 3.3 Operation of a bowl cutter.

Photo 3.8 Bowl cutter.
Photo courtesy UltraSource/Koch Equipment, Kansas City, MO.

Both the speed of the turning anti-clockwise bowl and rotating knives are adjustable. The stainless steel bowl turns about 14-16 times per minute and the knives rotate about 3,000 times per minute. The resulting friction generates so much heat that the meat will boil and cook. To keep the temperature down the flaked ice is added to the mixture. As the meat is finely comminuted, a lot of protein is released which in combination with salt and phosphates can easily absorb melting ice and resulting water. The mixture becomes a fine paste which after stuffing becomes hot dog, bologna or any emulsified sausage. The bowl cutter can be employed to make any kind of a sausage. No ice or water is added when making fermented sausages given that the technology of making these products is based on the removal of moisture. The temperature is controlled by adding frozen fat and cold meat. Bowl cutters are expensive. At home, emulsified paste can be produced by grinding meat several times through a small grinder plate.

Photo 3.9 Adding spices. The built-in thermometer permits to control temperature of the sausage mass.
Photo courtesy UltraSource/Koch Equipment, Kansas City, MO.

Emulsifying

Emulsion breakdown occurs at 18° C (64° F) and obviously this temperature should not be crossed. A big advantage of using a bowl cutter is that mixing becomes a part of the process.
Basic processing steps during bowl cutting:

- Cut lean meat.
- Add seasonings and ice.
- Add extenders and binders (starch, rusk).

A large amount of meat proteins (mainly *myosin)* are extracted during cutting. They combine with salt and form a protein solution (exudate). *Myosin* is the protein most instrumental for making emulsion, *actin* exhibits preference for binding water. This solution provides the following benefits:

- It immobilizes the added water (ice) and binds it inside meat.
- It coats the particles of fat with a fine layer of protein so they don't clump together.

Proteins are also extracted from collagen rich tissues (skin, sinews, membranes) during the comminution process forming the protein solution. This solution can coat fat particles as well although it is less stable than the *myosin* solution. When heat is applied, collagen shrinks and forms a gelatin which results in some fat particles losing their protective coat. During heat processing the layer of protein solution that covers the fat particles coagulates and firmly entraps them into a newly created lattice. This prevents fat particles from unifying with each other. The ice which was added during cutting is absorbed by meat and the protein solution.

Photo 3.10 Rotating knives generate heat.

Photo 3.11 Flaked ice or cold water is added to control emulsion temperature.

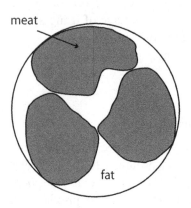

Fig. 3.4 Regular sausage. Coarsely ground lean meat and fat particles are naturally separated.

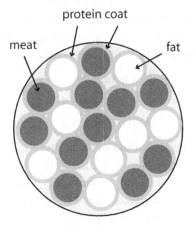

Fig. 3.5 Emulsified sausage. Finely cut lean meat and fat particles are suspended in protein solution.

Chapter 4

Mixing and Stuffing

Mixing introduces spices and flavorings into the previously minced meat. Home based sausage makers use a grinder to mince the meat which is then mixed by hand with other ingredients. The mixer is a must when over 50 lb of sausage is produced as the task is physically demanding. It takes about five minutes to manually mix 10 lb of ground meat. Mixing is not just moving meat and ingredients around, but rather a combination of forceful kneading and squeezing of meat paste until the paste becomes sticky. Some water is usually added to combine dissolved in salt proteins, meat juice and meat paste together.

There are small manually cranked mixers designed for a hobbyist and they will accomodate 25-50 lb of meat. Keep in mind that for limited home production a small mixer has some short comings as it must be washed before and after use and needs a storage space. It makes little sense to go into all this trouble to mix 15 lb of minced sausage mass when the same task can be accomplished in 10 minutes using hands and any suitable container.

Photo 4.1 Koch KFM-220, 220 lb capacity mixer.

Photo courtesy UltraSource/Koch Equipment, Kansas City, MO.

Massaging and Tumbling.

Originally whole cuts of meat were either dry cured or immersed in brine. This required an investment in time and storage space. Today the majority of meats are injected with a solution of salt, nitrite, phosphates, sodium erythorbate and other ingredients and flavors. The operation is performed by a bank of about 30 needles which inject a solution under pressure into the meat. There is a limit to how many needles can be inserted as this procedure creates holes and affects the internal structure of the meat. To evenly distribute the injected solution inside, the tumblers come into play. They offer the following advantages:

- Curing solution is distributed evenly inside of the meat.
- Curing times are greatly reduced.
- Mechanical action leads to stronger extraction of meat proteins and more exudate is created which helps in binding meat cuts together.

All tumblers employ a similar principle of operation: a set of paddles rotate inside of a tank moving meat pieces around. There are units that operate under a vacuum that further improve the results.

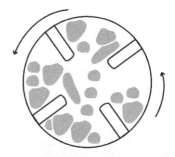

Photo 4.2 Koch LT-60 Vacuum tumbler, 1000 lbs. capacity. *Photo courtesy UltraSource/Koch Equipment, Kansas City, MO.*

Fig. 4.1 Tumbler operation. A good tumbler must have a diameter of at least 3 feet, otherwise there is little impact to falling meat pieces.

The tumbler is a machine with a rotating drum. The meat pieces bounce around its moving walls providing better brine distribution inside of the meat. Tumblers normally are horizontal units where meats are struck by the paddles, fall down and are moved up again by the rotating paddles. A tumbler resembles a cloth dryer which moves wet clothing around by means of a rotating drum with paddles.

Through the use of vacuum tumbling, meat, poultry, fish, and seafood processors can produce ready to cook, value added products while reducing labor content and increasing product yields. Vacuum tumbling offers improvements to product sliceability, curing color, and overall product juiciness and tenderness which results in higher profitability. Small products (below 2.5 inches in diameter) can be *marinated and tumbled* within minutes. Large (2.5 inches or larger) products can be marinated using a combination of injection and tumbling. Large whole muscle meats are normally injected with brine. The primary purpose of tumbling these products is the optimal protein extraction which will allow individual pieces of meat to stick together during the cooking process. Due to renewed public interest in making quality products at home, smaller tumblers (8 and 15 lb) are carried by distributors of sausage making equipment and supplies.

Massagers generally are vertical units and offer more delicate action than tumblers. Meat pieces rub against each other or the surface wall of the massager without loss of contact. Although the actual massaging or tumbling time is only about 1-3 hours, this action is continuously interrupted and meats are allowed to rest. The process generally continues for about 24 hours at low temperatures. The machines are normally loaded 1/2 - 2/3 capacity. Due to their gentler mode of operation, massagers need more time than tumblers to perform the same task.

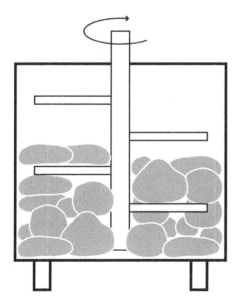

Fig. 4.2 Massager.

Photo 4.3 Koch equipment stainless steel Magnum Series 6000 massager with 6000 liter capacity.

Photo courtesy UltraSource/Koch Equipment, Kansas City, MO.

The machine comes standard with cooling and is equipped with a uniquely designed baffle that rotates and slides the product throughout the drum during processing. This results in the product remaining against the walls and baffles of the drum versus the actual tumbling delivered by competitor models. The advantage is a more gentle massaging action while extracting protein in a highly efficient manner under constant vacuum.

Benefits:

- Improved product quality (juicier, more tender, and flavorful).

- Increased profit margins through the delivery of ready-to-cook, value-added products.

- Increased productivity through reduced handling/processing time.

Stuffing. There is a distinct difference between stuffing requirements of a commercial meat plant, little butcher shop and a home sausage maker.

- Meat plants need a machine that will stuff, link and portion sausages in one cycle. Sausages must be of the same length and weight otherwise it would be impossible to estimate costs and run the business. Such machines are very expensive and can stuff thousands of pounds of sausage in one hour. The piston is powered by hydraulic pressure and the machine is controlled with a foot or a knee.

- Butcher shops do not care much about linking and portioning sausages as the experienced sausage maker can fast link sausages by hand. Drawing on his experience he can estimate the weight of one foot of a particular diameter sausage. In addition the salesperson will weigh each order on a scale. What is important is that the stuffer performs faultlessly and is easy to operate and maintain. Such stuffers can be manually operated or can be hooked up to a motor.

- Home sausage makers are concerned with the cost of the equipment and end up stuffing sausages with a grinder and the attached stuffing tube. This is a labor consuming operation that requires two persons. Recently, many manually operated piston stuffers (5-20 lb capacity) have entered the market-place. They are inexpensive, reliable and some of them can be motorized.

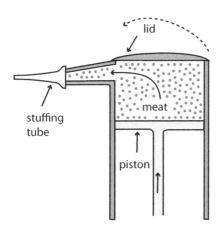

The lid is raised and the meat mass is loaded. Knee operated switch supplies hydraulic pressure to the piston which forces meat up to the stuffing tube.

Fig. 4.3 Hydraulic piston stuffer.

Photo 4.4 - left. SC-50 Hydraulic piston stuffer.
Photo 4.5 - top. Volumetric portioner for constant sausage weight. *Photos courtesy Ultra-Source/Koch Equipment, Kansas City, MO.*

Photo 4.6. Stuffing and linking in progress.
Photo courtesy UltraSource/Koch Equipment, Kansas City, MO.

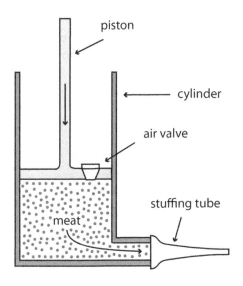

Fig. 4.4 Manually cranked piston stuffer.

Piston is manually raised up and the cylinder is detached from the base for loading. There isn't any lid on top of the cylinder. The cylinder is inserted back into the base and the piston is lowered down. By cranking the handle the gear forces the piston down the cylinder pushing meat in through the stuffing tube. Any air that might be compressed by the piston and delivered into the sausage escapes through the air valve.

Photo 4.7 - top, stuffing tubes.

Photo 4.8 - left, 15-lb capacity manual stuffer.

Vertical stuffers come from 5 lb to 25 lb capacity. Bigger units can be equipped with an electrical motor.

There are also small capacity horizontal piston stuffers, usually 5 lb capacity, but they are less popular.

The majority of hobbyists stuff sausages using grinders and the attached stuffing tube. This arrangement has served us well for centuries, but it is a labor consuming operation normally requiring two persons.

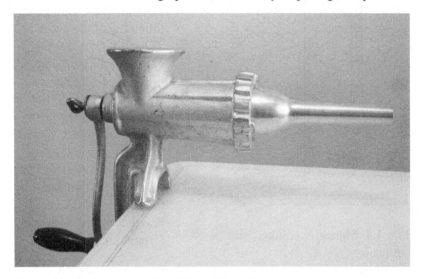

Photo 4.9 Number 10 grinder with stuffing tube.

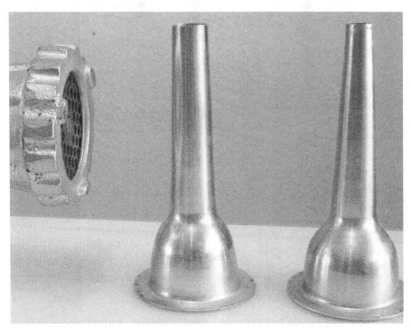

Photo 4.10 Number 10 grinder accepts different sized tubes.

Fig. 4.5 Spacer. Knife and grinder plate are always removed for stuffing. It is a good idea to insert the spacer, although not absolutely necessary. Spacers hold the auger shaft and prevent the unit from wobbling.

There is a small (3-5 lb) vertical elbow shaped stuffer which we do not recommend. It is our opinion than a serious hobbyist should invest in a *vertical piston stuffer* which will make stuffing faster and more enjoyable. The money that is saved by not buying an electrically operated grinder can be reinvested into a purchase of a piston stuffer. By all means if you can afford it, buy all top of the line industrial automated equipment, but keep in mind that a manual grinder is an incredibly efficient device that can be successfully deployed in any production that requires 20 pounds or less of sausage.

Casings. Casings can be divided into two groups:

- Natural casings.
- Synthetic casings.

It is impossible to match the quality of natural casings. They can be used for almost any product. The biggest advantage of using natural casings is that they shrink equally with the meat and thus are great for making dry or semi-dry salami or sausages. That leaves their use to smaller butchers or sausage makers and it is the preferred choice for a home producer. Another advantage is that they are edible and you don't even feel them when eating a well made smoked sausage.

The main reason that commercial manufacturers cannot use natural casings is the fact that they are not uniform and have a different diameter, texture and length. They also have a tendency to produce a curved sausage, especially beef rounds. The meat plant even knowing the length of the sausage, cannot precisely estimate the weight of meat it contains and by the same token cannot arrive at the correct price. And you cannot run a business when no two samples are alike. Natural casings are usually packed and stored in salt. Before use they should be rinsed on the outside and flushed out with water inside. Then they should be left for 30 minutes in a water filled container.

That removes more salt from the casings and makes them softer and easier to work with. Natural casings are usually obtained from pigs, cattle and sheep and can be generally classified as:

Small intestine casings	Large intestine casings	Other
hog and sheep casings, beef rounds (runners)	hog and beef middles, bungs	stomach, bladder

Hog Casings

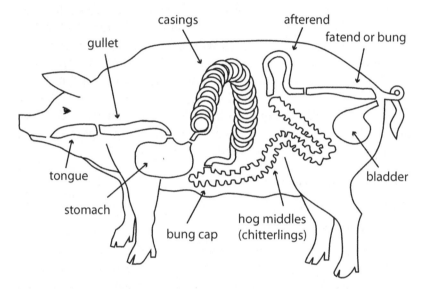

Fig. 4.6 Hog casings.

Casings	Middles	Bungs or fatends
30-32 mm, frankfurter, break-fast sausage, Italian sausage	45 - 50 mm, Italian salami (frisses), blood sausage, sopressata	50 - 90 mm, liver, Braunschweiger
32-35 mm, bratwurst, bock-wurst, Italian sausage	50-60 mm, dry salami, liver sausage	
35-38 mm, knockwurst, Polish sausage, bratwurst, pepperoni	60-70, cooked Braunschweiger	
38-44 mm, Polish sausage, summer sausage, ring bolo-gna, liverwurst, pepperoni		

Hog casings are sold in "bundles" or "hanks." This unit of measure equals approximately 91 meters. One bundle of 38 mm casing will accommodate about 132 lbs. (60 kg) of meat.

Beef Casings

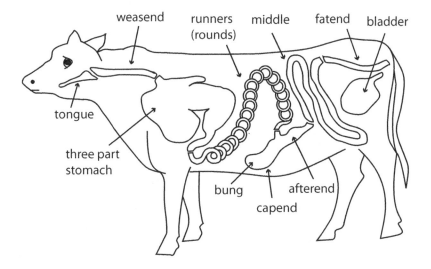

Fig. 4.7 Beef casings.

Rounds	Middles	Bung Caps
35-46 mm, ring Bologna, ring liver, blood sausage, Polish Sausage, Holsteiner	45-65 mm, Bologna, dry and semi-dry cervelats, dry and cooked Salami	76-126 mm, large Bologna, Lebanon Bologna, cooked salami, Mortadella

Beef casings are tougher than hog casings and should be soaked in water longer. When making fermented sausages beef casings also have a higher tendency to become slimy during fermentation or the drying stage. This is a minor inconvenience and the slime is simply wiped off.

- Beef rounds - are the small intestines and derive their name from their characteristic "ring" or "round" shape.

- Beef middles - are the large and straight intestines.

- Beef bungs - are used for making large sausages like mortadella or large bologna.

• Beef bladders - are the largest casings and will hold up to
14 lb (6.5 kg) of sausage. They are used for mortadella,
pepperoni and minced ham sausages.

Sheep Casings

Sheep casings are the highest quality small diameter casings used for
sausages such as: Bockwurst, frankfurters, wieners, Polish Kabanosy
and breakfast sausage links. These casings combine tenderness with
sufficient strength to withstand the filling, cooking and smoking
operations. Their diameter varies from 18 - 28 mm.

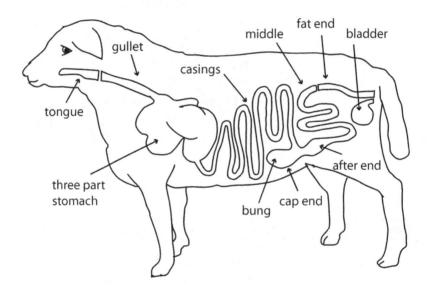

Fig. 4.8 Sheep casings.

For a hobbyist natural casings are hard to beat. They are tender, they
can be used for any type of a sausage, and will last almost indefinitely
when salted and kept under refrigeration. Natural casings can be
reused even if they have been soaked. Just apply regular table salt to
the casings, place them in an air tight container such as a zip-lock and
refrigerate. Don't freeze as this will damage their structure and will
weaken them.

Typical use for natural casings

Hog casings

- Small casings - fresh sausage, Bockwurst, Polish sausage, frankfurters, and chorizos.
- Hog middles - are the large intestines of a pig, also called chitterlings. They are used for making dry sausages.
- Hog bungs - are the colon of the pig. They are used for liver sausage and dry sausages such as milano, gothaer, and salami Arles.
- Hog stomachs - head cheese.
- Hog bladders - luncheon meats.

Beef casings

- Round (small casing), middle, and bung (blind end).
- Bladders - luncheon meats and mortadella.
- Rounds - ring bologna, holsteiner, mettwurst.
- Middles - bologna, cervelat, blood sausage.
- Weasands (the lining of the esophagus or passage to the stomach) - long bologna and salami.

Sheep casings

- Casings - meat sticks, kabanosy, wieners.

Note that beef and sheep possess a three part stomach making it difficult for use. Pork stomach consists of a one chamber with two entrances and has been traditionally used for making head cheeses. One opening would be sewn with butcher's twine, the casing would be stuffed and the second opening would be sewn off.

Synthetic Casings

Artificial casings are inedible and don't require refrigeration. They can be made in a variety of colors and diameters. White casings can be used for liver sausage, red for bologna, some casings come pre-printed, for example casings with deer antlers can be used for sausages made from wild game meat. Before use cellulose casings and other artificial casings should be immersed for 30 minutes in room temperature water to facilitate stuffing.

Synthetic casings are straight, consistent in diameter, require less preparation and are easier to stuff. Those are good reasons why they are used by commercial manufacturers.

Name	Description	Use
Collagen 16-140 mm	made from collagen which is the main ingredient of connective tissue, skin and bones. The casings are made from beef hides. There are several types of collagen casings on the market today. There are edible casings for making fresh and smoked sausages. Can be used for *smoked or dried sausages.*	**Edible:** breakfast links, wieners, frankfurters, fresh sausages. **Non-edible:** ring style sausages, salami, good substitute for beef middles.
Cellulose 15-44 mm	strong, can be used for *smoked or air dried sausages.*	**Non-edible:** skinless hotdogs and frankfurters.
Fibrous 38-198 mm	come in different colors and are popular among processors who don't smoke sausages with natural wood but instead add liquid smoke. A mahogany colored casing looks like if it were smoked. Casings exhibit excellent permeability for smoke penetration and moisture evaporation and can be used *for smoked or dried sausages.*	**Non-edible:** summer sausage, salami, pepperoni, bologna.
Plastic 18-152 mm	provide barriers to moisture, smoke and oxygen to maximize shelf life and minimize off flavors of prepared foods. They can be used for cooked products such as liver sausage, ham or cooked salami. Can NOT be used for *smoked or dried sausages.*	**Non-edible:** Liver sausage, Mortadella, Cooked Salami.
Hukki 40-200 mm	available in different net patterns for a traditional look of the products. Hukki are made as collagen (edible and not), cellulose, fibrous or plastic casings and the definition does not imply a new material but an unusual and decorative shape of the casing.	**Non-edible** (plastic): for cooked products. **Edible:** (fibrous) for smoked or dried products.

Chapter 5

Smoking Process

Smoking - Reasons

Man discovered that in addition to salting and curing with nitrates, smoking was a very effective tool in preserving meats. Besides enhancing the taste and look, it also increases its longevity by slowing down the spoilage of fat and growth of bacteria. Smoking meat leads to more water loss, and results in a saltier and drier product, which naturally increases its shelf life. The advantages of smoking meat are numerous:

- Slows down the growth of bacteria.
- Prevents fats from developing a rancid taste.
- Extends the shelf life of the product.
- Develops a new taste and flavor.
- Changes the color; smoked products shine and look better.

Smoked fish develops a beautiful golden color. The meat on the outside becomes a light brown, red, or almost black depending on the type of wood used, heating temperatures, and total time smoking. The smell in an ethnic meat store specializing in smoked products can be overwhelming. This experience is not shared with our supermarkets since their products are rarely naturally smoked and they are vacuum-sealed to prolong shelf life. This unfortunately locks the aroma in.

The main reason to smoke meat at home today is to produce a product that cannot be obtained in a typical store. One can order traditionally made products on the Internet, but they will be very expensive. It is estimated that in the USA smoked meats account for about 30% of meats sold. And hot dogs and frankfurters constitute the largest portion of this number, though few people ever think of them as a smoked product.

Understanding Smoking Process

Smoking meat is exactly what the name implies: *flavoring meat with smoke. Using any kind of improvised device* will do the job as long as the smokehouse is made from environmentally safe material. As long as smoke contacts the meat surface it will impart its flavor to the meat. The strength of the flavor depends mainly on the time and density of the smoke. *Smoking may or may not be followed by cooking.* Generally we may say that smoking consists of two steps:

1. Smoking.

2. Cooking - this step determines the design and quality of your smokehouse as it needs temperature controls, a reliable heat supply and good insulation to hold the temperature when the weather gets cold. After smoking is done we increase the temperature to about 170° F (76° C) to start cooking. The smoked meats must be cooked to 155° F (69° C) internal temperature and here the quality and insulation of the smoker plays an important role. Nevertheless, the main smoking process is performed below 160° F (71° C). Smoked meats are usually eaten cold at a later date. Many great recipes require that smoked products hang for a designated time to lose more weight to become drier. It is only then that they are ready for consumption. We know now that the smoked meat must be cooked, but *does that mean that it must be cooked inside of the smokehouse?* Don't we have factory built electrical or gas stoves inside every kitchen? They are insulated, have built-in temperature controls and are almost begging for these smoked sausages to be baked inside. How about putting your smoked meats into a pot full of hot water and cooking these products on top of the stove?

Smoking Methods

Cold Smoking

Continuous smoking at 52-71° F (12-22° C), from 1-14 days, applying *thin smoke* with occasional breaks in between, is one of the oldest preservation methods. We cannot produce cold smoke if the outside temperature is 90° F (32° C), unless we can cool it down, which is what some industrial smokers do. *Cold smoking is a drying process* whose purpose is to remove moisture thus preserving a product. You will find that different sources provide different temperatures for cold smoking. In European countries where most of the cold smoking is done, the upper temperature is accepted as 86° F (30° C). The majority of Russian, Polish and German meat technology books call for 71° F (22° C), some books ask for 77° F (25° C). Cold smoking assures us of total smoke penetration inside of the meat. The loss of moisture also is uniform in all areas and the total weight loss falls within 5-20% depending largely on the smoking time. Cold smoking is not a continuous process, it is stopped a few times to allow fresh air into the smoker. In XVIII century brick built smokehouses a fire was started every morning. It smoldered as long as it could and if it stopped, it would be restarted again the following morning.

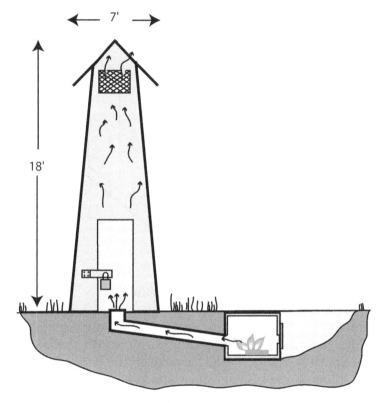

Fig. 5.1 Old Polish smokehouse.

Cold smoked meats prevent or slow down the spoilage of fats, which increases their shelf life. The product is drier and saltier with a more pronounced smoky flavor and very long shelf life. The color varies from yellow to dark brown on the surface and dark red inside.

Cold smoked products are not submitted to the cooking process. If you want to cold smoke your meats, bear in mind that with the exception of people living in areas with a cold climate like Alaska, it will have to be done in the winter months.

Fig. 5.2 American XVIII century smokehouse.

Dry wood should be used for cold smoking. Once the moisture content drops low enough, the salt present in the meat will further inhibit the development of bacteria and the products can hang in the air for months losing more moisture as time goes by.

Lox (salmon) is smoked with cold smoke for an extended period of time. In general, fish starts to cook at 85° F (29.4° C), so exceeding this temperature will cook the salmon: the flavor will change and we will not be able to slice it so thin anymore. Cold smoking is a slow process and the hams, which lend themselves perfectly to this type of smoking, can be smoked from 2 to even 6 weeks. During smoking they will acquire a golden color along with a smoky flavor.

Photo 5.1 & 5.2 Cold smoking at its best. Waldemar Kozik is making meat products of the highest quality at the Catskill Mountains of New York. There is no room for chemicals, binders or colorants here, just quality meats, Mother Nature and the art of smoking of Mr. Waldemar. The same way it has been done for centuries, the right way.

Warm Smoking

Continuous smoking at 73-104° F, (23-40° C), from 4-48 hours depending on the diameter of the meat, humidity 80%, and *medium smoke*. The weight loss varies between 2-10%, with the difference being largely dependent on the time spent smoking. The surface of the product becomes quite dry but the inside remains raw. Because of the warm smoke, the product receives more smoke in its outside layers. This dry second skin helps increase shelf life, as well as prevent the loss of its natural juices. The color ranges from yellow to brown and has a little shine due to some fat moving outwards.

Warm smoke temperatures lie within the The Danger Zone (40-140° F, 5-60° C), which is the range of temperatures where all bacteria grow very fast. Optimum growing conditions for the infamous *Clostridium botulinum* are 78-95° F, (26-35° C), but will still grow at 113° F, 45° C. To avoid the possibility of the growth of *Cl. botulinum* sodium nitrite (Cure #1 or 2) should always be added to smoked meats.

Hot Smoking

Continuous smoking at 105-140° F, (41-60° C), 0.5-2 hours, 5-12% weight loss, *heavy smoke*. This is not recommended for large pieces of meat that are expected to be stored for a long time. Although it is the fastest method, there is not enough time for adequate smoke penetration. This results in higher moisture content, reducing the product's shelf life. This type of smoking can be divided into three separate phases:

1. Drying out the surface of the meat for 10-40 min at 112-130° F, (45-55° C), without smoke, although some very light thin smoke is acceptable. If stuffed sausages are kept for 1-2 hours at room temperature, their surface may be sufficiently dry to receive hot smoke. Besides drying out the surface of the meat, the temperature speeds up nitrite curing. Keep in mind that the draft controls must be fully opened to eliminate any moisture residing inside of the smoker. Applying smoke at temperatures higher than 130-140° F, (54-60° C) will prematurely dry out the casings on the surface of the meat and will create a barrier to smoke penetration.

2. This is the proper smoking stage at 112-140° F, (45-60° C)   for 30-90 min, using medium to heavy smoke. The color becomes a light yellow to dark brown with a shade of red. In this state, the natural casings become strong and fit snugly on the sausages.

3. Baking the sausage at 140-176° F, (60-80° C) for about 10-20 min. Temperatures as high as 194° F (90° C) are permitted for a short period of time. Proteins are denatured in the outside layers of the product, but the inside remains raw with temperatures reaching only 104° F (40° C). Natural casings fit very snugly, become shiny, and develop a few wrinkles. This is a welcomed scenario; lots of smoked products are subsequently slow cooked in water. Acting like a barrier, the drier and stronger casings prevent the loss of juices. This type of cooking (poaching) is more economical to baking (less weight loss).

If a smoker is used, the temperature in the last stages of the hot smoking process is increased to 167-194° F (75-90° C) until the inside of the meat reaches 154° F (68° C). This is the fastest and most common method of smoking. Because of a relatively short smoking time, hot smoked products should be kept in a refrigerator and consumed relatively quickly. The above smoking times apply to a regular size sausage (32-26 mm) and smoking times for a thin meat stick or a large diameter sausage, have to be accordingly readjusted. There is no fixed rule dictating the length of smoking; it depends on the diameter of the sausage and the desired color.

Wet Smoking

Smoked meats lose around 10% moisture during the smoking process. This depends on temperature, the length of smoking and humidity in the smokehouse. Eliminating moisture was important when the products were cold smoked for preservation purposes. Nowadays, the importance of preserving meats by dehydration plays the secondary role, as losing moisture means decreasing weight that in turn leads to decreased profits. To prevent this loss, commercial manufacturers pump meats with water and recirculate moist air through the smokehouse. Ready made charcoal briquettes or electric heating elements produce no moisture, thus placing a water filled pan inside of the smoker is of some help. This method is very common when barbecuing or smoking meats in commercially produced little smokers.

Fresh air contains moisture which cools sausage casings or the surface of the meat. When smoking with an open fire, lots of fresh air enters the smoker and keeps the meat from drying out. No matter how pretty a small factory unit may be, it will not be able to perform the same duty without a little help from a water pan. Given that at the sea level water boil at the constant temperature of 212° F (100° C), placing a water filled pan inside of a small smoker will also help regulate temperature inside. Bear in mind that this is too high a temperature for smoking quality meats and sausages. In short, *wet smoking is the type of smoking that employs a water dish placed inside of the smoker to increase humidity levels.* Dampening wood chips before smoking will produce a similar effect.

Wood contains always at least 20% moisture, even when perfectly dried on the outside. During the first stage of combustion this wood dries out and any remaining moisture evaporates with the smoke into the chamber. Once the wood has burned out, the remaining charcoal has no water left, and the only moisture the smokehouse gets is brought by the outside air. In dry climates known for little humidity the smoked product will benefit from extra moisture. Keep in mind that the surface of smoked meats or sausages *must not be wet* during the smoking process.

Smoking Without Nitrates

Sodium nitrite (Cure #1) is the most effective agent for preventing the growth of *Clostridium botulinum. Clostridium botulinum* bacteria need moisture, warm temperatures and the *absence of oxygen* in order to grow. For those who smoke meats without cures, it will be advisable to smoke them at temperatures well above the danger zone (>160° F, 72° C). The end product will not be pink but will exhibit a typical grayish color of cooked meat. Barbecued meats are smoked at much higher temperatures which eliminates the danger of *Clostridium botulinum* producing toxins. Those who insist on smoking meats without nitrates, should be aware that the internal meat temperature trails the temperature of the smokehouse by about 25° F and to be on the outside of the danger zone, the smoking must be performed at temperatures higher than 170° F (77° C) which becomes *cooking with smoke.* These are prevalent conditions in a small self contained smoker, where incoming air is kept at minimum in order for the sawdust to smolder and not to burst into the flames.

A large outside smokehouse with a separate fire pit is at a smaller risk as there is an ample flow of *fresh air* that enters smoking chamber together with the smoke. Using dry wood increases safety as less moisture will be created.

Note: replacing nitrate with celery powder is covered in Chapter 2 Curing and Nitrates - Curing with Celery Powder.

Smoke Generation

Smoke can be generated by:

- Burning firewood. Due to the danger of flames this method is limited to smokers with a separate fire pit.
- Heating wood chips or sawdust with an electrical wire (barbecue starter). Once started they will keep on smoldering and the wire starter is not needed anymore.
- Heating wood chips or sawdust over a gas flame or placing wood chips over hot coals. This method is commonly used when barbecuing meats.

Photo 5.3 Hot plate.

Photo 5.5 Gas burner.

Photo 5.4 Barbecue starter.

Photo 5.6 Smoke Daddy™ air pump smoke generator.

The preferred method to handle wood chips or sawdust is to place them in a stainless steel pan, about 10-12" in diameter, not higher than 4", otherwise smoke may be too hot. To sustain smoke production more wood chips must be added. The wood chips should be kept together in a conical pile so that they will smolder and not burn. The moment they spread they come in contact with more air and are more inclined to burn. The same applies when adding wood chips directly on hot coals or ashes, keep them in a pile and if the flames start to grow bigger, add more wood chips to cut off the supply of fresh air. After a while a natural rhythm of adding sawdust will be established and the whole process will go on smoothly.

If smoking stops, the barbecue starter or hot plate is reconnected again. If the sawdust bursts into flames, any common spray bottle can bring it under control. All small and medium size factory made smokers use these methods to generate smoke. Commercial units employ a free standing smoke generation unit that is connected with the smoker by a short pipe and an electrical blower blows the smoke into the smoker. Industrial smokehouses choose different methods of smoke generation but that does not necessarily mean that the quality is better. One method involves pressing blocks of pressed sawdust against rotating wheels. The resistance creates high temperatures and the block of wood starts to smoke. It's like cutting a piece of wood with a dull saw blade; it starts to smoke because of the heat generated.

Wood For Smoking

The wood used for smoking should be relatively new and kept in a well ventilated but covered area. A freshly cut tree contains 50% moisture, the dried wood about 25%. That level of dryness requires about 6–9 months of drying. Wet wood can be recognized immediately because of the hissing sound it creates when burned. This is escaping vapor and boiling particles of water. To achieve moisture contents of 20% or less, the wood must be oven dried.

Any hardwood is fine, but evergreen trees like fir, spruce, pine, or others cause problems. They contain too much resin and the finished product has a turpentine flavor to it. It also develops a black color due to the extra soot from the smoke, which in turn makes the smoker dirtier, too. This wood will burn quickly and cleanly, but will not be suitable for smoking. However, there is a region in Germany called Bavaria where they have been using evergreen for centuries.

They have acquired this taste in childhood and they are very fond of it even though most people don't like it. And of course you cannot use any wood that was previously pressure treated, painted, or commercially manufactured. The type of wood used is responsible for the final color of the smoked product and it can also influence its taste. All fruit and citrus trees have a light to medium sweet flavor and are excellent with poultry and ham. Many say that cherry wood is the best. *Oak, available all over the world, is probably the most commonly used wood for smoking.* It produces a brown color. If hickory is used, the color will have a more vivid red tint in it. Wood types can be mixed to create custom flavors. For instance, walnut, which has a heavy smoke flavor, can be mixed with apple wood to create a milder version. For practical reasons a home sausage maker will probably use oak or hickory most of the time. Some sausages like German or Polish Hunter Sausages develop their characteristic flavors and aromas by adding juniper branches or berries to the fire. Juniper is the main ingredient for making gin, so we know it has to be a fine element.

Dry or Wet Wood

Here is another question that never seems to go out of fashion: "what's better, wet or dry". Wet chips or sawdust, seem to produce more smoke but this is not true. The extra amount of smoke is nothing else but water vapor (steam) mixed with smoke. This does make a difference when hot smoking at 105-140° F, (40-60° C) and the smoke times are rather short. That extra moisture prevents the sausage casings from drying out during smoking. Besides, wet chips are not going to be wet for very long; the heat will dry them out anyhow. Wood chips produce good smoke when wet and they decrease temperature, but the moment they become dry, they burst into flames and the temperature shoots up. The grease from the sausage drops down on the little flames, the temperature goes up, and the once little flames are now big flames. In one minute we may have a raging fire inside the smoker.

When a smoker has a separate standing fire pit, large pieces of wood can be burned as the resulting flames will never make it inside the smoker. As you already know, we don't use wet wood for cold smoking because we want to eliminate moisture, not bring it in. Cold smoke warms the surface of the meat up very finely, just enough to allow the moisture to evaporate. Applying cold smoke for two days with wet wood will impede drying the meat. When hot smoking, the smoke along with the air is drying out the casings, which develops a harder surface. The surface of the meat will become drier, too. By using wet wood when hot smoking, we moisten the surface of the product, aiding the smoking.

Wood Pieces, Wood Chips or Sawdust

The type of wood used will largely depend on the smoker used, and the location of the fire pit. With a separately located fire pit it makes little difference what type of wood is burned as this design can take a lot of abuse and still provides efficient and comfortable smoke generation. Most people that use these types of smokers don't even bother with chips or sawdust and burn solid wood logs instead. Burning wood inside of small one-unit smokers creates the danger of a fire erupting so a safety baffle should be installed. This would also prevent fat from dripping down on the wood chips and starting a fire. When preparing sawdust, do not throw it into water, but place it in a bucket and then moisten it using a spray bottle.

Mix sawdust by hand until it feels moist. Sawdust burns longer and at lower temperatures than other woods and is the material of choice in small electrical smokers. When smoking in a home made barrel smoker with a fire pit in the bottom part of the drum, it is much easier to control the smoking process by using dry chips. These smolder and burn in a more predictable manner.

To Bark or Not to Bark

Bark of the birch tree produces a lot of soot when it burns. Alder or oak bark is fine. Powdered bark of some trees have been used for medicinal purposes: (willow tree-aspirin, cinchona tree - source of quinine to fight malaria or to make tonic water) and they all taste bitter. When in doubt remove the bark.

Smoking Temperatures

Smoking temperature is one of the most important factors in deciding quality. There is no steadfast rule that dictates exact temperature ranges for different types of smoking. A few degrees one way or the other should not create any problem as long as the hot smoking upper temperature limit is not crossed. Crossing this limit will significantly affect the look and the taste of the product. When smoking, the inside temperature of the smoker cannot exceed 170° F (78° C) for any extended time. At this temperature, fat starts to melt quickly. Once it melts, the sausage inside will be a mass of bread crumbs, have a greasy outside, will lose its shine, and will have an inferior taste. If your sausage:

- Is greasy on the outside.
- Contains spots of grease under the sausage.
- Is too shriveled and wrinkled.
- Has lost its shine and looks opaque.
- Is crumbly inside with little empty pockets.

- it means that the internal temperature of the sausage was too high during smoking or cooking. The fats start to melt at very low temperatures and we don't want them to boil and leak through the casings. When faced with excessive temperatures, they begin to melt, and there is no way to undo the damage.

Smoke Deposition

The amount of smoke deposited on a product is influenced by:

- Smoke density - the thicker the smoke, the faster the rate of smoke deposition.
- Smokehouse relative humidity - high humidity favors smoke deposition but inhibits color development.
- The surface condition of the product - moist surface favors smoke but limits color development.
- Smokehouse temperature - higher temperature favors smoke deposition rate.
- Air draft - sufficient air velocity is needed to bring smoke inside. Too fast air might reduce smoke density, not enough air speed and product may be over smoked.

Humidity Control

Meat weight loss (moisture) is directly linked to the temperature and humidity and it is of great importance that we learn how to manipulate those two factors. Regulating humidity in a home made smokehouse can be done indirectly, and is relatively simple and cost free. When smoking in a home made smokehouse the humidity can be controlled by:

- Choosing the time of smoking.
- Placing a water filled pan inside the smoker.
- Using moist wood chips or sawdust.

The amount of needed humidity is dictated by:

- Type of a product - hot smoked sausage, cold smoked sausage, smoked and air-dried ham, or just air-dried ham.
- The smoking method that will be employed.

There is more humidity in areas containing many lakes, rivers or being close to the sea shore. Arid areas such as deserts or mountains have less water and subsequently less humidity. As you cannot change the physical location of the smokehouse, you have to learn how to go around it and how to choose the time of smoking to your maximum advantage. The most important rule to remember is that *when the temperature goes up, the humidity goes down.* When the temperature goes down, the humidity goes up (night). When the clouds come in and it starts to drizzle, the humidity will go up immediately.

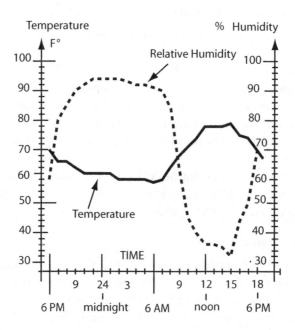

Fig. 5.3 Humidity and temperature changes recorded in Florida on November 10/11, 2006.

Photo 5.7 -7 AM, fog,
90% humidity.

Photo 5.8 - 8 AM, clear,
84% humidity.

In a home refrigerator the humidity remains at about 45% at 40° F (4° C) and in a freezer it is about 70% at 0° F (-18° C). In an air-conditioned room the humidity remains at 40-45%. Different smoking methods require different humidity levels; in dry climates like Nevada, New Mexico or Arizona the relative humidity stays low at 15-20% during the day so the solution is to place a water pan inside of the smoker and use moist wood chips. The best solution is to smoke at night time when the temperature will drop and the humidity will increase.

Photo 5.9 Simple humidity tester.

How Long to Smoke?

There isn't one universal time, use your own judgement and keep records. When cold smoking, the times are very long, days or even weeks as the purpose of cold smoking is to preserve the product for future use by removing moisture. There are not many people today that will have the time or patience to smoke products in this manner but those that will try it will be richly rewarded by creating products of different texture and flavor.

When hot smoking, the times are short as we smoke and then cook the product trying to achieve the best flavor. The diameter of the meat piece or sausage will be a deciding factor here but you can estimate smoking time by checking the color of the smoked piece as well. Sausages have a small diameter so the times are relatively short. For example, Kabanosy meat stick is stuffed into 24-26 mm sheep casings and 1 hour smoking time is plenty. Polish Smoked sausage stuffed in 36 mm hog casings will need about 1-2 hours. If the color of the sausage is yellow it is lightly smoked, if it is light brown the sausage is nicely smoked, if the color becomes dark brown the sausage is heavily smoked.

Smoking Meats

Traditionally smoked meats come almost always from cured parts of pork. The most popular large cuts used for smoking are ham, bacon, butt, loin, back fat and smaller parts such as hocks and jowls. Ribs are usually barbecued. Due to their large size those popular cuts require longer curing times although those times can be somewhat shortened when needle pumping precedes the common wet curing method. Hams can be dry or wet cured, butts and loins are normally wet cured and bacon and back fat are commonly dry cured. Trimmings end up for making sausages. Poultry tastes great when smoked, but nothing improves the looks and taste of a product more than smoking fish.

Photo 5.10 Cold meats are usually eaten cold.

Building Smokehouse

A smokehouse is just a tool but smoking is time, temperature, and humidity, and how you control those parameters. The tool does not make a quality product - YOU DO! If you understand the smoking process you will create a top quality product in any smoker and in any conditions. And making quality products depends on meat selection, curing, smoking, cooking temperatures and other processing steps. Each step influences the step that follows, and all those steps when performed correctly will, as a final result, create the quality product. Almost any smokehouse will do for home production. If you see smoke sipping through your cardboard box, *you are smoking meat*, it is that simple. It does not have to be perfectly tight if the cooking process will be performed somewhere else. Commercial manufacturers make thousands of pounds of product an hour and they work by different rules to be cost effective. They have to produce a constant quality product that will be accepted every day by the supermarkets. They need fancy computerized equipment which costs millions of dollars. A hobbyist is not bound by those rules as he has plenty of time to watch smoke going out of his paper box smoker.

Any design will do as long as it supplies smoke. Things get more complicated if you want to cook meats inside the smokehouse. There are books about building smokers that offer plans and detailed information, for example our own "Meat Smoking and Smokehouse Design." All distributors of sausage making equipment and supplies offer smokers designed for home use.

Basic Parts of a Smoker

Every smoker, no matter how simple or sophisticated, consists of the following parts:

- A source of smoke (fire pit).
- A smoking chamber (enclosure that confines smoke inside).
- Smokesticks, hooks or screens.
- Draft controls (dampers).

The most important parts are the smoke generator (fire pit) and the smoke chamber. They could be part of the same unit or they could stand separately. With smaller smokers it is difficult to control the heating process by burning wood unless an electrical heating element or a gas burner is used.

Without a doubt the most popular design is the 55 gallon drum smoker. Its well deserved popularity is due to the fact that it is:

- Easy to find and is practically free.
- Almost finished with the hardest work done by the factory.
- Very strong, made of metal.
- Versatile, can be used as a smoker, woodstove, or heating stove.
- Resistant to heat, lends itself to be used as a fire pit.
- Easy to work with – no need for technical skills nor specialized tools, the bottom can be cut out with a chisel and a hammer (top in many cases is removable).

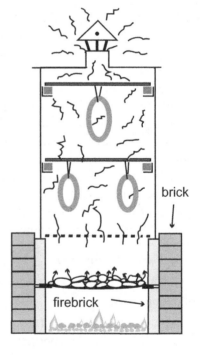

Photo 5.11 - top, the base. Vertical bricks are firebricks. Screen on top.
Fig. 5.4 - right, the base.

brick

firebrick →

Wood Fired Smoker

Using firewood to slowly bring the temperature to 170° F, (76° C) and maintain it at that level for about 30 minutes is extremely difficult. Irregular sizes of wood need to be constantly added on. One moment of negligence and the temperature soars over 200° F. Without a safety baffle, this can be disastrous for a smoked product. These little flames will not be little anymore. The fat inside the sausage will melt, leak through the casings, and drop on the small flames which will turn them into a raging fire. The sausage casings will become so dry and brittle that the sausages themselves will fall down into the fire pit.

Photo 5.12 Drum smoker. Burning wood.

Photo 5.13 Drum smoker. Hot plate inside, note the electrical cord.

Smokers with a Separate Smoke Generator

When the amount of air is limited severely, the resulting smoke is very dark as it contains a large number of unburned particles. Such smoke is generally undesirable for smoking meats and it can produce a bitter flavor. The design of a good smokehouse should provide for ample air supply during combustion. To fully utilize the little space small smokers have at their disposal, a separate smoke generator should be used. The benefits of a separate smoke generator are numerous:

- Ability to provide cooler smoke.
- Better flame control.
- Easier control of a smoking/cooking process.

In the woods, simply dig a trench. The sides and top must be supported somehow with rocks or pieces of plywood. Any small heat fluctuation coming from the smoke generator will not have much effect on the temperature inside the smoking chamber.

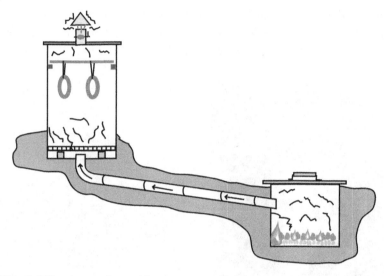

Fig. 5.5 Drum smoker with a separate firebox.

Concrete Block Smoker

An excellent smoker can be built in no time by using standard 8" x 8" x 16" concrete blocks. A firm support base is recommended and square patio stones of 12", 16", or 18" that are available at garden centers can be successfully used. The construction does not require using mortar, just arranging blocks in the manner that will be most practical. A separate fire pit built from blocks is attached to the smokehouse. This way the entire smoking chamber can be utilized for smoking meats and the process is easy to control. A permanent structure can be made, but a strong suggestion is to try it out a few times.

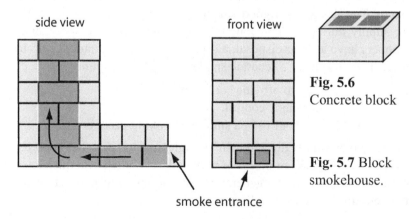

side view   front view

smoke entrance

Fig. 5.6 Concrete block

Fig. 5.7 Block smokehouse.

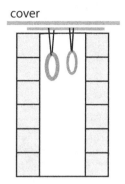

Fig. 5.8 Smokesticks on top.

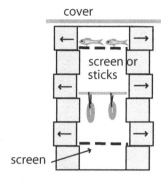

Fig. 5.9 Smokesticks on blocks.

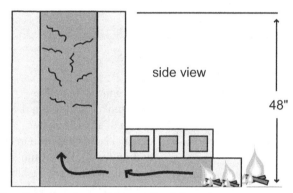

Fig. 5.10 Smoker with attached fire pit.

Top view at smoker and firepit

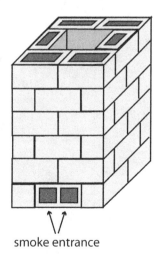

Fig. 5.11 & 5.12 Top view.

Photo 5.14 - top. Fish being inserted on smokesticks.
Photo 5.15 - bottom. A fire pit burning wood logs.

Most unusual but effective smoker made from the stump of an old oak tree. This original set up has been in operation for 20 years. Smoker located on Poliwoda Fishing Grounds, Opole, Poland. Smoked trout ends up on a dinner plate in a popular tourist restaurant which is located on the same grounds.

A sheet of metal covers the smoke delivery channel and the bricks lying on top provide stability. It is connected with a smoker by an underground pipe. Black item lying on the ground to the right of the smoker is an old potato burlap bag that is used as the smoker's cover. Note that a potato burlap sack makes an excellent cover allowing just the right amount of smoke to sip through.

Two Box Smoker

This is definitely the easiest smoker that can be built. It is popular in Asian countries. Disposable, yet fully functional, it can be built without any costs. This smoker may be the best introduction for the beginner to the world of smoking. Materials needed: 2 cardboard boxes of the same size, masking tape, smoke sticks, metal pan for sawdust, and kitchen colander or a suitable baffle. A higher box will make a bigger smoker, although the size is not of real importance.

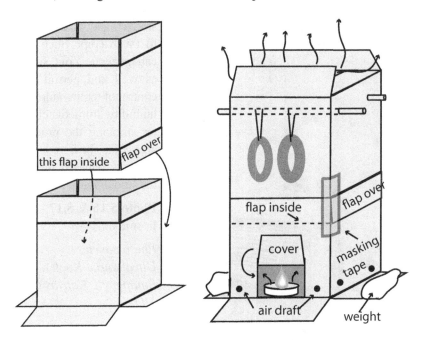

Fig. 5.13 Two equal size boxes.

Fig. 5.14 One box inserted into another.

Smoke exhaust can be adjusted by placing different weights on top covers. The cover flaps act as a spring and tend to open up. At the bottom a few holes may be punched out to supply air or the firebox cover may be left open. All corner joints should be reinforced with masking tape. A kitchen colander may be placed over the pan with sawdust. This is to prevent the possibility of sawdust bursting up in flames when grease drips down from the meat.

Commercial Smokehouses

When properly set, steam, water spraying, and other microprocessor controlled functions take care of the entire smoking and cooking operations. The smoke generator is a separate unit standing outside of the smoker and is connected to it with a pipe. Such units can generate cold smoke as well and permit easy control of temperature and humidity. Immediately after smoking the products are cold showered. The water is released through the smokehouse drain.

Photo 5.16 & **5.17** - 600 lb smoker.

Photo courtesy UltraSource/Koch Equipment, Kansas City, MO.

The smokehouses used for commercial applications are big in size and the economy of running efficient day to day operations plays the major role in their design. Those factors are of lesser importance for a home sausage maker who smokes meats for himself a few times a year. It doesn't make much sense to blindly build a smoker to impress your friends and then later find out that it is ill suited for a particular climate because it can not generate enough heat to cook your products.

Chapter 6

Cooking

Cooked meat is without a doubt more palatable, but the main reason for cooking is to kill bacteria and make meat safe for consumption.

The factors that influence cooking are:

- Temperature - the higher the temperature the shorter the cooking time.

- Size and weight of meat: it takes some time for the heat to reach inside of the large meat piece and it will cook slower.

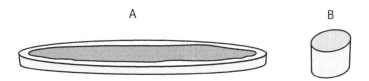

Fig. 6.1 Meat piece A weighs more than B, but due to its small thickness, it will cook much faster.

Cooking produces meat loss which is of major importance for commercial producers but less for a hobbyist who's major concern is making the highest quality product.

The main losses are:

1. Fat. Once the temperature of the meat reaches about 100° F (38° C) all fat tissues, regardless from which animal they come, become liquid. Connective tissue that surrounds them softens up but still holds them within. This tissue is composed from collagen and elastin protein, and if the temperature goes over the 100° F (38° C) mark, the connective tissue breaks down and the liquid fat particles are able to move around (this does not mean that they will leave the meat).

There is very little fat loss between 150 - 190° F (66 - 88° C) or even up to the boiling point of water 212° F (100° C). There is a significant fat loss at temperatures over 248° F (120° C). This is the range that covers barbecuing, grilling or roasting. At those temperatures the fat leaks out of the meat.

2. Water. Depending on a particular meat cut and the animal it came from, meat can contain up to 20% of protein. Those proteins bind molecules of water and they are enveloped by connective tissues. Some of them start to cook at 120° F (49° C), though most of them start to cook fast between 140° F (60° C) and 155° F (69° C). The effect is squeezing out the water and some loss of water soluble proteins. The meat shrinks. This loss depends on the meats internal temperature and happens regardless of what cooking media is used.

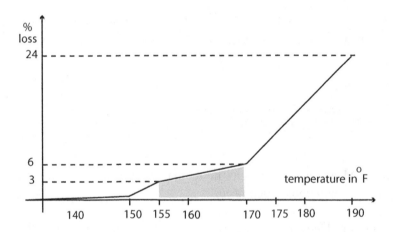

Fig. 6.2 Meat cooking loss.

The shaded area in the drawing shows that the smallest cooking loss occurs when meat is cooked to 155 - 170° F (69 - 77° C) internal meat temperature. Cooking meat to 140° F (60° C) will result in an even smaller loss, but the majority people prefer the taste of meat, especially hams, when they are cooked to 155 - 169° F (69 - 77° C). A great way to cut down on losses is to save the meat stock and use it for soups or gravies.

Methods of Cooking

It is important that meat reaches the safe internal temperature. There are basically two methods:

- Cooking in water. A large pot plus thermometer is needed. The process can be simplified by using an electric water cooker, soup cooker or turkey fryer as these devices come with an automatic temperature control.
- Cooking in a smoker or an oven.

Fat melts down at quite low temperatures and although it solidifies again, it doesn't look the same. There is no reason to intensify the problem by creating unnecessarily high temperatures. When the source of heat is switched off, the product's internal temperature will still increase by a few degrees. This is due to the heat transfer from the surface into the inside of the meat. The temperature of the surface of the cooked product is higher than the temperature inside of it.

Cooking in Water. We usually assume that meats and sausages are fried, baked or grilled. However, majority of smoked products are cooked in water as this is a fast, precise and cost effective method that offers many advantages:

1. It is accurate. At the sea level, water boils always at 212° F (100° C), providing the vessel is uncovered. We may get hung up on the phone, watch television or even fall asleep, but as long as there is water in the pot the temperature will not go higher than 212° F (100° C). It is easy to hang on the pot a candy thermometer, lower the heat and maintain the temperature at 176° F (80° C). Most electrical stoves will not even go below 200° F (93° C) as they were not designed for cooking smoked meats and sausages.

2. Water conducts heat much faster than air. Pizza cook can insert his hand briefly to a hot 450° F (232° C), but he will never insert his hand into boiling water that boils at merely 212° F (100° C). A 25 mm diameter smoked sausage will cook in 20 minutes in water, but will take much longer in a smokehouse or in the oven.

3. Water cooking methods results in a smaller moisture loss what simply translates in a bigger product and higher profits for the manufacturer.

4. It works with different fuel sources, be it gas, electric, or burning wood over the camp fire.

Baking in the Oven

You can bake your meat or sausages in the oven as long as your unit can maintain temperatures of 190° F (88° C) or lower. Gas home ovens are usually capable of delivering such low temperatures, but the electric ones are not. If the oven's lowest temperature will be higher than 190° F (88° C) switch to the water method.

Photo 6.1 Checking internal meat temperature.

Cooking Pork

Sausages, hams and other pieces of meat are considered raw products and must be cooked after smoking. A sausage smoked at 100° F (38° C) for 3 hr, will have a great smoky taste, flavor and color but it will still be a raw sausage like a fresh sausage that was only ground, mixed with spices, and stuffed into casings. Both of them must be cooked to safe temperatures before consumption. The U.S. Department of Agriculture recommends cooking fresh pork to an internal temperature of 160° F (71° C) and The National Pork Producers Council recommends an internal cooking temperature of 155° F (69° C) for maximum juiciness and flavor. Those extra 5° F (between 155° and 160° F) might kill a few more microbes and as a result the sausage might have a few hours longer shelf life, which is more important from a commercial point of view.

For a home sausage maker the inside temperature of the meat should fall between 155-160° F (69-72° C). We can stop cooking at 155° F (69° C) as most products will be of smoked variety and thus *previously cured with salt and nitrite* which gives us considerably more safety. Meats, which were not previously cured, will not be smoked, just cooked before consumption and the recommended temperature of 160° F should be observed. The lower the cooking temperature, the juicier and tastier the product is and the weight loss is also smaller.

Cooking Beef and Poultry

There are some sausages made entirely of beef though in most cases beef is mixed with pork. As beef can develop *Salmonella*, the Food Safety and Inspection Service of the United States Department of Agriculture has issued the following guidelines in June, 1999:

"Cooked beef and roast beef including sectioned and formed roasts, chunked and formed roasts, and cooked corned beef can be prepared using one of the following time and temperature combinations to meet either a 6.5-log10 or 7-log10 reduction of Salmonella":

F°	C°	6.5-log10 lethality	7-log10 lethality
130	54.4	112 minutes	121 minutes
140	60.0	12 min	12 min
145	62.8	4 min	4 min
150	65.6	67 seconds	72 seconds
152	66.7	43 sec	46 sec
154	67.8	27 sec	29 sec
158	70.0	0 sec	0 sec

*"Cooked poultry rolls and other cooked poultry products should reach an internal temperature of at least 160° F (71° C) prior to being removed from the cooking medium, except that **cured and smoked** poultry rolls and other **cured and smoked** poultry should reach an internal temperature of at least 155° F (69° C) prior to being removed from the cooking medium". (FSIS, June, 1999).*

Cooking Fish

Fish is considered done when cooked to 145° F (63° C) internal temperature. A reliable test is to insert a fork or knife into the thickest part of the fish and twist. The flesh should "flake" (separate).

Summary

- The thermometer should be inserted in the thickest part of the meat.
- Cured meat will develop the best color when heated to 160° F (72° C). Most sausage recipes contain smoking instructions on required temperatures and times. At higher cooking temperatures sausage shrivelling will be more pronounced.

- In many poorly insulated smokers the cooking temperature must be almost 25° F higher than the corresponding meat temperature to notice any practical progress (the meat temperature follows the smoker's temperature but is behind by about 25° F).
- The advantage of cooking in the smokehouse is that smoke may be applied at the same time.
- Cooking losses are smaller when meat is boiled as opposed to baking in the oven.
- The surface area of a cooked product exhibits a higher temperature than the inside and even after the heat source is switched off, the heat will continue to transfer towards the inside. The internal temperature of the meat will still advance by a few degrees.

Meats that were not cured and smoked should be cooked to the following temperatures:

- Fish should reach 145° F (63° C) as measured with a food thermometer.
- All cuts of pork to 160° F (72° C).
- Ground beef, veal and lamb to 160° F.
- All poultry should reach a safe minimum internal temperature of 165° F (74° C).
- Leftovers to 165° F (74° C).

Photo 6.2 Cooking in the wild.

Photo courtesy Waldemar Kozik

Chapter 7

Cooling, Freezing and Thawing

The following standards come from the Food Safety and Inspection Service (FSIS), United States Department of Agriculture (USDA):

Compliance Guidelines for Cooling Heat-Treated Meat and Poultry Products (Stabilization)

It is very important that cooling be continuous through the given time/temperature control points. Excessive dwell time in the range of 130° to 80°F is especially hazardous, as this is the range of most rapid growth for the clostridia. Therefore cooling between these temperature control points should be as rapid as possible.

1. During cooling, the product's maximum internal temperature should not remain between 130°F and 80°F for more than 1.5 hours nor between 80°F and 40°F for more than 5 hours. This cooling rate can be applied universally to cooked products (e.g., partially cooked or fully cooked, intact or non-intact, meat or poultry) and is preferable to (2) below.

2. Over the past several years, FSIS has allowed product to be cooled according to the following procedures, which are based upon older, less precise data: chilling should begin within 90 minutes after the cooking cycle is completed. All product should be chilled from 120°F (48°C) to 55°F (12.7°C) in no more than 6 hours. Chilling should then continue until the product reaches 40°F (4.4°C); the product should not be shipped until it reaches 40°F (4.4°C). This second cooling guideline is taken from the former ("Requirements for the production of cooked beef, roast beef, and cooked corned beef", 9 CFR 318.17(h)(10). It yields a significantly smaller margin of safety than the first cooling guideline above, especially if the product cooled is a non-intact product.

If an establishment uses this older cooling guideline, it should ensure that cooling is as rapid as possible, especially between 120°F and 80°F, and monitor the cooling closely to prevent deviation. If product remains between 120° F and 80° F more than one hour, compliance with the performance standard is less certain.

3. The following process may be used for the slow cooling of ready-to-eat meat and poultry cured with nitrite. Products cured with a minimum of 100 ppm ingoing sodium nitrite may be cooled so that the maximum internal temperature is reduced from 130 to 80° F in 5 hours and from 80 to 45° F in 10 hours (15 hours total cooling time).

This cooling process provides a narrow margin of safety. If a cooling deviation occurs, an establishment should assume that their process has exceeded the performance standard for controlling the growth of *Clostridium perfringens* and take corrective action. The presence of the nitrite, however, should ensure compliance with the performance standard for *Clostridium botulinum*.

The cooked product should pass the "danger zone" (40-140° F, 4 - 60° C) as fast as possible. *The most dangerous part of this range is between 130 and 80° F (54-27° C)* and should be passed within 1.5 hours.

In cafeteria buffets cooked foods are held at 140° F, (60° C) or higher. Holding foods at such temperature has detrimental effects on their quality. If they are to be stored for longer periods they must be held at < 40° F (4° C).

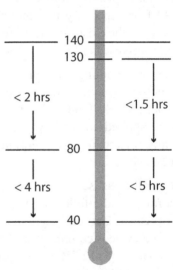

Fig. 7.1 Cooling standards.

Cooked meats that would be subsequently stored are usually showered with cold water. Water removes heat much faster than air and hot products will drop their temperature fast. If a product was smoked such showering also cleans the surface from any remaining smoke particles and prevents shrivelling.

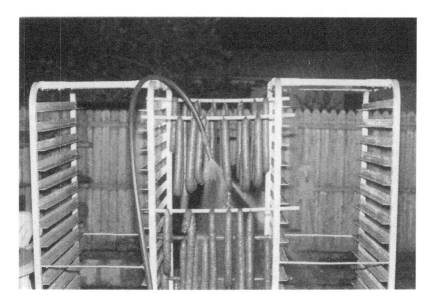

Photo 7.1 Showering sausages.

From FSIS Directive 7117.0

1. Heat-resistant food-poisoning bacteria can grow from 38°F up to approximately 125° F; however their range of rapid growth is from approximately 80°F to 125° F. *Thus, cooling product quickly through the rapid growth range is more important than cooling through the slow growth range.*

2. The rate of heat transfer (cooling rate) from the product's center to its surface is directly proportional to the difference in temperature between those two points. Thus as the product temperature approaches the coolant temperature, the cooling rate diminishes.

3. *Traditional cured products*, containing high amounts of salt and nitrite, together with low moisture content *are more resistant to bacterial growth* than similar newer products; some are even shelf-stable. Thus rapid cooling of these traditional products is not always necessary. However, manufacturers are making fewer products of this type today. Instead, to meet present consumer tastes, most of their cured products contain less salt and more moisture. These changes minimize the inhibitory effect of added nitrite and increase the need to rapidly cool these products.

Pre-cooling

There is no need to grab a water hose the moment the sausage was cooked in a smokehouse to 155° F (69° C) as this temperature lies outside the danger zone (40 - 140° F (4 - 60° C). U.S. regulations permit restaurants to hold cooked food at 145° F (63° C) or higher temperatures. However, once when the temperature of the product drops to 140° F (60° C), it should be cooled fast. The surface of a product such as a head cheese or smoked sausage both will benefit from a brief hot shower or immersing them in hot water. This will remove any possible grease from the outside and the product will look better. Then it will be showered with cold water. Some pork products may be cooked to > 137° F (58° C) just to eliminate the danger of contracting Trichinae. Such products should be cold showered immediately as they are already laying within the danger zone.

A question may arise as to why not to place a cooked product straight in a refrigerator? Well, you could and nothing will happen to your product but you may lose your expensive refrigerator. At first, when the hot product is placed in a refrigerator, the initial rate of cooling is fast. How fast it is depends on the difference between the temperature of the hot meat and the temperature inside the refrigerator. Both, the temperature of the food and the temperature of the refrigerator will drop lower and the rate of cooling will slow down. If a large amount of hot food was placed inside, it may severely test the capacity of the refrigerator to do its job. The temperature of the refrigerator and the temperature of the meat will come closer together and *other foods will start warming up*. For those reasons it is recommended to pre-cool the food.

At home conditions the best solution is to shower products with cold water or place them briefly in cold water. They may be kept in cold water (or ice bath) even longer but they should be placed in plastic bags first, to prevent unnecessary loss of meat flavor or salt migration. Then when the product goes into the refrigerator, there should be some space around it to facilitate cooling.

A home unit is designed to hold foods at 36-40° F (2 - 4° C) and not to cool large amounts of very hot products. For this purpose we have industrial blast chillers which have large capacity compressors that blow cold air over the meats and chill them quickly.

Freezing

To understand the concept of freezing it is necessary to remember the fact that the meat consists of up to 75% of water. When water is placed in a freezer it freezes but also *increases in volume.*

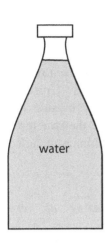

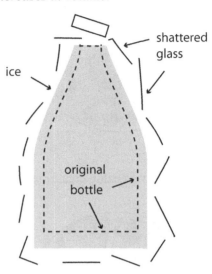

Fig. 7.2 Bottle of water is placed in a freezer. Water becomes ice and expands by about 10%.

Fig. 7.3 Expanding ice puts pressure on the bottle and ruptures the glass. The ice remains in one solid block but the glass shatters into pieces although it still clings to the ice.

The same applies to meat – it contains water everywhere, inside the muscle cells, in sarcoplasm, in connective tissues of membranes and in smaller amounts in fats.

The water inside of the meat, like the water inside of a bottle, will become ice and because of its increased volume will expand and do damage to the meat protein, resulting in a loss of elasticity and its ability to hold water. How much damage is created depends directly on the temperature and speed of freezing.

When freezing is slow, water molecules that get frozen first are the ones that reside between individual muscle fibers. Water inside cells contains more salt, it is under higher pressure and lower temperature. As a result water molecules leave muscle cells and diffuse towards connective tissues. Crystals grow large, mainly outside the cells and damage the structure of the meat, membranes included.

Fig. 7.4 Slow freezing creates large ice crystals.

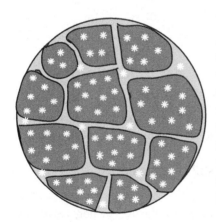

When freezing *at very low temperatures* water has no time to leave cells and move into areas with lower pressure. Freezing is almost instantaneous, the formed ice crystals are very small and there is no damage to the internal meat structure. The crystals are formed inside and outside the cells, water in myofibrils is the last to freeze.

Fig. 7.5 Fast freezing creates small ice crystals.

It shall be noted that the curing process progresses somewhat faster in meat that was previously frozen due to the disrupted cell structure that was created by ice crystals. Meat freezes at 28° F (-2° C) but to freeze all water present inside of the meat cells we have to create temperatures of -8°-22° F (-22°-30° C), which is well beyond the range of a home refrigerator. The temperature of a home freezer is set to 0° F (-18° C) which fits into the slow freezing process described earlier. A butcher's freezer -25° F (-32° C) is more effective, but to really fast freeze the meat an industrial unit is needed.

They freeze meat by blasting fast moving cold air over the product that drops the temperature to -40° F (-40° C). Freezing prevents the spoilage of sausage, however, keeping it in a freezer for longer than 6 weeks will lower it's flavor, though it will still be nutritious and safe to eat. Fish contains more water than other meats and its cells are more susceptible to damage by ice crystals.

Storage time of some meats		
Method	Refrigerated at: 28-32° F (-1.5-0° C)	Frozen at: -22° F (-30° C)
Pork halves	1-2 weeks	12 months
Beef quarters	4-5 weeks	18 months

Color of Frozen Meat

The color of frozen meat depends on the size of the crystals that formed during freezing. Fast freezing rate creates small ice crystals which scatter most light leaving the meat looking opaque and pale. Of course color of the meat is influenced by the species and the amout of myoglobin they carry. In frozen meat, light accelerates discoloration. Meats kept in freezers should therefore be covered.

Freezer Burn

Freezer burn is the appearance problem that affect meat in frozen storage. The problem occurs in unwrapped or poorly covered meat which is stored at low humidity. Such meat starts to dry out fast leaving unattractive spongy layer. Meats kept in freezers should therefore be covered as a precaution against freezer burn.

Thawing

Meat conducts heat very poorly. Smaller meat cuts will freeze and thaw much faster than large pieces. Thawing is a much slower process than freezing and is usually done in refrigerator. The process would be faster if performed at higher temperature, but that would create favorable conditions for the growth of bacteria. During thawing a liquid leaks out from the meat being thawed.

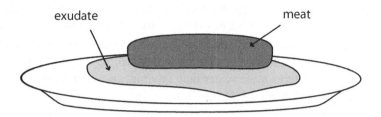

exudate   meat

Fig. 7.6 Thawing of meat.

Most people think of this liquid as blood as it is red in color. Actually, this exudate is a very valuable liquid and it should be saved. This liquid is the combination of extracted meat proteins, meat juice, minerals, water, collagen, blood, and other components. This is the result of ruptured meat cells and connective tissues by ice crystals. If the meat was submitted to fast freezing, smaller crystals were produced and less damage was made to the meat's structure. As a result the drip loss would be smaller.

Thawing Methods

- Refrigerator. The air exhibits very poor conductive properties and the thawing process is slow.

- Water. Water transfers heat or cold much faster than air and the meat immersed in ice cold water will thaw out much faster. There would be loss of meat juice unless a plastic bag is used.

- Microwave. Make sure the meat cuts are of uniform size.

Frozen meat will start thawing on the outside first. This results in moisture and favorable conditions for the growth of bacteria and that is why thawing should be performed at refrigerator temperatures.

Re-freezing

Thawed meat can be re-frozen. What must be noted is that spoilage bacteria has already begun working on the meat in the thawing stage. Depending on how and where it was kept during thawing, its shelf keeping qualities will be shortened, even if re-frozen again.

Chapter 8

Food Safety and Meat Microbiology

Meat of a healthy animal is clean and contains very few bacteria. Any invading bacteria will be destroyed by the animal's immune system. Once the animal is slaughtered these defense mechanisms are destroyed and the meat tissue is subjected to rapid decay. Although unaware of the process, early sausage makers knew that once the animal was killed, it was a race between external preservation techniques and the decomposition of the raw meats to decide the ultimate fate of the issue.

Most bacteria are present on the skin and in the intestines. In a stressed animal bacteria are able to travel from the animal's gut right through the casing into the meat. The slaughtering process starts introducing bacteria into the exposed surfaces. Given time they will find their way inside anyhow, but the real trouble starts when *we* create a new surface cut with a knife. This creates an opening for bacteria to enter the meat from the outside and start spoiling it. We must realize that they don't appear in some magical way inside of the meat, they always start from *the outside and they work their way in.*

Meat Surface Area and Volume Relationship

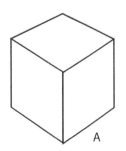 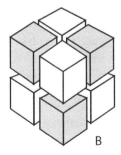

Fig. 8.1 Relationship of surface area and volume.

A. Cube A is 1 inch on each side and has a volume of 1 cubic inch and the surface area of 6 square inches. **B.** Three complete cuts (two vertical and one horizontal) produce eight small cubes with a volume of 0.125 cubic inch. Total *volume remains the same* - 1 cubic inch, but total *surface area has doubled* and is 12 square inches.

This is what happens when the meat is cut, the surface area increases. Now imagine what happens when the grinder cuts meat through a 1/8" (3 mm) plate, it creates an infinite number of small particles. The more cuts, the more spoils of meat, the more air and free water available to bacteria. This is the reason why *ground meat has the shortest shelf life*. In a large piece of meat the outside surface serves as a natural barrier preventing access to bacteria. *They have a long distance to travel to reach the center of the meat*. Meat muscles are surrounded with a connective tissue which also *acts as a protective sheath and so does the outside skin*. Duties like cutting meat, grinding, mixing or stuffing all increase meat temperature and should be performed in the kitchen at the lowest possible temperatures as fast as possible. Otherwise we create conditions for the growth of bacteria and that will decrease the shelf life of the product.

All About Bacteria

Food safety is nothing else but the control of bacteria and to do it effectively first we have to learn how bacteria behave. Once one knows what bacteria like or dislike, it will be very simple to produce safe products with a long shelf life. Let's make something clear: it is impossible to eliminate bacteria altogether, life on the planet will come to a halt. They are everywhere: on the floor, on walls, in the air, on our hands and all they need to grow is moisture, nutrients and warm temperature.

All microorganisms can be divided into the following classes:

- Bacteria
- Yeasts
- Molds

They all share one thing in common: they want to live and given the proper conditions they will start multiplying. They don't grow bigger, they just divide and divide and divide until there is nothing for them to eat, or until conditions become so unfavorable that they stop multiplying and die.

Meat contains about 75% of water and this moisture is the main reason that it spoils. Bacteria love temperatures that revolve around the temperature of our body (36.6° C, 98.6° F). Holding products at higher temperatures (greater than 130° F, 54° C) restricts the growth of bacteria. Increasing temperatures over 60° C (140° F) will start killing them. Most bacteria need oxygen (aerobic), others thrive without it (anaerobic). All of them hate cold, and around 32° F, (0° C) they become lethargic and dormant when the temperature drops lower. *Keeping them at low temperatures does not kill them, but only stops them from multiplying.* Once when the conditions are favorable again, they will wake up and start growing again.

Some bacteria tolerate the presence of salt better than others and we take advantage of this when curing meats. Other bacteria (e.g. *Clostridium botulinum*) are able to survive high temperatures because they form spores. Spores are special cells that envelop themselves in a protective shell and become resistant to harsh environmental conditions. Once conditions become favorable, the cells return to their actively growing state.

Given favorable conditions bacteria can double up in numbers every 20 minutes. In a refrigerator their number will also grow, albeit at a reduced pace, but they can double up in 12 hours. Short of deep freezing, it is impossible to stop bacteria from contaminating meat, but we can create conditions that will slow down their growing rate. At room temperatures bacteria will grow anywhere they have access to nutrients and water. Microorganisms which are of special interest when processing meats:

- Food spoilage bacteria.
- Dangerous (pathogenic) bacteria.
- Beneficial bacteria.
- Yeasts and molds.

Food Spoilage Bacteria

Spoilage bacteria break down meat proteins and fats causing food to deteriorate and develop unpleasant odors, tastes, and textures. Fruits and vegetables get mushy or slimy and meat develops a bad odor. Most people would not eat spoiled food. However, if they did, they probably would not get seriously sick. Bacteria such as *Pseudomonas spp.* or *Brochotrix thermosphacta* cause slime, discoloration and odors, but don't produce toxins. There are different spoilage bacteria and each reproduces at specific temperatures. Some can grow at the low temperatures in the refrigerator or freezer.

Pathogenic Bacteria

It is commonly believed that the presence of bacteria creates an immense danger, but this belief is far from the truth. The fact is that a very small percentage of bacteria can place us in any danger, and most of us with a healthy immune system are able to fight them off.

Pathogenic bacteria cause illness. They grow rapidly in the "Danger Zone" - the temperatures between 40 and 140° F (4-60° C) - and *do not generally affect the taste, smell, or appearance of food.* Food that is left too long at warm temperatures could be dangerous to eat, but smell and look just fine. *Clostridium botulinum, Bacillus cereus* or *Staphylococcus aureus* infect food with toxin which will bring harm to us in just a few hours. Still others, like *Salmonella* or *Escherichia coli* will find their way with infected meat into our intestines, and *if present in sufficient numbers*, will pose a serious danger. Pathogenic bacteria hate cold conditions and lie dormant at low temperatures waiting for an opportunity to jump into action when the conditions get warmer again. They all die when submitted to the cooking temperature of 160° F (72° C), but some sausages are never cooked and different strategies must be implemented to keep them at bay. Fighting bacteria is a never ending battle, but at least we can do our best to turn the odds in our favor.

Beneficial Bacteria

Without beneficial bacteria it will not be possible to make fermented sausages. They are naturally occurring in meat but in most cases they are added into the meat in the form of starter cultures. There are two classes of beneficial (friendly) bacteria:

- Lactic acid producing bacteria - *Lactobacillus, Pediococcus.*
- Color and flavor forming bacteria - *Staphylococcus, Kocuria* (previously known as *Micrococcus*).

Although lactic acid producing bacteria are used mainly to produce fermented products, color and flavor forming bacteria are needed to brake Nitrate into nitrite and are often added to develop a stronger red color of meats.

Yeasts and Molds

Yeasts and molds grow much slower than bacteria and they develop later in the drying process. This means they are normally part of the traditionally made sausage process. Yeasts need little oxygen to survive, and live on the surface or near the surface inside of the sausage. Molds are aerobic (need oxygen) and will grow on the surface of the sausage only. On fermented European sausages, the development of mold is often seen as a desired feature as it contributes to the flavor of the sausage.

Smoking sausages during or after fermentation, will prevent the growth of mold. If mold develops and is not desired, it can be easily wiped off with a cloth saturated in vinegar. Because molds can grow only on the outside of the sausage, there is nothing wrong with the meat itself.

Effects of Time and Temperature on Bacteria Growth

Under the correct conditions, spoilage bacteria reproduce rapidly and the populations can grow very large. Temperature and time are the factors that affect bacterial growth the most. Below 45° F bacteria grow slowly and at temperatures above 140° F they start to die. In the so called "danger zone" between 40-140° F (4-60° C) many bacteria grow very well. Most bacteria will grow exponentially at temperatures between 70-120° F (21-121° C). When bacteria grow, they increase in numbers, not in size. Let's see how fast bacteria grow at ideal temperature:

Number of bacteria	Elapsed time
10	0
20	20 minutes
40	40 minutes
80	1 hour
160	1 hour 20 min
320	1 hour 40 min
640	2 hours
1280	2 hours 20 min
2560	2 hours 40 min
5120	3 hours
10,240	3 hours 20 min
20,480	3 hours 40 min
40,960	4 hours
81,920	4 hours 20 min
163.840	4 hours 40 min
327,680	5 hours
655,360	5 hours 20 min
1,310,720	5 hours 40 min
2,621,440	6 hours

Looking at the table it becomes evident what happens to a piece of meat left out on the kitchen table for many hours on a beautiful and hot summer day. The thermometer drawing that follows below has been compiled from the data we found at the College of Agriculture, Auburn University, Alabama. It shows the time that is required for one bacteria cell to become two at different storage temperatures. Looking at the drawing we can see that once the temperature rises above 50° F (10° C), bacteria will double up every time we raise the temperature by about 10° C.

From the above examples we can draw a logical conclusion that if we want to process meats *we should perform these tasks at temperatures not higher than 50° F (10° C)*. And those are the temperatures present in meat processing plants. You might say that lowering the temperature of the room will be better still. Of course it will be better, but people working in such conditions for 8 hours a day will find it very uncomfortable.

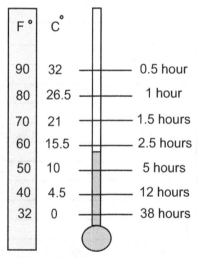

It can be seen that at 32° F (0° C) bacteria needs as much as 38 hours to divide in two. That also means that if our piece of meat had a certain amount of bacteria on its surface, after 38 hours of lying in a refrigerator the amount of bacteria in the same piece of meat will double. If we move this meat from the refrigerator to a room having a temperature of 80° F (26.5° C) the bacteria will double up every hour (12 times faster). At 90° F (32° C) they will be dividing every 30 minutes.

Fig. 8.2 Bacteria growth with temperature.

After cooking, meats are free of bacteria, but leaving them warm for an extended time *will invite new bacteria* to settle in and start growing. For this reason smoked and subsequently cooked meats are submitted to cold showers to pass through the "danger zone" as fast as possible.

Destruction of Bacteria

Most pathogenic bacteria, including *Salmonella, Escherichia coli 0157:H7, Listeria monocytogenes*, and *Campylobacter,* can be fairly easily destroyed using a mild cooking process. Maintaining a minimum temperature within the range of 130-165° F (54 -74° C) for a specific amount of time will kill them. However, cooking at low temperatures will not destroy these toxins once they have formed in food.

Spoilage bacteria (*Pseudomonas* spp.) need oxygen to survive and applying a vacuum (removing air) during mixing and stuffing is an effective way to inhibit their growth. At home, a precaution must be made so that the sausage mix is stuffed firmly and any air pockets which are visible in a stuffed casing are pricked with a needle. Oxygen also affects the development of proper curing color and promotes rancidity in fats.

Toxins

Toxins of most concern are produced by *Clostridium botulinum, Clostridium perfringens, Bacillus cereus*, and *Staphylococcus aureus.* All are the result of the growth of bacteria in foods that have been mishandled. These bacteria are common in the environment and are often found on carcasses. Proper cooking, fermentation, cooling, and storage of food can prevent the growth of these bacteria and more importantly, the production of their toxins. Thermal processing (canning) at temperatures of greater than 240° F (115° C) for a specific amount of time is necessary to destroy most spores and toxins.

What is Botulism?

Botulism, once known as a sausage disease, is a rare but serious food borne disease that can be fatal. The symptoms of botulism include difficulty swallowing, talking, breathing, and double vision. Without medical care, respiratory failure and death are likely. Botulism symptoms typically appear within 18 to 36 hours of eating the contaminated food, although it can be as soon as four hours and last up to eight days. Food borne botulism can be especially dangerous because many people can be poisoned at once. Sausages are the second biggest source of food contamination and food poisoning, second only to home-canned food products. The optimal temperature range for the growth of botulinum bacteria is 78-95° F (26-35° C) and it significantly slows down at 118° F (48° C).

When these bacteria feel threatened, they envelop themselves in protective shells called "spores" which can only be killed by boiling in water at 212° F (100° C) for at 5 hours or heated in a pressure canner at 240° F (116° C) for 2 minutes. At 140° F (60° C), botulinum spores do not develop into toxins, although they are heat resistant.

Where Does Botulism Come From?

Cl. botulinum is found in soil and aquatic sediments all over the world. Like plant seeds, they can lie dormant for years. They are not threatening until they encounter an adequate environment for growth. The spores that germinate produce the deadly botulinum toxin. To grow, they require a slightly acidic, oxygen free environment that is warm and moist. That is exactly what happens when smoking meats:

1. First of all, meats contain a lot of moisture. Water is then also added to sausages to facilitate stuffing. Hams and other meats are pumped up with water.

2. Lack of oxygen – when smoking we intentionally decrease the amount of available air. This allows our sawdust or wood chips to generate lots of smoke.

3. Temperatures between 40° and 140° F - most smoking is done at this temperature range. The most dangerous range is from 78-95° F (26-35° C), and that fits into the "warm smoking" method. Bacteria thrive at this temperature range and smoking process creates ideal conditions for *Cl. botulinum* to grow.

How to Prevent Botulism

Adding *Nitrates/nitrites* prevents the transformation of *C. botulinum* spores into toxins. It is almost like applying a vaccine to eliminate a disease. By curing meats with nitrites, we protect ourselves from possibly contracting a deadly disease. Nitrites are cheap, commonly available, and completely safe in amounts recommended by the Food and Drug Administration. So why not use them? All commercial plants do. Nitrites are needed only when smoking meats or making fermented sausages. You don't need nitrites when barbecuing or grilling, as the temperatures are high enough to kill all bacteria.

Trichinae

There are some cold smoked pork products and sausages that will not be submitted to the cooking process and they can be at risk of being infected with trichinae.

Trichinae is an illness caused by the consumption of raw or under cooked pork or wild game meat infected with *"trichinella spiralis."* Deers are herbivores; they eat leaves from trees, bushes and shrubs and they don't contract the disease. Trichinae is a parasitic nematode (round worm) that can migrate from the digestive tract and settle in the form of cysts in various muscles of the body. The disease is almost non-existent in American pigs due to their strictly controlled feed, but it can still be found in meats of free roaming animals. The illness is not contagious, but the first symptoms appear within 1-2 days of eating contaminated meat. They include nausea, diarrhea, vomiting, abdominal pain, itchy skin, and may be mistaken for the flu. Trichinae in pork is killed by raising its internal temperature to 137° F (58° C). The U.S. Code of Federal Regulations requires pork to be cooked for 1 minute at 140° F (60° C). Traditionally made fermented sausages, also called dry or slow-fermented sausages are normally never cooked and the heat treatment does not apply here. They are cured with a higher percentage of salt which kills *trichinae* too. Fortunately, *storing pork at low temperatures also kills trichinae.*

The U.S. Department of Agriculture's Code of Federal Regulations, Title 9, Volume 2, Cite: 9 CFR318.10 requires that pork intended for use in processed products be frozen at:

Group 1 - comprises product in separate pieces not exceeding 6" (15 cm) in thickness, or arranged on separate racks with layers not exceeding 6" (15 cm) in depth, or stored in crates or boxes not exceeding 6" (15 cm) in depth, or stored as solidly frozen blocks not exceeding 6" (15 cm) in thickness.

Group 2 - comprises product in pieces, layers, or within containers, the thickness of which exceeds 6" (15 cm) but not 27" (68 cm) and product in containers including tierces, barrels, kegs, and cartons having a thickness not exceeding 27" (68 cm).

Table 1. Required Period of Freezing Indicated			
Temperature		Days	
° F	° C	Group 1	Group 2
5	-15	20	30
- 10	-23.3	10	20
- 20	-28.9	6	12

The product undergoing such refrigeration or the containers thereof shall be so spaced while in the freezer as will insure a free circulation of air between the pieces of meat, layers, blocks, boxes, barrels, and tierces in order that the temperature of the meat throughout will be promptly reduced to not higher than 5° F (-15° C), -10° F (-23.3° C), or -20° F (-28.9° C), as the case may be. In lieu of the methods prescribed in Table 1, the treatment may consist of commercial freeze drying or controlled freezing, *at the center of the meat pieces*, in accordance with the times and temperatures specified in Table 2 which can be found in Appendix A.

Microwaving, curing, drying or smoking is not effective in preventing Trichinae. It should be noted that *freezing will not kill larval cysts in bears and other wild game that live in Northwestern U.S. and Alaska.* That meat has to be cooked to 160° F (72° C) internal temperature.

Trichinae Control in Dry Meat Products

Pork products which are not cooked such as slow fermented and dried sausages are at risk of being infected with *trichinae*. Cured hams and butts fit into the same category and must be dealt with differently. Although it is possible to obtain certified pork trichinae free it is not something that is universally done as it requires laboratory tests. Curing meats with salt according to USDA regulations takes care of the problem. Hams were cured with salt long before USDA came to be and the procedures used in the past took care of the trichinae problem. As explained earlier, freezing pork meat is an approved method for treating trichinae and it can be applied at home. It is not practical for large scale production as it will require investment in time and space plus additional electricity costs. In addition frozen meat exhibits damaged sell structure due to the growth of ice crystals. That will affect the texture and sliceability of the finished ham. The best solution is to use enough salt what will remove moisture, slow the growth of bacteria and will eliminate *trichinae* problem.

Most prescribed procedures call for 3.3% salt for dry sausages and 4-5% salt for large whole meats like shoulders and hams. Those amounts, which are usually applied anyhow, will cure meats and will treat it for *trichinae* at the same time. There are detailed USDA instructions on preventing *trichinae* by curing pork with salt in Appendix A. Keep in mind that pork used in fermented spreadable sausages should be treated for *trichinae* by freezing.

Good Manufacturing Practices that Can be Applied in the Everyday Kitchen

Home made sausages are produced at kitchen temperature and a dose of common sense is of invaluable help:

- Take only what you need from the cooler.
- When a part of the meat is processed put it back into the cooler.
- Keep your equipment clean and cold.
- Work as fast as possible.
- Try to always keep meat refrigerated.
- If your premises are not temperature controlled, limit your production to late evening or early morning hours.
- Wash your hands often.

The presented hurdles increase our defense against the growth of bacteria and by implementing those simple recommendations we greatly increase our chances for producing quality sausages.

Temperature Control

If you live in a tropical climate without air conditioning, try to process meat in the evening or early morning hours and work with a small portion of meat at one time. Other factors which influence your product quality and can eliminate the danger of any food poisoning are the 4 C's of Food Hygiene:

- Cleanliness-wash hands, prevent insects, use clean equipment.
- Cooking-cook meat, poultry and fish to proper internal temperature.
- Chilling and storage-keep food at refrigerator temperature.
- Cross-contamination-don't mix raw and cooked meats, use clean knives, keep separate cutting boards for cooked and raw meat.

Storing Meat

All uncooked meats or sausages should be treated as fresh meat. We can keep on hand an amount that will be consumed within a few days and the rest should be frozen. A ready to eat product should not be stored for more than 7 days if held at 41° F (45° C), or 4 days at 45° F (7° C).

This practice will help control the growth of *Listeria monocytogenes*, a harmful bacteria. Meats should be stored at 32-40° F (0-4° C). We should bear in mind that there are differences between home and commercial refrigerators and freezers:

Home refrigerator	Butcher's cooler
36° - 40 F° (2° - 4° C)	32 F ° (0° C)
Home freezer	Butcher's freezer
0° F (-18° C)	-25° F (- 32° C)

Meat products stored for a long time in a freezer will start developing inferior taste due to the oxidation of fat. Those chemical changes known as "rancidity" occur spontaneously and are triggered by light or oxygen. Meats stored in a freezer will turn rancid more slowly than meats stored in a refrigerator. Rancid meat is noticeable more with frozen meat than chilled meat because bacteria can spoil meat in a refrigerator well before rancidity begins. To prevent fat oxidation and to prolong shelf-life of the product, antioxidants such as BHA, BHT, TBHQ and rosemary extracts are commonly used.

Chapter 9

Additives and Ingredients

Additives and especially water retention agents play the most important role in today's methods of producing meat products. If you examine the list of machinery which is produced by an average factory, you will see that half of the products are related to pumping water and distributing it within the meat. To perform those operations fast and to produce a product that will be visually appealing with a long shelf life, the number of additives, some natural and some of chemical nature, are added.

Soy Products

Soybeans were cultivated in Asia about 3,000 years ago. Soy was first introduced to Europe in the early 18th century and to British colonies in North America in 1765, where it was first grown for hay. Benjamin Franklin wrote a letter in 1770 mentioning bringing soybeans home from England. Soybeans did not become an important crop outside of Asia until about 1910. Soy was introduced to Africa from China in the late 19th Century and is now widespread across the continent. Although the USA is the biggest producer of soy, soy was considered an industrial product only and not used as a food prior to the 1920's. Traditional non-fermented food uses of soybeans include soy milk, and from the latter tofu and tofu skin. Fermented foods include soy sauce, fermented bean paste, natto, and tempeh, among others.

Originally, soy protein concentrates and isolates were used by the meat industry to bind fat and water in meat applications and to increase protein content in lower grade sausages. They were crudely refined and if added at above 5% amounts, they imparted a "beany" flavor to the finished product. As the technology advanced, the soy products were refined further and exhibit a neutral flavor today. Today, soy proteins are considered not just a filler material, but a "good food" and are added to processed meats all over the world.

They are used by athletes in diet and muscle building drinks or as refreshing fruit smoothies. The dramatic increase in interest in soy products is largely credited to the 1995 ruling of the Food and Drug Administration allowing health claims for foods containing 6.25 g of protein per serving. The FDA approved soy as an official cholesterol-lowering food, along with other heart and health benefits. The FDA granted the following health claim for soy: "25 grams of soy protein a day, as part of a diet low in saturated fat and cholesterol, may reduce the risk of heart disease."

Soybean Nutrient Values(100 g)					
Name	Protein (g)	Fat (g)	Carbo-hydrates (g)	Salt (g)	Energy (cal)
Soybean, raw	36.49	19.94	30.16	2	446
					Source: USDA Nutrient database

Soybeans are considered to be a source of complete protein. A complete protein is one that contains significant amounts of all the essential amino acids that must be provided to the human body because of the body's inability to synthesize them. For this reason, soy is a good source of protein, amongst many others, for vegetarians and vegans or for people who want to reduce the amount of meat they eat. They can replace meat with soy protein products without requiring major adjustments elsewhere in the diet.

Photo 9.1 Soy beans. From the soybean many other products are obtained such as: soy flour, textured vegetable protein, soy oil, soy protein concentrate, soy protein isolate, soy yoghurt, soy milk and animal feed for farm raised fish, poultry and cattle.

In the past the soybean industry begged for acceptance, but today soybean products start to shine and become the sparkle of the food industry. Differently flavored soy milk can be found in every supermarket and roasted soybeans lie next to almonds, walnuts and peanuts.

Photo 9.2 A variety of soy products.

Soy flour is made by milling soybeans. Depending on the amount of oil extracted the flour can be full-fat or de-fatted. It can be made as fine powder or more coarse soy grits. Protein content of different soy flours:

- Full-fat soy flour - 35%.
- Low-fat soy flour - 45%.
- Defatted soy flour - 47%.

Generally, soy flour is not added to processed meats due to its flavor profile.

Textured soy flour (TSF) is obtained from regular soy flour which is processed and extruded to form products of specific texture and form, such as meat like nuggets. The formed products are crunchy in the dry form and upon hydration become moist and chewy.

Soy Proteins

Soybeans contain all three of the nutrients required for good nutrition: complete protein, carbohydrate and fat, as well as vitamins and minerals, including calcium, foolish acid and iron. The composition of soy protein is nearly equivalent in quality to meat, milk and egg protein. Soybean oil contains no cholesterol. *Soy concentrates and isolates are used in sausages, burgers and other meat products.*

Soy proteins when mixed with ground meat will form a gel upon heating, entrapping liquid and moisture. They increase firmness and juiciness of the product, and reduce cooking loss during frying. In addition they enrich the protein content of many products and make them healthier by reducing the amount of saturated fat and cholesterol that otherwise would be present. Soy protein powders are the most commonly added protein to meat products at around 2-3% as the larger amounts may impart a "beany" flavor to the product. They bind water extremely well and cover fat particles with fine emulsion. This prevents fats from lumping together. The sausage will be juicier, plumper and have less shrivelling.

Soy protein concentrate (about 60% protein), available from most online distributors of sausage making supplies is a *natural product* that contains around 60% protein and retains most of the soybean's dietary fiber. SPC can bind 4 parts of water. However, *soy concentrates do not form the real gel* as they contain some of the insoluble fiber that prevents gel formation; *they only form a paste.* Before processing, soy protein concentrate is re-hydrated at a ratio of 1:3.

Soy protein isolate (80-90% protein), is a natural product that contains at least 80-90% protein and no other ingredients. Given that it is made from de-fatted soy meal by removing most of the fats and carbohydrates, soy protein can form *clear gel.* Therefore, soy protein isolate has a *very neutral flavour* compared to other soy products. As soy protein isolate is more refined, it costs slightly more than soy protein concentrate. Soy protein isolate can bind 5 parts of water. Soy isolates are excellent emulsifiers of fat and their *ability to produce the real gel* contributes to the increased firmness of the product. Isolates are added to add juiciness, cohesiveness, and viscosity to a variety of meat, seafood, and poultry products. This enhances both the nutritional quality and taste of meat products.

For making quality sausages the recommended mixing ratio is 1 part of soy protein isolate to 3.3 parts of water. SPI is chosen for delicate products that require superior flavor such as yoghurt, cheese, whole muscle foods and healthy drinks. Soy protein isolates sold by health products distributors online usually contain 92% of protein.

In reduced fat sausages animal fat can be partly or completely replaced with a vegetable oil. In such a case the protein : oil : water emulsion can be made.

Binder	Binder/fat/water ratio	Average amount	Added as
Milk caseinate	1:5:5 to 1:8:8	2% in relation to meat mass.	Dry powder or pre-mixed emulsion
Soy protein isolate	1:4:5	2% in relation to meat mass.	Dry powder or pre-mixed emulsion

In the past soy protein isolate cost twice as much as soy protein concentrate and the concentrate became an obvious choice for the majority of products. Soy protein isolate it still costlier today, but not as much, so a hobbyist's decision will be based not on economics, but on the application. Soy isolates are excellent emulsifiers of fat and their ability to produce gel contributes to the increased firmness of the product. For these reasons they may be chosen over soy protein concentrate for making liver and emulsified sausages.

Soy protein concentrates do not form the real gel as they contain some of the insoluble fiber; they only form a paste. This does not create a problem as the sausage batter will never be emulsified to the extent that the yoghurt or smoothie drinks are. Soy protein concentrate is carried by all distributors of sausage making equipment and supplies online.

Protein rich powders, 100 g serving					
Name	Protein (g)	Fat (g)	Carbo-hydrates (g)	Salt (mg)	Energy (cal)
Soy flour, full fat, raw	34.54	20.65	35.19	13	436
Soy flour, low fat	45.51	8.90	34.93	9	375
Soy flour, defatted	47.01	1.22	38.37	20	330
Soy meal, defatted, raw, crude protein	49.20	2.39	35.89	3	337
Soy protein concentrate	58.13	0.46	30.91	3	331
Soy protein isolate, potassium type	80.69	0.53	10.22	50	338
Soy protein isolate (Supro®) *	92.50	2.8	0	1,400	378

Source: USDA Nutrient database
* Data by www.nutrabio.com. Soy isolates sold by health products distributors online usually contain 92% of protein.

Commercially processed meats contain soy protein today throughout the world. Soy proteins are used in hot dogs, other sausages, whole muscle foods, salamis, pepperoni pizza toppings, meat patties, vegetarian sausages etc. Hobbyist have also discovered that adding some soy protein concentrate allowed them to add more water and improved the texture of the sausage. It eliminated shrivelling and made the sausage plumper. Soy proteins play a very crucial role in making reduced fat sausages.

Textured Vegetable Protein - TVP

Textured vegetable protein, also known as textured soy protein (TSP), soy meat, or soya meat has been around for more than 50 years. It contains 50% protein, little fat, no cholesterol and is very rich in fiber fiber. It is an excellent filler material for *ground meat and sausages*. TVP is made from defatted soy flour, a by-product of extracting soybean oil, and is relatively flavorless. Its protein content is equal to that of the meat, and it contains no fat.

Photo 9.3 Textured vegetable protein (TVP) flakes. TVP must be rehydrated with water/liquid before use. TVP flakes are the size of the finely ground meat and they have the texture and the bite of the meat.

Textured vegetable protein is cheaper than meat and is used to extend meat value. It adds an unexpected bonus - the final product contains less fat and cholesterol and still retains its full nutritional value.

Textured Vegetable Protein (100 g = 1 cup)					
Name	Protein (g)	Fat (g)	Carbohydrates (g)	Salt (mg)	Energy (cal)
TVP	50	0	30	8 mg	333
					Source: Bob's Red Mill

Gums

Gums, technically referred to as hydrocolloids, originate from different sources. They can immobilize water and contribute viscosity. Two gums that are pretty familiar are gelatin and corn starch. If you look at processed food, you see all sorts of other gums like carrageenan, xanthan gum, cellulose gum, locust bean gum, gum arabic, agar, and so on. The value of gums is not as a fat replacer but as a thickener which can combine with water and create gel. Gums fulfil several functions in food products:

1. They thicken things - ice cream, syrups.
2. They emulsify things - mixed liquids stay together without separating.
3. They change the texture - a gum will make something thicker.
4. They stabilize crystals - a gum might help prevent sugar or ice from crystallizing.
5. They help to reduce cooking loss which results in a higher yield and more succulent product.

The most popular gums are:

- Agar
- Alginate
- Carrageenan
- Gum Arabic
- Guar Gum
- Locust Bean Gum
- Konjac Gum
- Xantham Gum

While at first glimpse, such exotic names may discourage consumers from ever considering such products, the truth is that they are natural products which we consume all the time. The are added to ice creams, puddings, sauces and processed foods that require a creamy texture. Without gums sugar crystals will separate from ice cream and many products would turn into a watery mess.

We take for granted that manufactured foods should always look good and taste well, but there is more to that than meets the eye. Food products are made in one location, then stored in a different one, and then transported many miles to a supermarket where they will sit on a shelf for some time. *Gums hold those products together.* The reason that we dedicate so much space to gums is that they become more popular every day.

Originally, only food technologists understood the subject and they were the ones to add them into food products. Today gums are commonly available and used in general cooking. For example traditional jams were made by stirring the mixture of fruit and sugar for hours until it lost enough moisture to gel. Pectin shortens the process to minutes and the product looks better and has a better consistency.

Let's make something clear-an occasional cook or a sausage maker does not need to use things like carrageenan, Konjac flour or xanthan gum because the sausage needs a superior texture. Commercial producers need to use gums, as their products, for example thinly sliced and packaged ham, must hold its shape together for a long time. A hobbyist can also use less expensive things like gelatin, flour, eggs or protein concentrate, because the time between making the product and consumption is usually very short. Nevertheless, the information presented in this chapter, will enable the reader to have a better understanding of the subject and will make it easier to further expand his knowledge by reading more technical books. The gums most often used in processed meats are: *carrageenan, xanthan and konjac*.

Carrageenan is a natural extract from red seaweeds used in processed foods for stabilization, thickening, and gelation. During the heating process carrageenan can absorb plenty of water and trap it inside. This results in a higher cooking yield and less purge during storage. About 0.01% (1 g per kg of meat) can increase the yield of the finished product up to 8%. Usually, up to 1.0% (10 g/kg) of carrageenan is added to processed meats.

Carrageenan forms a solid gel during cooling and improves sliceability. Many vegetarians use carrageenan in place of products like gelatin, since it is 100% vegetarian. There are three types of carrageenan employed in the food industry:

- Kappa - meat products, very strong gel. It is currently the most used type of carrageenan in meat products. It improves sliceability of thinly cut meat and helps to peel off casings in low fat sausages.
- Iota - meat products, medium strong gel.
- Lambda - sauces and dressings. Does not gel.

Kappa carrageenan gels better in the presence of alkali agents such as potassium chloride (KCL). Enough potassium chloride is usually added to the carrageenan blend to create a strong gel.

Potassium chloride is the same salt that is added to Morton's Low Salt, at 50% level, thus the salt itself promotes the development of strong gel. In addition milk protein is a strong promoter of carrageenan gels. Adding caseinate (milk protein) or non-fat dry milk will assist in the development of strong carrageenan gel. Kappa and Iota carrageenan are only partially cold water soluble and need to be heated for full activation. Lambda carrageenan is fully cold water soluble.

Konjac Gum

Konjac flour also called konjac gum or konjac glucomannan is produced from the konjac plant root and can form meltable or heat stable gels. Konjac flour is rich in soluble fiber, but does not contain starch or sugar so it does not have calories. It is also gluten free. Its thickening power is 10 times greater than cornstarch. Konjac has the highest water holding capacity of any soluble fiber-up to 100 times its own water weight. One part of glucomannan can absorb 50 parts of liquid. About one teaspoon of konjac flour can gel about one cup of liquid, which may be water, meat stock or wine. Konjac powder can be used as a thickener for smooth gravies, sauces, glazes, soups, stews and casseroles. Konjac interacts synergistically with carrageenan, xanthan gum, locust bean gum. Konjac interacts with most starches increasing viscosity and allowing improvement of texture.

As a gelling agent, konjac exhibits *the unique ability to form thermo-reversible and thermo-irreversible gels under different conditions:*

- Reversible gum- konjac mixed with xanthan gum.
- Non-reversible gum-when heated at a pH of 9-10.

With addition of a mild alkali such as calcium hydroxide, Konjac will set to a strong, elastic and thermo-irreversible gel. This gel will remain stable even when heated to 100° C and above. Konjac will form a reversible gel when it is mixed with xanthan gum. Due to the thermo-irreversible property of the konjac gum, it has become popular to make a great variety of foods such as konjac cake, konjac noodles, and *foods for vegetarians.*

Preparing Konjac gel:

If konjac flour is added directly to food it may create lumps. Konjac powder thickens slowly when mixed with cold water, but quickly thickens when it's heated. Mix konjac flour with cold water or other liquid first, stirring often until fully dissolved. Then add konjac flour to a hot liquid or food that is cooking. It has no taste of its own so it inherits the flavor of the product. Konjac flour can be mixed with other gums or starches. If you have not used konjac powder as a thickening agent before, it is best to experiment with it by beginning with lesser amounts, and adding as necessary until the desired consistency is reached. The addition of 0.02-0.03% konjac to 1% xanthan gum will raise its viscosity by 2-3 times under heating. Konjac is usually added at 0.25-0.50%.

Xanthan Gum

Xanthan gum is produced by *fermentation* of glucose, sucrose (corn sugar), or lactose by bacteria. During fermentation, a strain of bacteria (*Xanthomonas campestris*) turns sugar into a colorless slime called xanthan gum. Xanthan gum is most often found in salad dressings and sauces. It helps to prevent oil separation by stabilizing the emulsion, although it is not an emulsifier. Xanthan gum also helps suspend solid particles, such as spices. Also used in frozen foods and beverages, xanthan gum helps create the pleasant texture in many ice creams, along with guar gum and locust bean gum Xanthan gum is soluble in cold water but in order to eliminate lumps, it should be well agitated.

Xanthan gum does not gelatinize when used alone, but it can form gel at any pH when used with konjac gum. At a ratio of 3 (xanthan) : 2 (konjac) the strongest gel is obtained. The gel is thermo-reversible: it is in solid state at temperatures below 40° C (104° F), but it will be in a semi-solid or liquid state at temperatures of 50° C (122° F) or above. When the temperature drops back to the ambient temperature <40° C (<122° F), it will resume the solid state.

Gum Blends

It is often desirable to use a combination of gums to create a synergistic effect. Synergy means that a combined effect of two or more ingredients is greater than it would be expected from the additive combination of each ingredient. In this case the viscosity or gel strength will be greater if the following combinations are created:

• Konjac with carrageenan.
• Konjac with xanthan.

The above combinations may be used at a one-to-one ratio with each other. This effect is also present when a gum is combined with starch.

- Konjac with starch.
- Carrageenan with starch.

Adding modified starch and gum to food produces a similar effect. However, modified starch is less expensive than a gum. Adding starch to ground meat is a universally accepted method. On the other hand 1 part of gum will produce a similar effect as 10 parts of starch, so the result balances out.

Extenders and General Binders

Non-fat dry milk powder is an extender that binds water very well and is often used in making sausages. It is produced by removing fat and water from milk.

Ingredient (100 g serving)	Protein (g)	Fat (g)	Carbo- hydrates (g)	Salt (mg)	Energy (cal)
Non-fat dry milk	36.16	0.77	51.98	535	362
Source: USDA Nutrient database					

Non-fat dry milk powder is a good natural product and it does not affect the flavor of the product. It is added at about 3% and effectively binds water and emulsifies fats. Its action is very similar to that of soy protein concentrate. Non-fat dry milk powder can bind water and is often used in making sausages, including fermented types. Dry milk powder contains 50% lactose (sugar) and is used in fermented sausages as a source of food for lactic acid producing bacteria. It also contains around 35% of protein, about 0.6 - 1% fat and may be considered a healthy high energy product. Dry milk powder greatly improves the taste of low fat sausages.

Sodium caseinate, a milk protein, is an excellent emulsifier that was commonly used to stabilize fat and water emulsions. Caseinate allowed to emulsify different types of fats from different animals. However, the price of milk proteins was increasing and soy proteins took over the dominant spot. Caseinate is about 90% protein and is added at 1-2% per kg of meat. Milk protein will lighten up the sausage and will make it slightly softer. It is added to meat batter as dry powder or as prepared emulsion. The emulsion is usually set at milk protein/fatty trimmings/water in the ratio of 1:5:5.

Whey protein is made by drying liquid whey, which is a byproduct obtained during cheese making. Similarly to soy products, whey protein comes as:

- Whey protein concentrate, 30-89% protein.
- Whey protein isolate, 90% or more.

Whey is essential in the bodybuilding world today because of its ability to be digested very rapidly. It can be used for making processed meats, though it faces strong competition from soy products which are less expensive.

Egg is often added to sausages to increase binding ingredients. It should be noted that only the egg white possesses binding properties and egg yolk contributes to more fat and calories. One large egg weighs about 50 grams, of which the yolk accounts for around 20 grams and white for 30 grams.

Egg white is often added (1-3%) to frankfurters with low meat content. It increases protein content, forms stable gel and contributes to a firm texture of the sausage. Powdered egg whites are also available and you generally mix 2 teaspoons of powder with 2 tablespoons of water for each white.

Powdered gelatin (1%) helps to bind de-boned meat together or stuffing individual cuts of meat which are not perfectly lean. The strength of gelatin is measured in Bloom numbers (after inventor of the system Oscar T. Bloom). The higher the Bloom number the stiffer the gelatin will be. Gelatin used in food usually runs from 125 Bloom to 250 Bloom; the unflavored gelatin sold in supermarkets is at the higher end of this range.

Flours

Adding 2-3% of potato flour to minced meat was widely practiced in the past and it offered many advantages. It made sausages cheaper what was important after the II World War ended and it improved the mouthfeel of low fat products.

Semolina flour is the coarsely ground endosperm of durum, a hard spring wheat with a high-gluten content and golden color. It is hard, granular and resembles sugar. Semolina is usually enriched and is used to make couscous and pasta products such as spaghetti, vermicelli, macaroni and lasagna noodles. Except for some specialty products, breads are seldom made with semolina. Durum wheat is considered the gold standard for pasta production; the wheat kernel's density and high protein and gluten content result in firm pasta with a consistent cooking quality and golden color. Semolina has been used as a filler in many European sausages, for example Polish Semolina Liver Sausage.

De-fatted soy flour clearly is the nutritional winner. It contains the most protein and dietary fiber, and it is the lowest in calories. The reason that its use in meat products is not widespread is that it has a little "beany" flavor. Its derivative - Textured Vegetable Protein is used in processed meats as it has a neutral flavor, particle size similar to minced meat and its texture and bite resemble those of real meat.

Starch and Starch Derived Products

Starch is often added to sausages with low meat content. Starch is added when making sauces, to trap moisture and to make the sauce heavy. In sausages starch is used for its properties to bind water and to improve texture of the product. The most common sources are potato, wheat, corn, rice and tapioca. You can add as much as you like but around 10% (100 g per kilogram of total mass) will be the upper limit. Starch is a common additive in extended injected products like a ham. It is usually applied at 10 - 50 g/kg (1-5%) of finished product. Many Russian sausages were made with 2% potato starch.

Another advantage is that unlike flour-thickened sauces it doesn't separate when frozen. Starch has the ability to swell and take on water. The swelling of the starch occurs during the heating stage. A combination of *starch and carrageenan* produces a synergistic effect. Most commercial fat replacers derived from starch carry label designations of either *modified starch, dextrin or maltodextrin.*

Modified starch

Properties of starch can be altered by physical, enzymatical or chemical processes to obtain a modified starch that will be more suitable for a particular application. Modified starches are used in practically all starch applications, such as in food products as a thickening agent, stabilizer or emulsifier; in pharmaceuticals as a disintegrant; or in paper as a binder. Modified starches remain stable at many temperatures, allowing foods to be frozen and then thawed without losing texture and taste. Because of that modified starches are used in frozen and instant foods. A suitably-modified starch is used as a fat substitute for low-fat versions of traditionally fatty foods, e.g., reduced-fat hard salami having about 1/3 the usual fat content.

When using corn starch, first mix it with cold water (or another liquid) until it forms a smooth paste, then add it to whatever is being thickened. Adding starch directly into the cooking food will form lumps that are then difficult to mash out. A good idea is to put starch and cold water into a jar with a screw on lid and vigorously shake the sealed jar until the solution is smooth. This method can be applied to a flour/water mixture. It allows greater control when slowly adding it to a soup, sauce, or gravy.

Is Potato Starch the Same as Potato Flour?

Potato starch	Potato Flour
A very fine flour, neutral taste, made by removing potato skin, then made into a watery slurry, and dehydrated to form potato starch powder. It is not cooked and it *does not absorb much water, unless it is heated*. When heated with liquid, it will make an excellent sauce or gravy.	Potato flour is made from the potato, including the skin, and it is cooked. It has a slight potato flavor. Potato flour contains protein, the starch does not. It can absorb large amounts of liquid. Adding small amounts of potato flour (2%) to a sausage mix helps to increase the water holding capacity and hold the product together.

In food applications a starch is twice as effective as the flour it was made from.

100 g serving	Protein (g)	Fat (g)	Carbohy-drates (g)	Salt (mg)	Energy (cal)	Choles-terol (mg)
Potato flour	8.82	1.47	79.4	0	353	0
Potato starch	0	0	83.3	0	333	0
						Source: Bob's Red Mill Natural Foods

Rusk is a popular baked and ground product, made from wheat flour. It can be ground to different diameters and there is a coarse, medium or fine rusk. Rusk can absorb water at 3 - 4 times its weight.

Other popular binders are: oatmeal, bread crumbs, general flour, cornflour, potatoes, rice, farina, and semolina. Rusk and oatmeal (steel cut groats) are especially popular in England. Popular extenders are: rice, potatoes, and barley or buckwheat groats.

Starch Sugars - Dextrins and Maltodextrins

Starch can be hydrolyzed into simpler carbohydrates known as *dextrins* by acids, various enzymes, or a combination of the two. The extent of conversion is typically quantified by dextrose equivalent (DE), which is roughly the fraction of the glycosidic bonds in starch that have been broken. These starch sugars include:

- *Dextrose* (DE 100), commercial glucose, prepared by the complete hydrolysis of starch. This is the simplest form of sugar and is the preferred sugar for making fermented sausages (salami) as bacteria can feed on them without a delay. Dextrins provide 4 cal/g of energy.

- Various glucose syrup / *corn syrups* (DE 30–70), viscous solutions used as sweeteners and thickeners in many kinds of processed foods.

- *Maltodextrin*, a lightly hydrolyzed (DE 10–20) starch product used as a bland-tasting filler and thickener.

Dextrose equivalent (DE) is the relative sweetness of sugars, *compared to dextrose*, both expressed as a percentage. Dextrose is about 70% as sweet as common sugar (sucrose). For example, a maltodextrin with a DE of 10 would be 10% as sweet as dextrose (DE = 100), while sucrose, with a DE of 120, would be 1.2 times as sweet as dextrose. For solutions made from starch, it is an estimate of the percentage reducing sugars present in the total starch product.

Dextrose Equivalent (DE) of Different Carbohydrates	
Starch	0
Dextrins	1 - 11
Maltodextrins	3 - 20
Dextrose (glucose)	100
Sucrose (sugar)	120

The U.S. Food and Drug Administration classifies potato starch maltodextrin as a direct food ingredient. *There are no limits to the concentrations of maltodextrins allowed in foods.* As other carbohydrates they provide 4 cal/g. However, when used as fat replacements, they are mixed with a water to maltodextrin ratio of 3:1, which reduces the calories further to 1 cal/g.

Phosphates are the most effective water holding agents. Salt and most water binding agents force meat protein to swell which helps them trap and hold more water. Phosphates are able *to open the structure of the protein* which helps them to hold even more water.

This increased water holding capacity of the protein is what prevents water losses when smoking and cooking. Originally many countries in Europe such as Germany or Poland did not allow the use of phosphates, but after joining the European Common Market had to conform to the same regulations and were forced to accept their use. The case of liquid smoke in Germany is very similar. The country did not allow its use but now adding of liquid smoke is permitted. Needless to say, the products were better and healthier before.

Phosphates are the strongest water binders and protein extractors and all commercial producers use them. Most countries permit 0.5% of phosphates (5 g per kilogram of meat). Today, the whole meat industry operates on this principle, inject the maximum allowed amount of water and make sure it does not leak out.

There is tetrasodium pyrophosphate, there is tripolyphosphate, hexametaphosphate, there are diphosphates and they all exhibit different properties. American emulsified sausages can hold up to 40% of fats and water over the initial weight of the meat mass. If your starting sausage mass weighed 100 lb, then you have lost 15% during smoking and cooking and you should end up with 85 lb of product, right? Not a commercial plant, they will add up 10% fat trimmings, 30% of water and the final product will weigh 125 lb. Pure profit thanks to phosphates. In some countries there are no rules at all, a manufacturer can boost up the original weight of meat mass (100 lb) to 160 lb by using phosphates and water.

Curing accelerators speed up color formation. These substances accelerate the reaction of sodium nitrite with meat's myoglobin resulting in the development of the red color.

Ascorbic acid (vitamin C) - should not be added with sodium nitrite at the same time as they react violently creating fumes. Therefore, ascorbic acid should be added last. A vitamin C tablet may be pulverized and applied to meat. It is usually applied at 0.1%.

Sodium ascorbate - sodium salt of ascorbic acid.

Sodium erythorbate (isoascorbate) - salt of erythorbic acid.

Ascorbate is added at 0.4 - 0.6 g per kilogram of total mass, ascorbate or erythorbate are added at 0.5 - 0.7 g per kilogram of total mass.

Curing accelerators are of little use in air dried products as by increasing nitrite reaction they deplete its amount. As a result less nitrite is available for long time curing.

Antioxidants prolong the products shelf life by preventing fat rancidity and color changes that are caused by exposure in oxygen in the air. Sage, rosemary and oregano are known to delay rancidity.

Flavor Enhancers

MSG (monosodium glutamate) is a very effective flavor enhancer which is produced by the fermentation of starch, sugar beets, sugar cane, or molasses. Although once chiefly associated with foods in Chinese restaurants, it is now found in many common food items, particularly processed foods. MSG is commonly available in food stores.

Ribonucleotide is a much stronger flavor enhancer than MSG and is carried by commercial producers.

Yeast Extract is a natural food flavoring made from the same yeast used to make bread and beer. It is used to create savory flavors and umami taste sensations and can be found in a large variety of packaged food. In Italy it is often added to meat products and salami sausages.

Preservatives

Sodium metabisulphite and **sodium sulphite** are added to keep food safe for longer by preventing the growth of spoilage and pathogenic bacteria.

Sodium lactate or **potassium lactate** are used to increase the shelf life of the product in the amount of 3% (30 g/kg).

Acetate can be added to increase shelf life at around 3%. Larger amounts may impart a vinegar-like taste to the product.

Potassium sorbate is an effective mold inhibitor.

Meat Glue - Transglutaminase (TG), better known to chefs as "Meat Glue," has the wonderful ability to bond protein-containing foods together. Raw meats bound with meat glue are strong enough to be handled as if they were whole muscles. Transglutaminase was discovered in 1959 but was not widely used as it was hard to produce and was expensive. Only in 1989 the Japanese company Ajinomoto (best known for the production of MSG) made it cost efficient. Meat glue is primarily used for:

- Binding smaller cuts of meat into a larger ones. Small fish fillets can be bound together to form a large diameter roll.
- Making formed hams which are produced from individual cuts of meat.

- Making formed hams which are produced from individual cuts of meat.

Although meat glue will glue different meats together, for example fish and chicken, it is not such a good idea as they exhibit different textures and are cooked to different temperature requirements. Meat glue can be sprinkled on like a powder, mixed in water to make a slurry, or added directly into meat mixtures. About 0.1% is all that is needed to improve cohesion between the meat pieces.

Additives Typical Usage Amounts

Name	Common amount
Soy protein concentrate	1-3%
Soy protein isolate	1-3%
Non-fat dry milk	1-3%
Milk caseinate	2%
Whey protein concentrate	1-3%
Whey protein isolate	1-3%
Agar	0.2-3.0%
Alginate	0.5-1%
Carrageenan-Kappa	0.02-1.5%
Konjac	0.25-0.50%
Xanthan	0.02-0.03%
Locust bean gum (LBG)	0.1-1.0%
Gellan	0.4-0.7
Guar gum	0.1-0.7%
Gum Arabic	10-90%
Microcrystalline cellulose (MCC)	0.5-5%
Carbomethyl cellulose (CMC)	1.0-2.0%
Low methoxy pectin (LM Pectin)	0.5-3.0%
Gelatin	0.5-1.7%
Textured vegetable protein (TVP)	0.1-15%
Starch	1-5%
Monosodium glutamate	0.2-1.0%
Phosphate	0.1-0.5% (0.5% is the max allowed)
Ascorbate and erythorbate	0.03-0.05% (0.05% is the max)

Chapter 10

Sausage Types and Names

Sausages come in many shapes and different combinations of meat and spices. In some countries they are classified by the degree of comminution, ie. coarse grind or fine grind sausages which adds only to confusion. The following American system is very simple and practical:

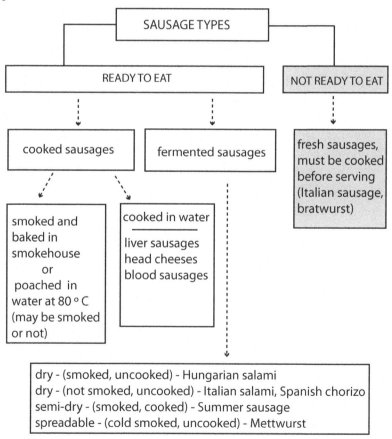

Fig. 10.1 Types of sausages.

Not Ready to Eat sausages are fresh sausages that are made normally from pork, but sometimes also, beef or veal. The meat is not cured, sausages must be refrigerated and fully cooked before serving. Examples: Italian Sausage, American Breakfast Sausages, German Bratwurst, Mexican Chorizo. They may be fried with eggs for breakfast or grilled at the party.

Ready to Eat Sausages is the main group of sausages that covers almost every sausage. With the exception of fermented and air dried sausages, all sausages that belong to this group are *cooked* in hot water or baked in a smokehouse or in the oven. Some sausages are hot smoked and cooked, others are not smoked, only cooked.

There is a special group of sausages that consists of *liver sausages, blood sausages, and head cheeses.* They are normally made from pork only although on occasion lean beef is added to liver sausages. Head cheeses and liver sausages are usually prepared from fresh uncured meats, although occasionally meats are cured for the development of a pink color, not for the safety reasons. Head cheese made with tongues looks much better when the meat is red and not grey. Meats used in these sausages are first precooked in hot water, then stuffed into casings and then they are cooked in hot water until the safe internal meat temperature is obtained. In simple words the cooking is performed twice. These sausages are usually not smoked although cooked liver sausages are occasionally briefly treated with cold smoke. Those products are fully cooked and kept under refrigeration.

Fermented sausages can be classified as:

◊   Fermented/dried, smoked, uncooked - Hungarian salami
◊   Fermented, smoked, uncooked - spreadable raw sausages German Mettwurst, Italian Nduja
◊   Fermented/dried, uncooked - Italian salami, Spanish chorizo
◊   Fermented/semi-dried, smoked, partially or fully cooked semi-dry sausages - Summer Sausage, Pepperoni, Salami

There are sausages called "non-fermented salami" (for example Koch Salami) which are neither fermented nor dried, but fully cooked. They only look like salami given that they have similarly looking texture with well defined small particles of meat and fat, and they are stuffed in a large diameter casings.

Smoked Sausages

All sausages can be smoked or not. What was once an important preservation step has become a matter of personal preference. If you like the smoky flavor, smoke the sausage, it's that simple. After smoking, most sausages enter the cooking process which can be an extension of the smoking step or may be performed in a different unit such as an oven or in a different media (hot water). Smoked sausages can be divided as:

◊ Cold smoked sausages. These sausages are not cooked and must be refrigerated. They may be dried at about 54° F (12° C) and after losing sufficient moisture they will not require refrigeration as long as kept at this temperature in a dark, lightly ventilated room at 65% humidity or less.

◊ Hot smoked sausages. Those sausages are fully cooked following smoking.

The Small World of Sausages

There are less original sausages than one might think. Many sausages have similar compositions but carry a different name due to the particular language that is used to name them. For example, the blood sausage which has been made for centuries:

• Blood sausage - USA
• Black pudding - UK
• Blutwurst - Germany
• Morcilla - Spain and South America
• Boudin Noir - France
• Kaszanka - Poland

Any sausage can be called "wurst" in German and it is correct. Or "kielbasa" in Polish, "chorizo" in Spanish or "chouriço" in Portuguese. The point we are stressing here is that once you understand how a particular type of a sausage is made, a head cheese for example, the name becomes less relevant and you can call it anyway you like, but it will still be a head cheese. One day you may call it "My Head Cheese" and the next time you add some vinegar to it and the name becomes "My Souse" although it is basically the same product. It is like making one sausage and calling it by different names.

You can make up your own recipe and call it My Kielbasa, My Wurst or My Chorizo and it will still be the same sausage. Polish Krakowska sausage (from the city of Krakow) is called Krakauer sausage in German, but that does not mean it is a different sausage as they both contain solid chunks of cured meat. You can create your own recipe and call it Thüringer Salami, or My Salami or American Salami and it will still be the same sausage. The point is that *there are much less original sausages that people like to think.*

And adding raisins, pineapples, prunes, peanuts and other ingredients hardly qualifies a sausage to be the new classic. Some sausages change names because the meat was ground with a different plate, but that is hardly a new sausage. Take all those recipes with a proverbial grain of salt and do not imagine that it must be a great recipe just because it was published in the book or on the Internet.

There are books written by known and recognized professors in the field of meat science that list thousands of recipes, but no instructions on how to make them. There is a book which lists 22 Polish Sausage formulations like this: Polish Sausage A, Polish Sausage B, Polish Sausage V, yet the book does not mention even one sausage by name, although all Polish sausages have their own names.

Every country has a farmer sausage or a countryside sausage. These are regular sausages which contain meat that is ground with a larger plate or cut with a knife. In many countries little sausages are called "Tourist" sausage, better quality liver sausages are often called "Delicatessen Liver Sausage."

European Certificates of Origin

The sausage gets its individual character when it is supported by the name of the region it has originally come from. Throughout Europe there is a huge assortment of great foods. When a product acquires a reputation extending beyond national borders, it can face competition from other products which may pass themselves off as the genuine article and take the same name.

Our hats go off to the French who invented the idea in the 1930's to protect their regional wines. The system used in France from the early part of the twentieth century is known as the Appellation d'Origine Contrôlée (AOC).

Items that meet geographical origin and quality standards may be endorsed with a government-issued stamp which acts as an official certification of the origins and standards of the product to the consumer. In 1992, the European Union created the following systems to promote and protect food products:

Photo 10.2 Protected Designation of Origin (PDO) - covers the term used to describe foodstuffs which are produced, processed and prepared in a given geographical area using recognized know-how.

Example: Italy - Prosciutto di Parma

Photo 10.3 Protected Geographical Indication (PGI) - the geographical link must occur in at least one of the stages of production, processing or preparation.

Example: France - Boudin blanc de Rethel

Photo 10.4 Traditional Speciality Guaranteed (TSG) - does not refer to the origin but highlights traditional character, either in the composition or means of production.

Example: Spain - Jamon Serrano

This system is similar to the French Appellation d'Origine Contrôlée (AOC) system, the Denominazione di Origine Controllata (DOC) used in Italy, and the Denominación de Origen system used in Spain. The law (enforced within the EU and being gradually expanded internationally via bilateral agreements of the EU with non-EU countries) ensures that only products genuinely originating in that region are allowed in commerce as such. The purpose of the law is to protect the reputation of the regional foods and eliminate the unfair competition and misleading of consumers by non-genuine products, which may be of inferior quality or of different flavor.

These laws protect the names of wines, cheeses, *hams, sausages,* olives, beers, and even regional breads, fruits, and vegetables. As such, foods such as Gorgonzola, Parmigiano Reggiano, Asiago cheese, Camembert de Normandie and Champagne can only be labelled as such if they come from the designated region. To qualify as Roquefort, for example, cheese must be made from the milk of a certain breed of sheep, and matured in the natural caves near the town of Roquefort in the Aveyron region of France where it is infected with the spores of a fungus (*Penicillium roqueforti*) that grows in those caves. Fresh meat and meat based products (cooked, salted, smoked, etc.) are also covered by the law and many countries have already filed their products with the European Commission.

European Certificates of Origin *don't come easy* and only a few countries were able to obtain them. Countries which were granted most Certificates of Origin for Meat Products and Sausages are: Portugal, Italy, Spain, France, and Germany. It shall be noted that countries that have joined the European Union at later dates still have products pending approval.

Any product that bears a certificate is certified as being unique and of the highest quality. It can be said that those certified products represent the best traditionally made products that the world has to offer. The products which were granted certification can be searched by the name or country of origin. There are details about the product and a brief description of its manufacturing process.

Country	Product Name	Type	Registration Date
Germany	Thüringer Rotwurst	PGI	18/12/2003
Hungary	Szegedl szalámi	PDO	15/12/2007
Italy	Prosciutto di Parma	PDO	05/02/2008
Poland	Kielbasa Lisiecka	PGI	13/10/2010
Spain	Jamón Serrano	TSG	13/11/1999

German Sausages

When seeing the name Bratwurst, Kochwurst, or Rohwurst, one might think that each represents a particular sausage. Well this is not the case and you have to break up the name to find more about the sausage. The word "wurst" denotes a sausage, nothing else.
Bratwurst - chopped sausage (brät = chopped)
Kochwurst - cooked sausage (koch = cooked)
Rohwurst - raw sausage (Mettwurst, Teewurst, salami), (roh = raw)
Leberwurst - liver sausage (leber = liver)
Sülzwurst - head cheese (sulz = jellied meat)
Blutwurst - blood sausage (blut = blood) Nürnberger Bratwurst (Bratwurst from Nürnberger region).
Münchener Bratwurst (Bratwurst from Münchener region).
Rheinische Bratwurst (Bratwurst from Rhein region).
Rheinische Leberwurst (liver sausage from Rhein region).
Thüringer Leberwurst - liver sausage from Thuringia region)
Frankfurter Leberwurst (liver sausage from Frankfurt region).
Berliner Sülzwurst (Head cheese from Berlin region).
Thüringer - sausage from Thuringia region

This sausage-by-region classification is not a new concept and we have been using it without even thinking when choosing salamis: Salami Genoa, Salami Milano, Salami Lombardia, Salami Sorrento etc. In most cases the recipes are very similar. The word "würstchen" means little sausage and the wiener sausage will be called "Wienerwürstchen" in German. By the same token Bratwürstchen denotes a little grill type sausage. When you come across this new intriguing recipe you may discover nothing else but the sausage that you have made before. Take for example "Knoblauchwurst." Knoblauch = garlic and "wurst" = sausage. What we have is a "garlic sausage." In Polish it is known as Kielbasa Czosnkowa (czosnek = garlic) and the Spanish will say "Chorizo con Ajo" (ajo = garlic). The sausage may go by many names but it is still ground meat, salt, pepper and a large amount of garlic. It may include other spices but as long as garlic is the dominant spice we have a garlic sausage.

Italian Meat Products *(Salumi)*

1. Sausages - *salame, cotechino, soppressata, luganiga, zampone, mortadella.*

2. Whole meat cuts - ham (*prosciutto*), shoulder (*spalla*), neck (*capocollo*), belly (*pancetta*), an aged fillet of rump (*culatello*), smoked flank (*speck*).

The meat products that have managed to obtain certifications are listed above, but keep in mind that there are hundreds of similar products which are not registered and they are all good. For example there are seven Prosciutto Ham registrations but thousands of prosciutto hams are made every day by meat processors and home sausage makers. They may differ slightly in their formulations but after all they are all dry hams.

Can anyone produce an equivalent ham, let's say Spanish Jamón Serrano or Italian Prosciutto di S. Danielle? Well, ham imitation can certainly be made but it will be almost impossible to produce an exact replica. With our modern computerized climate control chambers we can simulate the atmospheric conditions that prevail anywhere in the world, so depending on the climate is of lesser importance.

The factor that we can not replicate is the flavor of meat that comes from pigs that grow in a particular region. A pig grows very fast and the texture and flavor of its meat depends largely on its diet. Most of those animals graze freely in fields being fed a strictly controlled natural feed. Spanish pigs roam in oak forests and eat plenty of oak acorns. This alone affects the structure and color of the fat and the proportion of fat to lean.

A person living in a large city is at the mercy of a local supermarket where he obtains his meat. This meat has come from pigs that were raised on a commercial, supplemented with antibiotics diet, and the pigs were raised in different areas in the fastest possible way in order to obtain the highest return on investment. The quality of the meat will not compare to that which was produced on a small farm in Spain or Italy. This does not mean that one can not produce a wonderful ham at home. The point we are trying to make is that it will be impossible to exactly copy one of those registered European products. The main reason that those products have obtained those certificates is that they are so unique.

Spanish Meat Products

Classical Spanish sausages are Longanizas, Chorizos and Sobrasadas. It shall be noted that those sausages may be made differently in South and Latin America. Mexican Chorizo is also much hotter and vinegar is often used and in the Dominican Republic (Carribean) orange juice is added.

Two characteristics make those three sausages distinctly Spanish:

- Use of pimentón - Spanish grown and smoked paprika which gives it its deep red color and unique flavor (don't confuse with Hungarian sweet paprika). The paprika itself can be found as either sweet (dulce), bittersweet (agridulce) or hot (picante). After harvesting the little peppers are placed in drying houses where they are smoke-dried with oakwood for about two weeks. Pimentón although not generally available, even in gourmet shops, have no substitute for use in authentic Spanish cooking. It can be ordered on the Internet.

- The sausages are air dried (not cooked).

These sausages are almost always made from high quality pork, the butt being the preferred choice. The main spices are pimentón and garlic. There is very little difference between longanizas and chorizos as far as production methods are concerned. Chorizos vary in length from 6-8" to one foot long. They contain a slightly higher dosage of pimentón than longanizas but not as much as sobrasadas.

Sobrasadas are sausages from the Balearic Islands (Majorca and Menorca islands) which are similar to chorizos but are spiced very heavily with pimentón. The islands have a warm semi-tropical climate with more humidity and under such conditions it is difficult to dry-cure meat. This is the reason that sobrasada is cured by mixing it heavily with a locally grown paprika and sea salt. Pork casings are used and the sausages are hung to cure in the open air, usually for between one month and eight months, with the timing dependent on the size and shape of the casing. Sobrasada is a soft textured sausage (like a soft pâté) that can be spread on bread or added to simmered dishes. Since 1993 it has been recognized by the European Union with the quality seal of the Protected Geographical Identity.

Longanizas	Chorizos	Province
Andalusian	Andaluz	Andalucia
Calendaria	Calendario	
	Cantipalo	
Castellana	Castellano	Castilla-La Mancha
Extremeña	Extremeño	Extremadura
Navarra	Navarro	La Navarra
	Riojano	La Rioja
	Salamantino	Salamanca (Castilla-Leon)
	Sobrasada	Balearic Islands

La Morcilla (*Blood Sausage*) is used in virtually every Spanish kitchen. It is commonly added to most other meals and stews, but you can also slice and fry it, or cook it on your outdoor grill.

Butifarras (*La Morcilla Blanca - White Blood Sausage*) is made almost identically as the original blood sausage (*Morcilla*) but without blood. It is commonly called butifarra or white blood sausage (*La Morcilla Blanca*). Blood sausages made in other countries are classified in a similar manner: English Black or White Pudding, French **Boudin Noir** (*Blood Sausage*) or **Boudin Blanc** (*White Blood Sausage*). White blood sausages are often made with rice and milk.

Sometimes butifarras will contain blood as well but will be made correspondingly:

Butifarra Negra Catalana (*Black Catalan Butifarra*). Butifarra is perhaps the most popular Catalan (Barcelona area) sausage of them all. When you stop to eat at any restaurant in the countryside, invariably you will be served butifarra in one form or another.

Salchichas are common sausages that borrow recipes from known sausages from other countries. For example, Salchicha *Polaca* will be one of Polish sausages, Salchicha *Turca* (Turkish Sausage) or Salchicha *Inglesa* (English Sausage). Those sausages are about 4-5" (10-15 cm) long.

Salchichones (*Los Salchichones*) differ from regular sausages (salchichas) in that they are to be stored for a long time, often until the next slaughter. They are stuffed into larger diameter hog casings and ox casings are also used.

There is very little smoking employed when making Spanish sausages. There are a few salchichas or salchichones which are smoked but most sausages are air dried. Little smoke that is applied can be considered to be part of the drying process which was always performed in North European Countries such as Poland or Germany where meats were cold smoked for a long time. Needless to say those sausages developed a different style and much more pronounced smoky flavor. The climate in North Europe was ill suited for air drying meat products and thus the smoking art has developed. Almost all meat products in Poland are of the smoked variety. The Spanish climate was perfectly suited for drying meat products and there was less need to apply smoke to preserve meats. What is similar is that almost all meat products in Spain and Poland are made from pork.

South American - Latin American - Caribbean and Philippines Sausages

All these countries owe much of their culture to mother Spain and culinary arts are not an exception. Not surprising, all Spanish sausages are popular there although different climatic conditions have a profound influence on the methods of their manufacture. Most sausages made in Spain were air dried as the country was blessed with dry prevailing winds for most of the year which were ideally suited for air drying products. There is no vinegar present in Spanish recipes as that would unnecessarily add moisture and the purpose of drying is preserving a product by eliminating the moisture from it. The products were hung in dry cool areas for a year or two without any adverse effect to its quality.

In other Spanish speaking countries the climate is hot and humid and air drying would be severely limited. An exception would be Argentina and Chile which are large countries and contain many climatic zones. Countries situated in the Caribbean Basin are part of the tropics and are hot and humid and that will create unwelcome mold on sausages. All those countries add vinegar (sometimes wine) as these acidic fluids help to preserve food at least to a certain degree. Mexican sausages are much hotter than those made in other countries and recipes call for a hefty dose of hot peppers. Many countries (Cuba, Dominican Republic, Philippines) always faced energy problems and a large percentage of the population did not own refrigerators. A very common method was to keep sausages in barrels filled with lard (rendered pork fat).

Russian Sausages

During the Second World War the meat industry was wiped out and about 17 million cattle and huge quantities of poultry and pigs were killed. In 1945 about 2.6 million tons of meat (slaughter weight) was processed, the number which has increased to 8.7 million times in 1960. At the peak of the communist system, Russia produced about 200 different sausages and 65 types of smoked meats.

Hams: Moscow, Sibir, Soviet, and Tambov hams are made from hind legs. Voronezh ham is made from shoulder.
Rolled hams are made from boned hind and front legs after rolling the flesh with the skin outside. The popular types: Leningrad, Rostov, Soviet.

Types of Russian sausages:

1. Cooked sausages - Belorussian, Kharkov, Krasnodar, Metropolitan, Moscow, Doctor's, Teewurst.
2. Frankfurters.
3. Semi-smoked sausages - Poltava, Cracov, Lithuanian, Polish, Ukrainian, Kiev, Arzamas, Minsk, Tbilisi, Drogobych, Donbas, Semipalatinsk.
4. Smoked sausages - Moscow, Soviet, Tambov, Metropolitan, Orsk, Uglich, Maikop, Neva, Minsk, Tourist, Hunter's.
5. Special sausages - liver, head cheese and blood sausages.
6. Dietetic sausages.
7. Meat Loaves.
8. Pâtés.

Depending on the quality of meat and fat used, the cooked and smoked sausages were classified into: higher class, Class 1, and Class 2.

Polish Sausages

During WWII (1939 - 1945) most meat plants were destroyed and the rebirth was very slow. The country's currency "zloty" was not convertible, the government needed hard currency and the only way to get it was to export raw (coal) materials or finished goods (vodka, meat products). The government spared no effort to create the best meat industry. In 1945 someone came up with a brilliant idea of standardizing Polish meat products using traditional time proven recipes. The official list of products was drawn and the Department of the Meat Industry started to work out details.

In 1959 the first official guide for making meat products and sausages was issued. Its name was # 16 Collection of Recipes and Instructions for Making Meat Products and Sausages and it was reserved for internal use only. It was 300 pages long and had sections on meat curing, making brines, grinding and emulsifying, cooking, methods of smoking, the whole factory process was described in details. Then in 1964 the Polish Government issued an expanded version called # 21 Collection of Recipes and Instructions for Making Meat Products and Sausages. It was 760 pages long and included: 39 smoked products (hams, loins, bacon, ribs), 119 sausages, 12 headcheeses, 19 liver and blood sausages and 11 pâtés and meat loaves. In total 200 meat products were covered and ONLY ONE chemical was used. The additive was potassium nitrate which is still used today although it has been replaced by its easier to administer cousin - "sodium nitrite".

Those manuals were written by the best professionals in meat science the country had. The project was government funded and no effort or money was spared. This standardization allowed Poland to produce sausages of high and *consistent* quality. All meat plants and retail stores belonged to the government and meat inspectors rigidly enforced the regulations. Those government standardized recipes became legally binding documents that could not be changed. The government meat inspectors enforced the newly issued standards and the sausages tasted exactly the same even when produced in different regions of the country.

Some sausage makers were lucky and rich enough to bribe their way out to getting a passport, others simply defected crossing the border between Yugoslavia and Italy, those people brought the taste of Polish sausages to the USA and other countries. At that period, *between the end of the war and collapse of the communist system in 1989, Polish meat products were made the best ever.* The decline in Polish meat products is synonymous with the fall of the Berlin Wall and the subsequent collapse of communism. This opened Polish borders to free trade with the West and created new business ventures between Poland and other European countries.

Poland became a new undeveloped market and the capital started to flow in. Soon many meat processors established joint ventures loaded with capital and new partners. That allowed them to bring the latest technological meat machines and products were made faster and cheaper. Factory made curing solutions were injected by brine injectors into meat to shorten curing time and to increase the gain of the product. This peaceful revolution came so suddenly that the new government was caught by surprise and not able to control all that was happening. The meat industry imported the latest machinery and chemicals from other European countries and started to follow the new standards of production which were much lower than those that were enforced by the former Polish regime.

When Poland officially joined the Common Market in 2004 the situation deteriorated even further. Now the country had to conform to new European regulations and that did not make sausages any better. For example, in the 1900's the Polish government allowed 1.5 mg (150 parts per million) of phosphates to be added to 1 kg of meat (phosphates increase meat's water holding capacity). New standards allowed 5 mg of phosphates and of course manufacturers loved the idea as it amounted to higher profits. On the other hand now an average Polish consumer had to swallow three times more chemicals than before and was buying a product with more water in it. Common Market policies have affected other countries as well. For instance, Germany never allowed the use of liquid smoke in its products. When the country became a member of the European Common Market it had to conform to new regulations and liquid smoke is now added to meat products. Unfortunately, hundreds of smaller sausage makers who made wonderful products, could not compete with larger companies and went out of business. Very few managed to survive by charging higher prices for their superior products and catering to a more demanding consumer.

The Mystery of Polish Sausage - What is Kielbasa?

Without a doubt the word "Kielbasa" has worldwide recognition yet it is just one of many wonderful meat products that have been produced for centuries in Poland. It is also often misunderstood. Kielbasa is the Polish general name for "a sausage". You can not walk into a Polish store and say: "please give me a pound of kielbasa". The sales lady surrounded by 50 different kinds of kielbasa will inevitably reply: "yes, but which one"? It is like going into a deli and asking for some cheese. Sure, but which one: American, Provolone, Swiss, Gorgonzola, Gouda, Muenster - you have to provide some details.

As the most popular Polish sausage is without a doubt Polish Smoked Sausage, (Polska Kielbasa Wędzona) we are willing to speculate that this is what people have in mind. This is probably what the first immigrants brought with them to America. The little problem we face here is that you can find Polish Sausage in almost every supermarket in the USA and no two are made the same way. The Polish Smoked Sausage has been well defined for centuries and almost everybody in Poland knows what goes inside.

We do not intend to become judges in this matter. Instead, *we are going to rely on Polish Government Standards for Polish Smoked Sausage* as those rules have remained unchanged for the last 60 years. *This way if any reader does not agree with our recipes* he is welcome to contact the Polish Meat Industry in Warsaw, which still publishes the latest standards for meat products and sausages through the Polish Bureau of Standards (*Polski Komitet Normalizacyjny*).

Before we anger many people who have been making Polish Smoked Sausage in their own way for many years, let's clarify something further. If you add an ingredient that you or your children like into your sausage it is fine and you have the full right to say that you have made a better sausage than the famous Polish Smoked Sausage. You may say that your grandfather who came from Poland made the best Polish sausage in the world and we honor that. Maybe he used chicken stock instead of water or maybe he added something else.

What we are trying to say is that he was making *his own version* of the known classic or some other Polish sausage and it could have tasted better for you and your family. We do not dispute that fact. You can of course add anything you like to your sausage, but it will no longer be the original Polish Smoked Sausage (Polska Kiełbasa Wędzona) or another sausage. Once you start changing ingredients you create your own recipe and you may as well come up with your own name. Let's unravel some of the mystery:

1. For centuries Polish Smoked Sausage was made entirely of pork. Then in 1964 the Polish Government introduced a second version of the sausage that was made of 80% pork and 20% beef. All other ingredients: *salt, pepper, sugar, garlic*, and marjoram remain the same in both recipes. The marjoram is optional but the garlic is a must.

2. The meat is cured before it is mixed with spices.

3. The sausage is stuffed into a large hog casing: 36 - 38 mm.

4. The traditional way was to cold smoke it for 1 to 1.5 days (it had to last for long time).

5. In most cases it is hot smoked today.

For curiosity sake let's see how large American manufacturers make Polish Smoked Sausage. Four sausages called Polish Kielbasa were bought at the American supermarket and each of them were produced by a large and well known meat plant. Let's see how they compare with the original Polish recipe.

Name	Meat used	Ingredients
Authentic Polish Smoked Sausage Natural hardwood Smoked	Pork	salt, pepper, sugar, garlic, marjoram, *sodium nitrite*
Polish Sausage Natural Hardwood Smoked	Pork, beef, turkey	salt, water, corn syrup, 2% or less dextrose, *flavorings,* ground yellow mustard, autolyzed yeast, hydrolyzed whey protein, monosodium glutamate, potassium and sodium lactate, sodium diacetate, *sodium nitrite*, starch, (modified food, potato starch), Vitamin C (Ascorbic Acid, Contains: milk
Polish Sausage *Natural Smoke Flavoring Added*	pork, turkey, beef (2% or less)	salt, turkey broth, water, corn syrup, starch (potato, modified starch), dextrose, hydrolyzed milk protein, *smoke flavoring,* Vitamin C (Ascorbic Acid), autolyzed yeast, gelatin, sodium phosphate, sodium diacetate, *sodium nitrite,* potassium lactate, potassium chloride, granulated garlic, oleoresin of paprika, *flavorings,* ingredients not found in or in excess of amount permitted in regular smoked sausage, Contains: milk
Polish Sausage Naturally Hickory Smoked	Pork, beef	salt, water, dextrose, *natural spices,* garlic powder, paprika, monosodium glutamate, sodium erythorbate, *sodium nitrite*
Polska Kielbasa Fully Cooked	Beef	salt, water, corn syrup, 2% or less of: natural spices, natural flavors, dextrose, monosodium glutamate, isolated soy protein, Vitamin C (Ascorbic Acid), sodium phosphates, **sodium nitrite**, Contains: soy

Looking at the above sausage recipes we tried to come up with a name of an equivalent Polish sausage that might fit the description but we couldn't. It becomes quite clear that different manufacturers put different ingredients inside of the casing and the name Polish Kielbasa is used just for credibility and to gain the trust of the consumer. It seems that for some manufacturers *any sausage that is smoked and stuffed in a 36 mm casing* will qualify to be called the Polish Smoked Sausage or Polish Kielbasa. With all due respect to the Polish meat industry we can say that *although today the recipes remain basically correct, binders, fillers and chemicals are widely used in order to improve yield and profits.* That is why there is such an interest in home made products as people want the old quality and taste. It is not realistic to expect that a person will make sausages all the time, but it is feasible that he might do it once for Christmas and another time for Easter, exactly as it was done 100 years ago.

Although we do love the latest achievements in science and technology, we feel that the simple time proven methods of sausage manufacturing will still create higher quality products. It may not last as long on the shelf or in a refrigerator, it may lose its pink color sooner, *but it will definitely taste better.* I do not care much how pretty and plump they are, as they will not hang on the wall among my paintings and photographs. I am going to eat my sausages and I want them to be good. As mentioned earlier the best quality sausages were made in Poland until the collapse of the Berlin Wall in 1989. Then in 2004, Poland joined the European Common Market and the situation deteriorated even further. Polish sausages were never the same again.

Many great cold smoked products were made in the past in Poland and Russia. When thinking about Russia, a picture of a poor farmer laboring his land often comes to mind. Well, there was also an aristocrat, Tzar family and royalty who liked good food, sausages not being an exception. The same happened in Poland and continued during the communist regime when the privileged class (party members) had access to the special state run stores where everything was available: the best locally made foods and sausages, American cigarettes, French cognac, and other fancy items. Farmers and miners were miserable and hungry but the party members were having a ball. Lithuania was the region that developed a reputation for making wonderful and long lasting products. One of the most famous products was "Kindziuk" ("Skilandis" in Lithuanian) but today most unfortunately it is a thing of the past. It is not made commercially for the mass market as the costs would be too high, but it can be made at home. The end product was microbiologically stable, and had an almost indefinite shelf life. Looking at those recipes and keeping in mind the scientific advance in meat science, it is conclusive that these were naturally fermented products. If these products were made in Italy, we would have called them salamis today. The procedure was as follows:

- Top quality meats were selected and cured with salt and nitrate for 3-4 days at low temperatures. This is the same as the curing process where the purpose is to develop a larger number of beneficial bacteria (*Lactobacilli* and *Micrococci*).

- Sausages were smoked with cold smoke (below 22° C, 72° F) for weeks at the time. This allowed natural fermentation and drying to take place inside of the smokehouse.

- Sausages were left hanging in a smokehouse for a long time which created proper conditions for lowering water activity (drying) and ripening (development of flavor). Due to the action of the smoke, there was no mold on the sausages and if it developed it would be wiped off.

All those times and temperatures fall precisely into the principles of making traditional products as practiced in Southern Europe. The only difference was that due to a favorable climate, Mediterranean products were made in the open air and North European sausages were made during the cold season inside of a smokehouse.

Why Have We Made Better Sausages in the Past?

Well, there are three answers to this question and one can be found already in the first step of sausage making - *the meat selection process.* Good meat cuts make good meat products, everybody knows that.

1. Meat quality. The flavor of the meat, especially the pig, depends on its diet. If the animal eats a lot of barley its meat is firm and fat. If the same pig will be fed with corn, its meat will be softer and fatter. Meat of pigs that were fed with kitchen meal leftovers or fed mainly with potatoes or beets, will contain more water in it. Even today famous Spanish Serrano hams are still made from pigs that graze freely on grass and eat a lot of oak acorns. Change that diet and you will change the quality of the ham. Old sausage makers were well aware of those factors and for them meat was quality food and they strived for the best. Today all pork tastes the same as it is mass produced, growth hormones and antibiotics are added, and the pigs movement is restricted in order for the animals to grow as fast as possible.

Living in large metropolitan centers, there is little we can do about choosing our meat as we depend entirely on a local supermarket that we buy it from. That large piece of meat that we buy from a supermarket will be most likely already individually packed and injected with liquid. If you read the label it will say: "up to 12% of patented solution was added *to improve tenderness and juiciness*". And the ingredients are listed on the label: potassium lactate, sodium phosphates, salt, sodium diacetate.

Pig meat was perfect for thousands of years and now suddenly our plants want to improve it? Well, the truth is that this patented solution was added to improve the meat's shelf keeping qualities and preserve color, but that does not sound as nice as saying: to improve "tenderness and juiciness". Another factor which is completely beyond our control is that the pigs of today are fed a specially prepared diet to make their meat much leaner. You have to take that under consideration because the fat is what makes sausages succulent and those meats used in old recipes were much fatter. You may not agree with me, but when I eat my hamburger I want it to be good and juicy, and I intend to compensate for my cholesterol in another way. The same applies to sausages.

2. Adding water. It seems that today's meat technology is obsessed with adding the maximum amount of water that the meat can hold inside. Entire labs with college educated scientists are working on better and more efficient ways of trapping water inside. Check out any meat equipment supplier and you will see that half of all equipment manufactured today is related to injecting meat with curing solutions and shaking it in tumblers to uniformly distribute this liquid. And the final result? Of course more juiciness, after all you are eating more water now. But what happened to the original meat flavor?

Well, it's gone now so you have to use all kinds of flavor enhancements to compensate for it. Here is a simple example to follow. Let's assume that for many years you have been drinking your favorite Earl Grey tea and you have always used one tea bag per cup of water. What will happen if you still will use one tea bag but add 50% more water to your tea? *Will it taste the same or will it taste weaker?* The answer is self explanatory. The same happens to the quality of meat, it may be juicier but it will have a watered down flavor.

3. Extra ingredients. Looking at the original recipes you will see how little spice was needed to impart a required flavor to a particular sausage. And this is how they were made and they were great. No binders, fillers or chemicals were used, *only meat, salt, pepper, sugar and spices.* The only chemical that was used was potassium nitrate and that ingredient was mandated by law in Poland and everywhere else in the world. Nitrates are still used in every country, although in its different form called nitrite. If you look at the label of any commercially produced sausage, you will see how many ingredients go inside. All those extras have a certain cumulative value and will distort the flavor of the sausage. *To compensate for that we have to increase the amount of spices and use flavor enhancers.*

We are not picking on meat plants that make those products as we understand that they have to walk a very thin line between profits and quality. Our aim is to convince you that *you can make those sausages at home the way they were once made.* To stress the point that you can make a superior product without adding chemicals, let's look at the example of the famous Polish ham "Krakus" brand that was made during the Communism rule.

The main reason Polish Ham "Krakus" brand was the best ham in the world was that it was produced from carefully selected young hogs and no water was added. The consumer enjoyed the full taste and flavor. The ham was cured in water, salt and nitrate only. *Nothing else was added.* This cure (1.5 - 7%) was injected into an artery and then the ham was immersed in cure for 10 days. Then it was rinsed, dried, smoked and cooked. The ham was canned, it had its own certificate of authenticity and its own serial number. It was so good it grabbed 30% of the American market share and was displayed in every supermarket.

Later, the Krakus brand was purchased by Polish concern "Animex" which was owned by the biggest American meat processor Smithfield Foods which was founded in Smithfield, Virginia, in 1936. In 2013 Hong Kong-based WH Group acquired Smithfield Foods. The Krakus brand ham still exists today, however, we have no details about how those hams are manufactured today as the brand is owned by the Chinese.

Chapter 11

Sausage Making Process

Making Sausages

Sausages require some extra work as the meat has to be ground, mixed and stuffed into the casing. Making sausage is like making hamburger - the meat is ground, salt, pepper and the required spices are added, and then it is cooked until it is safe for consumption. If this prepared meat were stuffed into casings it would become a sausage. While various recipes usually get the spotlight (there are thousands on the Internet), the technical know-how behind preparing sausages is far more important. These basic rules will dictate how to make your meal both delicious and safe. Basically, a sausage is meat, salt and pepper. Most sausages will include a dominant spice plus other spices and ingredients.

The proper amount of salt in meat (tastes pleasant) is between 1.5-2% and 3.5-5% will be the upper limit of acceptability; anything more and the product will be too salty. There is less room for compromise when making fermented sausages where salt is used as a safety hurdle to prevent the growth of bacteria in the first stage of processing. Dry sausages require about 3% of salt and semi-dry around 2.5%. Usually, most home sausage makers omit the curing step. This can be attributed to the lack of information available on curing meats for sausages as many recipes on the Internet are very amateurish at best.

A commercial plant might avoid the traditional way of curing meats in order to save time and space but they make up for it by injecting larger cuts with curing solution or adding salt, nitrite, and curing accelerators during meat chopping and mixing. As a result the meat still cured and red although by using different methods. What is missing is *"curing flavor"* which could not be obtained in such a short time. For example, a frankfurter which is a smoked sausage is cured, smoked, peeled and packed in about 30-45 minutes.

The sausage making process:

- Meat selection
- Curing
- Grinding
- Mixing
- Stuffing
- Conditioning (pre-drying)
- Smoking
- Cooking
- Cooling
- Storing

There are some exceptions to the above process:

- Fresh sausages-manufacture ends with stuffing.
- Boiled sausages (liver, head cheese and blood sausages) - meats are cooked, the sausage is stuffed and then cooked. The cooking process is performed twice.
- Fermented sausages - cooking step is usually absent.
- Smoking and conditioning step may be employed or not.

Meat Selection

All cuts of good meat make good sausages. The trick is to know when and how to use them. Trim out all gristle, sinew, blood clots, and excess fat but save suitable trimmings for later. They can be used for making emulsified sausages or head cheeses. Those lower quality trimmings are hard to grind through a grinder but a food processor will chop them fine. If you choose only lean cuts, your sausage will definitely be healthier, but you will miss out on the taste.

Most sausages are made of either pure pork, or a combination with other meats, most often beef. Sausages made entirely from beef will be drier with a harder texture. In Germany sausages are often made from equal amounts of pork and beef, in Poland pork is more popular. Hungarian, Italian and Spanish sausages contain mostly pork.

Sausages need about 25-30% of fat in them and when it comes to selecting pork meat for sausages, the majority of books and recipes mention the same magical word: "use a pork butt" as it has the right lean meat to fat ratio of 70/30 so pork butt is an excellent choice.

What about a guy with a big family who buys the whole hog - there are only two pork butts and he certainly can make some sausages but what about the rest of the meat? He should have nothing left, cuts like ribs, chops, and loins will be eaten right away. The rest can be processed to make products like hams, butts, smoked bacon, back fat, blood sausage, liverwurst, head cheese and dozens of different sausages.

Veal makes a light colored sausage and has excellent binding properties. Mutton can also be used in sausage. It has poor water holding properties and its distinctive flavor is not appreciated by many. For this reason it should be limited to around 15% in any recipe.

Emulsified sausages (finely comminuted) such as high quality frankfurters usually contain more beef (40-60%) due to its excellent water holding capacities. Cheaply produced commercial versions incorporate machine separated meat, different trimmings, and phosphates which are known for their strong water binding properties. You can mix fresh and previously frozen meats together but for the best results there should be no more than 20-30% frozen meat.

Geographical locations have often dictated what animals can grow in a particular climatic zone. High altitudes establish the vegetation that will grow at those levels which will attract only animals that like such a diet. Lamas have adapted well to the high Andes of South America and will be popular meat in Bolivia and Chile. Goats generally prosper well in mountainous locations. Ostrich is commonly consumed in South Africa.

People living in off beaten track areas, (i.e. Central Alaska) might use wild game meats like moose, bear, elk, reindeer, caribou or rabbit, however, it is still recommended to mix these lean meats with pork fat to achieve better texture and flavor. Local custom and religious beliefs greatly influence which meats will be selected. Norway is known for using different meats such as moose, reindeer, mutton, lamb, goat, horse, offal (heart, liver) and blood. Norwegian sausages such as Faremorr, Sognemorr gilde, Stabbur and Tiriltunga contain beef, lamb and horsemeat and are heavily smoked.

The second important factor is a religious belief and many people stay away from pork, depriving themselves from eating the best quality products.

The third factor will be simple economics which is to reserve the consumption of higher value meats to the upper class and those less fortunate have to look at other combinations of meats. Sausages are made from sheep, goats, camels, horses and other meats, but those materials will hardly appeal to the majority of Western consumers.

Sausages can be made from all kinds of meats, some of them quite exotic, but we limit our choices to meats that are common. Chicken is the most popular meat which is consumed worldwide as it is easy to raise and can be cooked and eaten by the average family at one sitting. Other meats of value are fish, venison and wild game.

Meat Type	Advantages	Disadvantages
Chicken	Cheap, contains little fat, available every-where.	High pH: breast 5.6-5.8, thigh 6.1-6.4. Poor fat characteristics, very low fat melting point temperature. Low myoglobin content (light meat, especially breast) results in a poor final color. Skin often contains a large number of pathogenic bacteria.
Fish	Cheap raw material. Easy to process. All varieties can be used, including de-boned meat.	Needs to be combined with pork or other meats. No myoglobin (white or grayish color). The final flavor is always fishy even when other meats were added.
Venison	Good color, good price. Popular meat in Northwestern U.S. and Alaska.	Available during hunting season. Often infected with trichinae worms. Very lean, needs some pork fat.

Meat Classes

Imagine a butcher cutting pork into pieces until nothing is left on the table. Before he can carve out a ham from the leg he has to separate it from the body, then cut off the lower leg, remove the bones, tendons, gristle, sinews, skin, pieces of fat etc. To get a clean piece of meat like a ham, butt or pork loin a lot of work has to be performed first in order to separate scraps of meat that cannot be sold in one piece.

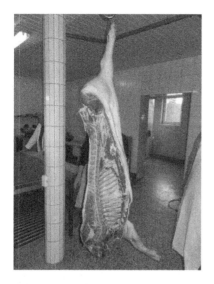

Photo 11.1

Photo 11.2

Photo 11.4

Photo 11.3

Photo 11.6

Photo 11.5

As carving progresses only smaller cuts and trimmings remain. These are grouped into different classes and will be used for making sausages.

Keep in mind that the meat plant was established to bring profits to its owners, and every little piece of meat, fat, and blood included is money. A commercial recipe does not call for pork butt, lean ham or beef chuck. The recipe asks for pork class 1, beef class 2 or back fat class 1 or 2. It may call for jowl or belly fat. It really *does not matter whether this meat comes from ham, butt, picnic or from the container with little meat pieces* as long as it fulfills the requirements of the recipe. Only after all those scraps of meats are depleted, then a meat plant may resort to using noble parts such as ham or loin for sausages.

All those trimmings end up in a cooler in labelled containers. Names such as ham, picnic or butt lose their meaning as one can only see cuts of meat with different fat contents. They have to be classified in some logical manner so they can be picked up from a cooler by any operator and transferred to production.

Photo 11.7 Pork class I.

Photo 11.8 Pork class II.

Photo 11.9 Pork class III.

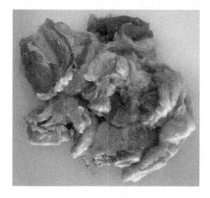

Photo 11.10 Pork class IV.

For orientation purposes we provide a glimpse at the meat classification system that has been used in Poland. Germany uses a similar system.

Pork	
Meat Class	Market Equivalent
I - No bone, lean, no sinews. Fat between muscles up to 2 mm. No more than 15 % fat.	**Ham** (rear pork leg). *You can obtain all meat grades from pork leg.*
II - A, No bone, medium fat, little sinews. Fat between muscles up to 10 mm. No more than 30 % fat.	Pork **butt** also known as Boston butt. *You can obtain all meat grades from pork shoulder.*
II - B, No bone, little sinews. Fat between muscles up to 10 mm. No more than 45 % fat.	Pork picnic (pork shoulder). Other cuts.
III - Lean or medium lean, *a lot of sinews.* No more than 25% fat.	Pork picnic, legs. Other cuts.
IV - No bone, traces of blood, tendons, glands. No more than 36% fat. Other criteria not defined. Lowest quality meat.	Pork picnic, legs. Other cuts.
Beef	
I	No bone, lean, no tendons. Fat between muscles - none. No more than 7 % fat.
II	No bone, lean, some tendons. Fat between muscles up to 2 mm. No more than 16% fat.
III	Fat beef. Fat between muscles up to 10 mm. No more than 45% fat.
IV	No bone, traces of blood, tendons, glands. No more than 40% fat.

Looking at meat class III or IV that contains a lot of sinews one can develop the feeling that it is a low quality meat. After all who wants to chew meat with sinews. The truth is that *this is a very important meat class as it contains a lot of collagen* that is necessary for binding meats and ingredients together. When slow cooked in a little water collagen will turn into liquid gelatin which will solidify again upon cooling, and will hold everything together.

When meat is ground and placed for sale in a supermarket it is labeled as 85% lean, 70% lean or even 90% lean. When this meat is ground the calculations are made as to its fat content and more lean meat or more fat are added in order to comply with the requirement of a particular label. *It is a great idea to get into the habit of thinking in terms of meat classes or grades when making your own products.* Once we become familiar with this way of thinking we will be able to look at the cut of the meat and decide what will be the best product to use it for. All the time different meats are on sale and they can be bought at a good price and stored in a freezer until needed.

A pig has only two pork butts weighing together about 15 pounds but the farmer is left with an additional 250 pounds of meat that must be used. Without a doubt pork butt is a lovely cut for making sausages and the best choice for someone living in a large city as it is widely available and is economically priced. Its little blade bone is easy to remove and we are left with six pounds of meat *that can be graded into all classes.* There is lean meat, meat with some fat, meat with a lot of fat, some pure fat and the skin.

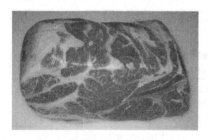

Photo 11.12 Pork butt, fat. A butt's surface fat is a hard fat which leads itself for making any sausage, for example salami.

Photo 11.11 Pork butt.

Save the skin as it can be frozen and used later to make liver sausage.

Picnic (front leg) contains very little true lean meat (class I), but contains a lot of connective tissue (collagen) and *is great for making a head cheese.* It is next to impossible to get pork head meat for a person living in a large city and picnic is a fine substitute. We may think of all those little scraps of meats with gristle and sinews as inferior meats, but they are rich in collagen and will produce gelatin for head cheeses or will help to bind fats and water in liver sausages.

Photo 11.13 Picnic consists of a leg bone and many individual muscles which are surrounded with connective tissue.

Picnic is a poor choice for a beginner but a great cut for someone who can make different types of sausages. It contains a lot of trimmings that can be used for making emulsified sausages, liver sausages and head cheeses. It requires much more work to trim it down into suitable pieces. In addition it contains a lot of connective tissue which will put a regular home grinder to a serious test. A bowl cuter or kitchen food processor is needed to effectively cut such trimmings.

Photo 11.14 Pork picnic muscle surrounded with connective tissue (silver screen).

Knowing meat classes will help you immensely when shopping for better deals at large supermarkets. You will understand what quality meat you will be buying, regardless what's on the label. Next time when trimming pork chops, loins or hams for roasting, save all those little meat pieces and put them into a freezer. You can use them to make sausages at a later date. All professional books that list sausage recipes list materials using concept of meat classes.

When making sausages from pork butt, save the skin and fat for later use in a head cheese or liver sausage. When carving ham or butt you will get all meat classes, of course in different proportions. Picnic which is mainly class III, will also provide class II or even a piece of meat class I. It is a good substitute for pork head meat.

Let's assume that tripe is on sale. Well, there is nothing wrong with a tripe stew, ask anybody in Europe or any person of Spanish descent. Buy the tripe, precook it, grind it, add 20% into any sausage and your sausage will taste great, will cost you less and will have a lighter color. Tripe has poor binding qualities so you won't be able to add too much water.

After the best cuts of meat are selected for steak, hams, bacons and loins, there is a large number of trimmings such as fat and meat trimmings, heads, skins, and offal meat such as liver, heart, kidneys, lungs, tripe and whatever remains leftover. All those leftovers end up in bologna, hot dogs and frankfurters.

People living on a farm have more control over the meat when the animal is slaughtered. They can process still warm meat and thus obtain the highest quality product. It will be unrealistic to expect that on the farm the entire animal will be processed in a few hours, but at least meat cuts that are prone to spoil such as liver or blood should be immediately processed, unless they can be frozen. It is more practical to throw split pork head, hocks, feet, and leftover ribs into a stock pot and slow boil it for 3-4 hours. Then, this pre-coked meat can be used for making head cheeses, blood and liver sausages on the same or on the following day.

Fat. There are different types of fat and they will all be used for different purposes. There are hard, medium and soft fats and they have a different texture and different melting point. Some head cheese and emulsified sausage recipes call for dewlap or jowl fat that may be hard to obtain. Bacon looks similar and it seems like a good replacement, but it is not. Bacon is a soft belly fat and dewlap/jowl is a hard fat. Fatter cuts from a pork butt are a much better choice that contain hard fat and meat.

Pork fat is preferred for making sausages as it is hard, white and tastes the best. It exhibits different degrees of hardness depending from which animal part it comes from. Back fat, jowl fat, or butt fat (surface area) have a very hard texture and higher melting point. They are the best choice for making products in which we expect to see the individual specks of fat in a finished product such as dry salami. Soft fat such as belly fat and fat trimmings are fine for spreadable sausages such as fermented mettwurst or fine liver sausages. For most sausages any fat pork trimmings are fine providing they were partially frozen when submitted to the grinding process.

This prevents fat smearing when temperature increases due to the mechanical action of knives and delivery worm on fat particles.

Beef fat has a higher melting temperature than pork but is yellowish in color which affects the appearance of the product in which discrete particles of fat should be visible. Besides, beef fat does not taste as good as pork fat. If no back fat is available, use fat pork trimmings or meats which contain more fat and grind them together. Instead of struggling with fat smearing when processing meats at higher than recommended temperatures, it is better to use cuts that contain a higher proportion of fat. Partially frozen back fat may be manually diced with ease into 3/16" (5 mm) pieces.

Chicken fat is neutral in flavor and is suited for making chicken sausages although it presents some problems. It is soft and melts at such low temperatures that it is hard to work with. Softer fats can be used for making emulsified or liver sausages where it will become a part of emulsified paste. For instance, vegetable oil can be successfully mixed with liver and fat when producing liver sausage.

Curing Meat For Sausages

Let's make something absolutely clear, you don't need to cure meat to make your sausage. Grind the meat, mix with spices and stuff the mass into a casing. Grill it, hot smoke it, or place it in a refrigerator, the product is still called a sausage. Curing is an extra process that requires more time, designated containers and a space in a refrigerator.

The reason we advocate the curing procedure is that *this book is about making quality products* and quality takes time. Meat for quality smoked sausage *should be cured.* Curing imparts a certain peculiar flavor which is in demand by the consumer and if we cure hams, bacon, chops, butts, and fish because they taste better, so why not cure meat for sausages? The fact that we grind meat makes it only easier on our teeth to chew it - it does not improve the color, texture or the flavor of the sausage.

Someone might say: but I've mixed nitrite and spices with ground meat before stuffing so that's OK. Well, it's not ok, the problem is that *not enough time* was allocated and although the sausage has developed an acceptable red color, its curing flavor is missing.

The curing time depends on:

- Diameter of the meat - making cuts smaller or grinding them increases the meat's surface area and speeds up curing.
- Temperature - usually set by the refrigerator setting. In the past when Nitrates were used, curing temperatures were higher (42-46° F, 6-8° C) which promoted the growth of curing bacteria.
- Additives - curing accelerators speed up curing which is of great importance for commercial producers.

Meat should be cut into smaller pieces, about 1-2 inches (2.5-5 cm). Then the pieces are thoroughly mixed with salt, Cure #1 (salt, nitrite), packed tightly in a container, covered with clean cloth and stored in a refrigerator. There are chemical reactions taking place inside meat and the cloth allows the gases to evaporate through. It also prevents the surface of the meat from reacting with oxygen which creates gray color areas on the surface. This is normal, the meat is fine and there is nothing to worry about. With the use of ascorbates and erythorbates it is possible to cure meats at even lower temperatures, which is commonly practiced by commercial establishments. The curing times at 40° F (4° C) (refrigerator temperature) are as follows:

- Meat pieces size: 2" - 72 hours, 1" size - 48 hours
- Ground meat - 24 - 36 hours, depending on a plate size

What will happen to smoked sausages if the meat is not cured? Basically nothing as long as you add salt and Cure #1 (sodium nitrite) to meat during mixing (you are still curing meat). The final color might not be as good as the properly cured sausage but it will still be a great sausage.

Photo 11.15 Dry and wet cured meats in a cooler.

Alternative curing methods

If you don't want to cure meat using the traditional method, use the alternative curing method described below.

Method 1. Grind each meat through a proper plate (as dictated by the recipe). Salt and sodium nitrite will penetrate tiny pieces of ground meat much faster. Mix meat with salt and Cure #1. Pack tightly (to remove air) and separately, place each type of ground meat in a container and cover it. Let it "set" for 3-4 hours at room temperature 20-22°C (68-71°F). Chemical reactions proceed much faster at higher temperatures and so does curing. Add spices, mix and stuff casings.

Method 2. Grind each meat through a proper plate (as dictated by the recipe). Mix meat with salt, Cure #1 and other ingredients. *Stuff sausages and place in a cooler* for 12 hours before smoking. When removed from a cooler they have to be conditioned at room temperature for a few hours to remove moisture from the surface.

Method 3. Grind each meat through a proper plate (as dictated by the recipe). Mix meat with salt, Cure #1 and other ingredients. *Stuff sausages and hang at room temperature* for 2 hours. Transfer to a smokehouse. Apply smoke when sausages feel dry.

As you can see in all instances *we are buying extra time* to allow curing inside the meat. A commercial producer will not perform curing at higher than cooler temperature as this will affect the shelf life of the product. Commercial processors cure meat faster and at lower temperatures by using ascorbic acid, erythorbic acid, or their derivatives, sodium ascorbate and/or sodium erythorbate. These additives speed up the chemical conversion of nitrite to nitric oxide which in turn will react with meat myoglobin to create a pink color. They also deplete levels of meat oxygen which prevents the fading of the cured meat color in the presence of light and oxygen.

Bear in mind that those "simplified" curing methods can not be used when curing whole pieces like hams, butts or loins. Due to the insufficient curing time there will be uneven pink, red or even gray areas inside. That would be easily noticeable when slicing those meats. As sausage is made from comminuted meat any variations in color cannot be spotted, unless larger chunks of meat are added. When making less than 5 pounds of sausage it is perfectly acceptable to make curing a part of the mixing and conditioning process. This way the sausage is stuffed, cured and smoked in one operation.

Processing large amounts of sausage may be separated into parts:

1. The first day - meat selection and trimming. The skin and bones are removed, all sinews, gristle and glands are discarded. Meat is cut into small pieces, mixed with salt and nitrite and placed in a refrigerator for 24 hours where it will cure properly.

2. The second day - cured meat goes into the grinder and the sausage making process continues.

Grinding

The lean meat should be separated from the fat. As a rule, lean meat is ground coarsely while fatty cuts are ground very finely. This way our sausage is lean looking and the fat is less visible. It is much easier to grind cold meat taken directly out of the refrigerator. The question may arise, why do we grind different grades of meat through different plates? It will be much easier to use 3/8" plate for everything. You could do just that if you had only high grade lean meats. With such fine meats you would not get any pieces of bone, gristle or sinews that would stick between your teeth.

Large grinder plate advantages

Larger grinder plate produces larger meat particles which retain more meat juices and water, thus providing a more satisfied mouthfeel. Many sausages contain "show meat" which are large chunks of meat or fat and these are supposed to be seen. Examples: Mortadella Bologna (fat cubes), Krakowska Sausage (lean meat chunks). Such show meat can be manually cut with a knife or ground through a large hole plate.

Small grinder plate advantage

Lower grade meats, especially the ones with connective tissue would be hard to chew if they were not finely ground. Lean pork, more so lean beef, when ground through small plate holes release more protein which dissolves in salt and water. This improves the binding of all ingredients. The smaller and cleaner the grind the stronger the binding power of the meat. A grinder, manual or electrical, cuts meat and *pushes meat* through plate holes, cutting meat but also mechanically breaking it at the same time. A bowl cutter cuts cleanly without tearing up the meat's structure. It generates a lot of heat so ice or cold water are added to cool down the meat and rotating knives. That allows the meat to emulsify into a consistency of fine paste that is able to trap all this ice and water and hold it inside.

A customer may be reluctant to purchase a sausage with a large amount of visible fat. By grinding fat through a fine plate the fat will will be less noticeable. Emulsified sausages such as hot dog or bologna include plenty of fat, but all a customer sees is a meat paste.

There is not any rigid, fixed rule in regard to grinder plates and that the plate selection depends greatly on the type of sausage that you decide to make. For hundreds of years we chopped meat with knives and stuffed it with fingers through a horn. And the sausages were great. Queen Victoria of England had her own very strict rules about making her sausages:

- The meat had to be chopped, not ground to prevent natural juices from leaking out.
- The casings had to be filled by hand, the mixture pressed down through a funnel with the thumbs.

The fat is usually ground through a plate with very small holes and if it is not partially frozen a smeared paste will be produced. The locking ring on a grinder head should be tight and the knife must be sharp, otherwise the meat will smear. This will become a big problem when making salami as the fat will clog the pores in the casing and the moisture will be trapped inside. Ideally, meat should always be chilled between 32-35°F (0-2° C) for a clean cut. After we are done cutting the meat, we should separate it into different groups: lean, semi - fat, and fat. Then they should be placed back into the refrigerator. Since refrigerator temperatures are roughly 38-40°F (3-4° C), we should place the meat in a freezer for about 30 min just before grinding. In hot conditions, we could choose to cut the meat either during the early hours of the morning, or during late evenings when temperatures are not higher than 70°F (21°C).

Mixing

If the meat was previously cured, then salt and nitrite were already added. Lean meat should be mixed with spices first, and the fat comes last as mixing raises the temperature of the meat dough. It takes roughly about 5 minutes to thoroughly mix 10 lbs. of meat. The time is important because fat specks start to melt at 95-104° F (35-40° C). We want to prevent this smearing to keep the sausage texture looking great.

The ingredients may be premixed with cold water in a blender, and then poured over the minced meat. The water helps to evenly distribute the ingredients and it also helps soften the mass during stuffing. We can easily add 1 cup of cold water to 5 lbs. of meat because it is going to evaporate during smoking anyhow. A rule of thumb is about 8% of water in relation to the weight of the meat.

In fermented sausages the addition of water to the sausage mass should be cut down to a minimum, as this creates favorable conditions for the growth of bacteria and will prolong drying. Some recipes call for wine or vinegar which seems to contradict the above statement. Both of those liquids are very acidic in nature and although they bring extra water they make up for it by increasing the acidity (lowering pH) of the sausage mix which inhibits bacteria growth.

The temperature of the sausage mix should be between 0-5° C (32-40° F). If this temperature increases, the sausage mix should be cooled down in a refrigerator before proceeding to the stuffing step. When mixing meat with ingredients, it is best to follow this sequence:

1. Minced meats, starter culture, nitrite/nitrate, salt, spices.
2. Minced fat.

There are some people that like to add spices to meat during the grinding step. Then they will mix it again. Some don't mix at all but grind meat through a big plate 3/4" - 1", then add spices to ground meat and regrind it again through a 1/8" plate. Some say that placing salt in a grinder has a detrimental effect on a cutting knife and that it should be avoided. The easiest procedure for someone using a manual grinder is to grind the meat first and then mix it well with all ingredients.

Apply some force when mixing, kneading might be a good word for it. *This will help to extract proteins* which will combine with salt and water and will create a sticky meat mass. This will hold meat particles together very well and will result in a good texture.

Stuffing

Taste the sausage before it's stuffed as there is **still** time for last minute corrections. People make mistakes when reading recipes, they get confused with ounces and grams, they use different size spoons to measure ingredients, etc. Just make a very tiny hamburger, throw it on a frying pan and in two minutes you can taste your sausage.

After the meat is ground and mixed it has to be stuffed into a casing, preferably as soon as possible. Allowing the meat to sit overnight causes it to set up and absorb all this moisture that we have added during mixing and stuffing. It will take more effort to stuff the casings the next day, however, this can corrected by remixing the mixture. Although sausage should be stuffed as tightly as possible, nevertheless for practical reasons different sausage types are stuffed to a different degree of firmness:

Sausage type	Firmness	Remarks
Rope sausage	Tight	Meat shrinks in time due to evaporation of the moisture.
Individual links, tied with twine or enclosed with clips	Tight	Meat shrinks in time due to evaporation of the moisture.
Rope sausage manually linked into individual links by twisting	Loosely	If stuffed tight, twisting will be difficult to perform.
Liver sausage, Blood sausage, Head cheese	Loosely	These products are heated in water and casings may burst open. They often contain filler material (rice, oats, barley etc) which expands in volume.

The casing should have about a third of a cup of water inside as it acts as a lubricant for the entering meat. By the same token pouring water over the stuffing tube is recommended to increase lubrication. Some people grease the tube lightly. Use the largest stuffing tube which fits the casing but make sure it goes on loosely otherwise the casing might break. It is important to stuff sausages firmly and without air as the resulting air pockets might fill with water or become little holes later.

In fermented and dry products, such moisture pockets may become breeding grounds for bacteria. The air also creates unnecessary resistance during stuffing. Most piston stuffers come equipped with an air valve that allows accumulating air to escape outside. After the sausage is stuffed, any accumulated air pockets visible to the naked eye are simply pricked with a needle. Commercial producers solve this problem by mixing and stuffing under a vacuum, but this requires expensive equipment.

Recommended stuffing tube diameters

Tube size	Casing diameter
1/2"	22-28 mm
3/4"	30-36 mm
1"	38 mm and over

Natural casings may look solid but in reality they contain minute holes (pores) that permit smoke or moisture to go through.They cling to meat and shrink with it as it goes through the drying process. After the first sausage session they become easy to work with and are always ready to be used at a moment's notice. Any remaining casings should be packed with salt and stored at refrigerator temperature (38 - 40° F) where they will last indefinitely. Natural casings come salted and they must be soaked in water for 30 minutes before use to eliminate salt and to make them pliable.

Do not:

- De-salt casings with hot water.
- Store casings at high temperatures.
- De-salt casings for a prolonged period of time.

Steps such as meat cutting, grinding, mixing and stuffing should be done at temperatures below 12° C (54° F). If working at higher temperatures, try to plan and organize your work in such a way that the meats will be processed as fast as possible and then placed in a refrigerator.

Whether a sausage is stuffed into 32, 36 or 38 mm hog casings, its taste will obviously remain the same. The smoking and cooking times will change slightly but it will still be the same sausage. The casing is just a packing material and although some traditionally made products may look unusual when stuffed into casings we are not accustomed to. For example, pepperoni will look odd if stuffed into 24 mm sheep casings but it will still be pepperoni and you may as well call it a pepperoni stick. The same applies for using synthetic casings, a liver sausage will remain a liver sausage whether it is stuffed into a hog, cellulose or fibrous casing.

How Hard to Stuff

There are two factors to consider:

1. Type of the sausage. Fresh, cooked and fermented sausages do not expand after stuffing and cooking so they so they can be stuffed firmly. Sausages which include filler material such as rice, oats, buckwheat groats, for example blood sausages are known to expand during cooking and should not be stuffed too hard.

2. Method of linking - sausages that are stuffed in natural casings into one continuous coil and then twisted into individual links must be stuffed loosely as the twisting consumes certain amount of casing.

Linking Sausages

The easiest way to stuff the sausage is to work it off the stuffing tube in one long section which is called a rope. Then it can be coiled and placed in a refrigerator or hung on a smokestick. Before serving or sale the rope sausage is cut or twisted into desired sections. This may be the fastest way to stuff the sausage but such a shape is hard to handle or sell to a consumer. A small store can manually link sausages but a large plant needs the final product to be of a consistent length and diameter. This of course calls for artificial casings and linking equipment. In most cases a hobbyist will use natural casings and the following estimates provide some idea on the weight of a sausage.

Casing type	Diameter in mm	Links to a pound
Sheep	22	16
	26	14
Hog	32	8
	36	6

Keep in mind that if the linking is performed by twisting a long stuffed sausage, the sausages must be filled loosely. The sections will be pinched between thumb and index finger in every spot where a link would begin. Twisting sausages into many links will take up any slack and the ends will be tied with twine.

- twist each link in a direction opposite to that of the preceding link to keep the casing from untwisting.

- twist only every *second link* in the same direction. Most people use this method to save casings.

Large sausage such as bologna in beef bungs is heavy and must be reinforced by wrapping it two or more times with twine. A hanging loop must also be provided. Large traditionally produced Italian salamis are long and stuffed into a large diameter natural casings what makes them very heavy. As they will hang for a month or more they must be reinforced with butcher twine or placed in netting.

After sausages are stuffed any visible air pockets should be pricked with a needle. This is especially important when making fermented sausages as air pockets might become a source of bacterial contamination. To eliminate this the casings are often pricked with needles regardless of whether air pockets are present or not.

Photo 11.16 Clips and rings are used for synthetic casings but can be applied to natural casings as well. The clips are normally used to seal the bottoms of the casings. The tops are usually tied with twine or clipped with hog rings. The end of sausage casing can be tied up with a secure knot.

Butcher's twine or regular cotton twine of different thickness can be employed. Heavier gauge is recommended for large diameter sausages which are heavy and must be reinforced by wrapping them around with twine. A hanging loop must also be provided. If the sausage is large and long like a salami it is a good idea to reinforce the casing with twine. Two lengthwise loops and a few loops across will make it stronger. In addition a hanging loop should be provided.

Conditioning

This pre-drying step at the first look seems insignificant, but is very important when smoking sausages. Stuffed sausages may contain meat that was not cured at all or only partially cured. Leaving sausages for 12 hours at 2-6°C (35-42°F) or for 1-3 hours at room temperature provide extra time to cure the meat. Moderate use of a fan will definitely be of some help. Air-fan should not be used for an extended period of time as it may harden the surface of the product. Conditioning is a short, hardly noticeable process and when making a lot of sausages, before the last casings are stuffed, the first ones are ready for smoking.

Photo 11.17 Stuffed sausages that are subject to smoking follow a drying procedure which can last from 0.5-2 hr at 68-86° F (20-30° C). This drying process is often performed inside the smoker and lasts about 1 hr (no smoke applied) at 40-54°C (104-130°F) until the casings feel dry.

Conditioning prepares sausages for the smoking step that follows. The time depends on the diameter of the sausage and the amount of moisture it contains. Moist surface attracts large soot particles which black and not welcome. Conditioning dries out the surface of the casing so it can develop proper smoking color. Draft controls or the top of your smoker should be fully open to let the moisture out. If natural wood is used for fuel, enough wood must be burned to produce sufficient amounts of hot embers that would be releasing heat without creating smoke to dry out the casings. Preheating a smoker to eliminate the humidity inside is a must step for the smoking process that follows.

Smoking

Nothing improves the flavor of a sausage in a such a rapid and inexpensive way as smoking process. In countries such as Poland and Germany smoked meats account for 60% of all ready to eat meat products. In the USA the variety of sausages carried in supermarkets pale in comparison with their European counterparts. Statistically, smoked sausages control a large share of the American market but most of the credit goes to emulsified and lightly smoked sausages such as hotdogs, frankfurters or bolognas. Today, the manufacture of smoked sausages conforms to different criteria and smoke is added purely for the love of the flavor. Some products are not smoked at all but receive liquid smoke during mixing, are immersed in smoke solution or sprayed with liquid smoke mist. As the synthetic casings can be ordered in mahogany color, to the untrained person such a liquid smoke enriched sausage can easily pass as the original.

In the past sausages were smoked for different reasons. Our ancestors did not care much about the flavor of the meat or the sausage. What they needed was a method that would preserve food for later.

They tried different ways to preserve meat and this eventually lead to methods like salt curing, drying, smoking and fermenting. It was discovered that salted meats could be air dried and would keep for a long time. Soon two different methods of drying developed.

In **Northern Europe**, winters were cold and the only way meat could be dried at low temperatures was placing them close to the fire. Originally that took place in caves where fire was the center of all social activities. Later, separate enclosures (smokehouses) were built for drying and storing meats. As the temperature had to be higher than freezing temperatures outside, the fire was slowly burning on the ground providing suitable temperatures for drying. Given that fire produces smoke the meats and sausages were dried and smoked at the same time. They were just flavored with cold smoke which not only further preserved the product but gave it a wonderful aroma. Those advantages of applying smoke were not ignored by our ancestors and smoking became the art in itself. This does not deny the fact that the main method was *drying* and the benefits of smoke was just an added bonus.

In **Southern Europe** the climate was warmer and less humid with the ever present blowing winds what created perfect conditions for drying food in the open air for most of the year. There was hardly any need for burning fires and hams and sausages were produced by salting drying. There was no need for smoking meats and the occasional application of cold smoke was limited to preventing the growth of mold. Smoked meats had never become popular in Italy or Spain as in the North.

Smoked Sausages Cured with Nitrite

The step which differentiates smoked sausages from others is the addition of sodium nitrite (Cure #1). This is a must procedure when smoking meats below 170° F (77° C) smoke temperature. Although cases of food poisoning by *Clostridium botulinum* are very rare, they have one thing in common: they are fatal. Smoking is done at temperatures from 50° F (10° C) to 140° F (60 °C) and depending on a particular smoker, the humidity levels and the amount of fresh air varies too. The combination of low temperature. the moisture from the sausages and the absence of oxygen creates the right conditions for the growth of the *Cl. botulinum*.

Photo 11.18 A variety of smoked products.

Smoking Sausages Without Nitrite

A common question is: can I smoke meats without nitrite? Of course you can. As explained earlier, you have to smoke/bake your sausage at above 185° F (85° C) or higher which will affect its texture and make it greasy on the outside.

Many people say they don't use nitrites when smoking meats, however, most of them barbecue or grill meats at high temperatures which kill all bacteria, including *Clostridium botulinum*. Replacing sodium nitrite with *celery powder* is just repacking sodium nitrite into a different package as celery powder contains the same nitrite.

Color of a Smoked Sausage

Cold smoked products develop a yellow-gold color. As the smoking progresses the color will become light brown and then dark brown. Keep in mind that cold smoking continues for days, even weeks at a time with occasional breaks in between.

Hot smoked products are smoked in a matter of hours. The color depends mainly on the length of smoking. The color will start changing from light brown to dark brown. The type of wood will influence it as well, oak smokes in brown color, hickory smokes reddish-brown. Heavy smoke will increase the amount of smoke deposition.

Sausages owe their characteristic flavors to the different spices they contain. *Long smoking with heavy smoke can overpower these subtle spice aromas.* Smoking a thin 1/2" piece of meat like jerky for 3 hours applying heavy smoke might make it bitter and non-palatable. When smoking, the rule "easy goes a long way" holds very much true. Large pieces of meat such as hams, bacon, and loins will require longer smoking times and should be smoked until the typical dark color is obtained.

Using softwood from evergreen trees will make casings much darker, even black due to the deposits of tar and resin that this wood contains.

The Length of Smoking

This criteria is very loosely defined. Smoking today is just a flavoring step which is done *when the desired color is obtained.* Preservation is accomplished by *cooking* and keeping the product in a refrigerator. In the past, cold smoking/drying continued for weeks as it was the preservation method. Hot smoking is performed with a dense smoke and smoke deposition is more intense at higher temperatures. About one hour of smoking for 1" (25 mm) of sausage diameter is plenty. If your sausage is stuffed into 36 mm casing 1-2 hours is fine. If it is smoked for 2 or 3 hours, the smoky flavor will be more intense. Smoking much longer with a heavy smoke might create a bitter flavor.

Rearranging Smoke Sticks or Smoke Carts During Smoking.

In the past the most common smokehouse was the so called gravity smokehouse which sometimes was quite large. Meats were hung on different levels in a smoking chamber and the smoke would rise up using a natural draft. Sausages hanging higher will pick up moisture from the sausages below and they will become wetter which will affect the color and flavor. Being wet they will attract more soot and other unburned smoke particles. Smoke and heat distribution would differ in different areas of the chamber especially if the smokehouse was of a large size. If smoking continued for a long time those would become serious problems if left untreated. Periodic rearranging of the smokesticks would correct those problems. A large smokehouse had many levels of smokesticks that were loaded with sausages or fish, but the fire pit generating smoke or supplying heat was located at the bottom. Smoke carts were reversed as well, as there was higher temperature in a back. In today's units electrical blowers force smoke or hot air into all areas of the smokehouse and the temperature and relative humidity are easily controlled.

Cooking Sausages

Fats start to melt at 95-104° F (35-40° C) and going over 170° F (76° C) internal meat temperature will decrease the quality of the sausage. Staying within 154-160° F (68-72° C) will produce the highest quality product. Special sausages such as blood sausage, liver sausage and head cheese have their ingredients pre-cooked before being minced, mixed and stuffed. As different cuts like skins, tongues, or jowls for example, will call for different cooking times it may seem that many pots might be needed. The solution is to use one pot but place the meats in separate bags made of netting. Each bag is removed as soon as the meat in it is cooked sufficiently.

Photo 11.19
Placing cuts in a bag facilitates their removal from hot water.

The leftover stock should be saved and used as a cooking medium for cooking sausages. If not enough stock remains, add more water. After sausages are cooked the remaining stock may be used for a soup or to cook filler material such as barley or buckwheat groats..

Cooking in a Smoker

It makes a lot of sense to cook smoked meat in the smoker as it is already there. Besides, it will have a slightly better taste than by using the poaching method and it will shine more. On a downside, it will lose more weight than by other methods. It is also the slowest and the most difficult method that largely depends on the technical possibilities of the smoker. A slowly increasing temperature inside the smoker will achieve the best effects. The smoking process is relatively fast and a typical 36 mm sausage will be smoked in about 1-2 hours.

While it takes 1-2 hours to smoke a sausage, it may take an additional 3 hours to cook it inside the smoker. It will largely depend on the inside temperature of the meat when smoking was stopped. If it was 100° F (38° C) we have a long way to go, if it was 150° F (66° C) we are almost there. That shows a need for some intelligent planning and it is advisable to slowly *increase the smoking temperature* to about 160° F. When smoking is done, the temperature should be increased to 176° F (80° C) and maintained at that level until the inside temperature of the smoked meat reaches 155-160° F (69-72° C). The product is both smoked and cooked. A lot will depend on *outside conditions and how well the smoker is insulated.* That may be difficult to achieve sometimes and we will have to increase the temperature of a smoker to about 185° F (85° C) to bring the internal temperature of the meat to the required level.

The other easier method is to set the temperature of the smoker to 77-80° C (170-176° F) and wait until the meat's inside temperature reaches 154° F, (68° C). Smokehouse temperature is around 25 degrees higher than the temperature inside of the meat, but that largely depends on the meat's diameter. Two thermometers are needed: one to monitor the temperature of the smoker and the other to monitor the inside temperature of the meat or sausage in its thickest part. It helps to have a thermometer with an alarm sounder in it, this way we get an audible warning when the meat has reached its pre-set temperature.

Cooking in Water

Cooking meats and sausages in hot water is more convenient than baking in hot air. Water in an open container at sea level always boils at 212° F (100° C) and no higher. This precisely controls the maximum temperature that can be obtained using the simplest equipment.

This method is easier and faster than baking in a smoker and the meat weight loss is smaller. This is due to the fact that *water conducts heat more efficiently than air*. Water cooking drastically lowers the technical expectations from the smokehouse. The smoker can be any kind of enclosure, even a corrugated cardboard box will do, as long as it can accommodate the meat inside and deliver the smoke. The smoker has to handle smoking temperatures which in most cases will stay below 140° F (60° C).

Cooking in water is an acceptable and professional way of cooking sausages. There are dozens of known products that are made this way: regular smoked sausages, liver and blood sausages, head cheeses, butts and hams. There are some smoked sausages that are baked in a smokehouse, for example Kabanosy or Mysliwska (Hunter's Sausage). Choosing cooking method is basically up to you, the dividing line may be the diameter of the sausage and the technical possibilities of your smoker.

Water is brought to the temperature of 158-194° F, (70-90° C) and the meats or sausages are immersed in it. For instance, home made hams are poached at 176° F (80° C) and this temperature is maintained until the meat's inside temperature reaches 155° F (69° C). Some recipes call for preheating the water before adding the sausages and some call for adding the sausages to cold water, however, it makes more sense to add *hot smoked* sausages to pre-heated water, given the fact that they are already hot. They will lose all heat in cold water and the cooking process will be longer. . A product taken out of the hot vessel might still increase its internal temperature by one or two degrees. A cooking pot remains uncovered during water cooking.

The poaching method is the preferred choice for sausages that are smoked with hot smoke. The short hot smoking process creates a dry layer on the outside of the sausage, similar to a second skin, that prevents the migration of moisture and juices from inside of the sausage to the water. Exact times and temperatures of poaching are given with particular recipes.

A rule of thumb calls for about 30 minutes per pound, depending, of course on the cooking temperature. It is generally accepted that at 176° F (80° C) about 10 minutes are needed for each 1 cm of the diameter of the sausage.

Poaching times for products up to 60 mm in diameter:

- Typical sausage - 10 min per 1 cm. Sausage 30 mm diameter is cooked 30 minutes.
- Liver sausage - 12 min per 1 cm. Sausage 50 mm in diameter is cooked 60 minutes.
- Blood sausage - 15 min per 1 cm. Sausage 40 mm in diameter is cooked 60 minutes.

Photo 11.20
Cooking ham and sausages in the same pot. The ham, will of course cook much longer.

Photo 11.21
Tying sausages into bundles helps to move them in and out of the hot water. The string is usually tied up to the pot's handle.

Once the diameter of the sausage is larger than 60 mm, the above times are less accurate and should be increased. Double up the time, it is better to be safe than sorry. For example pork stomach may be cooked for 2-3 hours. *The best solution is to use a meat thermometer.* A sausage may contain air which sneaked in during the stuffing process. Such a sausage will swim up to the surface and the remedy is to prick it with a needle. This unfortunately results in the loss of some meat juice. A good solution is to construct a grid shaped wooden float-cover that will be fit to the diameter of a cooking vessel. Such a cover is placed on top of sausages and keeps them submerged all the time. The cover can be used during cooling sausages as well.

Baking Sausages

Baking sausages in a smokehouse is less efficient that poaching them in water, but they look better having a glossy look on the outside. This is due to the fat that has melted under the surface of the casing and moved to the surface where it resides as a thin coat of grease. It is like putting grease on a pair of boots, they are going to shine and look better. Besides the looks, the flavor of a baked sausage is also slightly better as there was no loss of meat juices which in the case of poached sausages will migrate to the water. However, the baked sausage loses more weight than the same sausage poached in water and the process itself is much longer, given the fact that air conducts heat very poorly.

Cooling Sausages

After cooking the sausages should be showered or immersed in cold water to drop their internal temperature outside the danger zone (40 - 140° F, 4 - 60° C). At home, a cold shower is normally practiced. As most smokehouses are located outside of the house the common method employs the use of a garden hose. Sausages cooked in water should be placed in another vessel filled with cold water (50-60° F, 10-15° C). Cooling sausages with water offers the following advantages:

- Cleans the surface from grease.
- Extends product's shelf life.
- Decreases time of air cooling which subsequently follows.

Photo 11.22 Sausages being cooled.

Photo 11.23 Smoked sausages showered with water.

Sausages should remain at temperatures between 140° - 40° F (60° - 4° C) for the shortest time possible as this temperature range facilitates the growth of bacteria. Although bacteria have been killed during the cooking process, new bacteria is anxious to jump back into the sausages surface. Cooling time depends on the diameter of the product but it may be estimated as:

- Small diameter sausages such as frankfurters - 5-10 min.
- Large diameter sausages - 15-20 minutes.

When the sausages have cooled down it is recommended to rinse them briefly with hot water to wash down any grease that might have accumulated on the surface. Then they should be wiped off with a moistened cloth until they are clean and dry. Once the temperature drops below 68° F (20° C) it is safe to hang sausages for air cooling. The sausages will develop a darker color and better looks but may also become more shriveled, though some shriveling is normal. The solution is to poach it again for 30-60 seconds with hot water (194° F, 90° C) and then cool as before.

During this cooling/drying process a smoked sausage will further improve its shine, color, and will develop a darker shade of brown. Some call it "blooming" but this is the air drying we are writing about. Sausages should be hung in a dark place with a newspaper on the floor to catch any grease dripping down. After that, the sausage can be refrigerated. The official recommendation of the Food Safety and Inspection Service of the USDA (June 1999) issues the following guidelines:

"During cooling, the product's maximum internal temperature should not remain between 130° F (54° C) and 80° F (27° C) for more than 1.5 hours nor between 80° F (27° C) and 40° F (4° C) for more than 5 hours" (6.5 hours total time). "Products cured with a minimum of 100 ppm ingoing sodium nitrite may be cooled so that the maximum internal temperature is reduced from 130° F (55° C) to 80° F (27° C) in 5 hours and from 80° F (27° C) to 45° F (7 C) in 10 hours" (15 hours total time).

Sausage Color

Different meats exhibit different colors and a sausage containing beef will be darker than a pork sausage. A sausage containing more fat will be lighter than a lean one. Adding cure with nitrite guarantees the pink color of the finished product.

Some sausages such as fresh sausage, head cheese, blood sausage or liver sausage are normally prepared without nitrite and the resulting color will be that of a cooked meat. Livers from different animals will create liver sausages of different color. Adding 20% of white tripe will make any sausage lighter. Use of dark spices such as black pepper, cinnamon or nutmeg makes sausages darker. The smoking process will affect the color of the sausage casing. Although it is possible to manipulate the final color of the sausage, this is not what sausage making is about. We have to create a product that looks appetizing and tastes great. Natural colorants:

- Paprika - orange
- Turmeric - yellow
- Beet juice - burgundy
- Annatto - red

Show Meat

Some sausages, besides head cheeses, exhibit solid chunks of meat or fat inside, including even nuts or olives. For example Mortadella is often made with pistachio nuts, some sausages contain whole peppers. Sopressata contains large pieces of fat inside. There are liver sausages that contain cubes of fat or ham sausages with solid chunks of meat inside. This is done for a decorative purpose only and such a sausage does not contain more fat than others. Were this fat emulsified with the rest of meat we would not be able to see it, though it would still be inside.

Photo 11.25 Sopressata sausage - fat used as show material.

Photo 11.24 Krakowska sausage - chunks of lean meat used as show material.

Those effects are easily obtained by grinding meats through a fine plate and grinding or cutting display material (meat or fat) with a larger plate. It is easy to cut frozen fat into uniform pieces with a knife. Such diced fat is then placed in a refrigerator and is added at the last moment during the mixing process. In order for it to look visually pleasing such filler material should be cut into the same size cubes.

Making Rectangular Shaped Sausages

Certain products such as hams which are made from many individual pieces or sausages like Austrian Kantwurst and some German Hunter sausages, are molded in special press devices to give them the rectangular shape. You may build yourself a few shaping devices to impress your friends with square sausages.

Photo 11.26 Wooden press for making square sausages.

Photo 11.27 The slider allows to position linked sausages. The connecting casing is inserted into the grove of the slider.

Photo 11.28 Sausage forced into the channel.

Photo 11.29 Cover secured with rubber band.

Photo 11.30 Squared sausage.

Equipment

Knives. Knife and knife sharpener.

Cutting board. Once popular wooden boards have been replaced by plastic cutting boards. Wooden boards were harder to clean. In addition when not used often, they allowed bacteria and molds to develop.

Buckets, containers and bowls. They are needed to store meat cuts, ground meats and to cure meats. A mixing bowl should be large enough to permit comfortable mixing with both hands.

Colander is needed to strain meats which were boiled for making head cheeses or liver sausages.

Weighted boards. If you plan on curing meats with the immersion method, a wooden board cut to the shape of the pot will make your work easier. Such a board will prevent the meat from raising to the surface during curing or cooking in hot water.

Ladle is needed for filling head cheeses, liver and blood sausages.

Filling horn is needed to stuff head cheeses, blood and liver sausages using a ladle. A set of different size plastic funnels will do.

Stirring spoon with a long handle is needed to stir sausages during cooking.

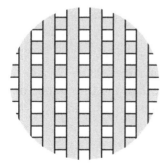
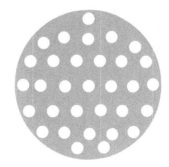

Fig. 11.1 Weighted cover made from wooden planks.

Fig. 11.2 Weighted wood cover with holes.

Meat pump. A good grade meat pump for injecting curing solution can be obtained from distributors of sausage making supplies. A smaller pump can be purchased in department stores.

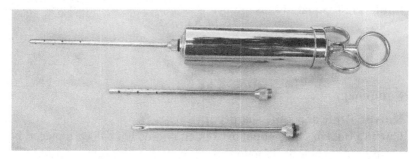

Photo 11.31 Meat pump.

Grinder. Manual grinder is sufficient for occasional production. If it doubles as a stuffer, a set of stuffing tubes is needed.

Photo 11.32 General scale. The size depends on production needs.

Spice scale - a highly accurate scale that is needed for reading cultures and spices. It can read with the accuracy of 0.01 g (0.001 oz.).

AWS Compact Digital Scale v2.0 by *American Weigh Systems*

www.awscales.com
Capacity: 100 g
Accuracy: 0.01 g (0.001 oz)
Units: grams, ounces, carats, grains
Size: 5.6 x 4.9 x 0.5"
Warranty: 10 years

Photo 11.33 Weighing whole cloves.

Sausage stuffer. The piston sausage stuffer is a very practical device. It makes the job of stuffing much easier and it develops less heat during operation.

Spice mill. Spices are normally ground. Certain spices for example juniper berries and allspice usually come whole and you may want to grind them.

Photo 11.34 The old fashioned brass mortar and pestle is a great device allowing total control of a particle size. You may crack peppercorns any way you want, for example a very coarse grind for Cotto Salami.

Photo 11.36 The old fashioned coffee grinder/spice mill.

Photo 11.35 Small spice mill. There are of course electric spice grinders.

Thermometers. A thermometer for checking water temperature when cooking sausages plus another thermometer to check the internal meat temperature during cooking.

Cooking pot. A large pot can be placed on a gas or electrical burner and a hang-on thermometer will display the temperature. Water temperature is normally maintained at around 176° F (80° C). There are electrical water cookers, soup cookers and turkey fryers which provide adjustable temperature control and can be found in department stores.

Making Sausages in the Past

The processing steps in the past were not much different from the ones employed in home production today. The main difference was in equipment as grinders and stuffers were not available then. Keep in mind that the kitchen knife is much sharper than the grinder's knife, the difference lies in speed. Meat for sausages was cut with a knife and stuffed with fingers into casings. Any funnel resembling device was used for that purpose, monks in monasteries used the eye of massive door keys as the stuffing device. The casing would be pulled through the ring, flipped over and the sausage mass will be pushed down. Head cheeses or liver sausages made today at home are stuffed loosely and the common method is to use a funnel, even if a stuffer is available.

In old European homes the meats were hung on top of the chimney. Two strong nails were hammered into the walls of the chimney and a strong wire was stretched between them. The serious drawback was that the meat had to accept any kind of smoke produced by the kitchen stove.

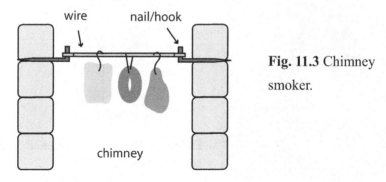

Fig. 11.3 Chimney smoker.

A much better design was attaching a smokehouse to the chimney on the second floor. Two holes were made in the chimney: one for the smoke to enter the chamber and another to allow it to escape. On the other side a flat damper was pushed in or out of the chimney allowing the smoke to go straight up or forcing it to flow into the smokehouse.

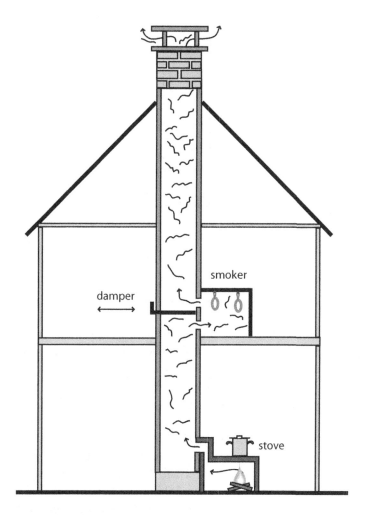

Fig. 11.4 Home chimney smoker.

In many cases sausages were not smoked at all but dried for a few hours over a hot stove plate and then kept in a cool place. Then they were boiled in water before serving. Another solution was to attach a wooden box to the bread stove or any wood burning appliance.

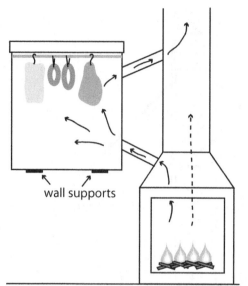

wall supports

Fig. 11.5 Box on the wall smoker.

Needless to say a meat grinder was either not invented yet, or only a few lucky ones happened to own it. The majority of people had to chop meat manually with a knife. That required a careful meat selection and removal of all inedible parts like sinews, gristle, parts of tendon, etc. Today a grinder will cut and mechanically tenderize meat at the same time but in those times meat was cut into little chunks. The product was definitely juicy and first class.

This is how sausages were made in the past and a great deal of improvisation was employed. Back fat was normally cut into long and narrow strips. Wood for smoking was often wet and the final product was very dark. After smoking the sausages were oven baked or poached in water.

Butcher's twine was an item not available to everybody and people invented a quite clever method of tying casings with little pieces of wood picks. A wooden toothpick is an ideal instrument for that purpose. The method is illustrated in Appendix A.

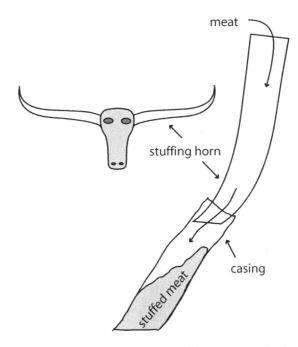

Fig. 11.6 Sausage casings were stuffed with any suitable device.

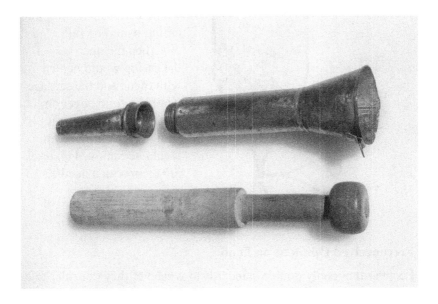

Photo 11.37. An early manual stuffer.

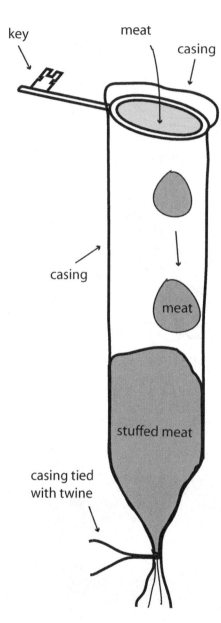

key   meat   casing   casing   meat   stuffed meat   casing tied with twine

Old keys were massive pieces of metal and the loop of the key would be inserted into the end of the casing. The casing would be held around the key loop with fingers. The other end of the casing would be tied with butcher's twine.

Meat would be pushed down through the loop of the key and from time to time the casing would be removed and meat would be pushed down further by squeezing the casing on the outside. The process would eliminate most of the air which was important as most sausages were smoked and air dried. This operation would be repeated until the casing would be full.

Then the open end of the casing would be tied with twine and the sausage would be rolled over on a flat surface to make it straight. Any air pockets would be removed by pricking them with a needle.

Fig. 11.7 Key method of stuffing a sausage.

Preconceived Opinions on Food

People often apply double standards to whatever they consider to be good food. Mention smoked eel to a friend and he is already shaking seeing in his mind a nasty rattler going after him. He does not even want to hear that smoked eel can be spread on a roll like butter.

Until the 1970's one could not find a single eel in a fish store in New York City. Then an influx of immigrants from the Far East had brought new customs and cuisines and eels are swimming in fish tanks everywhere. Take the "carp" for example, the fish originally came from Japan to China, then to Europe and finally to the USA. Served in aspic or cooked Jewish style, in Poland carp has been the traditional Christmas Eve dish for centuries. In 1985 when I was trained in New York as a scuba diver, my manual stated that carp was non-edible. The probable cause was that the fish being a bottom dweller, acquired a slight muddy flavor especially as it grew larger. It also contains more bones than other species and ourselves being a busy species today, we expect to order our meal, swallow it and rush out to watch a baseball game. In Poland there were no stores nor proper distribution systems when the war ended and live carp was sold on street corners before Christmas. People would buy a few fish a week earlier and keep them swimming in a bathtub full of water until they were ready to process and cook them. The kids loved the fish, besides, there was no talk about taking a bath.

A few hundred years ago we had cases of blood sausage poisoning that was attributed to our insufficient knowledge of meat technology but recently people are afraid to eat fresh leafy vegetables. Which is not surprising given that many food recalls involve vegetables. If you eat salads, corn flakes and canned food throughout your life your stomach is not what it used to be and most likely you will be afraid to order "steak tartare." You are a city fellow now. People are afraid and confused to eat food that has been around for a long time.

Mention to someone that skins, ears, and snouts are used to make a head cheese and he'll never touch it, however, if it is packed in a form and called a meat jelly it will be accepted. We eat hot dogs not realizing that they are made from tongues, skins, organs, head meat, and machine separated meats by emulsifying those ingredients. Special machines are designed to scrape off pieces of meat from the bones until they are bare. One cannot find a blood sausage in American supermarket because of the word "blood", though the blood is fully cooked and a little of it. On the other hand, one eats medium rare steak that's dripping raw blood. Blood sausage can be found in every meat store in Europe. As well as rabbits, venison, wild boar and even horse meat. Somehow, Europeans don't form opinions on quality of meats by studying the name, they establish quality by eating the product.

Finger Sausage
(Palcówka)

One of the oldest known sausages that gets its name from the method used to fill the casing. The casings were stuffed with fingers (palce) by means of any suitable device like a pipe, funnel or a stuffing horn. Needless to say a meat grinder was either not invented yet, or only a few lucky ones happened to own it. The majority of people had to chop meat manually with a knife.

Meat	Metric	US
pork butt	400 g	0.88 lb.
ham (or lean beef)	400 g	0.88 lb.
back fat or bacon	200 g	0.44 lb.

Ingredients per 1000 g (1 kg) of meat:

salt	18 g	3 tsp.
Cure #1	2.5 g	½ tsp.
pepper	2.0 g	1 tsp.
sugar	2.5 g	½ tsp.
marjoram, ground	2.0 g	1 tsp.
coriander	2.0 g	1 tsp.
allspice	2.0 g	1 tsp.
cold water	60 ml	¼ cup

Instructions:
1. Cut meat into ½-¾" (1-2 cm) pieces. Bacon can be cut into smaller pieces to make it less visible.
2. Mix meat pieces with salt and Cure #1. Add sugar now. Mix very well and leave in a cool place (preferably in a refrigerator) for 48 hours.
3. Stuff into casings.
4. Smoke for 1-2 days with cold smoke or for a few hours with hot smoke.
5. Hot smoked sausages were usually poached in water. Cold smoked sausages were left in a dry cool place (54° F, 12° C) to dry.

Back fat was usually cut into long and narrow strips. Wood for smoking was often wet and the final product was very dark. After smoking the sausages were oven baked or poached in water.

Chapter 12

Creating Your Own Recipes

It is mind boggling to see people clicking for hours and hours on a computer keyboard to find magic recipes on the Internet. Searching for the Holy Grail of a sausage. Then when they find something they like, they mess it up by applying too high smoking or cooking temperatures. The recipe of course, gets the blame. Then they look for another magic recipe again.

Recipe is what the word says: "the recipe", it does not imply that one will produce an outstanding sausage. Making quality sausages has little to do with recipes, *it is all about the meat science and the rules that govern it.* All sausage making steps, especially temperature control, are like little building blocks that would erect a house. It is like the strength of the chain, which is only as strong as its weakest link. *Each step in sausage making influences the step that follows, and all those steps when performed correctly will, as a final result, create the quality product.* Let us quote Madame Benoit, the famous Canadian cookery expert and author who once said:

> *"I feel a recipe is only a theme, which an intelligent cook can play each time with a variation."*

A good chef is not looking at his notes when making chicken soup and an experienced sausage maker knows how to make a good sausage. We could fill this book with hundreds of recipes but that won't make you more knowledgeable. *There isn't one standardized recipe for any of the sausages.* The best meat science books, written by the foremost experts in this field list different ingredients for the same sausage. Salami Milano and Salami Genoa are basically the same sausage, the difference lies mainly in meat particle size. Replacing mace with nutmeg, using white or black pepper, adding/removing a particular spice will have little final effect on a sausage.

Grinding cold meat or frozen fat is more important for making a quality sausage than a pretty arrangement of expensive spices. It's all about the technology. By adhering to the guidelines outlined in this book, you have to make a great sausage. By all means look at different recipes but be flexible and not afraid to experiment. Use ingredients that you personally like as in most cases you will make a sausage for yourself, so why not like it? When making a large amount of the product a wise precaution is to taste the meat by frying a tiny piece. After mixing meat with all ingredients there is still time for last minute changes to the recipe. There is not much we can do after a sausage is stuffed. Tasting should always be performed when mixing ground meat with spices to make a sausage. *A recipe is just a recipe and let your palate be the final judge.*

General Guidelines

Use spices that you and your kids like, after all you will end up eating it. Basically a sausage is meat, salt and pepper. I will never forget when I made my first Polish smoked sausage that turned out very well and I proudly gave it to my friend - professional sausage maker Waldemar to try. I have included salt, pepper, garlic, and added optional marjoram. I also added nutmeg and other spices that I liked. Well my friend's judgement was as follows:

"Great sausage, but why all those perfumes?"

For him it was supposed to be the classical Polish Smoked Sausage and all it needed was salt, pepper and garlic. The moral of the story is that putting dozens of spices into the meat does not guarantee the best product. Another real example is when the owner of a popular Texas barbecue restaurant was asked this question: "what do you put inside your sausages that they taste so great?" The answer was: *"it is not what I put into them, but what I don't put is what makes them so good."* Keep it simple. Combining meat with salt and pepper already makes a great sausage providing that you will follow the basic rules of sausage making. It's that simple. Like roasting a chicken, it needs only salt, pepper, and it always comes out perfect. If you don't cure your meats properly, grind warm fat or screw up your smoking and cooking temperatures, all the spices in the world will not save your sausage.

There is one rule though which is obeyed by professionals who keep on winning barbecue contests: *cook it low and slow.*

The same principle applies to traditional methods of smoking meats and sausages. It is all about temperatures and patience, other factors such as marinades, sauces, and different woods for smoking are just a dressing.

Sausage Recipe Secrets

1. Fat. The meat for a sausage should contain about 25 - 30% fat. This will make the sausage tender and juicy, without fat it will feel dry. This is not such a big amount as it might seem so at first. Fresh sausages made in the USA can legally contain 50% fat and this is what you get in a supermarket. The fat is cheap and the manufacturer is not going to replace it with a higher priced lean meat. This is where the main advantage of making products at home comes to play: you are in control. Avoid beef fat which is yellow and tastes inferior to pork fat. Fat from lamb or wild game should not be used either, unless you make original sausages like Turkish Sucuk or Scottish Haggis. Sheep or goat fat has a specific odor which lowers quality of the sausage.

2. Salt

The sausage needs salt. Salt contributes to flavor, curing and firmness, water holding and juiciness, binding and texture, safety and it prevents water cooking loss. In general sausages contain 1.5-2% salt. About 3.5-5% will be the upper limit of acceptability, anything more and the product will be too salty. Get the calculator and punch in some numbers. Or if you use the metric system you don't even need the calculator: You need 2 grams (2%) of salt per 100 grams of meat. If you buy ten times more meat (1 kg) you will also need ten times more salt (20 grams). Now for the rest of your life you don't have to worry about salt in your recipes. If you want a consistent product, weigh out your salt. Estimating salt per cups or spoons can be deceiving as not all salts weigh the same per unit volume.

Salt perception can be an acquired taste. If you decide to go on a low sodium diet and start decreasing the amount of salt you consume, in about three weeks time you may reach a point when your food tastes enjoyable, though you use less salt than before. This is fine as long as you prepare those meals for yourself. When making sausages for your friends, try to adhere to the amount of salt the original recipe calls for, as other people might like a different amount of salt.

Remember that a large piece of finished product that is kept in a refrigerator *will keep on drying out. Salt will, however, remain inside and your sausage will now taste saltier and will be of a smaller diameter.* The meat flavor will also be stronger now. In such a case you may use less salt than originally planned for. There are different types of salt and people often speculate which kind is the best. Well, probably the cheapest salt that is known as rock or canning salt might be the best as it is very pure. Salt was originally mined and transported in huge slabs to different areas. It was a valuable commodity and was named after the mine which had produced it. Different mines produced salt with different impurities content. If a particular salt contained more Nitrate, it would impart pink color to the meat and improve its keeping qualities. Such salt would be popular for meat preservation.Table salt that we use for general cooking contains many added ingredients such as iodine (there is a non-iodized salt, too) and anti-caking agents   such as sodium silicoaluminate or magnesium carbonate that prevent salt from acquiring moisture. Pure rock salt will lump together and will not shift from a salt shaker. Salt lumping is of a minor inconvenience as the hardened salt can be reversed to its original powdery form by shaking the container. Cleaner salt will produce cleaner gelatin in a head cheese. Some salts are finely ground and some are flaked. A finely ground salt will be more suitable for curing fish in brine. Due to a short time involved finely pulverized salt will penetrate fish flesh faster. On the other hand dry cured products such as ham or bacon which cure for weeks at the time, might benefit from a coarsely ground salt.

For brining purposes both table salt and kosher salt will work equally well in terms of providing the desired effects, though kosher salt – and in particular Diamond® Crystal kosher salt dissolves more readily. What is important to remember is that kosher salts are less dense than ordinary table salts and measure quite differently from a volume standpoint. Kosher salt has larger crystals and is bulkier. A given weight of Diamond® Crystal takes up nearly twice the volume as the same weight of table salt. One teaspoon of table salt weighs 6 g but 1 teaspoon of Kosher salt weighs 4.8 g. Five tablespoons of Diamond® Kosher Salt (72 g) or five tablespoons of Morton® Table Salt (90 g) will add a different percentage of salt to your product as the former salt is much lighter. Yet when you weigh 90 g of salt on a scale it makes no difference what kind of salt you choose.

Ninety grams of table salt equals to 90 g of flaked salt regardless of the volume they might occupy. The table below shows approximate equivalent amounts of different salts:

Table Salt	1 cup	292 g (10.3 oz)
Morton® Kosher Salt	1⅓ to 1½ cup	218 g (7.7 oz)
Diamond® Crystal Kosher Salt	1 cup	142 g (5 oz)

As you can see it is *always advisable to weigh out your salt.* The above table proves how misleading a recipe can be if listed ingredients are measured in volume units only (cups, spoons, etc).

Sea salt is made by evaporating sea water and what is left is the salt plus *impurities* which were in sea water. Those impurities include different minerals and chemicals such as magnesium, calcium or nitrate. If a substantial amount of Nitrate is present, such salt will somewhat cure meats and make them pink. Due to impurities sea salt may taste a bit bitter. Sea salt is occasionally added to dry cured and air dried products which are made without Nitrates. Nevertheless such a manufacturing process is not recommended for an amateur. Each gallon of sea water (8.33 lb) produces more than 1/4 pound of salt.

3. Pepper (*Piper nigrum*)

It is available as whole seeds but you have to grind it which results in a fresher aroma. It is available as coarse grind, sometimes called butcher's grind or fine grind. Black pepper is normally used in fresh sausages and blood sausages, and white pepper is used in others. Polish sausage might need coarse grind black pepper, but a hot dog, Bologna or Krakowska sausage will call for a fine grind white pepper. The dividing line is *whether you want to see the pepper in your product or not.* Otherwise it makes no difference and you can replace black pepper with the same amount of white pepper, although the black pepper is a bit hotter. Pepper is added at 0.1-0.4% (1.0-4.0 g per 1 kg of meat). The definition of pepper can be confusing at times as it comes in different colors: black, white, green and pink, however, they all come from the same plant. Depending on a harvest time and methods of production peppers of different color, taste and hotness can be obtained. This offers benefit of creating special effects by including colored peppercorns in emulsified sausages, for example in Bologna.

Red Pepper - a common name used for all hot red peppers.

Capsicums family of peppers - includes hot red pepper, cayenne pepper, chili pepper and paprika. Chili *powder* is a combination of chili pepper, cumin, oregano and garlic. Interestingly, the smaller the fruit of pepper is, the stronger the pepper.

Peperoncino - these peppers have a spicy, mildly fruity taste and aroma and come from Calabria in southern Italy. They are used in Italian sausages, for example in fermented spreadable Nduja.

Pimentón - it is quite common to come across the definition of pimentón as smoked paprika, which is not correct. Pimentón is Spanish paprika which is usually not smoked unless the label states it is smoked. Only *Pimentón de La Vera is always smoked.* Spanish sausages such as chorizo, sobrasada and others display a unique vivid red color which is due to pimentón. Sweet paprika used for general cooking may be Hungarian, Californian, or South American but Spanish pimentón is darker and has a more intense flavor.

4. Sugar. As a flavoring ingredient, sugar plays a little role in making sausages and is added for other reasons:
   - to offset the harshness of salt, Adding some sugar can correct the problem but only to a some degree. No more than 3 g (3%) of sugar is added to 1 kg of meat otherwise it can be noticeable. Chinese sausages may be an exception as Chinese recipes contain a lot of sugar, however, they mix it with soy sauce and the taste is quite pleasant. Adding too much sugar to a sausage that is smoked for a long time may trigger fermentation by lactic bacteria naturally occurring in meat. This may lead to a sourly flavor.
   - to help bacteria produce lactic acid in fermented sausages. Process of making semi-dry fermented sausages depends on adding sugar.
   - adding 1 - 2 g sugar per 1 kg of meat helps to preserve the color of the sausage.

Dextrose is the sugar of choice for making fermented sausages as it can be immediately consumed by lactic acid bacteria and other sugars must be broken down to glucose first.

In Europe beet sugar is commonly used, in the USA cane sugar is readily available. Often dextrose is used, but keep in mind that it is only 70% as sweet as sugar. Brown sugar carries more flavor than a regular sugar due to the addition of molasses.

5. Spices and Herbs. Throughout history spices were known to possess antibacterial properties. *Cinnamon, cumin, and thyme* were used in the mummification of bodies in ancient Egypt. It is hard to imagine anything that is being cooked in India without curry powder (*coriander, turmeric, cumin, fenugreek* and other spices). *Spices alone can not be used as a hurdle against meat spoilage* as the average amount added to meat is only about 0.1% (1 g/1 kg). To inhibit bacteria, the amounts of spices will have to be very large and that will alter the taste of the sausage. *Rosemary, mace, oregano and sage* have antioxidant properties that can delay the rancidity of fat. *Marjoram* is a pro-oxidant and will speed up the rancidity of fats. *Black pepper, white pepper, garlic, mustard, nutmeg, allspice, ginger, mace, cinnamon, and red pepper* are known to stimulate *Lactobacillus* bacteria to produce lactic acid. *Curcumin* has been shown to be active against *Staphlococcus aureus* (pus-producing infections). An ointment based on turmeric is used as an antiseptic in Malaysia. Spices such as *mustard, cinnamon,* and *cloves* are helpful in slowing the growth of *molds, yeast, and bacteria.* Most cases of illness associated with *Campylobacter* are caused by handling raw poultry or eating raw or under cooked poultry meat and *only garlic* offers some protection. During the last few years a number of studies were undertaken to investigate its antibacterial and antiviral properties. It is widely believed that garlic contributes positively to our cardiovascular and immune systems and a number of on-the-shelf drugs have entered the market. Detailed research was done on the antioxidant and antimicrobial effects of garlic in chicken sausage (Kh.I. Sallam, M. Ishioroshi, and K. Samejima, *Antioxidant and Antimicrobial Effects of Garlic in Chicken Sausage,* Lebenson Wiss Technol., (2004); 37 (8): 849-855.) and the conclusion follows:

"This study concluded that fresh garlic, garlic powder and garlic oil provide antioxidant and antimicrobial benefits to raw chicken sausage during cold storage (3° C, 38° F) and the effects are concentration dependent. Among the garlic forms studied, fresh garlic at a concentration of 50 g/kg demonstrated the most potent effect, but such a high concentration may not be acceptable by many people because of its strong flavor. However, the addition of fresh garlic at 30 g/kg or garlic powder at 9 g/kg, did not result in a strong flavor and at the same time, they produced significant antioxidant and antibacterial effects and extended the shelf life of the product up to 21 days."

What is very significant is that for centuries Thai fermented pork sausage "Nham" and Balinese fermented sausage "Urutan" have been made with 5% of fresh garlic that corresponds to 50 g/kg - the amount found to be effective in the above study.

Spices are more forgiving than salt and you have more space to maneuver when choosing the amounts. The most popular spices in the manufacture of sausages are: pepper, garlic, sage, allspice, marjoram, thyme, rosemary, fennel, anise, cinnamon, mace, mustard, nutmeg, ginger, cardamom, coriander, oregano, and are normally added at around 0.1-0.2% (1-2 g/kg). To weigh spices and starter cultures accurately, specialized digital scales are recommended. Spices are very volatile and lose their aroma rapidly which is more pronounced in slow-fermented sausages that take three months or longer to make. Dark spices such as nutmeg, caraway, cloves, and allspice can darken the color of the sausage.

Allspice *(Pimenta dioica)* - originally from Jamaica, now cultivated in many warm parts of the world. It gets its name because it has flavor similar to the combination of cinnamon, cloves and nutmeg. Allspice can be used in any meat product or sausage.

Mace and Nutmeg *(Myristica fragrans)* - come from the same tree that grows in Malaysia. Nutmeg is the hard nut found inside the ripe fruit and the membrane that surrounds the seed is mace. Nutmeg can leave a bitter taste when more than 1.0 gram per 1 kg of meat is used. As a rule they are not used in fresh sausages as their aroma is easily noticeable. Mace is often used in *liver sausages, frankfurters, hot dogs* and *bologna*.

Cinnamon *(Cinnamomum Casia)* - is the dried bark of the tree which grows in India and China. Often added to *blood sausages* and *bologna*. Better quality and much thinner cinnamon comes from the inner bark of *Cinnamomum Laurel* tree that grows in Sri Lanka (formerly Ceylon), Java and Sumatra. These are tightly rolled thin tubes that we find in supermarkets.

Paprika *(Capsicum annuum)* - is of two different kinds: Hungarian which is sweet, or Spanish pimentón paprika which is slightly pungent. It comes as sweet, medium or hot variety and is used in the highest quality *chorizos*. Paprika is a well known colorant and will give the sausage an orange tint. It agrees well with *emulsified sausages (hotdogs, bologna)* or any pork sausage.

Ginger *(Zingiber officinale)* - is used in cooked sausages, often added to head cheeses and liver sausages.

Clove *(Syzygium aromaticum)* - means nail (clavo) in Spanish and the dried flowers resemble a nail with its sharp point. The trees grow in the Moluccas Islands (Indonesia) and in Madagascar. Cloves are one of the most intensely flavored spices. Cloves go well with *emulsified sausages, head cheese, liver* and *blood sausages.* Cloves are usually inserted into hams which are baked.

Oregano *(Origanum vulgare)* - widely used in Spanish, Italian and French cuisine.

Rosemary *(Rosmarinus officinalis) or (Salvia rosmarinus)* - is native to the Mediterranean region. Rosemary leaves are used as a flavoring in roast lamb, pork, chicken, turkey and wild game.

Tarragon *(Artemisia dracunculus)* - also known as estragon, has a flavor similar to anise. It is widespread in the wild across much of Eurasia and North America, and is very popular in French cuisine.

Aromatic Herbs and Seeds

Anise *(Pimpinella anisum)* - also called *aniseed* is a flowering plant native to the eastern Mediterranean region and Southwest Asia. Its flavor resembles that of fennel and of course it is added to fresh *Italian sausage* or dry sausages such as *Mortadella* or *Pepperoni.* Anise has a very similar flavor to licorice. But they are slightly different. Anise isn't as sharp and bitter as licorice.

Star Anise - despite its name and flavor which is similar to anise, star anise, shaped like a star, is not related to anise and grows in northeast Vietnam and southwest China.

Cardamom *(Elettaria cardamomum)* is the fruit that consists of a shell containing the seeds. Cardamom seeds are used in *liver sausages* and *head cheese.*

Celery seeds *(Apium graveolens)* are used in pork sausages.

Coriander *(Coriandrum sativum)* seed is the dried fruit of the cilantro herb. Used in *emulsified sausages, Polish sausages, minced hams* and *pastrami.*

Cumin *(Cuminum cyminum)* seed is principally used for making curry and chili powders. Similar to caraway, but milder.

Caraway *(Carum carvi)* seed is the dried fruit of caraway plant which grows in Europe and the United States. An aromatic seed, somewhat resembling the cumin seed, often added to rye bread, sauerkraut, pickles and some sausages, for example *Kabanosy.*

Fennel *(Foeniculum vulgare)* i- s the dried seed of the fennel plant. It is added to fresh and other Italian sausages.

Juniper Berries *(Juniperus communis)* - The taste of juniper berries is fresh and tangy with a strong aroma of pine and citrus. Usually added to wildgame, often with rosemary together. Juniper gives gin its unique flavor.

Mustard *(Brassica alba)* - the seed of the white/yellow mustard plant which is grown all over the world. There are brown and black mustard seeds.

Herbs:

Sage *(Sylvia officinalis)* - is used in pork sausages, for example in American breakfast sausage.

Savory *(Satureia hortensis)* - is good with any sausage.

Bay leaf *(Laurus nobilis)* - is principally used in vinegar pickles in products such as pigs feet, and lamb and pork tongues.

Marjoram *(Maiorana hortensis)* - is added to liver sausages, head cheese and many Polish sausages.

Thyme *(Thymus vulgaris)* - is added to liver sausage, head cheese, bockwurst and other pork sausages. Thyme is similar to marjoram but stronger.

Onion *(Allium capa)* - fresh onion is to many sausages, however, to soften its bitter taste, the onion is often fried in fat until glassy and yellow. This caramelizes sugar the onion contains and the onion tastes sweeter. It also comes in dehydrated powder which is preferred as it saves storage and eliminates chores such as peeling and chopping. If using onion powder use about 1/3 of the weight of fresh onion.

Garlic *(Allivum sativum)* - is cultivated all over the world. After pepper it may be considered the most popular ingredient added to sausages. It also comes in dehydrated powder which is preferred as it saves storage and eliminates chores such as peeling and chopping. If using garlic powder use about 1/3 of the weight of fresh garlic. Although the flavor of fresh or granulated garlic is basically the same, fresh garlic has a much stronger aroma.

Turmeric *(Curcuma domestica)* - is the rhizome or underground stem of a ginger-like plant. It is available as a ground, bright yellow fine powder. It is the principal ingredient in curry powder. Turmeric is a natural yellow colorant. Turmeric is used extensively in the East and Middle East as a condiment and culinary dye. It is added to Asian sausages, for example to Balinese Urutan dry sausage.

Guidelines for Spice Usage

The following is a very valuable table which will help you create your own recipes. This is how much spices the professional sausage maker adds to 1 kilogram (2.2 lbs) of meat.

Spice in grams per 1 kg of meat	
Allspice	2.0
Bay Leaf	2 leaves
Cardamom	1.0 - 2.0
Caraway seeds	2.0
Caraway powder	0.5
Celery salt	1.0
Chillies	0.5
Cinnamon	0.5 - 1.0
Cloves	1.0 - 2.0
Coriander	1.0 - 2.0
Cumin	1.0
Curry powder	1.0
Fennel	2.0
Fenugreek	2.0
Garlic paste	3.0 - 5.0
Garlic powder	1.5
Ginger	0.5
Juniper	2.0
Mace	0.5
Marjoram	3.0
Mustard	2.0
Nutmeg	1.0
Onion (fresh)	10.0
Onion powder	2.0 - 10.0
Paprika	2.0
Pepper-white	2.0 - 3.0
Pepper-black	2.0 - 3.0
Thyme	1.0
Turmeric	2.0 - 4.0

Ingredients in g per 1 kg of meat	
non fat dry milk powder	4.0
soy powder	1.0 - 3.0
sugar	1.0 - 2.0

Useful Information

1 US Tablespoon (Tbs) = ½ US fl. oz. = 14.8 ml
1 metric tablespoon = 15 ml (Canada, UK, New Zealand)
1 metric tablespoon = 20 ml (Australia)
1 Tablespoon = 3 teaspoons in both the US and the UK.
1 tsp salt = 6 g
1 tsp Cure#1 or Cure #2 = 6 g
1 tsp sugar (granulated) = 4.1 g
1 tsp sugar (brown) = 4.6 g
1 Tbs water = 15 ml (15 g)
1 cup oil = 215 g
1 Tablespoon of oil = 13.6 g
1 Tbs of butter = 14.19 g
1 cup of all purpose flour = 120 g (4.2 oz).
1 Tbs of flour = 9.45 g
1 cup finely ground bread crumbs = 120 g
1 small onion = 60 g
16 tablespoons = 1 cup
1 dry ounce = 28.3495 grams.
1 cup of water weighs 8.3454 ounces.
There are 236.588 ml in one cup so 1 cup of water weighs 236.588 g.
1 liter = 1.0567 US quart
1 ml water = 1 g

How many grams of spice or ingredient in one flat teaspoon			
Allspice, ground	1.90	Marjoram, dried	0.60
Aniseed	2.10	Marjoram, ground	1.50
Basil	1.50	Milk powder	2.50
Bay leaf, crumbled	0.60	Mustard seed, yellow	3.20
Basil, ground	1.40	Mustard, ground	2.30
Caraway, seed	2.10	Nutmeg, ground	2.03
Cardamom, ground	1.99	Onion powder	2.50
Cayenne pepper, ground	2.50	Oregano, ground	1.50
Celery seed	2.50	Paprika, ground	2.10
Cilantro, dry	1.30	Parsley, dry	0.50
Cinnamon, ground	2.30	Pepper-black, ground	2.10
Cloves, ground	2.10	Pepper-white, ground	2.40
Coriander, ground	2.00	Pepper, flakes, red	2.30
Coriander, seed	1.80	Pepper. whole	4.00
Cumin, ground	2.00	Poppy seed	2.84
Cumin seed	2.10	Rosemary, leaf	1.20
Cure #1 or Cure #2	6.00	Saffron	0.70
Curry powder	2.50	Sage, ground	0.70
Dill, whole	2.42	Savory	1.72
Fennel, whole	2.00	Salt	6.00
Fenugreek, ground	3.70	Soy powder	3.00
Garlic powder	2.80	Sugar	5.00
Ginger, ground	1.80	Tarragon, dry	1.00
Juniper berries	1.53	Thyme, crumbled	0.60
Mace, ground	1.69	Turmeric, ground	3.00

General rule: *1 tsp of dried ground spice weighs 2 grams.*

You don't need a magical recipe to make a good sausage, you need to know how. There are books which list thousands of sausage recipes such as *Sausage and Processed Meat Formulations* by Herbert Ockerman, but don't tell you how to make a great product. Once, you know *the how*, you will transform any recipe into a wonderful sausage.

Dominant Spices Used in Different Sausages

Most sausages will include a dominant spice plus other spices and ingredients. There are some Polish blood sausages *(kaszanka)* that add buckwheat grouts or rice, there are English blood sausages *(black pudding)* that include barley, flour or oatmeal. Some great Cajun sausages like Boudin also include rice, pork, liver and a lot of onion. Let's see what goes besides salt and pepper into some well known sausages that have a recognized flavor.

Name	Meat	Dominant Spice
Dry Chorizo	Pork	Smoked Pimentón
Hunter's Sausage-Polish	Pork, beef	Juniper
Italian Sausage-Sweet	Pork	Fennel
Italian Sausage-Medium	Pork	Fennel plus cayenne
Italian Sausage-Hot	Pork	Fennel plus more cayenne
Italian Nduja	Pork	Peperoncino
Kabanosy	Pork	Nutmeg, caraway
Knoblauchwurst	Pork	Garlic
Polish Smoked Sausage	Pork	Garlic
American Breakfast Sausage	Pork	Sage
Hungarian Smoked Sausage	Beef	Paprika-sweet
Andouille	Pork	Garlic, thyme, cayenne
Swedish Potato Sausage	Pork	Allspice
Nham-Thai Fermented Sausage	Pork	Garlic, hot chillies

All those sausages contain salt, pepper and more spices in smaller doses, but the dominant spice is what gives them their characteristic flavor. Take for example two great Polish classics: Polish Smoked Sausage and Mysliwska Sausage (Hunter's Sausage). The amount of salt and pepper is exactly the same and they both contain garlic. The difference is that Mysliwska has 10% of beef and juniper. And that gives it a different color and, taste and flavor. Then, if you add more juniper into Mysliwska sausage it becomes the Juniper Sausage although all processing steps remain exactly the same. Some sausages are named after the dominant spice they carry: **Juniper** Sausage, **Garlic** Sausage, **Knoblauch**wurst (*Knoblauch* means garlic in German), **Caraway** Sausage etc,.

Vinegar though not a spice is used in some sausages like *white head cheese* or Mexican *chorizo. What is the difference between 50, 100, and 200 grain vinegar? The grain strength of vinegar indicates the acetic acid content. The grain strength is ten times the acetic acid content, so 50 grain vinegar is 5% acetic acid (common variety), 100 grain is 10% acetic acid, and 200 grain is 20 % acetic acid.*

Cold water is often added during mixing and is absorbed by extracted proteins. The finer degree of comminution the more water can be absorbed by the meat. This also depends on meat type and for example beef can absorb much more water than pork. Crushed ice or cold water is added when making emulsified products and the amount depends on the type of device used for emulsifying. A bowl cutter is more effective than a kitchen food processor and the last one is better than a regular grinder.

Wine - red or white dry wines are often added to fermented sausages.

Garlic-in-wine infusion - Italian salami recipes often ask for garlic-in-wine infusions. Chopped garlic is immersed in red wine, then the marinade is filtered and about 5 ml (1 tsp) of infusion is added to 1 kg of ground meat.

Creating Your Own Recipe

1. Choose the sausage type you want to make (fresh, smoked, fermented, cooked, uncooked etc). This step will influence the amount of salt and nitrite (if any) added and the processing steps that will follow. In case a specialty sausage such as liver sausage, head cheese or blood sausage is chosen, different meats and fillers will be selected. Choose whether you want to make a classical sausage such as Italian Sausage, Polish Smoked Sausage, Swedish Potato Sausage or Hungarian Salami. If you decide on a known sausage, add spices which are typical for this sausage.

2. Weigh in your spices and salt. Consult the spice guidelines table. You are in command so *decide how much salt you want to add.* All you need is a calculator. For example you have 11 pounds (5 kg) of meat and you would like to have 1.8% of salt in your sausage.

0.018 x 11 pounds = 0.198 lb
OR make it simple and use metric system:
0.018 x 5000 grams = 90 g

1 tablespoon of regular table salt weighs around 18 g and you need about 5 tablespoons of salt. Let's say you are on a low sodium diet so you want to use 1.2% salt only.

0.012 x 5000 g = 60 g (3.3 Tbsp)

Salt for 1 kg (2.2 lbs) of meat				
1%	1.2%	1.5%	1.8%	2%
10 g	12 g	15 g	18 g	20 g

Most sausages contain between 18 and 20 g salt per 1 kg of meat. One teaspoon contains 6 g of salt.

3. Choose the amount of Cure #1. *You can be flexible* with sodium nitrite (Cure #1), too. Although the maximum allowed by law limit for comminuted meats is 156 ppm (parts per million), there is no established lower limit. European limit is 150 ppm. Denmark has won a concession from the European Common Market and their max nitrite limit is only 100 ppm.

You want at least 50 ppm for any meaningful curing to take place but whether the amount is 150 ppm, 120 ppm or 100 ppm you will be fine. Let's assume that you need 6 g (1 tsp) of Cure #1 to cure 5 lbs of meat. One flat teaspoon will provide the right amount but if it is only 3/4 full the meat will be equally cured, although the pink color might be less intense. If you make a mistake and apply a full teaspoon instead of a flat teaspoon of cure there is no need to despair and don't throw away your sausage. Just don't make it a habit. Nitrite dissipates quite rapidly and after cooking and a brief period of storing, there will be little of it left in a sausage.

There is an important exception to this reasoning:

You should not decrease the amount of salt and nitrite when making traditionally fermented sausages. In those sausages salt and nitrite provide the only protection during the initial stages of the process against spoilage and pathogenic bacteria and they should be applied at the maximum allowed limits.

By now you should be aware that you don't need nitrite for sausages which will not be smoked. Nevertheless, some products such as head cheese or blood sausage, although not smoked, might incorporate nitrite to cure meats such as tongues, in order to develop the red color expected by the consumer. Keep in mind that *nitrite does not cure fat* and if your sausage is on the fat side, *less nitrite will do the job.* The reason we deal with nitrite and cures in this book in such detail is that many people are unnecessarily afraid of them.

U.S. Cure #1 (6.25% sodium nitrite) for 1 kg (2.2 lbs) of meat			
75 ppm	100 ppm	120 ppm	156 ppm - max
1.2 g	1.6 g	1.9 g	2.5 g

European Peklosol (0.6% sodium nitrite) for 1 kg (2.2 lbs) of meat			
75 ppm	100 ppm	120 ppm	150 ppm - max
12.5 g	16.6 g	20 g	25 g

European Peklosol can be substituted for salt and the nitrite limits would be observed. For example adding 20 g Peklosol to 1 kg of ground meat would result in 120 ppm (parts per million) of sodium nitrite and 2% saltiness. Increasing nitrite levels (ppm) higher would result in a slightly salty product, for example adding 25 g of Peklosol results in 150 ppm limit but the percentage of salt becomes 2.5%.

This problem is not present with Cure #1 which contains 6.25% sodium nitrite. *Adding 2.5 g of Cure #1 (½ tsp) to 1 kg of ground meat results in 156 ppm.* This corresponds to adding 1 teaspoon of Cure #1 to 5 pounds of meat. This is still the safe amount and you may make it your standard formula. For those who like to be perfect, it must be noted that adding Cure #1 brings an extra salt into the sausage mass as Cure #1 contains 93.75% salt. This amount can be subtracted from the salt that is added to the recipe. On the other hand this amount is so small that it makes little sense to bother. Nevertheless it is good to understand this fact in case someone is producing a large quantity of sausages.

Examples

Let's create some great sausages which are based on a simple recipe.

Example 1 - My Fresh Sausage

Meat

pork	1000 g	2.20 lbs

Ingredients

salt, 1.8%	18 g	3 tsp.
pepper	2.0 g	1 tsp.
garlic	3.5 g	1 clove
marjoram	1.0 g	½ tsp.

1. Grind meat through 3/8" (10 mm) plate.
2. Mix meat with all ingredients. Knead the mass well until sticky.
3. Stuff into 36 mm hog casings.
4. Refrigerate. Cook before serving.

Example 2 - My Hot Smoked Sausage

You can add beef to the recipe which has excellent water binding properties. Now you can add even more water, making your sausage juicier and more of it.

Meat

pork	800 g	1.76 lb.
beef	200 g	0.44 lb.

Ingredients

salt, 1.8%	18 g	3 tsp.
cure #1	2.5 g	½ tsp.
pepper	2.0 g	1 tsp.
garlic	3.5 g	1 clove
marjoram	1.0 g	½ tsp.
water	120 ml	1/2 cup.

1. Grind meat through 3/16" (5 mm) plate.
2. Mix meat with all ingredients including water. Knead the mass well until sticky.
3. Stuff into 36 mm hog casings.
4. Hang for 60 minutes at room temperature.
5. Smoke at 140 - 150° F (60 - 65° C) for 60 min.
6. Cook to 160° F (72° C) internal meat temperature.
7. Immerse in cold water for 10 minutes.
8. Dry in air to evaporate moisture and refrigerate.

How about making a frankfurter out of it. Add mace, paprika, and coriander to the above recipe. After grinding emulsify meats and stuff the mixture into 26 mm sheep casings. Then smoke, cook and eat your frankfurters.

Example 3 - My Cold Smoked Sausage

Meat

pork	800 g	1.76 lb.
beef	200 g	0.44 lb.

Ingredients

salt, 3.0%	30 g	5 tsp.
cure #1	2.5 g	½ tsp.
pepper	2.0 g	1 tsp.
garlic	3.5 g	1 clove
marjoram	1.0 g	½ tsp.

1. Grind through 3/16" (5 mm) plate.
2. Mix meat with all ingredients including water. Knead the mass well until sticky.
3. Stuff into 36 mm hog casings.
4. Hang for 2 days in a cool place (around 50° F, 10° C).
5. Smoke with cold smoke for 3 days. It does not matter much whether you smoke it for 2, 5 or 7 days. This will only affect the smoky flavor. The purpose of cold smoking is to dry meat and to provide some protection against bacteria. Think of cold smoking as the first part of the drying step that follows.
6. Dry sausage in a cool, ventilated area (50-54° F, 10-12° C) for about 25 days to lose about 30% of its original weight. A degree one way or the other will not make much difference. People did not have thermometers before and the sausages were great. You must not go over 59° F (15° C) because this is when the *Staphylococcus aureus* pathogen starts to multiply fast.
7. Store in a cool, dry area.

Note: the sausage is basically dry salami.

By adding sugar and starter culture to the above recipe you can make semi-dry fermented sausage.

You can come up with your own names for these sausages. Imagine now what will happen if you start changing meat combinations and naming each sausage differently. Or adding different spices and creating even more names. This is exactly what is out there on the Internet - thousands of recipes that differ very little from each other.

Once you have mastered the basic rules of sausage making you will be able to make up hundreds of your own recipes. Furthermore, you will be able to recognize a good recipe from an amateurish one.

The Recipes in This Book

There are 172 recipes in this book and there was a question about the best way to present them. The recipes in many books are listed for different amounts of meat from 2-10 lbs and ingredients are given in pounds, ounces, tablespoons, teaspoons, quarts, pints, cups etc. Although it required some recalculations on our part, we have decided to choose the system which is very popular in German books.

All materials and ingredients are listed for 1 kg of meat (2.2 lbs). This way if one needs to make 2 kg (4.4 lbs), 3 kg (6.6 lbs) or 5 kg (11 lbs) of sausage, all that is needed is to multiply the amount of each ingredient by a factor of 2, 3, or 5. Most professional books list the amount of spice in grams/per kg of meat. This is of great advantage and after a while the sausage maker knows exactly how much spices are needed in each recipe. He can not only create his own properly designed recipe, but he can also easily spot a faulty one. Just look at the recipe and break it down into components. Are the ingredients listed in grams (ounces) or do they call for cups, teaspoons or whole onions? If they do, they are very amateurish and you can do better.

Most recipes call for 16-18 g salt per 1 kg (1000 g) of meat. This corresponds to 1.6-1.8% salt content which provides enough saltiness, yet is less salty that sausages that were made in the past. Those sausages contained 2% (or more) of salt, which was needed to provide additional safety. Refrigeration was not widely available and the product had to keep well at room temperatures. When we mention "room temperature" we mean European climate room temperatures (around 59° F, 15° C) and not the sub-tropical tropical temperatures in Southern Europe or in American states like Florida or Louisiana.

Keep in mind that *by varying processing steps you can create different sausages although the recipe will remain basically the same.* Ending processing on the stuffing step creates a not-ready-to-eat fresh sausage but if we cook the same sausage, the result will be a ready-to-eat-sausage.

Useful Information

- For best quality sausage cure meats in a refrigerator. You can add 20-25% of water into beef.
- When mixing meats by hand, don't just mix but knead the mass with some force. You want to extract proteins which were cut during the grinding/cutting process. You will know when it happens as the mixture becomes sticky.
- After stuffing, hang sausages intended for smoking for 1-2 hours (depending on diameter) at room temperature or place them in a pre-heated smokehouse.
- When smoking sausages in a large smokehouse it is a good idea to periodically re-arrange the smokesticks inside. This compensates for uneven smoke, heat and moisture distribution.
- You can emulsify meat using a manual grinder. After first grind place meat dough for 30 minutes in a freezer, then run it again through 1/8" (3 mm) plate adding a little water. For even smoother texture place it again for 30 min in the freezer
- and grind it again.
- Recipe might say: make 6" long links but it is up to you what links you want. Leave it in a continuous rope if you like.
- Add diced back fat for this special look in emulsified or liver sausages. The pieces of fat will stand out like in mortadella.
- For unusual flavor, instead of water add chicken or beef bouillon, tomato juice, or wine into sausages. Don't do this when making fermented products.
- You can use different cultures than those mentioned in the book when making fermented sausages.
- Lean pork: shoulder, leg (ham part), loin or any lean pork cut that comes from any part of the pig.

Chapter 13

Fresh Sausages

Fresh sausages are embarrassingly simple to make and the procedure resembles making a meal. A fresh sausage is not cooked nor smoked and that explains the ease of its production. Everybody knows how to make a hamburger and if you stuff ground and spiced hamburger meat into a casing it becomes a sausage. Somehow this classical definition has been twisted in recent years and many ordinary meat dishes such as meat patties are also called sausages. The best example is McDonald's® Sausage Mc Muffin which is a meat patty served on a bun.

Whether you chop meat with a knife or use a grinder is of lesser importance. The same applies to the stuffing process, you may use grinder with a stuffing tube, a self-contained piston grinder, or stuff the mixture with your fingers through a suitable funnel. Once the sausage is finished it goes into the refrigerator where it remains a day or two. Of course it has to be fully cooked before consumption.

The taste of the sausage will depend on meats that were selected and spices which were added to the mix. If you want to make Italian sausage use fennel which is the dominant spice in the recipe. To create a medium hot or hot version of the sausage add more or less of red pepper or cayenne. Polish white sausage requires garlic and marjoram (optional), other sausages call for different dominant spice combinations. The best advice is to use spices that you like, after all you are the one that will eat the sausage.

The Internet is loaded with millions of recipes which were invented by creative cooks. You will find sausages with apples, arugula, pineapples, and other ingredients. Many large recipe oriented web sites must provide new content on a continuous basis to stay alive. They employ people with writing skills on a paid by article or recipe basis and those creative persons look everywhere to find an original or rather unusual recipe.

In our opinion this has little in common with serious sausage making and rather fits into the general cooking category, which makes sense as many recipes are written by restaurant chefs who always think in terms of cooking a meal. A fresh sausage will end up on a breakfast plate with fries and ketchup or on a grill in the back yard.

Providing that fresh meat is obtained and the safety practices are implemented, there is little to worry about *Salmonella, E.coli* or *Clostridium botulinum* as high heat during cooking takes care of those pathogens. Store fresh sausages in a refrigerator for 2-3 days or up to 2-3 months in the freezer. They must be fully cooked before serving.

Fresh sausages contain much fat which is shown in the table that follows. The data comes from U.S. CFR 319. 140.

Name	Max Fat in %	Max Water in %
Fresh Pork	50	3
Fresh Beef	30	3
Breakfast	50	3
Italian	35	3

Manufacturing Process

Making of a fresh sausage follows the basic steps described in the previous chapter:

1. Cutting/grinding
2. Mixing
3. Stuffing
4. Storing in refrigerator.

There is no need to cure meat, unless pink color in the finished product is desired. Although making fresh sausages is easier it is still a *great introduction* into the art of sausage making.

Andouille

Andouille sausage is a classical Louisiana smoked sausage which is used in meals like gumbo or jambalaya. The regional cooking style known as Cajun employs many hot spices and vegetables and is famous for its original sausages: Andouille, Boudain, Chaurice (local version of Spanish chorizo) or Tasso (smoked butt). It is not easy to come up with a universal Andouille sausage recipe. Some recipes include dry red wine, others bay leaves, allspice, sage, paprika, crushed red peppers, sugar, onion powder, pequin pepper, mace, nutmeg, sage, ancho chili or file powder. So which one is the real Andouille Sausage? As nearly all recipes agree on the following ingredients: pork butt, salt, cracked pepper, garlic, thyme and cayenne pepper, we have decided to keep it simple and to include only those mentioned and nothing else. But please feel free to improvise and include any spices that you like.

Meat	Metric	US
pork butt	1000 g	2.20 lb.

Ingredients per 1000 g (1 kg) of meat:

salt	16 g	2¾ tsp.
Cure #1	2.5 g	⅓ tsp.
cracked black pepper	6.0 g	3 tsp.
chopped garlic	10.0 g	3 cloves
dried thyme	2.0 g	1½ tsp.
cayenne pepper	4.0 g	2 tsp.
cold water	100 g	⅜ cup

Instructions:

1. Grind all meat with 1/4" (5 - 6 mm) plate.
2. Mix meat with all ingredients, including water.
3. Stuff into 38 - 40 mm hog casings. Leave as a rope or make 12" (30 cm) links.
4. Dry for two hours at room temperature or preheat smoker to 130° F (54° C) and hold without smoke for one hour.
5. Apply hot smoke for 2 hours.
6. Shower for 5 minutes with cold water.
7. Store in refrigerator and fully cook before serving.

Notes: to make a ready to eat sausage increase smoker temperature to 170° F (76° C) until internal temperature of 155° F (69° C) is obtained. You may poach it in water at 175° - 185° F (80° - 85° C) until internal temperature of 155° F (69° C) is obtained.

Bockwurst

Bockwurst (Munchner Weisswurst) is a German white sausage made of pork and veal. White pepper, parsley, nutmeg (or mace) and lemon flavor are typical ingredients.

Meat	Metric	US
pork	500 g	1.10 lb.
veal	300 g	0.66 lb.
back fat	200 g	0.44 lb.

Ingredients per 1000 g (1 kg) of meat:

salt	18 g	1 Tbs.
white pepper	3.0 g	1½ tsp.
ginger, ground	0.5 g	⅓ tsp.
fresh parsley, chopped	10 g	1 bunch
onion powder	6 g	2 ½ tsp.
grated lemon peel	¼ lemon	¼ lemon
egg	1	1
whole milk	100 ml	3 oz. fluid

(instead of whole milk you may use 40 g (1.4 oz) of non fat dry milk)

Instructions:
1. Grind meat through 3/16" plate (3 mm).
2. Beat eggs in a food processor.
3. Add to the processor ground meats, milk and all ingredients and emulsify.
4. Stuff into 28-32 mm hog casings forming 4" (10 cm) links.
5. Keep in a refrigerator (very perishable product) or freeze for later. Cook before serving.

To make ready to eat cooked sausage:
6. Poach in water for 30 min at 176° F, 80° C. Keep refrigerated or freeze for later use.

Notes:
Eggs are used to bind everything together.
Non fat dry milk has good binding properties.
One stalk of chopped scallions or chives may be added.
Grate the outside of the lemon only, not the inner white skin.

Boudin

Boudin is a Cajun sausage (not to be mistaken with French Boudoin Blanc) stuffed with pork and rice. Boudin needs pork liver to be really good. Boudin is the most popular sausage in southwest Louisiana and can be purchased from just about every supermarket, convenience store and restaurant.

Meat	Metric	US
pork	700 g	1.54 lb.
pork liver	300 g	0.66 lb.

Ingredients per 1000 g (1 kg) of meat:

salt	18 g	1 Tbs.
cracked black pepper	6.0 g	3 tsp.
dried thyme	2.0 g	1½ tsp.
cayenne pepper	2.0 g	1 tsp.
parsley, finely chopped	60 g	½ bunch
1 small onion, cut up	60 g	4 Tbs.
1 stalk green onions, chopped	15 g	1 stalk
1 rib celery, cut up	75 g	1 rib
bay leaf, crushed	1	1
1 cup rice	150 g	1 cup
cold water	100 ml	⅜ cup

Instructions:

1. Place pork meat, liver, chopped onion, chopped celery, bay leaf and black peppercorns in 1 quart (950 ml) of water and bring to boil. Reduce heat, skim as necessary and simmer for 1 hour until meat separates from the bone.
Remove the meat, discard the vegetables, strain the stock and save for cooking rice and for mixing.
Bring stock to boil and add rice. Simmer until rice is very tender.
2. Grind all meat through 1/4" plate.
3. Mix ground meat with chopped green onions, chopped parsley, salt, white pepper, cayenne and rice. Add enough stock until mixture does not stick to your fingers. Taste it and add more salt or cayenne if necessary.
4. Stuff into 36 mm casings.
5. Refrigerate. Cook before serving.

A good stock plays a very important role in making this sausage. You can use chicken parts like leg quarters along pork meat and liver. When thoroughly cooked remove the skin, dice the meat off the bones, grind it and mix it with the rest of the ingredients.

You can fry liver with a few strips of bacon for additional flavor. First fry bacon until crisp, remove it (it does not go into the sausage), then add green onion bottoms, some extra chopped onion and cook shortly until the onions are translucent. Then add liver and cook until tender. Add 1/2 cup of stock and simmer for 15 more minutes. Grind liver with fried onions. Don't discard the frying pan drippings, they are added during mixing for the extra flavor.

Boudin is served hot:

- Baked for 10 min at 350° F (180° C) in the pre-heated oven.
- Boiled for 10 min in hot water.
- Heated in a microwave.

Fresh sausages are normally neither smoked nor cooked. They have useful life of just a few days and must be stored in a refrigerator, and cooked before serving. Making fresh sausages ends with stuffing the sausage mass into the casing. This does not mean that this is the only way they can be manufactured.

What follows below is the example of how easily a fresh sausage recipe can be changed into a cooked one:

Smoked *fresh* sausage - if you want to smoke the sausage add 2.5 g of Cure #1 (1/2 tsp.) per 1 kg of meat when mixing ingredients. Stuff the sausage and then apply smoke at 140-150° F (60 - 65° C) for 60 minutes. You will get a smoky flavor but the sausage is still not ready-to-eat. Refrigerate and fully cook before serving.

Smoked *cooked* sausage *If you follow the smoking step with the cooking step, you will get a ready-to-eat sausage*:

a. increase the smokehouse temperature to 185° F (85° C) and bake the sausage (without smoke) for 30 minutes *OR*

b. cook in water at 176° F (80° C) for 30 minutes.

The sausage still has to be refrigerated, though it will last much longer. You can eat it cold at any time, make sandwiches or serve it hot.

Bratwurst

Bratwurst is a German sausage which is usually fried or grilled. It can be made from pork and beef, though most bratwursts are made from pork and veal. Depending on the region where the sausage was made and the combination of spices which were added, we may find bratwursts with many names, such as: Thuringer Bratwurst, Nurnberger Bratwurst, Rheinishe Bratwurst and many others.

Meat	Metric	US
pork	700 g	1.54 lb.
veal	300 g	0.66 lb.

Ingredients per 1000 g (1 kg) of meat:

salt	18 g	1 Tbs.
white pepper	3.0 g	1½ tsp.
marjoram, dry	1.0 g	1 tsp.
caraway	1.0 g	½ tsp.
nutmeg	1.0 g	½ tsp.
ginger, ground	0.5 g	⅓ tsp.
white of an egg	2	2
cold water	100 g	⅜ cup

Instructions:
1. Grind meat through 3/16" plate (3 mm).
2. Whisk the eggs.
3. Mix meats and all ingredients together.
4. Stuff into 32-36 mm hog casings forming 4" (10 cm) links.
5. Keep in a refrigerator or freeze for later use.
6. Cook before serving.

Note: adding white of an egg is optional. It is common in Germany to add eggs into fresh sausages to increase the binding of ingredients.

Breakfast Sausage

Breakfast sausage is without a doubt the most popular sausage in the world. Served by fast food restaurants, given in the form of sausage links to patients in hospitals, sold at supermarkets. Made like most sausages of pork, salt and pepper with *sage being the dominant spice.*

Meat	Metric	US
pork butt	1000 g	2.20 lb.

Ingredients per 1000 g (1 kg) of meat:

salt	18 g	1 Tbs.
pepper	2.0 g	1 tsp.
sage (rubbed)	2.0 g	2 tsp.
nutmeg	0.5 g	¼ tsp.
ginger	0.5 g	⅔ tsp.
thyme (dried)	1.0 g	1 tsp.
cayenne pepper	0.5 g	¼ tsp.
cold water	100 g	⅜ cup

Instructions:
1. Grind meat with 1/4" (5-6 mm) plate.
2. Mix meat with all ingredients, including water.
3. Stuff into 22-26 mm sheep or 28-30 mm hog casings. Tie into 4" links. Refrigerate.

Notes:
Cook before serving. Recommended for frying or grilling.

Chaurice

Chaurice is a pork sausage that is Creole Cajun in origin and has a hot and spicy flavor. Chaurice sausage is popular in Creole Cajun cooking both as a main dish and as an ingredient in dishes such as gumbo and jambalaya. It came originally to Louisiana as the Spanish chorizo but was adapted to local customs and ingredients. Chaurice sausage is popular as a main dish but it also goes well with beans or as an ingredient in dishes like gumbo, jambalaya or even potatoes with sauerkraut. Chaurice with eggs makes a good breakfast too.

Meat	Metric	US
pork butt	1000 g	2.20 lb.

Ingredients per 1000 g (1 kg) of meat:

salt	18 g	1 Tbs.
dried thyme	2.0 g	1½ tsp.
cayenne pepper	2.0 g	1 tsp.
red pepper flakes	1.0 g	1 tsp.
bay leaf, crushed	1	1
garlic	7 g	2 cloves
parsley, finely chopped	60 g	½ bunch
onions, finely diced	60 g	1 cup
cold water	100 g	⅜ cup

Instructions:
1. Grind all meat through the 3/8" - 1/2" (10 - 12 mm) plate.
2. Mix meat with all ingredients, including water.
3. Stuff into 32 - 36 mm hog casings and make 8" long links.
4. Refrigerate.

Notes:
Cook before serving.

Chicken Curry

Very original, yet simple to make sausage.

Meat	Metric	US
chicken	700 g	1.54 lb.
pork back fat,	300 g	0.56 lb.
belly or fat trimmings		

Ingredients per 1000 g (1 kg) of meat:

salt	12 g	2½ tsp.
white pepper	3.0 g	1½ tsp.
curry powder	2.5 g	1 tsp.
garlic	3.5 g	1 clove
white wine	50 g	1/5 cup

Instructions:
1. Grind meat and fat through 3/8" plate (8 mm).
2. Mix meats with all ingredients.
3. Stuff into 32-36 mm hog casings forming 4" (10 cm) links.
4. Keep in a refrigerator or freeze for later use.

Notes:
Cook before serving.

Chorizo - Argentinean

Original Spanish chorizo is a fermented sauage which is made of cured pork and is air dried until ready for consumption. South American chorizos are fresh sausages which are cooked on a grill. They contain more hot spices and are often seasoned with nutmeg, fennel and cloves. Another difference is that South American chorizos are made with wine or in the case of Mexican chorizo with vinegar which makes them much moister.

Argentinian chorizo is a fresh sausage and like other sausages made in Chile, Uruguay, Paraguay, Peru or Bolivia, it has its distinctive character. When sold on street corners or soccer stadiums they are served on a long French bread that in the USA will be called a subway sandwich. When served this way they go by the name of Choripan which is a combination of two words: **Chori**-zo (sausage) and **pan** (bread). The roll is cut lengthwise on one side and the sausage is placed on one of its halves. The second half is always covered with chimichurri which is Argentinian steak sauce. Sometimes the sausage is split lengthwise which is known as butterfly (mariposa) style. In Uruguay it will be served with mayonnaise and ketchup.

Meat	Metric	US
beef	250 g	0.55 lb.
lean pork	500 g	1.10 lb.
pork back fat, belly or fat trimmings	250 g	0.55 lb.

Ingredients per 1000 g (1 kg) of meat:

salt	18 g	3 tsp.
pepper	3.0 g	1½ tsp.
paprika or sweet pimentón	10 g	5 tsp.
garlic	7 g	2 cloves
red wine	125 ml	½ cup

Instructions:
1. Grind meat through 1/2" (12 mm) plate.
2. Smash garlic cloves and mix with a little amount of wine.
3. Mix meat, infused garlic, salt and all ingredients together.
4. Stuff into hog casings, 32-36 mm and form 6" (15 cm) links. Refrigerate.
Notes: cook before serving.

Chorizo - Mexican

Original Spanish chorizo is made from coarsely chopped pork and seasoned with paprika and garlic. It is a dry cured and air dried sausage. Most South American chorizos are of a fresh type which is fried for breakfast or grilled on a fire. Mexican Chorizo Sausage is made from pork that is ground and seasoned with chile peppers, garlic and vinegar). It is moister and much hotter than the Spanish chorizo.

Meat	Metric	US
pork butt	1000 g	2.20 lb.

Ingredients per 1000 g (1 kg) of meat:

salt	18 g	3 tsp.
pepper	4.0 g	2 tsp.
cayenne pepper	4.0 g	2 tsp.
oregano, dry	1.0 g	1 tsp.
garlic	7 g	2 cloves
white vinegar	50 ml	1/5 cup
water	50 ml	1/5 cup

Instructions:
1. Grind meat through 1/2" (12 mm) plate.
2. Smash garlic cloves and mix with a little amount of water.
3. Mix meat, all ingredients and vinegar together.
4. Stuff into 32 - 36 mm hog casings and make 8" long links. Refrigerate.

Notes:

Cook before serving.
Chorizo with eggs is often served for breakfast: insert pieces of chorizo into scrambled eggs and blend them together.

Greek Sausage

Greek sausage made from lamb, pork fat and cheese.

Meat	Metric	US
lamb	700 g	1.54 lb.
pork back fat, jowl, fatty pork trimmings	300 g	0.66 lb.
goat or sheep cheese	60 g	0.13 lb

Ingredients per 1000 g (1 kg) of meat:

salt	15 g	2½ tsp.
pepper	2.0 g	1 tsp.
cayenne pepper	2.0 g	1 tsp.
coriander, ground	2.0 g	1 tsp.
thyme, dry leaf	2.0 g	1½ tsp.
mint, dry leaf	2.0 g	1½ tsp.
red wine	100 ml	⅜ cup
cornstarch	10 g	1 Tbs.

Instructions:
1. Grind meat and fat through 3/8" plate (8 mm).
2. Cut cheese into little cubes.
3. Mix cheese with all spices. Mix salt with wine and then pour over meat. Add cheese and spices and mix. Add cornstarch and mix everything together.
4. Stuff into 32-36 mm hog casings forming 4" (10 cm) links. Refrigerate or freeze for later use.

Notes:
Cook before serving.

Hurka Hungarian Sausage

Hurka is a well known Hungarian water cooked sausage made originally from organ meats such as pork liver, lungs, head meat, rice and onions. Blood is occasionally added.

Meat	Metric	US
pork liver	300 g	0.66 lb.
pork butt	600 g	1.32 lb.
fat pork trimmings, belly		
or lard	100 g	0.22 lb

Ingredients per 1000 g (1 kg) of meat:

salt	12 g	2 tsp.
pepper	2.5 g	1 tsp.
garlic	3.5 g	1 clove
½ small onion	30 g	2 Tbs.
cooked rice (15%)	150 g	1 cup
cold water	125 ml	½ cup

Note: Hurka was originally made with 30% pork liver, 30% pork tongues and 10% pork back fat, belly or lard.

Instructions:

1. Boil all meats (except liver) for about 2 hours. Poach liver in hot water until no traces of blood are visible (cut the liver to test). Cool meats and remove the skin from tongues.
2. Grind meats through 3/16" plate (5 mm). Grind liver through a smaller plate.
3. Cook rice for about 15 minutes. Place some bacon fat or lard on a frying pan and fry onions until light brown.
4. Mix everything together, adding 125 ml (½ cup) water. You may substitute some water with white wine.
5. Stuff loosely into large hog or synthetic casings.
6. Cook for 4 minutes in boiled water or poach in water for 8 minutes at 85° C (185° F). Refrigerate. Serve hot.

Frozen Hurka sausage can be baked at 180° C (350° F) for about 50 minutes (leave the lid on or cover with aluminum foil). Then uncover the sausage and continue baking for 5 more minutes until brown. Fresh Hurka sausage can be pan fried or grilled. Goes well with pickles.

Italian Sausage *(Sweet)*

Italian Sausage is a wonderful sausage for frying or grilling and can be found in every supermarket in the USA. The dominant flavor in fresh Italian sausage is fennel and by adding (or not) cayenne pepper we can create sweet, medium or hot variety. Fried on a hot plate with green bell peppers and onions, it is sold by street vendors everywhere in New York City. Don't confuse it with cheap poached hot dogs on a bun, Italian sausage is bigger and served on a long subway type roll. It is leaner than other fresh sausages and the US regulations permit no more than 35% fat in the recipe. *Fennel,* sometimes added with anise, is the dominant spice in this sausage.

Meat	Metric	US
pork butt	1000 g	2.20 lb.

Ingredients per 1000 g (1 kg) of meat:

salt	18 g	1 Tbs.
sugar	2 g	½ tsp.
coarse black pepper	2.0 g	1 tsp.
cracked fennel seed	3 g	2 tsp.
coriander	1 g	½ tsp.
caraway	1 g	¼ tsp.
cold water	100 g	⅜ cup

Instructions:
1. Grind meat with ⅜" (10 mm) plate.
2. Mix meat with all ingredients, including water.
3. Stuff into 32 - 36 mm hog casings and tie into 5" (12 cm) links.
4. Cook before serving. Recommended for frying or grilling.

For **Medium Hot Italian Sausage** add 2 g (1 tsp) cayenne pepper.
For **Hot Italian Sausage** add 4 g (2 tsp) cayenne pepper.

Italian spices such as basil, thyme and oregano are often added.

Jalapeño Sausage

Jalapeño is a medium-hot pepper rated around 6,000 heat units on Scoville scale, less hot than Serrano (20,000 SHU) or Tabasco (50,000 SHU), and it can be consumed raw. Fully matured jalapeño is red, however, green pepper is milder and more visible inside the sausage.

Meat	Metric	US
beef	700 g	1.54 lb.
back fat, fatty pork trimmings or bacon	300 g	0.56 lb.

Ingredients per 1000 g (1 kg) of meat:

salt	18 g	3 tsp.
white pepper	2.5 g	1 tsp.
cilantro, crumbled	0.6 g	1 tsp.
cumin, ground	1.0 g	½ tsp.
garlic,	3.5 g	1 clove
½ onion,	30 g	2 Tbs.
green jalapeño, diced	20 g	1
white wine,	50 ml	1/5 cup
water	50 ml	1/5 cup

Instructions:
1. Grind meat through 3/16" plate (3 mm).
2. Add all ingredients to wine and mix. Pour over ground meat and mix everything well together.
3. Stuff into 32-36 mm hog casings forming 4" (10 cm) links. Keep in a refrigerator or freeze for later use.

Notes:
Cook before serving.

Longanisa

Longanisa is a Philippine version of a Spanish Longaniza sausage. Longaniza is also popular in Argentina, Chile, Mexico and all other Spanish speaking countries including the Caribbean Islands like Cuba and the Dominican Republic. And of course there are different varieties of Longaniza.

In 1565 Spanish Conquistador, Miguel López de Legazpi arrived in Cebu, Philippines from Mexico (New Spain) and established the permanent Spanish settlement that lasted over three hundred years. This brought Catholic Religion, Spanish law, administration, and the new culture. Culinary arts were no exception and Spanish sausages were introduced as well. They had to be somewhat modified due to a different, hot and humid climate, but their names remained the same. The most popular sausage in the Philippines is Longanisa (in Spain called Longaniza) and it has a distinctive flavor in each region of the country: Lucban is heavy on garlic and oregano, Guagua is saltier with more vinegar, or finger-sized ones from Guinobatan. Traditional Longanisa may be dried (conditions permitting) and sometimes smoked, however, it can be kept fresh or frozen and cooked. Unlike Spanish chorizos, Longanisas can also be made of chicken, beef, or even tuna.

Meat	Metric	US
pork	1000 g	2.20 lb.

Ingredients per 1000 g (1 kg) of meat:

salt	18 g	3 tsp.
black pepper	2.5 g	1 tsp.
sugar	2.5 g	½ tsp.
paprika	6.0 g	3 tsp.
garlic,	7.0 g	2 cloves
½ onion,	30 g	2 Tbs.
oregano, dry leaf	2 g	2 tsp.
white vinegar	50 ml	1/5 cup
water	50 ml	1/5 cup

Instructions:

1. Cut pork into small cubes or grind through a coarse plate, 3/8" - 1/2" (10 - 12 mm).
2. Mix all ingredients in water and pour over ground meat. Mix all together.
3. Stuff into 32 mm or smaller hog casings and twist them into 4-5" (10-12 cm) links. Using cotton twine, tie the ends of each sausage link tightly, then cut between each link to separate.
4. Store in refrigerator.

Notes: cook before serving - fry on a frying pan until golden brown.

Loukanika

Loukanika Sausage is a Greek fresh sausage made with lamb and pork and seasoned with orange rind. The Greek mountainous terrain is ill suited for raising cattle but perfect for animals such as goats and sheep. The best example is the famous Greek "Feta" cheese which is made from goat and sheep milk. Most recipes include spices like garlic, oregano, thyme, marjoram, and allspice. Dry red or white wine is often used.

Meat	Metric	US
pork	700 g	1.54 lb.
lamb	300 g	0.56 lb.

Ingredients per 1000 g (1 kg) of meat:

salt	18 g	3 tsp.
pepper	2.0 g	1 tsp.
garlic	3.5 g	1 clove
allspice, ground	1.0 g	½ tsp.
thyme, dry leaf	2.0 g	1½ tsp.
oregano, dried	2.0 g	2 tsp.
orange peel, grated		2 tsp.
red wine	100 ml	⅜ cup

Instructions:
1. Grind meats through ⅜" (10 mm) plate.
2. Mix ground meat with wine and all ingredients.
3. Stuff into 32-36 mm casings, forming 6" links.
4. Store in refrigerator or freeze for later use.

Notes: cook before serving. The sausage can be fried, baked or boiled. You may place it in a skillet with water to cover, bring it to a boil and then simmer on lower heat for about 20 minutes. Keep the cover on.

Merguez

Merguez, the French transliteration of the Arabic word mirqaz, is a spicy, short sausage from North Africa made with lamb or beef, and flavored with spices. Spices such as paprika, cayenne or harissa, a hot chili paste that gives Merguez sausage its red color. Sold by street vendors in Paris, can also be found in London, Belgium and New York.

Meat	Metric	US
lamb	1000 g	2.20 lb.

Ingredients per 1000 g (1 kg) of meat:

	Metric	US
salt	18 g	3 tsp.
pepper	4.0 g	2 tsp.
garlic	7.0 g	2 cloves
cayenne pepper	4.0 g	2 tsp.
allspice, ground	1.0 g	½ tsp.
paprika	4.0 g	2 tsp.
cumin, ground	1.0 g	½ tsp.
olive oil	14 g	1 Tbs.

Instructions:
1. Grind through 1/4" (6 mm) plate.
2. Mix ground meat with all ingredients and olive oil.
3. Stuff into 24-26 mm sheep casings. Leave as one long rope or make 5" links.
4. Store in refrigerator.

Notes:
Cook before serving.
Some recipes call for a mixture of lamb and beef.
Merguez owes its red color due to the high amount of paprika.
Some recipes call for Harrisa Paste which is nothing more than a combination of the spices that are already listed above (garlic, cumin, olive oil, hot chili peppers) plus coriander.

Making Harrisa paste:

Making Harrisa paste:

1. Place 4 oz of red hot chilies in a bowl and cover with hot water for two hours, then drain.

2. Process in a blender 1/4 cup garlic cloves, 1/4 cup ground cumin, 1/2 cup ground coriander, 1/4 cup salt, drained chilies and 1/2 cup olive oil. Add olive slowly until a thick paste is produced. *For a finer consistency rub paste through a sieve.*

• You can make a smaller amount of paste: 1 garlic clove crushed and finely chopped, 1/2 Tbs. salt, 2 Tbs. olive oil, 1 tsp. cayenne pepper, 1/2 tsp. ground cumin, 1/4 tsp. ground coriander. Mix ingredients in a jar and shake well. Cover with a lid.

• There are Merguez sausage recipes that include coriander, oregano, fennel seeds (used in Italian sausages) and even ground cinnamon. This is a spicy sausage and in addition to the spices listed in the ingredients above, please feel free to add any spices that you personally like.

• Merguez is often made into hamburger patties or meat balls. It is served by frying in olive oil until well browned or grilled.

Potato Sausage

Potato Sausage with non-fat dry milk is very similar to Swedish Potato Sausage. It is much easier to make as instead of boiling potatoes it calls for the addition of potato flour. Non fat dry milk effectively binds water and greatly improves the taste of low fat sausages. Adding potato flour, non fat dry milk, onions and water increases the yield by 40% making it not only great tasting but also a great value added product.

Meat	Metric	US
pork	700 g	1.54 lb.
beef	300 g	0.56 lb.

Ingredients per 1000 g (1 kg) of meat:

salt	18 g	3 tsp.
white pepper	6.0 g	3 tsp.
marjoram, ground	1.5 g	1 tsp.
ginger, ground	1.8 g	1 tsp.
nutmeg, ground	1.0 g	½ tsp.
cardamom, ground	1.0 g	½ tsp.
cloves, ground	1.0 g	½ tsp.
allspice, ground	1.0 g	½ tsp.
small onion, chopped	30 g	½ onion
potato flour,	80 g	1 cup
non fat dry milk,	80 g	1 cup
water	200 ml	¾ cup

Instructions:
1. Grind pork and onions through 3/8" (10 mm) plate.
2. Grind beef through 3/16" (5 mm) plate.
3. Add salt, spices, 1/2 of the water and start mixing with meat sprinkling potato flour and non fat dry milk powder. You could mix all ingredients with half of the water in a blender and then pour over the meat.
4. Add remaining water and keep on mixing until absorbed.
5. Stuff into large hog casings 36-40 mm or beef rounds.
6. Keep under refrigeration.

Notes:
Cook before serving.

Swedish Potato Sausage

Swedish Potato Sausage *(Potatis Korv)* is a fresh sausage made with ground pork and beef that is mixed with potatoes, onions, salt and pepper. Most Swedish potato sausage recipes include allspice and the proportion of beef and pork vary from 75/50 - 50/50 - 50/75 pork to beef.

Materials	**Metric**	**US**
pork	500 g	1.10 lb.
beef	500 g	1.10 lb.
potatoes	500 g	1.10 lb.

Ingredients per 1000 g (1 kg) of meat:

salt	25 g	4 tsp.
white pepper	6.0 g	3 tsp.
allspice, ground	2.0 g	1 tsp.
½ small onion,	30 g	2 Tbs.
water	125 ml	½ cup

Instructions:

1. Grind meats, potatoes and onions through ⅜" plate.
2. Mix water with salt, pepper and allspice and mix everything well together.
3. Stuff into 36 mm casings.
4. The sausage can be fried, baked or boiled. You may place it in a skillet with water to cover, bring it to a boil and then simmer on lower heat for about 20 minutes. Keep the cover on.
5. Store in refrigerator or freeze for later use.

Notes:
Cook before serving.

Tomato Sausage

Tomato sausage is made from pork and veal and it derives its flavor from tomatoes. Cracker meal or bread crumbs are used as fillers and a lot of sausage can be made from a few pounds of meat.

Materials	**Metric**	**US**
pork	700 g	1.54 lb.
fat pork: back fat, jowls, belly	100 g	0.22 lb.
veal	200 g	0.44 lb.

Ingredients per 1000 g (1 kg) of meat:

salt	18 g	3 tsp.
white pepper	3.0 g	1½ tsp.
sugar	5.0 g	1 tsp.
nutmeg	2.0 g	1 tsp.
ginger	1.0 g	½ tsp.
cracker meal	60 g	2 oz.
canned tomatoes	200 g	7 oz.
cold water	100 ml	⅜ cup

Instructions:
1. Grind all meat through 3/16" plate (5 mm).
2a. Mix all ingredients with ground meat in a food processor, adding 1 cup cold water.
2b. If no processor is available, refreeze meats and grind again through 1/8" (3 mm) plate. Then mix everything together.
3. Stuff into 26-28 mm collagen, hog or sheep casings and form 5" (12 cm) long links.
4. Store in a refrigerator or freeze for later use.

Notes:
Cook before serving.
The flavor comes from tomatoes so don't overpower with spices.
Cracker meal: crumbled or smashed crackers that are either used as topping or as breading. May be substituted with bread crumbs.

White Sausage

White Sausage (*Kiełbasa Biała Surowa*) is a popular Polish fresh sausage, always to be found on Easter tables and very often added into soups (*"żurek"*) with hard boiled eggs. Adding sausages into soups has been a long tradition, in Louisiana, sausages are added into everything. The recipe consists of the same ingredients and spices as in Polish Smoked Sausage the only difference is that the White Sausage is not smoked. An easy to make, excellent sausage, a real treat. As no nitrite is used the sausage turns grayish white after cooking.

German equivalent - Weisswurst (white sausage) is made from veal and fresh pork belly. It is flavored with parsley, onions, mace, ginger, cardamom, lemon zest and stuffed into 22 mm sheep casings.

Meat	Metric	US
pork butt	900 g	1.98 lb.
beef	100 g	0.22 lb.

Ingredients per 1000 g (1 kg) of meat:

salt	18 g	1 Tbs.
pepper	2.0 g	1 tsp.
garlic	2.0 g	½ clove
marjoram	2.0 g	1 tsp.
cold water	100 g	0.4 cup

Instructions:
1. Grind pork with 1/2" (12 mm) plate. Grind beef (preferably twice) with the smallest plate - 1/8" or 3/16" (3-5 mm). Add 45% of cold water (in relation to beef) which comes to 45 g (3 tablespoons) and mix with ground beef adding all ingredients.
2. Add 6% of cold water (in relation to pork) to ground pork which comes to 54 g (¼ cup). Now mix everything well together.
3. Stuff the mixture hard into 32 - 36 mm hog casings making one long rope sausage. Tie both ends with twine and prick any visible air pockets with a needle. Refrigerate.

Notes:
Cook in water before serving. Place sausage in hot water and simmer at 176° F (80° C) until the sausage reaches an internal temperature of 160° F (72° C) which will take approximately 30 min.

Chapter 14

Cooked Sausages

This is a huge group of sausages, some are minced through a large or medium size grinder plate, others through a fine plate or emulsified in food processor. They may be smoked or not, however, they all have one similar characteristic: *they are ready to eat at any moment without need for full cooking.* Smoked sausages will usually be consumed cold, others in most cases will be heated. Many sausages include filler material such as: rice, potatoes, barley, buckwheat groats, pumpkin, bread crumbs, soaked white rolls, rusk, or tomatoes. There is also a special group of cooked sausages such as liver and blood sausages, and head cheeses which use slightly different method of preparing materials.

Photo 14.1 An assortment of cooked sausages.

Bacon Sausage

Bacon Sausage is a smoked sausage with a great taste and flavor. For all bacon lovers here is another classical Polish sausage.

Meat	Metric	US
beef	400 g	0.88 lb.
pork	350 g	0.77 lb.
pork belly	250 g	0.55 lb.

Ingredients per 1000 g (1 kg) of meat:

salt	18 g	3 tsp.
Cure #1	2.5 g	½ tsp.
pepper	2.0 g	1 tsp.
sugar	1.0 g	1/5 tsp.
garlic	3.5 g	1 clove
paprika	1.0 g	½ tsp.
coriander	1.0 g	½ tsp.
ginger	0.5 g	⅓ tsp.
water	100 ml	⅜ cup

Instructions:

1. Cut belly into ½" (12 mm) cubes. Grind other meats twice with ⅛" (3 mm) plate.

2. Add all ingredients to the 1¼ cup of cold water and mix thoroughly with ground meat. At the end of mixing add diced belly and mix together until mixture feels sticky.

3. Stuff mixture into 70 mm synthetic fibrous casings and form straight links 35 - 40 cm (12-13") long. Tie both ends with butchers twine and make a hanging loop on one end.

4. Hold for 2 hours at room temperature.

5. Smoke with hot smoke for 120 minutes.

6. Cook in water at 160 - 167° F (72 - 75° C) until the internal temperature of the sausage reaches 155 - 158° F (69 - 70° C). That will take approximately 80 min.

7. Shower with cold water (or dip in cold water) for 15 min.

8. Hold in air to evaporate moisture.

9. Store in a cool place < 52° F (12° C) or refrigerate.

Note: in the past Bacon Sausage was made with potassium nitrate and a small amount of sugar was added *as food for* naturally present in meat *curing bacteria* which caused potassium nitrate to produce *nitrite* and cure the meat. This sugar did not affect the taste of the sausage.

Chinese Sausage

Chinese sausage is a dried, hard sausage usually made from fatty pork. The Chinese name for sausages is "Lap Chong" which means the "winter stuffed intestine" or "waxed intestine" because "chong" not only means "intestine" but also "sausage". This sausage is normally smoked, sweetened, and seasoned. It is used as an ingredient in many dishes in some parts of southern China, including Hong Kong and countries in Southeast Asia. It is for example, used in fried rice, noodle and other dishes. Chinese sausage formulations are unique, based on long tradition.

Ingredients like monosodium glutamate, soy sauce and sugar are added to the sausages in very high levels. The addition of selected Chinese rice wines or even scotch or sherry are common for certain quality products. The most popular spice is cinnamon since Chinese manufacturers believe that it acts as a preservative. Chinese sausages may be divided into meat sausages (Yuen Chong) and liver sausages (Goin Chong). A special class of sausages are chicken liver sausages containing chicken livers or chicken livers combined with selected young pork livers.

Meat	Metric	US
pork	1000 g	2.20 lb.

Ingredients per 1000 g (1 kg) of meat:

soy sauce	30 ml	1 oz fl.
Cure #1	2.5 g	½ tsp.
sugar	50 g	4 Tbs.
monosodium glutamate	3 g	½ tsp.
cinnamon	1 g	½ tsp.
rice wine	30 ml	2 Tbs.
pepper	2.0 g	1 tsp.
garlic	3.5 g	1 clove
cold water	80 ml	⅓ cup

Instructions:

1. Grind pork through the 3/8" (10 mm) plate.
2. Mix ground meat with all ingredients.
3. Stuff into 28 diameter hog or sheep casings and make 5" - 6" long links. Tie both ends with a light butcher twine. Hang sausages at room temperature for one hour.
4. Smoking:

  • hot smoke for 50-60 min.
  • bake for about 20 min until the meat reaches a temperature of 154-160° F (68-71° C inside. The color of the casings should be dark brown.

Total smoking and cooking time about 70 - 90 min. This is a rather short time due to the small diameter of the meat sticks. The sausage is done and ready to eat.

5. Shower with cold water.
6. Keep under refrigeration.

Notes:

  • The traditional Chinese way, still applied today, is a time consuming operation of cutting meat and fat by hand into small cubes.
  • Popular Chinese wine is Mei Kwei Lo.
  • The sausage color is dark reddish-brown. Its surface is normally shrivelled due to quick drying.
  • Traditional Chinese method of tying sausage casings uses pieces of straw. This is the same technique as the Polish method of using wooden picks (see Appendix A).

Ham Sausage

Called ham sausage because solid chunks of lean meat are imbedded in its texture.

Meat	Metric	US
lean pork, leg (ham part) or butt	850 g	1.87 lb.
pork jowls or fatty		
pork trimmings	150 g	0.33 lb.

Ingredients per 1000 g (1 kg) of meat:

salt	18 g	3 tsp.
Cure #1	2.5 g	½ tsp.
pepper	2.0 g	1 tsp.
sugar	2.5 g	½ tsp.
nutmeg	1.0 g	½ tsp.
coriander	2.0 g	1 tsp.
cold water	60 ml	¼ cup

Instructions:

1. Manually dice lean pork into 2" (5 cm) cubes. Mix with 2 tsp of salt and 2.0 g of Cure #1. Cover and place in a refrigerate for 48 hours.

2. Grind pork trimmings through ⅛" (3 mm) plate. Add 1 tsp salt and 0.5 g Cure #1 and mix together. Cover and place in a refrigerate for 48 hours..

3. Emulsify ground pork adding cold water. Add remaining ingredients when emulsifying.

4. Mix diced lean pork until sticky, then add emulsified mixture and mix everything well together.

5. Stuff firmly into 100-120 mm (4-5") beef bungs or synthetic fibrous casings and tie the ends with twine forming a hanging loop on one end. Make 14-16" long sections. Lace up sausages with two lengthwise loops and loops across the casing every 2 inches. Prick any visible air pockets with a needle.

6. Hang at room temperature until casings feel dry.

7. Smoke with hot smoke for 120-150 min until casings develop a light brown color with a pink tint.

8. Poach sausages at 72-75°C (161-167°F) until meat reaches internal temperature of 69-70°C (155-158°F). This will take about 2 hours.

9. Shower with cold water for about 10 min, evaporate moisture and place in refrigerator.

Notes:

Cure diced pork for 48 hours, otherwise it may develop uneven color. This will be visible when the sausage is sliced.

Jadgwurst
(*German Hunter's sausage*)

Hunter sausage can be found in most countries, Mysliwska)Poland), Salamini Italiani alla *Cacciatora* (Italy), in Germany the sausage is known as Jagdwurst.

Meat	Metric	US
lean pork butt	500 g	1.10 lb.
lean fresh belly	500 g	1.10 lb.

Ingredients per 1000 g (1 kg) of meat:

salt	18 g	3 tsp.
Cure #1	2.5 g	½ tsp.
pepper	1.0 g	½ tsp.
mace	0.5 g	⅓ tsp.
coriander	1.0 g	½ tsp.
mustard, ground	2.0 g	1 tsp.
ginger, ground	0.5 g	½ tsp.
water	60 ml	¼ cup

Instructions:
1. Grind all meat through 3/8" (10 mm) grinder plate.
2. Mix meat with all ingredients.
3. Stuff into 50 mm (2") fibrous casings.
4. Hang at room temperature for 30 min.
5. Place sausages in smokehouse pre-heated to 130° F (54° C) for 1 hour (no smoke applied).
6. Hot smoke for 30 minutes only.
7. Increase smokehouse temperature (no smoke applied) to 170° F and cook sausages until internal temperature of 155° F (69° C) is obtained OR
cook in water at 167-172° F (75-78° C) for about 1 hour.
8. Cool sausages in cold water and hang at room temperature.
9. Refrigerate.

Kabanosy

Kabanosy is a famous Polish sausage and probably the finest meat stick in the world. The name Kabanosy comes from the nickname "kabanek" given to a young fat pig no more than 120 kg (264 lbs.) that was fed mainly potatoes in the Eastern parts of XIX Poland (Lithuania today).

Meat	Metric	US
pork	1000 g	2.20 lb.

Ingredients per 1000 g (1 kg) of meat:

salt	18 g	3 tsp.
Cure #1	2.5 g	½ tsp.
pepper	2.0 g	1 tsp.
nutmeg	1.0 g	½ tsp.
caraway	1.0 g	½ tsp.
water	100 ml	⅜ cup

Instructions:
1. Grind lean pork with 3/8" plate, fatter pieces with 3/16" plate.
2. Mix ground meat and all ingredients together until the mass feels sticky.
3. Stuff mixture into 22-26 mm sheep casings. 22 mm diameter. Link sausage into 60-70 cm (24-27") links so when hung on a smoking stick the individual links (half of the meat stick) will be about one foot long. Don't separate stuffed sausage into short individual links, leave it linked, but as one long rope.
4. Hang on smoke sticks in a cool place at 35-42° F (2-6° C) for 12 hours. It is permitted to dry it at room temperature for 30-60 min and then smoke it.
5. Kabanosy are smoked in two stages:

- smoking with hot smoke 104-122° F (40-50° C) for 50-60 min
- baking for about 20 min at 140 → 190° F (60 → 90° C) until the meat reaches a temperature of 155-160° F (69-72° C) inside. The color of the casings should be dark brown.

Total smoking and cooking time about 70 - 90 min. This is a rather short time due to the small diameter of the meat sticks. The sausage is done and ready to eat.

6. Shower with cold water, separate into links and keep refrigerated.

Notes:

In the past, when refrigerators were scarce, the following step was performed after smoking to create semi-dry sausages that could be stored at room temperatures.

- Place Kabanosy for 5-7 days in a room at 54-59° F (12-15° C), relative humidity of 75-80%, until the weight is reduced by 45%. If during this drying period you will see a slight accumulation of mold on the outside surface just wipe it off, this is normal.

- Separate links into individual pieces and keep it in a cool place, no need to refrigerate. In Europe the sausages hang in the kitchen and were consumed as needed.

In the past Kabanosy were made with potassium nitrate and a small amount of sugar was added *as food for* naturally present in meat *curing bacteria* which caused potassium nitrate to produce *nitrite* and cure the meat. This sugar did not affect the taste of the sausage.

Nowadays, Kabanosy after being stuffed are hot smoked at 140-150° F (60-65° C) for 30 minutes and cooked in water at 176° F (80° C) for 25 minutes.

Krakowska Sausage

(Kielbasa krakowska krajana)

This sausage has always been one of the top sellers in Poland. The name relates to the city of Krakow, one of the oldest cities in Europe. The middle part of the name "krajana" implies that the meat was manually cut into pieces. It goes by many similar names for example Krakauer Sausage.

Meat	Metric	US
lean pork, leg or shoulder	900 g	1.98 lb.
pork jowls or fatty		
pork trimmings, picnic meat	100 g	0.22 lb.

Ingredients per 1000 g (1 kg) of meat:

salt	18 g	3 tsp.
Cure #1	2.5 g	½ tsp.
pepper	2.0 g	1 tsp.
sugar	2.5 g	½ tsp.
nutmeg	1.0 g	½ tsp.
cold water	30 ml	2 Tbs.

Instructions:

1. Manually dice lean pork into 2" (5 cm) cubes. Mix with 2 tsp of salt and 2.0 g of Cure #1. Cover and place in a refrigerate for 48 hours.
2. Grind pork trimmings through 1/2" (12 mm) plate. Add 1 tsp salt and 0.5 g Cure #1 and mix together. Cover and place in a refrigerate for 48 hours..
3. Grind pork trimmings with 1/8" (3 mm) plate adding cold water or emulsify in food processor. Add remaining ingredients when emulsifying.
4. Mix diced pork cubes until sticky, then add emulsified mixture and mix everything well together.
5. Stuff firmly into 75 mm (3") hog middles or synthetic fibrous casings. Stuff casings firmly and tie up both ends. Form 16-18" long sections. Prick any visible air pockets with a needle.
6. Hang at room temperature for 2 hours.
7. Smoking/Cooking is done in three steps:
   - Dry sausages using thin smoke, 113-131°F (45-55°C) for 20 min.
   - Smoke with a thick smoke, 113-131°F (45-55°C) for 150 min.
   - Bake with a thin smoke, 167-194°F (75-90°C) for 20-30 min.

Total time about 3 hours until the internal meat temperature reaches (155-158°F) 69-70°C and casings are dark brown.

8. Shower with cold water for about 5 min and place in refrigerator.

Notes:

Cure diced pork for 48 hours, otherwise it may develop uneven color. This will be visible when the sausage is sliced.

Moscow Sausage

This is a hot smoked version of the Moscow sausage which was originally cold smoked and not cooked.

Meat	Metric	US
beef	750 g	1.65 lb.
pork back fat or fat	250 g	0.55 lb.
pork trimmings		

Ingredients per 1000 g (1 kg) of meat:

salt	18 g	3 tsp.
Cure #1	2.5 g	½ tsp.
pepper	2.0 g	1 tsp.
sugar	2.0 g	½ tsp.
nutmeg	1.0 g	½ tsp.
potato starch, 2%	20 g	2 Tbs.
water	100 ml	⅜ cup

Instructions:
1. Grind beef with 3/8" (10 mm) plate. Manually cut back fat into ¼" (6 mm) cubes.
2. Mix all ingredients with meat, adding water. Mix until all water is absorbed by the mixture. Then add fat and mix everything together.
3. Stuff into beef middles or fibrous synthetic casings 40-60 mm and form 12" (30 cm) long links.
4. Hang at room temperature for 60 min.
5. Apply hot smoke for 110-130 min until casings develop brown color or a red tint.
6. In the last stage of smoking the sausage is baked at 75→90° C (167→194° F) until internal meat temperature is 69-70° C (155-158° F).
7. Shower with cold water for about 5 min, then lower sausage temperature below 12° C (53° F).
8. Store in refrigerator.

Mysliwska - Hunter's Sausage

Myśliwska Sausage - Hunter's Sausage is made of pork and beef and prolonged smoking and juniper berries give the sausage its unique character. Hunting always was a popular sport in Poland practiced originally by the nobility and even then by only well to do people. A hunter carried a big hunting bag where he kept the necessary tools and food that had to last for a number of days. Myśliwska Sausage was a relatively short, well smoked sausage that would make an ideal food or snack in those circumstances.

Hunter's Sausage is popular in many countries, for example in Germany it is called Jadgwurst and in Italy Salamini Italiani alla *Cacciatora*.

Meat	Metric	US
pork,	900 g	1.98 lb.
beef, lean	100 g	0.22 lb.

Ingredients per 1000 g (1 kg) of meat:

salt	18 g	3 tsp.
Cure #1	2.5 g	½ tsp.
pepper	2.0 g	1 tsp.
garlic	3.5 g	1 clove
juniper	1.0 g	½ tsp.
water	100 ml	⅜ cup

Instructions:

1. Grind lean pork with ½" (13 mm) plate, fat pork with ¼" - ⅜" (8 mm) plate. Grind beef twice through ⅛" (2 - 3 mm) plate.
2. Add 20-25% of cold water in relation to the weight of the beef (about 1½ tablespoon) into the ground beef and mix well with remaining ingredients (juniper, garlic and pepper). Mix all pork together until the meat becomes sticky. Finally mix everything together adding remaining water.
3. Stuff mixture into 32 mm hog casings and form 7 - 8" (18-20 cm) links.
4. Hang sausages at room temperature for 2 hours.
5. Smoke sausage:

5. Smoke sausage

- At about 122° F (50° C) for 80-90 min. You can keep on increasing the smoking temperature gradually up to 176° F (80° C).
- Smoke/bake at 176 → 194° F (80 → 90° C) for 25 min until the internal temperature of 155 - 158° F (69 - 70° C) is reached. The color of the sausage should be brown.

Though the above listed cooking temperatures may seem to be high, the sausage is baked for a while only and the inside should only reach 154 - 158° F. Myśńliwska sausage is somewhat baked on the outside. The sausage is done and ready to eat.

In the past the following steps were added:

6. The sausage was air-cooled at room temperature to 86° F (30° C) inside temperature. It hung on smoke sticks in the room until the next day allowing more moisture to escape from inside.

7. The sausage was smoked again the next day with warm smoke, 86° F (30° C) from 3 - 12 hours until it developed the dark brown color. This eliminated more moisture.

8. The sausage was stored at 60° - 65° F (16° - 18° C), in a dark place for 6 - 8 days (until the sausage obtained 60 - 65 % of its initial weight).

The finished product was the dry sausage that did not have to be refrigerated.

Note: in the past Myśliwska Sausage was made with potassium nitrate and a small amount of sugar was added *as food for* naturally present in meat *curing bacteria* which caused potassium nitrate to produce *nitrite* and cure the meat. This sugar did not affect the taste of the sausage.

Podhalanska

Podhalańska Sausage is made with lamb and pork. This sausage comes from the Southern part of Poland known as "Podhale" where the Tatry Mountains are located. For centuries it was a region where mountain men ("górale") raised sheep for their skins. The leather and sheepskin industry operated there and some of the finest master furriers came from that area. Sheep were wandering everywhere and it comes as no surprise that the regional cooking was based on that meat.

Meat	Metric	US
lamb, lean	200 g	0.44 lb.
lamb, fat	400 g	0.88 lb.
pork	300 g	0.66 lb.
pork back fat or fat trimmings	100 g	0.22 lb.

Ingredients per 1000 g (1 kg) of meat:

salt	18 g	3 tsp.
Cure #1	2.5 g	½ tsp.
pepper	2.0 g	1 tsp.
herbal pepper *	2.0 g	1 tsp.
allspice	2.0 g	1 tsp.
garlic	3.5 g	1 clove
cold water	100 ml	⅜ cup

Instructions:
1. Grind pork and pork back fat through a 3/8" (10 mm) plate. Grind lean lamb through 1/2" (13 mm) plate.
Grind fat lamb at least two times through 1/8" (2 mm) plate. Add water, salt and all ingredients and emulsify together. This can be done in a food processor.
2. Mix lean lamb with pork until sticky. Then add emulsified lamb that was already mixed with spices. Mix everything well together.
3. Stuff tightly into 32-42 mm hog casings and make a long rope with 1 foot (30-35) cm individual links.
4. Hang for 12 hours at 35-42° F, (2-6° C) or for 1-2 hours at room temperature.
5. Smoke with hot smoke 105-140° F (41-60° C) for 80-100 min until light brown color is obtained. In the last 30 minutes of smoking

increase the temperature to 140 → 176° F (60 → 80° C) while still applying smoke. Temperature as high as 194° F (90° C) is allowed for a short time as you are baking the sausage on its outside only. The sausage is done when an internal meat temperature of 155-158° F, (69-70° C) is obtained.

6. Divide links into pairs. Keep refrigerated.

OR:

Hang sausages for 2-3 days at 53-59° F (12-15° C) at <70% humidity. They will start losing moisture and will become dry sausages.

Notes:

* Herbal pepper is a mixture of mustard, caraway, marjoram, chili, sweet Hungarian paprika, hot paprika and bay leaves. There are different combinations of spices on the market, so choose something you like.

Another combination: coriander, caraway, marjoram, cayenne, mustard, dried horseradish, powdered onion.

Polish Hot Smoked Sausage

Polish Smoked Sausage consists of pork, salt, pepper, garlic and optional marjoram. This is the hot smoked version known all over the world which is much easier and faster to make than the cold smoked version that was more popular in the past.

Meat	Metric	US
pork	1000 g	2.20 lb.

Ingredients per 1000 g (1 kg) of meat:

salt	18 g	3 tsp.
Cure #1	2.5 g	½ tsp.
pepper	2.0 g	1 tsp.
garlic	3.5 g	1 clove
marjoram	1.0 g	⅔ tsp.
cold water	100 ml	⅜ cup

Instructions:

1. Grind the lean meat with a 3/8" grinder plate and the fat meat through 3/16" plate.
2. Mix everything together adding cold water.
3. Stuff mixture into 32 - 36 mm hog casings and form links 12 - 13" 30 - 35 cm.
4. Hang on smoke sticks for 1-2 hours at room temperature OR
5. Place sausages in a preheated smoker at 130° F (54° C) with draft dampers fully open (no smoke applied).
6. When casings are fully dry apply heavy hot smoke for 60-90 minutes. Keep on increasing the smoking temperature until you reach 160 → 170° F (71 → 76° C) range. Sausage is done when the meat reaches 155-160° F (672° C) internal temperature.
7. Remove from smoker and shower with water or immerse sausages in water.
8. Store in refrigerator.

Note: in the past Polish Smoked Sausage was made with potassium nitrate and a small amount of sugar was added *as food for* naturally present in meat *curing bacteria* which caused potassium nitrate to produce *nitrite* and cure the meat. This sugar did not affect the taste of the sausage.

Romanian Sausage

Meat	Metric	US
lean pork	750 g	1.65 lb.
pork trimmings	250 g	0.55 lb.

Ingredients per 1000 g (1 kg) of meat:

salt	18 g	3 tsp.
Cure #1	2.5 g	½ tsp.
pepper	2.0 g	1 tsp.
sugar	2.0 g	⅓ tsp.
coriander	2.0 g	1 tsp.
garlic	3.5 g	1 clove
ginger	0.5 g	¼ tsp.
cold water	100 ml	⅜ cup

Instructions:

1. Grind all pork meat through 3/8" (10 mm) plate.
2. Mix all ingredients adding water.
3. Stuff into 36 mm hog casings.
4. Hang sausages at room temperature for 1-2 hours to dry OR place for 30 minutes in a pre-heated smokehouse (no smoke applied) at 110-120° F (43-49° C) to dry the surface of the sausages. Keep the vent fully open to facilitate the removal of moisture.
5. Adjust vent 1/4 open and apply heavy smoke increasing temperature to 140-145° F (60-65° C) until desired color is obtained. This should take about 2 hours.
6. Increase temperature to 170° F (77° C) until an internal meat temperature of 155° F (69° C) is reached.
7. Shower sausages or immerse in cold water for 15 minutes. Hang in air to evaporate moisture.
8. Keep refrigerated.

Note: in the past Romanian Sausage was made with potassium nitrate and a small amount of sugar was added *as food for* naturally present in meat *curing bacteria* which caused potassium nitrate to produce *nitrite* and cure the meat. This sugar did not affect the taste of the sausage.

Russian - Hot Smoked

This is a hot smoked version of the Russian sausage which was originally cold smoked and not cooked.

Meat	Metric	US
lean pork	500 g	1.10 lb.
pork back fat	300 g	0.66 lb.
beef	200 g	0.44 lb.

Ingredients per 1000 g (1 kg) of meat:

salt	18 g	3 tsp.
Cure #1	2.5 g	½ tsp.
pepper	2.0 g	1 tsp.
cardamom	2.0 g	1 tsp.
allspice	2.0 g	1 tsp.
Madeira wine or brandy	60 ml	¼ cup
cold water	60 ml	¼ cup

Instructions:

1. Grind meats with 3/8" (10 mm) plate. Cut back fat manually into ⅛" (3 mm) cubes.

2. Mix all ingredients with meat adding wine until all wine is absorbed by the mixture. Then add diced fat and mix everything together.

3. Stuff into beef middles or fibrous synthetic casings 40 - 60 mm and form 12" (30 cm) long links.

4. Hang at room temperature for 1-2 hours.

5. Apply hot smoke for 110-130 min until casings develop brown color with a red tint.

6. In the last stage of smoking the sausage is baked at $167 \rightarrow 194°$ F ($75 \rightarrow 90°$ C) until internal meat temperature is 69-70° C (155-158° F).

7. Shower or immerse sausages in cold water for 10 min. Hang in air to evaporate moisture.

8. Store at < 12° C (53° F) or refrigerate.

Note: in the past Polish Smoked Sausage was made with potassium nitrate and a small amount of sugar was added *as food for* naturally present in meat *curing bacteria* which caused potassium nitrate to produce *nitrite* and cure the meat. This sugar did not affect the taste of the sausage.

Salami - Polish
(*Salami Krakowskie*)

Salami Krakowskie is a dry cured, smoked and baked sausage. Although salami is of Italian origin, almost every country has its own version and Poland is no exception. Salami Krakowskie like Krakowska sausage owes its name to the region of Kraków (Cracow), one of the oldest cities in Poland.

Meat	Metric	US
lean pork (ham, butt)	750 g	1.65 lb.
pork fat trimmings (ham, butt, back fat)	250 g	0.55 lb.

Ingredients per 1000 g (1 kg) of meat:

salt	18 g	3 tsp.
Cure #1	2.5 g	½ tsp.
pepper	2.0 g	1 tsp.
garlic	3.5 g	1 clove

Instructions:
1. Cut meat and fat into 2" (5 - 6 cm) pieces. Add salt, Cure # 2, garlic and pepper and mix well.
2. Grind above mixture through 3/16" (4 mm) plate.
Pack ground meat tightly into suitable containers (stainless steel, food grade plastic) and cover with a layer of skins or butcher paper. Keep for 10 - 14 days at 35 - 39° F (2 - 4° C).
3. Stuff into 60 mm beef middles or synthetic fibrous casings, make straight links 40 - 45 cm long. Pack the meat very tightly to eliminate air pockets. Make 10 - 12 cm loop at one end for hanging.
4. Hang for two hours in a well ventilated area.
5. Smoking:
A. Smoke/dry with thin smoke for 20-40 min at 113-122° F (45 - 50° C)
B. Smoke with thick smoke for 90-140 min at 104-122° F (40- 50° C)
C. Bake with thin smoke for 70-100 min at 167→194° F (75 → 90° C)
6. Hang in a shaded well ventilated area at 10-12° C, 80 - 85 % humidity for 5 - 6 weeks until salami develops white mold on outside. In case the mold becomes wet and green in color wash the sausages with warm salty water and wipe them dry. Dry salami until it loses 35 % of its original weight.
7. Hold in a dry place.

Note: this sausage fits into non-fermented cooked salami category and has not much in common with salami because salami is a non-heated product. Another well known sausage of this type is Koch Salami.

Tambov

This is a great highly nutritional sausage made of pork, beef, pork bellies and basic spices like pepper and nutmeg.

Meat	Metric	US
beef	400 g	0.88 lb.
pork	200 g	0.44 lb.
pork bellies	400 g	0.88 lb.

Ingredients per 1000 g (1 kg) of meat:

salt	18 g	3 tsp.
Cure #1	2.5 g	½ tsp.
pepper	2.0 g	1 tsp.
nutmeg	1.0 g	½ tsp.
water	100 ml	⅜ cup

Instructions:
1. Grind meats with 3/8" (10 mm) plate. Grind belly through ⅛ " (3 mm) plate.
2. Mix all ingredients with meat adding water. Mix until all water is absorbed by the mixture.
3. Stuff into hog casings 32-36 mm and form 12" (30 cm) long links.
4. Hang at room temperature for 60 minutes.
5. Apply hot smoke at 140-145° F (60-62° C) for 110-130 min.
6. In the last stage of smoking the sausage is baked at 167 → 194° F (75 → 90° C) until the meat reaches 155-158° F (69-70° C) internal temperature.
7. Shower or immerse in cold water for 10 min, then lhang in air to evaporate moisture.
8. Store below 53° F (12° C) or refrigerate.

Note: in the past Tambov Sausage was made with potassium nitrate and a small amount of sugar was added *as food for* naturally present in meat *curing bacteria* which caused potassium nitrate to produce *nitrite* and cure the meat. This sugar did not affect the taste of the sausage.

Tatar Sausage

The name Tatar initially appeared amongst the nomadic Turkic peoples of northeastern Mongolia in the region around Lake Baikal in the beginning of the 5th century. As various of these nomadic groups became part of Genghis Khan's army in the early 13th century, a fusion of Mongol and Turkic elements took place and the invaders of Rus and Hungary became known to Europeans as Tatars (or Tartars). After the break up of the Mongol Empire, the Tatars became especially identified with the western part of the empire, which included most of European Russia and was known as the Golden Horde. This is a hot smoked version of the Tatar sausage which was originally cold smoked and not cooked.

Meat	Metric	US
lamb	900 g	1.98 lb.
lamb hard fat	100 g	0.22 lb.

Ingredients per 1000 g (1 kg) of meat:

salt	18 g	3 tsp.
Cure #1	2.5 g	½ tsp.
pepper	2.0 g	1 tsp.
allspice	2.0 g	1 tsp.
caraway seed	2.0 g	1 tsp.
nutmeg	1.0 g	½ tsp.
garlic	3.5 g	1 clove
cold water	60 ml	¼ cup

Instructions:
1. Grind meats with 3/8" (10 mm) plate. Cut fat manually into ⅛ " (3 mm) cubes.
2. Mix all ingredients with meat adding water. Then add diced fat and mix everything together.
3. Stuff into sheep casings 24-26 mm and form rings.
4. Hang at room temperature for 1 hour.
5. Apply hot smoke at 140-145 (60-65 C) for 60-90 min until casings develop a brown color with a red tint.
6. In the last stage of smoking the sausage is baked at 167 → 194° F (75 → 90° C) until the meat reaches 155-158° F (69-70° C) internal temperature.
7. Shower or immerse in cold water for 10 min, then hang in air to evaporate moisture.
8. Store at <53° F (12° C) or in refrigerator.

To make a cold smoked version, increase salt to 28 g, replace Cure #1 with Cure #2, replace water with Madeira wine and follow instructions for Russian-Cold Smoked sausage.

Tourist

This is a small sausage designed for tourists and travelers. Meats are the same as in Tambov sausage but different spices are employed. Similar to Polish Kabanosy meat stick which is made of pork only.

Meat	Metric	US
beef	400 g	0.88 lb.
pork	200 g	0.44 lb.
pork belly	400 g	0.88 lb.

Ingredients per 1000 g (1 kg) of meat:

salt	18 g	3 tsp.
Cure #1	2.5 g	½ tsp.
pepper	2.0 g	1 tsp.
caraway	1.0 g	½ tsp.
garlic	3.5 g	1 clove
water	100 ml	⅜ cup

Instructions:
1. Grind meats with 3/8" (10 mm) plate. Grind bacon through ⅛ " (3 mm) plate.
2. Mix all ingredients with meat adding water. Mix until all water is absorbed by the mixture.
3. Stuff into sheep casings 24-26 mm and form 12" (30 cm) long links.
4. Hang at room temperature for 30 minutes.
5. Hot smoke for 60 min.
6. In the last stage of smoking the sausage is baked at 167 → 194° F (75 → 90° C) until the meat reaches 155-158° F (69-70° C) internal temperature. This will take about 30 min.
7. Shower or immerse in cold water for 5 min, then hang in air to evaporate moisture.
8. Store at < 53° F (12° C) or in refrigerator.

Note: in the past Tourist Sausage was made with potassium nitrate and a small amount of sugar was added *as food for* naturally present in meat *curing bacteria* which caused potassium nitrate to produce *nitrite* and cure the meat. This sugar did not affect the taste of the sausage.

Ukrainian Sausage

A traditional heavily smoked sausage that is cooked in water from the Poland's neighbor in the East.

Meat	Metric	US
beef	700 g	1.54 lb.
pork jowls, hard fat trimmings,		
belly	300 g	0.66 lb.

Ingredients per 1000 g (1 kg) of meat:

salt	18 g	3 tsp.
Cure #1	2.5 g	½ tsp.
pepper	2.0 g	1 tsp.
paprika	2.0 g	1 tsp.
allspice	2.0 g	1 tsp.
garlic	3.5 g	1 clove
marjoram	2.0 g	1½ tsp.
water	150 ml	⅝ cup

Instructions:
1. Grind fat pork (jowl or equivalent) with 3/8" (13 mm) plate. Grind beef with 1/4" (5 mm) plate. Grind lower class beef (sinews, gristle) twice through 1/8" (2-3 mm) plate. You may emulsify it in a food processor.
2. Add 20 - 25 % of cold water in relation to the weight of the beef (about 150 ml) into the emulsified beef, add all spices and mix well together. Then mix the mass together with ground fat until the mass feels sticky.
3. Stuff mixture into 36 mm hog casings or beef rounds and form rings about 12" long.
4. Hang at room temperature for 1 hour to dry.
5. Smoke with hot smoke at 140-145° F (60-62° C) for 90-110 minutes until the color of the casing is light brown with a red tint (paprika makes it red).
6. Cook in water at 160-167° F (72-75° C) until the meat reaches 155-158° F (69-70° C) internal temperature.
7. Shower or immerse in cold water. Hang in air to evaporate moisture.
8. Store at < 53° F (12° C) or in refrigerator.

Originally the sausage was made with the preservation in mind and after the cooking step (6) this procedure followed:

Sausage was hung for 12 hours at < 64° F (18° C).
It was cold smoked for 24 hours which might be considered a drying process. Then it was smoked with warm smoke 75-90° F (24-32° C) for an additional 12 hours. The casings developed a brown color with a tint of red.
Sausages were dried at 53-64° F (12-18° C), 75-80% humidity until about 80% yield was obtained (sausage lost 20% of its original weight). If mold appeared it was simply wiped off. *A dry sausage* was created that could be stored at room temperature.

White Pudding

White pudding is a sausage popular in Ireland, Scotland and some parts of England. It consists of beef suet, oatmeal, and leeks or onions. If blood was added, the sausage could be called black pudding which is a blood sausage. In many cases it is not stuffed into casings becoming a breakfast dish which is served with bacon, fried eggs and often with black pudding.

Materials	Metric	US
beef suet	400 g	0.88 lb.
oatmeal (steel cut groats)*	600 g	1.32 lb.

Ingredients per 1000 g (1 kg) of meat:

salt	20 g	3½ tsp.
pepper	2.0 g	1 tsp.
cold water	100 g	0.4 cup
small onion, finely chopped	30 g	½ onion
OR		
leeks, finely chopped	60 g	½ leek
1 fresh egg		

Instructions:
1. Cut suet into 1/4" (6 mm) pieces or grind through 1/4" (6 mm) plate.
2. Soak oatmeal in milk overnight.
3. Drain oatmeal, add an egg and all other ingredients. Mix well.
4. Stuff into 26-32 mm hog casings.
5. Simmer in hot water 80-85° C (170-185° F) for 30 minutes.
6. Keep refrigerated.
7. Heat before serving. Serve by frying.

Notes:
White pudding sausage is often made with pork trimmings or bacon. Cloves and mace are often added.
In the past a traditional white pudding was made with chopped dates, currents and Spanish saffron.
*Don't confuse oatmeal with instant oats that are served for breakfast. Those are steel cut oat groats, which are quite hard. They can be obtained in large supermarkets.

Chapter 15

Emulsified Sausages

Emulsified sausages are cooked sausages that have been finely comminuted to the consistency of a fine paste. Hot dog, mortadella, bologna, frankfurter, liver sausage, pâté are typical examples. In most cases they are smoked and cooked with moist heat (steamed or in hot water).

The first emulsified sausage was probably the German frankfurter, followed by the Austrian wiener. In the 1800's German immigrants brought these recipes to America and originally these sausages were served like any other. The story goes that in 1904, a street vendor in St. Louis was selling his wieners on small buns. They were nicknamed the "red hots" as they were too hot to handle by his customers. Suddenly he got this great idea of making a bun that will fit the shape of the sausage and an all American favorite "hot dog" was born.

Emulsified sausages can be divided in two groups:

1. High quality products made at home such as Austrian wiener or Polish Serdelki which are made from high quality meats and without chemicals. Beef, veal and pork are the meats commonly used. Beef frankfurter contains beef only. High quality products contain enough lean meat to absorb the necessary water without help from water retention agents.

2. Commercial products made from all types of meat trimmings (pork, beef, chicken, turkey), including machine separated meat. Chicken hot dogs, turkey hot dogs and all possible combinations can be found in a supermarket. A large number of chemicals, water binding agents, fats and water are added during manufacturing to compensate for lower meat grades.

The public prefers moist emulsified sausages and it is hard to imagine a hot dog or frankfurter that will feel dry. In commercial production meat is chopped in bowl cutters by rapidly moving blades that create lots of friction. This action develops a significant amount of heat which will encourage the growth of bacteria. To prevent that, the manufacturer adds crushed ice to the meat in the chopper.

Emulsification will be successful if the following criteria are met:

- Enough lean meat has been selected. The lean meat is the main source of *myosin*. The more myosin extracted, the thicker and stronger protein coat develops around particles of fat.

- Enough *myosin* has been extracted. This depends on how vigorous the cutting process was and how much salt (and phosphates) was added.

Too much fat, especially when finely comminuted, will create such a large surface area that *there will not be enough protein solution to coat all fat particles*. As a result pockets of fat will form inside of the sausage. Some moisture is lost during smoking, cooking, and storing, and this factor must be allowed for in the manufacturing process. To make up for those losses more water is added during chopping/ emulsifying. Experienced sausage makers know that the meats used in the manufacturing of sausages exhibit different abilities at holding water. Lean meat can hold more water than fatty tissue. Organ meats such as heart, glands, pork and beef tripe, pork skin, or snout all have poor water holding capabilities. Red meat found in pork head exhibits good water holding capability. Generally speaking any lean red meat holds water well although beef is on top of the list.

- Beef- high
- Veal – medium
- Pork – medium

Beef meat can absorb significant amounts of water:

- Bull meat – up to 100%
- Shank meat – up to 70%
- Cow meat - up to 60%
- Cheek meat – up to 40%

In simple terms 100 lb of cow meat can absorb 60 lb of water and 100 lb of bull meat can absorb 100 lbs. of water. An average beef piece bought in a local supermarket should hold about 30-40% of added water. To make top quality emulsified sausages at home a combination of lean red muscle meats should be used. This does not mean that only best lean cuts of meat must be employed.

Using meat trimmings is in fact encouraged. A typical frankfurter recipe consists of about 60% beef and 40% pork trimmings. Those trimmings may consist of cheaper grades of meat such as heart, jowls, kidneys, snouts, pork or beef tripe, and fats. As long as lean beef is used to bind water, other "filler" meats may be added.

A commercial manufacturer can not afford the luxury of using only top quality meats and to keep the costs down he has to use second grade meat trimmings. Keep in mind that there is nothing wrong with such meats from a nutritional point of view, but in order to success-fully incorporate them in a sausage we have to resort to water binding agents which will help to absorb and hold water within the meat struc-ture. If you study original instructions for making emulsified sausages from earlier times when chemicals were not yet widely used, you will see that beef was always ground with a smaller plate than pork. This was done in order to fully extract meat proteins which allowed meat to absorb more water.

As finer meat particles are obtained, more protein is extracted and more water can be absorbed by the meat. The fats are not going to hold water and it makes little sense to emulsify them as fine as lean meat. That is why fat is added to the bowl cutter at the end. If show meats (larger pieces) or chunks of fat (Mortadella) are required, they will be mixed with an emulsified sausage mass in a mixer.

Water

Water plays an important part:

- It helps to extract water soluble proteins (*actin* and myosin) which contribute to better meat binding and strong emulsion.

- It helps to keep temperature down by adding ice to the bowl cutter.

Manufacturing Process

Meat selection. Lean beef, veal, lean pork. Keep in mind that the color of the sausage will depend on the type of meat used (*myoglobin* content) and to a smaller degree on spices.

Fat

About 20% of fat is needed for good texture, taste and flavor. Hard and soft fats can be used. Pork fat, beef fat, mutton fat, chicken fat or even vegetable oils can be utilized. Beef and lamb fat have a very strong flavor which can be masked by a careful choice of spices.

Examples of typical low cost meat formulas:

Formula A. Beef trimmings 60% (80% lean, 20% fat),
Pork trimmings 40% (80% lean, 20% fat).

Formula B. Beef trimmings - 50% (80% lean, 20% fat),
Pork trimmings - 50% (80% lean, 20% fat).

Traditional curing. Meats should be properly cured with salt and sodium nitrite (Cure #1) using the dry curing method. This will produce a pink color so typical to frankfurters or bologna. The smaller meat particle size results in a shorter curing time and emulsified meats are often cured using the faster "emulsion curing" method.

Emulsion curing. Salt, spices, binders and sodium nitrite are added directly into a bowl cutter where they are mixed with minced meat. Crushed ice or ice cold water is slowly added and as a result an emulsified paste is obtained. This emulsified mix is then stuffed into casings but cannot be submitted to smoking as the curing color has not developed yet. In this particular case meats have not been cured and more time is needed in order for the sodium nitrite to react with the meat. As the meat has been very finely comminuted, it is sufficient to hang stuffed sausages overnight in a refrigerator (38° F, 3-4° C). Then they are kept for 1-2 hours at room temperature or in a warm smokehouse at around 50° C (122° F) without smoke. The reason is to dry out the sausage casings which may be moist when removed from a cold refrigerator into a warmer room. It also provides an extra time for curing as sodium nitrite cures even faster at such high temperatures. The normal 2-3 days curing period has been eliminated. The "emulsion curing" may not be the best choice at home conditions, unless an extra refrigerator is available.

To lower costs, a commercial manufacturer tries to accomplish the entire curing process during meat cutting and emulsifying. This is possible due to the addition of sodium erythorbate or ascorbic acid, which accelerates the production of nitric oxide (NO) from sodium nitrite (Cure #1). Nitric oxide reacts with meat myoglobin rapidly producing nitrosomyoglobin (NOMb). As a result the cured red color is obtained much faster and is more stable.

Grinding/Emulsifying. Commercial producers will perform the first stages of production entirely in a bowl cutter. This saves time and space, simplifies equipment and allows the introduction of huge amounts of water.

A typical emulsifying process:

1. Add beef to a bowl cutter rotating on low speed.
2. Add salt, sodium nitrite (Cure#1), phosphates (if used) and ingredients and 1/3 of finely crushed ice (less wear on knives). Cut on high speed.
3. Add lean pork trimmings and another 1/3 of ice.
4. Add last part of ice, all spices, color enhancers (ascorbic acid, sodium erythorbate etc), fat and fat pork trimmings. Cut and mix together.

Notes:

- Fat is added last as it does not absorb water and has tendency to smear when warmer.
- Ascorbic acid reacts violently when in direct contact with sodium nitrite. This is why sodium nitrite is added at the beginning and ascorbic acid last.
- About 2 - 3% salt and 0.3 - 0.5% phosphates should be added for maximum protein extraction.
- Salt soluble proteins are most effectively extracted from lean meat at 36 - 38° F (2 - 4° C).

Home Production

Grinding. Grind all meats with a coarse plate 3/8" (10 mm), refreeze and grind again through 3/16" (5 mm) or 1/8" (3 mm). Refreeze the mixture briefly and grind the third time through 1/8" (3 mm) plate.

Using Food Processor

A food processor is the smaller brother of a commercial bowl cutter. It allows to effectively chop meat trimmings that contain a lot of connective tissue, the task which will be hard to perform with a manual grinder. The meat should be first ground in a grinder through 1/8" (3 mm) plate and then emulsified in a food processor. The grinding process can be performed a day earlier. Most processors come with a single cutting blade, some are equipped with two knives. In both cases a lot of heat is generated and crushed ice should be added.

Making ice. Fill any suitable container with water and when frozen insert warm water to remove a block of ice. Wrap a towel around it and break into smaller pieces. For preparing smaller quantities of ice the ice holding tray will suffice. *The smaller ice particles the less wear and tear on the cutting knife.*

Adding ice flakes extends the life of the cutting blade and keeps down the meat's temperature. Different meats can absorb different amounts of water, but adding 25% of crushed ice may be a good estimate. This will result in 10% sausage yield. If the sausage mass weighed 1 kg, the finished cooked sausage should weigh about 1.1 kg. Chop meat and fat gradually adding crushed ice until it is completely absorbed by the meat. If this process were performed at high temperatures the emulsion would be lost and the fat will separate from water.

A good comparison is the process of making mayonnaise or some butter sauces. For example, if oil is added too fast to egg emulsion while whisking, the emulsion will break apart and oil will come out of the solution. If butter is added to emulsion too fast or at too high temperatures, the emulsion will be lost. The remedy is to add ice and vigorously whisk again. Adding some non-fat dry milk (3%), although not necessary, will strength the emulsion and will help the finished sausage retain moisture.

Meat should be emulsified until its temperature reaches 57° F (14° C). *Above 60° F (15° C), the fat will separate from the meat.* In a properly emulsified meat there should be no distinction between meat and fat particles. In commercial operations the temperature of the emulsion is continuously monitored and is kept around 59° F, 15° C or lower. If making only one type of sausage you may add all ingredients into the food processor which will eliminate the mixing process.

Making Different Sausages

1. Often more than one sausage type is produced at the same time. In such a case the emulsified mixture becomes a sausage mass that becomes a base for different sausages. Of course besides salt and nitrite no other ingredients are added when making the base.

2. Lean meat is manually cut into desired size pieces or ground through a coarse grinder plate. The fat can be diced into 1/8" cubes. Those bigger parts will become the show meat in a finished sausage.

3. Emulsified sausage base is mixed with other ingredients and stuffed into casings. Ingredients such as olives, pistachio nuts, whole peppercorns may be added as well.

4. The sausage mass is stuffed into casings and cooked in water.

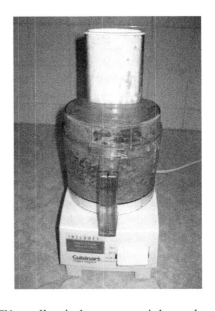

Photo 15.1 Cuisinart® Food Processors can chop a variety of foods, meat included.

Photo 15.2 Cusinart®Handy Prep™ small unit does a great job emulsifying meat. Adding cold water helps to emulsify meat and it keeps the temperature from rising.   *Photos courtesy Cusinart®.*

Photo 15.3 A small commercial bowl cutter.

Mixing. Mix all ingredients with a cup of cold water and pour over minced meat. Start mixing, gradually adding flaked ice or cold water until a well mixed mass is obtained. We have been making wieners and frankfurters long before food processors came to be and there is no reason why we can't process them in the same way again.

Stuffing. Stuff hot dogs or frankfurters into sheep casings making 4-5" (10-12 cm) links. Hang them for 1 hour at room temperature to dry out the casings and then place the sausages in a smokehouse. The smoking step is very important during commercial manufacturing as sausages such as hot dogs or frankfurters are skinless (no casings). They are stuffed into cellulose casings and then smoked. This creates a hardened surface which becomes a sort of artificial casing. After smoking and cooking, sausages go through the machine that cuts cellulose casings lengthwise and then the casing is peeled off. The hardened surface of the sausage is strong enough to hold a sausage mass in one piece. At home the sausages are stuffed into sheepskin casings which are edible and it is entirely up to you whether to remove the casings or not. If it comes off clean and easy without attached meat you may remove it. A skinless fresh sausage can be produced by stuffing meat into cellulose casings. The sausage is then frozen and the casing stripped off.

Smoking. Freshly stuffed sausages are left for 1-2 hrs at room temperature or in a warm smokehouse at around 50° C (122° F) without smoke. The purpose of this step is to dry out the casings which should feel dry or tacky to the touch. Sausages are smoked at 60-70° C (140-158° F) until a reddish-brown color is obtained. Smoking and cooking should be considered as one continuous operation.

Cooking. Cooking time depends directly on the temperature when the smoking has ended. For small diameter sausages such as hot dogs or frankfurters it should not be longer than 15 minutes. Emulsified sausages are heat treated with steam or hot water. At home conditions they will be submerged in hot water at 75° C (167° F). Frankfurters are thin sausages and 15 minutes cooking time is plenty. Keep in mind that they have been smoked at 60-70° C (140-158° F) for about 60 minutes and are already warm and partly pre-cooked. If a sausage diameter is larger, let's say 60 mm Mortadella, you may cook it at 75 – 78° C (167 – 172° F) for 60 minutes. A very large bologna sausage may be smoked for 3-5 hours and cooked for 5 hours more.

A rule of thumb dictates 10 min of poaching in water for each 1 cm (3/8") of the diameter of the sausage. There is no need for estimating time when a thermometer is used and cooking stops when the internal temperature of the sausage reaches 69-70° C (155-158° F).

Cooling. Dip sausages in cold water to cool them down. You may have to change the water once or twice depending on the size of the container and the size of production. If possible shower or dip them very briefly in hot water to remove any grease on the surface. Hang sausages and wipe off any fat with a wet cloth. The reason for cooling is to bring the temperature down outside the Danger Zone (60-4° C, 140-40° F) when most bacteria find favorable conditions to grow. Although the cooking process kills 99% of bacteria, nevertheless new bacteria which are present all around will start multiplying again on the surface of the sausage. It is in our interest to bring the temperature below 60° C (140° F) as soon as possible. The sausages can be hung between 25-30° C (77-86° F) as at those temperatures moisture and heat evaporate from the surface rapidly. Then the sausages may be placed in a refrigerator.

Storing. In refrigerator.

Spices and additives. Aromatic seeds such as cloves, ginger, allspice, cinnamon, and nutmeg are commonly added to emulsified sausages. Other popular spices are white pepper, coriander and celery seed. The following additives can be used in emulsified products: non-fat dry milk, starch, soy protein isolate or concentrate, egg whites, phosphates and ascorbates.

Manufacture of Commercial Emulsions

The following set of technical papers is reprinted with permission courtesy Koch Equipment, Kansas City, MO. In 2012 Koch Equipment LLC and Ultravac Solutions combined to become UltraSource LLC, www.ultrasourceusa.com

Introduction

The purpose of this document is to educate meat processors and sausage makers about the advantages of using a bowl cutter to emulsify, coarse chop, or fine chop products such as bologna, hot dogs, brats, kielbasa, summer sausage, snack sticks, or any European style sausage.

Problem Statement

In spite of the fact that many meat processors and sausage makers want to remain competitive and take their business to the next level by increasing their productivity and product quality, some still utilize a grind/mix/regrind process to produce their meat and sausage products. Not only is this process time consuming, processors are also missing an opportunity to extract protein from their meat mixtures so they can produce high-quality, value added products.

Solution

Bowl cutting offers benefits far beyond grind/mix/regrind systems, including:

- Reduced labor costs - bowl cutting takes half the time of grind/mix/regrind process
- Improved product quality - bowl cutting extracts up to 92% available protein. Protein is the binder for water and fat in your product. One pound of properly extracted protein binds four pounds of fat and/or moisture through the cooking process. The result is a firmer or snappier, more flavorful product with improved particle definition, better color during shelf-life, and a "clean cut" with no smear.
- Increased profits - maximum protein extraction translates to increased binding and weight retention, which equals less cookout and increased yields. Bowl cutting also enables product line expansion - from emulsified products to summer sausages and snack sticks using least-cost formulations.

GRINDER Ingredient cost		BOWL CUTTER Ingredient cost	
100-lbs. meat	$150.00	100-lbs. meat	$150.00
12-lbs. water	$1.00	30-lbs. water	$1.00
2.5-lbs. salt	$0.50	2.5-lbs. salt	$0.50
1.5-lbs. misc.	$7.20	1.5-lbs. misc.	$7.20
Total batch: 116-lbs.	$158.70	Total batch: 134-lbs.	$158.70
Grinder nets 101-lbs. finished product		Bowl cutter nets 123-lbs. finished product	
Savings of $0.28 per pound or 17%			

In the above table there is a cost comparison between a mix/grind/ regrind system and a bowl cutter utilizing protein extraction. Due to the differences in the amount of added moisture and shrink during the cooking process, bowl cutting results in a 17% decrease in product cost.

Base Emulsion Manufacturing Procedure
(Meat temperature 36 to 38° F)

A base emulsion program simplifies inventory control and reduces inventory costs without sacrificing product variety or quality.

25-lbs. 85% lean beef trimmings   Note: 100-lbs. raw materials
25-lbs. 75% lean pork trimmings   = 35.5% fat in material and
25-lbs. skinned pork jowls   26.52% fat in emulsion blend
25-lbs. flaked ice
1-lb. salt
2-oz. 6.25 sodium nitrite
4-oz. phosphate blend

Under refrigeration, this emulsion will last up to seven days.

- Calculate the percentage of emulsion to coarse material adding a balance of salt, cure, and spices.
- Cut together until desired particle definition is obtained.
- Transfer to stuffer.

Coarse Emulsion Formula
(Meat temperature 36 to 38° F)

20-lbs. 80/20 beef, ground 1/2-in.
30-lbs. 80/20 pork, ground 3/8-in.
20-lbs 80/20 pork, ground 1/8-in.
30-lbs. 50/50 pork, ground 3/16-in.
4-oz. 6.25% sodium nitrite 2-lbs. salt
8-oz. dextrose
4-oz. phosphate blend
7/8-oz. sodium erythorbate
15-lbs. flaked ice
1 ½-oz. celery seed, ground
1 ½-oz. coriander
4-oz. garlic powder
2-oz. nutmeg
5-oz. ground white pepper
Black pepper, coarse ground (optional)

288 Home Production of Quality Meats and Sausages

Coarse Emulsion Manufacturing Procedure

The emulsion base for this sausage will be 20% of the meat total. This manufacturing procedure provides the benefit of properly extracted protein in a coarse sausage with particle definition from the various sizes of meat up to the ½ -in. cut beef (shine through the casings for eye appeal).

- Place the 20-lbs. of 80/20 1/8-in. ground pork into the bowl cutter on low speed.
- Add salt, nitrite, dextrose, phosphate blend, and half of the flaked ice.
- Cut on high speed approximately 10 to 15 revolutions.
- Add the remaining flaked ice and cut until a fine emulsion and a shiny appearance is realized.
- While cutting on slow speed, add dextrose, all spices, and sodium erythorbate.
- Allow 2 to 3 bowl revolutions until all is well distributed.
- Add 80/20 ½-in. ground beef, 80/20 ⅜-in. pork and 50/50 3/16-in. pork.
- Cut until desired particle definition is obtained.
- Transfer to stuffer.

Note: It is not necessary to pre-grind material before placing in a bowl cutter. However, pre-grinding does remove a predominance of bone chips, gristle, and sinew providing clean meat to further process.

Fine Emulsion Formula
(Meat temperature 36 to 38° F)

60-lbs. 80/20 beef, ground ⅛-in.
20-lbs. 80/20 pork, ground ⅛-in.
20-lbs. 50/50 pork, ground ⅛-in.
4-oz. 6.25% sodium nitrite
2-lbs. salt
8-oz. phosphate blend
7/8-oz. sodium erythorbate
25-lbs. flaked ice
7-oz. ground white pepper
3-oz. paprika 120 astor
1-oz. coriander
1-oz. onion powder

Calculated composition 10% shrink:

Moisture	62.0
Fat	18.8
Protein	14.5

Properties

% Collagen (maximum 35)	22.1
Bind Points (minimum 1.8)	3.7
Color Points (minimum 2)	5.6

Fine Emulsion Manufacturing Procedure

You are working with two types of protein at this point: salt soluble and water soluble. Beef has the highest percentage of protein available.

- Place 60-lbs. of beef into the bowl cutter on low speed.
- Add salt, nitrite, dextrose, phosphate blend, and one-third of the total flaked ice.
- Cut on high speed approximately 15 revolutions.
- Add another third of the flaked ice and 80/20 pork and cut approximately 10 revolutions until meat starts to show a good protein extraction. The consistency of the product should be fine and have a shiny surface appearance.
- Add remaining flaked ice to drive the meat temperature down before adding the fat pork.
- Add the 50/50 pork, all spices and sodium erythorbate.

Reducing the temperature allows the extracted proteins (mainly myosin) to encapsulate the fat molecules thus holding them in suspension. Otherwise, you run the risk of smearing or fat separating during the cooking process (i.e., fat caps).

Bologna

Bologna and frankfurter are smoked and cooked emulsified sausages which are similar. Many producers use the same formula and processing steps for both sausages. The main difference is the size of the casings as bologna is a much bigger sausage. It is an American equivalent of Italian Mortadella with no visible pieces of fat.

Meat	Metric	US
beef	700 g	1.54 lb.
pork trimmings	300 g	0.66 lb.

Ingredients per 1000 g (1 kg) of meat:

salt	18 g	3 tsp.
Cure #1	2.5 g	½ tsp.
paprika	2.0 g	1 tsp.
allspice	2.0 g	1 tsp.
white pepper	2.0 g	1 tsp.
coriander	2.0 g	1 tsp.
water	150 ml	⅝ cup

Instructions:

1. Grind meats through 3/16" plate (5 mm). Keep lean meats separately from fat trimmings. Refreeze and grind again. Refreeze again and grind through 1/8" (3 mm) plate.

2. Mix lean beef with all ingredients adding ⅓ (50 ml) of cold water. Add lean pork and ⅓ of cold water and mix well. Add fat trimmings and the last ⅓ of water and mix everything well together.

3. Stuff firmly into 40-60 mm beef middles or fibrous casings. Form 18" (40 cm) long sections. Use butchers twine to reinforce the ends and form a hanging loop.

4. Hang on smokesticks for one hour.

5. When sausages feel dry to touch, apply hot smoke 50-60° C (120-140° F) for 2 hours.

6. Gradually increase smokehouse temperature to 70-77° C (160-170° F), until internal meat temperature reaches 155-158° F(69-70° C). This should take 45-60 minutes or more depending on the size of casings.

7. Shower with cold water for about 10 minutes.

8. Hang for 2 hours at room temperature and then place in a refrigerator.

Notes:

There are many varieties of bologna which are made the same but stuffed differently:
- Long bologna - stuffed in beef middles, smoke for 1-2 hours.
- Ring bologna - stuffed in beef rounds, smoke for 2-3 hours.
- Large bologna - stuffed in beef bungs, smoke for 3 hours.

Coney Island Frank

This sausage was very popular in the Coney Island amusement park and other parks in New York City where it was roasted over charcoal fires.

Meat	Metric	US
beef	700 g	1.54 lb.
pork trimmings	300 g	0.66 lb.

Ingredients per 1000 g (1 kg) of meat:

salt	18 g	3 tsp.
Cure #1	2.5 g	½ tsp.
pepper	2.0 g	1 tsp.
red pepper	1.0 g	½ tsp.
nutmeg	1.0 g	½ tsp.
water	150 ml	⅝ cup

Instructions:

1. Grind meats with 3/16" plate (5 mm). Keep lean meats separate from fat trimmings. Refreeze and grind again. Refreeze again and grind through 1/8" (3 mm) plate.

2. Mix lean beef with all ingredients adding ⅓ (50 ml) of cold water. Add lean pork and ⅓ of cold water and mix well. Add fat trimmings and the last ⅓ of water and mix everything well together.

3. Stuff firmly into 24-26 mm sheep casings. Form 4-5" (10-12 cm) long links.

4. Hang on smokesticks for one hour.

5. When sausages feel dry apply hot smoke 60-70° C (140-158° F) for about 60 minutes until brown color develops.

6. Cook in hot water, at 75° C (167° F) until internal meat temperature reaches 155-158° F(69-70° C). This should take about 15 minutes.

7. Shower with cold water for 5 minutes.

8. Keep in a refrigerator.

Frankfurter

The frankfurter is a cured, smoked and cooked sausage. It is a ready to eat sausage or it may be boiled, fried or grilled for serving. The frankfurter originated some 350 years ago in Frankfurt, Germany and German immigrants brought the technology to the USA. The terms frankfurter, wiener or hot dog are practically interchangeable today. When the term "beef frankfurter" is used, the sausage is made of pure beef only.

Meat	Metric	US
beef	600 g	1.32 lb.
regular pork trimmings	200 g	0.44 lb.
fat pork trimmings	200 g	0.44 lb.

Ingredients per 1000 g (1 kg) of meat:

salt	18 g	3 tsp.
Cure #1	2.5 g	½ tsp.
paprika	2.0 g	1 tsp.
white pepper	2.0 g	1 tsp.
coriander	2.0 g	1 tsp.
nutmeg	1.0 g	½ tsp.
cold water	150 ml	⅝ cup

Instructions:
1. Grind meats with 3/16" plate (5 mm). Keep lean meats separately from fat trimmings. Refreeze and grind again. Refreeze again and grind through 1/8" (3 mm) plate.
2. Mix lean beef with all ingredients adding ⅓ (50 ml) of cold water. Add lean pork and ⅓ of cold water and mix well. Add fat trimmings and the last ⅓ of water and mix everything well together.
3. Stuff firmly into 24-26 mm sheep casings. Form 4-5" (10-12 cm) long links.
4. Hang on smokesticks for one hour.
5. When sausages feel dry apply hot smoke 60-70° C (140-158° F) for about 60 minutes until brown color develops.
6. Cook in hot water, at 75° C (167° F) until internal meat temperature reaches 155-158° F(69-70° C). This should take about 15 minutes.
7. Shower with cold water for 5 minutes.
8. Keep in a refrigerator.

Hot Dog

The origin of the word "hot dog" stirs much debate as everyone wants to claim ownership of the America's favorite food. German immigrants brought not only the sausage with them in the late 1800s, but also dachshund dogs. The name hot dog probably began as a joke about the Germans' small, long, thin dogs. As the legend goes, Tad Dorgan, the cartoonist of New York Journal, observed vendor Harry Stevens selling the "hot dachshund sausages" during a game at the New York Polo Grounds and shouting "get your red-hot dachshund sausages." Dorgan illustrated this scene with a dachshund dog nestled in a bun with the caption "get your hot dogs."

Meat	Metric	US
beef	400 g	0.88 lb.
pork	350 g	0.77 lb.
back fat	250 g	0.55 lb.

Ingredients per 1000 g (1 kg) of meat:

salt	18 g	3 tsp.
Cure #1	2.5 g	½ tsp.
paprika	1.0 g	½ tsp.
white pepper	2.0 g	1 tsp.
mace	0.5 g	⅓ tsp.
garlic	3.5 g	1 clove
crushed ice/cold water	120 ml	½ cup

1. Grind all meats through ⅛" (3 mm) plate.
2. Dissolve all other ingredients in a little water and stir well. Mix all ingredients with meats.
3. Emulsify ground meat in a food processor adding crushed ice.
4. Stuff into 24-26 mm sheep casings. Hang for 1 hour at room temperature.
5. Smoke for 1 hour at 140° F (60° C).
6. Poach in water at 162° F (75° C) until the internal temperature reaches 155 - 158° F, (69 - 70° C). That should take about 15 minutes.
7. Shower with cold water, then place in a refrigerator.

Using a manual grinder

Grind beef and pork with 3/8" (10 mm) plate 2-3 times.
Grind fat pork with 1/8" (3 mm) grinder 2-3 times but keep fat separate.
Add about 100 g (⅜ of a cup) of icy cold water to ground beef and pork and mix together until water is fully absorbed by the meat.
Add fat and all ingredients and mix everything well together. Then continue with step # 4 above.
Notes:
You can use all beef (25% fat) or different combinations of meats; pork, veal, chicken, and beef.

Mortadella di Bologna

The name mortadella originates from the Latin words myrtle (mirtatum) and mortar (mortario) and the sausage was made the same way in Italy for hundreds of years. This is not an American pre-packaged and sliced bologna product. It is an emulsified sausage with cubes of white fat, whole peppercorns and pistachio nuts. This sausage is the pride of the Italian city of Bologna.

Meat	Metric	US
pork	700 g	1.54 lb.
jowls, bacon or fat trimmings	200 g	0.44 lb.
back fat (10-15%)	100 g	0.22 lb.

Ingredients per 1000 g (1 kg) of meat:

salt	18 g	3 tsp.
Cure #1	2.5 g	½ tsp.
white pepper	2.0 g	1 tsp.
whole peppercorns	4.0 g	1 tsp.
coriander	0.5 g	¼ tsp.
garlic powder	1.5 g	½ clove
anise	1.0 g	½ tsp.
mace	1.0 g	½ tsp.
caraway, ground	0.5 g	¼ tsp.
pistachios, whole	35 g	¼ cup
cold red wine	60 ml	¼ cup

Instructions:
1. Dice back fat into ¼" cubes for use as *show meat*.
2. Grind all meats through ¼" (6 mm) plate, refreeze and grind again through ⅛" (3 mm) plate.
3. Mix ground meats with all ingredients (except whole peppercorns and pistachios).
4. Emulsify sausage mass in a food processor adding cold red wine.
5. Mix emulsified meat paste with cubed fat, pistachios and whole peppercorns.
6. Stuff into large diameter fibrous casings.
7. Poach sausages in water at 176° F (80° C) to an internal meat temperature of 155° F (69° C).

Mortadella Lyoner

Mortadella Lyoner is a French version of mortadella. It is finely emulsified meat without any visible show pieces like pistachios and fat cubes (Italian Mortadella di Bologna), bell peppers (German Mortadella) or olives (Spanish Mortadela Cordobesa).

Meat	Metric	US
pork	300 g	0.66 lb.
beef	300 g	0.66 lb.
back fat, jowls or		
fat pork trimmings	400 g	0.88 lb.

Ingredients per 1000 g (1 kg) of meat:

salt	18 g	3 tsp.
Cure #1	2.5 g	½ tsp.
white pepper	2.0 g	1 tsp.
mace	0.5 g	¼ tsp.
coriander	0.5 g	¼ tsp.
ginger	0.5 g	¼ tsp.
cardamom	0.5 g	¼ tsp.
sweet paprika	1.0 g	½ tsp.
onion powder	2.0 g	1 tsp.
crushed ice or cold water	150 ml	⅝ cup

Instructions:
1. Grind all meats with ⅛" (3 mm) grinder plate.
2. Mix ground meats with all ingredients adding crushed ice (water).
3. Emulsify sausage mass in food processor.
4. Stuff into 60 mm plastic waterproof casings.
5. Poach sausages in water at 167° F (75° C) for 60 min to an internal meat temperature of 155-158° F (69-70° C).
6. Cool in cold water and refrigerate.

Mortadella - Polish

Polish Mortadella like Italian original and Spanish versions is made with visible cubes of fat inside. Mortadella has its roots in the Italian city of Bologna. The sausage was made popular by Italian immigrants settling in many parts of the world and it became known in Spanish countries as "Mortadela", in the USA as "Bologna", Iran as "Martadella" and in Poland as "Mortadella". It is often served by dipping it in egg, then covering both sides with breadcrumbs and frying in oil or butter on a frying pan.

Meat	Metric	US
pork	600 g	1.32 lb.
beef	250 g	0.55 lb.
back fat or		
fat pork trimmings	150 g	0.33 lb.

Ingredients per 1000 g (1 kg) of meat:

salt	18 g	3 tsp.
Cure #1	2.5 g	½ tsp.
white pepper	2.0 g	1 tsp.
nutmeg	1.0 g	½ tsp.
white mustard seeds (whole)	1.0 g	½ tsp.
sugar	2.0 g	½ tsp.
cold water	150 ml	⅝ cup

Instructions:
1. Manually dice back fat into 6 mm (1/4") cubes. Grind pork, beef and fat pork trimmings through 1/8" (3 mm) plate. Refreeze and grind again adding water. You can emulsify using food processor:
a. emulsify ground beef and pork adding ice cold water.
b. add fat pork trimmings and continue emulsifying until thoroughly mixed.
2. Mix diced back fat with emulsified mixture until fat cubes are evenly distributed.
3. Stuff firmly into 120 mm cellulose or synthetic fibrous casings. Tie the ends with butcher's twine and make 10-12 cm (4-5") hanging loop on one end.
4. Hang for 60 min to dry.
5. Apply hot smoke for 100-135 min.
6. Poach sausages in water at 72-75° C (161-167° F) for 90-120 min until internal meat temperature of the sausage becomes 69-70° C (155-158° F).
7. Shower with cold water for about 10 min and place in a cooler.

Pork Curry Sausage

Pork curry sausage is an emulsified and cooked sausage which is basically frankfurter flavored with curry. You may add beef to the recipe if you like or even make an all beef curry sausage.

Meat	Metric	US
lean pork	600 g	1.32 lb.
fat pork	200 g	0.44 lb.
fat pork trimmings	200 g	0.44 lb.

Ingredients per 1000 g (1 kg) of meat:

salt	18 g	3 tsp.
white pepper	2.0 g	1 tsp.
curry powder	2.0 g	1 tsp.
mace	0.5 g	⅓ tsp.
ginger	0.5 g	⅓ tsp.
cardamom	2.0 g	1 tsp.
coriander	2.0 g	1 tsp.
nutmeg	1.0 g	½ tsp.
grated lemon peel	1.0 g	½ tsp.
non fat dry milk	28 g	1 oz.
cold water	120 ml	½ cup

Instructions:

1. Keep lean meats separate from fat trimmings. Grind lean meats through 3/16" plate (5 mm). Refreeze and grind again. Refreeze again and grind through 1/8" (3 mm) plate. Grind fat trimmings through 1/8" (3 mm) plate, refreeze and grind again.
2. Mix lean ground pork with all ingredients adding 50 ml of cold water. Add ground fat pork and 50 ml of cold water and mix well. Add fat trimmings and the last 20 ml of water and mix everything well together.
3. Stuff firmly into 28-32 mm hog casings. Form 4-5" (10-12 cm) long links.
4. Cook in hot water, at 167° F (75° C) until internal meat temperature reaches 155-158° F (69-70° C). This should take about 30 minutes.
5. Shower with cold water for 5 minutes.
6. Keep in a refrigerator.

Sausage Links - Polish

Polish Sausage Links (*Parówki*) are little sausages, kind of a hot dog and of similar fine texture and taste. Those fully cooked small sausages are often served hot for breakfast by boiling them shortly in hot water. Then when placed on a plate they are known to emit steam ("para" in Polish) and since the name parówka.

Meat	Metric	US
pork butt	700 g	1.54 lb.
beef	300 g	0.66 lb.

Ingredients per 1000 g (1 kg) of meat:

salt	18 g	3 tsp.
Cure #1	2.5 g	½ tsp.
white pepper	2.0 g	1 tsp.
sugar	2.0 g	½ tsp.
nutmeg	1.5 g	1 tsp.
garlic	3.5 g	1 clove
cold water	150 ml	⅝ cup

Instructions:

1. Grind pork through 3/16" (5 mm) plate, refreeze and grind again through 1/8" (3 mm) plate. Repeat procedure with beef.
2. Mix everything together adding water and all ingredients. You can use a food processor.
3. Stuff mixture medium hard into 22 - 24 mm sheep casings and form 5 - 6" (12 - 14 cm) links. Prick any visible air pockets with a needle. Keep the total number of links an even number as it will be easier to divide them later into pairs.
4. Leave it hanging on smoke sticks at room temperature, 64 - 68° F, (18 - 20° C) for 30 min.
5. Hot smoke at 104 - 140° F, (40 - 60° C) for 70 min until the color becomes light pinkish with some yellow tint in it.
6. Poach in hot water at 167° F (75° C) until the internal temperature reaches 155 - 158° F (69 - 70° C).
7. Shower with cold water and let it cool.

Notes:
The best way to serve this sausage is by reheating it in hot water.

Serdelki

Serdelki is the Polish equivalent of a wiener. This is a fine textured emulsified sausage like a hot dog or frankfurter.

Meat	Metric	US
pork	500 g	1.10 lb.
beef	250 g	0.55 lb.
fat pork trimmings	250 g	0.55 lb.

Ingredients per 1000 g (1 kg) of meat:

salt	18 g	3 tsp.
Cure #1	2.5 g	½ tsp.
white pepper	2.0 g	1 tsp.
nutmeg	1.5 g	1 tsp.
garlic	3.5 g	1 clove
cold water	120 ml	½ cup

Instructions:

1. Grind pork and pork trimmings through 3/16" (5 mm) plate, refreeze and grind again through 1/8" (3 mm) plate. Repeat procedure with beef.
2. Mix everything together adding water and all ingredients. You can use a food processor.
3. Stuff firmly into 32-34 mm hog casings, or 28-30 mm sheep casings. Make a continuous rope but form links about 4" (10 cm) long. You may form links using butchers twine.
4. Place sausages on smoke sticks and hang for 30-60 minutes.
5. When sausages feel dry to the touch, apply hot smoke 60-70° C (140-158° F) for about 100 minutes until a light reddish - brown color develops.
6. Poach in water at 75° C (167° F) for about 15 minutes. The internal meat temperature should be 69-72° C (155 - 160° F).
7. Place under running tap water for 3 minutes.
8. Store in a refrigerator.

Wiener

The wiener is a cured, smoked and cooked sausage. It is a ready to eat sausage or it may be boiled, fried or grilled for serving. The wiener originated about 300 years ago in Vienna, Austria. German immigrants brought this technology to the USA. The terms frankfurter, wiener or hot dog are practically interchangeable today.

Meat	Metric	US
lean beef	400 g	0.88 lb.
veal	300 g	0.66 lb.
back fat, pork jowl		
or fat pork trimmings	300 g	0.66 lb.

Ingredients per 1000 g (1 kg) of meat:

salt	18 g	3 tsp.
Cure #1	2.5 g	½ tsp.
paprika	2.0 g	1 tsp.
white pepper	2.0 g	1 tsp.
coriander	2.0 g	1 tsp.
mace	0.5 g	⅓ tsp.
onion powder	1.0 g	½ tsp.
cold water	150 ml	⅝ cup

Instructions:

1. Grind meats 3/16" plate (5 mm). Keep lean meats separately from fat trimmings. Refreeze and grind again. Refreeze again and grind through 1/8" (3 mm) plate.
2. Mix lean beef with all ingredients adding ⅓ (50 ml) of cold water. Add lean pork and 50 ml of cold water and mix well. Add fat trimmings and the last part (50 ml) of water and mix everything well together.
3. Stuff firmly into 24-26 mm sheep casings. Form 4-5" (10-12 cm) long links.
4. Hang on smokesticks for 30 minutes.
5. When sausages feel dry apply hot smoke 60-70° C (140-158° F) for about 60 minutes until a brown color develops.
6. Cook in hot water, at 75° C (167° F) until internal meat temperature reaches 155-158° F(69-70° C). This should take about 15 minutes.
7. Shower with cold water for 5 minutes. Keep in a refrigerator.

Chapter 16

Boiled Special Sausages

This group of sausages covers the following products:
- Liver sausages
- Head cheeses
- Blood sausages

What makes them unique is that meats are pre-cooked in water, then *stuffed into a casing and cooked again.* Their production is more time consuming as it requires additional cooking. In liver sausages the liver is added raw or only scalded otherwise it loses its emulsifying properties. This secondary cooking is not performed for the safety of the product as the meats were already cooked. *The secondary heating of the sausage creates a proper bond between meat and gelatin.* Take head cheese as an example, cold meats were stuffed into the casing and the gelatin started to solidify. If left to itself, there might be little binding between meat pieces and gelatin.

These products are very popular in Europe and anywhere in the world except the USA where only liver sausages can be found in supermarkets. A head cheese can be sometimes found but in order to get a blood sausage, one must shop in ethnic butcher shops be it German, Polish, Russian, Irish and others. These sausages were always made on the farm when the pig was slaughtered and any meat cuts that would not be used for making regular sausages were incorporated in their production. This fact probably induced many people not to believe that those materials were inferior but nothing could be further from the fact. First of all those cuts such as pork head meat, snouts, skin, hocks, jowls, tongues, back fat, liver and kidneys are used for making emulsified sausages like hotdogs and frankfurters. Secondly, they are good meats, some of them like pork head meat are very flavorsome.

A feasible explanation for the lower popularity of these sausages is that manufacturers see less profit in their manufacture as they require cooking meats, separating them from bones, filtering stock, stuffing them in casings and cooking them again. It involves a lot of labor and the product has to be sold at the price that would justify the investment. These above conclusions do not negate the fact that these are delicious products to eat. General considerations for making special sausages:

- Pork - all parts are suitable.
- Lean beef is sometimes added to liver sausages. Beef fat should not be added at all.
- Veal - can be successfully used but it is pricey.
- Sheep and goat - may be used, but should be selected from younger animals.
- Wild game - discard fat, use meat and add pork trimmings.

The manufacturing process

- Meats are rinsed/soaked in cold water to eliminate traces of blood.
- Meats are simmered below the boiling point for 3-4 hours until they can be separated from bones. As you may cook different size sausages in the same vessel some stirring is required to expose cooked products to uniform temperatures. A wooden spoon with a long handle will perform this duty neatly. The resulting stock should be saved for two reasons:
  ◊   It is added to head cheese and forms the jelly.
  ◊   It is used as a cooking medium.
- Meat is separated from bones and cut manually.
- Liver is ground and emulsified. Livers must not be cooked. They may be scalded with hot water. Back fat should be diced into ⅜" (1 cm) pieces and then boiled for about 30 minutes. Skins should be boiled until soft but not overcooked. Tongues are scalded for a few minutes in hot water in order to remove the skin and to clean them. Then they are boiled.
- Meats are mixed with other ingredients, often the meat stock is added.
- Sausages are stuffed loosely with a horn and a ladle.
- Sausages are poached at about 176° F (80° C).
- Sausages are cooled and stored under refrigeration.

Photo 16.1 Cooking leftover meat trimmings.

A lot of meat is left over on bones from the prior processing of items such as hams, ribs, loins, butt, head and other cuts. A significant amount of skin remains, too. All those trimmings are slow cooked in water and will end up in special sausages.

Photo 16.2 Cooking leftover meats.

Photo 16.3 Cooked meat trimmings.

Photo 16.4 Meat, when still warm, is carefully separated from bones, then selected for a particular type of a sausage. The operation seems to be messy, but the finished product presented below looks appetizing.

Photo 16.5 Arrangement of different meat, including headcheese.

Chapter 17

Liver Sausages

Liver sausages can be classified as:

- Regular liver sausages - coarsely comminuted through 5 mm grinder plate.
- Delicatessen type liver sausages - finely comminuted through 2 mm grinder plate and emulsified.
- Pâtés - liver sausages which are not stuffed, but placed in molds and baked or cooked in water. Molds are often lined with pastry and pâtés are covered with decorations and gelatin.

Composition of a Liver Sausage

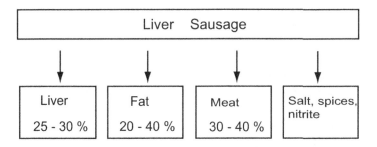

Fig. 17.1 Composition of a liver sausage.

Liver is an organ that works hard by filtering blood and as an animal grows older, the liver becomes darker and might develop a slightly bitter taste. Think of it as it were a filter that would become dirtier in time, the difference is that not the dust, but atoms of heavier materials like iron or copper will accumulate in time within its structure. Calf are slaughtered at the age of 4 months, a pig at 6 months, but a cow may live a few years. Because it is older, the cow's liver and blood are darker and will induce a darker color to a finished sausage.

306   Home Production of Quality Meats and Sausages

On the other hand veal, pork or poultry liver will make a sausage lighter and will make it taste better. This does not mean that you can not use beef liver at all; up to 25% of beef liver may be mixed with other livers without compromising the final taste. As the name implies a liver is an essential ingredient in the recipe but which one is the best?

Liver source	Description
Veal	Excellent. Light color, great taste, more expensive.
Pork	Very good.
Lamb and goat	Good. Up to 50% can be mixed with pork liver.
Beef	Poor. Tougher and dark. Can be mixed with other livers but should not account for more than 25% of the total liver mass. Dark color.
Goose	Excellent.
Turkey, duck	Good. Can be mixed with pork liver in any proportions.
Chicken	Good, but slightly bitter. Mix with pork liver.
Rabbit	Very good. Can be mixed with pork liver in any proportions.
Venison and wild game	Good.

The quality and color of the sausage is largely determined by choosing the liver. The way the liver, fat and meats are processed will have the biggest impact on the quality of the sausage. A careful selection of spices will give the sausage its final character. Best liver sausages are made from livers of young animals.

Liver must NOT be cooked as it will lose its emulsifying properties. In many recipes liver is blanched briefly in hot water for a few minutes to remove any leftover blood, but there is no need for that when the liver is clean. Blanching will cook some of the liver proteins and less of them would be available for emulsifying fat and water. Instead, liver can be rinsed and soaked in cold water for one hour to get rid of any traces of blood and remaining gall liquid. Soaking liver in milk is an old remedy for the removal of some of the liver's bitterness which can be noticeable in beef liver.

Meat Selection

Meats used for commercially made liver sausages are first cured with sodium nitrite to obtain a pinkish color and the characteristic cured meat flavor. Sodium nitrite has some effect on extending the shelf life of the product and for that reason alone it is used by commercial processors. Liver sausages made at home in most cases employ meats that are not cured with sodium nitrite and the color of the sausage will be light or even white as some sausages include cream. That will largely depend on the type of liver and spices used.

It is advantageous, especially when making coarse type liver sausage, to use meats with a lot of connective tissues such as pork head meat, jowls (cheeks) or skin. Those parts contain a lot of collagen which will turn into gelatin during heat treatment. During subsequent cooling this gelatin will become a gel and that will make the sausage more spreadable with a richer mouthful texture. Meats commonly used in commercial production are pork head meat, jowls, meat trimmings and skin. Although pork head meat may not appeal to most people as a valuable meat, it is high in fat and connective tissues and contains more meat flavor than other cuts. Between 5-10% of pork skins may be added, however, adding more makes the texture of the sausage feel rubbery. As long as the proper proportion of liver and fat are observed the remaining meats can be of any kind.

Fat

Liver sausages contain a large percentage of fat (20-40%) which largely determines their texture and spreadability. If pork fat is used it makes no big difference whether a hard fat (back fat), soft fat (belly) or other fat trimmings are utilized. Beef fat or pork flare fat (kidney) are not commonly used as they are hard and not easy to emulsify.

Adding soft fat results in a finer *spreadable* liver sausage. Generally, the harder fat is found in the center of the animal and the softer fat is located towards outside. A thick piece of fat such as pork back fat or belly consists of many layers containing different amounts of connective tissue. The next-to-the skin fat is much softer than the fat in the inner layer.

Salt, Spices and Other Ingredients

Liver sausages contain less salt than other sausages, the average being 12-18 g (1.2-1.8%) of salt per 1 kg of meat. Those sausages are of a much lighter color and for that reason white pepper is predominantly used. Given that most liver sausages are not smoked there is no need to use nitrite in home production. Sometimes, after cooking and cooling, liver sausages are cold smoked for a short time to add some smoky flavor. This short process has no effect on the preservation of the product which happens to be highly perishable.

Fresh onions are frequently used in home made liver sausages but are a poor choice in canned products and can create a sour taste. Onions become much sweeter when chopped and slow-fried in fat until glassy and straw like yellow color, but when browned, they become bitter. Milk or sweet cream is often added for a milder taste. Like in other sausages, sugar may be added to offset the salty taste. Liver likes aromatic spices such as nutmeg, mace, allspice, marjoram, white pepper, sweet paprika and ginger. Vanilla is often added to create an aromatic sweet taste. Port or brandy are often added.

Home Production

Precooking meat. Commercial plants cure meats with sodium nitrite regardless whether they will be smoked or not. Liver sausages made at home contain meats that are traditionally not cured although if a smoked product is desired, sodium nitrite can be added. Pork skin should be clean without any remaining hair or excess fat. They are slowly cooked at 85-90° C (185-194° F). If the skins are under cooked, they will be hard to emulsify and hard pieces will be visible in a finished sausage. If overcooked they will break into pieces. When the skins are properly done they should hold their shape but you should be able to put your finger through them.

Pork heads are normally cut in halves and are cooked at 85-90° C (185-194°F) until all meat and fat can be removed by hand. If they fall off the bones by themselves that means that the pork head was overcooked. All cartilage and gristle must also be removed. If pork head meat will not be used the same day it should be frozen. If jowls came attached to the head, they must be removed and cooked separately as different times are involved. Fats and other meats are cooked at 85-90° C (185-194° F) until the meat reaches 70° C (158° F) internal temperature.

Don't discard leftover meat stock (from cooking meats), it can be added to meat mass during emulsifying or grinding at 100-200 ml (1/4-1/2 cup) per 1 kg of meat.

Grinding. Warm pre-cooked meat should be minced with a small grinder plate 3-5 mm (1/8-3/16"). Liver is ground cold. As it contains a lot of water and blood, the ground liver is easily emulsified. Grinding of meats, especially liver with a small plate increases the surface area and improves spreadability.

Emulsifying. The sausage will have a more delicate texture and will be more spreadable if grinding is followed by emulsifying. As raw liver is a natural emulsifier, this task is greatly simplified. During the comminution process the fat cells become ruptured and the free fat is released. Fat does not dissolve in water or mix with it well. The purpose of emulsion is to bond free fat, meat and water together so they will not become separated. Previously ground meats are emulsified in a kitchen food processor until a smooth paste is obtained.

Liver is emulsified separately until air bubbles appear on the surface. Even if meat and fat are ground only, it is a good idea to at least emulsify the liver. If no food processor is available, grind meats and liver twice through the fine grinder plate.

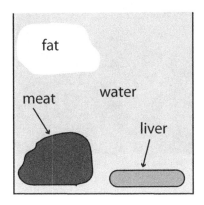

Natural emulsifiers that help to emulsify sausages are: egg protein, blood plasma, soy and sodium caseinate. Commercial plants use chemical emulsifiers such as monoglycerides and diglycerides. More on the emulsification process can be found in Chapter 15.

Fig. 17.2 Components of liver sausage which must be mixed together.

If emulsification is not done right, the finished product might display pockets of fat. To prevent fat deposits experienced sausage makers massage gently warm sausages between their thumb and index fingers.

Mixing. Meat, fat and liver are mixed together with salt and spices. Between 10-20% meat stock may be added now. This can be performed in a food processor.

Stuffing. Meat mass should be warm (35-40° C, 95-104° F) and not too dense. The casings are filled rather loose and can be stuffed with a stuffer or a funnel. Beef middles or natural hog casings are often used, synthetic waterproof casings can be used as well but will not allow smoke to go through. The density of the stuffed casing can be regulated by braking the slide of the casing from a nozzle.

Photo 17.1 Stuffing liver sausages.

Photo 17.2 Stuffing liver sausages.

Photo 17.3 Filling casings.

It may be impractical to use a manual grinder with a stuffing tube to stuff casings when the sausage mass is very thin. The preferred solution is to attach a casing to a funnel and to pour the sausage mass from a large cup or use a ladle. Due to its weight the sausage mass will fall down into the casing and no pushing is required. This way one continuous coil of loosely filled sausage can be made and then it can be subdivided into individual links or rings.

Photo 17.4 Liver sausages are usually made into a ring.

Photo 17.5 Liver sausage.

Cooking. Sausages stuffed into natural casings can be cooked in the stock that has been obtained during cooking meats. Cooking temperature stays below the boiling point, usually about 176° F (80° C) otherwise casings might burst open. After a while the layer of fat would accumulate on the surface of the stock. It is a good idea to remove this fat when using stock for poaching sausages, given that the fat's temperature is higher than that of water. Cooking water absorbs meat flavor and the resulting stock is usually saved for making soup.

Photo 17.7 Checking internal temperature.

Photo 17.6 Cooking sausages.

Times between grinding/emulsifying, mixing and stuffing should be kept to the minimum. Longer delays will lower the temperature of the sausage mass considerably, which should stay at least at 35° C (95° F). Below this temperature fat particles will clump together. That prevents them from being properly coated by emulsified liver protein and increases the risk of fat separation during the cooking process. Another reason for keeping short processing times is that a warm sausage mass surface area is high in moisture and sugar (liver may contain up to 8% of glycogen which is glucose sugar) that makes a perfect breeding ground for bacteria. If pre-cooked meats are to be processed at a later date they should be frozen. Then they should be thawed and re-heated in hot water before going into the grinder. Fresh or chilled liver tastes better than a frozen one.

Beef tripe is white in color and tripe stews are popular in many countries: "flaczki" in Poland or "Sopa de Mondongo" in any Spanish speaking country. Although tripe has practically no meat binding nor water holding properties, it is a nutritious material.

About 10% cooked and finely ground beef tripe can be added to liver sausage. As the tripe is white, the sausage will develop a lighter color.

Cooling. Sausages are usually rinsed with tap water and then placed in cold water. Then they are spread on the table to cool. Finely comminuted liver sausage may be gently massaged at this stage between the thumb and index finger. This will prevent the possibility of accumulating pockets of fat inside of the sausage. When the sausages are cool, they are placed in a refrigerator.

Photo 17.8 Cooling sausages.

Smoking. Once the sausages have cooled down to 30° C (86° F) they are occasionally *cold smoked* at 20-30° C (68 - 86° F) for 1-2 hours, depending on the diameter of a casing. This will provide an additional degree of preservation on the surface of the sausage against bacteria and its shelf life will increase. The casing develops yellow color and the sausage gains smoky flavor. After smoking, sausages must be placed in a refrigerator.

Storing. Liver sausages should be kept at the lowest temperatures above the freezing point possible: 0-2° C (32-34° F) although in a home refrigerator the temperatures of about 3 - 4° C (38 - 40° F) can be expected.

Kosher Liver Sausages. People who object to eating pork on religious reasons can still make liver sausages utilizing poultry and beef livers and replacing pork fat with vegetable oil. The rules remain the same: you need liver, fat (oil), meat and spices. There is no need to worry about fat particles clumping together when the temperature drops below 35° C (95° F) as above freezing point the oil remains in its liquid state.

Liver sausages are quite easy to make and they taste delicious. Although they require more time due to precooking meats, nevertheless all labor is done within boundaries of the kitchen and that makes it easy and enjoyable.

Pâtés (French for "pie") is a type of liver product whose composition resembles a liver sausage but the product is much finer in texture and packed in any shaped container. Very often those molds are inserted in a bigger dish filled with water and then baked. Some are placed in molds lined up with pastry and the pastry lid is placed on top. Often gelatin and decorative fruits are added and brandy or port wine are incorporated. As they are not stuffed in casings, we don't consider them to be sausages. They are quite easy to make as the materials are cooked only once, them emulsified, placed in containers and chilled. Then they can be served. For those interested in learning more, the best advice is to get a good cook book that will cover the subject of "charcuterie".

   Foie Gras (in French "fat liver") is made only with 80% of goose or duck liver with no other meats added.

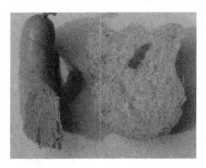

Photo 17.9-top, veal liver sausage.
Photo 17.10-right, all chicken liver sausage.

Both sausages were stuffed in natural casings. Veal liver sausage is visibly lighter and has a superior taste.

Photo 17.11 Liver sausage stuffed in plastic casing.

Braunschweiger Liver Sausage

Braunschweiger is a spreadable liver sausage that gets its name from a town in Germany called Braunschweig.

Meat	Metric	US
pork liver	500 g	1.10 lb.
pork jowls, belly	500 g	1.10 lb.
or fat pork trimmings		

Ingredients per 1000 g (1 kg) of meat:

salt	18 g	3 tsp.
pepper	2.0 g	1 tsp.
marjoram	2.0 g	1 tsp.
nutmeg	1.0 g	½ tsp.
onion, finely chopped	60 g	1 onion

Instructions:

1. Cut back fat into ¼" (6 mm) pieces.
2. Soak liver in cold running water for 1 hour, remove sinews, cut into slices and place in hot water (194°F, 90°C). Poach liver 5 min stirring frequently. This is done to eliminate any traces of blood. Cool liver in cold water for about 5 minutes and leave to drain water away.
3. Grind liver through 2 mm plate and emulsify. Grind fat pieces through 2 mm plate and emulsify.
4. Add salt, spices, onions, emulsified fat and liver and mix everything together.
5. Stuff loosely into pork bungs, pork middles or 65 mm synthetic cellulose casings. Tie the ends with twine and make a hanging loop.
6. Immerse sausages in boiling water and poach at 176°F (80°C) for 50-90 min until the internal meat temperature reaches 155-158°F, (69-70°C).
7. Cool sausages in cold running water for about 10 min, then hang them in air to evaporate moisture.
9. Store in refrigerator.

Note: if smoky flavor is desired, the sausages may be *cold smoked* for a few and then cooled down again.

Liver Sausage

An interesting liver sausage that utilizes any leftover piece of meat. Almost like a commercially made frankfurter or hot dog, the exception being a large proportion of liver.

Meat	Metric	US
pork, beef or lamb liver	300 g	0.66 lb.
brains, tongues, hearts, kidneys	200 g	0.44 lb.
lungs, beef or lamb tripe,		
stomachs, veal casings, beef, veal		
or lamb boiled head meat, boiled		
bones meat, pork trimmings	200 g	0.44 lb.
fat trimmings	300 g	0.66 lb.

Ingredients per 1000 g (1 kg) of meat:

salt	18 g	3 tsp.
pepper	2.0 g	1 tsp.
marjoram	2.0 g	1 tsp.
onion, fresh	60 g	1 onion

Instructions:

1. Soak liver in cold running water for 1 hour, remove sinews, cut into slices and place in hot water (194°F, 90°C). Poach liver for 3-5 minutes stirring frequently. This is done to eliminate any traces of blood. Cool liver in cold water for about 5 min and drain.

2. Cook meats (except liver and brains) in a small amount of water:
   - kidneys and lungs at 176-185°F, 80-85°C.
   - other meats (except fat) at 203°F, 95°C until soft.
   - fat trimmings at 185°F, 85°C until medium-soft.

Save meat stock.

3. Grind liver and brains through 2 mm plate and emulsify. Grind other meats through 2 mm plate and then emulsify.

4. Add salt, spices, all other meats, lastly fat pieces and keep on emulsifying everything together. During emulsifying add about 10% of the stock (in relation to the weight of poached meats) that remained after poaching.

5. Stuff mixture loosely into pork bungs, beef middles or synthetic casings.

6. Immerse sausages in boiling water and poach at 176-185°F (80-85°C) for 50-90 min until the meat reaches 155-158°F (69-70°C) internal temperature.

7. Cool sausages in cold running water for about 10 min then hang in air to evaporate moisture.

8. Store in refrigerator.

Liver Pâté Sausage

Liver Paté Sausage is a quality liver sausage. Most good liver sausages will contain pork liver, some recipes ask for veal liver which is a great choice though expensive. Beef liver is tougher and makes sausages darker. After the meats are emulsified or ground through a fine plate a few times the product can be spreadable like a pâté.

Meat	Metric	US
lean pork or veal	125 g	0.27 lb.
regular pork		
(butt or trimmings)	175 g	0.38 lb.
pork or veal liver	250 g	0.55 lb.
fat pork trimmings	400 g	0.88 lb.
back fat	50 g	0.11 lb.

Ingredients per 1000 g (1 kg) of meat:

salt	18 g	3 tsp.
pepper	2.0 g	1 tsp.
marjoram	2.0 g	1 tsp.
onion, fresh	60 g	1 onion

Instructions:

1. Cut back fat into ¼" (6 mm) pieces.
2. Soak liver in cold running water for 1 hour, remove sinews, cut into slices and place in hot water (194°F, 90°C). Poach liver 3-5 min stirring frequently. This is done to eliminate any traces of blood. Poach diced back fat for 5 minutes. Cool liver in cold water for about 5 min and drain water away.
3. Grind liver through 2 mm plate and emulsify. Grind pork, veal, and fat pieces through 2 mm plate and emulsify.
4. Add salt, spices, pork, veal and keep on emulsifying everything together. Mix the emulsified mixture with ¼" back fat pieces until uniformly distributed. They will stand out in the finished sausage.
5. Stuff loosely into pork bungs, pork middles or synthetic cellulose casings 65 mm. Tie the ends with twine and make a hanging loop.
6. Immerse sausages in boiling water and poach at 176-185°F (80-85°C) for 50-90 min until the meat reaches 155-158°F (69-70°C) internal temperature.
7. Cool sausages in cold running water for about 10 min then hang in air to evaporate moisture.
8. If a smoky flavor is desired, the sausages may be cold smoked for a few hours and then cooled down again.
9. Store in refrigerator.

Liver Sausage - White

White liver sausage exhibits a much lighter color than other sausages due to the careful selection of meats.

Meat	Metric	US
veal or pork livers	300 g	0.66 lb.
veal	100 g	0.22 lb.
pork trimmings, pork jowls,		
picnic, pigs feet	300 g	0.66 lb.
skins	200 g	0.44 lb.
beef tripe, cooked	100 g	0.22 lb.

Ingredients per 1000 g (1 kg) of meat:

salt	18 g	3 tsp.
white pepper	4.0 g	2 tsp.
sugar	2.0 g	½ tsp.
coriander	2.0 g	1 tsp.
cardamom	2.0 g	1 tsp.
nutmeg	1.0 g	½ tsp.
cinnamon, ground	1.0 g	½ tsp.
onion, chopped	30 g	½ onion

Instructions:

1. Cut blood veins out of livers and place them in cold water until all traces of blood are removed. Poach pork liver at 167° F (75° C) for 8 minutes. Scald veal liver with hot water. This is done to eliminate any traces of blood.

2. Cook other meats at 212° F (100° C). Cook beef tripe in hot water (1-2 hours) until soft. Cook pork skins (if used) until soft. Cook pork trimmings, picnic leg and feet meat for 30 minutes (save this stock).

3. Be sure all meats are cold. Grind all meats through a 2 mm (⅛") plate. Refreeze and grind again. Grind liver twice with a 2 mm (⅛") plate until you achieve paste consistency.

4. Combine all meats, liver, spices and mix everything together adding 10 % meat stock in relation to the meat total, which comes to 100 ml (3.3 oz fl).

Note: using food processor. Grind all meats and liver only once when using food processor. Place liver in food processor and emulsify, add a little meat stock if needed. Then add ground meats, 100 ml (10%) of meat stock, salt, spices and emulsify/mix all together..

5. Stuff loosely into 38 - 42 mm diameter hog casings, make straight links about 10 - 14" long. You can use natural beef casings or beef middles up to 3" (8 cm) in diameter.

6. Place sausages into boiling water, let the temperature drop and simmer at 176 - 185° F (80 - 85° C) until the meat reaches 155- 158° F (69 - 70° C) internal temperature. This takes about 50 - 90 minutes, depending on the diameter of the casing.

7. Shower or immerse in cold water cold water for 10 minutes, then hang in air to evaporate moisture.

8. Store in refrigerator.

Liver Sausage with Rice

Liver sausage with rice is a popular sausage in many East-European countries. Rice is a common filler in many Asian sausages.

Meat	Metric	US
pork 70/30 (picnic, butt)	700 g	1.54 lb.
pork liver	300 g	0.66 lb.

Ingredients per 1000 g (1 kg) of meat:

salt	18 g	3 tsp.
pepper	2.0 g	1 tsp.
marjoram	2.0 g	1 tsp.
ginger	0.5 g	⅓ tsp.
nutmeg	1.0 g	½ tsp.
allspice	2.0 g	1 tsp.
onion, chopped	30 g	½ onion
rice	150 g	5 oz.
meat stock	100 ml	3.3 oz fl.

Instructions:

1. Cover meats (not livers) with water and cook in simmering water until soft, save meat stock.
2. Cut blood veins out of livers and place them in cold water until all traces of blood are removed. Poach livers in simmering water at around 167° F (75° C) for 8 - 10 min.
3. Cook rice (don't overcook), then rinse in cold water and drain.
4. Fry onions in oil or lard until golden. Do not make them brown.
5. Be sure all meats are cold. Grind all meats and fried onions through 2 mm plate (1/8"). Slice liver in smaller pieces and grind through 2 mm (1/8") plate.
6. Mix everything with spices and meat stock
7. Stuff not too hard into 38 - 42 mm diameter hog casings, make links about 10 - 14" long. You can use natural beef casings or beef middles up to 3" (8 cm) in diameter.
8. Cook sausages in preheated water at 176-185° F (80-85° C) until the meat reaches 155-158° F (69-70° C) internal temperature. The will take about 50 - 90 minutes depending on the diameter of the casings.
9. Shower or immerse in cold water for 10 minutes then hang in air to evaporate moisture.
10. Store in refrigerator.

Chapter 18

Head Cheeses and Meat Jellies

In English, the name *head cheese* doesn't sound appealing which prevents many people from trying the product. In other languages it is called in a friendlier manner, without the word *"head"* being part of the name. When vinegar is added, it is called "souse" and this already sounds much better. Head cheese, brawn, or souse are not cheeses, but rather jellied loaves or sausages that may or may not be stuffed into the large diameter casing. They can be easily found in places that cater to Central Europeans, Eastern Europeans and Italians.

Traditionally head cheese was made entirely from the meat of the head of a hog, cured and stuffed in large beef bungs or in pork stomachs. We may find this choice of meat today less appealing, forgetting at the same time the fact that pork head meat is highly nutritional and flavorsome. Bear in mind that the head is slow boiled first until the meat easily separates from the bones and then it looks like any other meat. Let's look back into the history of making head cheese. The following comes from an old booklet "Meat Production on the Farm" by the E.H.Wright Company, Lt., Kansas City, Missouri.

"Head cheese is supposed to be better when made from the head of the hog alone; but the odds and ends can be included without harming the product. The head must be shaven clean, the snout skinned and the nostrils cut off just in front of the eyes. The eyes and ear drums should be removed and the fattest part of the head cut away for lard. Great care must be taken in soaking and rinsing the head to free it from all dirt. Boil the head until the meat comes off the bones. The heart and tongue may also be included, if desired. Take out the meat and chop it fine, saving the liquor which will be needed again.

For every twenty-five pounds of meat, use three-fourths pound of salt, one and one-half ounces of black pepper, one half ounce of red pepper, two ounces of ground cloves and one gallon of the liquor in which the head was cooked.

Mix these thoroughly with the finely ground meat and stuff into large casings, boil them again in the liquor in which the head was cooked, until they float. Place them in cold water about fifteen minutes, drain and lay away in a cool place. If the meat is not stuffed it should be packed in shallow vessels and kept cool until used."

Persons living in metropolitan areas cannot buy pork head anyhow but still can make a great tasting product by using pork picnic and pigs feet. Nowadays head cheese can include edible parts of the feet, tongue, and heart. Many of us have made a head cheese before without even realizing it, although pork head meat was not a part of the recipe.

Every time we cook meat stock or chicken soup based on bones we are making a weak version of a head cheese. The reason the soup does not become a meat jelly is because there is too much water in it.

If this stock would simmer for a long time, enough water will be lost, and the resulting liquid, when cooled, will solidify and become a jelly. In the past, after the first and second World War, or even in most countries today, people had no opportunity to buy a commercially made gelatin. And this is why those unappealing cuts of meat like pork head, jowls, skins, hocks, legs and fatty picnic legs started to shine. You cannot make the real head cheese by using noble cuts like hams, tender loins or other tender lean meats. Those cuts don't contain enough connective tissues (collagen) in order to make natural gelatin. *You can use them, but a commercial grade gelatin must be added* and of course the taste and flavor of the finished product will be less satisfactory, although the resulting jelly will be very clear. Making head cheese is quite easy as the procedure does not involve the use of specialized equipment like a grinder or stuffer. Every kitchen contains all utensils that will be needed.

Any professional cookbook lists wonderful meat jellies that incorporates different cuts of meats. They are often garnished with fruits and vegetables. Don't your kids eat fruit jello? You can make your own by mixing commercial gelatin with water and adding fruit to it. Gelatin and glue are derived from a protein called collagen. You may not realize it, but every time you lick quality ice cream, you eat gelatin that came from hides, bone, tendon, skin and connective tissues rich in collagen.

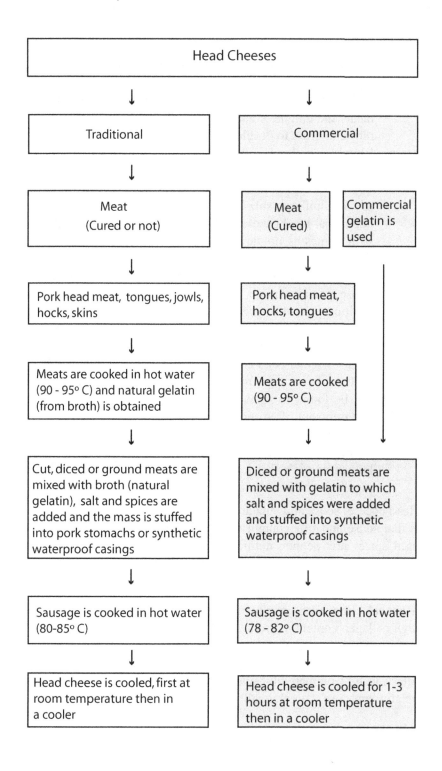

Head Cheeses

Traditional | Commercial

Meat (Cured or not) | Meat (Cured) | Commercial gelatin is used

Pork head meat, tongues, jowls, hocks, skins | Pork head meat, hocks, tongues

Meats are cooked in hot water (90 - 95° C) and natural gelatin (from broth) is obtained | Meats are cooked (90 - 95° C)

Cut, diced or ground meats are mixed with broth (natural gelatin), salt and spices are added and the mass is stuffed into pork stomachs or synthetic waterproof casings | Diced or ground meats are mixed with gelatin to which salt and spices were added and stuffed into synthetic waterproof casings

Sausage is cooked in hot water (80-85° C) | Sausage is cooked in hot water (78 - 82° C)

Head cheese is cooled, first at room temperature then in a cooler | Head cheese is cooled for 1-3 hours at room temperature then in a cooler

Types of Head Cheeses

- Regular head cheese - pork head meat, jowls, skins, snouts, pigs feet, gelatin.
- Tongue head cheese - in addition to the above mentioned meats the tongue is added. It should be cured with salt and nitrite in order to develop a pink color.
- Blood head cheese - head cheese made with blood. Such a head cheese is much darker in color.
- Souse - a typical head cheese to which vinegar has been added. Similar to sulz but not limited to pig's feet only. Most people eat head cheese with vinegar or lemon juice anyway, so it comes as no surprise that vinegar would be added to during manufacturing. It also increases the keeping qualities of the sausage as all foods containing vinegar last longer. Souse contains more jelly than a regular head cheese. In addition pimentos, green peppers or pickles are often added for decoration. Both sulz and souse contain about 75% of meat, 25% of jelly and around 3% of vinegar.
- Sulz - original head cheese made of pigs feet with the bone in. Later bones were removed to facilitate slicing. This name can be found in some older books. It was made with pig's feet only, but often snouts and pig skins were added as well. Meat jellies made from pig's feet are still popular in many European countries, for example in Poland where they are known as pig's feet in aspic (*Nóżki w Galarecie*). Pickled pigs feet which are sold today are basically sulz in vinegar.

Head cheese, souse and sulz are all very similar, the main difference is that souse and sulz contain vinegar and more gelatin. Commonly used spices are: pepper, nutmeg, mace, allspice, cloves, marjoram, cardamom, onions, garlic, caraway, thyme, ginger.

Manufacturing Process

Meat selection. Traditionally made head cheese requires meats with a high collagen content to produce a natural gelatin. Meat cuts such as pork head, hocks and skins are capable of producing a lot of natural gelatin. In addition tongues, hearts, snouts and skins are also used as filler meats. Commercially made products don't depend on natural gelatin and use commercially produced gelatin powder instead.

It is a natural product which is made from bones (pork and beef) and skins. Before meats will be submitted to cooking in hot water a decision has to be made whether the meats will be cured or not. Commercial producer will invariably choose to cure meats with nitrite in order to obtain a typical pink color. Meats that were traditionally used for head cheeses were:

Pork heads (cured or not), usually split in half - boiled in hot water at about 194° F (90° C) until meat was easily removed from bones by hand. The raw heads should be first soaked for 1-2 hours in cold water to remove any traces of coagulated blood.

Pork hocks (cured or not) - boiled at about 194° F (90° C) until meat is easily removed from bones by hand. Pork shanks with meat (picnic), cured or not - boiled in hot water at about 194° F (90° C) until soft.

Skins. Pork skin should be clean without any remaining hair or excess fat. They are cooked at 185-194° F (85-90° C) until soft, requiring a longer cooking time.

Lean pork trimmings (cured or not) - boiled in hot water at about 194° F (90° C) until soft.

Hearts (cured or not) - boiled in hot water at about 194° F (90° C) until soft. Hearts are first cut open and any remaining blood is rinsed away in cold water. The heart is a very hard working muscle and will be of a dark red color due to its high content of *myoglobin*. It should be diced into small diameter pieces (1/4", 5-6 mm) otherwise it will stand out.

Tongues (cured or not) - boiled in hot water at about 194° F (90° C) until soft. Pork or beef tongues are very often used but the outer skin on the tongues must be removed due to its bitter taste. It is easily accomplished once the tongues are submerged for a few minutes in hot water.

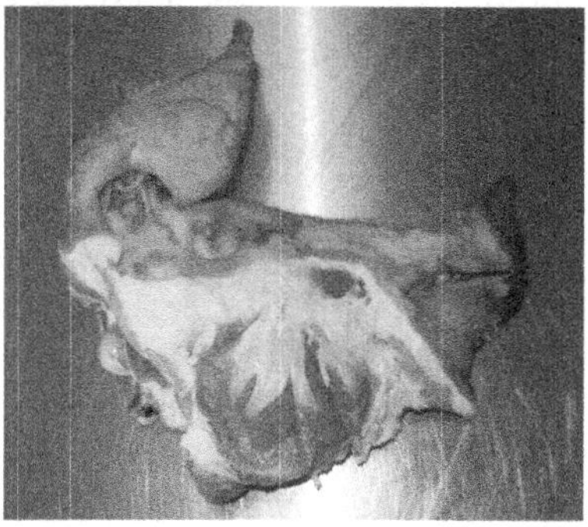

Photo 18.1 The head meat was the main ingredient of head cheese.

Curing meats. Traditionally made products may employ meat curing with nitrite or not. If meats are not cured with sodium nitrite the product will be of grey color, a matter that is of a little concern to a hobbyist. Curing pork head or legs is a hassle that requires an extra space in a cooler, needs dedicated containers and will take some time.

Head cheeses are not smoked so there is very little need for sodium nitrite at least for safety reasons. A commercial producer will cure meats as he is mainly concerned with the profit. The product must look pretty and must have a long shelf life otherwise supermarkets will not carry it. As a customer judges a healthy looking meat product by its red or pink color (poultry meat is an exception) the commercial producer must cure meats and add nitrite to get this pink. Another incentive for a commercial plant to cure meats is that they gain weight and that leads to increased profits.

Cooking meats and making broth. This is basically one easy process but certain rules must be observed. Head cheese differs from other sausages in that meats are cooked before stuffing:

Cover meats with 1-2 inches of water and simmer *below the boiling point* for 2-3 hours. Vigorous boiling creates cloudy stock. The skins should be boiled separately until soft, but still in one piece. When still warm, meats are easily removed from bones. They can be shredded with fingers without using knife. The skins are cut into strips. The resulting meat stock should be strained or filtered though 1-2 layers of cheese cloth. The better clarity obtained, the better looking cheese head will be produced.

When too much water is added it is possible to end up with a broth that will contain not enough gelatin and will not set. This may be corrected by additional boiling of the meat stock. As more water evaporates from the stock, the denser meat broth becomes and upon cooling it will become a jelly. If this does not work you will have to re-heat the weak jelly, strain it and add a packet of a commercial gelatin. Then re-arrange meats on a plate and pour the hot gelatin over them. This will become a serious issue if the meat was already stuffed into the casing. When in doubt, it is safer to add powdered gelatin straight from the beginning than to create unnecessary extra work for yourself.

Note: if you add powdered gelatin directly to hot liquid, it might stick together and form lumps. It is safer to stir powdered gelatin into cold water so that it dissolves easily. Then pour slowly the gelatin into hot broth stirring it at the same time.

As an extra precaution you may test your meat broth before it is added to the casing. Place some of it in a refrigerator and see whether it solidifies within one hour. If not enough collagen is present, for example mainly lean meats were used, little gelatin will be produced and the resulting meat stock will not solidify. This can be easily corrected by adding commercial gelatin. For best results mix powdered gelatin with the cold meat broth and not with water. Water will dilute the flavor of the broth.

Photo 18.2 Cooking head.

Photo 18.3 The meat is separated from bones.

Photo 18.4 Cooked meat trimmings.

Photo 18.5 Cooking head cheeses.

Cutting meats. The grinder is not employed as this will extract proteins and will break the fat's structure. *As a result a cloudy stock will be obtained.* Meats are much easier to cut into smaller pieces when chilled. After they are cut, it is a good idea to rinse them briefly in hot water as *this will eliminate unnecessary grease that would normally cloud the jelly.* Until this point, the process of making head cheese or meat jelly has been the same. What differentiates them is that head cheese is stuffed into a casing and meat jelly is not.

Mixing. Meats are mixed with all other ingredients. Although the recipe provides the amounts of all ingredients, nevertheless due to precooking meats in water, then washing them with hot water later on, it is recommended to taste the mixture and refine the recipe if needed. *Do not mix meat and broth together before stuffing.* The hot jelly will draw some of the juices out of the meat and the jelly will become cloudy. A good idea is to first scald meat with hot water to remove any grease that might cloud the gelatin.

Stuffing. Head cheese was traditionally stuffed into pig stomach. Pig stomach is a one unit chamber of uniform oval shape with two easy to saw openings. Stomachs of a cow or a sheep are three chambers in one unit. The shape of those stomachs is irregular and not easy to fill. After filling, the stomach's opening had to be sewn with butcher's twine.

Photo 18.6
Turning stomachs inside out for cleaning.

Photo 18.7 Scraping off fat.

Photo 18.8 Washing stomachs.

In most cases stomachs you buy will be pre-washed. All you will need is to reverse them, scrape off the fat and wash them.

In the USA pig stomachs are hard to obtain. The best advice is to visit Asiatic meat markets. Today, head cheese is stuffed into a large diameter synthetic casing, preferably a plastic one that will prevent loss of aspic during cooking.

The tied or clipped at the bottom casing is held vertically and meat pieces are placed first. Then a gelatin, from naturally produced meat broth or made from a commercial powder, is carefully poured down into the casing. This is normally done through a big funnel using a ladle. The casing is tied or clipped on the top and head cheese is ready for cooking.

Photo 18.9 Filling up the stomachs.

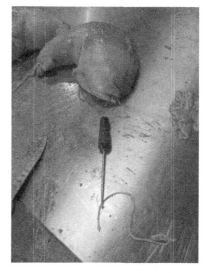

Photo 18.1 Basic tools are required.

Photo 18.11 After filling, the stomachs are stitched up and tied with twine.

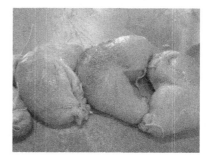

Photo 18.12 Filled stomachs.

Cooling. After cooking head cheese should be left at room temperature for a few hours. After that, the head cheese is placed between two wooden boards. The top board is weighted and the sausage is stored overnight in a refrigerator. This permanently flattens the head cheese and gives him the rectangular shape with rounded corners.

Photo 18.13 Cooked head cheeses cooling off.

Photo 18.14 A head cheese is a big piece of a sausage.

Photo 18.15 Head cheeses cut into smaller portions.

Photo 18.16 Head cheese with a lot of aspic.

Photo 18.17 Head cheese.

There are many variations of head cheeses. Some contain more jelly as more broth was added. Ingredients like red peppers, olives, garlic or vinegar may be added. They all share a common factor, they are delicious.

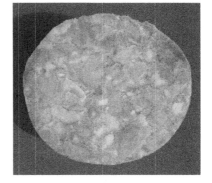

Photo 18.18 Head cheese with tongues.

Photo 18.19 Head cheese with smaller size filler meat.

Meat jellies

Meat jellies are much easier to make than head cheeses as they don't have to be stuffed which greatly simplifies the procedure. In addition no secondary cooking is needed. Cooked meats are arranged on the bottom of the container, meat broth is carefully poured over it and left for cooling. It basically becomes a meat jelly.

Meat jelly although technically not a sausage, follows the same rules of production as a head cheese. They fit more into general cuisine and many fancy products can be created based on one's ingenuity and imagination. They are basically more refined products where looks of the products play an important role. Because of that, they contain solid chunks of lean "show meat" and are made with a commercial gelatin in order to obtain perfectly clear jelly. Different meats can be incorporated in meat jellies, for example fish fillets, skinless and boneless chicken breast, diced ham etc. As a rule meat jellies don't include low value meat products like skins, snouts, or hearts. Chicken breast or fish fillet will make a great show meat in any meat jelly.

Meat jellies are easily decorated:

- A thin layer of hot gelatin is placed in a form or deep plate and allowed to set in a cooler.
- Decorative items are placed on top of the set gelatin.
- A new layer of gelatin is poured on top and allowed to set in a cooler.
- Meat and the remaining gelatin are placed on top and allowed to set in a cooler.
- When ready for consumption the form is briefly placed in hot water which melts a thin layer of gelatin around it. Turning the form upside down will release the meat jelly with decorations being on top.

Decorative pieces such as slices of oranges, apples or hard boiled eggs are used. Herbs, cubed cheese, cracked pepper, slices of pickle, carrots, peas, corn, green scallions are often used in meat jellies.

Photo 18.20 Diced ham jelly made with commercial gelatin. Sliced hard boiled eggs used for decoration.

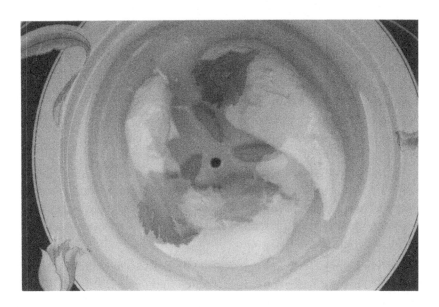

Photo 18.21 Chicken jelly made with commercial gelatin.

Photo 18.22 Fish jelly made with commercial gelatin.

Gelatin

Natural gelatin is produced from meat stock such as the one used for head cheese manufacture. Natural stock will not be as clear as the one made by dissolving commercial gelatin powder with water. The main reason the natural stock is often cloudy is that it is boiled and not simmered. *Do not to boil the stock, always simmer.* If you cook your stock gently, below the boiling point, the fat will not emulsify in water and the stock will remain clearer.

The natural gelatin that is obtained from the natural stock has a superior taste and flavor that comes from boiling meats and ingredients that were put with meats into the pot. The ingredients such as peppercorns, bay leaf, pimentos, and soup greens are often added to create a better flavor.

Clarifying stock. The natural stock can be clarified to obtain a clearer version. This is a basic cooking technique that every cook is familiar with.

1. Once when the stock cools down a little, the fat will accumulate on the surface and can be easily scooped up and discarded.

2. Then the liquid can be strained through a cheese cloth.

3. For every quart of stock, lightly beat 3 egg whites with 2 Tbsp of water and 1 tsp of vinegar.

4. Add the egg white mix to the stock. Bring stock to boil, then reduce heat and simmer for 20 minutes. Stir constantly with the soup ladle. Do not boil. The egg white will attract fat and impurities and will coagulate. It may float on top of the stock, which should be much clearer now.

5. Let it cool for 15 minutes.

6. Put several layers of cheese cloth in colander and pour the stock carefully over it.

7. Refrigerate stock overnight. Skim any remaining fat off the top. Now you have crystal clear stock with great flavor.

Note: number 3 & 4 steps are optional, but will further clarify the stock.

Photo 18.23 Home made meat jelly with natural gelatin. The fat layer on top is left on purpose as it will be spread on bread. This is very tasteful fat that has been obtained by boiling meats with vegetables and spices.

Commercial gelatin is a powder that is obtained from skins, hooves, and other meat cuts that contain a lot of connective tissue. It has no flavor, but is very clear and convenient to apply. A little salt and white vinegar should be added to give it some character. Packets of powdered gelatin are available in every supermarket and all that is required is to mix it with water. Gelatin use is not limited to meats, and you can use it with fruits and juices as well. The size of the packet will dictate how much water is needed. Usually, 1 part of gelatin to 6 parts water will produce a good jelly. If more powder is added the jelly will be much thicker.

To make a jelly:

1. Pour the gelatin into a container with *cold water* and let it stand until the gelatin absorbs the water. Do not stir.
2. Place this container inside another vessel filled with hot water.
3. Heat the water until the gelatin solution reaches 160° F (72° C).

Useful Information

Head cheeses, liver sausages and blood sausages belong to a special group of products that incorporate less noble cuts of meat that will be much harder to sell to the public at least in their original form. What separates those products from other common sausages is the fact that meats are precooked before being stuffed into casings and then they are submitted to a hot water cooking process. Another peculiarity is that all those products are often made *without being stuffed into casings.*

- Head cheeses are placed in forms, boiled in water and they become meat jellies.
- Head cheese is usually eaten cold or at room temperature as a luncheon meat.
- Head cheese freezes very well.
- Diced meats must be washed with hot water to remove any fat particles from the surface and then drained. This will make them look sharp in jelly.
- Gelatin should be soaked in cold (room temperature) water for about 15 min to swell and then mixed with hot water.
- Commercial gelatin produces a very clean, transparent jelly. Traditionally made meat jelly of pork and beef meat may use natural gelatin (broth) as the looks of the product are less important. Lean cuts of meat such as hams, pork loins, chicken breast or fish fillet will look much better in a clean, commercially made gelatin. On the other hand the natural meat broth may be sometimes cloudy but has superior taste.
- Commercial gelatin packets come with instructions and are available in every supermarket, for example Knox® brand. If jelly does not want to set in because gelatin was made too thin, reheat your weak jelly, strain it and reinforce it with an extra packet of gelatin. Then pour your stronger and warmer gelatin over the meat.

- Meat jellies can be made of lean meats and will taste good even if little salt is added (1.0 %)
- The gelatin is often made with wine, brandy and other spirits to create a high quality product.
- Show meat, for example tongues, may be cured in order for meat to develop a pink color.

Traditionally made head cheese or meat jelly may look less pretty but will be a product of much higher quality due to the following reasons:

- No chemicals are added.
- No water is pumped into the product (stronger meatier flavor).
- It contains the natural broth. Commercially prepared gelatin is a combination of neutrally flavored powder (natural glue) and water and natural broth is a combination of natural glue plus highly flavored meat stock that remains after cooking bones. On cooling this gelatin will subsequently become a jelly and accounts for about 30% of the total weight of the product. What would you prefer to have in your head cheese or meat jelly: 30% of water or 30% of meat broth?
- meat jelly is a fat free and rich in protein product.

Note: if gelatin solution is heated above 160° F (72° C), it will lose its binding power.

Chicken Meat Jelly

Meat
chicken breast,
fully cooked

Instructions:
1. Make 1 liter/quart gelatin. Add 1 Tbs white vinegar and 1 Tbs white wine.
2. Pour a small amount of hot gelatin on the bottom of container, then place it in a refrigerator.
3. Once the solution hardens, place a slice of orange, hard boiled egg, carrot, apple or any decoration of your choice on top of solid gelatin.
4. More hot gelatin is added again to set the slices of fruit in place and the container is placed in the refrigerator again.
5. Once the solution solidifies it is removed from the refrigerator and the whole pieces of cold chicken breast are placed into the container.
6. The container is filled with gelatin and placed in the refrigerator overnight for the jelly to solidify.
7. Before serving the container is flipped upside down so that the entire product drops out. It helps to dip the container first for a short while in hot water to melt a tiny amount of gelatin that is attached to the container inside.

Farmer Head Cheese

Countryside Head Cheese is one of the easiest head cheeses to make. You can substitute pork heads with picnics. Blood may be omitted.

Meat	Metric	US
pork heads (with bones)	800 g	1.76 lb.
pork legs (with bones)	180 g	0.40 lb.
blood	20 g	0.04 lb.

Ingredients per 1000 g (1 kg) of meat:

salt	18 g	3 tsp.
pepper	2.0 g	1 tsp.
allspice, ground	2.0 g	1 tsp.

Instructions:

1. Wash pork heads and legs in cold running water.
2. Poach heads and legs in separate containers at 185° F, (85° C) until meat can be removed from the bone (try not to cook the meat). Save some of the left over stock liquid for later. Spread all cuts on a flat surface to cool.
3. Cut head meat into 1/2" (12 mm) cubes. Grind leg meat with 3/16" (3 mm) plate.
4. Mix all meats with salt, spices, blood and add some of the saved stock.
5. Stuff mixture not too tight into hog stomachs or beef bungs about 12" (30 cm) long, 8" (20 cm) wide and 3" (8 cm) thick. Saw the ends with butchers twine.
6. Cook in water at 180° F (82° C) for about 90-120 min (depends on a size) until internal temperature of 154°-158° F (68°-70° C) is obtained. If stuffed bungs swim up to the surface prick them with a needle to release air.
7. Place head cheeses on a flat surface to cool them down and let more moisture evaporate. Then cool them down to below 42° F (6° C), place in refrigerator and put some weight on top of it (determines the shape and the thickness of the finished product).
8. After cooling clean head cheese of any fat and aspic that accumulated on the surface, even them out and cut off excess twine.
9. Store in refrigerator.

Haggis

Haggis is a traditional Scottish dish that resembles Pennsylvania Scrapple originally made by early German settlers in America.

Haggis	Scrapple
sheep offal (heart, liver, lungs)	pig offal (heart, liver, lungs)
oatmeal	cornmeal
in casings (originally in sheep stomachs)	meatloaf
boiled	fried

Haggis was a popular meal for the poor, as it was made from cheap leftover parts of a sheep, the most common livestock in Scotland. Meats are minced with fat, onions, oatmeal, spices, meat stock, and traditionally boiled in the animal's stomach for about three hours. Cooked Haggis is normally served with Scotch whisky.

Meat	Metric	US
sheep (or beef, pork) heart	500 g	1.10 lb.
sheep (or beef, pork) liver	300 g	0.66 lb.
suet (beef or pork back fat)	200 g	0.44 lb.
oatmeal	300 g	10.5 oz

Ingredients per 1000 g (1 kg) of meat:

salt	18 g	3 tsp.
pepper	4 g	2 tsp.
nutmeg	1 g	½ tsp.
onion, finely chopped	60 g	1 onion

Instructions:
1. Simmer hearts in hot water, 180° F (82° C) until tender. Simmer liver for 10 minutes. Save meat stock.
2. Grind meats and fat through ¼" (6 mm) grinder plate.
3. Bring stock to a boil and add all meats and other ingredients, stirring often.
4. Stuff into beef caps or water proof plastic casings and cook in water at 170° F (77° C) until internal temperature reaches 160° F (71° C).
5. Cool and refrigerate.

Notes: don't confuse oatmeal with instant oatmeal that we eat for breakfast. For sausages we use *steel cut oats* which are very hard and must be soaked overnight. They are available in food supermarkets.

Head Cheese - City

Head cheese also known as brawn or souse is a jellied meat sausage that is stuffed in a large diameter casing or it may be placed in a form becoming a jellied meat loaf. Traditionally made head cheese incorporated meats that were rich in collagen which was required to produce a natural gelatin (broth) that after cooling became a jelly. The best meat was highly flavored pork head meat and pork legs and feet (hocks). A person living in a large city may not be able to find these cuts anymore but intelligent substitutions can easily be made by buying commonly available supermarket carried meats. The final product will be of very high quality yet much easier to make. The easiest way to make a head cheese is to think in terms of cooking a heavy meat broth which will be stuffed into casings.

Meat	Metric	US
pork picnic, hocks	1000 g	2.20 lb.

Ingredients *per 1000 g (1 kg) of meat:*

salt	18 g	3 tsp.
white pepper	2.0 g	1 tsp.
garlic	3.5 g	1 clove

Instructions:
Making Broth
1/2 pork picnic (front leg) or pork butt. The amount of boiled meat available for further processing will be about 2.2 lbs. (1 kg). Picnic meat is fattier with more connective tissues (collagen) and will produce more gelatin than a butt. The butt has only one little bone and less connective tissue. Its meat is leaner than a picnic and a commercial gelatin (natural product made from bones and skins) will have to be added.
Two pig feet (hocks). If you use hocks and picnic enough natural gelatin (broth) should be produced to create jelly on cooling.

3 bay leaves
1 stalk celery
1 carrot
Salt and pepper to taste
1 package of gelatin (if needed)

1. Place meats and other ingredients in a pot and cover with about two inches of water. Cook below boiling point for about 3 hours or until meat separates easily from bones. Strain liquid and save for later.

2. Separate meats from bones. It is easier to perform this task when meats are still warm. Cut meats into smaller pieces. It is easier to cut them when they are chilled. Normally the leaner the meat the larger diameter the cut. Fatter meats and fat will be chopped into smaller pieces.

3. Dissolve gelatin in 1/4 cup room temperature water and add to your hot meat broth.

4. Mix meats with meat broth/gelatin and add garlic and salt and pepper to taste. Head cheese does not require much salt and a low sodium product can be made.

5. Now you can go two different ways:

a. pour your head cheese into containers, let them sit for 2 hours at room temperature and then place in a refrigerator. Keep it there for 12 hours to give the head cheese time to set. The result is the meat jelly.

b. stuff with a ladle into large diameter waterproof casings, clip the ends and cook (simmer) in hot water at about, 185° F (85° C). A rough estimate will be about 20 min for each ½" (12 mm) of diameter of a casing. Or using a thermometer cook to 160° F (72° C) internal meat temperature. Then place at room temperature for about 2 hours for gelatin to set. Place for 12 hours in a refrigerator.

Notes:

Don't add garlic when making broth as it loses its flavor very rapidly when being cooked. Add garlic when mixing meats with gelatin.

It is easy to add a degree of sophistication to your product by decorating your gelatin.

Meat jelly is usually removed from a container and turned upside down. This way any decoration will rest on top of the product. It is eaten cold with bread and some vinegar or lemon juice is sprinkled on top of it.

Head cheese that was stuffed in casings is sliced and eaten like any other regular sausage.

Head Cheese - Italian

Although of Italian origin this head cheese has been always popular in Poland.

Meat	Metric	US
pork heads (with bones)	750 g	1.65 lb.
beef (with bones)	120 g	0.26 lb.
pork skins	130 g	0.28 lb.

Ingredients per 1000 g (1 kg) of meat:

salt	18 g	3 tsp.
pepper	4.0 g	2 tsp.
caraway seeds	4.0 g	2 tsp.

Instructions:

1. Poach meats in a small amount of water
   * pork heads at 185°F, 85°C.
   * beef head meat and pork skins at 203°F, 95°C.
   * After poaching remove meat from pork heads and spread all meats apart on a flat surface to cool.
   * Save meat stock.
2. Boiled pork head meat: cut into strips 1.5 x 2 cm (⅝ x ¾") by 7-10 cm (2 x 4")
   * Boiled beef head meat: cut into strips 1 x 5 cm (⅜ x 2")
   * Boiled skins and tougher meat parts: grind with 3 mm (⅛") plate.
3. Mix all meats with spices adding 10% of meat stock in relation to the weight of pork heads with bones. The meat stock is the result of boiling pork heads.
4. Stuff mixture not too tight into hog stomachs or beef bungs about 12" (30 cm) long, 8" (20 cm) wide and 3" (8 cm) thick. Saw the ends with butchers twine.
5. Poach head cheeses at 180°F (82°C) for 90-150 min (depending on size) until the internal temperature of the meat reaches 15-158°F (69-70°C). Remove air with a needle from pieces that swim up to the surface.
6. Spread head cheeses on a flat surface at 2-6°C (35-43°F) and let the steam out. Then flatten them with weight and cool them to below 6°C (43°F).
7. After cooling clean head cheeses of any fat and aspic that accumulated on the surface, even them out and cut off excess twine. Store in refrigerator.

Notes:
Commercial producers will cure heads with nitrite in order for meat to develop a pink color.

Head Cheese - Tongue

Meat	Metric	US
pork or veal tongues	350 g	0.77 lb.
skinless pork jowls	400 g	0.88 lb.
pork skins	50 g	0.11 lb.
pork liver	100 g	0.22 lb.
blood	100 g	0.22 lb.

Ingredients per 1000 g (1 kg) of meat:

salt	18 g	3 tsp.
pepper	4.0 g	2 tsp.
marjoram	4.0 g	2 tsp.
garlic	3.5 g	1 clove
cloves, ground	2.0 g	1 tsp.

Instructions:

1. Blanch tongues with hot water and remove the skin.
2. Cut tongues into 1-1¾" (25-40 mm) cubes. Mix thoroughly with 0.87 g (⅓ tsp.) Cure #1, cover with a cloth and place in a refrigerator for 72 hours. You may skip this curing step but the tongues in your head cheese would be of a poor gray color instead of vivid pink.
3. Except liver, poach other meats in water until soft:
   - tongues at 185° F (85° C).
   - skins at 203° F (95° C).
   - jowls at 185° F (85° C).
3. Cut boiled skinless dewlap into 5 mm (¼") cubes. Dice or cut boiled pork or veal tongues into 4 cm (1¾") cubes (They were previously cut for curing, if this step was employed). Grind boiled skins through 2-3 mm plate. Grind raw pork liver through 2-3 mm plate.
4. Add salt and spices to cut and ground meats and mix thoroughly with blood.
5. Stuff into middles or bladders loosely and sew the ends with twine. You may use large diameter waterproof casings.
6. Poach at 82°C (180°F) for 90-120 min (depending on size) until the internal temperature of the meat reaches 68-70°C (154-158°F). Remove air with a needle from pieces that swim up to the surface.
7. Spread head cheeses on a flat surface at 2-6°C (35-43°F) and let the steam out. Then flatten them with weight and cool them to below 6°C (43°F).
8. After cooling clean head cheeses of any fat and aspic that accumulated on the surface, even them out and cut off excess twine.
9. Store in refrigerator.

Meat Jelly

Meat	**Metric**	**US**
lean pork, ham or lean pork butt	1000 g	2.20 lb.

Ingredients:

salt	18 g	3 tsp.
Cure #1	2.5 g	½ tsp.
white vinegar	15 g	1 Tbsp.
gelatin	see manufacturer's instructions	

Instructions:

1. Cut lean meat into 1" (5 cm) cubes. Mix with salt and Cure #1. Pack tightly in a container, cover with a cloth and place for 2-3 days in refrigerator.
2. Cook meat until 154-160° F (68-72° C) internal temperature is reached.
3. Make 1 liter/quart gelatin. Add 1 Tbs. white vinegar and 1 Tbs. white wine.
4. Pour a small amount of hot gelatin on the bottom of the container, then place it in a refrigerator.
5. Once the solution hardens, place a slice of orange, hard boiled egg, carrot, apple or any decoration of your choice on top of the solid gelatin.
6. More hot gelatin is added again to set the slices of fruit in place and the container is placed in the refrigerator again.
7. Once the solution solidifies it is removed from the refrigerator and the diced lean meat cubes are placed into the container.
8. The container is filled with gelatin and placed in the refrigerator overnight for the jelly to solidify.
9. Before serving the container is flipped upside down so that the entire product drops out. It helps to dip the container first for a short while in hot water to melt a tiny amount of gelatin that is attached to the container inside.

Notes:

Whole pieces of meat such as pork butt or loin can be cured in brine and then cooked. Then they can be sliced and used as "show meat" in meat jellies.

Cure #1 may be omitted but the color of the product will be gray.

Pennsylvania Scrapple

Pennsylvania Scrapple, also known as Pennsylvania Dutch Scrapple or Philadelphia Scrapple, is a delicious pork dish that was created by German settlers in Eastern Pennsylvania. The word scrapple comes from "scraps" which is the definition for leftover bits of food and pieces of animal fat or cracklings. The original Pennsylvania Deutsche (name changed in time to Pennsylvania Dutch) immigrants were hard working people that used less noble parts of a butchered pig (pork skins, jowls, snouts, ears, heart, tongue, brains, kidneys, head meat, liver, pork bones, some claim that pork neck bones are the best) to make scrapple. Those leftover meats were used for making original scrapple though today's recipes often call for parts like loin or picnic. Originally buckwheat was an essential part of the recipe although many of today's recipes call for a mixture of cornmeal and buckwheat half and half.

Meat	Metric	US
pork meat (heart, tongue, liver, head meat, brains, kidneys, jowls, picnics, legs)	1000 g	2.20 lb.

Ingredients per 1000 g (1 kg) of meat:

salt	18 g	3 tsp.
pepper	4.0 g	2 tsp.
chopped onion	60 g	1 onion
buckwheat flour	80 g	1 cup

Optional spices:

marjoram, crumbled	2 g	3 tsp.
thyme, crumbled	2 g	3 tsp.
nutmeg	2 g	1 tsp.
sage, crumbled	2 g	3 tsp.
mace	0.5 g	⅓ tsp.
red pepper	0.5 g	⅓ tsp.

Instructions:
1. Cover the meat and bones with cold water, add salt, pepper and onions and bring to a boil. Reduce heat, skim off the foam cover with lid and simmer for 1-2 hours until meat is tender.
2. Remove the meat, scrape off the meat from the bones. Discard bones but save the stock.
3. Chop the meat very fine by hand or grind through 3/16" (4 mm) plate.

4. Place meat in stock, mix and taste. Add more salt or pepper if needed. Many recipes call for additional spices, now is the time to add them.

5. Make sure the stock with meat is hot and start slowly adding buckwheat flour stirring the mixture with a paddle. Make sure it is smooth and thick - the paddle should stand up in the pot.

6. Pack the mixture into baking pans about 8 x 4 x 2" or 9 x 4 x 3". The pans should be either oiled or lined up with wax paper. Cover and place in the refrigerator for at least 4 hours.

7. Cut into 1/2" individual slices. To freeze, place the slices between pieces of butcher paper.

Notes:

Serve in a large skillet, brown scrapple slices on both sides in a hot oil until brown and crisp on each side. You can dredge the slices with flour and fry them.

Pickled Pigs Feet

Pickled feet are usually cured in brine with sodium nitrite (Cure #1).
There are two methods:

Method I.

1. Pigs feet are immersed for 12 days in 1 gallon 80° SAL brine

water	1 gal.	3.80 kg
salt	2.2 lb.	1.00 kg
Cure #1	4.2 oz.	120 g

2. Pigs feet are removed from brine, skinned and the entire foot is cooked for 3-4 hours at 200° F (94° C), (below boiling point) until meat separates from bones.
3. Feet are rinsed in cold water, then placed in a refrigerator.
4. Feet are split and semi-boned.
5. They are placed in jars with white vinegar. Whole peppercorns and bay leaves are added for flavoring.

Method II.

1. Pigs feet are immersed in brine for 4 hours.
2. Temperature of the brine is increased to 180°F (82°C) and the feet are cooked for 3-4 hours.
3. Then they are cooled in cold running water and packed in white vinegar in glass jars.

Notes:
Feet can be bone-less or semi-boneless depending on preference.

Souse

Souse also known as Sulz is a head cheese to which vinegar has been added. It is a jellied meat sausage that is stuffed in a large diameter casing or simply as a jellied meat loaf. As most people add vinegar or squeeze some lemon juice into head cheese when eating it, so it should not be a surprise that producers add vinegar (5%) into the mix. This added the benefit of a longer shelf life of the product as all foods containing vinegar last longer. The reason is an increased acidity of the product which inhibits the growth of bacteria.

Meat	Metric	US
pigs feet	730 g	1.60 lb.
meat broth (from cooking pigs feet)	220 g	0.48 lb.
vinegar (5%)	50 g	0.11 lb.

Ingredients per 1000 g (1 kg) of meat:

salt	18 g	3 tsp.
pepper	2.0 g	1 tsp.

Instructions:

1. Place pigs feet, salt and pepper in a pot and cover with about two inches of water. Cook below the boiling point for about 2 hours or until meat separates easily from bones. Head cheese does not require much salt and a low sodium product can be made.

2. Strain liquid and save for later.

3. Separate meats from bones. It is easier to perform this task when meats are still warm.

4. Cut meats into smaller pieces. It is easier to cut them when they are chilled.

5. Now you can go two different ways:

a. pour your souse into containers, let them sit for 2 hours at room temperature and then place in a refrigerator. Keep it there for 12 hours to give the souse time to set.

b. stuff with a ladle into large diameter waterproof casings, clip the ends and cook in hot water below the boiling point at 185° F (about 85° C). A rough estimate will be about 20 min for each 1/2" (12 mm) of diameter of a casing. Then place at room temperature for about 2 hours for gelatin to set. Place for 12 hours into refrigerator.

Notes:

Green peppers, pimentos or pickles are often added to souse to make it visually pleasing. You may add garlic, allspice, caraway, marjoram or other spices you like.

Sulz

Meat
pigs feet

Ingredients:
salt, whole pepper, bay leaf, soup vegetables.

Instructions: think in terms of cooking a meat stock that is based on bones.

1. Place pigs feet in cold water, add whole peppercorns, bay leaf, carrot, onion and cook pigs feet until meat separates from bones. Use enough water to cover the feet. This might take 3 hours.
2. Remove feet but save the stock. Remove fat from the top, then clarify meat stock by filtering it through cheese cloth. Add about 1.5% of vinegar which comes to about 1 Tsp per liter of stock.
3. Separate meat from bones when feet are still hot.
4. Pour a little stock into the container.
5. Place meat on the bottom of the container.
6. Pour stock carefully into the container.
7. Place in refrigerator.

Notes:
Green peppers, scallions, pickles, pimentos, carrots, or sliced boiled eggs are often added to increase the attractiveness of a product.
The Polish popular product *"Nóżki w Galarecie"* is processed in the above manner, the only difference is that vinegar is not added to stock. Instead each customer sprinkles his portion with vinegar or lemon juice according to his liking.

Chapter 19

Blood Sausages

Blood sausages have been made for thousands of years and every country has its own recipes. The oldest ever reference to a sausage mentioned in written literature comes from Homer's Odyssey written in the ninth century B.C., book XX, verse 25:

"And as a man with a paunch pudding, that has been filled with blood and fat, tosses it back and forth over a blazing fire, and the pudding itself strains hard to be cooked quickly; so he was twisting and turning back and forth, meditating how, though he was alone against many, he could lay hands on the shameless suitors."

Different cultures and/or regions have their own versions of blood sausage. These recipes are generally variable takes on a similar theme. Whatever the name – Black pudding (UK, Ireland), Boudin noir (France), Blutwurst (Germany), Morcilla (Spain), Jelito (Czech), Kaszanka (Poland), or Mustamakkara (Finland), the main ingredients are as follows: blood – either from pig, sheep, lamb, cow, or goose; a filler that varies with region (e.g., oatmeal, buckwheat, bread crumbs, barley, or other grains); onions and regional spices. All of these are typically smashed together and stuffed into a sausage casing.

Unfortunately many people hearing the word blood imagine a blood sucking vampire circling over their heads and they assume that this is not a healthy sausage. I have asked for a blood sausage in the large supermarket in Florida and the sales lady did not know what it was. Being a friendly person she submitted the question to her manager who came over but he also did not have the slightest idea what I was talking about. Mention blood sausage or head cheese to an average American consumer and he is looking the other way. Yet mention blutwurst to a German, black pudding to an Englishman or morcilla to a Spaniard and you will see a spark in the eye. In all areas of the world people love those products as they taste great. Unfortunately many of us display a preconceived opinion on some products.

When they hear blood sausage they imagine that blood is bad they look the other way. Then, they go to a restaurant, order a medium rare steak and lick the every drop of blood that is on the plate. Fully cooked blood in a sausage is not acceptable but raw fresh blood in a steak is fine...

Meat selection

Blood sausages were originally made from inexpensive raw materials such as pork head meat, jowls, tongues, groins, skins, pork or veal lungs, pork liver, beef and lamb liver, pork snouts, beef and liver lips, udders, beef and lamb tripe, veal casings, pork stomachs, pork heart, boiled bone meat and of course blood. This way any part of the animal was utilized and a highly nutritional product was made. In times of war and other hard times when meat was scarce, fillers were added to increase the volume of the sausage.

Generally speaking a blood sausage is composed of diced, cooked fat pork and finely ground cooked meat and gelatin producing materials, mixed with beef or pork blood. The whole is spiced and stuffed into a casing. Sometimes pork or lamb tongues are included, in which instance the product is known as tongue and blood sausage.

Fat. Back fat, belly, jowls, fat trimmings or even lard are suitable for blood sausage. Sliceable blood sausages look much nicer with visible pieces of white fat in it. To achieve this effect hard fat such as pork back fat should be cut into 4-5 mm (about 3/16") cubes which should be blanched briefly (5 min) in hot water (90°-95° C, 194°-203° F). *This seals the surface of fat cubes and prevents blood from entering and discoloring it.*

Skins. Skins are a very important ingredient as they contain a lot of collagen which will turn into gelatin during heat treatment. During subsequent cooling this gelatin becomes gel and that creates a better texture of the sausage. In sliceable blood sausages which are usually consumed cold, this will positively contribute to the sliceability of the sausage. Don't discard skin when trimming pork cuts, but freeze it for later use in head cheeses, blood or liver sausages.

Fillers. Many countries have their own traditionally preferred fillers that are incorporated in sausages:

England and Ireland - rusk, barley, rice, potatoes, flour, oatmeal.
Poland - buckwheat groats, barley, bread crumbs, rice, semolina.
Spain - milk, rice, eggs, cheese.

Germany - barley, rye and potato flour, oats, pumpkin, white bread
France - bread crumbs
Sweden - rye meal,
Argentina - wheat gluten (seitan), corn flour, flour.

Filler material such as rice, barley or buckwheat groats must be pre-cooked. Groats can be found in supermarkets, but they have been factory processed and are often modified to make them attractive to a buyer. The real natural groats can be ordered from online distributors such as the Sausage Maker, Bulk Foods or Bob's Red Mill. Many recipes call for oatmeal, but don't confuse this with instant oats which are served for breakfast. For sausages we use steel cut oats, which are tough groats which must be soaked overnight. They can be pre-cooked as well, but don't make them mushy.

The addition of filler material makes a sausage very economical, the fact of importance for those making sausages for profit.

Photo 19.1 Buckwheat groats. Barley is also often used.

Photo 19.2 Buckwheat groats added to water.

Photo 19.3 Filtering cooked groats.

With such variety of filler materials, different meats that can be selected, and spices that can be chosen, it is hardly surprising to see the huge number of recipes floating around. And they are all good, but as we often repeat, it is not only the recipe that makes a great sausage, but the way you make it.

Blood. Blood from any animal including poultry can be used for making blood sausage, although pig and cow bloods are most often used. Pork blood is a better choice than beef blood as it is much lighter in color. Beef blood can be very dark red or almost black in color and was traditionally used in England. The amount of blood in a sausage typically vary from 5%-60%, however, there are sausages for example Spanish "Morcilla Lustre Malagueña" which is made with blood only (100%) plus salt and spices. The more blood added, the darker the cooked sausage.

Blood coagulates easily and is stirred frequently when collected during the slaughter. It must be refrigerated and used within 1-2 days or frozen for later, given the fat that being a great food for bacteria it spoils rapidly. Before use it must be stirred again and filtered, otherwise the sausage may contain lumps of blood. Adding salt or nitrite is not effective in extending blood's shelf life. In time blood plasma separates from the blood and water accumulates on top and the blood must be stirred before use. Commercial producers add anticoagulation chemicals like trisodium citrate to prevent the coagulation of blood. It is not easy to obtain blood in a metropolitan area. The best advice is to talk to the local butcher or visit an Asian supermarket. They make blood sausages and order frozen blood for themselves. In most countries of the world, not including the USA, dry blood powder is available for human consumption and after mixing with water is used for making blood sausages.

Note: blood is not just an ingredient, but a very effective binder that holds all ingredients within a sausage together.

Photo 19.4 Dry blood powder.

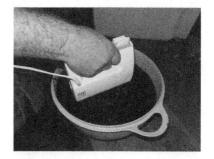

Photo 19.5 Mixing dry blood with water.

Photo 19.6 Adding blood to buckwheat groats.

Photo 19.7 Frozen blood.

Photo 19.8 Partially frozen blood is ground and mixed with other ingredients.

Salt, Spices and Other Ingredients. Blood sausages are perishable products and contain a large amount of water (blood). Adding salt will have little effect on the preservation of the product so salt is given mainly as a flavoring ingredient at 1.5 - 2.2%).

Onions. The majority of blood sausages include onions. Fresh onions are commonly added, but if added in larger quantities, they can impart a sourly taste to the product. In Spanish sausages onions are boiled for 30-40 minutes, then strained and ground. Such onions lose plenty of water and may be added to sausage that will be dried.

However, blood sausages exhibit the best flavor when onions are slow-fried in fat until they become glassy and light yellow like a straw. This is due to *caramelization* which is the browning of sugar, a process that takes place at 302-338 °F (150 to 170 °C). Given that onions contain 4% of sugar, frying them changes their color and induces sweet nutty flavor.

Spices. Blood sausages like highly aromatic spices such as: pepper, thyme, marjoram, caraway, pimento, cloves, nutmeg, allspice and coriander. Often apples, pine nuts, chestnuts, raisins and cream are added.

Manufacturing process

1. Cooking. Meats and fillers are pre-cooked. The fat is not cooked but only scalded and diced into cubes. The blood is not pre-cooked.

2. Grinding. Except fat, all other pre-cooked meats are cooled, ground through 1/4" (5 mm) plate and mixed together.

3. Mixing. Diced fat, blood, salt, and spices are added and everything is mixed together.

4. Stuffing. The blood sausage mass is much softer than the mixture for regular sausages. It can be stuffed with a stuffer or ladled into the casing through any suitable funnel. Traditionally blood sausages were stuffed into beef bungs or hog middles, but any natural or synthetic casings will do. Prick any visible air pockets with a needle otherwise the sausages will swim up to the surface during cooking.

5. Cooking. The sausages are cooked in water for about 1 hour at 176-180° F (80-82° C).

6. Cooling. Chill in cold water, refrigerate or freeze for later.

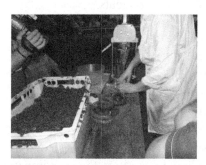

Photo 19.9 Stuffing blood sausages.

Photo 19.10 Cooked blood sausages.

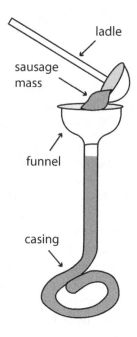

Fig. 19.1 Stuffing blood sausage through a funnel.

Smoked blood sausages are not common, but ff a smoked flavor is desired, smoke the sausages for 30 minutes after cooking. Then cool and refrigerate. A simpler solution is to add liquid smoke during mixing.

Countries where blood sausages are very popular:

Germany-*Blutwurst,* Poland-*Kaszanka,* Russia-*Krovianka,* Chech-*Jelito,* Hungary-*Veres Hurka,* Sveden-*Blodkorv*, Finland-*Musta Makkara,* Norway-*Bloodpolse,* Belgium-*Beuling,* Iceland-*Blodmor,* Croatia and Serbia, *Slovenis-Krvavica,* Estonia-*Verivorst,* England and Ireland-*Black Pudding,* France-*Boudin Noir,* Spain, South and Latin America-*Morcilla,* Portugal-*Chourico de Sangre,* Mexico and Columbia-*Rellena* or *Moronga,* Chile-*Prieta.*

In Asian Countries (China, Taiwan, Korea, Vietnam, Philippines) there is an enormous variety of blood pudding products which are not stuffed into casings but served as blood cakes.

When cooked blood changes its color to dark brown, almost black. In some countries, for example in England, black colorants like Black PN or Brilliant Black (E151) were added, since the name "black pudding." Those colorants, however, are no longer permitted in the EU.

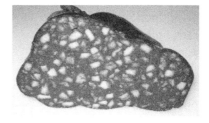

Photo 19.11 Blood sausages with diced fat.

Photo 19.12 Blood sausage with buckwheat grouts.

Sliceable blood sausages contain less than 10% blood what makes them much lighter than non-sliceable sausages (30%- 60% of blood). If an excessive amount of blood is added to a sliceable sausage, solid chunks of meats will have a tendency to sink down and accumulate in one area of the sausage. Blood sausages with filler material don't face this problem as the filler material acts like a sponge and more blood can be added.

White Blood Sausage

A white blood sausage is made from pork *without* blood. Many countries have their own versions:

England - White Pudding - diced pork, oats or bread, suet, sugar, onions, cinnamon.
France - *Boudin Blanc* - pork, milk, parsley, rice, pepper, onions. *Boudin blanc de Rethel* carries PGI certificate and must be made without filler material. Pork meat, fresh whole eggs and milk.
USA - *Boudin Blanc, Cajun Style* - pork meat, pork liver, rice, onions, parsley, garlic, pepper.
Poland - *White Blood Sausage* - pork meat, pork liver, rice, onions, marjoram.

Photo 19.13 White blood sausage (no blood added) with rice.

Although blood sausages, notably sliceable type, can be eaten cold, nevertheless, the majority of blood sausages taste best when they are fried or baked. They are usually served with fried onions, potatoes, bread/rolls, pickles and mustard.

Photo 19.14 Blood sausage fried with sliced onions.

Black Pudding

Black Pudding is a blood sausage, very popular in Northern England, Scotland and Ireland.

Materials	Metric	US
pork blood	500 g	1.10 lb.
diced fat (beef suet, pork flare fat or belly)	250 g	0.55 lb.
cooked oatmeal, barley or both	250 g	0.55 lb.

Ingredients per 1000 g (1 kg) of material:

salt	20 g	3 ½ tsp.
black pepper	2.0 g	1 tsp.
mace	1.0 g	½ tsp.
ground coriander	2.0 g	1 tsp.
onion, finely chopped	30 g	½ onion

Instructions:
1. Mix diced fat with blood and other ingredients.
2. Stuff loosely into 32 - 36 mm hog casings. Make 12" rings.
3. Cook in a hot water at 176° F (80° C) for about 40 minutes. Any sausage that floats to the top should be pricked to remove air. Don't increase temperature as the casings may burst.
4. Store in refrigerator.

Notes:
The color of the sausage should be dark brown or black, with white pieces of fat.
Suet is raw beef fat especially the hard fat found around the loins and kidneys. It is a solid at room temperature, and melts at about 70°F (21°C). Pork flare is the fat found around intestines, stomach, heart or kidneys. Belly fat is the softest of the three.

Drisheen

Drisheen is an Irish blood sausage similar to English black pudding, very popular in specialty stores in Cork or Dublin.

Materials	Metric	US
sheep blood	500 g	1.10 lb.
full cream milk	250 g	1 cup
cooked oatmeal or		
bread crumbs	250 g	1 cup

Ingredients per 1000 g (1 kg) of material:

salt	18 g	3 tsp.
black pepper	2.0 g	1 tsp.
mace	1.0 g	½ tsp.
thyme	2.0 g	1 tsp.

Instructions:
1. Add salt to blood and stir it.
2. Mix blood with cream, then add bread crumbs and other ingredients. Mix all together well.
3. Stuff into largest hog casings (38 - 42 mm), pork stomachs or beef bungs.
4. Place sausages into boiling water and poach at 176 - 185° F (80 - 85° C) for about 60 - 90 minutes to reach internal sausage temperature of 155 - 158° F (69 - 70° C). Stomach will require longer cooking time. When sausage casings are not available bake in oven like a meat loaf. Put into greased glass pan and bake at 300 - 350° F (149 - 177° C) for about 1 hour.
5. Cool and keep in refrigerator.
6. Drisheen is sliced and either fried or grilled, often with bacon, eggs and other sausages.

Notes:
If sheep blood can be hard to obtain use pork, veal or beef blood.

Kaszanka - Polish Blood Sausage

Materials	Metric	US
pork meat	500 g	1.10 lb.
pork liver	50 g	0.11 lb.
pork skins	50 g	0.11 lb.
blood	200 g	0.44 lb.
buckwheat or barley groats	200 g	0.44 lb.

Ingredients per 1000 g (1 kg) of material:

salt	18 g	3 tsp.
black pepper	2.0 g	1 tsp.
allspice	1.0 g	½ tsp.
marjoram	2.0 g	1 tsp.
chopped onion	30 g	½ onion

Instructions:
1. Poach meats (except liver) in small amount of water:
   - skins at 203°F (95°C) until soft.
   - other meats at 176-185°F (80-85°C) until soft.

Spread meats apart on a flat surface to cool. Save stock.
2. Boil buckwheat or barley grouts in left over stock or water until semi-soft. Boil for about ½ hr continuously stirring. After boiling leave for ½ to 1 hr covered.
3. Chop onions and slow-fry in fat in frying pan glassy and golden, but not brown.
4. Grind pork through 10 mm plate. Slice boiled skins into strips and grind with pork meat through 3 mm plate. Grind *raw* liver through 3 mm plate.
5. Add salt and spices to ground meats, mix barley or buckwheat grouts with blood and then mix everything well together.
6. Stuff mixture loosely into pork middles, beef rounds or synthetic casings.
7. Place sausages in boiling water and poach at 176-185°F (80-85°C) for about 60-90 min until internal meat temperature reaches 69-70°C (155-158°F).
8. Place sausages for 5 min in cold running water, then spread them on a flat surface to cool down.
9. Store in refrigerator.

Morcilla

Morcilla is a blood sausage, very popular in Spain and Latin America.

Materials	Metric	US
pork blood	250 g	0.55 lb.
fat (beef suet, pork back fat, hard pork fat trimmings or bacon)	250 g	0.55 lb.
rice	250 g	0.55 lb.
diced onions	250 g	0.55 lb.

Ingredients per 1000 g (1 kg) of material:

salt	18 g	3 tsp.
black pepper	2.0 g	1 tsp.
Spanish paprika, sweet	10.0 g	5 tsp.
Spanish paprika, hot	10.0 g	5 tsp.
cinnamon	1.0 g	½ tsp.
cloves, ground	2.0 g	1 tsp.
oregano, ground	2.0 g	1 tsp.

Instructions:
1. Peel off onions and chop them finely. Mix them with rice and leave overnight in a suitable container. The rice will absorb onion juice and will increase in volume.
2. Dice fat into 1/2" cubes.
3. Stuff loosely into 32 - 36 mm hog casings as the rice will still increase in volume during cooking. Make 12" rings.
4. Cook in a hot water at 176° F (80° C) for about 60 minutes. Any sausage that floats to the top should be pricked to remove air. Don't increase temperature as the casings may burst.
5. The color should be dark brown - red with white pieces of fat.

Notes:
The remaining morcilla stock known as "calducho" is used for cooking.
There is a morcilla variety where instead of the rice the bread crumbs are used. Everything else remains the same.
Pimenton is Spanish Smoked Paprika that gives chorizos or morcillas this particular flavor and deep red color.

Morcilla Blanca

Morcilla Blanca is Spanish sausage which is related to blood sausages, but it is made without blood. You may translate it as White Blood Sausage and this sausage type is quite common in countries such as England, France, Germany, Poland and Spain.

Meat	Metric	US
lean pork	700 g	1.54 lb.
fat (beef suet, pork back fat, hard pork fat trimmings or belly)	300 g	0.66 lb.

Ingredients per 1000 g (1 kg) of meat:

salt	20 g	3 ½ tsp.
white pepper	3.0 g	1 ½ tsp.
cinnamon	1.0 g	½ tsp.
cloves, ground	1.0 g	½ tsp.
nutmeg	1.0 g	½ tsp.
whole egg	1	1
cream	250 g	1 cup
onion, finely chopped	60 g	1 onion
parsley, finely chopped	1 Tbsp	1 Tbsp

Instructions:

1. Grind pork and back fat through 3/16 (3 mm) plate.
2. Mix the eggs, cream and all ingredients in a blender. If no blender available, mix manually.
3. Pour over meat and mix everything well together.
4. Stuff into 32-36 mm hog casings, make 6" (15 cm) links.
5. Place sausages into warm water, increase the temperature to 185° F (85° C) and simmer for 25 min. Do not boil the water, the sausages may burst open.
6. Store in a refrigerator.
7. To serve: fry in a skillet or grill.

Navajo Blood Sausage

Navajo Blood Sausage is a blood sausage, very popular among Navajo Indians in the USA. The Navajo Indians lived in Arizona, New Mexico, and Utah. During the 1600's the Navajo Indians began to raise sheep and this animal became a part of their diet. All of the sheep is eaten. A butchered sheep's blood is caught and mixed with corn meal, bits of fat, and potatoes to make blood sausage. The Navajo Indians in Utah reside on a reservation of more than 1,155,000 acres in the southeastern corner of the state.

Materials	Metric	US
sheep blood	500 g	1.10 lb.
fat, diced	200 g	0.44 lb.
cornmeal	200 g	0.44 lb.
cooked and diced potato	70 g	1
onion, finely chopped	30 g	½ onion

Ingredients per 1000 g (1 kg) of material:

salt	18 g	3 tsp.
black pepper	2.0 g	1 tsp.
mace	1.0 g	½ tsp.
green chile	20 g	1

Instructions:
1. Add salt to blood and stir it.
2. Mix blood with all ingredients.
3. Stuff into sheep stomachs or large hog casings (38 - 42 mm).
4. Place sausages into boiling water and poach at 176° - 185° F (80° - 85° C) for about 60 - 90 minutes to reach internal sausage temperature of 155° - 158° F (69° - 70° C). Stomach will require longer cooking time.
5. Cool and keep in refrigerator.

Notes:
If sheep blood can be hard to obtain use pork, veal or beef blood.

Chapter 20

Fermented Sausages

Introduction

Cold smoked and fermented sausages are grouped together as they are so closely related. For example fermented spreadable sausage such as Mettwurst can also be called a cold smoked sausage. Polish Cold Smoked Sausage is basically cold smoked salami or cold smoked dry sausage. All cold smoked sausages once sufficiently dried become North European versions of traditionally made Italian salami which is dried, but not smoked.

Traditionally, the production of fermented meats relied on bacteria present at the butcher's premises. The facility developed its own microbiological flora in which microorganisms lived all over the establishment. Meat brought from outside had already been infected with bacteria. At some places the slaughter of the animal was performed right on the premises, which also contributed to new bacteria infecting the meat. Summing it up there was no shortage of microorganisms and this combination of bacteria from the meat and from the premises often created favorable conditions for making fermented sausages.

Plants developed different bacterial flora and sausages of different qualities were made depending on the location. In the past meat facilities were not sanitized as scrupulously as the ones of today, which helped create more favorable conditions for the bacteria to survive in the plant. These conditions were unique to each establishment and it was impossible to duplicate them somewhere else. By the same token, sausage makers were unable to produce a fermented sausage in two different locations that would have exhibited the same quality.

Some places in Italy developed a specific flora which was instrumental in producing a high quality product of a peculiar taste and flavor. Such establishments suddenly developed fame and a brand name for making wonderful meat products.

They probably were not better sausage makers than their counterparts working in different locations. They were lucky to have their shop located in the area which was blessed by mother nature for making fermented sausages. They did not have much clue as to what was happening, but passed this empirical knowledge to their sons and it worked like magic.

Until the second half of the XX century, the manufacture of fermented sausages was covered with a shroud of secrecy. One of the secrets was known as *back slopping,* which was reusing a part of the sausage mass from the previous batch. Such inoculation helped to produce a sausage of the same quality as the one previously made. Unfortunately any defects that were acquired in following productions would be passed along, and the method is seldom used today.

Climatic differences were a significant factor in the development of different methods of smoking, drying, and preserving meat products. The best time of year was when temperatures were cooler and mildly humid. In the summer, higher temperatures and lower humidity did not favor the production of high quality sausages. The South had a drier climate with steady winds, and the best air-dried hams and salamis originated there. In the North, the weather was less predictable with cooler temperatures and higher humidity. Those conditions were ill suited for making air-dried products and smoking became the preferred method. For those reasons Mediterranean countries produced slow-fermented sausages that were only dried, and countries in Northern Europe produced fermented sausages which were smoked and dried.

Modern production is independent of outside conditions and parameters such as temperature, humidity, and air speed are computer controlled in sophisticated drying chambers. This latest technology, combined with a universal use of bacteria cultures, permit producing fermented sausages of constant quality at any time of the year. Even so, the manufacture of fermented products is still a combination of an art and technology.

The preservation of meats by fermentation has been practiced for centuries and traditional practices rely on indigenous bacteria present in meat and in the environment. These techniques are being replaced by the application of commercially grown starter cultures. Fermentation technology has become a huge part of food science and to be able to choose the right culture for a particular product, requires a basic understanding of microorganisms and their behavior.

How Fermented Sausages Differ From Others

Making a regular sausage is amazingly simple: the meat is ground, salt and spices are added, and the mass is stuffed into a casing. If this is a fresh sausage, the process ends right there and the sausage goes into the refrigerator. Then it is cooked and eaten. If making a smoked type, the sausage goes into a smokehouse and then is cooked and consumed. This is a simple and fast manufacturing process and there is no health risk present at any time if basic safety precautions are in place. On the other hand it takes a lot of effort to produce a high quality traditional fermented sausage.

There is a serious investment in time and a lot of care is needed by the sausage maker. It is almost like planting a tomato plant in the garden, a lot of pruning and watering is needed within the next three months. Or like making wine, it has to ferment, clarify, mature, and only then it is ready to be consumed. In many cases fermented sausages are not submitted to heat treatment and *this separates them from other sausage types*. This one missing step (lack of cooking), forces upon a sausage maker a completely new manufacturing technology in which the knowledge of microbiology plays a crucial role. Although the first steps of sausage making such as meat selection, curing, grinding, mixing and stuffing seem to be the same, under closer examination it becomes clear that they have to be finely tuned to new safety requirements. All tasks involved in the manufacture of fermented sausages must always be performed in such a way that meat safety is **never compromised.** A mistake in any of the processing steps can later spoil the sausage or bring harm to the consumer.

A recipe can be downloaded from the Internet and with some luck, one may produce quality salami at home. The problem is that the next time one attempts to make the same sausage, it will turn out completely different even if the same ingredients were used. There are a few stages of making a fermented sausage and a serious violation of established rules will spoil the product and may even make it dangerous to consume. As some sausages, notably slow fermented ones, take many weeks or even months to produce, it is a great loss to waste so much time and investment due to insufficient know-how or one's negligence. Making fermented sausages can be considered an advanced sausage making and to produce a consistant quality sausage some understanding of meat science and microbiology must be first acquired.

It's All About Bacteria

Making fermented sausages is a combination of the art of the sausage maker and unseen magic performed by bacteria. The friendly bacteria are working together with a sausage maker, but the dangerous ones are trying to wreak havoc. Using his knowledge the sausage maker monitors temperature and humidity, which allows him to control reactions that take place inside the sausage. This game is played for quite a while and at the end a high quality product is created.

The start of fermentation is nothing else but a war declaration by all bacteria residing inside the meat and the stuffed sausage becomes the battlefront. We have to protect the product at all costs and the two best weapons we have at our disposal are increasing meat acidity (lowering pH) and lowering its water content (Aw). We have to create conditions that will:

- Inhibit growth of spoilage and dangerous bacteria.
- Take a good care of friendly bacteria so they can prosper and work for us.

Water Activity

All microorganisms need water and the amount of water available to them is defined as water activity. Water activity (Aw) is an indication of how tightly water is "bound" inside of a product. It does not say how much water there is, but how much water is *available* to support the growth of bacteria, yeasts or molds.

Water activity of some foods	
Pure water	1.00
Fresh meat & fish	0.99
Bread	0.99
Salami	0.87
Aged cheese	0.85
Jams & jellies	0.80
Plum pudding	0.80
Dried fruits	0.60
Biscuits	0.30
Milk powder	0.20
Instant coffee	0.20
Bone dry	0.00

Below certain Aw levels, microbes can not grow.

USDA guidelines state:

"A potentially hazardous food does not include . . . a food with a water activity value of 0.85 or less."

Adding salt or sugar "binds" some of this free water inside of the product and *lowers the amount of available water* to bacteria which inhibits their growth. The most practical approach for lowering water activity is drying, although it is a slow process which must be carefully monitored, otherwise it may backfire and ruin the product. A simple scale is used to classify foods by their water activity and it starts at 0 (bone dry) and ends on 1 (pure water).

Meats were preserved throughout history and the technology was based on simple techniques of salting and drying. Both factors contribute to lowering the water activity of the meat. Freshly minced meat possesses a very high water activity level around 0.99, which is a breeding ground for bacteria. Adding salt to meat drops this value immediately to 0.96-0.98 (depending on the amount of salt), and this already creates a hurdle against the growth of bacteria. This may be hard to comprehend as we know that water does not suddenly evaporate when salt is added to meat. Well, this is where the concept of water activity becomes useful.

Although the addition of salt to meat does not force water to evaporate, it does something similar: it immobilizes free water and prevents it from reacting with anything else, including bacteria. It is like stealing food from bacteria, the salt locks up the water creating less favorable conditions for bacteria to grow and prosper. As we add more salt, more free water is immobilized, but a compromise must be reached, as adding too much salt will make the product unpalatable. It may also impede the growth of friendly bacteria, the ones which work with us to ferment the sausage. The same happens when we freeze meat though we never think of it. Frozen water takes the shape of solid ice crystals and is not free anymore. The manipulation of water content in processed meat is very important to the successful production of traditionally made slow-fermented sausages.

Removing water content by drying a sausage is a slow process which is not practical when we want to make a product safe to consume within a few days. We could dry sausages at higher temperatures by applying fast air speed, but that would only harden their surfaces, trapping the moisture inside causing the sausages to spoil. Slow, controlled drying is the method applied to traditionally made slow-fermented sausages which require three months or more to produce. As the process proceeds, water starts to evaporate making meat stronger against spoilage and pathogenic bacteria.

There eventually comes a point when there are no bacteria present and the meat is microbiologically stable. It will not spoil as long as it is kept at low temperatures and at low humidity levels. If the temperature and humidity go up, new bacteria will establish a colony on the surface and will start moving towards the inside of the sausage. The mold immediately appears on the surface.

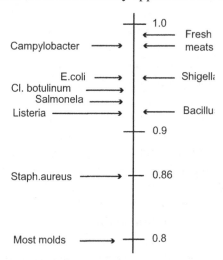

Fig. 20.1 Water activity minimum for growth of microorganisms.

From the graph on the left it can be seen that except *Staphylococcus aureus*, all other bacteria (spoilage and pathogenic) will not grow below 0.91. This is why drying is such an effective method of preventing bacteria growth and preserving foods in general.

Decagon Devices Inc presently known as Meter Group produces Aqualab instruments which are the fastest, most precise water activity meters available.

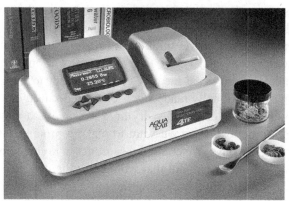

Photo 20.1 Aqualab 4TE water activity meter can measure water activity (Aw) in 5 minutes or less with 0.003 accuracy.

Photo courtesy: Meter Group, Pullman, WA,USA.

pH -The Measure of Food Acidity

Foods with a low pH value (high acidity) develop resistance against microbiological spoilage. Pickles, sauerkraut, eggs, pig feet, anything submerged in vinegar will have a long shelf life. Even ordinary meat jelly (head cheese) will last longer if some vinegar is added, and this type of head cheese is known as "souse." Next time when buying meat marinade look at the list of ingredients. The list invariably includes items like vinegar, dry wine, soy sauce, lemon juice, and ingredients which are acidic or salty by nature. Although those ingredients are added mainly to tenderize meat by unwinding the protein structure, they also contribute to inhibiting the growth of bacteria. *Bacteria hate acidic and salty foods* and this fact plays an important role in the production and stabilization of fermented sausages.

Bacteria prefer meats with a pH of 6.0-7.0 which falls in the neutral range of the pH scale. It is in our interest to increase the meat acidity (lower pH) as this inhibits the growth of bacteria. As a result the sausage is stable and safe to consume, although it has not been submitted to heat treatment, which in many cases follows anyhow. A pH drop is accomplished by lactic acid bacteria, which consume sugar and produce lactic acid. This increases the acidity of the meat. The acidity can also be increased by directly adding additives to the meat such as Gdl (glucono-delta-lactone) and/or citric acid.

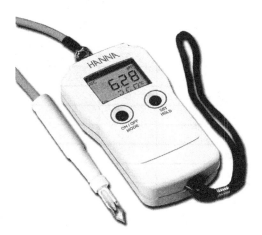

Photo 20.2 pH meat tester made by Hanna Instruments.

Photo courtesy Hanna Instruments, Woonsocket, RI, USA
www.hannainst.com/usa

From the pH scale on the facing page, it can be seen that adding vinegar to meat will increase the acidity but adding baking soda will produce an opposite effect. Of course such ingredients have to be carefully selected as they will alter the flavor of the sausage. Using different meats and fats will produce a sausage mass of a certain pH, and the pH meat tester will provide the initial value of the pH of the mix.

The table on the right shows a pH value below which the listed bacteria will not grow. In the majority of today's fermented sausages, increasing the acidity of the meat has become the main hurdle against bacteria. *Almost all fermented sausages produced in the USA today are manufactured by lowering the pH of the meat.* It is a profitable and risk free method for commercial producers, although the taste and flavor of the product leaves much to be desired.

Name	Min pH
Salmonella	3.8
Cl.botulinum	5.0
Staph.aureus	4.2
Campylobacter	4.9
Listeria	4.4
E.coli	4.4
Shigella	4.0
Bacillus	4.3

Effects of temperature, acidity (pH) and moisture (Aw) on bacteria behavior:

Name	Temperature in ° C			Min pH	Min Aw
	Min	Optimum	Max		
Salmonella	7	35 - 37	45	3.8	0.94
Cl.botulinum	3	18 - 25	45	5.0	0.97
Cl.perfringens	12	43 - 47	50	5.5	0.93
Staph.aureus	6	37	48	4.2	0.85
Campylobacter	30	42	45	4.9	0.98
Listeria	-1.5	37	45	4.4	0.92
E.coli	7	37	46	4.4	0.95
Shigella	7	35-37	47	4.0	0.91
Bacillus	4	30 - 37	55	4.3	0.91

Controlling pH and Aw is crucial when making fermented products, for the purpose of this book it is enough to know that bacteria hate high acidity (low pH) and low water levels (Aw).

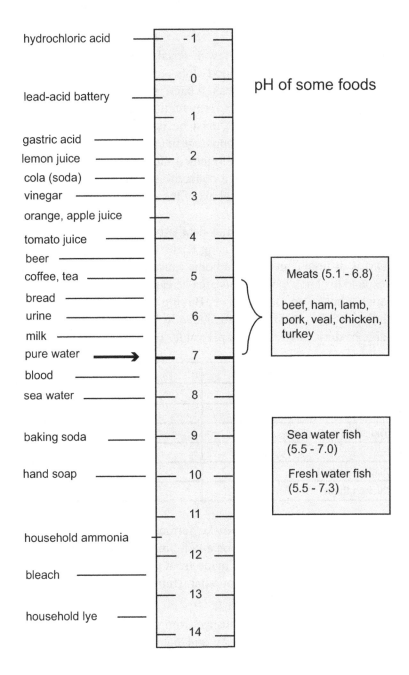

Fig. 20.2 pH of some foods.

Making Fermented Sausages

Meat selection. Only the best raw materials are chosen for making dry or semi-dry sausages. Any blood clots and glands must be removed as these may accumulate undesired bacteria. Those bacteria will then multiply during the curing or fermentation step and will affect the quality of the product. Meats must be well trimmed of gristle and sinews. Such defects are not apparent in emulsified sausages but will strike out in coarsely ground fermented sausages. The fact that fat has a lower acidity is not of grave concern as it accounts for the minor parts of a sausage and the initial pH of the sausage mass is the average of all meats.

We are not going to go into details on selecting meats the way commercial meat plants do. Using terms like PSE meat, or DFD, or MDM is of little concern for a home sausage maker, and if he wants to expand his knowledge in this area he can address any of the widely available books on meat science. Buying ground meat is not a good solution as it has the shortest life due to its large surface area and it has a large bacteria count. Typical pH values of raw meats follow below:

Raw material	pH
Pork	5.7 - 5.9
Back fat	6.2 - 7.0
Emulsified pork skins	7.2 - 7.8
Beef	5.5 - 5.8
Chicken breast	5.6 - 5.8
Chicken thigh	6.1 - 6.4

Different meats are used to make fermented sausages: pork, beef, lamb, goat, venison, poultry or a combination thereof. In Germany fermented sausages are often made from equal amounts of pork and beef, in Poland pork is more popular. Hungarian, Spanish and Italian sausages contain mostly pork.

Chicken. Trying to make a sausage from chicken meat only presents some problems: high pH, high Aw and that means favorable conditions for bacteria growth. *Campylobacter jejuni* is a typical pathogen found in poultry meat.

Fish. Fermented fish products are popular in countries such as the Philippines, Japan, and China. The products are not so much as fermented sausages but fermented fish paste and fish sauce which are used for general cooking. Rice is used as a filler and the source of carbohydrates for fermentation. Two known products are Balao Balao (fermented rice and shrimp) and Burong Isda (fermented rice and fish). There was research done on making fermented fish sausages and the customer acceptance in order of preference follows below:

- Fish-pork, the highest score.
- Fish-beef.
- Fish-chicken.

Non-fish beef-pork sausage was rated the highest of all. Using starter cultures and good manufacturing processes a semi-dry fish sausage can successfully be made at home.

Venison. Sausages made of venison are commercially made for sale in Canada and Alaska. Venison is lean meat and it should be mixed with pork back fat, fatty pork, or a combination of pork and beef. A proportion of 60% venison to 40% other meats is a good choice. Wild game meat (except venison) is at risk of being infected with *trichinosis* and the regular freezing methods as applied to pork may not be enough. *Freezing may not kill larval cysts in bears and other wild game animals that live in Northwestern U.S. and Alaska.* That meat has to be cooked to 160° F (71° C) internal temperature, but this step cannot be applied to fermented sausages which are not cooked. Curing meat with salt for prescribed times will prevent trichinosis as well (see Appendix A).

Fat

When making fermented sausages use pork back fat. It is hard, it has a higher melting point, and it will make a great sausage. Soft fat (belly) smears easily and may adhere to the inner casing surface, clogging up the pores and affecting drying. It may also coat meat particles which will affect the drying process. Although soft fat is a poor choice for making sliceable sausages, it can be successfully used for making fermented spreadable sausages (Mettwurst, Teewurst), especially the ones with a fine grind. Make sure the fat is partially frozen before it is ground or cut. Fat contains little water (10-15%), so if the sausage is fatty it contains less water. As a result *the drying step is shortened.*

Beef fat has a higher melting temperature than pork but is yellowish in color which affects the appearance of the product where discrete particles of fat should be visible. In addition beef fat does not taste as good as pork fat which makes it a secondary choice. There are some that may object to pork fat on religious grounds and beef fat (tallow) will have to do. In large metropolitan areas it may be difficult to obtain back fat. It may be easier to obtain back fat from ethnic butcher stores (Polish, German, Spanish, Thai) but it is often heavily salted. Some supermarkets carry heavily salted pork fat and it will have to be de-salted in cold water (48 hours) before grinding. A few water changes are necessary.

Chicken fat. Fermented sausages can be made of chicken but a big problem is chicken fat. It is too soft and melts at such low temperatures that it is of no practical use. Chicken fat contains more water and less collagen structure than other fats which makes it soft and semi-liquid at room temperature due to its low melting point. When submitted to heat treatment, chicken fat will melt inside the sausage creating oily pockets and make the sausage seem like a fat product. For those reasons pork fat should be added to a sausage but it can not be classified as an all chicken sausage anymore. Using starter cultures and good manufacturing processes, a semi-dry chicken sausage can successfully be made at home.

Smoking

Smoking may or may not be utilized in the production of fermented sausages. It has been used in countries in Northern Europe where due to colder climate and shorter seasons, the drying conditions were less favorable than in Spain or Italy. Smoking imparts a different flavor, fights bacteria, (especially on the surface of the product) and thus prevents the growth of molds on fermented sausages.

Mold is desired on some traditionally made Italian salamis and obviously smoking is not deployed. It should be pointed out, that *when making slow-fermented sausages only cold smoke should be applied* and its temperature should correspond to the fermentation or drying temperature present at a particular time. Applying smoke which is much cooler than the fermentation temperature will slow down fermentation.

Applying smoke which is much hotter than the fermentation or drying temperature will create favorable conditions for the growth of undesirable bacteria. When making traditional slow-fermented sausages we apply fermentation temperatures around 66° F, (18° C) and even less when drying. To match these values we have to apply cold smoke that falls more or less in the same temperature range < 72° F, 22° C. It is a known fact that smoke possesses antibacterial properties and smoking meats was one of the earliest preservation methods. Prolonged cold smoking is the most effective of all smoking methods as it thoroughly penetrates meat.

Smoke which is applied early in the fermentation stage will definitely inhibit the growth of lactic acid bacteria to some degree, especially *if the diameter of the sausage is small.* In such a case it will be wiser to wait until fermentation is over before the smoke is applied. Applying smoke during the fermentation period creates a barrier to the growth of *Staph.aureus* at the surface of the product where toxin production may be a problem.

Cold Smoke And Fermented Sausages

When smoking fermented products such as dry salami or German spreadable sausages it is of utmost importance to keep smoke temperature down. German meat technology books recommend applying cold smoke below 64° F , (18° C) for about 3-4 days. Slow fermented dry sausages and fermented spreadable sausages can be cold smoked only. The reason being that these sausages are never cooked and applying smoke at higher temperatures will create favorable conditions for the growth of undesirable bacteria. The product will spoil and might become dangerous to consume.

Spreadable sausages are neither dried nor cooked and after cold smoking must be kept in a refrigerator. The initial drying temperature for fermented sausages falls into 64 → 59° F, (18 → 15° C) range and cold smoke < 72° F (22° C) fits nicely into this range. Then drying continues at temperatures below 59° F (15° C). To sum it up the length of cold smoking is loosely defined, but the upper temperature should remain below 72° F (22° C).

Unfortunately, this rule puts some restraints on making slow-fermented sausages in hot climates for most of the year, when using an outside smokehouse. You can't produce cooler smoke than the ambient temperature around the smokehouse, unless some cooling methods are devised.

The quote from *"The Art of Making Fermented Sausages"* follows below:

"Think of cold smoke as a part of the drying/fermentation cycle and not as the flavoring step. If the temperature of the smoke is close to the fermentation temperature, there is very little difference between the two. The sausage will still ferment and the drying will continue and the extra benefit is the prevention of mold that would normally accumulate on the surface. Cold smoking is performed with a dry, thin smoke. If we applied heavy smoke for a long time, that would definitely inhibit the growth of color and flavor forming bacteria which are so important for the development of flavor in slow-fermented sausages (salamis). As drying continues for a long time and cold smoking is a part of it, it makes little difference whether cold smoke is interrupted and then re-applied again."

Semi-dry sausages, which are of fast-fermented type, are fermented at higher temperatures. These sausages can be smoked with warmer smoke as they are subsequently cooked.

Fermentation and Conditioning. In commercial plants the process of grinding, mixing and stuffing is undertaken at a low temperature (32° F, 0° C) and as the cold sausage is placed in a warmer fermenting room, the condensation will appear on the surface of the sausage. To prevent this the sausage must remain in the fermentation chamber at a prevailing temperature for 1-6 hours (depending on its diameter) at low humidity (60%, no air speed) until the moisture evaporates. If air draft is applied at such low humidity, excessive drying will develop and case hardening will occur. This would affect subsequent fermentation and the drying processes.

In simple terms *meat fermentation is spoilage of meat by bacteria*. If this process is left to itself, the meat will spoil, but if it is properly controlled, the result is a fermented product. Meat fermentation is accomplished by lactic bacteria, either naturally present in meat or added as starter cultures. These bacteria feed on carbohydrates (sugars) and produce lactic acid and small amounts of other components.

Fermentation is required not only to produce a highly desirable product, but also to prevent the growth of spoilage and pathogenic bacteria. When a sausage is introduced into a fermentation chamber, the bacteria hold all cards in their favor:

- Warm temperature - right inside of the Danger Zone.

- Moisture - meat contains 75% water.

- Sugar (food) - little sugar is present in the meat itself (glycogen) but extra amounts are usually added.

- Oxygen, present in air. Food spoilage bacteria require oxygen to grow, but there are bacteria that thrive without oxygen.

When a sausage is stuffed *the only barrier that protects the meat from spoiling is salt and nitrite which were introduced during curing or mixing.* The selected meat always contains some bacteria and they will grow in time. It is of the utmost importance to process meats with a bacteria count that is as low as possible. Commercial producers add chemicals such as Gdl (glucono-delta-lactone) or citric acid into a sausage mass to rapidly increase the acidity of the meat and to create an extra margin of safety. Unfortunately, this introduces a sourly flavor to the sausage typical of fast fermented salamis. There is a fierce competition among different groups of bacteria for food. Bacteria that are beneficial to us slowly but steadily gain the upper hand in this fight by eliminating the food spoilage and pathogenic types. "Survival of the fittest" at its best. The reason that beneficial bacteria get the upper hand in this war is that they are:

- Stronger competitors. This becomes much more pronounced when starter culture is added which brings millions of beneficial bacteria into the mix.

- Better tolerate exposure to salt, nitrite and decreased water levels. Salt is always added to meat and depending on the amount added, it binds some free water which would normally be available to bacteria. As a result the Aw water activity level of a sausage mix drops from 0.99 (fresh meat) to 0.96-0.97.

Although the addition of salt, nitrite and starter cultures to a sausage mix creates favorable fermentation conditions, nevertheless undesired and dangerous pathogenic bacteria such as *Listeria monocytogenes, Salmonella, Staphylococcus aureus* and *E. coli 0:157:H7* are still able to grow, albeit at a much slower pace.

When a sausage is placed in a warm fermentation chamber, *all bacteria* types spring into action and start to multiply, but they react to the new environment differently:

- **Spoilage bacteria** (*Pseudomonas*) which are aerobic (need oxygen), start to choke as there is little air inside of the sausage. The salt and lowered moisture further inhibits their growth. Once lactic acid bacteria start to produce lactic acid, the increased acidity inhibits spoilage bacteria even more.

- **Lactic acid bacteria** (*Lactobacillus* and *Pediococcus*) are quite resistant to salt and function well at slightly reduced water levels. *After a short lag phase* they start to metabolize sugar and produce lactic acid which starts to create a barrier against undesirable types. As they grow in numbers, they eat more sugar and multiply again.

- **Color fixing and flavor producing bacteria** (*Staphylococcus* and *Kocuria*) tolerate increased salt levels very well, but they grow slowly. They can grow in the presence of oxygen or without it. They don't like increased acidity and at pH below 5.5 they become less effective. In fast-fermented sausages a drop of pH 5.0 can be achieved in just 12 hours giving them no chance to perform. They need not days, but months of time to break meat proteins and fats in order to produce all those aroma releasing enzymes.

- **Pathogenic bacteria** are kept in check primarily by salt and nitrite. Once lactic acid bacteria start making lactic acid, this increasing acidity starts to inhibit pathogenic bacteria, especially *Staphylococcus aureus,* which is very sensitive to acidity though it can function very well at low moisture levels .

- In addition, some lactic acid bacteria strains (*Pediococcus acidilactici, Lactobacillus curvatus*) can produce bacteriocins that are very hostile towards wild and unwanted lactic bacteria strains and pathogenic *Listeria monocytogenes.*

The main product of fermentation is lactic acid and the main cause is an increased acidity of meat (lower pH). The more sugar that is metabolized by the lactic acid bacteria, the more lactic acid is produced and the higher acidity of meat is obtained. This increased acidity of meat known as pH drop, erects the barrier against the growth of spoilage and dangerous bacteria.

The speed of fermentation is due to the temperature and higher temperatures produce faster fermentation. If the fermentation temperature drops to <12° C (53° F), the lactic acid bacteria may stop metabolizing sugar. *How acidic the sausage becomes depends on the amount and type of sugar introduced.* If more sugar is added, a higher acidity (lower pH) is obtained and the sausage gains a more sourly flavor.

In traditionally made dry products the proper fermentation can take place only if there is a sufficient number of lactic bacteria in the meat to begin with. To increase their number a long curing step was performed. Unfortunately, spoilage and pathogenic bacteria were growing as well, although at a much slower rate due to the preventive effects of salt and Nitrate. In the latest production methods, huge numbers of lactic acid bacteria (starter cultures) are introduced into the meat right at the beginning of the process and that guarantees healthy and strong fermentation. These armies of beneficial bacteria start *competing for food* with other undesirable bacteria types, decreasing their chances for growth and survival. Fermentation stops when no more lactic acid is produced by bacteria. This happens when:

- No more sugar is available to lactic acid bacteria.

- There is not enough free water (Aw < 0.95) available to lactic acid bacteria. This can happen when a sausage dries too fast during fermentation due to low humidity and fast air speed.

- Temperature is lowered (53° F, < 12° C) or product is heated (> 120° F, 50° C).

Fermentation is performed by *Lactobacillus* or *Pediococcus* lactic acid bacteria. *Lactobacillus* and *Pediococcus* require different temperatures for growth and this is what basically separates them. Depending on the type of a sausage desired (slow, medium or fast-fermented), different amounts and types of sugars will be chosen and in each case fermentation will run differently. In the past, it was all very simple as traditional sausages were manufactured with very little (sometimes none) sugar. Nitrate was always added, and we were not even aware of the fact that there was something called "nitrite" that cured meat. Today, the commonly available starter cultures help us to produce fermented sausages of many types such as slow or fast fermented, dry or semi-dry, sliceable or spreadable, with mold or without.

Choosing a type of sausage to make, decides the fermentation type and parameters of the fermentation chamber. Based on that choice, the proper type and amount of sugar will be added into the mix. The process of meat fermentation in slow or fast-fermented products varies slightly depending on the sausage type that is produced. The processing steps prior to the fermentation stage such as meat selection, curing, grinding, mixing and stuffing remain the same in both cases. The only difference is that different amounts of sugar and different cultures are used. Nowadays, starter cultures are added regardless of what sausage type is produced.

The temperature of the sausages should increase to the recommended fermentation temperature of a particular culture *as fast as possible*, to create the best starting conditions for the growth of starter culture bacteria. If the temperature is increasing slowly, the bacteria that is naturally present in meat will have favorable conditions to grow before culture bacteria start competing with them.

Fermentation starts at a high humidity (> 90%) to slow down the moisture removal from the sausage. Adding 3% salt will drop Aw water activity to 0.96-0.97 (salt immobilizes some of the free water) and drying too quickly may drop Aw to < 0.95 which will have a detrimental effect on the growth of lactic acid bacteria and fermentation will be inhibited. *All bacteria types need free water to survive and lactic acid bacteria are not an exception.* If humidity is high, but air speed is restricted, too little drying will take place which is indicated by slime that forms on the sausage. Once the fermentation has taken place the drying can be more aggressive.

As to when fermentation stops and drying begins, there is no easy answer especially in the case of slow-fermented products that are made with little sugar, which leads to a slow and small pH drop. pH will have to be periodically monitored and once it is at its lowest, it means that there is no more lactic acid production and no more fermentation. *The sausage pH, not the time, is the factor that determines when the fermentation is completed.* It should be noted that when yeasts and molds appear on the sausage during the drying process, "reversed" fermentation will take place as these microorganisms consume some of the lactic acid that was produced during fermentation. This will lower acidity (increase pH) further contributing to a milder flavor in the slow drying sausages. There are processors of dry products that limit the entire process to one long drying step.

The stuffed sausage is introduced into the drying chamber at 6-15° C, 42-58° F, where it remains for the rest of the process.

In general, faster fermentation results in a lower pH even if the same amount of sugar is added. According to Chr. Hansen a 5° C increase in temperature, if close to the optimum growth temperature for the specific lactic acid bacteria, doubles the rate of lactic acid formation.

The factors affecting fermentation:

- Temperature.
- Type of sausage (fast, medium or slow-fermented), the time can be from 12 hours to 8 days.
- The method of production (chance, back slopping or starter cultures).
- Sugar type.
- pH lowering ingredients (Gdl, citric acid).
- Salt concentration.
- Meats used, pork ferments faster than beef (lower starting pH).

Drying

When the sausage is stuffed its Aw should not be lower than Aw 0.96 as bacteria need some moisture to grow. Color and flavor forming bacteria (*Staphylococcus, Kocuria*) are aerobic (need oxygen to survive) and are concentrated close to the surface of the sausage (area with most oxygen). They are sensitive to changing water activity levels and fast drying at low humidity levels will rapidly remove moisture from the surface area of the sausage. This will inhibit the action of color and flavor forming bacteria and will affect the development of proper color and flavor. A gray surface ring is a typical example. Lactic acid bacteria are less sensitive to water activity and perform well until water activity drops down to 0.92.

Drying is normally performed at 66 → 54° F, 18 → 12° C with decreasing humidity, from about 85% to 65-70%. Higher temperatures and humidity over 75% will promote the development of mold on the surface of the sausage. When making slow fermented sausages without starter cultures, drying temperatures should fall in 54-59° F, 12-15° C range as *Staph.aureus* starts growing faster at 15.6° C (60° F) and obviously it is best to avoid this and higher temperatures.

Sausages dry from inside out and and to have a correct drying process, there must be a balance between moisture diffusion towards the surface and moisture evaporation from the surface. If diffusion is faster than evaporation, moisture will accumulate on the surface of the sausage, causing it to be slimy and yeasts and molds will follow. If evaporation is faster than diffusion, the outside surface area of the sausage will dry out and harden creating a barrier to subsequent moisture removal. As a result moisture will be trapped inside of the sausage, creating favorable conditions for the growth of spoilage and pathogenic bacteria.

Water activity can be lowered faster in a sausage which contains more fat than a leaner sausage. Meat contains about 75% of water but the water content of fat is only about 10 - 15%. Having less water the fat sausage will dry out faster.

Drying basically starts already in the fermentation stage and the humidity is kept at a high level of about 90-95%. Air flow is quite fast (0.8 m/sec) to permit fast moisture removal but the high humidity level moisturizes the surface of the casing preventing it from hardening. One may say why not to dry a sausage very quickly which will remove moisture and be done with all this pH stuff and bacteria. Well, there are basically two reasons:

1. The outside layer of the sausage must not be hardened as it may prevent the removal of the remaining moisture. It may affect the curing of the outside layer which will develop a gray ring that will be visible when slicing the sausage.

2. Bacteria naturally found in meat and/or introduced in starter cultures need moisture to grow. Once, when a sufficient pH drop is obtained, lactic acid bacteria are not needed anymore and more moisture can be removed.

Drying is affected by the following factors:

- Humidity - higher humidity, slower drying.
- Temperature - higher temperature, faster drying.

For the perfect drying the humidity of the drying room should be 5% lower than the water activity (Aw) within the sausage. This requires water activity measurements and computer operated drying chambers where parameters such as temperature, humidity and air speed are continuously monitored and readjusted.

This relationship remains constant and every time the water level drops, the humidity is lowered accordingly. At home we have to improvise, and do our best under circumstances which are present during production. And it can be done as the best proof lies in the fact, that we have been making those products without sophisticated equipment in the past. Increasing the acidity of the meat (lower pH) facilitates drying and the movement of moisture towards the surface is much smoother. As the pH drops, it approaches the *isoelectric point* of the myofibrillar proteins (*actin* and *myosin*) *where their ability to bind water reaches a minimum*. This happens around pH of 4.8-5.3. In simple words, *lowering pH aids in the removal of moisture*. Depending on the method of manufacture, diameter of a casing and the content of fat in a sausage mass, fermented sausages lose from 5 - 40% of their original weight.

Drying continues after the fermentation stage and more moisture is removed from the sausage. This becomes easier as the acidity increases as the forces binding water inside, lose some ot their holding power. As the Aw (water activity) keeps dropping lower, the humidity level is decreased to about 0.85-90%. *Maintaining previous fast air flow may harden the surface of the casing so the air speed is decreased* to about 0.5 m/sec (1.8 miles/per hour-slow walk). And the process continues until the desired amount of dryness is obtained. There is less available water to bacteria and the sausage becomes more stable.

- The length of the sausage has no influence on drying time.
- Sausage diameter - bigger diameter, slower drying.
- Sausages should be dried at a rate not higher than the moisture losing ability of the sausage.
- Traditionally made sausages have pH of about 5.3 and Aw about 0.88 at the end of the drying process.
- The drying chamber should not be overloaded as a uniform air draft is needed for proper drying and mold prevention.
- Air speed - higher air speed, faster drying.
- Casing type (pore size) - bigger pores, faster drying.
- Amount of fat - more fat in sausage, faster drying.
- Meat particle size - bigger size, faster drying.
- A medium diameter sausage should loose about *0.5-0.7% of its weight per day* when in a drying chamber.

- Load capacity of the drying room-fully loaded chamber will dry slower as air movement is restricted.
- Molds will develop more quickly if there is no air draft at all. Excessive drying hardens the surface and closes the casing pores.
- If the outside of the sausage becomes greasy, it should be wiped off with a warm cloth otherwise it may inhibit drying.

Starter Cultures

Although lactic acid bacteria are naturally present in meat, their quantity and qualities are hard to predict. In most cases they are of a hetero-fermentative type and that means that they not only produce lactic acid by metabolizing carbohydrates, but also create many different reactions which can produce unpleasant odors and affect the entire process. *Starter cultures are of a homo-fermentative type and will produce lactic acid only.*

The addition of up to 10 millions of bacterial cells per gram in a lactic acid culture assures microbial dominance over other undesirable microorganisms that might be present. Those other microorganisms might be unwelcome lactic acid bacteria that were naturally present in meat or pathogenic bacteria that must be eliminated. Although commercially grown starter cultures have been around since 1957, it is only recently that sausage equipment and supplies companies carry them in catalogs.

Storing

Slow-fermented sausages can be stored at 10-15° C (50-59° F), 75% humidity. If humidity is lower, the sausage will lose more moisture and weight which will amount to a lower profit. Higher humidity will invite molds to grow on the surface. Spreadable sausages which are neither dried nor cooked, must be refrigerated.

In time, there will be some flavor deterioration in dry fermented meats due to fat oxidation, also known as *rancidity*. Oxidation is usually started by the action of a catalyst, which includes heat, light, or oxygen. Rancidity can develop in fermented products rapidly if fermentation proceeds very slowly, which can be an issue in slow fermented products that are made without starter cultures and with little sugar. Sodium nitrite is a powerful antioxidant and *nitrite cured meats have a longer shelf-life.* Applying smoke also retards the onset of rancidity. *Rancidity is a quality issue, not a safety issue.*

Culture Types

Cultures can be classified into the following groups:

- Lactic acid producing cultures (fermentation).
- Color fixing and flavor forming cultures (color and flavor).
- Surface coverage cultures (yeasts and molds).
- Bio-protective cultures (producing bacteriocins). You may think of bacteriocins as some kind of antibiotics which kill unwanted bacteria. Some of the lactic acid cultures, for example, (*Pediococcus*) possess antimicrobial properties which are very effective in inhibiting not only *Staph.aureus,* but also *Salmonella*, *Cl.botulinum* and other microorganisms including yeasts.

The advantages of starter cultures are numerous:

- They are of known number and quality. This eliminates a lot of guessing as to whether there is enough bacteria inside the meat to start fermentation, or whether a strong curing color will be obtained.
- Cultures are optimized for different temperature ranges that allow production of slow, medium or fast-fermented products. Traditionally produced sausages needed three (or more) months to make, starter cultures make this possible within weeks.
- Production of fermented sausages does not depend on "secrets" and a product of constant quality can be produced year round in any climatic zone, as long as proper natural conditions or fermenting/drying chambers are available.
- They provide safety by competing for food with undesirable bacteria thus inhibiting their growth.

There are many manufacturers of starter cultures that are used in Europe and in the USA, for example cultures made by the Danish manufacturer "Chr. Hansen". Their products demonstrate superior quality and are easily obtained from American distributors of sausage making equipment and supplies. Some of the popular cultures are listed below:

Bactoferm® T-SPX-slow-fermented culture for traditional fermentation profiles applying fermentation temperatures not higher than 24° C (75° F). 25 g of culture ferments 200 kg of meat.

Bactoferm® F-LC - bio-protective culture capable of acidification as well as preventing growth of *Listeria monocytogenes*. Controlling *Listeria monocytogenes* is not easy as it is so widespread. It can be found in livestock, in humans, on processing equipment and in other locations of meat processing plants. To prevent its growth, proper sanitation and proper temperature control is needed in all steps of the manufacturing process. The culture works in a wide temperature range. Low fermentation temperature < 77°F (25° C) results in a traditional acidification profile whereas high fermentation temperature 95-115° F (35-45° C) gives a US style product. 25 g of culture ferments 100 kg of meat. *Use dextrose as this culture ferments sugar slowly.*

F-RM-52 - Fast culture targeted for fermentation temperatures 70-90° F (22-32° C).

LHP - Extra fast cultures targeted for fermentation temperatures 80-100° F (26-38° C).

Bactoferm® MOLD 600 - White mold cultures for surface coverage.

There is not one universal temperature for fermenting, drying or even storing. There is an acceptable range of temperatures that correspond to each particular process. When starter cultures are used, the fermentation temperature can vary from the minimum to the maximum setting recommended by the manufacturer and as long as we follow this advice the sausage will turn out fine. Technical information sheets provide the recommended temperatures for fermentation, however, *bacteria will also ferment at lower temperatures, just more slowly.* For example, the technical information sheet for T-SPX lists temperatures as 26-38° C, optimum being 32° C. T-SPX will ferment as well at 20-24° C which is not uncommon for "European" style sausages and 48 hours or more is not atypical.

When freeze-dried cultures are used it is recommended to disperse them in water. Adding 25 grams of powdered culture to 200 kg (440 lbs.) of meat makes uniform distribution quite challenging. That comes to about 1/2 teaspoon to 4.5 kg (10 lbs.) of meat and the culture must be very uniformly dispersed otherwise defects will occur later on. It is then advisable, especially at home conditions, to dissolve culture in a little amount of *chlorine free* water, wait 15-30 minutes and then pour down over the meat. Mixing cultures with water before use allows them to cross the "lag phase" faster and to react with meat sooner. Cultures distributed by Internet online companies are of the freeze dried type.

Most people mix all ingredients together, sometimes with little water in a blender as this allows better distribution of ingredients during mixing. *Starter cultures should not be mixed with salt, nitrite or spices in advance* as unpredictable growth of culture bacteria may occur (all they need is a bit of moisture from spices). As a result starter cultures with different characteristics will be introduced into the sausage. Starter cultures should be added to the sausage mass just before stuffing. They may be mixed with other ingredients at the same time, but the stuffed sausage should enter the fermentation stage as soon as the sausages reach room temperature. Once fast-fermented starter culture or Gdl has been added to the sausage mix, the mix should be immediately filled into casings.

Safety Hurdles

Think of safety hurdles as a sophisticated alarm system. It consists of many components: perimeter protection (switches on doors, foil on windows, switch mats, trap wire etc), then a second line of defense comes into play: (motion detectors, glass breakage detectors, photo-electric eyes etc). Fermented sausages are like a sophisticated alarm - they need many security measures (hurdles) to stop undesirable bacteria. Using a combination of different hurdles is more effective that relying on one method only.

For example the first hurdle is an application of salt and sodium nitrite which slows down spoilage and keeps pathogenic bacteria at bay. This first hurdle is a temporary one, and if we don't follow up with additional hurdles, such as lowering pH and then lowering water activity Aw, the product will spoil. Typical safety hurdles:

- Selecting meats with a low bacteria
- Processing sausages at low temperatures
- Adding salt and nitrite/Nitrate
- Lowering pH of the meat to < 5.3 by adding sugar
- Lowering Aw (water activity) by drying to < 0.91
- Using starter culture
- Smoking
- Cooking
- Spices
- Cleanliness and common sense

Salt

When making fermented sausages use between 2.5-3.5 % salt as this combined with nitrite, is your first line of defense against undesirable bacteria. Almost all *regular* sausage recipes, regardless of whether fresh or cooked, contain 1.5-2% of salt which is added to obtain a good flavor. These amounts are *not high enough* to provide safety against bacteria and *there is no room for compromise.* When adding salt to fermented sausages try to think of salt as a *barrier* against undesirable bacteria. Use 3.0 - 3.5% salt when making traditionally fermented dry sausages and 2.5% for fast-fermented and spreadable types. Although starter cultures assure proper fermentation, nevertheless to inhibit undesirable bacteria in the beginning of the process, the salt level should remain high (2.5-3%).

Nitrates

You must not make fermented sausages without nitrite/Nitrate as they provide protection against pathogenic bacteria. For your own safety nitrates should be applied at the maximum allowable limits. Research that was done on the flavor of traditionally produced sausages concluded that sausages made with Nitrate exhibited superior quality to those that were made with nitrite only. A panel of professional testers-judges has made this finding (*A. Marco, J.L. Navarro. M. Flores, The Sensory Quality of Dry Fermented Sausages as Affected by Fermentation Stage and Curing Agents, Eur Food Res Technol, (2008), 226:449-458.*).

In the past, Nitrate was predominantly used as a curing agent as most sausages were of the dry type. Those sausages were made slowly and at low temperatures, which provided sufficient time for color and flavor forming bacteria to reduce Nitrate to nitrite. With today's faster production times sodium nitrite (Cure #1) is used as it *does not depend on microbial action and works better than Nitrate at low temperatures.* Employing only Nitrate during low temperature curing does little for the color as curing bacteria work best at 8° C (46° F) or higher. For these reasons a combination of nitrite and Nitrate (Cure #2) is applied to slow-fermented products, as nitrite starts reacting with meat at low temperatures and Nitrate guarantees a stable color during long term drying. Fast or medium-fast fermented sausages are made with nitrite (Cure # 1) only.

Sugar

Fresh meat contains very little glucose (0.08-0.1%), which is not enough for lactic acid bacteria to produce any significant amount of lactic acid. Adding sufficient amounts of sugar is of great importance for fast-fermented sausages which rely on acidity as a main safety hurdle. About 0.3-1% dextrose (glucose) must be introduced into meat when making a fast fermented product.

For slow-fermented sausages the amount of added sugar is much smaller (0.1-0.3%), as the microbiological safety is achieved by drying products and not by increasing acidity. Many traditional long dried sausages do not employ any sugars at all. In general, increasing sugar levels up to 1% decreases pH proportionally. In specific products (e.g. American pepperoni), limiting sugar to 0.5-0.75% creates adequate fermentation with no residual carbohydrate present after fermentation. *A lower pH is obtained with increasing temperature at the same sugar level.*

Amount of sugar in %	final pH
0.3	more than 5.0
0.5 - 0.7	less than 5.0
1.0	4.5

Carbohydrate (1%)	Lactic acid produced (%)	Final pH
Glucose	0.98	4.08
Saccharose	0.86	4.04
Maltose	0.72	4.24
Maltodextrin	0.54	4.54
Galactose	0.31	4.83
Raffinose	0.08	6.10

Lactic acid production and final pH achieved by *Lactobacillus pentosus* during growth in MRS-broth at 86° F, 30° C for 12 hours.

Data of Chr. Hansen

The types of sugar which may be used in making fermented sausages are listed below:

Glucose - also known as *dextrose,* is sugar refined from corn starch which is approximately 70% as sweet as sucrose.

It is the simplest form of sugar that serves as a building block for most carbohydrates and because of its simplicity it can be directly fermented into lactic acid by all lactic bacteria. It is the fastest acting sugar for lowering pH. As lowering pH is the main hurdle against bacteria growth *in fast-fermented sausages, dextrose is the sugar of choice.*

Sucrose - common sugar (also called saccharose) made from sugar cane and sugar beets but also appears in fruit, honey, sugar maple and in many other sources. Sucrose is composed of 50% glucose and 50% fructose and is the second fastest acting sugar. It can be used with Gdl in medium-fermented sausages. In slow-fermented sausages common sugar can be used as it has been used for hundreds of years. Addition of glucose and common sugar contributes to the safety of the sausage, strong curing color and better flavor.

Fructose - commonly found in fruits and honey. It can be obtained in a supermarket.

Maltose - malt sugar is made from germinating cereals such as barley which is an important part of the brewing process. It's added mainly to offset a sour flavor and to lower water activity as its fermenting qualities are poor.

Lactose - also referred to as milk sugar, makes up around 2–8% of milk (by weight) and has poor fermenting qualities. It is composed of glucose and galactose. Non fat dry milk contains about 52% of lactose. Lactose binds water well. Non fat dry milk can be obtained in a supermarket.

Galactose - makes up half of lactose, the sugar found in milk.

Raffinose - can be found in beans, cabbage, broccoli, asparagus, other vegetables and whole grains.

Maltodextrin - type of sugar usually made from rice, corn, or potato starch. It is commonly used for the production of natural sodas.

Spices

Without a doubt *black pepper is the most popular spice* added to fermented sausages (0.2-0.3%, 2-3 g/kg). The most popular spices in the manufacture of fermented sausages are *pepper and garlic*. Spices added to the sausage also contribute to the flavor, more so in fast-fermented products. Spices lose their aroma rapidly and their contribution to flavor in slow-fermented sausages is weaker.

Use of fresh spice in fermented products is generally not a good idea. Fresh spices being moist may contain bacteria, insects, and molds, which may negatively affect the manufacturing process.

Flavor

Dry sausages made with *pepper only* will have the wonderful mellow cheesy flavor, *which is created in time by the reaction of bacteria with meat.* Fast-fermented sausages will always exhibit this tangy and sourly flavor as flavor forming bacteria don't get sufficient time to work with meat. In this case a variety of spices, sugars and syrups can somewhat off set the acidity of the meat.

The metabolism of sugar by bacteria and lactic acid production is directly responsible for the tangy or sour taste in fast fermented sausages. The lower pH the more sourly flavor especially noticeable in fast-fermented products. The true salami flavor of a slow-fermented sausage depends mainly on the breakdown of sugars, fats and proteins through the fermentation and drying process. These reactions are products of microbiological action of color and flavor forming bacteria, which need sufficient time in order to develop a true salami flavor.

The little fermentation that takes place in dry products, is due to lactic acid bacteria reacting with small amounts of sugar (glycogen) present in meat. Even today, in true Hungarian salami, the addition of starter cultures and sugars is not permitted in order to eliminate any possibility of the acidic taste of the sausage. The commercial salami flavor is influenced by the acidity of the sausage and addition of spices and flavorings.

As the sausage matures, its flavor becomes more mellow due to a slight decrease in acidity. This also happens to wines and brandy, as they mature the taste improves and brandy in time becomes cognac. The noticeable difference in flavor between South European, North European and American fermented sausages is not due to spice combinations, but to different manufacturing methods which are used for making sausages. These methods influence the choice of starter cultures, fermentation temperatures, amounts and types of sugars, and the resulting pH drop.

Another huge factor is the presence or absence of color and flavor forming *Micrococcaceae* bacteria, which are responsible for the sausage aroma. It should be pointed out that *as the sausage slowly dries out, it loses moisture, but not the original amount of salt which remains inside.* That will change the proportion of salt in regards to the new weight of the meat and the sausage will taste saltier. The truth is that this is hardly noticeable due to the bacterial action on proteins and fats which somehow cover up this saltiness.

The supermarket variety of semi dry sausages is made in a few days at the lowest cost possible. There is no time for flavor forming bacteria to start breaking proteins and fats; the rapidly dropping pH prevents them from doing so. During fermentation the main bacterial action is due to lactic acid bacteria which are producing lactic acid. The faster acidity is achieved, the faster the sausage becomes microbiologically stable and sooner it can be distributed into stores. This technology is popular in North Europe and especially in the USA.

Without starter cultures it will be very risky to attempt making fast-fermented (semi-dry) sausages which will not be subsequently cooked, as the safety of this type of sausages relies heavily on a fast pH drop to 5.3 or less in about 48 hours. Without starter cultures such a fast pH drop is difficult to achieve unless Gdl is introduced.

Choosing Sausage Type

Choosing the sausage type is the first step as it determines fermentation and drying temperatures, total production time, amount and type of sugar used, type of starter cultures and other factors. *By now you should realize that with one recipe you can make different sausage types (slow or fast-fermented) and it is entirely up to you which way you want to go.* Twenty years ago a hobbyist had only one choice, and that was a slow-fermented sausage. Today, starter cultures are easily obtainable and all types of fermented sausages can be produced at home. Let's say you have a recipe for a fresh Italian sausage and you want to make a fermented sausage out of it. All you need is to increase the percentage of salt, add sodium nitrite, starter culture and decide whether you want to wait 3 months before you can eat it, or whether you want to take it with you on a hunting trip that happens in one week time.

Classical dry fermented sausages are the hardest to manufacture. They also require the most time and care. Therefore, it is advised to start with semi-dry sausages first, which are faster, easier and safer to produce. After they are fermented, smoked and cooked they become great snacks, which can be taken everywhere. They can be left hanging in the kitchen and even though they will lose more moisture in time, they will still be safe to consume. Then, as more experience is gained, more difficult sausages can be attempted.

Adapting Known Sausage Recipes

There are many sausages, for example Soviet, Moscow or Tambov, which technically speaking are dry salami. The meat was cured with salt and nitrate for 5-7 days at 40° F (4° C), then cold smoked for 3-5 days below 71° F (22° C) and then dried for 25-30 days at 54-56° F (12-14° C). Of course, no starter cultures were used. Those were naturally fermented sausages as some fermentation took place during the cold smoking stage. With starter cultures, these sausages can be much safer to produce today at home. By using different cultures and adjusting the fermentation and drying temperatures, the same sausage recipe can produce a semi-dry or dry sausage. Information presented in this chapter is by no means complete and should be thought of only as an introduction to the science of making fermented products. It is paraphrased from our book *The Art of Making Fermented Sausages* where a reader will find more detailed information on the subject.

The recipes are calculated for 1 kg of meat. This requires 0.12 g T-SPX starter culture or 0.25 g of F-LC, or LHP culture. A compact digital scale with an accuracy of 0.01 g is needed. Another solution is to make 5 kg of sausage at the time and the amount of culture may be estimated using a teaspoon: 0.6 g (¼ tsp.) of T-SPX and 1.2 g (½ tsp.) of F-LC.

Air Dried Sausages

Air dried sausages such as Spanish chorizo or cold smoked and dried sausages, conform to the same safety rules as fermented sausages. In many cases they are made without starter cultures and all safety hurdles as explained in this chapter must be obeyed. Fresh meat, processing at low temperatures, and a high percentage of salt and sodium nitrite will offer protection in the initial stages of production. Then as the sausage keeps on drying, it loses more moisture and becomes more stable in time. Needless to say, the production of fermented and air dried sausages require more skill and knowledge on the part of a sausage maker.

Equipment

To be able to precisely control temperature, humidity, and air speed requires expensive computer controlled drying chambers, however, a hobbyist must use his ingenuity in order to come up with suitable solutions. Making fermented sausages at home definitely presents some difficulties, which we don't have to face when making other types of sausages. It is very helpful to have a system capable of automated temperature and humidity adjustments, but those with limited funds will have to improvise a bit. Without a doubt the precise control of such a vast range of temperatures 50-104° F (10-40° C) and humidity (60-95%) is not easy. There are no small drying chambers designed for home production of fermented sausages, and one has to assemble his own system. Commercial producers use huge rooms with air conditioning ducts supplying air at the right temperature, humidity and speed. There is a refrigerator in every kitchen and that appliance can be quite easily adapted for fermenting and drying sausages. A used refrigerator can be obtained everywhere and as long as it works it will fit our purpose. Most refrigerators are made with a separate freezer door which is normally located in the upper part of the unit. Well, this unit is not needed and will not become part of the system. If a one door refrigerator can be found it works even better.

Temperature Control

There is a problem with the refrigerator's temperature range as its thermostat is made to control temperatures between 0-4° C (32-40° F). Such temperatures are not needed during fermenting and drying sausages. Fortunately, there is a commonly available device called a line voltage thermostat. It is an electronic temperature control or rather a combination of a temperature sensors, switches and electronic controls that can transform an ordinary refrigerator into a wonderful drying chamber. It is made by a few companies (see Links of Interest).

Line Voltage Thermostat - Single Stage

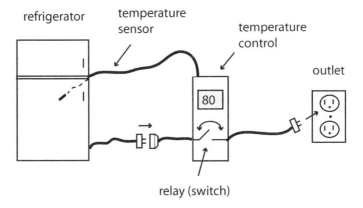

Fig. 20.3 Electronic temperature control in *cooler* mode.

A refrigerator is *unplugged* from the outlet and is then plugged into the temperature control which is plugged into the electrical outlet. The refrigerator's thermostat is not controlling the temperature anymore and is taken over by the temperature sensor in the controller, which is inserted into the refrigerator.

There is no need to drill a hole as the refrigerator door has rubber insulation and the sensor's cable is thin. In short terms, the micro-processor monitors the temperature through the sensor and when the temperature is warmer than the set point, the processor will energize the internal relay (switch).

This allows the refrigerator to draw the current from the controller and start cooling. The drawing is not to scale and the typical unit is about: 6.5" x 2.7" x 2.5". These units can control coolers, heaters or any electrical devices.

The unit depicted in Fig. 20.3 is *a single stage control which means that it can control only one device at a time.* A line voltage thermostat set to "cooling mode" can only decrease temperature lower than the temperature that remains outside the refrigerator. There are instances when the temperature inside the chamber must be higher:

• Fast fermented sausages made with starter cultures which require fermentation temperatures of around 86 -113° F (30 - 45° C).

• Drying chamber is located in a cool climate where temperatures are below 68° F (20° C) for a larger part of the year. Under such circumstances the same line voltage thermostat can be combined with a heater and used in the heating mode.

In such a case the temperature control is switched to "heating mode", *the refrigerator is disconnected* and *the heater is plugged* into the temperature control. The refrigerator becomes now a drying chamber.

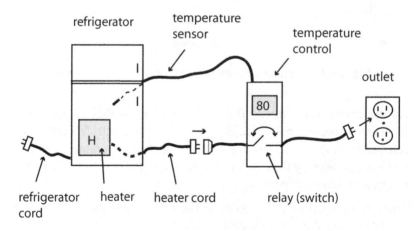

Fig. 20.4 Electronic temperature control in *heater* mode. Refrigerator not working but used as a fermentation/drying chamber. Any kind of box or chamber will work with this arrangement.

Any little heating element, ceramic heater, heat lamp or even a UL approved light fixture will easily raise the temperature in a small unit such as a refrigerator. Using an ordinary light bulb is not recommended as prolonged exposure to light creates rancidity in fat. Temperature control can be used in the heating mode during fermentation, which lasts on average about 1-2 days and even less for fast fermented products. Then, when a product enters the drying stage, the heater can be removed and the control unit is switched back into the cooling mode. When ambient temperatures are low and the heating mode is selected, the refrigerator can still be used as a drying chamber, even though it is disconnected from the power supply.

In cooler climates it is practical to build a large drying chamber (even a walk in unit) from any materials, as long as a good insulation is included. Then, not being limited by space, any kind of a free standing heater and humidifier can be placed inside providing there is electricity close by. These electronic temperature controls are very precise and can maintain the set temperature within 1 degree.

Line Voltage Thermostat - Two Stage

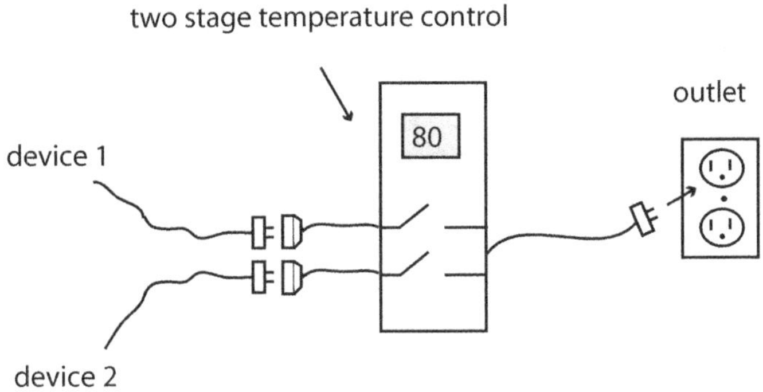

two stage temperature control

Fig. 20.5 Two stage line voltage thermostat.

The advantage of a two stage thermostat is that two independent devices such as a heater and a cooler, or a heater and the fan can be connected to only one temperature control. Two stage temperature control offers more possibilities but comes at a higher cost.

Humidity Control

Humidity control is much harder to accomplish than temperature. All those improvised arrangements such as placing salt covered with water in a shallow pan, or bringing more water filled pans into the chamber may increase the humidity level to 50-60%, which is nowhere close to the required humidity during fermentation.

The simplest way to control humidity is to install a small digital adjustable humidifier. A good unit should lock to the setting within a few percents. In industrial units increasing humidity is accomplished by steam injection but home units produce a cool vapor mist.

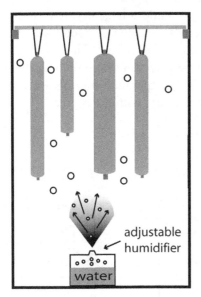

Fig. 20.6 Adjustable humidifier.

It should be noted that an average hygrometer is rated to indicate humidity plus or minus 3% at best. In reality they are even less accurate (10%) but there are more expensive calibrated units that are accurate within 1%.

Air conditioners and refrigerators dehumidify air until the relative humidity is around 40%. This is much too low for making fermented sausages, especially at the beginning of the fermentation stage when 90-95% humidity is recommended. If a sausage is fermented without humidity control, periodic spraying or immersing it in water will help a lot by providing 100% of humidity on its surface, if only for a short while.

There is a device called a line voltage humidistat which basically works like the temperature controls described earlier. When in "humidify" mode the device will increase humidity by switching on the humidifier. When in "dehumidify" mode the same device will switch on the fan to remove moist air from the chamber.

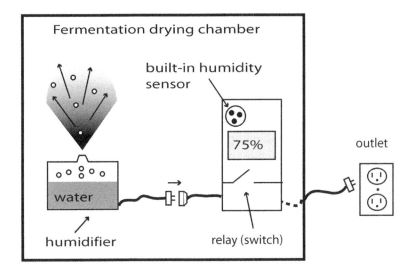

Fermentation drying chamber

built-in humidity sensor

75%

outlet

water

humidifier

relay (switch)

Fig. 20.7 Single stage humidistat.

The in line voltage humidistat depicted above comes with a built-in humidity sensor and must be installed within the drying chamber. There is a humidistat which comes with a remote humidity sensor and a control unit can be mounted outside of the drying chamber. Humidity control plays an important role in greenhouse production of flowers and vegetables and many clever devices can be obtained from green house equipment suppliers.

Air Speed

Air speed is a factor that helps remove moisture and stale air, and of course it influences drying. Sausages will dry faster at higher temperatures, but in order to prevent the growth of bacteria, drying must be performed at lower levels, generally between 59-53° F (15-12° C). The speed of drying does not remain constant, but changes throughout the process: it is the fastest during the beginning of fermentation, then it slows down to a trickle. At the beginning of fermentation humidity is very high due to the high moisture content of the sausage. *When starter cultures are used, the temperature is at the highest during fermentation* which speeds up moisture escape from the sausage.

The surface of the sausage contains a lot of moisture which must be constantly removed otherwise slime might appear. If the sausages are soaking wet during fermentation, the humidity should be lowered. At the beginning of fermentation the fastest air speed is applied, about 0.8 - 1.0 m/sec. *The speed of 3.6 km/h (2.2 mile/hour) corresponds to the speed of 1 meter/second.* Ideally, the amount of removed moisture should equal the amount of moisture moving to the surface.

To control air speed in improvised chambers such as a refrigerator is surprisingly easy. The most reliable device is a computer cooling fan as it is designed for working 24 hours a day. There is a huge variety of these fans and they come in different sizes, shapes and power outputs. The current draw of a typical 3" 12 VDC, 1.9 W fan is only 0.1 A. It runs from a 115 VAC adapter and the beauty of the design is that the adapter's output can be set to 12, 9, 7.5 or 6 VDC with a built in mini switch. Each voltage setting lets the fan run at a different speed and quite a sophisticated system is created.

If only a fixed DC output voltage adapter is available, a simple, inexpensive and universally available device called a "potentiometer" can be attached between the fan and the adapter. The device will control the fan's speed.

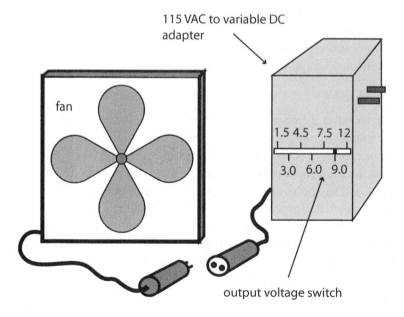

Fig. 20.8 Adjustable air speed fan.

Measuring pH

For someone who is serious about making fermented products, the pH meat tester made by Hanna Instruments (Photo 20.2) is of great help. Most people use disposable test strips such as the ones made by: *Micro Essential Laboratory, Inc., www.microessentiallab.com®*

Photo 20.3 pH testing strips, pH range: 3.9 - 5.7.

Photo 20.4 pH testing strips, pH range: 4.9 - 6.9.

These two strips will cover the entire range of pH values of fresh materials (meats and fats) and finished sausages. To use, mix 1 part finely chopped meat and 2 parts distilled water, tear off a strip of pH paper, dip into test solution, and match immediately to the color chart. No technical training is necessary. The results may be less accurate than those obtained with a pH meter, but the strips are very inexpensive. They can also be obtained online or at any pet store that sells fish.

Borenmetworst

Dutch specialty dry sausage, made without garlic.

Meat	Metric	US
pork	500 g	1.10 lb.
lean beef	200 g	0.44 lb.
back fat	300 g	0.66 lb.

Ingredients per 1000 g (1 kg) of meat:
salt, 3%

(salt in cure #2 accounted for)	28 g	5 tsp.
Cure #2	2.5 g	½ tsp.
dextrose (glucose)	3.0 g	½ tsp.
pepper	3.0 g	1½ tsp.
coriander	2.0 g	1 tsp.
mustard	2.0 g	1 tsp.
T-SPX culture	0.12 g	use scale

Instructions:
1. Grind pork and back fat through 3/16" plate (5 mm). Grind beef with ⅛" (3 mm) plate.
2. Mix all ingredients with meat.
3. Stuff firmly into large diameter (36-40 mm) hog casings. Form 24-30" long links, then tie ends together to make a ring.
4. Ferment at 20° C (68° F) for 72 hours, 90-85% humidity.
5. Cold smoke for 12 hours (<22° C, 72° F).
6. Dry at 16→12° C (60→54° F), 85-80% humidity. In about 6-8 weeks a shrink of 30% should be achieved.
7. Store sausages at 10-15° C (50-59° F), 75% humidity.

Notes:
Spices such as ginger and cloves are sometimes added.
Dry at 16→12° C signifies that the drying temperature should start at 16° C and decrease slowly to 12° C. Any temperature within 12-15° C is acceptable.

Cacciatore

Italian small dry sausage. Cacciatore means "hunter" in Italian and the story goes that hunters carried this sausage as a snack on long hunting trips.

Meat	Metric	US
lean pork	600 g	1.32 lb.
lean beef	100 g	0.22 lb.
back fat	300 g	0.66 lb.

Ingredients per 1000 g (1 kg) of meat:

salt, 3%		
(salt in cure #2 accounted for)	28 g	5 tsp.
Cure #2	2.5 g	½ tsp.
dextrose (glucose)	3.0 g	½ tsp.
pepper	3.0 g	1½ tsp.
coriander	2.0 g	1 tsp.
caraway	2.0 g	1 tsp.
red pepper	1.0 g	½ tsp.
garlic powder	1.5 g	½ tsp.
T-SPX culture	0.12 g	use scale

Instructions:

1. Grind pork and back fat through 3/16" plate (5 mm). Grind beef with ⅛" (3 mm) plate.
2. Mix all ingredients with meat.
3. Stuff firmly into large diameter 36-40 mm hog casings or beef rounds. Make 6" long links.
4. Dip into surface mold growing solution - Bactoferm™ M-EK-4.
5. Ferment at 20° C (68° F) for 72 hours, 95-90% humidity.
6. Dry for 2 days at 18→16° C (64→60° F), 90-85% humidity.
7. Dry at 16→12° C (60→54° F), 85 -80% humidity.
8. In about 6-8 weeks a shrink of 30% should be achieved.
9. Store sausages at 10-15° C (50-59° F), 75% humidity.

Cervelat

European semi-dry sausage, an equivalent of American summer sausage. Definition covers countless recipes and sausages with the name cervelat made in many countries. You can call Thuringer, the Thuringer Cervelat, or Summer Sausage the Cervelat Summer sausage and both names are correct describing the same type of sausage.

Meat	Metric	US
beef	700 g	1.54 lb.
pork	300 g	0.66 lb.

Ingredients per 1000 g (1 kg) of meat:

salt, 2.5%		
(salt in cure #1 accounted for)	23 g	4 tsp.
Cure #1	2.5 g	½ tsp.
dextrose (glucose)	10.0 g	2 tsp.
sugar	10.0 g	2 tsp.
ground black pepper	3.0 g	1½ tsp.
whole black pepper	2.0 g	1 tsp.
coriander	2.0 g	1 tsp.
whole mustard seeds	4.0 g	2 tsp.
ginger	1.0 g	½ tsp.
F-LC culture	0.24 g	use scale

Instructions:
1. Grind pork and beef through 3/16" plate (5 mm).
2. Mix all ingredients with meat.
3. Stuff into beef middles or fibrous casings about 60 mm diameter, form 30" links.
4. Ferment at 38° C (100° F) for 24 hours, 90-85% humidity.
5. Introduce warm smoke (43° C, 110° F), 70% humidity, for 12 hours. Gradually increase smoke temperature until internal meat temperature of 60° C, 140° F is obtained.
6. For a drier sausage: dry for 2 days at 22→16° C (70→60° F), 65-75% humidity or until desired weight loss has occurred.
7. Store sausages at 10-15° C (50-59° F), 75% humidity.

Chorizo

Spanish Chorizo is a dry sausage made from coarsely chopped pork seasoned with pepper, paprika and garlic. Spanish smoked paprika (sweet, bittersweet or hot) known as Pimentón gives it its deep red color.

Meat	Metric	US
lean pork, ham or butt (20% fat)	1000 g	2.20 lb.

Ingredients per 1000 g (1 kg) of meat:

salt, 3%		
(salt in cure #2 accounted for)	28 g	5 tsp.
Cure #2	2.5 g	½ tsp.
dextrose (glucose), 0.2%	2.0 g	⅓ tsp.
sugar, 0.2%	2.0 g	⅓ tsp.
pepper	6.0 g	3 tsp.
Spanish pimentón paprika, sweet	20 g	10 tsp.
Spanish pimentón paprika, hot	4.0 g	2 tsp.
oregano, rubbed	2.0 g	1 tsp.
garlic powder	2.0 g	1 tsp.
or chopped fresh garlic	7.0 g	2 cloves
T-SPX culture	0.12 g	use scale

Instructions:

1. Grind pork through ⅛" plate (3 mm).
2. Mix all ingredients with meat.
3. Stuff firmly into 32-36 mm hog casings, form 6" long links.
4. Ferment at 20° C (68° F) for 72 hours, 90-85% humidity.
5. Dry for 2 months at 16→12° C (60→54° F), 85-80% humidity.
7. Store sausages at 10-15° C (50-59° F), 75% humidity.

Fuet

Fuet is a Spanish pork sausage, dry cured, like salami. Sausage is frequently found in Cataluña, Spain. Unlike the Butifarra, another in the family of Catalan sausages, fuet is dry cured. The name fuet means "whip" in the Catalan language.

Meat	Metric	US
lean pork	700 g	1.54 lb.
back fat	300 g	0.66 lb.

Ingredients per 1000 g (1 kg) of meat:

salt, 3% (salt in cure #2 accounted for)	28 g	5 tsp.
Cure #2	2.5 g	½ tsp.
dextrose (glucose), 0.3%	3.0 g	½ tsp.
pepper	3.0 g	1½ tsp.
paprika	4.0 g	2 tsp.
garlic powder	3.0 g	1 tsp.
OR fresh garlic	7.0 g	2 cloves
T-SPX culture	0.12 g	use scale

Instructions:
1. Grind pork and back fat through 3/16" plate (5 mm).
2. Mix all ingredients with meat.
3. Stuff firmly into hog, beef middles or 38-50 protein lined fibrous casings.
4. Ferment at 20° C (68° F) for 72 hours, 90-85% humidity.
5. Dry at 16→12° C (60→54° F), 85-80% humidity for 1-2 months.
6. Store sausages at 10-15° C (50-59° F), 75% humidity.

Notes:
Some fuets are covered with white mold, others not. M-EK-4 Bactoferm™ mold culture can be applied.
The sausage is dried until around 30-35% in weight is lost.

Goteborg

Swedish dry sausage. Smoked.

Meat	Metric	US
pork (butt)	400 g	0.88 lb.
beef (chuck)	400 g	0.88 lb.
pork cheeks (jowls) or belly	200 g	0.44 lb.

Ingredients per 1000 g (1 kg) of meat:

salt, 3% (salt in Cure #2 accounted for)	28 g	5 tsp.
Cure #2	2.5 g	½ tsp.
dextrose (glucose), 0.2%	2.0 g	⅓ tsp.
sugar	2.0 g	⅓ tsp.
white pepper	3.0 g	1½ tsp.
cardamom	2.0 g	1 tsp.
coriander	2.0 g	1 tsp.
T-SPX culture	0.12 g	use scale

Instructions:

1. Grind pork and back fat through 3/16" plate (5 mm). Grind beef with ⅛" plate.
2. Mix all ingredients with meat.
3. Stuff firmly into 60 mm beef middles or protein lined fibrous casings. Make 16" long links.
4. Ferment at 20° C (68° F) for 72 hours, 90-85% humidity.
5. Cold smoke below 20° C (68° C) with thin smoke for 24 hours.
6. Dry at 16→12° C (60→54° F), 85-80% humidity, for 2-3 months. The sausage is dried until around 30-35% in weight is lost.
7. Store sausages at 10-15° C (50-59° F), 75% humidity.

Gothaer

German semi-dry sausage.

Meat	Metric	US
lean pork	800 g	1.76 lb.
beef	200 g	0.44 lb.

Ingredients per 1000 g (1 kg) of meat:
salt, 2.5% (salt in Cure #1

accounted for)	23 g	4 tsp.
Cure #1	2.5 g	½ tsp.
dextrose (glucose), 1%	10.0 g	2 tsp.
black pepper	3.0 g	1½ tsp.
F-LC culture	0.24 g	use scale

Instructions:
1. Grind pork through 3/16" plate (5 mm). Grind beef through 1/8" (3 mm) plate.
2. Mix all ingredients with meat.
3. Stuff into beef middles or fibrous casings 40-60 mm, 20" long.
4. Ferment at 24-30° C (75-86° F) for 24 hours, 90-85% humidity.
5. Introduce warm smoke (43° C, 110° F), 70% humidity, for 6 hours. Gradually increase smoke temperature until internal meat temperature of 140° F (60° C) is obtained.
6. For a drier sausage: dry for 3 days at 22→16° C (70→60° F), 65-75% humidity or until desired weight loss has occurred.
7. Store sausages at 10-15° C (50-59° F), 75% humidity.

Grassland Sausage
(*Kielbasa Kresowa*)

In many Eastern countries, Mongolia included, there are huge grasslands which are known as prairies in the USA. In Polish they are called "kresy" hence the name of the sausage. The following is the traditional recipe.

Meat	Metric	US
lean pork	600 g	0.1.32 lb.
lean beef or veal	200 g	0.44 lb.
pork back fat	200 g	0.44 lb.

Ingredients per 1000 g (1 kg) of meat:

salt	25 g	4 tsp.
Cure #2	2.5 g	½ tsp.
pepper	2.0 g	1 tsp.
allspice	2.0 g	1 tsp.
marjoram, ground	1.0 g	½ tsp.
cloves	0.5 g	¼ tsp.
bay leaf, crushed	1 leaf	1 leaf
rum	60 ml	¼ cup

Instructions:
1. Grind meats with 3/8" (10 mm) plate. Cut fat manually into ¾ " (20 mm) cubes.
2. Mix all ingredients with meat adding rum. Then add diced fat and mix everything together.
3. Stuff firmly into 45 mm beef middles or fibrous casings.
4. Place sausages between two wooden boards, place weight on top and leave in a cool place 50-54° F (10-12° C) for 2 weeks.
5. Remove boards and hang sausage in a ventilated cool place for 3 days.
6. Cold smoke for 7 days.
7. Store in a cool, dry place.

Notes: to make an easier and modern hot smoked version of the sausage, replace Cure #2 with Cure #1, decrease salt to 18 g, mix all ingredients, then hot smoke and cook the sausage. Store in refrigerator.

Holsteiner

German dry sausage.

Meat	Metric	US
beef (chuck)	600 g	1.32 lb.
pork butt	400 g	0.88 lb.

Ingredients per 1000 g (1 kg) of meat:

	Metric	US
salt, 3% (salt in Cure #2 accounted for)	28 g	5 tsp.
Cure #2	2.5 g	½ tsp.
dextrose (glucose), 0.2%	2.0 g	⅓ tsp.
sugar	2.0 g	⅓ tsp.
white pepper	2.0 g	1 tsp.
cracked white pepper	2.0 g	1 tsp.
T-SPX culture	0.12 g	use scale

Instructions:
1. Grind pork through 3/16" plate (5 mm). Grind beef with 1/8" plate.
2. Mix all ingredients with meat.
3. Stuff firmly into 60 mm beef middles or protein lined fibrous casings. Make 16" long links.
4. Ferment at 20° C (68° F) for 72 hours, 90-85% humidity.
5. Cold smoke below 20° C (68° C) with thin smoke for 24 hours. (Smoke can already be applied in the second half of the fermentation stage).
6. Dry at 16→12° C (60→54° F), 85-80% humidity, for 2-3 months. The sausage is dried until around 30-35% in weight is lost.
7. Store sausages at 10-15° C (50-59° F), 75% humidity.

Hungarian Smoked Sausage

Hungarian Smoked Sausage is a cold smoked, mettwurst style, naturally fermented spreadable sausage.

Meat	Metric	US
pork back fat or fat trimmings	700 g	1.54 lb.
beef	300 g	0.66 lb.

Ingredients per 1000 g (1 kg) of meat:

salt	24 g	4 tsp.
Cure #1	1.5 g	¼ tsp.
pepper	3.0 g	1½ tsp.
paprika	2.0 g	1 tsp.

Instructions:

1. Grind meat through 2 mm plate. Cut back fat into 15 mm (1/4") pieces.
2. Mix ground beef adding pepper until the mass feels sticky. Mix diced back fat with paprika, then mix everything together. Do not add water.
3. Stuff firmly into 40 mm beef rounds, 20-30" (50-75) cm long. Do not add water. Prick any visible air pockets with a needle.
4. Hang for 1-2 days at 2-6° C (35-42° F), 85-90% humidity. At this stage curing continues and beneficial curing and flavor forming bacteria start to grow.
5. Smoke with a thin cold smoke for 3-4 days until a yellow color with occasional red areas is obtained. At this stage natural fermentation takes place although pH drop (acidity increase) is insignificant as no sugar is added. Due to a large amount of fat (fat contains only 15% water), the sausage loses moisture rapidly.
6. Dry at 16→12° C (60→54° F), 85-80% humidity, for 1-2 months. The sausage is dried until around 30-35% in weight is lost.
7. Store sausages at 10-15° C (50-59° F), 75% humidity.

Kantwurst

Kantwurst is an original Austrian dry sausage, very unique in its characteristic square shape.

Meat	Metric	US
lean pork	800 g	1.76 lb.
back fat	200 g	0.44 lb.

Ingredients per 1000 g (1 kg) of meat:

salt, 3%		
(salt in Cure #2 accounted for)	28 g	5 tsp.
Cure #2	2.5 g	½ tsp.
dextrose (glucose), 0.3%	3.0 g	1 tsp.
pepper	3.0 g	1½ tsp.
coriander	2.0 g	1 tsp.
caraway	2.0 g	1 tsp.
garlic powder	1.5 g	½ tsp.
T-SPX culture	0.12 g	use scale

Instructions:
1. Grind pork and back fat through 3/16" plate (5 mm).
2. Mix all ingredients with meat.
3. Stuff loosely (80% capacity) into large diameter fibrous casings (70 mm). Place stuffed sausage between two boards, with some weight on top to flatten the sausage. Then move to a fermentation room.
4. Ferment at 20° C (68° F) for 96 hours, 95-90% humidity.
5. Remove boards and wipe off any slime that might have accumulated under boards.
6. Dry at room temperature until casings are dry to the touch. Hang square shaped sausages on smokesticks.
7. Cold smoke at 20° C (68° F) for a few hours to prevent growth of mold.
8. Dry for 2 days at 20→18° C (68→64° F), 90-85% humidity. Apply smoke from time to time.
9. Dry at 16→12° C (60→54° F), 85 -80% humidity. In about 8 weeks a shrink of 30% should be achieved.
10. Store sausages at 10-15° C (50-59° F), 75% humidity.

Notes:

To make a semi-dry version of the sausage, add total of 1% dextrose and ferment at 24° C (75° F) for 48 hours.

Kindziuk

Kindziuk - known in Poland as Kindziuk and in Lithuania as Skilandis, is an almost legendary product, famous for its long keeping properties. The sausage made from pork and beef is smoked and dried, but not cooked. It may be considered a traditionally fermented product.

Meat	Metric	US
lean pork	850 g	1.87 lb.
lean beef	150 g	0.33 lb.

Ingredients per 1000 g (1 kg) of meat:

salt, 3.5% (salt in Cure #2 accounted for)	33 g	6 ½ tsp.
Cure #2	2.5 g	½ tsp.
sugar	1.0 g	¼ tsp.
pepper	2.0 g	1 tsp.
herbal pepper*	1.0 g	½ tsp.
garlic	3.0 g	1 clove

Instructions:

1. Cut meat into 2" pieces. Rub in salt, Cure # 2 and sugar and leave on a screen for 3-4 days at 3-4° C (37-40° F).
2. Cut pork into 20-30 mm (¾-1¼") by 10-15 mm (3/8-5/8") pieces.
3. Grind beef through 2-3 mm (1/8") plate.
4. Mix beef with all spices. Add pork and mix everything together.
5. Stuff firmly into pork stomach, bladder, 60 mm beef middles or 60 mm fibrous casings. Reinforce with butcher's twine: two loops lengthwise and loops across the casings every 2" (5 cm). Form 10-12 cm (4-5") hanging loop on one end.
6. Hang for 2 months at 2-4° C (35-40° F).
7. Apply cold smoke 18-22° C (64-72° F) for 8 hours.
8. Hang in a cool place for 2 weeks.
9. Apply cold smoke again at 18-22° C (64-72° F) for 8 hours.
10. Dry for 2 months at 8° C (46° F) and 75% humidity. The sausage should lose about 35% of its original weight.
11. Store in a dark, cool and dry place.

Notes:

Meat should come from mature animals. Remove all sinews, glands and gristle. Originally all ingredients were stuffed into the pork stomach or bladder. The stomach was sewn and the bladder was tied off with butcher twine. Traditional Kindziuk was smoked with alder wood. Don't decrease the amount of salt. Salt and nitrite are the first line of defense against spoilage and pathogenic bacteria. Then as the sausage dries out it becomes more microbiologically stable every day.

* Herbal pepper is a combination of spices which is used in many countries such as French Quatre-epices (pepper, nutmeg, cloves, cinnamon) or Indian curry powder (turmeric, coriander, fenugreek, cumin and other spices). Italian seasoning (marjoram, thyme, rosemary, savory, sage, oregano and basil) is another known combination of herbs. In East European countries such as Poland or Lithuania herbal pepper is commercially made and available in supermarkets. A typical Polish herbal pepper contains: white mustard seed, caraway, marjoram, chili, hot and sweet paprika and bay leaf. You can buy pre-mixed spices or use your imagination for creating your own version. If you decide to go without herbal pepper, use 3 g (1½ tsp) of black or white pepper.

Photo 20.5 Kindziuk.

Photo courtesy Robert Winckiewicz

Landjager

Landjager is a German sausage similar to Austrian Kantwurst as both sausages are flattened during fermentation, which gives them a rectangular shape.

Meat	Metric	US
pork (70/30)	700 g	1.54 lb.
lean beef	300 g	0.66 lb.

Ingredients per 1000 g (1 kg) of meat:

salt, 3%		
(salt in Cure #2 accounted for)	28 g	5 tsp.
Cure #2	2.5 g	½ tsp.
dextrose (glucose), 0.3%	3.0 g	½ tsp.
pepper	3.0 g	1 ½ tsp.
cumin	2.0 g	1 tsp.
nutmeg	1.0 g	½ tsp.
T-SPX culture	0.12 g	use scale

Instructions:
1. Grind pork through 3/16" plate (5 mm). Grind beef through ⅛" (3 mm) plate.
2. Mix all ingredients with meat.
3. Stuff loosely (80% capacity) into 32-36 mm hog casings. Make links 8" (20 cm) long. Place stuffed sausage between two boards, with some weight on top, to flatten the sausage. Then move to a fermentation room.
4. Ferment at 20° C (68° F) for 72 hours, 95-90% humidity.
5. Remove boards and wipe off any slime that might have accumulated under boards.
6. Dry at room temperature until casings are dry to the touch. Hang square shaped sausages on smokesticks.
7. Cold smoke (< 20° C/68° F) for a few hours to prevent growth of mold.
8. Dry at 16→12° C (60→54° F), 85 -80% humidity. In about six weeks a shrink of 30% should be achieved.
9. Store sausages at 10-15° C (50-59° F), 75% humidity.
Notes:
To make a semi-dry version of the sausage, add total of 1% dextrose and ferment at 24° C (75° F) for 24 hours.

Lap Cheong

Chinese sausage is a dried, hard sausage usually made from pork meat and a high content of fat. The Chinese name for sausages is "Lap Cheong" which means the "winter stuffed intestine" or "waxed intestine" because "cheong" not only means "intestine" but also "sausage". This sausage is normally smoked, sweetened, and seasoned. It is used as an ingredient in many dishes in some parts of southern China, including Hong Kong and countries in Southeast Asia. It is for example, used in fried rice, noodles and other dishes. Chinese sausage formulations are unique, based on a long tradition. Ingredients such as monosodium glutamate, soy sauce and sugar are added to the sausages in very high levels. The addition of selected Chinese rice wines or even scotch or sherry are common for certain quality products.

Meat	Metric	US
pork butt	1000 g	2.20 lb.

Ingredients per 1000 g (1 kg) of meat:

salt, 2.5%		
(salt in Cure #1 accounted for)	24 g	4 tsp.
Cure #1	2.5 g	½ tsp.
dextrose (glucose), 1%	10.0 g	2 tsp.
sugar 4%	40 g	8 tsp.
cinnamon	2 g	1 tsp.
MSG (monosodium glutamate)	2 g	1 tsp.
rice wine	25 ml	1 oz.
F-LC culture	0.24 g	use scale

Instructions:
1. Grind pork and back fat through ⅜" plate (10 mm).
2. Mix all ingredients with meat.
3. Stuff firmly into hog or sheep casings 18-26 mm and form 5-6" (15 cm) long links.
4. Ferment at 38° C (100° F) for 12 hours, 90-85% humidity.
5. Apply light smoke at 45° C (115° F), 70% humidity for 6 hours. The sausage is still fermenting (F-LC culture is able to produce lactic acid at this temperature).
6. Gradually increase smoke temperature until internal meat temperature becomes 154° F (68° C).
7. Store sausages at 10-15° C (50-59° F), 75% humidity.
Notes: The traditional Chinese way, still applied today, is a time consuming operation of cutting meat by hand into small cubes. Chinese are fond of using MSG (monosodium glutamate), but it may be removed from the recipe.

Lebanon Bologna
(*Traditional method*)

This well known American sausage has its roots in the town of Lebanon, Pennsylvania, where it was made by German settlers. This is a semi-dry, fermented, heavily smoked, *all-beef* sausage which is not cooked. The traditional process (no starter cultures) calls for curing beef at 4-6° C (40-43° F) for 10 days.

Meat	Metric	US
beef	1000 g	2.20 lb.

Ingredients per 1000 g (1 kg) of meat:

salt, 3%		
(salt in Cure #1 accounted for)	28 g	5 tsp.
Cure #1	2.5 g	½ tsp.
sugar 3%	30 g	6 tsp.
dextrose (glucose), 0.3%	3.0 g	½ tsp.
pepper	3.0 g	1½ tsp.
allspice	2.0 g	1 tsp.
cinnamon	2.0 g	1 tsp.
cloves. ground	0.5 g	1/4 tsp.
ginger	0.5 g	⅓ tsp.

Instructions:

1. Curing. Grind beef with a large plate (3/4", 20 mm), mix with salt, Cure #1 and sugar and keep for 10 days at 4-6° C (40-43° F).
2. Grind cured beef through 1/8 - 3/16" (3-5 mm) plate.
3. Mix ground meat with all ingredients.
4. Stuff sausage mix into 40-120 mm casings. Natural beef middles, collagen or fibrous casings. The larger casings are tied and stockinetted or laced with butcher twine for support as this is a large and heavy sausage.
5. Cold smoke for 4-8 days at (< 22° C/72° F), 85% humidity.
6. For a drier sausage: dry at 16→12° C (60→54° F), 85-80% humidity.
7. Store sausages at 10-15° C (50-59° F), 75% humidity.

Notes:

Final pH: around 4.2-4.4, water activity 0.93-0.96, it is a moist sausage but extremely stable due to its low final pH. The sausage is often left for 3 days at 4-6° C (40-43° F) for additional ripening. The sausage was traditionally cold smoked for 7 days in winter months and 4 days in the summer.

Lebanon Bologna
(with starter culture)

Meat	Metric	US
beef	1000 g	2.20 lb.

Ingredients *per 1000 g (1 kg) of meat:*

salt, 3%		
(salt in Cure #1 accounted for)	28 g	5 tsp.
Cure #1	2.5 g	½ tsp.
sugar 3%	30 g	6 tsp.
dextrose (glucose), 0.3%	3.0 g	½ tsp.
pepper	3.0 g	1½ tsp.
allspice	2.0 g	1 tsp.
cinnamon	2.0 g	1 tsp.
cloves. ground	1.0 g	½ tsp.
ginger	0.5 g	⅓ tsp.
T-SPX culture	0.12 g	use scale

Instructions:
1. Grind beef through 1/8 - 3/16" (3-5 mm) plate.
2. Mix ground beef with all ingredients, including starter culture.
3. Stuff sausage mix into 40-120 mm casings. Natural beef middles, collagen or fibrous casings. The larger casings are tied and stockinetted or laced with butcher twine for support as this is a large and heavy sausage.
4. Ferment at 24° C (75° F) for 72 hours, 90-85% humidity.
5. Cold smoke for 2 days at (< 22° C/72° F), 85% humidity.
6. For a drier sausage: dry at 16→12° C (60→54° F), 85-80% humidity.
7. Store sausages at 10-15° C (50-59° F), 75% humidity.

Notes:
Final pH around 4.6, water activity 0.93-0.96, it is a moist sausage but extremely stable due to its low final pH. The sausage is often left for 3 days at 4-6° C (40-43° F) for additional ripening.
If no cold smoke is available, smoke with hot smoke for 6 hours. Start at 110° F (43° C), then gradually increase temperature and smoke at 120° F (49° C) for 3-4 hours.
Traditionally made Lebanon Bologna is not cooked. To comply with increasingly tougher government regulations for preventing the growth of *E. coli 0157:H7*, most manufacturers subject this sausage to a heat treatment.

Lithuanian Sausage

Lithuanian cold smoked sausage.

Meat	Metric	US
pork butt	500 g	1.10 lb.
beef chuck	150 g	0.33 lb.
rabbit	200 g	0.44 lb.
back fat	150 g	0.33 lb.

Ingredients per 1000 g (1 kg) of meat:

salt	30 g	5 tsp.
Cure #2	2.5 g	½ tsp.
pepper	4.0 g	2 tsp.
marjoram	1.5 g	1 tsp.
allspice	2.0 g	1 tsp.
cloves	2.0 g	1 tsp.
rum	60 ml	¼ cup

Instructions:

1. Grind all meats with a 3/8" grinder plate. Manually cut back fat into and ⅛ x ⅛ x ¾" strips.
2. Mix everything together.
3. Stuff firmly into 45 mm beef middles or fibrous casings.
4. Place sausages between two wooden boards, place weight on top and leave in a cool place 50-54° F (10-12° C) for 2 weeks.
5. Remove boards and hang sausage in a ventilated cool place for 3 days.
6. Cold smoke for 7 days.
7. Store in a cool, dry place.

Loukanka

Loukanka is a very well known Bulgarian dry sausage. It is formed into a traditional flat shape and it has great keeping qualities.

Meat	Metric	US
lean pork	800 g	1.76 lb.
pork back fat or fat trimmings	200 g	0.44 lb.

Ingredients per 1000 g (1 kg) of meat:

salt, 3% (salt in Cure #2 accounted for)	28 g	5 tsp.
Cure #2	2.5 g	½ tsp.
dextrose (glucose), 0.2%	2.0 g	⅓ tsp.
cumin	2.0 g	1 tsp.
garlic powder	3.0 g	1 tsp.
OR fresh garlic	10.0 g	3 cloves
T-SPX culture	0.12 g	use scale

Instructions:
1. Grind lean pork and fat through 3/16" plate (5 mm).
2. Mix all ingredients with meat.
3. Stuff firmly into 28-30 mm hog casings.
4. Ferment at 20° C (68° F) for 72 hours, 90-85% humidity. At the beginning of the fermentation process place weight on sausages to flatten them out.
5. Dry at 16→12° C (60→54° F), 85-80% humidity for about 1-2 months.
6. Store sausages at 10-15° C (50-59° F), 75% humidity.

Notes:
Loukanka has very little tang due to the small amount of sugar introduced into the mix. For this reason fermentation temperature is low and 0.2% dextrose will create a small pH drop, just enough to provide a safety hurdle during the beginning of the process.

Medwurst

Swedish sausages are characterized by the addition of potatoes and this semi-dry Medwurst is no exception.

Meat	Metric	US
pork	800 g	1.76 lb.
pork back fat or bacon	200 g	0.44 lb.

Ingredients per 1000 g (1 kg) of meat:

salt, 2.5% (salt in Cure #1 accounted for)	23 g	4 tsp.
Cure #1	2.5 g	½ tsp.
dextrose (glucose), 1%	10.0 g	2 tsp.
sugar 0.5%	5.0 g	1 tsp.
white pepper	3.0 g	1½ tsp.
allspice	4.0 g	2 tsp.
boiled potatoes	200 g	7 oz.
F-LC culture	0.24 g	use scale

Instructions:
1. Boil potatoes.
2. Grinding. Grind all meats through 3/16" (5 mm) plate. Re-freeze and grind again through ⅛" (3 mm) plate.
3. Mix everything well together, add 1 cup water.
4. Stuff into 36-40 mm hog casings, beef middles or fibrous casings.
5. Ferment at 24° C (75° F), 80% humidity for 72 hours.
6a. Apply smoke for about 1 hour every day. Cook to 140° F (60° C) internal meat temperature, OR
6b. Smoke for 6 hours at 115° F (46° C) gradually increasing temperature until internal meat temperature of 140°F (60° C) is obtained.

Notes:
Potato contains about 2% carbohydrates (sugars).
pH of fresh potato is 7.5

Metka

Metka Sausage is a cold smoked uncooked sausage and is often classified as a fermented spreadable sausage. When properly made, metka sausage can be spread with a knife like butter. The sausage derives its name from German Mettwurst Sausage. Metka sausages were not cooked and they were less popular in summer months due to higher temperatures. With the advent of refrigeration the storing problem has been eliminated.

Meat	Metric	US
pork	600 g	1.32 lb.
beef	400 g	0.88 lb.

Ingredients per 1000 g (1 kg) of meat:

salt	23 g	4 tsp.
Cure #1	2.5 g	½ tsp.
pepper	2.0 g	1 tsp.
paprika	2.0 g	1 tsp.
sugar	2.0 g	⅓ tsp.

Instructions:
1. Grind beef and pork at least two times through a 1/8" (2 mm) or 3/16" (3 mm) plate.
2. Add to meat all remaining ingredients and mix everything well together until feels sticky. Do not add water.
3. Stuff tightly into 36-40 mm hog casings, beef rounds, or synthetic fibrous casings.
4. Hang for 1-2 days at 35-42° F, (2-6° C) and 85-90 % humidity.
5. Smoke with a thin cold smoke (below 77° F, 25° C) for 1-2 days until brown-reddish color is obtained. Periodically re-arrange smoke sticks for even smoke distribution.
6. Cool down to less than 53° F (12° C).
7. Store in refrigerator.

Metka - Salmon Style

Salmon Metka Sausage (*Metka Łososiowa*) is made with beef and pork bacon. There is no salmon inside though the name might imply it. Metka sausage is a traditional sausage which is cold smoked and not cooked. Certain Polish meat products that call for an addition of bacon or pork loin have the salmon nickname added. For instance, Smoked Pork Loin-Salmon Style. The reason is that the loin is the best and the longest meat piece remaining in the shape of a salmon. Both pork loin and salmon are very popular in Poland and are considered delicacies. When properly made, metka sausages can be spread with a knife like butter.

Meat	Metric	US
pork belly, skinless	800 g	1.76 lb.
beef	200 g	0.44 lb.

Ingredients per 1000 g (1 kg) of meat:

salt	23 g	4 tsp.
Cure #1	2.5 g	½ tsp.
pepper	2.0 g	1 tsp.
paprika	2.0 g	1 tsp.
nutmeg	1.0 g	½ tsp.

Instructions:
1. Grind beef and pork at least two times through a 1/8" (2 mm) or 3/16" (3 mm) plate.
2. Add to meat all remaining ingredients and mix everything well together until feels sticky. Do not add water.
3. Stuff tightly into 36-40 mm hog casings, beef rounds, or synthetic fibrous casings.
4. Hang for 12 hours at 50° F (10° C) and 85-95 % humidity.
5. Smoke with cold smoke below 77° F (25° C) until gold-brown color is obtained. That should take 10-12 hours.
6. Cool down to less than 53° F (12° C).
7. Store in refrigerator.

Mettwurst - Braunschweiger

German spreadable sausage.

Meat	Metric	US
beef	300 g	0.66 lb.
pork butt	300 g	0.66 lb.
pork belly	400 g	0.88 lb.

Ingredients per 1000 g (1 kg) of meat:

	Metric	US
salt, 2.5% (salt in Cure #1 accounted for)	23 g	4 tsp.
Cure #1	2.5 g	½ tsp.
dextrose (glucose), 0.2%	2.0 g	⅓ tsp.
pepper	2.0 g	1 tsp.
paprika	2.0 g	1 tsp.
mace	0.5 g	⅓ tsp.
juniper extract*	1 g	⅓ tsp.
F-LC culture	0.24 g	use scale

Instructions:
1. Grind all meats through ⅛" (3 mm) plate. Re-freeze meats and grind again. You may grind once and then emulsify in the food processor without adding water.
2. Add all ingredients, starter culture included, during this step.
3. Stuff firmly into 40-60 mm beef middles or fibrous casings. Form 8-10" (20-25 cm) links.
4. Ferment for 48 hours at 18° C (64° F), 75% humidity.
5. Apply cold smoke for 12 hours at 18° C (64° F).
6. Store in a refrigerator.

Notes:
Cold smoking is drying with smoke and it is not a continuous process. Smoke is applied for about one hour, then the sausage "rests" for one hour. The cycle is repeated again and again.
* insert 20 g of crushed juniper berries into 120 ml (½ cup) vodka or cognac and leave in a closed jar for 2-3 days. Filter the liquid from berries.

Nham

Nham is an uncooked, fermented semi-dry Thai sausage very popular in Asia. It is made from fresh lean pork, pork skins, cooked rice, fresh garlic and eye bird chillies. The sausage is wrapped in banana leaves or synthetic casings and fermented for 3-5 days (depending on the season) at about 30° C (86° F) and 50% humidity.

Rice serves not only as a value added filler but as a source of carbohydrates for lactic acid production during fermentation. Many Asian products employ rice as a fermentation source, for example "saki" - the rice wine. The fermentation is performed at high Thai ambient temperatures and there is a danger of growth of undesirable bacteria if no lactic acid is produced during the first stage of the process. For this reason glucose (dextrose) is added to jump start fermentation as cooked rice is metabolized very slowly. The pH of boiled rice is about 7.4. If stored at room temperatures (20-30° C, 68-86° F) the sausage has a shelf life of less than a week but its life can be extended by keeping it under refrigeration. Then it is served as a dish or eaten raw.

It is important to keep in mind that natural fermentations are difficult to replicate in other settings. For example, the meat mixture for Nham is traditionally wrapped in small banana leaf packets. The leaves contribute to the surface flora of the sausage, which no doubt changes the fermentation pattern.

Traditional Nham is made with Bird's Eye Chili Peppers, which are tiny very hot chillies that can be found in Malaysia, Brunei, Indonesia, Philippines and in Thailand. Although small in size compared to other types of chili, they are very hot at 50,000 to 100,000 on the Scoville pungency scale. Tabasco and cayenne peppers are rated slightly lower at 30,000-50,000 Scoville units.

Meat	Metric	US
lean pork	700 g	1.54 lb.
pork skins	300 g	0.66 lb.

Different ratios of lean pork to skins may be used: 80/20, 70/30, 60/40, 50/50 or 40/60.

***Ingredients** per 1000 g (1 kg) of meat:*
salt, 2.5%		
(salt in Cure #1 accounted for)	23 g	4 tsp.
Cure #1	2.5 g	½ tsp.
dextrose (glucose), 1.0%	10.0 g	2 tsp.
cooked rice, 3%	30 g	1 oz.
Bird Eye Chilies or Tabasco peppers	20 g	0.71 oz.
garlic, minced 5%	50 g	14 cloves
F-LC culture	0.24 g	use scale

Instructions:
1. Trim all connective tissue and fat. Grind through a small plate (1/8-3/16",
3-5 mm). Remove any visible fat and cook in water for about 1 1/2 hours.
Cut de-fatted skin (rind) into 2-3 mm (⅛") thick and ¾" (20 mm) long
strips. Cut Bird Eye Chillies 3-5 mm thick.
2. Mix meat, skins, rice and all other ingredients well together.
3. Stuff tightly into synthetic casings, about 30 mm diameter and 6-8" (15-
20 cm) long.
4. Ferment at 30° C (86° F) for 46 hours, high humidity.
5. For a drier sausage: dry for 3 days at 22→16° C (70→60° F), 65-75%
humidity or until desired weight loss has occurred.
6. Store sausages at 10-15° C (50-59° F), 75% humidity.

Notes:
Cooked rice is commonly used between 2.5 and 4%.
Sausage contains a lot of garlic (5%).
Ground pepper may be added at 0.1%
Don't replace pork skins with fat. The texture and flavor of this sausage
depends largely on pork skins.
Tabasco or cayenne peppers are common everywhere.

If made traditionally (without starter culture):
- *Increase salt to 3% (140 g).*
- *Increase fermentation temperature to 30° C (86° F).*
- *Ferment for 3 days at 30° C (86° F) or for 5 days if temperature is
lower (> 24° C, 75° F).*
- *Refrigerate.*

Pepperoni
(Slow fermented-dry)

Dry sausage, smoked, air dried, sometimes cooked. Pepperoni can be made from beef, pork or a combination such as 30% beef and 70% pork. Pepperoni is a lean sausage with fat content < 30%. Cheaper, fast-fermented (semi-dry) and cooked types end up as toppings to pizzas worldwide to give flavor. Traditionally made Italian pepperoni was not smoked.

Meat	Metric	US
pork	700 g	1.54 lb.
beef	300 g	0.66 lb.

Ingredients per 1000 g (1 kg) of meat:

salt, 3% (salt in Cure #2 accounted for)	28 g	5 tsp.
Cure #2	2.5 g	½ tsp.
dextrose (glucose), 0.2%	2.0 g	⅓ tsp.
sugar, 0.3%	3.0 g	½ tsp.
black pepper,	3.0 g	1½ tsp.
paprika	6.0 g	3 tsp.
anise seeds, cracked,	2.5 g	2 tsp.
(or fennel seeds)	3.0 g	2 tsp.
cayenne pepper	2.0 g	1 tsp.
T-SPX culture	0.12 g	use scale

Instructions:
1. Grind pork and beef through 3/16" plate (5 mm).
2. Mix all ingredients with meat.
3. Stuff firmly into beef middles or 2" fibrous casings.
4. Ferment at 20° C (68° F) for 72 hours, 90-85% humidity.
5. Optional step: cold smoke for 8 hours (<22° C/72° F).
6. Dry at 16→12° C (60→54° F), 85-80% humidity. In about 6-8 weeks a shrink of 30% should be achieved.
7. Store sausages at 10-15° C (50-59° F), 75% humidity.

Pepperoni
(Fast fermented-semi-dry)

Meat	Metric	US
pork	700 g	1.54 lb.
beef	300 g	0.66 lb.

Ingredients per 1000 g (1 kg) of meat:

salt, 2.5% (salt in Cure #1 accounted for)	23 g	4 tsp.
Cure #1	2.5 g	½ tsp.
dextrose (glucose), 1.0%	10.0 g	2 tsp.
sugar, 1.0%	10.0 g	2 tsp.
black pepper,	3.0 g	1½ tsp.
paprika	6.0 g	3 tsp.
anise seeds, cracked,	2.5 g	2 tsp.
(or fennel seeds)	3.0 g	2 tsp.
cayenne pepper	2.0 g	1 tsp.
F-LC culture	0.24 g	use scale

Instructions:
1. Grind pork and beef through 3/16" plate (5 mm).
2. Mix all ingredients with meat.
3. Stuff into beef middles or fibrous casings about 60 mm.
4. Ferment at 38° C (100° F) for 24 hours, 90-85% humidity.
5. Optional step: introduce warm smoke (43° C, 110° F), 70% humidity, for 6 hours.
6. Gradually increase smoke temperature until internal meat temperature of 140° F (60° C) is obtained.
7. For a drier sausage: dry for 2 days at 22→16° C (70→60° F), 65-75% humidity or until desired weight loss has occurred.
8. Store sausages at 10-15° C (50-59° F), 75% humidity.

Notes:
Original Italian pepperoni is not smoked.

Polish Smoked Sausage
(Cold Smoked)

This is the predecessor of the Polish Smoked Sausage as it came to be known all over the world. When it was originally made food preservation was of the utmost importance and that is why it was cold smoked. Today its hot smoked version is better known as it requires less time to make.

Meat	Metric	US
pork	1000 g	2.20 lb.

Ingredients per 1000 g (1 kg) of meat:

salt	28 g	4½ tsp.
Cure #2	2.5 g	½ tsp.
pepper	2.0 g	1 tsp.
sugar	2.5 g	½ tsp.
garlic	3.5 g	1 clove
marjoram	1.0 g	⅔ tsp.

Instructions:
1. Grind the lean meat with a 3/8" grinder plate and the fat meat through 3/16" plate.
2. Mix everything together.
3. Stuff mixture into 32 - 36 mm hog casings and form links 12 - 13" 30 - 35 cm. Leave links in long coils.
4. Hang for 1-2 days at 2-6°C (35-42°F) and 85-90% humidity.
5. Apply thin cold smoke for 1-1.5 days until the casings develop yellow-light brown color. Re-arrange smoke sticks or smoke carts during smoking.
6. Dry at 10-12°C (50-53°F) and 75-80% humidity until the yield is 87% in relation to the original weight of the meat.
7. Divide into pairs.
8. Store in refrigerator or continue drying.

Russian Sausage
(*Cold Smoked*)

This is the original cold smoked version of the Russian sausage.

Meat	Metric	US
Lean pork	500 g	1.10 lb.
Pork back fat	300 g	0.66 lb.
Beef	200 g	0.44 lb.

Ingredients per 1000 g (1 kg) of meat:

salt	28 g	4½ tsp.
Cure #2	5.0 g	1 tsp.
pepper	2.0 g	1 tsp.
sugar	2.0 g	⅓ tsp.
cardamom	2.0 g	1 tsp.
allspice	2.0 g	1 tsp.
Madeira wine or brandy	60 ml	¼ cup

Instructions:
1. Cut meat and fat into 5-6 cm (2") pieces, mix with salt, sugar and Cure # 1 and place in a cool area for 4 - 5 days.
2. Grind beef with 3/8" (10 mm) plate. Manually cut back fat into ¼" (6 mm) cubes.
3. Mix all ingredients with meat adding wine. Mix until all wine is absorbed by the mixture. Then add diced fat and mix everything together.
4. Stuff into dry beef middles or synthetic fibrous casings 40-60 mm and form 12" (30 cm) long links.
5. Hang for 2 days in a cool place.
6. Cold smoke for 6 days.
7. Dry for 25 - 30 days in a cool, dry and drafty area.

Salami - Genoa

Salami Milano and Salami Genoa are very similar and they both incorporate different proportions of raw materials. Some typical combinations: 50/30/20, 40/40/20 (this recipe) or 40/30/30. Salami Genoa is also known as Salami di Alessandra. Salami Milano is chopped somewhat finer than Salami Genoa.

Meat	Metric	US
lean pork trimmings (butt)	400 g	0.88 lb.
beef (chuck)	400 g	0.88 lb.
pork back fat or fat trimmings	200 g	0.44 lb.

Ingredients per 1000 g (1 kg) of meat:

salt, 3% (salt in Cure #2 accounted for)	28 g	5 tsp.
Cure #2	2.5 g	½ tsp.
dextrose (glucose), 0.2%	2.0 g	⅓ tsp.
sugar, 0.3%	3.0 g	½ tsp.
white pepper	3.0 g	1½ tsp.
garlic powder	1.0 g	⅓ tsp.
OR fresh garlic	3.5 g	1 clove
T-SPX culture	0.12 g	use scale

Instructions:

1. Grind pork and back fat through ⅜" plate (10 mm). Grind beef with ⅛" plate.
2. Mix all ingredients with ground meat.
3. Stuff firmly into beef middles or 46-60 mm protein lined fibrous casings. Make links 16-20" long.
4. Ferment at 20° C (68° F) for 72 hours, 90-85% humidity.
5. Dry at 16→12° C (60→54° F), 85-80% humidity for 2-3 months. The sausage is dried until around 30-35% in weight is lost.
6. Store sausages at 10-15° C (50-59° F), 75% humidity.

Notes:

If mold is desired spray with M-EK-4 mold culture after stuffing.
The following spice and herb combination can be found in some recipes:
spices: 4 parts coriander, 3 parts mace, 2 parts allspice, 1 part fennel.
herbs: 3 parts marjoram, 1 part thyme, 1 part basil.

To make 1 kg sausage about 1.5 g of spices and 1 g of herbs are needed. Some recipes ask for the addition of red wine and you may add around 30 ml (⅛ cup).

Salami - Hungarian

The Hungarian salami is a unique sausage which is smoked and has mold. In the traditional process the use of starter cultures and sugars are not allowed. The sausage should not exhibit any acidity. The recipe below contains very little sugar, just to provide a margin of safety during the first stage of fermentation.

Meat	Metric	US
lean pork	800 g	1.76 lb.
back fat	200 g	0.44 lb.

Ingredients per 1000 g (1 kg) of meat:

salt, 3% (salt in Cure #2 accounted for)	28 g	5 tsp.
Cure #2	2.5 g	½ tsp.
dextrose (glucose), 0.2%	2.0 g	⅓ tsp.
white pepper	3.0 g	1½ tsp.
paprika	6.0 g	3 tsp.
garlic powder	2.0 g	½ tsp.
OR fresh garlic	7.0 g	2 cloves
Tokay wine (Hungarian sweet wine)	15 ml	1 Tbs
T-SPX culture	0.12 g	use scale

Instructions:
1. Grind pork and back fat through 3/16" plate (5 mm).
2. Mix all ingredients with ground meat.
3. Stuff firmly into beef middles or 3" protein lined fibrous casings.
4. Ferment at 20° C (68° F) for 72 hours, 90-85% humidity.
5. Cold smoke for 4 days (<22° C/72° F). You can apply smoke during fermentation.
6. Dry at 16→12° C (60→54° F), 85-80% humidity for 2-3 months.
7. Store sausages at 10-15° C (50-59° F), 75% humidity.

Salami - Milano

Salami Milano and Salami Genoa are very similar and they both incorporate different proportions of raw materials. Some typical combinations: 50/30/20 (this recipe), 40/40/20 or 40/30/30. Salami Genoa is also known as Salami di Alessandra. Salami Milano is chopped somewhat finer than Salami Genoa.

Meat	Metric	US
lean pork trimmings (butt)	500 g	1.10 lb.
beef (chuck)	300 g	0.66 lb.
pork back fat or fat trimmings	200 g	0.44 lb.

Ingredients per 1000 g (1 kg) of meat:

salt, 3% (salt in Cure #2 accounted for)	28 g	5 tsp.
Cure #2	2.5 g	½ tsp.
dextrose (glucose), 0.2%	2.0 g	⅓ tsp.
sugar, 0.3%	3.0 g	½ tsp.
white pepper	3.0 g	1½ tsp.
garlic powder	1.0 g	⅓ tsp.
OR fresh garlic	3.5 g	1 clove
T-SPX culture	0.12 g	use scale

Instructions:

1. Grind pork and back fat through 3/16" plate (5 mm). Grind beef with ⅛" plate.
2. Mix all ingredients with ground meat.
3. Stuff firmly into 80 mm protein lined fibrous casings. Make 25" long links.
4. Ferment at 20° C (68° F) for 72 hours, 90-85% humidity.
5. Dry at 16→12° C (60→54° F), 85-80% humidity for 2-3 months. The sausage is dried until around 30-35% in weight is lost.
6. Store sausages at 10-15° C (50-59° F), 75% humidity.

Notes:

If mold is desired spray with M-EK-4 mold culture after stuffing.
The following spice and herb combination can be found in some recipes:
spices: 4 parts coriander, 3 parts mace, 2 parts allspice, 1 part fennel.
herbs: 3 parts marjoram, 1 part thyme, 1 part basil.

To make 1 kg sausage about 1.5 g of spices and 1 g of herbs are needed. Some recipes ask for the addition of red wine and you may add around 30 ml (⅛ cup).

Salami Traditional

The following is the official Polish Government recipe for making traditional salami. When the war had ended, this recipe was used to make the salami that was sold in Poland to the consumers.

Meat	Metric	US
lean pork cuts	800 g	1.76 lb.
pork back fat or fat trimmings	200 g	0.44 lb.

Ingredients per 1000 g (1 kg) of meat:

salt, 3% (salt in Cure #2 accounted for)	28 g	5 tsp.
Cure #2	2.5 g	½ tsp.
sugar, 0.15%	1.5 g	⅓ tsp.
pepper	2.0 g	1 tsp.
garlic powder	1.0 g	⅓ tsp.
OR fresh garlic	3.5 g	1 clove
paprika	1.5 g	¾ tsp.

Instructions:

1. Cut meat into 10 cm (3-4") pieces and place in a slightly raised container with holes in the bottom to allow for draining of curing liquid. Leave for 24 hours at 1-2°C (33-35°F). Then grind with ¾" plate and leave for an additional 2-3 days following the above procedure. During that period turn meat around 1-2 times. Leave sheets of unsalted back fat for 2-3 days at -2° C (28° F) to -4° C (24° F) and then cut into 3 mm (⅛") pieces.
2. Mix meat, back fat, salt, nitrate and spices together. Grind through 3 mm (⅛") plate.
3. Leave the sausage mass for 36-48 hours at 2-4°C (35-40°F).
4. Stuff casings firmly. Do not add water. Prick any visible air pockets with a needle.
5. Hang for 2-4 days at 2-4°C (35-40°F), 85-90% humidity.
6. Smoke with thin cold smoke 16-18° C (60-64° F) for 5-7 days, until dark red color is obtained.
7. Hang in a dark, lightly drafty area at 10-12°C (50-53°F), humidity 90% for 2 weeks until salami develops white, dry mold on outside. If green and moist mold appears on salamis they have to be washed with warm salty water and wiped off dry with a cloth. Hang for 4-5 hours in a drier place, then move back to the original room and continue drying.
8. Place salamis covered with white mold for 2-3 months in a dark and lightly drafty area at 12-15° C (54-59° F), 75-85% humidity, until desired yield is obtained.

Notes:

In the original recipe 0.08 kg potassium nitrate was added to 100 kg of meat.

Sucuck

The Turkish Sucuk (Soudjouk) is the most popular dry fermented meat product in Turkey and other Middle Eastern Countries. As most of those countries practice Muslim it comes as no surprise that pork is not included in the recipe and the sausage is made from beef and lamb. The Turkish Food Codex (2000) states that high quality ripened sucuks should have pH values between 5.2 and 5.4.

Meat	Metric	US
lean beef	700 g	1.54 lb.
lean lamb/mutton	300 g	0.66 lb.

Ingredients per 1000 g (1 kg) of meat:

salt, 3% (salt in Cure #2 accounted for)	28 g	5 tsp.
Cure #2	2.5 g	½ tsp.
dextrose (glucose), 0.3%	3.0 g	½ tsp.
black pepper	5.0 g	2½ tsp.
red pepper	5.0 g	2½ tsp.
cumin	10 g	5 tsp.
garlic	10 g	3 cloves
allspice	2.0 g	1 tsp.
olive oil, 1%	10.0 g	2 tsp.
T-SPX culture	0.12 g	use scale

Instructions:
1. Grind beef and lamb through 3/16" plate (5 mm).
2. Mix all ingredients with meat.
3. Stuff firmly into 38 mm casings.
4. Ferment at 20° C (68° F) for 72 hours, 90-85% humidity.
5. Dry at 16→12° C (60→54° F), 85-80% humidity for 1 month.
6. Store sausages at 10-15° C (50-59° F), 75% humidity.

Notes:
Cinnamon and cloves are often added.
Original sucuks are made with sheep tail fat (40% beef, 40% lamb, 20% sheep tail fat).
Sucuk is a very lean sausage.
Olive oil (up to 5%) is often added as a replacement for beef fat, which has poor sensory qualities.

Summer Sausage

Summer sausage is an American semi-dry fermented sausage, made of pork and beef, although sausages made from beef alone are common. The sausage was made in the winter time and after drying and storing it was consumed in the summer when working in the field. Summer sausage displays a long shelf life without refrigeration and is often used as a component of food for gift baskets along with different cheeses and jams. Diameter of casings varies from 40-120 mm and so does the length of the sausage.

Meat	Metric	US
pork	700 g	1.54 lb.
beef	300 g	0.66 lb.

Ingredients per 1000 g (1 kg) of meat:

	Metric	US
salt, 2.5% (salt in Cure #1 accounted for)	23 g	4 tsp.
Cure #1	2.5 g	½ tsp.
dextrose (glucose), 1.0%	10.0 g	2 tsp.
sugar, 0.5%	5.0 g	1 tsp.
black pepper,	3.0 g	1½ tsp.
coriander	2.0 g	1 tsp.
whole mustard seeds	4.0 g	1½ tsp.
allspice	2.0 g	1 tsp.
garlic	3.5 g	1 clove
F-LC culture	0.24 g	use scale

Instructions:
1. Grind pork and beef through 3/16" plate (5 mm).
2. Mix all ingredients with ground meat.
3. Stuff into beef middles or fibrous casings about 60 mm.
4. Ferment at 30° C (86° F) for 24 hours, 90-85% humidity.
5. Introduce warm smoke 43° C (110° F), 70% humidity, for 6 hours. Gradually increase smoke temperature until internal meat temperature of 140° F (60° C) is obtained.
6. For a drier sausage: dry for 3 days at 22-16° C (70-60° F), 65-75% humidity or until desired weight loss has occurred.
7. Store sausages at 10-15° C (50-59° F), 75-80% humidity.

Notes:
Some sausages may contain around 10% diced cheddar cheese.

Teewurst

German spreadable sausage.

Meat	Metric	US
beef	200 g	0.44 lb.
lean pork	300 g	0.66 lb.
pork belly	250 g	0.55 lb.
back fat	250 g	0.55 lb.

Ingredients *per 1000 g (1 kg) of meat:*

salt, 2.5% (salt in Cure #1 accounted for)	23 g	4 tsp.
Cure #1	2.5 g	½ tsp.
dextrose (glucose), 0.3%	3.0 g	½ tsp.
white pepper,	3.0 g	1½ tsp.
allspice	1.0 g	½ tsp.
dark rum	5 ml	½ tsp.
T-SPX culture	0.12 g	use scale

Instructions:
1. Grind all meats through ⅛" (3 mm) plate. Re-freeze meats and grind again twice. You may grind once and then emulsify in the food processor without adding water. Add all ingredients, starter culture included, during this step.
2. Mix all together.
3. Stuff firmly into 40 mm beef middles or fibrous casings. Form 8-10" (20-25 cm) links.
4. Ferment for 48 hours at maximum 18° C (64° F), 75% humidity.
5. Apply cold smoke for 12 hours at 18° C (64° F).
6. Store in a refrigerator.

Notes:
Cold smoking is drying with smoke and it is not a continuous process. Smoke is applied for about one hour, then the sausage "rests" for one hour. The cycle is repeated again and again.

Thuringer

Semi-dry partially or fully cooked, smoked beef and pork sausage.

Meat	Metric	US
pork	700 g	1.54 lb.
beef	300 g	0.66 lb.

Ingredients per 1000 g (1 kg) of meat:

salt, 2.5% (salt in Cure #1 accounted for)	23 g	4 tsp.
Cure #1	2.5 g	½ tsp.
dextrose (glucose), 1%	10 g	2 tsp.
coriander	2.0 g	1 tsp.
whole mustard seeds	2.0 g	1½ tsp.
allspice	2.0 g	1 tsp.
F-LC culture	0.24 g	use scale

Instructions:
1. Grind pork and beef fat through 3/16" plate (5 mm).
2. Mix all ingredients with meat.
3. Stuff into beef middles or fibrous casings 40-120 mm.
4. Ferment at 30° C (86° F) for 24 hours, 90-85% humidity.
5. Introduce warm smoke 43° C (110° F), 70% humidity, for 6 hours. Gradually increase smoke temperature until internal meat temperature of 140° F (60° C) is obtained.
6. For a drier sausage: dry for 2 days at 22→16° C (70→60° F), 65-75% humidity or until desired weight loss has occurred.
7. Store sausages at 10-15° C (50-59° F), 75% humidity.

Urutan

Urutan is a Balinese traditional dry fermented sausage whose technology differs from the European sausages. No nitrite/nitrate is used in the process and the sausage owes its yellowish-brown color to turmeric (main ingredient of curry powder). Laos powder (*Galanga pinata*) and aromatic ginger (*Kaempferia galangal*) contribute greatly to its Eastern flavor. The climate in Bali is hot and the sausage is fermented at 25° C (77° F) at night and at 50° C (122° F) during the day. Such warm temperatures permit fast fermentation which is accomplished within 5 days. Urutan is not smoked.

Meat	Metric	US
lean pork	700 g	1.54 lb.
back fat	300 g	0.66 lb.
(OR 100% fatty pork butt)		

Ingredients *per 1000 g (1 kg) of meat:*

	Metric	US
salt, 3% (salt in Cure #2 accounted for)	28 g	5 tsp.
Cure #2	2.5 g	½ tsp.
dextrose (glucose), 0.5%	5.0 g	1 tsp.
black pepper	5.0 g	2½ tsp.
red chili pepper (cayenne family), 1%	10 g	5 tsp.
ginger	1 g	½ tsp.
garlic, 2%	20 g	6 cloves
turmeric, 1%	10 g	5 tsp.
Laos powder, 1.5%	15 g	7 tsp.
T-SPX culture	0.12 g	use scale

Instructions:
1. Grind meat and fat through 3/16" plate (6 mm).
2. Mix all ingredients with ground meat.
3. Stuff into collagen or sheep casings 24-26 mm and form 5" (12 cm) long links.
4. Ferment at 24° C (75° F) for 72 hours, 90-85% humidity.
5. Dry for two weeks at 16→12° C (60→54° F), 85-80% humidity.
6. Store sausages at 10-15° C (50-59° F), 75% humidity.

Notes:

Cure #2 has been added to the recipe to provide a safety hurdle. Traditional recipe calls for 5% garlic (similar to Thai Nham sausage) to provide extra safety.

Laos powder (*Galanga pinata*) the aromatic, peppery, ginger like spice is indigenous to Southeast Asia. Its pungent cardamom-like eucalyptus flavor enhances the overall flavor profiles of Thai and Indonesian cuisines. Used in pungent Thai curry pastes, meat marinades and stir-fries. Added to Indonesian spice pastes that are rubbed on duck and fish.

Chapter 21

Special and Kosher Sausages

Low Salt Sausages. It is a fact that a large percentage of the western population develops high blood pressure in later years. Once when we get it there is no way back and at best we can only try to control. We control it by suddenly paying attention to the amount of salt a particular food contains. We develop high blood pressure not by eating sausages but by consuming ready to eat products which we warm up at home on a stove or in a microwave. Just look at the amount of salt a canned soup, canned vegetable, or fish contains. *It is scary.* Salt is added in such a high amount to prevent the growth of bacteria. *We have no control over it unless we make our own chicken soup or other products ourselves.* By cooking at home we will add only as much salt as is required for good flavor and this amount will be well below what is added by commercial producers. The problem is that we lead such a hurried life that we have no time to cook and less and less people even know how.

Contrary to a popular belief, the sausages do not contain as much salt as we normally like to think. A typical range is from 1.5% to 2% salt in relation to the weight of a sausage mass. An average figure will be between 1.5% and 1.8%. In some sausages such as liver sausages, head cheeses, and blood sausages one can lower the salt content even further without affecting the flavor of the sausage. You can go as low as 1% and the sausages will still be of acceptable quality.

When World War II ended in 1945, there was no refrigeration in heavily damaged countries like Poland, Germany or Russia. Sausages were produced with food preservation in mind and they contained about 2.3% of salt. Those countries lay at a similar latitude like Quebec in Canada, which provides good conditions for keeping food at room temperatures most of the year. Everybody had a storage unit in the common basement of a building or a designated pantry in the apartment. Those conditions plus the right amount of salt, Nitrate and manufacturing procedures such as curing and cold smoking allowed the creation of meat products with a very long shelf life. We don't need to go over 2% salt today as everybody owns a refrigerator. If a person is on a low sodium diet, 1.5% salt will be fine too. The only exception are slow fermented dry sausages (salami type) or cold smoked spreadable fermented sausages, which will not be submitted to heat treatment. Those sausages need 3% salt to protect meat from bacteria and there is no room for compromise here. For people on a low sodium diet, the only way to reduce those amounts further is to substitute common sodium chloride salt (NaCl) with potassium chloride salt (KCl).

Potassium Chloride vs. Sodium Chloride

The salt we use for cooking is Sodium Chloride (NaCl) and sodium is what increases our blood pressure. Sea salt which is made by evaporating sea water includes traces of different minerals which were diluted in water and were too heavy to evaporate. But it is still sodium chloride salt which people on low sodium diets try to avoid. Potassium chloride does not contain sodium and is used by commercial manufacturers to make low sodium salts. It has a bitter metallic taste so it is mixed in varying proportions with regular sodium chloride salt.

Salt substitutes vary in their composition, but their main ingredient is always potassium chloride. For example, the listed contents of the NuSalt are: potassium chloride, cream of tartar, drier and natural flavor derived from yeast. Contains less than 20 mg of sodium per 100 grams. The contents of the NoSalt are: potassium chloride, potassium bitartrate, adipic acid, mineral oil, fumaric acid and silicon dioxide. A salt substitute does not taste exactly like sodium chloride, but it is similar enough, and it contains less or none of the sodium that some people are trying to avoid. You can reduce the amount of sodium in your diet by following these guidelines:

- Read labels carefully and choose foods that have less salt.
- Cook your own meals.
- Use salt substitutes.

Choosing salt substitute. The number one step is to pick up salt substitute which will be used and become familiar with it. Let's assume that a sausage will contain 1% of salt and that calls for adding 10 g of salt to 1 kg (1000 g) of meat. Mix 10 g of salt substitute (about 1½ teaspoon) with 1 kg of meat, make a tiny hamburger, cook it and see how you like it. Let your palate be the judge. Read the label carefully to see how much regular salt (sodium chloride) a particular salt substitute contains and you will know exactly how much salt your sausage contains. There are different brands of salt substitutes and they contain varying proportions of sodium chloride. For this reason we can not choose one for you and you must do your own shopping either in a local supermarket or online.

Curing. Best quality smoked products incorporate meat which is cured with salt and sodium nitrite (Cure #1 in the USA or Peklosol in Europe). To cure 1 kg of meat, introducing 150 parts per million of sodium nitrite, only 2.4 g of Cure #1 is required (about 1/3 of teaspoon). As Cure #1 contains 6.25% sodium nitrite and 93.75% of sodium chloride, 2.25 g of salt will be introduced. This comes to 0.2% salt, which is of little concern for people on low sodium diets.

Low Salt Recipes

If you have made it so far in this book you should be able to modify any existing recipe or create your own. Keep in mind that increasing the amount of spices will make up for using less salt, too. It will be a waste of paper to present a low sodium sausage recipe. It simply requires less salt or a different salt type. *Fermented/dry and cold smoked sausages should not be made with salt substitutes as sodium chloride (regular salt) provides safety in those products.*

Low Fat Sausages

Making low fat sausages is more complicated and requires some intelligent planning. Our government permits our processors to use a lot of fat, for example, a fresh sausage can contain 50% of fat. Italian fresh sausage is healthier as it can have only 35% fat. A home based sausage maker he can easily beat those numbers and by using 20-30% fat, he will create a great sausage. We understand that people with health problems may want to eat a healthier sausage even if this will affect the texture of it. Using no fat at all makes little sense as you will be limited to pork loins and lean cuts of ham. It will be wiser to cook entire loins or make formed hams.

Emulsions

Protein is needed to mix substances such as fat and water. Proteins are released from muscles during mechanical action such as cutting or grinding. Salt and phosphates greatly advance the release of proteins.

Protein and particles such as salt, protein, sugar, parts of fiber, muscles, and collagen create a liquid which coats each fat particle with a thin layer of soluble protein. Those coated fat particles combine with water and meat and the emulsion is created. The leaner the meat, the more protein it contains. If little or no fat is used, there will not be any real emulsion, and the proteins will simply hold the texture of the sausage together. Due to the high protein content (80-90%) soy protein isolate is a very strong emulsifying agent and will help to make quality liver and emulsified sausages (hot dog, bologna). In order to take full advantage of soy protein isolate capabilities, it should be cut in a bowl cutter. Milk protein (caseinate) is another binder that promotes a strong emulsion by interacting with water and fat particles.

Replacing animal fat with vegetable oil delivers good results, eliminates cholesterol and lowers calories. It is not easy to manually mix oil, meat, and water. It often results in poor binding and the texture may crumble. *Using pre-mixed oil emulsion provides the best texture and is strongly recommended.* Such an emulsion is easily made from soy protein **isolate**, vegetable oil and water. It has a consistency of a soft cream cheese, it is a white gel that looks and tastes like fat. Oil emulsion is easy and fast to make and can be stored in a refrigerator for up to 5 days.

Replacing Fat with Protein/Oil/Water Emulsion

Preparing protein/fat/water emulsion is practiced by commercial producers. Such emulsion is kept in a cooler until needed. It is a very practical solution for making reduced fat sausages. Think of it as a fat replacer solution that offers many advantages:

- It can be prepared in advance.
- Making emulsion is a clean and simple process.
- Its calorie content is well defined.
- It does not provide any cholesterol.
- It preserves the original texture and mouthfeel of the sausage.

soy protein isolate/oil/water emulsion 1 : 4 : 5			
	100 g	200 g	300 g
SPI (92% protein)	10 g	20 g	30 g
Vegetable Oil	40 g	80 g	120 g
Water	50 g	100 g	150 g
Calories	398 cal	796 cal	1194 cal

Oil emulsion is easy to administer and its calorie content is precisely defined. A 100 g chunk of emulsion provides 398 calories. One hundred grams of fat provides 900 calories.

Photo 21.1 Oil emulsion.

Sausage, 100 g (3.5 oz) serving		
Type and the amount of fat added	Meat	Total calories
Animal fat - 30% (30 g), 270 cal	lean pork, 70 g, 98 cal	368 cal
Oil - 4% (4 g), 36 cal	lean pork, 70 g, 98 cal	134 cal
Oil emulsion, 10% (10 g), 40 cal	lean pork, 70 g, 98 cal	138 cal
Oil emulsion is the mixture of soy protein isolate, oil and water.		

Soy protein concentrate (SPC, 70% protein) is commonly added to home made sausages, but will not produce an emulsion. Soy protein isolate (SPI, 90% protein) produces the real gel: a white, soft, cream cheese-like substance that tastes like fat. Soy protein concentrate (SPC) produces a yellowish paste at best. Even when the amount of SPC is increased the final product is still a paste. Soy protein isolate is pure protein with a very few impurities and that is why it makes such a great emulsion.

Making emulsion

1. Using a food processor start cutting cold water with *soy protein isolate* until a shiny paste is obtained. This takes about one minute.
2. Add chilled oil and cut at high speed until a stable emulsion is obtained. It should take about 2 minutes.
3. Place the emulsion in a shallow container and store in a refrigerator. It can be stored for up to 5 days.

Photo 21.2 Oil emulsion.

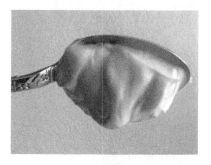

Photo 21.3 Oil emulsion sticks to the spoon.

Photo 21.4 Oil emulsion holds shape even when heated for 10 min at 176° F.

Meat selection. This is the crucial step and use your own judgement. This step starts when you choose meat in a supermarket. Select lean meat such as loin, ham, pork butt and lean beef. Don't buy other cuts such as picnic or fat trimmings, unless you plan on making different types of sausages. Keep in mind that such cuts as loin or ham cost more and your sausage will not be cost effective. Because you made it for yourself, it becomes a specialty product now and the cost is justified.

Non fat dry milk powder can bind water and is often used in making sausages, including fermented types. Dry milk powder contains sugar and is used in fermented sausages as a source of food for lactic acid producing bacteria. *Dry milk powder greatly improves the taste of low fat sausages.* Non fat dry milk powder is a good natural product and it does not affect the flavor of the product. It is added at about 3% and effectively binds water and emulsifies fats. Its action is very similar to that of soy protein concentrate.

Notes on reduced-fat sausages:

- The texture of sausages was adversely affected when 10-15% water was added. There is plenty of water present in the oil emulsion.
- Carrageenan made sausages firmer with great sliceability. Adding more than 0.5% carrageenan has resulted in a tough gummy texture.
- Using prepared oil emulsion produced not only better sausages than mixing ground meat with oil and water, but made the process simpler and faster.
- 100 g serving of a typical commercially produced sausage contains about 330 calories which are mainly derived from fat. Using emulsion cuts down calories by almost half and eliminates a lot of cholesterol by replacing animal fat with vegetable oil (emulsion).
- Adding 1% of powdered gelatin greatly improves texture of reduced-fat and non-fat sausages.

Head cheese or a nicer word for it would be meat jelly, will make a great low fat product. Although a traditional head cheese was made with parts such as pork head meat, skins and pork trimmings, most home made head cheeses are made with meats commonly available in a supermarket. You can choose two methods:

- Making your own gelatin.
- Buying powdered gelatin.

1. If you choose making meat jelly the traditional way, you need meat cuts that are rich in collagen tissue. Buy pork picnic which is very inexpensive, remove the skin, cut the picnic into smaller pieces and simmer for 2-3 hours. Use enough water just to cover the meat otherwise your gelatin will be too thin and will not solidify. You can boil the skin separately. Pig feet are also a very rich source of collagen. After meat is cooked, but still warm, select lean pieces for meat jelly and discard any fat trimmings as you are going to make low fat jelly.

2. Clarify your stock by filtering it through 2-3 layers of cheese cloth. This removes fat and leaves you with a protein rich source of gelatin.
3. Place lean meats in a container or in a large casing. You can add ready made diced ham pieces that are available in all supermarkets. Then carefully pour your gelatin which will set and become jelly.
4. You can simplify the entire process by using commercially made powdered gelatin. This eliminates making and filtering meat stock. This way you can use any lean meat such as chicken breast or fish and fill the container with gelatin.
5. With a bit of practice and clever decorations made from boiled eggs, sliced pickles, peppers, oranges, carrots, scallions or parsley, you can create wonderful low fat meat jellies or head cheeses.

Fat replacers. A hobbyist generally has no access to commercial fat replacers, but can achieve *the same results* with commonly available products such as soy protein, non fat-dry milk, carrageenan, potato starch or maltodextrin, gums or even the white of an egg. Any single or combinations of these additives will do a great job as long as it is properly administered and correctly chosen for the right sausage type.

All additives presented in the book are natural and classified as (GRAS-Generally Recognized As Safe) by the U.S. FDA, so there aren't any risks to the safety of the product. The safety will also not be jeopardized by adding too little or too much of any particular additive, in the worst case the taste and flavor of the product might suffer. For healthy individuals there is nothing wrong with eating moderate quantities of fat. People who are at cardiovascular risk may try to eliminate fat all together. This is where extended value added sausages start to shine as they are made with filler material. Because a significant amount of non-meat is added to the sausage, the amount of remaining meat, fat, cholesterol and calories becomes proportionally smaller. If all meat is removed, a vegetarian sausage will be created.

Extended Value Sausages

Sausages offer a great opportunity to create new products. Whereas whole meats such as hams, butts, loins, and bacon offer less room to improvise, sausages can be made from countless combinations of meats, spices and different fillers. Those fillers make it possible to produce nutritious, yet very inexpensive products. Take for example blood sausages which incorporate fillers such as rusk, barley, bread crumbs, or rice.

Make your own version without blood, which for people living in large cities may be difficult to obtain anyhow. Potatoes are much cheaper than meat and you get a lot of value when making Swedish potato sausage which tastes wonderful. Boudin, the Cajun classical sausage is made with rice. Cajun cuisine is a great example how local conditions dictate the way meat products and sausage are made. A bit of history might strengthen the point.

Acadia (what is known today as New Brunswick, Nova Scotia and Prince Edward Island in Canada) was the first permanent French settlement in North America, established at Port-Royal in 1607. In what is known as the Great Expulsion (le Grand Dérangement) of 1755-1763, during the Seven Years War between England and France (1755-1763) the British ordered the mass deportation of the Acadians. More than 14,000 Acadians (three-quarters of the Acadian population in Nova Scotia) were expelled by the British. Their homes were burned and their lands confiscated. Families were split up, and the Acadians were dispersed throughout the lands in North America; thousands were transported to France. Gradually, some managed to make their way to Louisiana, creating the Cajun population and culture after mixing with others there. The land they settled on was nothing like the fertile soil of Acadia. The climate was hot and humid, coastal areas abounded with swamps, alligators and snakes.

The popular crops were wheat, rice, sugarcane, sweet potatoes, peas, cabbage, turnips, apples, and raised maize as a secondary crop. Barley, oats, and potatoes were planted as feed for the livestock, including cattle, pigs, and poultry. These animals provided a steady supply of meat to the former Acadians, which they supplemented with fish. Living in such conditions Cajuns created a wonderful cuisine which combined the cooking art of Spanish, French, local natives, Filipinos and other ethnic groups. They have invented a unique style of cooking where fillers play an important part in a sausage formula. Often the sausage became a filler itself and became an ingredient of a more elaborate dish, for example gumbo or jambalaya.

Here presents itself a very attractive solution for making healthy sausages; why not to incorporate fillers into a sausage? This is not a new invention, sausages enriched with a filler material have been produced all the time. Emulsified sausages can easily incorporate fillers, vegetable proteins, and other ingredients which will blend in within the sausage mass.

Basically any combination of meats and filling material that can be stuffed into a casings, can be called a sausage. For example you have made a quantity of chili, which is basically ground meat, beans, and chili powder. If you stuff chili into a casing you will get chili sausage, won't you? If your chili is too thin, add some bread crumbs to it or flour. Throw it on the grill or frying pan and the kids are getting the same chili they have been eating, but in a different form.

In addition to typical flours that we are accustomed to, there is a great variety of flours that are utilized in tropical countries. Thanks to the Internet they all can be easily obtained online. This allows us to create even more different food combinations, each with a slightly different characteristic.

- Gram flour is a flour made from ground chickpeas. It is also known as chickpea flour, garbanzo flour, or bassoon. Used in many countries, it is a staple ingredient in Indian, Pakistani and Bangladeshi cuisines, and comes in the form of a paste mixed with water or yoghurt. When mixed with an equal proportion of water, it can be used as *an egg-replacer in vegan cooking*. Chila, a pancake made with gram flour batter, is a popular street and fast food in India.
- African gari and tufu flours are made from yam.
- Cassava flour is made from cassava (yuca).

Incorporating filler material into sausages was practiced throughout history. It was common in Europe after the end of World War II and has been practiced in poor countries in South America and Asia. What in the past was looked down as inferior food by the well to do Westerners, was actually a healthy sausage of the poor. They ate healthier food, being physically active they were thinner and fit. What's important is that they have had less problems with hypertension, cardiovascular diseases and cancer. The may live shorter than us, but that is not due to their diet, but to the lack of medical care that they don't have and which we take for granted. The time has come to rethink the way we look at meat in a supermarket display and to realize that combining meat with other ingredients can make a much healthier sausage. Our attitude towards foods has been recently changing and we start to accept and "love" foods on which we have looked in the past in disdain. The best example is a case of polenta.

From Wikipedia: Polenta is made with ground yellow or white corn-meal (ground maize), which can be ground coarsely or finely depending on the region and the texture desired. Polenta was originally and still is classified as a peasant food. Since the late 20th century, polenta has found popularity as a gourmet food. Polenta dishes are on the menu in many high-end restaurants, and prepared polenta can be found in supermarkets in tubes or boxes at high prices. Many current polenta recipes have given new life to an essentially bland and simple food, enriching it with meat and mushroom sauces, and adding vegetables, beans or various cheeses into the basic mixture.

Additives used in sausage production can be classified as:

1. Meat extenders - extend expensive meat proteins with cheaper plant proteins, like soy beans. Non-fat dry milk, sodium caseinate (milk protein) and egg white fit into this category, too. The main purpose of using meat extenders has been to lower the cost of a product. Extenders are usually added at 1-3%. They are capable of holding water and bind fats as well. The most cost effective meat extender is textured vegetable protein. The most commonly used meat extenders are:

- Soy protein isolate (SPI).
- Soy protein concentrate (SPC).
- Textured vegetable protein (TVP).
- Vegetable oil can be considered a meat extender as it replaces the animal tissue (fat).

In smaller caliber low-cost products such as hotdogs, larger quantity of extenders such as re-hydrated TVP and coarse fillers (bread crumbs, rusk, flour) are added during the chopping procedure. Finely cut fillers such as flours and starches are usually added dry. Coarse fillers such as bread crumbs, rusk and cereals are usually re-hydrated. Coarse extenders such as textured vegetable protein are usually re-hydrated before adding them to a mix.

2. Fillers - increase volume of the sausage. The result is a lower cost yet still nutritive product. Fillers are usually added at 2-15%. By using meat extenders and fillers together, the cost of the extended product can be lowered significantly.

Oats (steel cut type, not the instant type), barley, buckwheat groats and rice should be pre-soaked or pre-cooked.

Rice should be pre-cooked. Keep in mind that rice might swell inside stuffed casings and increase in volume. Because of that the casings should be stuffed loosely. Rice grains have strong cohesive properties. Rice can be added as flour.

Rusk is a popular filler in England. It is made from flour mixed with water, baked and crushed. It is a good binder and can absorb water at **3 - 4** times its weight.

Flours and starches make great fillers, water absorbers and binders. Flours such as corn, potato, wheat, soy and rice are in common use in the Western world. However there are tubers such as cassava that grow in very hot climates in Africa, South America or the Caribbean region. The Caribbean and the nations with populations of West African origin, such as Cuba, the Dominican Republic and Puerto Rico often use mashed plantains or yams which are then combined with other ingredients. Popular products are gari and tufu flour.

Potato flour and potato starch are well suited for making reduced-fat sausages. Potato flour's flavor agrees quite well with reduced-fat sausages, and improves their mouthfeel. Both flour and starch absorb water well. Potato starch has no taste, dissolves in cold water very well but does not thicken unless heated. Potato starch produces a very clear gel. Unmodified potato starch gelatinizes at 147° F (64° C) which is below the recommended meat internal temperature for cooked meats so a strong gel is always assured. Other starches gelatinize at temperatures from 165° F (73° C) to 178° F (81° C).

Potatoes are usually precooked and added at around 20% to meat barter. Dry flake potatoes can be re-hydrated and used as well.

Photo 21.5 Potato flour left, starch on the right. Both were mixed with 4 parts of water, then heated.

Photo 21.6 Potato starch produces a very clear gel.

Bread crumbs are ground and roasted bread particles absorb water very well, similarly to rusk. After World War II ended in Europe, people would save and dry bread rolls. Then they would be soaked in water or milk and used as a filler in meat products. Bread crumbs can absorb water at **2** times their weight.

Beans other than soybeans make a good filler too. Everybody likes burritos, which is ground meat mixed with bean paste. Beans can be soaked in water for a few hours, then simmered in a little water. The resulting bean paste can be used as a filler.

Banana is a good filler for chicken and pork sausages.

Textured Vegetable Protein (TVP) can be used in amounts up to 15% and can be considered a filler. Soy TVP can also be used as a low cost/high nutrition extender in comminuted meat and poultry products. Textured vegetable protein provides substance and taste to low fat meat products by imitating lean meat. Half a cup of soy TVP provides 126 calories, 25 g protein 14 g carbohydrates and 0 g fat. TVP flakes or powder are usually soaked in water (1 part of flakes to 2 parts of water) and then mixed with minced meat to a ratio of up to 1:3 (rehydrated TVP to ground meat). TVP has no flavor of it's own and is practical to use as a meat substitute or extender. Besides, it offers the best value for the money. You don't necessarily need to add TVP to your healthy sausage which would consist of mostly lean meat, but lean meat such as pork loin is expensive.

You may replace up to 30% of lean meat with re-hydrated TVP lowering the cost of the sausage and bringing down the cholesterol level. This may be less important when only a few pounds of meat are produced. However, when ten or more pounds of sausages are made to meet the needs of a large family, the savings are substantial. TVP is a great ingredient for making *vegetarian foods*. TVP is made from high (50%) soy protein, soy flour or concentrate, but can also be made from cotton seeds, wheat and oats. It is extruded into various shapes (chunks, flakes, nuggets, grains, and strips) and sizes, and is primarily used as a meat substitute due to its very low cost. The small granules of TVP are easy to rehydrate but hydration rates can further be improved by using warm water. However, the mixture must be cooled down before it can be blended with minced meat.

Rehydrated TVP must be refrigerated and treated like a meat. Usually 1 part of textured soy protein will absorb 2-3 parts of water. *Rehydrating TVP at a 2:1 ratio*, drops the percentage of protein to an approximation of ground meat at 16%. *TVP can be mixed with ground meat to a ratio of up to 1:3 (rehydrated TVP to meat)* without reducing the quality of the final product. Adding 3% re-hydrated TVP will result in a high quality sausage. Higher levels of TVP (3-10%) may result in sausages with a decreased meaty flavor. However, higher levels of up to 15% of TVP are accepted in burgers and patties.

3. Binders - are used to improve water and fat binding. They can be of animal or plant origin (soy, wheat and milk, egg white). Carbohydrate based binders such as flour and starch contain little protein but are able to bind fat and water. They also fit into the filler category. Binders are not used for volume increase, but to improve texture and are usually added at 1-3%. Popular binders are soy protein isolate and milk caseinate.

General Recommendations and Tips:

- Adding finely ground beef increases the water holding capacity of the sausage.
- You can add about 20% of precooked and minced tripe. This will make the sausage lighter.
- Good filler material: rice, potatoes, onions, bread crumbs, barley, rusk, oats, semolina flour. You can save natural bread rolls such as Portuguese rolls or French baquettes. They will dry out and will remain usable for a long time. Before use, soak them in water or milk. Then mix with ground meat and other ingredients. Add an egg to combine the mass better. Soy protein concentrate (or isolate) is a natural product and helps to bind water and retain moisture during cooking. The sausage will look plumper.
- Non-fat dry milk binds water very well.
- White of an egg binds all ingredients well together.
- *Textured vegetable protein (TVP) is an excellent filler and protein extender*. It is inexpensive, tasteless, feels like meat, contains more than twice the protein than meat and none of the cholesterol.
- Adding carrageenan results in a better texture and improved sliceability. Carrageenan works well in the presence of milk protein, so using it with non-fat dry milk is a good idea.
- Konjac flour mixes with cold water extremely well and gelatinizes easily. It provides a slippery, fatty sensation, but it does not create as firm of a texture as carrageenan does.

- Don't add salt to water when preparing rice, potatoes, barley or making meat stock. Salt will be added during mixing.

Kosher Sausages

Well, the meat selection is pretty much defined by the Jewish Bible:

- You may eat any animal that has a split hoof and chews the cud: the cow, the sheep, the goat, the deer, the antelope. The camel, rabbit and the coney can not be eaten.
- Of all the creatures living in the water, you may eat any that has fins and scales. That means no eels, oysters or lobsters.
- You may eat all clean birds: chicken, poultry. Eating birds of prey such as eagle falcon or nighthawk is not permitted.

Pork is not permitted and that includes pork fat which is normally added to venison, poultry or fish sausages. This puts certain limitations on the recipe as pork back fat is a superior ingredient that is added to most high quality products. This forces you to improvise and there are a few choices:

- Beef fat (suet).
- An emulsified olive oil at around 10%. Flax oil, sunflower oil or mixture of both can also be used at 6% or less otherwise there will be noticeable change in flavor. *Adding oils will lighten up the sausage.*

Don't use lamb or venison fat as they don't taste right. Chicken fat tastes good, the only problem is that it melts at room temperature and you may end up with pockets of melted fat inside your sausage. Adding vegetable or olive oil is a good choice and as long as you don't add more than 25%, the sausage will be of acceptable quality. Emulsifying olive oil with soy protein isolate is a great idea as it helps to hold the sausage together and increases its protein content. Vegetable fats (obtained from plants or vegetables) melt at lower temperatures than meat fats and they are liquid at processing temperatures. This may cause fat separation during processing and cooking with fat pockets as a result. Adding an emulsifier such as soy protein or caseinate will reduce the problem.

Chicken and fish look extremely attractive and taste wonderful when added to the natural clarified stock. It is easier to produce a natural chicken only gelatin when *chicken claws are added to meat broth.*

Concentrated chicken broth takes the first place in nutritional value compared with broths from other meats. It is also distinguished by a pleasant flavor. To produce fish stock with enough gelatin fish parts that contain collagen (skin, bone and fins) must be used in making broth. This implies that after filleting the fish, the rest of the body with the head included is added to the pot.

By now you should be able to take any recipe and modify it so it will conform to the requirements of Jewish rules and tradition. The manufacturing process will basically remain the same. In most cases beef will be the material of choice and more water can be added due to beef's excellent water holding properties. Sausages will also be darker during to the higher content of myoglobin in beef meat.

Additives

Konjac flour, carrageenan and microcrystalline cellulose are of plant origin so their use should not conflict with the rules of Kosher law. Xanthan gum is made by using bacteria to ferment sugars which should also be fine. Gelatin creates a problem; it is made from animal collagen, mainly pork skins and beef hides so it does not conform to the requirements of Kosher law.

Polish Smoked Sausage with Oil Emulsion
(Reduced-fat)

Polish Smoked Sausage consists of pork, salt, pepper, garlic and optional marjoram. This is the hot smoked version known all over the world which is much easier and faster to make than the cold smoked version that was more popular in the past.

Meat	Metric	US
lean pork	750 g	1.66 lb.
oil emulsion*	200 g	0.44 lb.
cold water	50 g	1/5 cup

Ingredients per 1000 g (1 kg) of meat:

salt	18 g	3 tsp.
Cure #1	2.5 g	½ tsp.
pepper	2.0 g	1 tsp.
sugar	2.5 g	½ tsp.
garlic	3.5 g	1 clove
marjoram	1.0 g	⅔ tsp.

Instructions:
1. Grind the lean meat with a 3/8" grinder plate.
2. Mix meat, salt, Cure #1 and spices together adding cold water.
3. Add oil emulsion and mix everything together.

4. Stuff mixture into 32 - 36 mm hog casings and form links 12 - 13," 30 - 35 cm.

4. Hang on smoke sticks for 1-2 hours at room temperature OR

5. Place sausages in a preheated smoker at 130° F (54° C) with draft dampers fully open.

6. When casings are fully dry apply heavy smoke and keep draft dampers 1/4 open. Smoke for 60-90 minutes. Keep on increasing the smoking temperature until you reach 160 - 170° F (71-76° C) range. Sausage is done when the internal temperature reaches 154° F (68° C).

7. Remove from smoker and shower with water or immerse sausages in water.

8. Store in refrigerator.

Note: *oil emulsion: soy protein isolate/oil/water at 1:4:5.

Kosher Beef Sausage

Meat	Metric	US
beef, beef trimmings,	750 g	1.65 lb.
brisket fat	250 g	0.55 lb.

Ingredients per 1000 g (1 kg) of meat:

salt	18 g	3 tsp.
Cure #1	2.5 g	½ tsp.
pepper	2.0 g	1 tsp.
paprika	2.0 g	1 tsp.
garlic	3.5 g	1 clove
cold water	60 ml	¼ cup

Instructions:

1. Grind meats with 3/8" (10 mm) plate.

2. Mix all ingredients adding water.

3. Stuff into beef middles or fibrous synthetic casings 40 - 60 mm and form 12" (30 cm) long links.

4. Hang at room temperature for 1-2 hours.

5. Apply hot smoke for 110-130 min until casings develop brown color with a red tint.

6. In the last stage of smoking the sausage is baked at 167-194° F (75-90° C) until internal meat temperature is 68-70° C (154-158° F).

7. Shower with cold water for about 5 min, then let it cool down.

8. Store in refrigerator.

Kosher Liver Sausage

Meat	Metric	US
veal	650 g	1.43 lb.
veal liver	250 g	0.55 lb.
brisket fat	100 g	0.22 lb.

Ingredients per 1000 g (1 kg) of meat:

salt	18 g	3 tsp.
white pepper	4.0 g	2 tsp.
coriander	2.0 g	1 tsp.
nutmeg	1.0 g	½ tsp.
ginger	0.5 g	⅓ tsp.
onion	30 g	½ onion

Instructions:

1. Scald veal liver with hot water.
2. Cook other meats at 212° F (100° C) until soft. Save stock.
3. Be sure all meats are cold. Grind all meats through 2 mm (⅛")
plate. Refreeze and grind again. Grind liver twice with a 2 mm (
⅛") plate until you achieve paste consistency, then add salt and
remaining ingredients including all meats. Meats can be ground only
once, then emulsified in a food processor (add 10%, 0.1 kg of the
stock).
4. Mix everything together, add 10 % meat stock in relation to the
meat total weight (0.22 lb., 0.1 kg) and grind again through 2 mm
plate. We are trying to chop meats very finely, without the use of the
bowl cutter. This is the reason for grinding meats three times. Don't
add stock if meats were emulsified (stock has been added during this
step).
5. Stuff loosely into 38 - 42 mm diameter hog casings, make straight
links about 10 - 14" long. You can use natural beef casings or beef
middles up to 3" (8 cm) in diameter.
6. Place sausages into boiling water but poach at 176 - 185° F (80
- 85° C) until internal temperature of 154 - 158° F (68 - 70° C) is
reached. The required time is about 50 - 90 minutes.
7. Shower with cold water for 10 min. then hang and cool down to
an internal temperature below 42° F (6° C).
8. Store in refrigerator.

Kosher Salami

Meat	Metric	US
beef chuck	750 g	1.65 lb.
brisket fat	250 g	0.55 lb.

Ingredients per 1000 g (1 kg) of meat:

salt	28 g	5 tsp.
Cure #2	2.5 g	½ tsp.
white pepper	4.0 g	2 tsp.
dextrose (glucose), 0.2%	2.0 g	½ tsp.
paprika	2.0 g	1 tsp.
Manischewitz sweet wine	15 ml	1 Tbs.
T-SPX culture	0.12 g	use scale

Instructions:

1. Grind meats through 3/16" plate (5 mm).
2. Mix all ingredients with ground meat.
3. Stuff firmly into beef middles or 3" protein lined fibrous casings.
4. Ferment at 20° C (68° F) for 72 hours, 90-85% humidity.
5. Cold smoke for 4 days (< 22° C, 72° F). You can smoke during last day of fermentation.
6. Dry at 16-12° C (60-54° F), 85-80% humidity for 2-3 months.
7. Store sausages at 10-15° C (50-59° F), 75% humidity.

Kosher Sausage With Oil

Meat	Metric	US
ground beef	1000 g	2.2 lb.

Ingredients per 1000 g (1 kg) of meat:

	Metric	US
salt	18 g	1 Tbs
pepper	4.0 g	2 tsp.
garlic	3.5 g	1 clove
marjoram, ground	2.0 g	1 tsp.
olive oil, 11%	112 g	½ cup
cold water	60 g	¼ cup

Instructions:

1. Grind beef with ⅛" plate.
2. Add cold water and all other ingredients and mix everything well together. Add oil and mix everything together.
3. Stuff mixture into 32-36 mm beef or fibrous casings.
4. Poach in water before serving. Poaching means placing sausage in water and simmering at 164° F (73° C) until sausage reaches inside temperature of 154 - 158° F (68 - 70° C) which will take approximately 35 min. Staying within these temperatures produces a sausage that is juicy and has a great flavor.
5. Cool and refrigerate.

Notes:

- You can finish with step #3, which will produce a fresh sausage that must be refrigerated and fully cooked before serving.

- You can smoke and cook the sausage. Use a regular olive or vegetable oil. Don't go much higher than 10-11% otherwise the taste of the sausage might suffer.

- A food processor may be used to chop and mix everything together which will result in the emulsified sausage type.

Chapter 22

Hams and Formed Meat Products

The ham has certainly evolved a long way. Traditionally associated with a cut from a hog's hind leg, it is made today in different shapes from a variety of meats such as pork, beef, turkey or chicken. There are bone-in hams, boneless hams, re-formed hams, dry hams, smoked hams, baked hams and hams cooked in water. A ham used to be one of the most valuable products, a cut with its own character and distinct flavor. Such a ham was made from a whole leg and was cured in brine or salted and dried in the air. The brine method was too slow and has been replaced by the combination of meat pumping and tumbling, although it is still practiced in home production. The method of making dry hams has basically remained the same with the exception of drying, which is performed in climate controlled chambers today.

Meat contains 25% of solid material and 75% of water. When we inject 50% or more water into the meat the same cut now contains 17% of solids and 83% of water. This extra water not only provides better conditions for bacteria to grow, but affects the flavor of the meat. One does not need to be a genius to understand that anything diluted tastes weaker.

Let's assume that the lady of the house serves chicken soup every Friday to her family which she always makes the same. What will happen if she adds an extra 50% of water to it? Everybody will taste the difference and there might be a complaint. She does not want to fight with her family and being smart she starts to think like a meat processor in order to cover up the diluted flavor.

She throws in two chicken cubes and saves her soup. This is basically how the manufacturing process looks; water is added, phosphate blend is introduced to hold this water, and the flavorings are added to boost up the flavor. It can be said that the *quality and the price of a ham is directly related to the amount of injected water.*

All those products are rosy pink and look pretty to convince the consumer that he is getting a top product. A ham today can be produced in one single day.

As a curiosity matter the Soviet hams were: salted, cured, soaked, air-cured for 10 days at 54-64° F, 12-18° C, and the relative humidity did not exceed 80%. Then they were smoked for 3 days at 86-95° F, 30-35° C or for 15 days at 18-20° C and dried for 10 days. The yield of the finished product was 70% of the original meat weight. Hams that are smoked today *after losing moisture* during smoking and cooking still weigh the same as what the original weight was. The present day ham might be juicier (extra water) than those old European products but its flavor does not even come close.

Ham Types

- Dry hams - smoked or not smoked but usually not cooked.
- Whole hams - partially or fully cooked. May be smoked or not. A bone-in ham can consist of a whole leg, half leg or just a butt portion. Boneless hams will have all bones removed. Bone-in hams are more flavorful and more attractive.
- Formed hams - made from individual cuts of meat and cooked in water. They can be smoked or not.

Adapted from CFR § 319.104

Country Ham, Country Style Ham, or Dry Cured Ham, and Country Pork Shoulder, Country Style Pork Shoulder, or Dry Cured Pork Shoulder:

The uncooked, cured, dried, smoked or unsmoked meat food products made respectively from a single piece of meat conforming to the definition of "ham," or from a single piece of meat from a pork shoulder. They are prepared by the dry application of salt or by salt and one or more optional ingredients: nutritive sweeteners, spices, seasonings, flavorings, sodium or potassium nitrate, and sodium or potassium nitrite. *They may not be injected with curing solutions nor placed in curing solutions.* The product must be treated for the destruction of possible live trichinae.

Product description	Protein in %	Water in %
Ham (Dry Cured)	20.5	0
Ham with Natural Juices	18.5	less than 8
Ham-Water Added	17	12-15
Ham & Water Products	15	more than 15

Looking at the official ham classification it is clear that *except country style hams (dry hams) all hams contain added water.* A typical consumer judges ham not by its flavor (he can't taste it) but by the color and its presentation. *If it look pretty and carries a good price, it is a good ham...*

Manufacturing Process - General Guidelines

1. Meat preparation - cutting and trimming the ham.
2. Curing/salting.
3. Equalizing.
4. Rinsing and soaking.
5. Drying.
6. Stuffing/Netting.
7. Smoking.
8. Cooking.
9. Cooling.

Photo 22.1 Carving ham.   **Photo 22.2** Removing bones.

It takes a considerable skill to make a boneless ham. Bones must be removed and the lean muscles must be carved out with the minimum damage.

Photo 22.3 Lacing ham. Large muscles must be laced tight with butcher's twine, otherwise poor bond will be created..

Photo 22.4 Smoked boneless ham. It can be seen how hard the ham was laced up.

Photo 22.5 Netting ham. Smaller muscles can be netted together.

Photo 22.6 Roast tyer helps with netting or even large diameter sausage casings.

Photo courtesy The Sausage Maker, Buffalo, NY.

Curing is the most important step that will affect the quality of the finished product. In a case of dry hams it also provides safety against spoilage. Hams are always cured and the procedure is different for a hobbyist and for a commercial plant. A home based sausage maker can employ time proven curing techniques such as brine, salting, salting and brine, needle injecting and brine, or needle injecting and salting wherein a commercial producer will inevitably choose needle stitching and tumbling as this is the fastest method.

A hobbyist can produce ham without chemicals, the meat plant can not afford such a luxury. A hobbyist is chiefly concerned with the quality, the meat plant must be cost effective in a highly competitive field.

Meat plant is forced to use chemicals in order to overcome problems which are of little concern for a hobbyist:

- deterioration of color - hams are exposed to fluorescent light

- fat rancidity - off flavor due to prolonged storage

- shelf life - this is a major concern as a supermarket wants a product that will last as long as possible.

Curing Method	Description
Dry	No water is used. Curing mixture is rubbed in and the meat is left to cure. This is the method for making dry hams.
Immersion - cover pickle	Meat is placed in a curing solution and left to cure. Traditional method.
Injection	The combination of the traditional method with modern technology. Meat is injected with pickle and: 1. Meat is placed in a cover pickle or rubbed with salt on the outside. Then it is left to cure. 2. The meat is placed in a tumbler (commercial method).

Most processed meats are cured today by injecting them with a solution of salt, nitrite, phosphate and ascorbate and then bouncing them around in a tumbler to distribute the curing solution uniformly.

There is no mystery about meat curing and successful curing requires:

- A two way cure, which works both from the inside out and from the outside in.

- Sufficient time.

It should be noted that only salt and nitrite perform the actual curing. Sugar is added for flavoring only or as food for bacteria if Nitrate is used (nitrite does not need sugar). Hams and bacon taste great when sugar and sweet flavorings are added to the recipe. Brown sugar is more flavorful than cane sugar. Regardless of the curing method employed, the curing principles remain the same, but the length of time a ham is cured will influence the final flavor most.

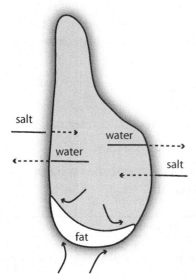

Fig. 22.1 The salt travels towards the inside, but the moisture evaporates towards the surface. The fat creates a barrier for both processes. This principle applies to all cured products, whether immersed in brine or dry cured.

Fig. 22.2, below. In a whole ham the individual muscles and intramuscular fat are left alone. Sufficient time must be allowed for curing as not all parts will cure at the same rate.

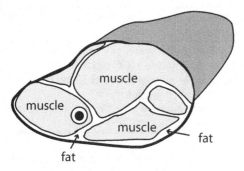

The intramuscular fat, the skin or any membrane surrounding the muscle, for example the silver skin on a pork loin, will not allow for uniform salt distribution.

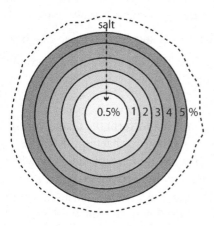

Fig. 22.3 A chunk of lean meat covered with salt. The salt will work from the outside drawing the moisture out of the meat. After the initial curing the outside area will contain 5% of salt but there will be only 0.5% of salt inside. The inside will contain more moisture as well. The solution is to continue curing without applying additional salt.

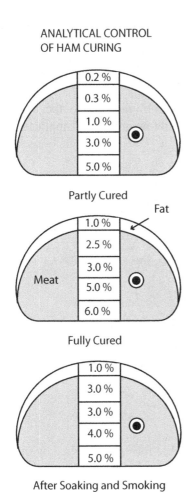

ANALYTICAL CONTROL
OF HAM CURING

Partly Cured

Fully Cured

After Soaking and Smoking

Rate of salt penetration in a traditionally cured ham *in brine solution*. The top drawing shows uneven distribution of salt in ham. Salt is working its way in *through the exposed lean meat surface first*. The fat under the skin inhibits curing.

The middle drawing shows a fully cured ham. The fat has acquired some salt but much less than other parts. The lean surface areas contain most of the salt.

The bottom drawing shows a ham after it was equalized or simply put rinsed and soaked. Salt is distributed almost evenly, the fat still contains little salt but the surface area is less salty.

Fig. 22.4 Salt penetration.

Adapted from Meat Through The Microscope, C.Robert Moulton, Ph.D and W. Lee Lewis, P.hD, Institute of Meat Packing, The University of Chicago.

Equalizing/Resting

After initial curing by a *dry or brine method*, the meat will contain more salt in its outside area than in the center. To distribute this salt uniformly an equalizing step is employed. A cured piece is rinsed in cold water and any crystallized salt that has formed on the surface is brushed off. If not removed, this salt would create a barrier to any smoking or drying procedure that might follow. Hams which would be cooked can be equalized in cold water. Dry hams would be either hung on hooks or placed on the shelf. The length of the equalizing period depends on the size of the meat. After equalization the hams will be submitted to smoking or cooking.

The following curing procedures provide more even salt distribution during curing:

- Meat pumping, followed by dry curing or wet curing (cover pickle).
- Meat pumping followed by tumbling. Due to the cost of machines this method is reserved for commercial applications.

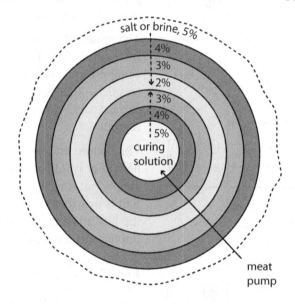

Fig. 22.5 The cure, either in dry or pickle form, is absorbed by the meat and penetrates from outside, mixing with the pickle which was previously distributed inside by stitch pumping. This combination provides faster and more uniform cure distribution and prevents over curing from outside.

Traditional Ham Production

Originally there were two methods of curing:

- Dry curing - explained in Dry Hams.
- Wet curing (cover pickle, also called brine).

Cover pickle hams. A ham was immersed in a solution of water, salt, nitrite, sometimes sugar was added, and left to cure. Historically, sugar was added to Nitrate to help catalyze the reaction with bacteria and release nitrite.

Depending on the size of a ham, the process could take from 4 to 6 weeks. As salt was slowly diffusing towards the center of the ham, there was a danger that in a large ham *the bone area would start spoiling from within before the curing solution would make it through*. That problem was known as bone sour and was well understood.

Bone areas contain a lot of connective tissue and blood vessels and offer favorable conditions for bacteria to grow. Depending on the shape of the ham, the leg is cut at the pelvis (aitch) and knuckle joint. This creates exposed areas which invite bacteria to follow. As the bone is located deep inside some time was required for the salt to reach it. At the beginning of the process the bone area contained no salt and offered little protection against spoilage bacteria. To compensate for that a method called "packing" was invented. Using a sterilized narrow knife or pointed stick, a number of insertions were made at the bone joints. Those openings were "packed" with a strong mixture of salt and saltpeter (nitrate).

Immersion curing is a fine method which offers even distribution of curing solution and as a result, very uniform and strong color. The only problem is that it is a slow method and in order to get the bone area safely cured we often ended up with a product that was over salted.

This method is greatly improved upon by *injecting some of the brine directly into the meat.* This is accomplished by a manually operated pump, that looks like a syringe with a very long needle with holes around it. Using the pump a strong curing solution can be injected right into the bone areas and into the muscle. The needle will be fully inserted into the meat and as it was slowly pulled out, the plunger was depressed injecting solution into the meat. There are many advantages to meat pumping:

- Curing times are greatly reduced.
- Solution can be precisely injected into any area, for example near the bone to eliminate the bone sour problem.
- Spices and flavoring ingredients can be added to the solution.
- There is no need to wait for the salt to migrate into the meat.
- Easy calculations of nitrite and other ingredients.
- Using meat tumblers it is possible to complete the entire curing process without submerging hams in brine.

After hams are injected with cure solution, they are usually immersed in the cover brine of similar or greater strength. This way the penetration of salt and curing ingredients will proceed to the inside as well as from the outside of the ham.

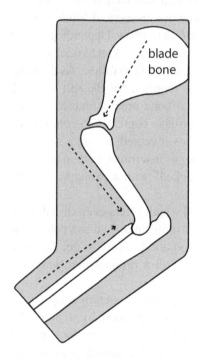

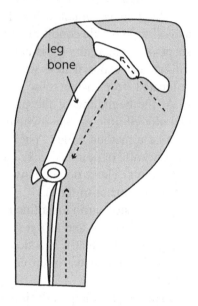

Fig. 22.7 Ham bone structure and direction of needle injection.

Fig. 22.6 Shoulder bone structure and direction of needle injection.

Pump the ham or shoulder along the bones. Fill the pump fully to prevent air pockets.

It is strongly recommended to pack some of the dry cure around the shank and hock bones. If curing is performed at higher than refrigerator temperatures, remove sugar from brine that will be injected into the bone areas. It may start fermentation and ruin the product. There is a variety of meat pumps for general cooking which are available in major department stores. Distributors of sausage making equipment and supplies carry stainless steel pumps, usually 4 oz. capacity with a selection of different needles.

Injection Methods

- Artery
- Stitch

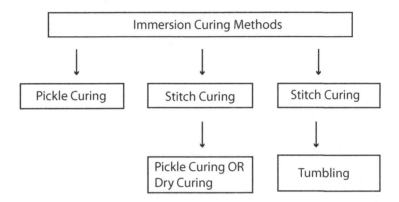

Fig. 22.8 Immersion curing.

The majority of today's hams are made by one of the above methods, most often by stitch pumping followed by cover pickle. A commercial producer may pump the meat and proceed directly to tumbling. *There is not one universal brine nor the time of curing that can be applied to a product.* As a rule, the more salt added to pickle, the stronger brine will be made and the longer the shelf life of a product will be obtained. Different amounts of brine can be injected and products of different quality will be produced. The more water added, a more diluted flavor is obtained and a cheaper product is produced which results in a higher profit for the manufacturer. Products of this nature are used for making sandwiches and their weak flavor is masked by extra toppings such as lettuce, tomato, or mayonnaise.

Making Brine (Cover Pickle)

There are thousands of recipes and they all call for different amounts of brine: gallons, liters, cups, ounces etc. To compound the matter further they ask for salt to be measured in pounds, cups, grams, spoons and teaspoons. To make the matter even worse they ask for table salt, Diamond Kosher Salt, Morton Kosher Salt, canning salt etc. This creates uncertainty and the poor hobbyist blindly follows an unknown recipe not having the slightest idea what he is doing.

Then if someone brings him 10 pounds of pork loins and asks him to prepare a brine, he will be lost because he has no recipe for a such an amount of meat. To avoid such a pitfall we cover the subject in such detail so that you will fully understand meat curing and you will be able to compose your own brine solutions.

Sugar. Sugar is normally added at 1-2% in relation to the weight of cover pickle. Sugar plays a small role in curing. It offsets the harshness of salt and combines with oxygen easily which helps to preserve the red color of meat.

Other ingredients. Cover pickle is not a marinade and it needs only water, salt, nitrite and occasionally sugar. You can add other ingredients such as garlic, pepper, bay leaf, although many experts frown at such procedures saying that it only distorts the ham's natural flavor.

How Much Brine

You have to cover the meats and a lot of brine will be wasted if you cure only 1 chicken in a 55 gallon drum. A basic rule of thumb dictates that *the amount of brine should come to about 40-50% in relation to the weight of the meat.* For 1.0 lb. of meat use 0.4-0.5 lb. of brine. Try to use a container whose size and shape will accommodate the meat piece snugly in order to use as little brine as possible.

Many professionals use the following weight ratio: from 30% to 40% of water to 100% of meat. That means that for 1 kg (2.2 lb) of meat we add 300 ml - 400 ml (10 oz fl-13.3 oz fl.)of water. Take a note that 400 ml of water = 400 g if you decide to use a scale. Then you choose the strength of the brine and keep on adding salt checking the reading with a salinometer. Let's say you want to cure two pork butts that weigh 10 pounds in total. A typical figure is to use 40% of water in relation to the weight of meat.

Example:
Green weight: 10 lb.
0.40 x 10 = 4 lb of water (1/2 gal). (1 gal of water weighs 8.33 lb).
Answer: Four pounds of brine will be the right amount.

These are rough estimates for orientation purposes only. What must be noted is that meat must be *fully covered with brine* so make just as much as is needed. Using more brine than necessary facilitates diffusion of protein and meat juices from meat into the solution. The loss will occur anyhow, but will usually stay at about 0.5% only.

Adding Ingredients

When adding ingredients to brine, the basic rule is to add ingredients that readily dissolve in water (phosphates, salt, sugar) first and then those that disperse (starch, carrageenan).

1. Add phosphates to water and dissolve.
2. Add sugars, soy proteins and dissolve.
3. Add salt and dissolve.
4. Add sodium nitrite and dissolve.
5. Add cure accelerator (sodium erythorbate) and dissolve.
6. Add starch and carrageenan.

Basic brine consisting of water, salt, sugar and nitrite may be prepared a day earlier and kept in a refrigerator. If there is any surface foam or bottom sediment it should be filtered. Chlorine in water impedes the action of nitrites so stay away from heavily chlorinated water. Ascorbic acid should not be added into brine containing nitrite as the two chemicals will react producing fumes. Liquid smoke may be added to brine at 0.1-0.5 g/kg but it is safer to stay on the low side as liquid smoke may impart an overpowering flavor.

Reusing brine is a bad idea as it may contain bacteria from the previous operation. Salt and cure mixes are inexpensive so it makes no sense to risk meat contamination. A meat plant employs qualified technicians who can run lab tests on brine in order to save costs but it makes little sense to take the risk at home. At the first suspicion of brine spoilage it should be replaced with a fresh one, in most cases there is nothing wrong with the meat itself. The accumulating foam on top of the brine should be periodically removed. In case the foam starts to give a foul odor, turn blue in color, or becomes a slime, what is known as "ropy" brine, we will have to remove the ham, wash it in cool water, and place it in a freshly made brine.

Strength of the Brine And Curing Times

There is no universal brine and its strength will be up to you. A brine tester is a must and a notebook for future reference will be of invaluable help. You can use a stronger brine and your curing time will be shorter or you can use a milder brine and the curing time can be longer. If you add sugar into your brine it will be heavier. For example, if we add 8 lb of salt to 5 gallons of water we obtain 61° brine but if we add 8 lb of salt plus 3 lb of sugar to 5 gallons of water, we get 75° brine.

All our calculations are based on salt and water only. What follows below is a part of complete tables for making brine which are listed in Appendix A.

Salometer Degrees	% of Salt by Weight	Pounds of Salt per Gallon of Water
0	0.000	0.000
10	2.640	0.226
20	5.279	0.464
30	7.919	0.716
40	10.588	0.983
50	13.198	1.266
55	14.517	1.414
60	15.837	1.567
65	17.157	1.725
70	18.477	1.887
75	19.796	2.056
80	21.116	2.229
90	23.756	2.595
100	26.395	2.986

The table shows that in order to create 60° SAL brine, we have to add 1.567 lb. of salt to 1 gallon of water.

Curing method used, curing times and brine strength all depend on each other:

- The strength of the brine – the stronger the brine the faster curing action.

- The size of the cured meat – a whole turkey requires more brining time than a shrimp.

- The method used – pumping and brining or just brining. Pumping meat shortens curing time.

Make sure you don't brine meats that have already been brined, such as supermarket stocked pork, which has been treated with sodium phosphate and water to make it juicier. The following brine strengths are for orientation purposes only and feel free to improvise your own solutions. Most meats like 70-75° brine, poultry likes a weaker solution of 21° and most fish are briefly cured in 80° brine.

Fish is cured for 1-2 hours only. Of course there are small diameter meat cuts and large ones, chicken breasts, whole chickens, turkeys, fish fillets, small fish, big fish and all these different meats and cuts will have different curing times. Products such as loins, hams, poultry, and spareribs taste good when some sugar is applied. *Sugar is not a curing agent and it has very little effect on the curing process.* Think of sugar in terms of flavoring.

Meat	Brine Strength in Degrees	Time of Curing
Poultry	21	overnight
Bacon	50 - 65	1½ - 2 days per pound
Spareribs	50 - 55	1 week
Loins	55 - 65	2 weeks
Ham, shoulders	65 - 75	4 days per pound
Fish	80	2 hours

If meat were stitch pumped with pickle first, these times would be shortened in half. Notice that sugar, though often added to brine after it is made, does not participate in the calculation for making a brine of a particular strength. That is due to the following reasons:

- A lot of brines do not call for sugar at all.

- A lot of brines call for different amounts of sugar (more sugar for bacon, less sugar for ham).

- People use different sugars, dextrose, maple syrup or honey.

How Long to Brine

Brine curing is slower than dry curing as you can add only about 26% of salt to water before the solution becomes saturated (100° SAL). Adding more salt will only cause it to settle down on the bottom of the container. On the other hand dry mix consists of 100% salt, although it may contain some sugar and other ingredients in small quantities. For this reason *dry salting is the fastest curing method* as *the more salt in a curing solution, the faster the curing process.* The disadvantage of dry curing is that the drawn out moisture is not replaced so the yield of the dry cured products is smaller.

Curing time estimates for the traditional wet cure method (brine strength 50–65 degrees) are as follows:

- 11 days per inch of thickness of the meat.
- About 3 ½ to 4 days per pound for 20 lb hams and picnics.
- 3 days per pound for smaller cuts.

Those curing times were practiced in the past when preservation was the main concern. Nowadays, these times may be shortened by 1 day per pound, i.e. a 15 pound ham will be cured for 45 days. Curing times may be further reduced if brine curing is preceded by stitch pumping.

Adding Nitrite

Making brine is very simple but calculating nitrites (Cure #1) is a bit harder. It is a straightforward procedure in the dry curing method used for comminuted products like sausages. We add the needed amount into the sausage mix, stuff the mix into casings and the amount of cure and other ingredients like salt is fully accounted for.

Now imagine adding Cure #1 into a solution of salt and water and then placing meat in it. The meat might be immersed 4, 5, 7, or 30 days in a brine, then the meat is removed but the brine remains. How much nitrite and salt diffused into the meat and how much has remained in a leftover brine is anybody's guess. There are only two ways to be sure:

- Weigh the meat before and after curing. This operation is time consuming and will have to be performed on each individual piece. Although the underlying theory is sound, it doubtful that any hobbyist is doing that.
- Pump the predetermined amount of solution inside of the meat and then don't immerse meat into leftover solution. Meats are usually placed in a tumbler to uniformly distribute solution.

To better estimate the amount of ingoing nitrite, the USDA recommends the following method for calculating nitrite in the cover pickle when curing large meats like hams, shoulders and bellies, as they require long time items to reach equilibrium. The method assumes that the meat or poultry does not absorb more than the level of nitrite in the cover pickle. Hence, the calculation for nitrite is based on the green weight of the meat or poultry (as is the case with pumped products), but uses percent pick-up as the percent pump. *The percent pick-up is the total amount of cover pickle absorbed by the meat or poultry.*

It is used in the calculation for immersion cured products in the same way the percent pump is used in calculations for pumped products. It sounds nice in theory but it still depends on the % pick-up of the cured meat. Does anybody know what would be the % pick-up of a 5 lb pork butt immersed for 10 days in 60° SAL brine? Without weighing the meat, the only way to determine % pick-up of cured meat is by an educated guess based on previous experience.

Calculation Formula (using % pick-up)

$$\frac{\text{lb. nitrite x \% pick-up x } 1{,}000{,}000}{\text{lb. pickle}} = \text{ppm}$$

It is generally accepted that immersion cured hams (60° SAL) pick-up about 4% weight. If we add 4.2 ounces (120 g) of Cure #1 to 1 gallon of brine, the solution will contain 1973 ppm of sodium nitrite. At first sight it may seem that there is an excessive amount of nitrite in water. The answer is that only a small percentage will be absorbed by meat during the immersion process. At 4% pick-up the ham will absorb 79 ppm which will be just enough for any meaningful curing. At 10% pump (needle pumping) the same ham will contain 197 ppm of sodium nitrite which is in compliance with the government standard of 200 ppm. Pumping more than 10% or increasing the amount of cure in the solution will of course cross the limit. Based on those findings we can come up with the general formula for 60° SAL brine:

water	1 gal.	3.80 kg
salt	1.32 lb.	0.60 kg
Cure #1	4.2 oz.	120 g
sugar	1.5 oz.	42 g

If you need stronger or weaker brine *change the amount of salt according to the salt tables.* Take note that Cure #1 contains 93.75% salt so this amount of salt should be accounted for, otherwise the brine will be slightly stronger than intended for. To eliminate the danger of uneven coloring, manufacturers add sodium erythorbate into the solution. This speeds up the nitrite reaction and more nitric oxide will be released. Nitric oxide will in turn react with the meat's myoglobin and the pink color will be created.

By now you should be fully aware that many solutions will do the job. Meat placed in a weaker solution will do as good a job as meat placed in a stronger solution as long as a proper curing time is allowed.

Meat Pumping

Meat pumping is the only method that allows for precise control of salt and nitrite distribution inside meat. A commonly used percentage of injection is 10%. Although after curing the meat may weigh 110% in relation to its original weight, some of the pickle will be lost during smoking and cooking. You can easily increase the gain of your product by adding a phosphate blend which is available from many distributors. This will allow you to pump more water which will be retained by the meat even during cooking. If you pump meat with a solution that contains 2000 ppm of nitrite, but you inject only 10% of solution in relation to meat's weight, the meat absorbs only 200 ppm of sodium nitrite. This is a true figure as long as the meat is not placed in curing solution anymore. Such pumped meat is usually placed in a meat tumbler and no more solution is added.

The percent pick-up or the percent pump is the total amount of cover pickle absorbed by the meat or poultry.

Example:
10 Percent injection.
Green weight (initial weight) = 5 kg (11 lb).
Percent injection = 10%
0.10 x 11 lb = 1.1 lb
Pounds of pickle to inject = 1.1 lb
The weight of injected ham:
11 + 1.1 = 12.1 lb

Formula for % pump is the same as the formula for % pick-up on the previous page.

$$\frac{\text{lb. nitrite x \% pump x 1,000,000}}{\text{lb. pickle}} = \text{ppm}$$

Pumping meat at 10% pump with the general brine formula from the previous page (4.2 oz Cure #1) results with 197 ppm of sodium nitrite which is in compliance with the government limit of 200 ppm. General guidelines for making brine:

General guidelines for making brine:

1. Choose the brine strength for your application.
2. Add Cure #1.
3. Add salt and check the brine strength with a brine tester.
4. Add other ingredients that you might like. Adding sugar and other ingredients increases the strength of the brine.
Note: Remember to account for the extra salt (93.75%) that Cure #1 contains when using brine tables.

You can immerse meat in this brine for pickle curing or you can use it for needle pumping. Let's assume you choose 10% pump. That means that your meat weighs 10 times more than the amount of brine that will be injected into it. For example, if you took 8.33 pounds (1 gal) of the brine and injected it into 83.3 pounds of meat, the total weight of your injected meat is 83.3 + 8.33 = 91.60 pounds.

To shorten the curing time in half, the meat is pumped with 10% pump and then immersed in the same solution. At home a good practice will be to pump meat with 7% pump and then immerse it in the remaining curing solution. At the end of curing the ham should gain about 7% in weight.

To calculate the strength of the brine using the floating egg or potato method makes very little sense as the readings are not reliable. There are books that advocate this method and each of them give different readings. The egg sinks in clean water and as the salt is added it should start lifting to the surface. Well, they do but in a very unpredictable manner. We have checked the floating egg method using five different size fresh eggs and the results were inconclusive.

All that information may look at first a bit confusing but remember that as long as you cure meat at refrigerator temperature, everything will be fine. The meat will be cured if your solution is 70, 60 or 50° SAL strong, but the curing times will be different. As the majority of hams are cooked to safe temperature there is not much to worry about.

Dry cured hams are not cooked and require stricter procedures and more attention. Having said that, be flexible and not afraid to experiment, and keep notes for future reference. A home processor can use a manual syringe to inject brine into the meat but I don't believe anybody wants to keep a tumbler machine in the kitchen. You could massage meat with your hands or pound it through a towel with a rubber mallet. Unfortunately, that will require a lot of time and at temperatures prevailing in an ordinary kitchen that will create more harm than good.

After losing moisture during smoking and cooking, commercially produced hams still weigh the same as what the original weight was. This miracle is due to the water that is injected into the meat and held there by phosphates.

Rinsing and Drying

After meat is taken from dry cure or brine, it must be rinsed and washed in cold water. A good idea is to soak meat for 2 hours under running water. Smaller pieces may be soaked for 30 minutes only. If a soaking container is used, water should be changed every 30 minutes. Soaking removes some of the salt which is concentrated in the outside area. After that the ham is hung for 12-24 hours to dry.

Stuffing/Netting

In the past products were laced with butcher's twine but today it is accomplished with netting that comes in an assortment of different sizes, patterns and colors. It also helps to hold meat together, after the removal of bones. The netting is the "casing" and the product has to be somehow stuffed into it. Netting sometimes clings to the surface of the finished cooked product and is hard to remove. To prevent that, the netting should be soaked in a releasing agent first until moist. The simplest remedy is to combine equal parts of liquid smoke and vinegar and soak the netting in it.

Below, there is a very ingenious method of stuffing ham which requires a common 3-5 gallon plastic bucket.

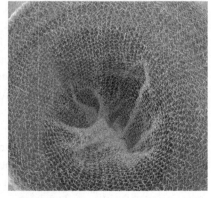

Photo 22.7 Netting flipped around the bucket.

Photo 22.8 Tied end of the netting inside the bucket.

Photo 22.9 Meat inside netting.

Procedure:

1. Flip netting around the bucket.
2. Pull the netting down on the outside of the bucket until the knot is centered and on top.
3. Place the butt end of the ham on top of the knot and let it drop into the bucket.
4. Tie the knot on top of the netting and make a hanging loop.

Photo 22.10 Meat inside netting hanging in smokehouse.

The 5 gallon bucket method works well with bone-in whole hams but for stuffing boneless ham that consists of a few individual muscles, a stuffing horn is usually employed. It is also known as the "roast tyer" and comes in two versions: a cheaper plastic unit and a better stainless steel model.

Hams which will be cooked in water can be stuffed into cook-bags or collagen foil. Then the foil is clipped and thermally treated. This prevents the loss of moisture and meat juices. Such hams are generally not smoked.

Smoking

Except formed products which are enclosed in a mold and cooked in water, all other meats such as hams, shoulders, loins, bacon, jowls and back fat can be smoked. The time of smoking will depend mainly on the diameter of the product, desired color and expected shelf life.

After the product has been rinsed or soaked, it has to dry until its surface becomes tacky. This will create proper conditions for smoke deposition. Products which will not be smoked can be submitted to the drying step.

Country hams must be cold smoked but the majority of products are smoked with hot smoke and then cooked inside of the smokehouse. It is a good idea to hold products at 110-115° F (44 - 46° C) without applying smoke for 30-60 minutes to dry the surface. The vents should be fully opened to allow for moisture removal.

Photo 22.11 Smoked ham

Then the vent is readjusted to 1/4 open position and hot smoke is introduced. The purpose of hot smoke is to flavor meat only and the process can be stopped at any time as long as we continue to cook the product to the FSIS recommended temperature. Generally hams are hot smoked between 3 and 5 hours. It is a good idea to keep on raising the smoking temperature as the process continues in order to shorten cooking time.

Cooking

Hams may be:

- Uncooked - hams which were not processed to 137° F (58° C), the temperature that kills Trichinae worm if present in pork. European hams are sliced thin and eaten uncooked. American country hams are often cooked before serving.

- Partially cooked - hams which are cooked to an internal temperature higher than 137° F (58° C) but less than 148° F (64° C).

- Fully cooked - hams which are thermally processed to more than 148° F (64° C), usually to about 155° F (68° C). They are ready to eat at any given time.

Many older butchers swear that hams should be first cooked in boiling water for about 15 minutes. This will cook the surface area of the ham preventing the loss of meat juices. The temperature is then lowered to 80° C and cooking continues at this setting. In their opinion this results in a more juicy ham with a better flavor. Meat technologists do not advocate this method and insist that a ham should be cooked at 167-176° F (75-80° C).

Photo 22.12 Cooking ham.

When ham is removed from hot water its internal temperature will still go up by a few degrees due to the heat transfer from the hot surface. Taking this under consideration, the cooking should be stopped about 2 degrees earlier before the desired internal temperature is obtained.

Cooling

Cooked hams like all other cooked meats and sausages are showered or immersed in cold water to bring the temperature down. In the case of a large ham the showering may continue for 30 minutes or longer. The need to pass through "danger zone" 140-40° F (60-4° C) fast. Given that after showering their internal temperature will still be too

high, they need to go to a cooler or be air cooled in the room or outside, weather permitting. Air ventilating fan will be of much help.

Photo 22.13 A large ham.

Painting Hams

Here is a nice professional trick for improving color of smoked ham.

Photo 22.14 Maggi liquid seasoning is mixed with ground sweet paprika.

Photo 22.15 The mixture is rubbed in all over the ham.

The orange-red tint of paprika in combination with black Maggi sauce result in a nice deep red color. Smoked paprika will make it even redder. Another spice which will work well is annatto.

Dry Cured Hams

Since dry curing draws out moisture, it reduces ham weight by at least 18%, usually 20 to 25%; this results in a more concentrated ham flavor. Dry hams are saltier than other products and before serving are often soaked in water for 6-12 hours in refrigerator. The 5-6% or more salt they contain is added for safety reasons, to eliminate the growth of spoilage and pathogenic bacteria. This salt plays a crucial safety factor in the initial stage of the process, when the product contains a lot of moisture. As curing and drying continues, the ham loses more moisture and less water remains available to bacteria. Dry-cured hams may be aged more than a year. Six months is the traditional process but may be shortened according to aging temperature.

Dry cured hams are not injected with a curing solution or immersed in it. They may be smoked or not. Today, dry cured hams may be marketed as items that need preparation on the part of the consumer to make them safe to eat. As with all meat products, it is important to read the label of hams to determine the proper preparation needed. These uncooked hams are safe stored at room temperature because they contain so little water that bacteria can not grow.

The way dry hams are made today is not much different from the process that was performed in the past. The difference lies mainly in climate control. In the past this process relied on understanding the local climate and the experience of the operator. He had to decide on a daily basis which windows to open or how much water bring inside. This empirical knowledge was not acquired overnight but was passed from father to son. Today the technology of making dry products depends on the same steps as in the past, the difference is that temperature and humidity of drying chambers are computer controlled. The manufacture of loins and shoulders is very similar to the process of making hams, the difference being the size of the product which influences the length of curing and drying.

The most popular hams:

Name	Description	Smoked	Country
Serrano	Ham made from white pigs, 110 kg, 6-7 months old.	No	Spain
Iberian	Ham made from black Iberian pigs, 160 kg, 18-24 months old, that grazed freely near oak trees. Fattened with oak acorns.	No	Spain
Parma	No nitrates allowed. Cured with salt. Pig weight 150 kg, 12-18 months old.	No	Italy
San Daniele	Ham, no nitrates allowed. Cured with sea salt.	No	Italy
Bayonne	White pigs, 110 kg, 6-7 months old, boneless.	No	France
Country style	The fastest production cycle of all dry hams. Usually made within 2-3 months.	Yes	USA
Westphalia	Smoked with beech wood.	Yes	Germany
York	Mild in flavor, smoked	Yes	England

The most popular Italian hams (prosciuttos in Italian) are: Prosciutto di Parma, Prosciutto di San Danelle, Prosciutto di Modena, Prosciutto di Carpegna, Prosciutto di Norcia, Prosciutto Toscano and Prosciutto Veneto Berico-Euganeo. Then there is Prosciutto Cotto which is Italian cooked ham. Cooked hams are easier to produce and every country makes their own.

Spanish Hams

There are two famous Spanish hams (jamón means ham in Spanish):

1. Jamón Iberico
2. Jamón Serrano

Iberico ham (*Jamón Iberico*), also called "pata negra", is a type of cured ham produced only in Spain. It is at least 75% black Iberian pig, also called the cerdo negro (black pig). According to Spain's Denominación de Origen rules on food products jamón ibérico may be made from cross-bred pigs as long as they are at least 75% ibérico. The pigs are allowed to roam in the pasture and oak groves to feed naturally on grass, herbs, acorns, and roots, until the slaughtering time approaches. At that point the diet may be strictly limited to acorns for the best quality jamón ibérico, or may be a mix of acorns and commercial feed for lesser qualities. Meat from those pigs exhibits a large amount of marbling which guarantees ham of the highest quality. Not surprisingly, Iberico hams are the most expensive hams in the world. Pigs are slaughtered at the age 8-9 months, having the weight of 150-170 kg (330-374 lb). Salt is added at 4-7% in relation to the weight of a ham.

Serrano Ham (*Jamón Serrano*) is made from the "Landrace" breed of white pig and are not to be confused with the much more expensive and entirely different Jamón ibérico. The manufacturing process remains similar to Iberico Ham, the main difference lies in the type of pork used.

Manufacturing process for Spanish Hams

1. Salting. Traditional production method uses only salt without adding nitrates, although often purified sea salt is mixed with common rock salt. Sea salt contains many minerals and can create different reactions with meat proteins and fats. The salt is added at 4-7% in relation to the weight of a ham. Using less salt may not prevent the growth of spoilage and pathogenic bacteria and will lower the final quality of the ham. Such an amount of salt immediately draws out some moisture from meat cells and this lowers the water activity of the meat. As a result a safety hurdle is created and the meat becomes bacteriologically stable in time. In order to prevent conditions for bacteria to grow, the salting process takes place at 40° F (4° C), 85-95% humidity. A rule of thumb calls for *2 days for each 1 kg of meat,* for example the 8 kg (17.6 lb) ham will be salted for 16 days.

After the salting stage hams are thoroughly brushed off to remove excess salt.

2. Equalization. Equalization, sometimes called post-salting takes place at 37-42° F (3-6° C), 85-95% humidity and continues for about 40 days. *Equalization is the time after the excess cure has been removed from the product, at the end of the cure contact period until the product is placed in the drying room and the drying period begins.*

3. Drying/Ripening. This is the longest stage that lasts 10-12 months. During this stage due to complex reactions between enzymes, meat proteins and fats, the ham develops its characteristic flavor and aroma. With time the ham loses moisture, but the salt remains inside increasing its proportional content. As the ham becomes more stable in time the temperatures are increased which increases the speed of internal reactions and decreases maturation time. The ripening continues in a few cycles: the temperature starts at 53-57° F (12-14° C), 60-80% humidity, and increases up to 75-93° (24-34° C), 70-90% humidity. The ripening takes about 5 months for Serrano Ham and 10 months for Iberico Ham. The high humidity creates better conditions for mold to develop which often happens. After ripening is completed, a mold covered layer of meat or fat is cut off from the surface of the ham.

4. Storing. Then the hams are stored at around 53° F (12° C), 75% humidity for up to a year. For the highest quality Iberico hams, the entire process may take up to 2 years.

Without a doubt the hardest product to make at home will be European dry cured hams due to their long curing and maturing times. This will require climate controlled drying chambers and a significant time investment. Another factor which is beyond our control is the meat quality. All great Spanish and Italian hams are produced from pigs that graze freely on a pasture and their diet is supplemented by natural foods only. No chemicals or antibiotics are permitted.

The manufacture of dry products such as hams, shoulders, butts or loins generally follows these steps:

1. Meat selection, cutting and trimming.
2. Salting/Curing/Overhauling.
3. Resting/Equalizing.
4. Drying and smoking (smoking is optional).

1. Dry hams are usually made from whole legs. It must be remembered that pork pork should be either certified free of Trichinosis or treated according to the USDA specifications.

2. In the past when meats had to be kept without refrigeration the curing times were longer. For example the standard curing time for large pieces as ham and shoulders was about 3 days per pound and 2 days for small pieces like bacon. Even then, those curing times would be shortened by 1/3 when a product would be consumed sooner.

A mixture of salt and nitrite is applied to the surface, then more salt is added on top and the meat is left top cure. A lot of salt is added as at this initial stage, this is the only protection against the growth of spoilage and pathogenic bacteria. Keep in mind that these products are not cooked and this is why more salt is needed. Since dry curing draws out moisture, it reduces ham weight by at least 18%, usually 20 to 25%; this results in a more concentrated ham flavor.

Overhauling. In the first days of curing, the salt rapidly extracts moisture from the meat. Some of the salt is absorbed by the meat, but some salt dissolves in the newly created liquid and drains off. This resulting liquid is not needed and is removed by storing hams in containers that have holes at the bottom or laying hams on slanted tables. To continue the curing process, more mixture must be added. In addition when many meat cuts are cured together, some pieces may press against each other, preventing the cure from penetrating the meat. Overhauling which is basically re-arranging the order of cured meat, takes care of the problem.

3. Equalizing/Resting. Hams are rinsed with tap water and any residual salt is brushed off from the surface. Then they are hung or placed on the shelf for salt equalization. This step takes 1-2 months depending on the size of the ham and other factors. The humidity is decreased as the drying continues. This step resembles drying fermented sausages. Due to the accumulation of salt inside, hams are bacteriologically more stable and will become more stable due to the continuous evaporation of moisture. Salt diffuses to all areas of the product and drying continues.

- Preventing spoilage of meat. This is accomplished by adding salt and nitrite into the meat and keeping the product at low temperature.

- Development of a proper color.

- Development of flavor. The flavor should depend on the natural flavor of the meat itself and not on adding a variety of spices. The aroma of spices will not last for six months or longer and those are the times needed to make those products. The final flavor is the result of naturally occurring reactions inside of the meat and fats as well.

4. Drying/Smoking is usually performed at 54-76° F (12-24° C) and every manufacturer has his own method, temperature range, humidity and air speed control. For products made at home, staying below 59° F (15° C) is the recommended setting as at this and higher temperatures pathogenic *Staphylococcus aureus* starts to grow faster.

Cold smoke (< 68° F, 20° C) can be applied during the drying process. Cold smoking is basically drying with smoke and can be applied for a few weeks for 3-5 hours every day. Smoking inhibits the growth of bacteria on the surface of the product and prevents molds from growing. It also imparts a different flavor to the product which is liked by many consumers. The factors affecting drying:

- Diameter of the meat.
- Amount of fat or skin on the surface (ham).
- Amount of intramuscular fat (ham) or fat trimmings in the sausage.
- Water content of the ham or sausage.

The drying is also affected by the temperature, humidity and the air flow. Growing molds can impede evaporation of water by closing the pores on the surface. One of the methods to slow down water loss in the later stage of the drying process is *to spread a thin layer of lard on ham's surface.* In a traditional meat plant producing hundreds of hams at a time, the quality control was based on visual inspection and sniffing techniques. A small probe, usually a thin horse bone 8 inches (20 cm) long and 1/8 in (3 mm) diameter was inserted into areas of the ham that are prone to spoilage. The probe was immediately sniffed by the expert to detect any unusual odor. With scientific advance in the field of instrumentation, there are electronic instruments that are able to sniff any off-odors as well.

European dry hams need almost one year to manufacture and the total weight loss in relation to the original weight is around 30 percent. The highest quality hams are usually produced with bones intact. Boneless hams, after drying, will have their bones removed by an expert and then compressed to obtain a desired shape.

American Country Hams

Only the hind legs of hogs can be called a country ham. *They may not be injected with curing solutions nor placed in curing solution.* The application of salt shall be a sufficient quantity to insure that the finished product has an internal salt content of at least 4 percent. For hams or pork shoulders labeled *"country" or "country style,"* the combined period for curing and salt equalization shall not be less than 45 days for hams, and shall not be less than 25 days for pork shoulders; the total time for curing salt equalization, and drying shall not be less than 70 days for hams, and shall not be less than 50 days for pork shoulders. During the drying and smoking period, the internal temperature of the product must not exceed 95 °F, provided that such a temperature requirement shall not apply to products dried or smoked under natural climatic conditions. The manufacturing process:

1. Salting. Salt and nitrite/nitrate are rubbed in all over meat and skin. Care should be taken to pack the salt deep into the exposed bone areas. The ham remains covered in salt for at least 30 days at 36-40° F (2-4° C). More curing solution is applied during that time. Any accumulated liquid is drained away. Then the hams are washed and the surface is brushed off to eliminate any crystalized salt. Such salt clogs the meat pores and will prevent proper drying or smoking.

2. Equalizing. Spices and sugar may be rubbed in. Hams are placed in cloth or net bags. In the past a wire was threaded through a hole cut in the hock. Occasionally, the hams were not hung but lied on a side on the shelves. This 2 weeks equalization period (3 days per pound) allows for more even salt distribution inside. The temperature varies from 50 - 54° F (10-12° C), 75% humidity.

3. Smoking. Hams are cold smoked for 24-30 hours.

4. Drying/Maturing. Hams lose more moisture and develop a characteristic flavor. This is also known as the ripening stage and it continues for 30-90 days. Temperature varies from 77-86° F (25-30° C), 65% humidity.

The production of American country hams is concentrated in the Eastern states such as Virginia or Tennessee. There are many local processors that produce excellent country hams, for example Benton's Smoky Mountain Country Hams in Madisonville, TN.

I made a decision early on in my country ham business that I would try to not make more hams; I would try to make better hams. - Allan Benton.

Mr. Benton has been involved with making hams since his childhood when he helped his family with pig slaughter and meat processing every year in early December in the Smoky Mountains. Since 1973 he runs a USDA approved and inspected country ham producing business. The hams are rubbed with ⅔ rd of a dry mix consisting of salt, brown sugar, and nitrite. Then they are left on maple shelves for 1 week at 38-40° F (3-4° C). After that, in about a week the remaining ⅓ rd of the cure is applied and the hams are restacked. They typically stay in that first stage of cure at thirty-eight to forty degrees for about two months - somewhere in the fifty-five to sixty day range. Then the hams are hung for 6 weeks in an equalization cooler at 42-50° F (6-10° C). From there they go into a smokehouse where they would hang until they are used up in the next fall. The average country ham that is made there is about nine months old.

Photo 22. 16 Allan Benton and his hams.
Photo courtesy Benton's Smoky Mountain Country Hams

Formulations From The Past

Hams

In the past the classical dry mix formula for 100 lbs. of meat was:

- 8 lb salt
- 3 lb sugar (optional)
- 3 oz Nitrate (saltpeter)

Using recent standards for dry curing 100 lbs. of meat, we can apply 453 g (1 lb) of Cure #1 (*or less*) to be in compliance with the maximum allowed level of 625 ppm.

Pepper or other spices may be added to the curing mix.

This formula was applied at the rate of 1¼ to 1½ ounces per pound of meat. One ounce of mix per one pound of meat was considered the minimum amount.

Application

The dry mix was divided into 4 equal parts and 2 parts were set aside for later use.

Day	Application
1	The first half (2/4) of the mixture was vigorously rubbed in all over the ham, taking special care to pack the mixture with thumbs along the bones as far as possible. The hams were placed an a slanted table or in containers with holes in the bottom to drain liquid away.
3	The meats were rubbed with ¼ th of the mixture and the stacking order was re-arranged. The pieces that were on top before were placed on the bottom and vice versa.
10	The meats were rubbed with the last ¼ th of the mixture and the stacking order was re-arranged. The pieces that were on top before were placed on the bottom and vice versa.
21	For best results large hams were overhauled again on the 21st day.

The hams were kept at 38-40° F (3-4° C), and at high humidity to prevent excessive drying and hardening of the surface which would have inhibited moisture removal during the drying process. Hams were placed fat side down and the curing continued for about 2-3 weeks. The general curing times were as follows:

- 2 days per pound for small pieces and the bacon.
- 3 days per pound for hams and shoulders.

Making Your Own Cure Mix

The allowed amount of nitrite that goes into dry products is 625 ppm. For comparison, the amount of permitted nitrite in regular comminuted products (sausages) is 156 ppm, which is four times lower. The reason is that dry products take much longer to make and nitrite dissipates in meat rapidly, especially at higher than refrigerator temperatures. Some of the mix falls off the meat during rubbing in, some mix is washed away by the draining liquid.

Dry Cure Mix for 1 kg (1000 g) of Meat			
Salt	Sugar (optional)	Cure #1	Sodium Nitrite in PPM
5-6%	2%	10 g (1%)	625

All you have to decide is how salty of a product you desire. Get the calculator and punch in some numbers.

Example:
How much dry cure is needed for 1 kg (2.2 lb) of meat?
Salt at 6% = 0.06 x 1000 g = 60 g
Sugar 2% = 0.02 x 1000 g = 20 g
Cure #1 = 0.01 x 1000 g = 10 g
The percentage of salt and sugar in the above table is not set in stone. You can use less salt or more sugar, depending on what product is produced. Dry cured ham that will not be refrigerated needs 5-6% salt, refrigerator kept loin or bacon will need less.

Dry Cured Loins, Shoulders and Butts

The technology of making shoulder and butts follows the rules for making hams, but the process is faster due to the smaller size of meat cuts.

1. Salting - about 7 days, 36-40° F (2-4° C).
2. Equalizing - 30 days at 46° F (8° C), 75% humidity.
3. Drying/Maturing - 21 days, 68-72° F (20-22° C), 65-70% humidity. When drying is performed at lower temperatures the time will be longer, for example at 54° F (12° C), 70% humidity it may take 6 weeks. Loins are ready when about 35% weight los has occurred.

Production of Formed Meat Products

When we purchase ready to eat ham we assume that it comes from a whole meat. This is due to our familiarity with images of country side hams hanging from the hooks or large hams lying in supermarket displays. This assumption is the correct one as traditionally made hams were after all a rear leg of a hog. This preconceived opinion is then applied to a boiled ham which looks as it were carved from a solid piece of meat. Although most one piece hams are smoked and then water cooked, they can be easily recognized by their characteristic shape. Yet the rectangular or oval shaped hams and individually sliced and packed ham packages *do not come from one leg of the hog.* They come from different animal parts, for example from the front and the rear legs or from different animals all together. In addition to hams, other products such as turkey or beef rolls may be produced. By choosing different shape forming molds, products can be made in the shape of pork chops, ham steaks and others.

The process for making formed products looks easy but there is more to it. First of all the individual meat cuts must stick together and when cooked, retain the shape of the mold without having any holes inside. This is accomplished by producing sticky exudate on the surface of meat pieces. Think of it as glue that binds the individual meat cuts together upon heating. *The exudate is formed when the muscle's cell structure is disrupted which releases protein called myosin.*

The disrupting of the muscle structure is accomplished by a physical action such as cutting or mechanically working meat pieces inside of the tumbler. For making formed meat products fine cutting or grinding is out of the question and massaging or tumbling is the preferred method. Using mechanical action by itself will tenderize meat but will not produce enough exudate. *To release more proteins salt and phosphates are injected to meat* prior to tumbling.

If a final product will consist of a few individual muscles the following must be observed:

- There must not be any fat on surfaces which are in contact with each other.
- All membranes or silver skin must be removed from each muscle or at least cut with a knife.

If those rules are not followed the final product will exhibit holes and will not hold its shape when sliced.

Meat selection. Lean meat contains more protein so selecting lean cuts will produce more exudate and the result will be better binding. A ham is a lean cut of meat and during the meat selection process the butcher removes lean whole muscles of meat and puts them aside. To bring exudate to the surface we have to eliminate the unnecessary obstacles such as sinews, external fat, skin, membranes and silver skin. The surface of the meat must be clean. *The meat cuts must be sorted by color* otherwise the final appearance will not be one of intact muscle. Grouping meats of similar diameter for the tumbler will result in a more uniform distribution of a curing solution and better protein extraction.

Curing. It is expected that adding about 3% of salt results in optimal protein extraction. Salt makes the cells swell and some proteins are released and a solution (exudate) of water, salt and protein is created. In order to produce even more exudate, more proteins must be released which is accomplished by adding 0.3-0.5% phosphates. Although phosphates are much more effective than salt in protein extraction, their effectiveness increases even more *when they are combined with salt.* Meats are pumped with solution containing salt, phosphates nitrite and color enhancer. If the meat is pumped with over 25% of the green weight (original weight) the meat protein solution will be weaker and the binding strength will decrease. There is a limit to how much water can be held by phosphates and the excess will be lost during cooking.

Color. Sodium nitrite is always added which results in a red color, better flavor and longer shelf life. Although sodium nitrite works with meat through chemical reactions, the time that is dedicated for making whole muscle formed meat products is still not sufficient for obtaining a strong color. It has been observed that after tumbling meat becomes paler, most likely due to oxygen reacting with meat structure during mechanical action.

This effect is largely decreased when a vacuum tumbler is employed as there is no air to react with meat. Foaming of the exudate on the surface of meat is also eliminated. Although holding meats for a few hours at room temperature will definitely help with curing color, such a procedure cannot be employed in commercial production as it leads to the growth of bacteria and subsequently to a decreased shelf life of the product. To make up for insufficient curing time ascorbic acid (vitamin C) is added to the curing solution.

Ascorbic acid forces sodium nitrite into producing more nitric oxide, which in turn reacts with myoglobin which is always present, although in different amounts in meat. This results in a strong red color which will be permanently secured by cooking.

Tumbling. The most efficient protein extraction is obtained at 36-38° F (2-4° C) working temperature. Boiled hams exhibit smaller weight loss than the baked ones. On the other hand baked hams look nicer due to the shiny and glazed surface which is due to the coating of brown sugar, honey or other ingredients. Experienced sausage makers swear by the fact that hams should be inserted into boiling water and kept at the boiling point for the first 10-15 minutes. Then the temperature should be lowered to 80° C (176° F) and remain at that level until the ham is fully cooked. The explanation is that the proteins in the outside area will be immediately cooked which leads to the development of a hardened surface. This in turn will prevent meat juices from migrating into water and the finished product will be juicier. The analogy will be grilling a steak when the surface area is seared first at very high temperature and then the steak is cooked at a lower temperature setting.

A commercial producer will place pumped meat in a tumbler and salt equalization will be performed inside of the machine. Meats are usually tumbled in two ways:

- 10 minutes "on" and 50 minutes "off" for each hour tumbled. Depending on the size of the ham it can take from 8-24 hours.
- 3 continuous hours, then let hams rest in the tumbler overnight. The next day the ham is tumbled for an additional 30 minutes before stuffing.

Those times are not set in stone and often hams are continuously tumbled for one hour and then submitted to thermal treatment. Such a ham can be manufactured in one single day.

Stuffing. Individual meat cuts are then stuffed rather loosely into a cook-in bag and the bag is vacuum sealed. If the meats were stuffed firmly, the bag may not conform to the shape of the mold. Then the bag is placed into a mold of a chosen shape. *The meat cuts must be pressed against each other* with some force, which is accomplished by adjusting the pressure of the top cover. The meat cuts may also be stuffed into a large fibrous casing. They should be stuffed rather loosely as the casing is often placed inside of a press to develop an oval shaped ham. Those presses are then cooked in hot water.

Photo 22.17 A popular ham press.

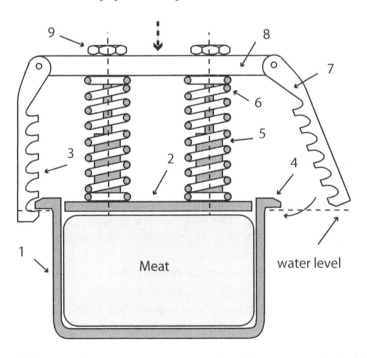

Fig. 22.9 A popular ham press. 1 - container, 2- top cover, 3 -locking teeth, 4 - retaining rim, 5 - rod-like guide , 6 - spring, 7 - securing arm, 8 - compression arm (strut), 9 - adjustable nut.

Operation of a ham press

A ham press consists of a container **1** and a top cover **2** which can be forced into the container **1** to compress the meat. The top of the container has a retaining rim **4**. A compression handle **8** which consists of a strut (handle) **8**, compression springs **6**, and the securing arm **7**, engages the retaining rim **4** and forces container **1** and cover **2** together compressing the ham. Strut **8** is penetrated by two upright rod guides **5**, such as with adjustable nuts or screws, attached to the cover **2** and enclosed in adjustable tension compression springs **6** that rest against the cover **2** and below the strut **8**. At each end of the strut **8** the securing arm **7** pivots toward and away from the container **1**. The edge of securing arm **7** that faces the container **1** has teeth **3** that engage below the retaining rim **4** of the container **1**. Pressure on the strut **8** compresses the springs **6** and forces the cover **2** into the container **1**. At the same time the teeth **3** on the securing arm **7** engage the retaining rim **4**. When the pressure on strut **8** is released, the cover **2** is retained in the position in which it is by the particular tooth **3** on each security arm **7** which engages below the retaining rim **4**. This engaged position is also ensured by the tension on the compression springs **6**.

Since the tension on the compression springs **6** also forces the cover **2** deeper into the container **1**, as the ham shrinks during the boiling process, the ham is always firmly compressed even as it shrinks. The securing arms **7** remain in the engaged position while the springs **6** force the cover **2** down.

Home Made Ham Presses

There is a great variety of home made presses and they all work very well. In many cases people don't use a ham press at all and they use a big waterproof casing. The simplest design we have seen is a tall stainless steel cylinder with a wooden cover and a large stone used as a weight.

Such long pots are known as *stainless steel vegetable insets* and are distributed by restaurant equipment suppliers. They are used to hold steamed or raw vegetables, or to keep soup warm in steam table pans adapters at buffets in restaurants. The same companies also sell different kinds of rectangular steam table pans which can be easily adapted for making ham presses.

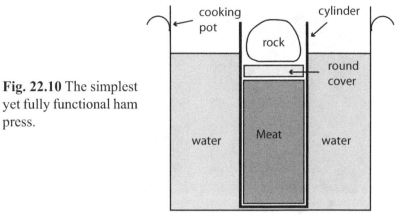

Fig. 22.10 The simplest yet fully functional ham press.

Depending on the diameter of a cylinder and amount of processed meat, a different rock (weight) will be needed. For example, a 6" (15 cm) x 10" (25 cm) cylinder may need around 2 kg (4.4 lb) weight.

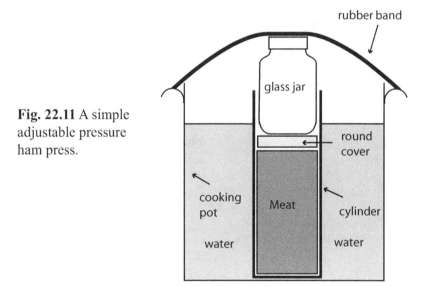

Fig. 22.11 A simple adjustable pressure ham press.

This is a different arrangement of the above mentioned method. A rubber band made from the inner tube tire provides pressure against a glass jar or a solid block of wood. A bungee cord will work too.

Note: water level in a cooking pot remains below the top of a ham press.

Photo 22.18 The simplest set up. Stainless steel cylinder, wooden cover and weight.

Photo 22.19 Cylinder with meat inside ready for cooking.

Photo 22.20 The same design using a rectangular steel pan.

There are adjustable pressure cheese presses that follow a clever but simple design. Cheese presses are not submitted to cooking temperatures and the cylinder is made from commonly available pvc. The pipe has no bottom in order for the water to drain away. Some designs use a cylinder with tiny holes just above the bottom.

A cylinder employed in a ham press is made from metal in order to efficiently conduct heat from water into the meat. Construction is very simple and all materials are available in any hardware store.

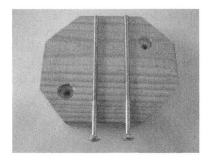

Photo 22.21 Base and ¼"
carriage bolts. The length of
bolts depends on the height of
the cylinder.

Photo 22.22 Meat press. Any
kind of wrench will apply
pressure to a spring.

The crucial element of the assembly is the threaded T-nut. Fortunately
it is available everywhere and is very inexpensive.

Photo 22.23 & 24 Threaded ⅜" T-nut. The nut allows the ⅜" threaded
center rod to move up and down and to apply pressure to the spring.

The nut has protruding spikes allowing it to be embedded in the bottom of the cylinder holding bar. The wooden bar rides on carriage bolts and is secured with wing nuts.

Photo 22.25 The nut, the center rod, the spring and the holding bar.

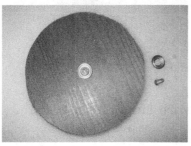

Photo 22.27 (above) #10 Finishing washer supports and holds the compression spring.

Photo 22.26 #10 Finishing washer is attached with a screw to the top of the meat cover and becomes a receiving base for the compression spring.

Photo 22.28 The compression spring fits over the bottom of the center rod and its play can be adjusted by two nuts above. The nut fits snugly over the rod and stays there.

Photo 22.29 Ham press based on a cheese press design.

In case you have no press at all, don't worry as not all is lost. There are people who tightly stuff meat cuts into large casings and they claim that the product is almost as good.

Smoking. You can not smoke formed ham as the meat is inside a metal ham press. There are special ham presses made of adjustable pressure screens which hold a boneless ham or a butt and they allow smoke to go through.

Cooking. The mold with the ham inside is placed in hot water 176-180° F (80-82° C) and cooked until meat reaches an internal temperature of 155-160° F (68-72° C). The higher the temperature, the shorter the cooking period. In order to destroy any trichinae that might be present, a ham should be cooked to at least 137° F (58.3° C), but such a ham is not considered very palatable. A temperature of 148-160° F (65-72° C) produces a product with better flavor and texture. The length of cooking time is based on the weight of the hams and 30 minutes per pound of meat is an average.

Cooling. The mold is taken out (meat remains inside) and is cooled down. Then it goes into a cooler overnight. The next day the mold is opened and the ham is removed. The ham permanently retains the shape of the mold it was in.

The Gel. When you cook any meat some of the fat and meat juices come out and are lost. In a frying pan this substance accumulates on the bottom and many people use it for making gravy. Since formed meat products are cooked in a sealed container, these juices have nowhere to go and when cooled they become a "gel." This gel is nothing else but the best that a ham can offer. For many years formed meat products contained the gel inside. Some people loved it, others hated it, most children cried at the site of this gluey substance.

Since 2001, in commercial products potato starch has been added as an absorbent material to prevent the formation of gel. You still eat the gel but it can not be seen now. So if your child objects to eating this delicious gel, just scrape it off.

Ham Flavor

With all due respect to the latest advances in meat science technology, it must be said that the flavor of today's commercially produced hams is just an echo from the past. They are nutritious, pretty and juicy, but exhibit little flavor. This is due to the following reasons:

Little fat. Hams in the past were produced with the skin and the underlaying layer of fat. Somehow this fat layer intensified and preserved the flavor and aroma of a ham. It is like monosodium glutamate (MSG) which is used during cooking. When added to meat it brings out the best of its flavor. The animals themselves were bigger and much fatter which also positively contributed to meat flavor.

A lot of water. With today's permissible injection rates of between 40 and 100% curing solution, the meat is juicy but has a diluted flavor. This juiciness is due not to the meat's natural juices but to the added water. Chemicals such as phosphates open a cell's structure and unwind the protein structure. These hold the added water not only during curing but also during the cooking process as well, which results in a smaller cooking loss but in a higher profit for the manufacturers.

Added ingredients. To make this gain possible, many ingredients such as soy protein isolate, phosphates, or ascorbates are added. Although they are added in small amounts they all taste bitter and this adds up. To compensate for that more flavorings and spices are added.

This is a chain reaction which results in a product which is still healthy and safe to a consumer, but is not the same ham which will be produced on a farm using traditional methods. The flavor of the ham also depends on the cooking method:

Cooking Method	Color	Flavor
Water	Light red color	Delicate, cooked meat flavor
Hot Air	Strong red color, shiny surface, smoky flavor, if smoking process is employed	Strong meat flavor

The difference in flavor between a commercially produced formed ham and a formed ham made at home is significant. The home made ham has a wonderful aroma that is easily noticed. It also has a strong meaty flavor as it was not injected and diluted with water. The slices of home made ham keep on losing moisture in the refrigerator and become drier. The slices of commercial made ham or other meat products feel wet when removed from the package. They become more slimy as time goes by due to the curing solution that is losing its holding power and beginning to leak out. The meat has no reason to feel slimy when held under refrigeration as there is only about 40% humidity present. Such meat will start drying out, even when kept in a container.

Luncheon Meats

Luncheon meats are finely ground meats which are usually cured and canned. They can be made at home following the technology for making formed meat products. This means that the meat is ground, cured, stuffed into the mold and cooked. The best example of a canned luncheon meat is American made SPAM® which became famous in 1937. The name SPAM is an acronym for "spiced ham" or "**S**-houlder **P**-ork h-**AM**."

American Country Ham

Meat	Metric	US
ham, bone-in	8 kg	9.6 lb

Ingredients for 1 kg of meat:

	Metric	US
salt	54 g	3 Tbs.
Cure #2	10 g	2 tsp.
sugar	20 g	4 tsp.
pepper	6 g	3 tsp.

Instructions:
1. Mix salt, Cure #2 and sugar together. Divide into three equal parts. Rub ham on all sides with ⅓ of the mixture. Place ham in refrigerator. Keep it covered with plastic wrap or a cloth to prevent drying. A good idea is to keep it in a ziploc bag. This prevents the ham from drying. The ham should be kept at around 90% humidity, but the humidity in a refrigerator is only about 40%.

2. After 3 days, rub the ham with another ⅓ mixture and place in a refrigerator.

3. After 10 days remove the ham from the refrigerator and apply the last ⅓ of the mixture. Place ham back in refrigerator.

4. After 40 days (total salting time) remove the ham from the refrigerator and briefly rinse with tap water. Brush off any salt from the surface.

5. Coat the surface of the ham with pepper and stuff the ham into the netting.

6. Keep for 14 days at 40-42° F (4-6° C), 75% humidity.

7. Apply cold smoke 77° F (25° C) for 24 hours.

8. Ripe (dry and mature) hams for 60 days at 77-86° F (25-30° C), 65% humidity.

Note:

Total time: 115 days.

Time can vary from 3-5 months. The actual time will depend on the size of the ham and processing temperatures.

Ham - Minced Butt

Meat	Metric	US
pork butt	1000 g	2.20 lb

Ingredients for 1 kg of meat:

salt	20 g	3½ tsp.
Cure #1	2.5 g	½ tsp.
sugar, finely pulverized	5.0 g	1 tsp.
water	100 ml	3.5 oz

Instructions:

1. Cut meat into 1" (25 mm) pieces. Grind skin with ⅛" (3 mm) plate.

2. Dilute salt, Cure #1 and sugar in 100 ml of water and pour over meat.

3. Stir meat pieces, kneading them lightly. Add spices and ground skin and mix everything together.

4. Stuff meat pieces into a cooking bag tightly, trying not to trap unnecessary air.

5. Place the bag inside the ham press. Apply slight pressure.

6. Place the ham press in a refrigerator for 48 hours. This is the curing step.

7. Apply pressure to the cover and place the ham mold in hot water. Cook for 60 minutes at 176° F (80° C). A five pound ham (2.5 kg) may need 3 hours cooking time.

8. Place the ham press for 2-3 hours in cold water to cool and then place overnight in a refrigerator.

9. Remove the ham from the mold. Keep refrigerated.

Ham - Minced Butt and Picnic

Meat	Metric	US
pork butt	300 g	0.66 lb.
pork picnic	700 g	1.54 lb.

Ingredients:		
salt	18 g	3 tsp.
Cure #1	2.5 g	½ tsp.
pepper	2.0 g	1 tsp.
coriander	2.0 g	1 tsp.
ginger	0.5 g	⅓ tsp.
nutmeg	1.0 g	½ tsp.

Instructions:

1. Remove skin. Cut meat pieces into 1" (25 mm) cubes.

2. Grind all meat through 3/16" (5 mm) plate.

3. Mix meat with salt and Cure #1. Pack tightly in a container, cover with cloth and leave in a refrigerator for 2 days.

4. Mix cured meat with all ingredients until mixture feels sticky.

5. Stuff mixture into cellophane bag whose size corresponds to the size of your ham press. Place the bag into the ham press and apply pressure to the cover.

6. Insert the ham press into boiling water but cook at 176° F (80° C) until meat reaches 155-160° F (68-71° C). In a small ham press, for example 4" diameter and 4-6" high, that will take about 2 hours.

7. Place ham press for 2-3 hours in cold water to cool and then place overnight in refrigerator.

8. Remove ham from the press.

Ham - Minced Picnic

Meat	Metric	US
pork meat, picnic, 97%	4,850 g	10.6 lb.
pork skins, 3%	150 g	0.33 lb.

Ingredients:

salt	90 g	5 Tbs.
Cure #1	12 g	2 tsp.
pepper	10 g	5 tsp.

Instructions:

1. Cut meat pieces into 1" (25 mm) cubes.

2. Add 90 g of salt and Cure #1 to meat and mix together. Pack tightly in a container, cover with cloth and leave for 3 days in refrigerator. Skins: make brine adding 2½ tsp of salt to 60 ml (¼ cup) of water. This will make 40° SAL brine. No nitrite is needed for curing skins. Leave skins in brine for 3 days in refrigerator.

3. Poach skins in hot water (just below boiling) for 30 minutes. Drain skins, then cool them.

4. Grind skins through ⅛" (3 mm) plate.

5. Mix cured meat pieces with pepper. Knead meat hard until feels sticky. Add ground skins and mix everything well together.

6. Stuff mixture into cellophane bag whose size corresponds to the size of your ham press. Place the bag into the ham press and apply pressure to the cover.

7. Insert ham press into boiling water but cook at 176° F (80° C) until meat reaches 154-160° F (68-71° C). In a small ham press, for example 4" diameter and 4-6" high, that will take about 2 hours.

8. Place ham press for 2-3 hours in cold water to cool and then place overnight in refrigerator.

9. Remove ham from the press.

Ham - Molded

Meat	**Metric**	**US**
lean pork	1000 g	2.2 lb.

Ingredients for 1 kg of meat		
salt	18 g	3 tsp.
Cure #1	2.5 g	½ tsp.

Instructions:

1. Cut lean pork into ¾" or larger pieces. Make sure that there is no fat or connective tissue left.

2. Mix meat pieces with salt and Cure #1. Pack meat tightly in a suitable container making the stack about 4" high. Place for 3 days in refrigerator. This is the curing process.

Photo 22.30 Freshly cut lean pork.

Cured meat pieces are red and sticky due to the exudate (protein extraction) that has formed on the surface. This will help to bind meat pieces together.

Photo 22.31 Cured pork.

3. Place Reynolds® plastic cooking bag inside of the 5" diameter stainless steel cylinder. It will help to remove the cooked ham. Insert meat pieces and pack them tightly. Flip over the top of the bag and cover the meat. Place the wooden cover on top of the meat and place a 2 lb weight on it.

Photo 22.32 Cylinder and the bag.

4. Cylinder with meat inside is placed in the water filled cooking vessel. Water level remains below the top edge of the cylinder. The weight is on top of the wooden cover. Meat cooked for 90 minutes at 194° F (90° C).

Photo 22.33 Cooking pot.

After cooking the cylinder is placed in tap water to cool and then placed overnight in a refrigerator. Then the bag is pulled from the cylinder and the ham is removed.

Photo 22.34 Finished ham.

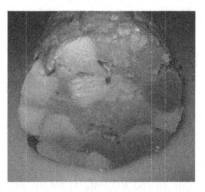

Lighter pieces are from the pork loin which exercises very little. It needs less oxygen and contains less myoglobin (oxygen carrier). That is why it is lighter in color. Darker pieces are from the leg (picnic) which exercises a lot and needs more oxygen. This results in a higher content of myoglobin and a stronger curing color.

The removal of cold ham will be difficult if a cooking bag is not used and the meat is packed directly in a cylinder. The gel will stick to the walls and the ham will not slide out. The remedy is to insert the cylinder for 30 seconds back into boiling water to melt down the gel.

Photo 22.35 Ham press for making 1.5 kg (3 lbs) product. The meat goes into cylinder, the spring goes on top, the cover with thermometer goes on top.

Smoked and Cooked Ham

Meat	Metric	US
ham, bone-in	5 - 8 kg	11.0 - 17.6 lbs.

Instructions:

1. Pump ham with 60° SAL brine:

Water	1 gal (3.8 kg)
Salt	1.32 lb (600 g)
Cure #1	4.2 oz (120 g)
Sugar	1.5 oz (42 g)

Note: Cure #1 contains 93.75% od salt. 120 g x 93.75/100 = 112.5 g.

The total amount of salt added to water is:

600 g (salt) + 112.5 g (salt in Cure #1) = 712.5 g (1.57 lb).

Percent injection: 7%.
The weight of cover pickle: 40% in relation to meat's weight.

2. Immerse pumped ham in cover pickle for 10-14 days at refrigerator temperature. Overhaul (turn around) hams every few days.

3. Soak for 3 hours in cold running water. Rinse in lukewarm water 86 - 104° F (30 - 40° C), using a brush to clean the surface.

4. Hang or place on a screen for 12 - 24 hours to dry.

5. Stuff in netting.

6. Smoke with warm smoke 86 - 104° F (30 - 40° C), for 4 hours until skin develops light yellow - light brown color.

7. Insert ham into boiling water and keep boiling for 15 minutes. Lower water temperature to 176-180° F (80-82° C) and continue cooking until the internal meat temperature becomes 154-158° F (68-70° C). A rule of thumb calls for 50 minutes cooking for 1 kg of ham.

8. Place on shelves/screens to cool down.

9. Keep refrigerated.

Ham - Smoked with Bone-in

Meat	Metric	US
ham, bone-in	5 - 8 kg	11.0 - 17.6 lbs.

Instructions:

1. Pump ham with 60° SAL brine:

Water	1 gal (3.8 kg)
Salt	1.32 lb (600 g)
Cure #1	4.2 oz (120 g)
Sugar	1.5 oz (42 g)

Note: Cure #1 contains 93.75% od salt. 120 g x 93.75/100 = 112.5 g.

The total amount of salt added to water:

600 g (salt) + 112.5 g (salt in Cure #1) = 712.5 g (1.57 lb).

Percent injection: 7%.
The weight of cover pickle: 40% in relation to meat's weight.

2. Immerse pumped ham in cover pickle for 10-14 days at refrigerator temperature. Overhaul (turn around) hams every few days.

3. Soak for 3 hours in cold running water. Rinse in lukewarm water 86 - 104° F (30 - 40° C) using a brush to clean the surface.

4. Hang or place on a screen for 12 - 24 hours to dry.

5. Stuff in netting.

6. Smoke with warm smoke 86 - 104° F (30 - 40° C), for 12 - 24 hours until skin develops a light brown color.

7. Cool down and keep refrigerated.

Note:
Cook before serving.

Chapter 23

Bacon, Butts, Loins and Lard

Those are smaller cuts of pork with their own distinct flavor and they are simply delicious. There is nothing that can compete with the smell of bacon which is served with eggs and home fries for breakfast. Pork butt is another flavorful cut and everybody loves pulled pork. No other animal can produce a leaner meat cut with such a flavor like a pork loin. These cuts are much smaller than a ham, and much easier to process at home where refrigerator space is at premium. Another advantage they carry is that they don't require time consuming steps like grinding and stuffing. Meats such as beef or lamb are leaner and they become harder in cure. Well known beef delicacies are corned beef and dry beef known as jerky. Corned lamb is as good as beef. In the past on farms without refrigeration, those noble cuts of meat were cured, then kept in dry cure or brine until consumed.

Bacon

Bacon is cured by two methods:

- Dry cure - a mixture of curing ingredients is rubbed all around bacon. Then the bellies are placed in a cooler for 10-14 days before smoking and cooking.

- Pickle cure - a common method which, in addition, allows pumping meats with an injector. Bacon may be immersed in pickle as well. After pumping bacon goes into the smokehouse.

The cooking smoking/process:

1. Bacon is dried for 1-2 hours at 122° F (50°C). Dampers are fully open.

2. Bacon is smoked and cooked for 3 hours at 130° F (55°C). Dampers are ¼ open. If trichinae free meat is used the cooking may stop when the internal meat temperature reaches 132° F (56° C), otherwise cook bacon to 140° F (60° C).

Because of problems associated with nitrosamine formation in bacon, *Nitrate is no longer permitted in any curing method for bacon.* Only sodium nitrite (Cure #1) is allowed at 120 ppm maximum level. Nitrate can still be used to cure other meat products. Regardless of the curing method used, restricted ingredient calculations for bacon are based on the green weight of the skinless belly. For *rind-on bacon,* e.g., where the skin is sold as part of the finished product, a restricted ingredient conversion calculation is necessary (explained below).

Bacon Curing Methods - Sodium Nitrite Limits					
Dry		Immersion		Pumped and/or Massaged	
Rind - **Off**	Rind - **On**	Rind - **Off**	Rind - **On**	Rind - **Off**	Rind - **On**
200 ppm	less 10% (180 ppm)	120 ppm	less 10% (108 ppm)	120 ppm	less 10% (108 ppm)
550 ppm sodium ascorbate or sodium erythorbate (isoascorbate), ingoing, is required in *pumped and massaged bacon,* in addition to any prescribed amount of nitrite.					

Pumped, Massaged, Immersion Cured, or Dry Cured Bacon (rind-On): The maximum limit for ingoing nitrite and sodium ascorbate or sodium erythorbate must be adjusted if bacon is prepared from pork bellies *with attached skin (rind-on).* A pork belly's weight is comprised of approximately 10 percent skin. *Since the skin retains practically no cure solution or cure agent, the maximum ingoing nitrite and sodium ascorbate or erythorbate limits must be reduced by 10 percent.* For example, the maximum ingoing limit for nitrite for pumped pork bellies with attached skin would be (120 ppm (limit) - 12 ppm (10%) = 108 ppm.

Bacon - Dry Cure Mix

The following tables are based on U.S. standards as presented above.

Dry Cure Mix for **1 lb** of Bacon using **Cure #1**					
Rind - **Off**, 200 ppm sodium nitrite			Rind - **On**, 180 ppm sodium nitrite		
3% Salt	4% Salt	Cure #1	3% Salt	4% Salt	Cure #1
0.48 oz	0.64 oz	0.05 oz	0.48 oz	0.64 oz	0.04 oz
13.6 g	18.1 g	1.45 g	13.6 g	18.1 g	1.30 g

Dry Cure Mix for **1 kg** of Bacon using **Cure #1**					
Rind - **Off**, 200 ppm sodium nitrite			Rind - **On**, 180 ppm sodium nitrite		
3% Salt	4% Salt	**Cure #1**	3% Salt	4% Salt	**Cure #1**
1.05 oz	1.41 oz	0.11 oz	1.05 oz	1.41 oz	0.10 oz
30 g	40 g	3.2 g	30 g	40 g	2.88 g

People in Europe use Peklosol for curing which contains only 0.6 sodium nitrite.

Dry Cure Mix for **1 kg** of Bacon using **Peklosol**					
Rind - **Off**, 200 ppm sodium nitrite			Rind - **On,** 180 ppm sodium nitrite		
3.28% Salt	4% Salt	**Peklosol**	3% Salt	4% Salt	**Peklosol**
0 g	0.23 oz	1.17 oz	0 g	0.35 oz	1.05 oz
0 g	6.7 g	33.3 g	0 g	10 g	30 g

Peklosol contains 99.4% salt and this has been accounted for in the above table. For example 3% salt in 1 kg (1000 g) is 30 g and not 0 g as shown in the table. Because 33 g of Peklosol (32.8 g salt) has been added to the mix, the total amount of salt is 32.8 g which is 3.28 %.

Dry Cured Bacon (*rind-off*): A maximum of 200 ppm of nitrite or equivalent of potassium nitrite (246 ppm) can be used in dry cured bacon.

Occasionally, instead of sugar, other sweeteners were eeployed. Keep in mind that honey is the sweetest of all sweeteners so if honey is substituted for sugar, reduce the amount by about 20 percent. Maple syrup is expensive, but an excellent syrup can be made by combining imitation maple syrup, brown sugar, corn solids and little water.

Using recent standards for dry curing 100 lbs. of whole cuts of meat, we can apply 453 g (1 lb.) of Cure #1 to be in compliance with the maximum allowed level of 625 ppm.

Caution: recent standards for immersion curing allow only 200 ppm for *bacon*. No Nitrate (Cure #2) is allowed.
To cure 100 lbs. of *bacon* we can apply 145 g (5.2 oz.) of Cure #1.

Bacon - Immersion Method

Bacon can be wet cured the same way hams are cured. The only difference is that less nitrite is allowed to go into brine.

1 US gallon (3.8 l) brine at **120 ppm** at 10% pump, Rind - **Off**			
Degrees SAL	**Amount of Cure #1**		
	Grams	Ounces	Teaspoons
40°	78	2.75	13
50°	79	2.78	13
60°	81	2.85	13-1/2
70°	82	2.89	13-1/2

1 US gallon (3.8 l) brine at **108 ppm** at 10% pump, Rind - **On**			
Degrees SAL	**Amount of Cure #1**		
	Grams	Ounces	Teaspoons
40°	70.3	2.4	11-4/4
50°	71.6	2.5	12
60°	73.0	2.5	12
70°	74.2	2.6	12-1/3
1 Tablespoon = 3 teaspoons. 1 tsp equals to around 6 g Cure #1.			

Formulations from the past

Small cuts - loins, butts, bacon

Basic formula for 100 lbs of meat:

    4 lbs. salt
    1½ lbs. sugar (optional)
    2 oz. nitrate (saltpeter)

Pepper or other spices may be added to the curing mix.

Application

The dry mix was divided into 3 equal parts.

Day	Application
1	The first ⅓ rd of the mixture was vigorously rubbed in all over the ham, taking special care to pack the mixture with thumbs along the bones as far as possible. The hams were placed on a slanted table or in containers with holes in the bottom to drain the liquid away.
3	The meats were rubbed with ⅓ rd of the mixture and the stacking order was re-arranged. The pieces that were on top before were placed on the bottom and vice versa.
6	The meats were rubbed with the last ⅓ rd of the mixture and the stacking order was re-arranged. The pieces that were on top before were placed on the bottom and vice versa.

Box Cured Bacon

A box cured method was a well known procedure for curing many slabs of bacon at the same time. A watertight box which can be thought of as a bacon press, was constructed from hardwood and lined up with galvanized steel. The weighted lid applied pressure to the bacon.

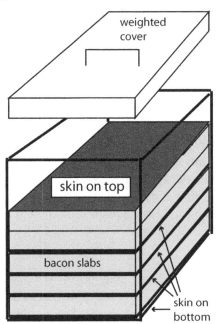

Fig. 23.1 Box bacon.

The slabs are placed skin down, except the last one which is placed skin up. During overhaul, the order is reversed. The top pieces are placed on the bottom and the bottom ones on top. The width and the length of the box would approximate the size of the bacon slab. The box would be high enough to accommodate 5-6 slabs, usually 24" high. If it were higher it did not matter much as the weighted lid was placed on top.

Rub bacon with 1/2 of the mix and place skin down in the container. After 7 days apply the second half of the mixture and overhaul the slabs. Leave the liquid in. If there are any significant gaps between slabs of bacon and the walls of the container, they can be filled with smaller cuts of trimmed meats. A natural brine will be created and the liquid will rise up to the surface. After curing is completed, soak bacon for one hour, brush the surface clean and hang until dry. Then smoke it with cold smoke.

Canadian Bacon

Canadian bacon is not manufactured from pork bellies as the name might imply. It is made from pork loin, which contains very little intramuscular fat. As a result, the finished product is very lean. The manufacturing process:

1. Boneless loins are stitch-pumped up to 10% green weight (original weight) and then placed in cover pickle for 2-5 days.
2. Then they are washed, stuffed into stockinettes and moved to a smokehouse for drying.
3. After they are dried the smoke is applied and the loins are smoked and cooked to an internal temperature of 150-155° F (66-69° C).

Canadian bacon is the version that is more popular in the USA. In Canada "peameal bacon" is common, which is cured but *not smoked* pork loin. It is rolled in yellow corn meal giving it the signature 'peameal' coating and par-baked to ensure uniformity. Peameal bacon is usually sliced and fried.

Wiltshire Bacon

Wiltshire bacon is an English term that usually refers to a side of pork consisting of the shoulder, loin, belly and ham as one piece. Wiltshire sides are cured by pumping and are then placed in cover pickle for 7-10 days. They are then removed and stored in a cooler from 2 - 14 days. They drain and dry for the first 2 days and then they mature which equalizes salt distribution inside. After equalization they may be smoked or sold without further processing.

Jowl Bacon

Jowl bacon's structure looks very much like a belly bacon, the main difference is that jowl fat is much harder. Jowls are a bit fatter than belly bacon. As the pig eats a lot, its jowls are exercised all the time and develop a lot of collagen and they become a good material for making boiled sausages such as head cheeses, liver and emulsified sausages. Trimmed jowls are squared to form jowl bacon slabs and are subjected to the same processing steps as is bacon made from bellies.

Photo 23.1 Jowl bacon looks like a regular belly bacon.

Photo 23.2 Sliced jowl bacon.

Beef Bacon

Beef bacon is made from boneless beef short plates. It is cured and processed similar to pork bacon. Its main advantage lies in the fact that it might be used in Kosher products.

Back Fat

Back fat, often called fatback is a heavy layer of hard fat taken from a pig's back (spinal region) that weighs about 20 lbs. It is cured by the pickle or dry cure method and is commonly referred to as salt pork. When dry cured, the slabs of back fat are rubbed with salt and stacked 3-4 feet high in coolers. The slabs are overhauled 2-3 times and the curing time generally is from 20 to 30 days, depending on thickness of a cut. If pickle method is chosen, the slabs are pumped and immersed in 90° SAL brine. Back fat does not contain *myoglobin* so there is no need to add nitrites. It is often cold smoked and used as a flavoring in many meat dishes. As a rule of thumb, back fat and bellies, both dry and pickle cured, remain in cure 1 day for each pound of weight.

Dry Cured Loins, Shoulders and Butts

The technology of making shoulders and butts follows the rules for making hams:

1. Salting - about 7 days, 36-40° F (2-4° C).
2. Equalizing - 30 days at 46° F (8° C), 75% humidity.
3. Drying/Maturing - 21 days, 68-72° F (20-22° C), 65-70% humidity

When drying is performed at lower temperature the time will be longer, for example at 54° F (12° C), 70% humidity it may take 6 weeks. Loins are ready when about 35% weight loss has occurred.

Pork Loin

Pork loins are usually pickle cured. They can be stitched pumped and then placed in cover pickle for 3-5 days or only immersed in cover pickle for up to 10 days. After curing loins are smoked and cooked to 142-152° F (62-67° C).

Photo 23.3 Smoked pork loins.

Photo 23.4 Commercially produced loins or butts would be pickle pumped and then tumbled.

Picnic

Picnics can be processed using the same procedures as hams. They contain a large amount of bone, fat and connective tissues which are rich in collagen. Picnic costs less than other cuts of meats but contains all meat classes in its structure and can be utilized for making different types of sausages.

Shoulder Butt

Shoulder butt, also known as Boston butt is cured, smoked and cooked similar to ham. They are the top part of the front leg (picnic) and taste great when smoked and cooked. They are usually cured in pickle for 7-10 days but may be 10% pumped and immersed in leftover brine for 3-5 days. After curing they are stuffed in a stockinette bag, dried and smoked. There are some well known butts, for example dry-cured and air dried Italian Coppa or immersion cured and smoked Polish baleron.

For a home sausage maker pork butts are perfect cuts as:

- They can be smoked whole, little blade bone intact, then sliced like ham for sandwiches or fried as a kind of leaner bacon.

- They are a great material for making sausages, having a lean to fat ratio of 75/25. The little blade bone is very easy to remove and after that there is very little trimming. The skin can be saved for making other types of sausages.

- They are inexpensive cuts of meat that are usually carried by every supermarket.

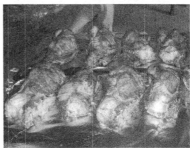

Photo 23.5 Smoked pork butts.

Pigs Feet

Due to their high collagen content pigs feet usually are used as:

- One of the meats for making head cheese.
- Principal meat for making souse (head cheese with added vinegar).
- Pickled pigs feet in vinegar.

Lard

Lard has always been an important cooking and baking staple in cultures where pork is an important dietary item, the fat of pigs often being as valuable a product as their meat. During the 19th century, lard was used in a similar fashion as butter in North America and many European nations. Lard was also held at the same level of popularity as butter in the early 20th century and was widely used as a substitute for butter during World War II.

Toward the late 20th century, lard began to be regarded as less healthy than vegetable oils (such as olive and sunflower oil) because of its high saturated fatty acid and cholesterol content. However, despite its reputation, *lard has less saturated fat, more unsaturated fat, and less cholesterol than an equal amount of butter by weight.*

Unlike many margarines and vegetable shortenings, unhydrogenated lard contains no trans fat (the consumption of trans fats increases the risk of coronary heart disease). It has also been regarded as a "poverty food". Many restaurants in the western nations have eliminated the use of lard in their kitchens *because of the religious and health-related dietary restrictions of many of their customers.* Many industrial bakers substitute beef tallow for lard in order to compensate for the lack of mouthfeel in many baked goods and to free their food products from pork-based dietary restrictions.

However, in the 1990's and early 2000's, the unique culinary properties of lard became widely recognized by chefs and bakers, leading to a partial rehabilitation of this fat among professionals. This trend has been partially driven by negative publicity about the trans fat content of the partially hydrogenated vegetable oils in vegetable shortening. Lard has become popular in the United Kingdom among aficionados of traditional British cuisine. This led to a "lard crisis" in early 2006 in which British demand for lard was not met due to demand by Poland and Hungary (who had recently joined the European Union) for fatty cuts of pork that had served as an important source of lard. Lard is one of the few edible oils with a relatively high smoke point, attributable to its high saturated fatty acids content. Pure lard is especially useful for cooking since *it produces little smoke when heated* and has a distinct taste when combined with other foods. Many chefs and bakers deem lard a superior cooking fat over shortening because of lard's range of applications and taste.

Because of the relatively large fat crystals found in lard, it is extremely effective as a shortening in baking. Pie crusts made with lard tend to be more flaky than those made with butter. Many cooks employ both types of fat in their pastries to combine the shortening properties of lard with the flavor of butter.

Butter consists mostly of *saturated fat* and is a significant source of dietary cholesterol. For these reasons, butter has been generally considered to be a contributor to health problems, especially heart disease. For many years, vegetable margarine was recommended as a substitute, since it is an unsaturated fat and contains little or no cholesterol. In recent decades, though, it has become accepted that the trans fats contained in partially hydrogenated oils used in typical margarines significantly raise undesirable LDL cholesterol levels as well.

Comparative properties of common cooking fats per 100 g (3.5 oz)						
	Total Fat	Saturated Fat	Mono-saturated Fat	Polyun-saturated Fat	Protein	Choles-terol
Vegetable shortening	71 g	23 g	8 g	37 g	0 g	0
Olive Oil	100 g	14 g	**73 g**	11 g	0 g	0
Butter	81 g	**51 g**	21 g	3 g	1 g	**215** mg
Tallow	100 g	50 g	42 g	4 g	0 g	109 mg
Lard	100 g	39 g	**45 g**	11 g	0 g	95 mg

Lard is rendered (heat melted) pork fat.
Tallow is a rendered suet.
Suet is a fresh beef or sheep fat.

Source: USDA Nutrient database

A higher proportion of monounsaturated fats in the diet is linked with a reduction in the risk of coronary heart disease. This is significant because olive oil is considerably rich in monounsaturated fats, most notably oleic acid. *Lard contains more monounsaturated fats than butter or tallow.*

Lard is one of the great products that is largely misunderstood today and has developed an undeserving reputation as an unhealthy product. To set the record straight we have listed some USDA data and statistics about lard and other animal fats. The conclusion is simple: *pork fat (lard) is much healthier than butter or tallow (beef or sheep fat).* Save on butter, eat more lard and you will live longer.

Home Production of Lard

Lard can be obtained from any part of the pig as long as there is a high concentration of fatty tissue. The highest grade of lard, known as leaf lard, is obtained from the "flare" visceral fat deposit surrounding the kidneys and inside the loin. Leaf lard has *little pork flavor*, making it ideal for use in baked goods, where it is treasured for its ability to produce flaky, moist pie crusts. The next highest grade of lard is obtained from *fatback*, the hard subcutaneous fat between the back skin and muscle of the pig. To extend the shelf life of pork fat (or any fat) it must be rendered (melted down). This offers the following advantages:

- removal of water.
- separation of impurities.
- it kills bacteria that would start the spoiling process.

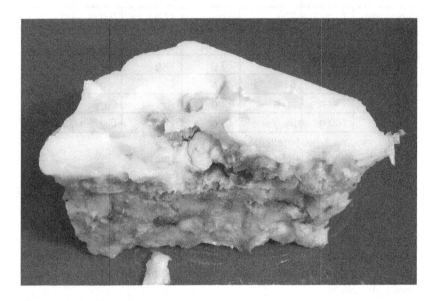

Photo 23.6 Home made lard.

Photo 23.7 Lard on bread.

Two types of lard can be produced:

1. Lard shortening that will be used for general cooking and frying. Such a lard can be made from any pork fat and even 20% of beef fat may be added. The leftover cracklings are normally saved for making liver or blood sausages. The easiest way to make lard is to mince fat with a grinder and that will produce the largest amount of lard.

Instructions:

- Cut fat into 1" pieces and grind through ⅛" (3 mm) plate.
- Add little water (½ cup to 4 quart skillet) to a skillet and place on a stove. Adding water prevents lard from sticking to the bottom of a skillet. Lard being a fat, will not mix with water anyhow and the water will evaporate during cooking.
- Add ground fat and stir often in order not to burn the fat.
- A by-product of dry-rendering lard is deep-fried meat, skin and membrane tissue known as cracklings. Once when cracklings develop a golden color and the lard becomes clearer, take off the skillet from the stove and let it stand for 20 minutes.
- Pour 75% of clear lard into jars. This is very clean lard that will last the longest. Filter the remaining lard (it contains cracklings) through a fine sieve or cheese cloth. Use cracklings for sausages.

2. Ready to eat lard (*smalec* in Polish) has been traditionally produced in Europe a sandwich spread.. Such lard is made *from pork fat only,* preferably from back fat. Belly fat may be used as well although it may be considered a waste as belly can be processed for bacon. The resulting cracklings are saved and become a part of lard. They may be added to boiled sausages (liver and blood). *The highest quality lard* will be obtained when the pork fat is manually diced into ¼" cubes which will produce a larger number of solid cracklings, known in Polish as *skwarki*. To add extra flavor, ingredients such as onion, garlic, apple or marjoram are often added.

Instructions:

- cut fat into 1" pieces and grind through ⅛" (3 mm) plate.

- add little water (½ cup to 4 quart skillet) to a skillet and place on a stove.

- add ground fat and stir often in order not to burn the fat.

- once when cracklings develop a golden color and the lard becomes clearer, take off the skillet from the stove and let it stand for 20 minutes.

- pour 75% of clear lard into jars. This is very clean lard that will last longest. Filter the remaining lard (it contains cracklings) through a fine sieve or cheese cloth. Use this lard first.

- add cracklings to each container or a glass jar. They will have a tendency to settle down on the bottom. To distribute them evenly, mix lard adding a new portion of cracklings. As the lard cools down it changes color to white. The cracklings will be trapped inside and uniformly distributed.

Adding flavors:

Follow the above procedure and when the lard is half-way done (becomes semi-liquid), add chopped onion. Add onion carefully as it contains water and the lard may boil over. Switch off the heat when onions become light yellow as the hot lard has high temperature and the onions and cracklings will continue to cook. The cracklings' color should be light brown, their flavor will become bitter when dark brown. When chopped onion is added to lard, the lard should be refrigerated. If lard will be kept at room temperature, add whole peeled onion and then discard the onion during filtering. If not kept under refrigeration, chopped onion will decrease the shelf life of the product.

Whole onions, apples cored and cut in halves, and a bay leaf are often added. Remove those ingredients during filtering. Add spices of your choice: marjoram, coriander or others. A few cloves of diced garlic may be added when lard is removed from the heat, given that garlic looses its aroma rapidly when heated. Lard consumed as a spread on bread was once very common in Europe and North America, especially those areas where dairy fats and vegetable oils were rare. When the II World War ended in 1945, it was the main staple in every household for these reasons:

- 100 g of lard provides 900 kcal of energy
- it tasted great. People ate lard sandwiches with tomatoes, pickles, it tasted even great when topped with sugar
- can be kept in a cool place for many months
- can be eaten with bread or used as fat shortening for cooking, for example when frying eggs

Photo 23.8 Modern back fat contains little fat.

Photo 23.9 In the past back fats were about 2" thick.

Photo 23.10 Diced back fat.

Photo 23.11 Melting fat.

Photo 23.12 Filtered lard.

Photo 23.13 Cracklings. May be added to lard or used in blood sausages.

Corned Beef

Corning means preservation of beef by salt. The word corn was synonymous with grain, and in England generally meant any small particle. In meat technology the word "corning" refers to meat preserved by sprinkling with grains or "corns" of salt. Beef is corned with similar pickle as hams and other pork cuts.

It is not unusual to include in curing pickle spices such as bay leaf, allspice and garlic. The meat is usually immersed in brine for about 2 weeks for cuts 3" or less in thickness. If meat is injected with 10% pump, it may be immersed in leftover brine for 5 days only. To be classified as a ready-to-eat product, corned beef should be cooked to 160° F (72° C) internal meat temperature.

Meat Loaf

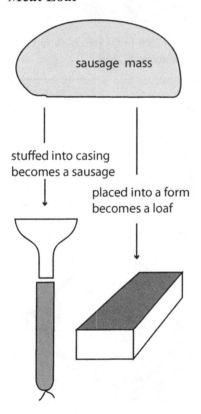

sausage mass

stuffed into casing
becomes a sausage

placed into a form
becomes a loaf

Fig. 23.2 Meat loaf and sausage.

Until the stuffing step the manufacture of sausage and meat loaf remains basically the same.

- When liver mass is packed into the pan, the liver loaf or pate is obtained.
- When head cheese materials are placed in a pan, the meat jelly is obtained.
- When sausage mass is packed into the pan, the meat loaf is produced.

Meat loaves are much easier to produce as time consuming steps such as stuffing, drying, smoking and showering are eliminated. Loaves come in different shape, firmness, texture and seasoning. They are often covered with attractive glazes and decorated with vegetables, pickles or even nuts.

Meat loaves are pressed into a shape that makes them just right size when sliced for topping sandwiches. Simple meat loaves can be made from typical sausage recipes but many fancy loaves employ ingredients such as chopped olives, pistachio nuts, diced cheese, cooked noodles, pimentos, pickles, etc. Water binding ingredients such as dry milk, potato starch, and soy concentrate are often added to retain moisture which helps to create juicier molds with good texture. Unless canned, meat loaves are not produced with preservation in mind and must be refrigerated and eaten relatively soon.

Bacon, Cured and Smoked

Bacon - Dry Cured

Recipe for 5 kg (11 lbs.) mild bacon with the skin on:

3%, 4.8 oz (150 g) salt
1.5%, 2.4 oz (68 g) sugar
7.8 g (0.02 oz) Cure #1

Rub in 1/2 of the mixture on all sides. After 7 days overhaul and rub in another half. Keep under refrigeration. The meat will be cured from 12 to 15 days (allow 2-2½ days per kg). Soak bacon for one hour in water, brush the surface clean and hang until the surface feels dry. Smoke with a thin *cold smoke* at 77° F (25° C) or lower for 1-2 days. Refrigerate.

Bacon - Brine Cured

Bacon slabs 5 kg (11 lbs.)
1 gallon 60° SAL brine,
81 g Cure #1 (2.8 oz)

Bacon is placed for 10 days in curing solution. The pieces are overhauled in the middle of the process. Then, it is soaked for one hour in fresh water and the surface brushed off clean. Bacon is hung in a cooler/refrigerator for 12 hours until the surface feels dry. It may be placed on a screen to drain the moisture away and turned over half way. Smoke bacon for 2 days at 77° F (25° C) or lower. Refrigerate.

Bacon - Injection Cured

Bacon is needle injected with the above 60° SAL curing solution at 10% pump. It is left in for 5 days in the same strength solution. Bacon is rinsed and hung in a cooler/refrigerator for 12 hours until the surface feels dry. It may be placed on a screen to drain the moisture away and turned over half way. Bacon is smoked for 2 days at 77° F (25° C) or lower. Refrigerate.

Note: some people may feel safer when bacon is fully cooked. It may be cooked in water at 176° F (80° C) or baked in oven at 212° F (100° C) until the meat reaches 145° F (62° C) internal temperature.

It may also be sliced and fried before serving.

Bresaola

Breasola is Italian dry cured beef.

Meat	Metric	US
beef sirloin	1000 g	2.20 lb.

Ingredients for 1 kg of meat:

salt	28 g	5 tsp.
cure #2	6 g	1 tsp.
pepper	6.0 g	3 tsp.
sugar	5.0 g	1 tsp.
cloves, ground	1.0 g	½ tsp.
garlic powder	1.5 g	1 tsp.

Instructions:

1. Remove all fat, connective tissue and silver skin.
2. Mix salt, Cure #2 and all ingredients together. Take ½ of the mixture and rub into the meat. Place in Ziploc® bag and put for 3 days into refrigerator.
3. Remove from the bag and apply the second half of the mixture. Drain away any liquid from the bag. Place in refrigerator for 3 more days.
4. Brush off excess mixture from the meat. Stuff into synthetic or collagen casings.
5. Hang for 4 weeks at 54° F (12° C) to dry and mature.

Canadian Bacon

The average weight of a pork loin is 12-14 pounds, however it can be cut into sections.

Meat
Pork loin   5-6 kg   11-13 lbs.

Making Brine:
To make 50° brine (10° Baumé) add
1.01 pound of salt to 1 gallon of water (3.8 liter).
Add 120 g (4.2 oz) of Cure #1*.
Add 226 g (½ lb) sugar.
This amount of brine will cure about 17 lbs (7.3 kg) of meat.

Instructions:
1. Remove all bones and trim down the fat until you reach the lean meat.
2. Immerse loin in brine and place for 10 days in refrigerator *OR* pump meat with 10% pump and then place it in leftover brine for 5 days only.
3. Remove from brine, wash and soak in cold water for 1 hour.
4. Stuff into synthetic casing or stockinette and hang in a preheated to 130° F (54° C) smokehouse to dry. This should take 3-4 hours with vents wide open. You can leave it in a cooler/refrigerator overnight.
5. When the loin feels dry apply smoke and smoke for 3 hours at 150° F (66° C).
6. Increase temperature (no smoke) to 170° F (77° C) and hold until the meat reaches 154° F (68° C) internal temperature.
7. Shower or immerse in cold water for 10 minutes.
8. Hang at room temperature until loin is dry.
9. Store in refrigerator.

Note: * the amount of salt in Cure #1 (112 g) has been accounted for when calculating brine strength.

Coppa

Coppa or Capocollo are Italian cured pork butts. Two well known Italian coppas are: Coppa Piacentina (Piacenza region) and Capocollo di Calabria (Calabria region), both have Protected Designation of Origin (PDO) status, which ensures that only products genuinely originating in those regions are allowed in commerce as such.

Meat	Metric	US
pork butt, boneless	1000 g	2.20 lb.

Pork butt weighs about 2.2 kg (5 lbs).

Ingredients for 1 kg of meat

salt	30 g	2¾ Tbs.
Cure #2	6 g	1 tsp.
black pepper	8 g	4 tsp.
sugar	25 g	2 Tbs.
garlic powder	2.5 g	1 tsp.
cumin, ground	2.0 g	1 tsp.
cloves, ground	2.0 g	1 tsp.
cinnamon	0.5 g	½ tsp.
paprika	2.0 g	1 tsp.
red pepper	1.0 g	½ tsp.

1. Trim excess fat all around the butt. Keep the butt in refrigerator to keep it cold.
2. Mix salt, Cure #2 and sugar together. Rub the meat on all sides with half of the mixture. Place the butt for 7 days in refrigerator. Keep it covered with plastic wrap or a cloth to prevent drying. You can place it in a zip lock bag too.
3. After 7 days, rub the butt with the remaining mixture and keep in refrigerator for an additional 10 days.
4. Remove from refrigerator, rinse the surface with tap water to remove any crystallized salt. Let it dry on the refrigerator's screen for 3 hours.
5. Mix all spiced together and rub the mixture into the butt.
6. Stuff the butt into beef bungs or 100 mm collagen casings. Prick air pockets to allow entrapped air to escape. Do this especially at the two ends, and anywhere you see pockets of air.
7. Hold butts for 21 days at around 55° F (14° C), 70% humidity to dry and mature. Do not go over 59° F (15° C).

Notes:
Original coppa is not smoked. If you like smoky flavor, you may apply cold smoke (< 65° F, 18° C) at any given time.

Liver Loaf

Meat	Metric	US
pork liver	400 g	0.88 lb.
pork trimmings	300 g	0.66 lb.
pork jowl or bacon	300 g	0.66 lb.

Ingredients		
salt	18 g	3 tsp.
white pepper	4.0 g	2 tsp.
nutmeg	1.0 g	½ tsp.
allspice	1.0 g	½ tsp.
sage, ground	1.0 g	½ tsp.
dry milk powder	60 g	1 cup
gelatin	10 g	2 tsp.
water	60 ml	¼ cup

Instructions:

1. Soak livers in cold water for 30 minutes, then grind them through ⅛" (3 mm) grinder plate or chop them in a food processor until bubbles appear on the surface of the emulsion which may take 5-10 minutes.
2. Grind meats through ¼" (6 mm) plate.
3. Dissolve gelatin in water.
4. Mix everything together.
5. Stuff into a ham press.
6. Transfer mold press to a cooking tank with hot water.
7. Let the temperature drop to 160°F (72° C) and hold this temperature until internal meat temperature reaches 154° F (68° C).
8. Chill loaves in cold water and then transfer to refrigerator over-night.
9. Remove loaf from the mold press.
10. Keep refrigerated.

Notes:

If a mold press is not available, tightly stuff the liver loaf into a pan and then bake in the oven.

Lomo Embuchado

Lomo embuchado is Spanish dry-cured pork loin.

The average weight of a pork loin is 12-14 lbs.

Meat	Metric	US
pork loin	5-6 kg	11-13 lbs.

Ingredients for 1 kg of meat:

salt	28 g	5 tsp.
Cure #2	6 g	1 tsp.
sugar	2.5 g	½ tsp.
pepper	8 g	4 tsp.
Spanish paprika	6 g	3 tsp.
garlic powder	2.0 g	1 tsp.

Instructions:

1. Remove all bones and trim down the fat until you reach the lean meat.
2. Mix salt, Cure #2 and all ingredients together.
3. Add little water to the mixture and rub the wet mixture into the loin.
4. Place into a plastic bag and leave for 7-10 days in refrigerator.
5. Remove loin from refrigerator and brush off the excess salt. Stuff into synthetic or collagen casings.
6. Hang loin at 46° F (8° C), 72-80% humidity for one month. This is the salt equalization stage.
7. Dry loins for 3 weeks at 68-72° F (20-22° C). Moisture removal and flavor development takes place at this stage.
8. Loin is ready when it loses about 40% of its original weight.

Meat Loaf

Meat	Metric	US
pork butt	700 g	1.54 lb.
beef chuck	300 g	0.66 lb.

Ingredients:		
salt	18 g	3 tsp.
Cure #1	2.5 g	½ tsp.
white pepper	4.0 g	2 tsp.
nutmeg	1.0 g	½ tsp.
onion powder	2.0 g	1 tsp.
dry milk powder	60 g	1 cup
cold water	120 ml	½ cup

Instructions:
1. Grind beef through ⅛" (3 mm) plate. Grind pork through ⅛" (3 mm) plate. Keep separate.
2. Mix ground beef with ½ water and dry milk. Add ground pork, all remaining ingredients including remaining water and mix everything well together.
3. Stuff into pans and bake at 212° F (100° C) until the internal temperature reaches 155° F (69° C).
4. Let cool in refrigerator before removing from the pan and slicing.

Note: for best results meat should be properly cured. Eliminating Cure #1 will result in a grey-brown color of a finished product.

538   Home Production of Quality Meats and Sausages

Pancetta

Pancetta is Italian bacon which is cured and air dried but not smoked. There are many varieties and each region produces its own type. Pancetta Placentina and Pancetta di Calabria have been protected by the PDO mark.

Meat	Metric	US
pork belly	1000 g	2.20 lb.

pork belly slab may weigh about 4.5 kg (10 lbs).

Ingredients for 1 kg of meat

salt	28 g	5 tsp.
Cure #1	3.2 g	¾ tsp.
sugar	5.0 g	1 tsp.
white pepper	4.0 g	2 tsp.
nutmeg	1.0 g	½ tsp.
fennel	2.0 g	1 tsp.
red peppers	1.0 g	½ tsp.
garlic powder	1.5 g	½ tsp.

Instructions:

1. Mix salt and Cure #1 together.
2. Rub ½ of the mix into the belly.
3. Place the belly in a zip lock plastic bag. Leave for 4 days in refrigerator.
4. Remove the belly from the bag. Mix all spices with the remaining half of the curing mixture (salt and cure #1). Rub the mixture into the belly. Refrigerate for 4 more days.
5. Wash belly with tap water and then soak it for 15 minutes in cold water.
6. Dry belly for 2 days at 54° F (12° C).
7. Remove the skin and divide the belly in two cutting along its length.
8. Soak 5" (120 mm) fibrous casing for 1 hour in water. Roll each belly into a tight roll and insert into the casing. Run butcher twine around the pancetta every ¾" and make a hanging loop. Remove any air pockets with a needle.
9. Hang for 3 weeks at 54° F (12° C).
10. Refrigerate.

Notes: Pancetta can be rolled or straight.

Pastrami

Pastrami is a cured smoked beef that was created by the Slavic Jews. It is related to pastrama, a highly seasoned smoked pork that is popular in Romania. The beef version of the product became very popular in the Jewish delicatessens in Europe and was brought to the USA by the Jewish immigrants. The "corn" in "corned beef" refers to the "corns" or grains of coarse salts used to cure it. The slab of beef is typically cured in a heavy, salty brine solution. After beef is removed from brine it drained and a combination of cracked black pepper and whole coriander is rubbed into it.

Meat	Metric	US
quality beef plates		
or brisket	1000 g	2.20 lb.

Ingredients per 1000 g (1 kg) of meat:

salt for making brine	333 g	0.73 lb.
Cure #1 for making brine	120 g	4.2 oz.*
black pepper, cracked	25 g	2 Tbs.
coriander seeds, whole	20 g	2 Tbs.

Note: * the amount of salt in Cure #1 (112 g) has been accounted for when calculating brine strength.

1. Making brine:
To make 40° brine (10° Baumé) add 0.73 lb of salt to 1 gallon of water (3.8 liter). Add 120 g (4.2 oz) of Cure #1. This amount of brine will cure about 17 lbs (7.3 kg) of meat.
To cure 1 kg meat about 500 ml (about 2 cups) of brine is required.

Pump briskets with the amount of brine equal to 10% of the original meat weight. After meats are injected with brine, pack them tightly in a suitable container. Add sufficient brine of the same formula and strength used for pumping to cover the meat. Cover with a weighted lid. Cure 4-5 days at refrigerator temperatures (38-40° F).
2. Remove meats from brine, wash for 2 minutes with cold water and drain. Rub thoroughly with cracked black pepper and whole coriander. Be generous with your rub, it should be applied in a thick coating.
3. Hang pieces in a preheated to 140° F (60° C) smokehouse. With dampers fully open, hold at this temperature until meat surface is dry.

4. Readjust dampers to 1/4 open and apply light smoke for 2 hours. Close dampers, shut off smoke and raise temperature to 200 - 220° F (93 - 104° C). Cook until an internal temperature of 165° F (74° C) is reached.

5. Remove pastrami from smokehouse and hang at room temperature for 1-2 hours to reduce internal meat temperature 110° F (43° C).

6. Place in refrigerator. When cooled, pastrami can be easily sliced.

Notes:

A light sprinkling of Spanish paprika over the top will give pastrami an attractive appearance.

A classical pastrami is covered with cracked black pepper and whole coriander seeds. In many cases it is covered with coarsely chopped spices.

Mustard seeds and garlic are often added.

A typical rub:

4 tablespoons (Tbsp.) salt. Optional, if meat was previously cured.
3 Tbsp. cracked black pepper
6 Tbsp. coriander seeds
2 Tbsp. yellow mustard seeds
4 Tbsp. paprika
8 cloves garlic, finely chopped

Pastrami may be dry cured. For 1 kg (2.20 lb.) beef use:

20 g salt (3½ tsp.)
100 g salt (8½ Tbsp.)
2.5 g (½ tsp.) Cure #1
2 tsp. cracked black pepper
5½ tsp. coriander seeds
5½ tsp. brown sugar
2 cloves garlic, finely minced

A. Mix all ingredients together and rub it into the meat. Massage it well and cover the meat's surface evenly.

B. Wrap the meat in aluminum foil and place in a plastic bag.

C. Hold in a refrigerator for 10 days, turning the package daily.

D. Remove meat from the package and let it dry for 2 hours at room temperature. Re-apply any spices that may have fallen off.

E. Go to Step 3 in instructions and follow steps 4, 5 and 6.

Pork Loaf

Meat	Metric	US
pork	1000 g	2.20 lb.

Ingredients:

salt	18 g	3 tsp.
Cure #1	2.5 g	½ tsp.
white pepper	4.0 g	2 tsp.
cloves, ground	1.0 g	½ tsp.
sage, ground	1.0 g	½ tsp.
dry milk powder	60 g	1 cup
cold water	120 ml	½ cup

Instructions:

1. Grind pork through ⅜" (10 mm) plate.
2. Mix ground meat with all ingredients.
3. Stuff into pans and bake at 212° F (100° C) until the internal temperature reaches 154° F (68° C).
4. Let cool in refrigerator before removing from the pan and slicing.

Notes: for best results meat should be properly cured. Eliminating Cure #1 altogether will result in a grey-brown color of a finished product.

Smoked Back Fat

This is an old classic which tastes great with bread, mustard and beer or it can be used as a flavoring to many other dishes.

Meat	Metric	US
back fat (not salted), with skin or without	5 kg	11.0 lbs.

back fat slab dimensions: about 10-12" long x 3-6" wide x 1" (no skin), 1¼" (with skin) thick.

Ingredients

salt	350 g	12.35 oz.

Instructions:

1. Salting. Take half of salt and rub into back fat on all sides. Spread salt on the bottom of container. Place back fat skin down in a container. Spread salt on top. Place another slab of back fat on top of the first one using the same procedure. Keep container under refrigeration 40-42° F (4-6° C).
2. After 7 days repeat procedure using second half of salt. Reverse order of slab placement: the slab that was previously on top goes on bottom now and vice versa. You can rub in any spices that you like for instance pepper, paprika, or coriander. Leave in a container for 1-2 weeks longer. This means that the total time is between 2 and 3 weeks.
3. Shake off excess salt from the surface of back fat and wash the slab in a lukewarm water. This removes any crystalized salt that has accumulated on the surface.
4. Make a hanging loop and hang at cool temperature for 12 hours to dry.
5. Smoke with a thin cold smoke for 2 days until back fat develops light brown or brown color.
6. Keep in refrigerator.

Notes: There is an excellent version of smoked back fat *(Słonina Paprykowana* in Polish) that employs paprika. After step #3, apply paprika generously all around the slab, patting the spice in slightly by hand. Then continue with steps 4, 5 and 6.
Sodium nitrite (Cure #1) is not used as there is no meat, just the fat.

Smoked Pork Butt

Pork butt, boneless or with bone, about 6 lbs.

Making 60° SAL brine:

water	1 gal.	3.80 kg
salt	1.32 lb.	0.60 kg
Cure #1*	4.2 oz.	120 g
sugar	1.5 oz.	42 g

This amount of brine cures about 17 lbs. of meat.

Note: * the amount of salt in Cure #1 (112 g) has been accounted for when calculating brine strength.

Mix all ingredients in 1 qt of cold water 40° F (4° C), then spray pump pork butts to 10% of the green (original) weight. Then leave them in the remaining brine for 3 - 4 days in a refrigerator. Take them out, wash briefly with cold water and let drain. Place them in stockinette bags. Hang them in a preheated to 130° F (54° C) smokehouse for 2-3 hours until dry. Then apply a medium smoke increasing temperature to 150° F (65° C) for about 3 hours. Then raise the temperature to 160–165° F (72- 74° C) and continue smoking until an internal temperature of 154° F (68° C) is obtained. Shower with cold water and hang them at room temperature to start cooling. Store in the refrigerator.

Smoked Pork Loin

Meat

pork loin without bone	2 kg	4.4 lb.
salt		

Making Brine:

60° SAL brine:

water	1 gal.	3.80 kg	This amount of brine cures about 17 lbs. of meat.
salt	1.32 lb.	0.60 kg	
Cure #1	4.2 oz.	120 g	
sugar	1.5 oz.	42 g	

Instructions:

1. Wet cure method. Mix all ingredients with cold water. Using a needle syringe, pump the loin to 3-4 % of its green weight. That means you are taking the amount of brine that equals 3-4% of the loin meat weight. In this case it comes to 60-80 g (2.1 - 2.8 oz) or 1/3 cup. The loin then is placed in the leftover brine and placed in a refrigerator for 5 days. If meat is not pump injected, leave it in brine for 10 days, overhauling every two days. Loins must be covered with brine, use some kind of weight on top of them.

2. Wash the outside of the loin briefly with tap water. It is wise to taste it now and if it is too salty place in cold water (refrigerator) for a few hours. If you want it saltier, stick it back into the brine for a few hours.

Let it drain and dry for 6-8 hours at room temperature. Then you can rub the dry loin all over with the yolk of an egg. That will give the loin a beautiful gold color on the outside after smoking.

3. Preheat the smoker to 130° F (54° C) and if the loin is dry, introduce smoke with dampers 1/4 closed and smoke for 1 hour at 122-140° F (50-60° C). Increase smoking temperature to 150° F (66° C) applying smoke all the time and stop when the meat's internal temperature reaches 142° F (61° C). Trichinae, almost non-existent in American pork, dies at 137° F (58° C).

4. Shower with cold water until the internal temperature is reduced to 110° F (44° C). Hang at room temperature for 1 hour then place in a refrigerator.

Notes:

Cooking is optional. The smoked loin was never submitted to high temperatures and has a characteristic color, taste and flavor. Nothing prevents you from increasing smoking temperature (keep the smoke on) to 160-170° F (71-77° C) until the meat's internal temperature reaches 154° F (68° C). There will be a difference in flavor between the cooked and uncooked version.

Soppressata

During treatment, natural flavors such as cumin, black pepper, red pepper and chilli peppers are added to the meat which is then aged. Depending on the type of product, the aging process may last from a minimum of thirty to a maximum of one hundred days.

Meat	Metric	US
pork butt	800 g	1.76 lb.
back fat	200 g	0.44 lb.

Ingredients for 1 kg of meat

salt	28 g	5 tsp.
Cure #2	2.5 g	½ tsp.
dextrose	10.0 g	2 tsp.
black pepper	2.0 g	1 tsp.
red peppers flakes	1.0 g	½ tsp.
whole peppercorns	2.0 g	1 tsp.
chili powder	1.0 g	½ tsp.
garlic powder	1.5 g	½ tsp.

Instructions:
1. Grind meat and fat through ½" (12 mm) plate.
2. Mix ground meat with all ingredients.
3. Pack tightly in a container, cover with cloth and refrigerate for 48 hours.
4. Grind through ⅜" (10 mm) plate.
5. Stuff into 60 mm, 8-10" hog middles.
6. Hang sausage at 68° F (20° C), 80-90% humidity for 2 days.
7. If smoky flavor is desired, apply cold smoke for 2 days.
8. Hold sausage at around 56° F (14° C), 80% humidity for about 2 months until it loses about 30% of its original weight.
9. If mold appears wipe it off with a cloth moistened with vinegar. You can cold smoke sausage again for a few hours which prevents the formation of mold.

Tasso

Tasso, intensely flavored and heavily smoked pork butt adds a unique flavor to many Cajun dishes. Tasso is seasoned with cayenne pepper and garlic and although it can be eaten alone, it is mainly used in vegetables, gumbos and soups.

Meat	Metric	US
pork butt	1000 kg	2.20 lbs.

Ingredients for 1 kg of meat:

salt	18 g	3 tsp.
Cure #1	2.5 g	½ tsp.
black pepper	4.0 g	2 tsp.
cayenne	1.0 g	½ tsp.
garlic	3.5 g	1 clove

Instructions:

1. Cut pork butt across the grain into 1" thick strips and remove excess fat. Mix together all ingredients and coat the pork strips on all sides. Place in a container (plastic Ziploc® bag is fine) and keep in refrigerator for 2 days. Turn pork strips over once a day or shake the bag.
2. Remove the pork pieces and hang them on S-hooks for 1-2 hours until dry.
3. Preheat smoker to 130° F, (55° C) and if meat feels dry apply smoke for 3 hours. If the surface of the tasso is still wet, hold it inside the smoker (no smoke) until it feels dry. Then in the last hour of smoking try to gradually increase the temperature to about 160° F, (71° C).
4. Increase temperature to 170°-180° F, 77°-82° C, (no smoke necessary) and cook tasso to an internal temperature of 155° F (69° C).
5. Store in refrigerator.

Notes:

1. Making tasso resembles making jerky. If you cut the pork pieces into 1/2" strips it will be much easier to dry them out after cooking. Once the moisture is gone the tasso pieces will be considered a dry product and like jerky will last a long time without refrigeration.

2. There are different Tasso recipes and some include sugar, allspice, cinnamon, sage, thyme. That we leave to your individual preference. Worcestershire sauce gives jerkys their specific tangy flavor and there are some Tasso recipes that include that sauce, too. You may mix all ingredients with 1 cup of Worcesterhire sauce and marinate tasso in it for 2 days. Make sure it is dry when you smoke it.

3. In case you decide to smoke an entire pork butt Tasso style, the wet curing method should be chosen and the curing times will be longer (5 - 7 days).

Chapter 24

Air Dried Meats

Preserving thinly sliced meat by drying was practiced in many areas of the world and the technology was basically the same. Even Eskimos who lived in the coldest climate on earth were preserving seal or whale meat by drying it in the open air. The well known air dried meats are:

- Hams
- Pork butts
- Jerky
- Pemmican
- Biltong

We all know that meat would spoil if not kept under refrigeration so the concept of drying meat seems to be very difficult and dangerous. And it is, unless proper steps are taken. This is not rocket science and if we could do it thousands of years ago when computers were not even around, we should be able to produce air dried meats without a sweat today. It is necessary to know the basics well, the good news is that the basics like many other things depend to a great extent on common sense and logic. Air dried, fermented and cold smoked meats are intimately related and follow the same guidelines. A reader is referred to the Chapter on Fermented Meats which includes a lot of information on drying and safety.

Take for example traditionally made Hungarian salami. The sausage is made without sugar so there is no fermentation. The small account of glycogen (sugar) that meat contains results in such a small fermentation, that for all practical purposes it can be considered negligible. The whole process of making this sausage depends on *drying*. The Spanish will call it chorizo and in Lithuania they will cold smoke sausages and after drying it will be called Cold Smoked Sausage. Of course it is more complicated to dry a huge piece of meat such as a ham than a thinly cut strip of meat that will become jerky, nevertheless the rules of the game remain basically the same.

You cannot just hang meat and let it dry as it will spoil. Even when left in a refrigerator it will spoil although at a slower rate. You have to prevent bacteria from growing and that is accomplished by:

- Applying salt. This prevents bacteria from growing and removes moisture. The less moisture remains, the harder it is for bacteria to grow.
- Adding nitrite/Nitrate. This prevents pathogenic bacteria, notably *Clostridium botulinum* from growing.
- Keeping meat at low temperature, especially at the beginning of the process.
- Drying in the air. Once the meat has lost some moisture it is safer to continue drying in the air at 50-54° F (10-12° C). We don't want to dry meat in the middle of the "danger zone" 40-140° F (4-60° C) when bacteria find optimal conditions to grow. When drying is accomplished in a dehydrator (jerky) the temperature should be 145° F (63° C) which is above the danger zone.

This leads to a common question "what if I don't want to use nitrates"? A commercial producer must conform to the Government standards and he has to use them. Replacing nitrite with celery powder is the marketing trick, as celery contains the same sodium nitrite. It is possible to obtain permission from the Food Inspection and Safety service to make products without nitrite, but this is a very costly and involved process. Needless to say such an establishment will be under great scrutiny of meat inspectors and most processors don't want to be bothered with such a waiver.

It is not expected that an Eskimo will cure seal or whale meat with nitrites. They would rather pound their meat pieces until thin, and dry them in windy and cold conditions that most of us will find impossible to duplicate. It also goes without saying that it takes longer to remove moisture from the inside of a 18 lb. ham than a 2 oz. strip of meat. More Nitrate can be safely applied to a meat that will dry for a year as the Nitrates dissipate slowly in time. For this reason you can apply 625 ppm of sodium nitrite to a dry product and only 156 ppm to minced meat.

The salt provides safety and is applied at around 6% to a country ham which needs plenty of protection, about 3-3.5% for a dry fermented sausage and 2.5% for semi-dry fermented sausage.

Jerky

Jerky is meat that is cut into long, thin strips and dried. Jerky was a popular snack with early trappers and soldiers because it kept well, was light and easy to carry. For the same reasons it is a popular food with today's hikers and is always on top of the list of the survival items. Jerky can be made from any lean meat such as beef, pork, poultry, fish or wild game. There is an unlimited number of flavors that may be created, for example smoky or not, hot and spicy, barbecue, Italian sweet and hot, and others. Best jerky is made from lean meat as fats become rancid in time, spoiling the flavor. Venison being very lean by nature, is great for making jerky.

Safety Concerns. Food Safety Regulations for Shelf Stability require jerky to lose moisture until its water activity (A_w) level is:

- A_w is equal or less than 0.85 (with packaging or other possible intervention).
- A_w is equal or less than 0.70 (without packaging - i.e. exposed to the air).

USDA guidelines state that: *"A potentially hazardous food does not include a food with a water activity value of 0.85 or less."* Although jerky is perfectly safe at A_w 0.85, nevertheless molds can still develop on its surface when the air is humid. At A_w 0.70 the molds will not grow.

Traditionally, jerky was only dried. In October 2003, in New Mexico, there was an outbreak of *Salmonella* that was traced to jerky production in one of the small plants. In response to this outbreak, the Food Safety and Inspection Service has initiated a series of policy changes and guidelines. What FSIS has concluded is that it is not enough to follow the time-temperature guidelines, but to also include the humidity factor in the cooking process. To make it short: *it is necessary to maintain the relative humidity of the oven at 90% or above for at least 25% of the cooking time and no less than one hour.*

This ruling has started a heated and ongoing debate between FSIS and small jerky manufacturers who claim that maintaining such high humidity in a smokehouse is difficult and may force them out of business. Another argument is that the humidity requirement changes the quality of jerky. Due to today's microbiological concerns, particularly *E.coli 0157:H7, Salmonella,* and *Listeria monocytogenes* jerky must be exposed to thermal processing.

A hobbyist is not bound by those rules but we believe it is beneficial to know about the latest safety requirements for making jerky products. The United States Department of Agriculture has divided jerky into specific categories:

1. Jerky - The product is produced from a single piece of meat. The product can also be labeled as "Natural Style Jerky" provided that the product name is accompanied by the explanatory statement "made from solid pieces of meat."

2. Jerky Chunked and Formed - The product is produced from chunks which are molded and formed and cut into strips.

3. Jerky Ground and Formed or Chopped and Formed. The meat is ground, molded, pressed and cut into strips.

Safety of Home Made Jerky

It must be noted that pork and wild game meat (except venison) is at risk of being infested with trichinae and should be either cooked or accordingly treated (see Appendix A). Commercially made jerky is monitored by inspectors of the U.S. Department of Agriculture's Food Safety and Inspection Service. Home made jerky, often made from venison, is often made in a hazardous way. Dried meat will keep for many years if kept at low humidity because bacteria will not grow under such conditions. That does not mean that all bacteria are dead. *E.coli* was found in dried but uncooked jerky that has been stored at room temperature for more than a year. Although curing salt (Cure#1) is not required in the manufacture of homemade jerky, *it is recommended that it be used.* Curing salt offers many advantages:

- Stabilizes and improves the color of meat.
- Contributes to the characteristic flavor of cured meat.
- Inhibits growth of spoilage and pathogenic bacteria.
- Slows down development of rancidity of fat.

Reprinted from FSIS - Food Safety of Jerky:

Why is Temperature Important When Making Jerky?

Illnesses due to *Salmonella* and *E.coli 0157:H7* from home made jerky raise questions about the traditional drying methods for making beef and venison jerky. The USDA current recommendation for making jerky safely is to heat meat to 160° F (72° C) *before the dehydrating process*. This step assures that any bacteria present will be destroyed by wet heat.

Most dehydrator instructions do not include this step, and a dehydrator may not reach temperatures high enough to heat meat to 160° F. After heating to 160° F (72° C) maintaining a constant dehydrator temperature of 130 - 140° F (54 - 60° C) during the drying process is important because the process must prevent jerky from spoiling; and must remove enough water that microorganisms are unable to grow.

Why is it a Food Safety Concern to Dry Meat Without First Heating it to 160° F (72° C) ?

The danger in dehydrating meat and poultry without cooking it to a safe temperature first is that the appliance will not heat the meat to 160° F (72° C) - a temperature at which bacteria are destroyed - *before it dries*. After drying, bacteria become much more heat resistant. Within a dehydrator or low-temperature oven, evaporating moisture absorbs most of the heat. Thus, *the meat itself does not begin to rise in temperature until most of the moisture has evaporated*. Therefore, when the dried meat temperature finally begins to rise, the bacteria have become more heat resistant and are more likely to survive. If these bacteria are pathogenic, they can cause food borne illness to those consuming the jerky.

Recent work at the University of Wisconsin has demonstrated that the following temperatures are effective at killing *E.coli 0157:H7* in jerky products. It is recommended that dehydrator temperature of 145° F (63° C) or higher be used.

Drying Temperature	Minimum drying time
125° F (52° C)	10 hours
135° F (57° C)	8 hours
145° F (63° C)	7 hours
155° F (68° C)	4 hours

Making jerky from a single piece of meat

Making safe jerky requires cooking the meat before placing it in the dehydrator or oven.

1. The leaner the meat, the better the jerky. Either fresh or frozen meat can be used. Meat should be trimmed of fat and connective tissue.

2. Slice partially frozen meat into 1/4" strips, 6" long x 1" wide.

3. Marinating. Home produced jerky made of sliced meat pieces is usually marinated for 8 hours or overnight. About 1/2 cup (120 ml) of marinade for each pound of meat sounds right. Drain the slices and pat them dry with paper towels. Sprinkle with black pepper and other spices you like.

Basic jerky marinade:

    1 cup soy sauce
    1/4 cup Worcestershire sauce
    1 Tbs. powdered garlic
    1 Tbs. black pepper
    1 tsp. liquid smoke

This amount of marinade is enough for 5-7 lb. of meat.
Commercially made jerky will not be marinated but mixed with salt, nitrite and spices in a tumbler. Then it will be dried.

4. Cook meat according to 160° F (72° C) as recommended by FSIS. You could bring the marinade with strips of jerky to a boil, but you may not have enough marinade. More water can be added into your marinade. Another fine solution is to make *a special dedicated brine* just for that purpose.

Bring half of the brine to a boil. Insert meat pieces, bring brine to a boil and cook for 2 minutes. Remove strips and let them dry. Change brine for the second half of meat and repeat the process.

5. Begin dehydrating immediately after cooking. Dry at 130-140° F (54-60° C) *until a test strip cracks but does not break when it is bent.* Jerky can be dried in the sun, oven, smokehouse or dehydrator.

6. Apply smoke if smoky flavor is desired. There is a danger when smoking very thin meat strips with heavy smoke *for too long.* If smoked longer than 60 minutes they might develop an unpleasant bitter flavor. Keep in mind that sausage meat is encased with casings which acts as a barrier to smoke penetration. The casings contain millions of tiny holes which let the smoke in. Thin jerky cuts have no protective barrier and accept smoke rapidly. If smoking temperature is maintained between 130-140° F (54-60° C), there is no difference between smoking and drying and it might be considered one process.

7. Let jerky cool and then place in a plastic bag. Remove air and seal tightly.

A typical jerky brine

Brine 21° SAL	USA	Metric
Water	1 gallon	3.8 liter
Salt	3/4 cup	220 g
Powdered garlic	1 Tbs	8.5 g
Powdered onion	1 Tbs	7.5 g
Sugar	1 Tbs	15 g
Liquid smoke	1/2 tsp	2.5 ml
Notes: Liquid smoke is not needed when natural smoke is provided. This amount of brine is sufficient for 5 lb of meat.		

Liquid smoke. The use of liquid smoke is beneficial when food dehydrators are used since the smoking process can not be performed inside of the unit. In these cases liquid smoke which comes in a variety of flavors can be added to marinade. Liquid smoke is very strong so be careful as *more is not necessarily better*.

Restructured jerky (*made from ground meat*). Making ground meat jerky resembles making sausage.

1. Grind lean meat through 1/4" (6 mm) plate.

2. Add all ingredients to meat and mix together. Adding Cure #1 is a good idea, as it inhibits the growth of pathogenic bacteria. You want the sausage mass to feel sticky, exactly like during making sausages. You may add some water to facilitate mixing and spice distribution. Leave the sausage mass overnight in a refrigerator. Cover the meat.

3. Stuff meat into flat strips using grinder attachments for making jerky or jerky gun. Use a plastic mat that prevents jerky from being easily removed.

4. Preheat oven to 325° F (162° C). Boiling it might break it apart and cooking in a oven or in a smokehouse is the preferred method.

5. Place the ground meat strips on a cookie sheet.

6. Heat to 160° F (72° C) internal meat temperature.

7. Begin dehydrating immediately after cooking. Dry at 130-140° F (54-60° C). Place the strips close together, but not touching. Jerky is done when a test strip cracks but does not break when it is bent. That should take about 8-10 hours.

8. Apply smoke if smoky flavor is desired. If smoking temperature is maintained between 130-140° F (54-60° C), there is no difference between smoking and drying, and it might be considered one process.

9. Let cool and then place in a plastic bag. Remove air and seal tightly.

Jerky made from wild game. Pre-cook wild game to 165° F (74° C). Game meats are often infected with trichinae and other parasites. If the meat will not be cooked, it should be frozen according to the USDA rules. Freezing meat takes care of *trichinae* but will not eliminate bacteria from the meat. The majority of recipes on the Internet do not mention the fact that jerky should be pre-cooked in order to be microbiologically safe. Some of us will refuse to accept this fact and will not cook jerky. Well, there are extra precautions that might be implemented to increase the safety of the product:

- Good manufacturing practices.
- Use at least 2% salt.
- Use sodium nitrite.
- Dry cure meat for jerky.
- If brine is used add acidic ingredients into your marinade.
- Don't make your strips thicker then 1/4". The thinner the strips are, the quicker they will dry.

People who like to decrease the amount of salt or use salt substitutes should pre-cook jerky. Salt prevents the growth of bacteria and helps to draw the moisture out of the meat.

Useful Information

- Ingredients that inhibit the growth of bacteria: salt, soy sauce, sodium nitrite, acidic liquids such as vinegar, lemon juice, ketchup, Worcestershire sauce, teriyaki sauce.
- Jerky strips heated in marinade will dry faster.
- Slice meat with the grain for chewy jerky.
- Slice meat across the grain for a more tender, brittle jerky.
- Be careful when applying liquid smoke as too much may make your product bitter.
- Worcestershire sauce agrees very well with jerky.
- It takes about 4 lbs. of fresh meat to make 1 lb. of dry jerky.
- Commercially produced and vacuum packed jerky can be stored for one year.

- Home made jerky should be refrigerated and should be consumed within 1-2 months. Its flavor will deteriorate in time. It is a good idea to store jerky in reusable plastic bags, removing as much air as possible.
- Dry seasoning mixes are available in a variety of flavors. They can be used as a basic formulation to which you can add additional spices making the project easier.

Procedures for making jerky outlined in this chapter are presented with safety in mind and they are based on the latest USDA requirements. Many people will continue making jerky without precooking meat, the way they have always done it. Whether you would follow them or make jerky in accordance with the USDA regulations is up to you although we strongly believe that safety is the most important step of any meat processing operation.

Pemmican

American Indians refined the process of making jerky further and created the perfect snack called "Pemmican." Pemmican is a naturally produced high energy bar that will last for years. There is a noted absence of pork in recipes and the explanation is that the pigs which came on board of Spanish ships had not been around yet.

Pemmican was made from thin slices of lean meat from large animals such as buffalo, deer, moose, and elk.

- The sliced meat would be dried in the sun or over a fire.
- The dried meat was pounded with a wooden mallet, or ground and shredded between the stones.
- Ground wild berries were mixed with the pulverized meat. Often dried peppermint leaves or wild onions were added for flavor.
- Melted fat and bone marrow grease was added to the mixture.

Originally pemmican was stored in the stomachs or large intestines of slaughtered animals, but later the hot mixture was poured into large buffalo-hide bags (parfleches) and allowed to cool and harden. Indian women made parfleche cases from folded rawhide. Buffalo hide was most commonly used, but as those animals grew scarce, women used elk, moose and later cattle hides. Holes were burned in the hide for rawhide strings to be threaded through that were used to open and close the bag. Paint for decoration was obtained from European traders. The bags were filled with hot tallow (melted fat).

They were generously greased along their seams to keep out air and moisture. As a result the containers were sealed and a huge vacuum bag was created which protected the product and kept it fresh for years. Before serving, the chunk of pemmican was chopped off with an axe and eaten raw or boiled. The Hudson Bay Company that had a monopoly on the fur trade in Canada for a few hundred years did a lot of trade with the Indians and pemmican was one of popular items.

Original Pemmican - The Perfect Snack & Survival Food		
Meat - 50%	Fat - 50%	Dried fruit & berries
Provided protein for sustaining muscles and body functions.	Provided calories that were needed for energy.	Provided vitamins which were so crucial in preventing scurvy.

How much dried fruit was added is a matter of speculation. It was probably added in the summer when widely available. European settlers started to add fruit and berries in larger quantities as flavoring. Pemmican became a perfect food for people on the move who needed high caloric food or were traveling in wilderness areas where food was not readily available. Today's health conscious consumer might say that it contained 50% fat. Well, every time we buy a fresh sausage in a supermarket it also contains 50% of fat, as allowed by the law. The manufacturer is adding fat all the way up to the allowed amount because fat is much cheaper than lean meat. Take note that a commercially produced sausage contains many chemicals which were not added to pemmican. Pork fat is not the best choice for making pemmican due to its low melting point. Beef fat (tallow) when cooled resembles candle wax in color and consistency and makes better pemmican.

Biltong

Biltong is South African dried meat. In 1652 the Dutch settlers came to the Cape of Good Hope and established a new country. The name biltong originates from the Dutch word Bil meaning buttock and Tong meaning strip. Biltong is not "beef jerky" and it is made by salting, spicing and curing selected cuts of beef, venison, kudu, springbok or ostrich.

Procedure	Jerky	Biltong
Heat applied	Yes	No
Vinegar	No	Yes
Smoked	Optional	No
Air dried	Yes	Yes
Note: biltong cuts are usually bigger and thicker than jerky. If you live in a warm, moist climate cut your strips of meat thin. The thicker the meat, the longer it will take to dry out, and the higher the risk to spoilage.		

A home made biltong will usually be made from the beef buttock. Great cuts are sirloin and steaks cut from the hip such as topside or silverside. The best biltong is made from the eye of the round muscles that run down both sides of the backbone. Ideally the meat is marinated in a vinegar solution (cider vinegar is traditional but balsamic also works very well) for a few hours, and finally poured off before the meat is flavoured. *Coriander* is the dominant spice.

Drying equipment. Drying jerky presents less of a problem than drying salami as the strips are much smaller and can be dried fast. Controlling humidity is not an issue. Quality salami has to dry slow in order to give time for flavor forming bacteria to react with proteins and fats. Jerky flavor is set by meat quality and the marinade. You can dry meat strips in a dehydrator, kitchen oven with the pilot light on, in the open air or in boxes and improvised containers. When drying jerky outside, cover openings with porch plastic screening fabric that is cheap, comes in a roll and can be easily cut. This will keep insects away. Remember to make holes at the bottom and the top of the box to create a natural draft. The bigger the height difference between the bottom and top holes, the stronger the draft.

You can build the wooden frame with supports for drying racks and hanging sticks and cover the sides and top with screening fabric. For starters even a cardboard box will do. If electricity is available you can place a light bulb (60 - 100 W) in the bottom to supply heat. Make a little shield over the light as the dripping grease might burst into flames. A little computer fan (described in the chapter on fermented sausages) will provide ample ventilation.

Beef Jerky
(*Traditional method*)

Meat	Metric	US
Beef	1000 g	2.20 lb.

Instructions:

1. Pre-freeze meat to be made into jerky so it will be easier to slice.
2. Cut partially thawed meat into long slices about ¼" thick and an inch or two wide. For tender jerky, cut at right angles to long muscles (across the grain). Remove visible fat to help prevent off-flavors.
3. Prepare marinade of your choice in a large sauce pan.

Sample marinade for 1 kg (2.2 lb) meat:

soy sauce	80 ml	⅓ cup
Worcestershire sauce	15 ml	1 Tbs.
powdered garlic	2.8 g	1 tsp.
black pepper	2.0 g	2 tsp.
dried juniper berries, crushed	1.5 g	1 tsp.

4. Pour marinade over the meat and marinate jerky 12-24 hours. Overhaul jerky pieces at least once.
5. Dry at 140-150° F (60-66° C) in dehydrator, oven or smoker. You can apply smoke for 30 minutes at this stage.
Test for doneness by letting a piece cool. When cool, it should crack but not break when bent.
6. Refrigerate and when cool check again for doneness. If necessary, dry further.

Notes:

If there is no dehydrator available, use traditional methods of drying:

- In the open air-use a fine screen to protect jerky from insects.
- In the attic - use a fine screen to protect jerky from insects.
- In the kitchen range using a pilot light only.

Using above methods jerky should be thoroughly dried in 3-4 days.

This traditional method of making jerky is not recommended by the USDA. The USDA current recommendation for making jerky safely is to heat meat to 160° F (72° C) *before the dehydrating process.*

Biltong

Meat	Metric	US
beef (London Broil)	1000 g	2.20 lb.

Ingredients per 1000 g (1 kg) of meat:

salt	23 g	4 tsp.
Cure #1	5.0 g	1 tsp.
brown sugar	10 g	2 tsp.
black pepper	6.0 g	3 tsp.
coriander, coarsely ground	10 g	5 tsp.

Instructions:

1. Cut the meat with the grain. When you cut the meat, remember that the finished product will be at least 50% smaller than the original cut.
2. Soak strips for 2 hours in vinegar. Remove strips and pat them dry.
3. Mix all ingredients together and sprinkle the mix on both sides of the meat. Make sure the ingredients are rubbed into the meat strips. Place strips in a covered container or plastic bag and leave for 12 hours in refrigerator.
4. Dry biltong strips. Depending on a method that might take from 4 hours to 4 days.
5. Keep in a dry, well ventilated area. To store longer, place biltong in a plastic bag and keep in refrigerator or a freezer.

Photo 24.1 Biltong.

Pastirma

Pastırma or bastırma is a highly seasoned, air-dried cured beef that is produced and consumed in a wide area of Eastern Europe and the Middle East. Though beef is the most common meat today, various meats are also used, including camel, pork, lamb, goat, and water buffalo, with camel being the most prized.

Pastırma is prepared by salting the meat, then washing it with water and letting it dry for 10-15 days. The blood and salt is then squeezed out of the meat which is then covered with a cumin paste prepared with crushed cumin, fenugreek, garlic, and hot paprika, followed by thorough air-drying. Depending on the variety of the paprika, it can be very spicy but not quite as hot as, for example, hot chili.

Meat	Metric	US
beef	1000 g	2.20 lb.

Ingredients per 1000 g (1 kg) of meat:

salt	25 g	4 tsp.
Cure #2	5.0 g	1 tsp.
fenugreek seeds	26 g	7 tsp.
cumin	4.0 g	2 tsp.
garlic, powdered	6.0 g	2 tsp.
black pepper	2.0 g	1 tsp.
red pepper	2.0 g	1 tsp.

Instructions:
1. Cut meat into 8 x 3 x 2" slices.
2. Mix salt with Cure #2 and rub the mixture into the meat.
3. Sprinkle some salt in a container and place meat slices on top of one another, separating them with salt. Place a wooden board on top of them and put a weight on top. *Pastırma is a noun derived from the verb pastırmak (bastırmak in modern Turkish), which means "to press".*
4. Keep for 1 week in refrigerator.
5. Remove meat from the refrigerator and wash with water. Brush off the surface of any salt. Place again in a container for 1 more day, covering meat with a weighted board. This will drain more liquid away.
6. Mix all ingredients adding 1 tsp of salt. Add a little water and make the mixture into a paste (known as *çemen*).
7. Cover the meat with the paste and hang in a dry, well ventilated area (50-59° F (10-15° C), 60% humidity). You can use hooks or netting. After about 5 days the paste has dried and Pastirma is ready although it may be further dried.

Pemmican

Meat	Metric	US
dry beef jerky	500 g	1.10 lb.
beef suet	500 g	1.10 lb.

Ingredients per 1000 g (1 kg) of meat:

raisins, dry cherries, blueberries, cranberries	1 cup

Instructions:

1. Chop jerky very finely with a knife or grind in a blender to a powder.
2. Grind/chop other ingredients and mix with pulverized jerky.
3. Mix jerky powder with powdered fruits.
4. Cut the fat (suet, also known as tallow) into chunks and melt down over *low heat,* until it becomes a yellow-brown liquid. Continue to heat, stirring often, until more moisture is removed. Strain it through the filter to remove any impurities and allow to cool - it will become white.
5. Reheat tallow over low heat and pour over jerky-fruit mixture. The tallow should be cool enough to touch but still liquid.
6. Place warm pemmican into suitable molds to make blocks or bars. If pemmican solidifies too fast, you can warm it up again in a microwave.
7. Wrap it up in wax paper or store in plastic bags.

Notes: to make pemmican from ground meat, double grind *lean* meat through a small plate. Spread it out thinly on a cookie sheet and dry (*don't cook*) at 180° F (82° C) overnight until crispy. Break it into powder in a blender.

Another option is to have the butcher slice meat as thin as possible and then to dry it overnight. Then powder these dehydrated strips in a blender.

A good combination is: 4 cups dried meat, 3 cups dried fruit (berries, apricots, apples, currents, 1 cups rendered beef fat. Unsalted nuts and honey are sometimes added.

Venison Jerky

Meat	Metric	US
venison	1000 g	2.20 lb.

Ingredients per 1000 g (1 kg) of meat:
Marinade:

soy sauce	80 ml	⅓ cup
Worcestershire sauce	15 ml	1 Tbs.
powdered garlic	2.8 g	1 tsp.
black pepper	2.0 g	2 tsp.
dried juniper berries, crushed	1.5 g	1 tsp.

Instructions:
1. Cut meat into strips about ¼" (6 mm) thick.
2. Bring the marinade to a full boil over medium heat.
3. Add a few meat strips, making sure there is enough marinade to cover them. Reheat to a full boil.
4. Remove quickly meat strips and place on a drying screen.
5. Repeat steps 3 & 4 until all meat strips have been precooked.
6. Dry at 140° F (60° C) in dehydrator, oven or smoker. You can apply smoke for 30 minutes at this stage.
7. Cool a sample piece of jerky and bend it. It should crack but not break.
8. When done, place jerky in a plastic bag and refrigerate.

Notes:
1 tsp. of liquid smoke may be added to marinade for a smoky flavor.

Chapter 25

Poultry

When overcooked, most meats will have an inferior taste, but poultry is particularly vulnerable because it is so lean. Fortunately, soaking birds in brine helps to produce a moister, juicier product.

Making Brine

Brine is a solution of water and salt. A sweetener such as brown or white sugar, molasses, honey, maple-flavored sugar, or corn sugar may be added to the solution for flavor. The salt has two effects on poultry, reports Dr. Alan Sams, a professor of poultry science at Texas A & M University. "It dissolves protein in muscle, and the salt and protein reduce moisture during cooking. This makes the meat juicier, more tender, and improves the flavor. The low levels of salt enhance the other natural flavors of poultry."

Curing and smoking imparts a unique, delicate flavor and pink color to poultry meat and increases its storage life. Mild cures with relatively low salt content are used in preparation for smoking to maintain the poultry flavor. A light smoke will add to the delicate flavor of the poultry, a heavy smoke will add flavor similar to smoked red-meat products. Poultry is cured by a wet method using mild cure. It is very easy to end up with a product that is too salty. One of the reasons is that the brine is prepared as if poultry were a piece of ham and no consideration is given to the fact that a large part of any bird consists of bones.

The bones are not going to absorb any salt so the curing times need to be shorter. It is safer to brine on the low end of the time range on the first attempt and keep notes for future reference. You can always brine longer the next time if required. To prepare a brine dissolve salt in cold water by mixing it thoroughly (salt dissolves much faster in hot water than in cold water). Cover and refrigerate before adding poultry.

The FSIS (Food Safety and Inspection Service) of the USDA (United States Department of Agriculture) recommends: *"To prepare a brine solution for poultry, add ¾ cup salt to 1 gallon of water, or 3 tablespoons of salt per quart of water. For best flavor use sodium chloride-table salt".*

Taking this as common table salt (non-iodized) works out as ¾ of a cup equals 219 g (0.49 lb.). This in turn works out to be a brine concentration of 5.55 % or salinometer reading of **21**. A noted expert on sausage making and meat curing, Parson Snows, recommends 1 part table salt to 16 parts water.

$1/1+16 = 1/17 = 0.0588$ (5.88%)

Using the ratio of 1 lb. of salt per 16 lbs of water (1.92 US gallons) or 0.52 lbs. of salt per US gallon of water equals a brine concentration of 5.88 % or a salinometer reading of **22.5** degrees.

Rytek Kutas presents the following formula in his book:

> 5 gal. water
> 2 lbs. salt
> 1 lb. Cure # 1 (there is 0.93 lb. salt in it)
> 1 ½ lbs. powdered dextrose

and that equals a brine concentation of 6.5% or a salinometer reading of **25** degrees (salt present in Cure #1 is included in calculations).

Dr. Estes Reynolds, a brining expert at the University of Georgia recommends using 9.6 ozs of salt for every US gallon of water for products that brine longer than several hours. This works out to be a brine concentration of 6.68% or a salinometer reading of **25** degrees. There are many sources that recommend using 1 lb of salt to 1 gallon of water. This works out a brine concentration of 10.71% or a salinometer reading of **40** degrees which is rather high if the bird will be brined for more than a few hours.

*With salt everyone's tastes are different, but it can be concluded that any salinometer reading between 17 and 26 degrees will work out fine with the **21 – 22** degrees being in the middle of the safe range. It should be noted that the higher salinometer reading, the saltier the brine.*

Products that are going to be smoked at low temperatures (below 200°
F, 93° C) need Cure # 1 to be added to the brine. Cure #1 contains
93.75 % of salt which has to be taken under consideration. Using ½
cup of salt and 3 oz. of Cure #1 for 1 gallon of water we obtain a brine
concentration of 5.6 % which corresponds to a salometer reading of
21 degrees.

A typical brine solution (with Cure #1) at 21 degrees salometer
reading:

> 1 gal. of cold water
> ½ cup (146 g) of salt
> 3 oz. (85 g) of Cure #1 – corresponds to 79 g of pure salt
> 3 oz. (85 g) sugar (brown or white).

A typical brine solution (no Cure #1 added) at 21 degrees salometer
reading:

> 1 gal. of cold water
> ¾ cup of salt
> 3 oz. (85 g) sugar (brown or white)

Curing time depends on the size of the bird:

Cornish Game Hens	1 - 2 hours
Chicken Pieces	2 – 4 hours
Whole Chickens (2 lbs.)	1 day
Whole Chickens (4 lbs.)	1 - 2 days
Turkey Breast	4 – 8 hours
Whole Turkeys (up to 10 lbs.)	1 - 2 days
Whole Turkey (over 10 lbs.)	2 - 3 days
A Very Large Turkey	4 - 5 days

To shorten curing time, poultry may be pumped with a brine mixture
in an amount equivalent to 10% of the bird's weight. A 10 lb turkey
should receive 1 lb of brine. Birds weighing less than 3 lb don't need
to be pumped and can be immersed in a brine mixture.

The poultry should now be placed in a stainless steel, clay or food
grade plastic container and covered fully with the remaining brine
(use weight plate if needed). It should be placed in the refrigerator
or in case the container is too large, ice should be added periodically
to the brine if the temperature goes over 40° F (4° C). Added ice
should be taken under consideration if we want to maintain the proper
proportion of ingredients in the brine.

Draining and Drying

After curing, the poultry should be rinsed in cold tap water for 5 minutes to remove any crystalized salt from its surface, then it should be left to drain. Poultry holds its shape after hanging in a smoker for many hours and it will look like a bat with spread wings and legs. To retain its original shape it should be placed in a stockinette bag.

Smoking

When the birds are dry or tacky to touch, they should be placed in a pre-heated smoker. Keep the damper wide open to allow moisture to escape. Once the birds feel dry, leave the damper in ¼ open position and smoke at 130° F (54° C) for about five hours. Then continue smoking slowly raising the temperature to 165-170° F (74-77° C) and hold until the inside temperature in the thickest part of the breast is 165° F (74° C). You could insert a thermometer close to the ball and socket joint of the thigh as this is also the last place the meat becomes fully cooked. If the thermometer is not available, you can check the turkey by twisting the leg slightly. If it moves easily, the cooking is done. Small birds like cornish game hens or small chicken will need shorter smoking and cooking times.

And be careful when making stuffing. Let's follow a beautifully presented scenario on stuffing a turkey from the 1984 classic "The Great Sausage Recipes and Meat Curing" by Rytek Kutas.

"The well-intentioned cook decides to make the dressing for the turkey the night before. This gives her more time to do many other important things the next day. She stuffs the turkey the night before, and places it in the refrigerator to be cooked the next day. Unfortunately, she doesn't know she is creating ideal conditions for food poisoning. Obviously, the stuffing that she put into the turkey is somewhere between 40° and 140° F. Because the various parts of dressing have some liquid in them, the moisture is also there. Lastly, she sews up the turkey to create a lack of oxygen in its cavity".

It is that simple to create food poisoning. You can make turkey stuffing a day earlier, just make sure it is left in a refrigerator.

Sodium nitrite (Cure #1) in the brine will cause the poultry meat to become pink when it is smoked. Keep in mind that nitrite cured meats develop a characteristic cured meat flavor and poultry will taste *ham-like.* To smoke turkey without Cure #1 higher temperatures are needed to eliminate food poisoning (botulism) that Cure #1 prevents.

The turkey should be placed in a smoker preheated to 180° F (82° C) for at least one hour. Then the temperature should be increased to 200-225° F (93-108° C) and smoke is introduced. The turkey breast should be smoked/cooked to an internal temperature of 165° F (74° C). We are now smoking/baking the turkey without worrying about food poisoning.

Duck and Goose

Duck and goose are more fatty than turkey and they taste very good when smoked. Follow procedures for smoking turkey.

Poultry Sausages

Making poultry sausages follows the same manufacturing procedure as production of other sausages: meat selection, curing, grinding, stuffing, smoking, cooking, cooling and storing.

The most popular meats on the market are:

- Chicken.
- Turkey.
- Duck.
- Goose.

This does not necessarily mean that chicken meat is superior to goose. Chicken occupies the # 1 spot as it is the most *profitable* poultry to raise. It needs less feed than other poultry types, its meat contains little fat and the bird is popular all over the world due to its egg producing capabilities. Everybody has eaten chicken in his life hundreds of times but how many times have we eaten a goose or a duck? The basic raw product is boned poultry meat. In addition to the ground meat, the stuffing often includes pork fat, eggs, butter and spices. About 2% starch is often added.

Chicken. Trying to make a sausage *from chicken meat only* presents some problems: high pH, high Aw and that means favorable conditions for bacteria growth. *Campylobacter jejuni* is a typical pathogen found in poultry meat. Chicken fat contains more water and less collagen structure than other fats which makes it soft and semi-liquid at room temperature due to its low melting point. When submitted to heat treatment, chicken fat will melt inside the sausage creating oily pockets and make the sausage seem like a fat product. For those reasons pork fat should be added to a sausage, but it can not be classified as an all chicken sausage anymore.

Chicken	Cheap, contains little fat, available everywhere.	High pH: breast 5.6-5.8, thigh 6.1-6.4. Poor fat characteristics, very low fat melting point temperature. Low myoglobin content (light meat, especially breast) results in a poor final color. Skin often contains a large number of pathogenic bacteria.

Turkey. Turkey is inexpensive and it has the biggest breast of all poultry. Turkey breast is a great cut for smoking. Being very lean, the breast should be pumped with curing solution. Other parts and turkey trimmings can be used for sausages.

Goose and Duck. These birds are much fatter, especially the skin which contains a lot of attached fat. As skin contains a lot of collagen, it can bind water and emulsify fats very well. Meats from those birds will make good sausages, in addition goose and duck livers are superior material for making liver sausages.

It is not recommended to make poultry fresh sausages (uncooked) as fresh poultry does not keep well. Although fermented sausages can be made from poultry why not use much better meats such as pork or beef. Poultry meat is fine for making emulsified sausages that would be cooked in water. The best example is a variety of poultry hotdogs and frankfurters that are carried in our supermarkets.

A basic 1 kg formula for emulsified poultry meat:

ground poultry meat	450 g
poultry skins	250 g
poultry fat	100 g
non-fat dry milk	30 g
salt	18 g
Cure #1	2.5 g
crushed ice (cold water)	150 g
spices - as you like	

A typical manufacturing process:

1. Grind meat through ⅛" (3 mm) plate.
2. Grind skins twice through a small plate ⅛" (3 mm).
3. Place ground skins in a food processor and emulsify, adding ½ ice/water. Add salt, Cure#1, all spices, ground meat and emulsify adding remaining ice/water.
4. Stuff into natural or synthetic casings.

5. Hang for 1 hour at room temperature.
6. Place in a preheated to 120-130° F (50-54° C) smokehouse.
7. If casings are dry apply hot smoke at about 150-160° F (66-72° C).
8. Cook in water at 176° F (80° C) until meat internal temperature reaches 165° F (74° C). Depending on a diameter of the casing that might take 15-120 minutes. A rule of thumb calls for 10 min for each 1 cm (10 mm) of the casing.
9. Cool in cold water until sausage temperature reaches 68-86° F (20-30° C). Dry in air to evaporate moisture.
10. Store in refrigerator.

Smoked Chicken

Materials: 1 chicken, 3 celery stalks, 1 bunch of green parsley

Instructions:

1. Prepare 21° SAL curing brine: 1 gal of water, 154 g (5.43 oz), 4 Tbsp Cure #1. This comes to about 221 g of salt total.

Note: * the amount of salt in Cure #1 (67 g) has been accounted for when calculating brine strength.
2. Immerse chicken for 18 hours in curing solution.
3. Remove the chicken from the curing solution and drain.
4. Stuff fully the chicken with parsley and celery.
5. Place chicken in 194° F (90° C) water. Pepper corns, bay leaf and wholespice may be added. Hold at that temperature for 10 minutes and then lower water temperature to 176° F (80° C). Cook at this temperature until the breast reaches 165° F (74° C) internal temperature. The chicken is fully cooked.
6. Carefully remove the chicken from the water, and place on a screen to drain and cool down to 77° F (25° C). Remove the parsley and celery. Save meat stock for soup.

Smoking
7. When chicken feels dry apply cold smoke at 64-77° F (18-25° C) for 4 hours.

Chicken Sausage

Chicken sausage is made from all chicken meat and then it is smoked and poached.

Meat	Metric	US
Chicken breast	400 g	0.88 lb.
Chicken legs	400 g	0.88 lb.
Chicken fat and skins	200 g	0.44 lb.

Ingredients per 1000 g (1 kg) of meat:

salt	18 g	3 tsp.
Cure #1	2.5 g	½ tsp.
pepper	2.0 g	1 tsp.
garlic	3.5 g	1 clove
cold water	100 ml	⅜ cup

Instructions:
1. Grind meats 3/16" plate (5 mm). Grind skins and fat through 1/8" (3 mm) plate. Refreeze skins and fat and grind again. You can emulsify them in food processor adding a little cold water.
2. Mix ground meats and fat with all ingredients adding cold water.
3. Stuff firmly into 32-36 mm hog casings. Leave in a continuous coil.
4. Hold for one hour at room temperature.
5. When sausages feel dry apply hot smoke 60-70° C (140-158° F) for about 120 minutes until brown color develops.
6. Poach at 176° F (80° C) until the meat reaches 160° F (72° C) internal temperature. This will take about 40 minutes.
7. Cool in cold water for 5 minutes and then continue cooling in the air.
8. Keep in a refrigerator.

Duck Sausage

Duck sausage is made from duck meat, pork and beef. Other poultry meats such as turkey or chicken breasts may be substituted for duck meat.

Meat	Metric	US
Duck meat	250 g	0.51 lb.
Duck fat	100 g	0.22 lb.
Pork, semi-fat	400 g	0.88 lb.
Beef	250 g	0.51 lb.

Ingredients per 1000 g (1 kg) of meat:

salt	18 g	3 tsp.
Cure #1	2.5 g	½ tsp.
pepper	2.0 g	1 tsp.
allspice	2.0 g	1 tsp.
coriander	2.0 g	1 tsp.
marjoram	1.0 g	⅔ tsp.
cold water	100 ml	3.3 oz fl.

Instructions:

1. Grind meats 3/16" plate (5 mm). Grind partially frozen fat through 1/8" (3 mm) plate. Refreeze and grind again.
2. Mix ground meats and fat with all ingredients adding 100 ml (3.3 oz fl) of cold water.
3. Stuff firmly into 32-36 mm hog casings. Leave in a continuous coil or make 1 foot (30 cm) links.
4. Hold for one hour at room temperature.
5. When sausages feel dry apply hot smoke 140-158° F (60-70° C) for about 120 minutes until brown color develops.
6. Poach at 176° F (80° C) until the meat reaches 160° F (72° C) internal temperature. This process will take about 40 minutes.
7. Shower or immerse in cold water for 5 minutes and then continue cooling in the air.
8. Keep in a refrigerator.

Goose Sausage

Goose sausage. This sausage is made from goose meat only.

Meat	Metric	US
Goose meat	700 g	1.54 lb.
Goose skins	200 g	0.44 lb.
Goose fat	100 g	0.22 lb.

Ingredients per 1000 g (1 kg) of meat:

salt	18 g	3 tsp.
white pepper	2.0 g	1 tsp.
cayenne pepper	0.5 g	⅓ tsp.
non-fat dry milk	40 g	1.5 oz.
cold water	100 ml	⅜ cup

Instructions:
1. Grind meat through 3/16" plate (5 mm). Refreeze and grind again. Grind skins through 3/16" (5 mm) plate and again through 1/8" (3 mm) plate.
2a. Place ground meat and skins in a food processor. Add ⅓ water and emulsify. Add poultry fat, salt and other ingredients including remaining ice cold water and emulsify everything together.
2b. If no food processor is available - grind fat through 1/8" (3 mm) plate. Mix ground meat, skins and fat with all ingredients adding 120 ml (½ cup) cold water.
3. Stuff loosely into 26-28 mm sheep casings forming 4" (10 cm) links. Hang for 30 min at room temperature.
4. Poach in water at 176° F (80° C) until internal meat temperature reaches 160° F (72° C). This process will take about 30 minutes.
5. Place in cold water for 5 minutes, then continue cooling in air.
6. Keep in a refrigerator or freeze for later use.

Notes:
Goose skins contain twice as much fat as chicken.
Non fat dry milk is used to bind water and meats together. Skins increase water holding capacity. Add water slowly to food processor. The color of the sausage will be light gray. If a pink color is desired, add 2.5 g (½ tsp.) of Cure #1.

Lithuanian Smoked Goose

Cold smoked goose or duck are delicious products that have always been popular in East-Northern Europe.

Meat	Metric	US
Goose breast, boneless and skinless	1000 g	2.2 lb.

Ingredients per 1000 g (1 kg) of meat:

salt	45 g	1.58 oz.
Cure #1	5.0 g	1 tsp.
pepper	4.0 g	2 tsp.
coriander	4.0 g	2 tsp.
cloves	1.0 g	½ tsp.
bay leaf, crushed		1 leaf

Instructions:

1. Mix salt, Cure#1 and all ingredients together. Rub the mix into breasts.
2. Place breasts in a container, sprinkle with any remaining mix and place a weight on top. Place container for 2 weeks in refrigerator.
3. Overhaul breasts every 2 days.
4. Remove breasts from the container and wipe off dry. Place in a stockinette bag and hang in a cool ventilated area for 12 hours.
5. Cold smoke at 64° F (18° C) for 7 days. Smoking does not have to be continuous, but the temperature must be maintained at 18° C.
6. The product can be stored for a few months in a dark, cool and lightly ventilated place.

Poultry Liver Sausage

Meat	Metric	US
Goose or other poultry meat	550 g	1.21 lb.
Goose or other poultry livers	150 g	0.33 lb.
poultry hearts and gizzards	150 g	0.33 lb.
Pork jowls or belly	150 g	0.33 lb.

Ingredients per 1000 g (1 kg) of meat:

salt	18 g	3 tsp.
Cure #1	2.5 g	½ tsp.
white pepper	2.0 g	1 tsp.
marjoram	2.0 g	1 tsp.
onion, chopped	30 g	½ onion
semolina flour	120 g	1 cup

Instructions:

1. Scald livers with hot water (do not boil).
2. Place all meats (except livers) in hot water and simmer below boiling point until semi-soft.
3. Grind all meats, liver and onions through ⅛" (3 mm) plate at least twice.
4. Mix everything with salt, pepper and semolina flour until smooth. Food processor will make it easier.
5. Stuff mixture into natural or synthetic fibrous casings.
6. Cook in water at 176° F (80° C) until meat internal temperature reaches 160° F (72° C). Depending on a diameter of the casing that might take 15-120 minutes. A rule of thumb calls for 10 min for each 1 cm (10 mm) of the casing.
7. Cool in cold water until sausage temperature reaches 68-86° F (20-30° C).
8. Optional: cold smoke at 64° F (18° C) for 2-3 hours.
9. Store in refrigerator.

Smoked Turkey

Instructions:

1. Make 21° SAL brine:

> 1 gal. of cold water
> ½ cup (146 g) of salt
> 3 oz. (85 g) of Cure #1*
> 3 oz. (85 g) sugar (brown or white).

If you need mor brine, for example 3 gallons, multiply above figures by 3.

2. Make sure that both the turkey and the brine are cold. Place large turkey in brine for 4-5 days,

OR

pump the turkey with brine using 10% meat pump (20 lb. turkey is pumped with 2 lbs. of brine). Place in brine for 2 days.

3. Wash the turkey with cold water, stuff into stockinette bag and hang in pre-heated to 130° F (54° C) smokehouse until dry. Keep dampers wide open. This drying process might take 2-3 hours.

4. When the bird feels dry apply hot smoke at 140° F (60° C) for about 5 hours. You may start raising the temperature slowly during the second half of the smoking process.

5. Raise smokehouse temperature to 170° F (77° C) and hold until the breast reaches 165° F (74° C) internal temperature. Raise the temperature of the smokehouse higher if needed.

6. Remove from the smokehouse and cool down.

Note: * the amount of salt in Cure #1 (79 g) has been accounted for when calculating brine strength.

Turkey Sausage

Turkey sausage can be made from turkey meat and pork back fat. Pork and beef trimmings may also be added.

Meat	Metric	US
Turkey breast	600 g	1.32 lb.
Turkey trimmings or other meats		
(pork, beef),	200 g	0.44 lb.
Pork back fat or		
fat pork trimmings,	200 g	0.44 lb.

Ingredients per 1000 g (1 kg) of meat:

salt	18 g	3 tsp.
white pepper	2.0 g	1 tsp.
paprika	2.0 g	1 tsp.
nutmeg	1.0 g	½ tsp.
garlic	3.5 g	1 clove
cold water	80 ml	⅓ cup

Instructions:
1. Grind meats and fat through 3/16" plate (5 mm). Refreeze and grind again.
2. Mix ground meats and fat with all ingredients adding 80 ml (⅓ cup) of cold water.
3. Stuff loosely into 50-60 mm fibrous casings forming 1 foot (30 cm) links.
4. Poach in water at 176° F (80° C) until internal meat temperature reaches 160° F (72° C). This process will take about 60 minutes.
5. Place in cold water for 5 minutes, then cool in the air.
6. Keep in a refrigerator or freeze for later use.

Notes:
The color of the sausage will be light gray. If a typical pink color is desired, add 2.5 g (½ tsp.) of Cure #1, then hang for 1 hour at room temperature. If meat can absorb more than 80 ml of water, add more. This will depend how much pork and beef (if any) will be used.

Chapter 26

Fish

Fish has always played a very important part in our diet being a precious commodity especially in areas without direct access to water. For those reasons the preservation played the main role and the taste was less important. Preservation was achieved by storing heavily salted fish in barrels where they were kept for months at the time. Caravans were able to move salted fish large distances and all the consumer had to do was to soak the fish in water to remove excess salt. Another technique relied on air drying to remove moisture from the meat thus eliminating favorable conditions for the growth of bacteria. Smoking fish was also effective as it prevented some bacteria from growing and removed moisture at the same time.

Most of the bacteria in the fish is present in the slime that covers the body of the fish and in its digestive tract. There are two reasons that fish spoils faster than other meat :

1. Its meat contains more water (bacteria need moisture)

Beef	-	60%	water
Veal, poultry	-	66%	water
Fat fish	-	70%	water
Lean fish	-	80%	water

2. Its meat contains very little salt (salt inhibits growth of bacteria). Both freshwater and saltwater fish have very low salt content in their meat (0.2-0.7% of salt).

Heavy salting of the fish is practiced today only in most undeveloped nations and everywhere else we strive to give fish the best taste and flavor. And there is no doubt whatsoever that smoked fish tastes the best. Fish like other meats can be smoked by different smoking methods and the taste and shelf life will depend on smoke temperature and the length of smoking. All fish may be smoked, but the fatty ones absorb smoke better, stay moister during smoking and taste better.

Fat content of different fish: lean fish < 2.5%, medium fat fish 2.5 – 6.5%, fat fish > 6.5%.

The same species of fish, depending where they live (Europe, Atlantic or Pacific Ocean), may have a significantly different fat content in their flesh. **Lean fish:** cod, flounder, grouper, haddock, hake, halibut, perch, pike, pollock, porgies, rockfish, snake eels, snapper, soles, tuna, whitting. **Fat fish:** bluefish, carp, freshwater eels, herring, mackerel, mullet, sablefish, salmon, shad, trout, and whitefish.

The process of smoking fish consists of the following stages: cleaning/washing → brining → drying → smoking → cooking → storing.

Cleaning Fish

Photo 26.1 A proper set up is crucial for processing many fish. Water hose, brush, sharp knife, container and plenty of ice.

The scales will fly everywhere so it is recommended to perform this operation either outside or inside a large clear plastic bag. Make note that the fish which will be smoked does not need its scales to be removed. After cleaning, the fish has to be washed again. Previously frozen fish can be thawed, then brined and smoked.

Small fish are not filleted, but only gutted and cleaned on the outside. The gills and all traces of blood are removed, especially the bloody kidney line along the back of the fish. Then depending on the size, the fish is either cut across into 2" pieces, filleted or hung in one piece. The flesh of fish is delicate by nature and they have to be handled gently when hanging them on smokesticks or hooks. There are a few commonly used methods of securing fish for smoking:

- Placing fillets or smaller pieces of fish on a screen, making sure they don't touch each other. Place small fish pieces on smoking screens right from the begining of the drying process. Brush screens lightly with oil to prevent sticking of the fish.

- Inserting sharp pointed sticks through fish gills.

- Inserting "S" shaped hooks through the gills of the fish and hanging them on smoking sticks.

- Nailing fish directly to smoke sticks.

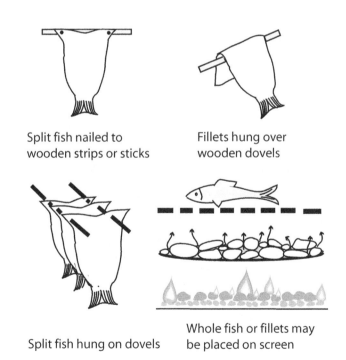

Split fish nailed to wooden strips or sticks

Fillets hung over wooden dovels

Split fish hung on dovels

Whole fish or fillets may be placed on screen

Fig. 26.1 Hanging fillets.

When hanging fillets it is advisable to leave the skin on, otherwise the fillets may break apart.

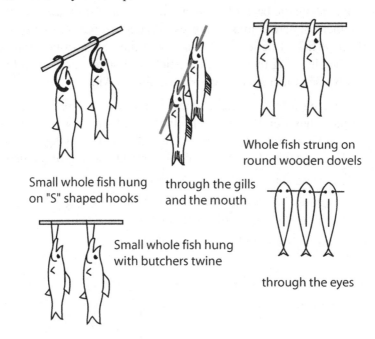

Small whole fish hung on "S" shaped hooks

through the gills and the mouth

Whole fish strung on round wooden dovels

Small whole fish hung with butchers twine

through the eyes

Fig. 26.2 Hanging small fish.

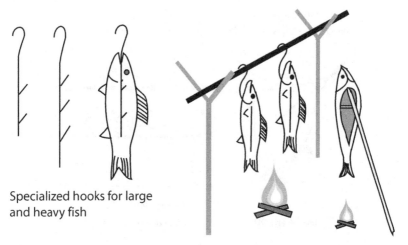

Specialized hooks for large and heavy fish

Fig. 26.3 Hanging large fish.

Fig. 26.4 Smoking over camp fire.

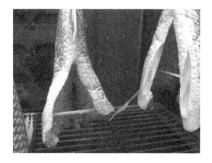

Photo 26.2 A toothpick will keep the belly from collapsing.

Making Brine

Fish that will be smoked must be salted or brined first. The stronger the brine the shorter time of brining. A large fish and fat fish absorb salt slowly. Only fine non-iodized salt should be used as the iodized salt can impart a bitter flavor to the fish. It is recommended to use a brine tester or the brine tables. The fish is normally brined with a heavy brine for the following reasons:

- Its meat contains very little salt and a lot of water. These are the ideal conditions for the development of meat spoiling bacteria.
- Fish is home to an unusually high concentration of bacteria.

Photo 26.3 Making brine.   **Photo 26.4** Testing brine.

A 70-80% brine can be employed for all the common types of fish. By placing fish in a strong degrees brine we are perfoming an all out attack on the bacteria preventing them from growing. Salt penetrates the flesh of fish very rapidly and the brining times are relatively short, between 1 and 2 hours. Brines stronger than 80 degrees can deposit salt crystals on the surface of the fish skin creating unattractive white patches that can be difficult to remove.

Fish brined in 90-100% brine will lose around 3% of its weight. We can get better and more uniform salt penetration if the brining times are longer, but that will require a 40 - 50 degree solution. In such a brine fish may be left overnight, but will pick up about 2-3% of water which will evaporate later during smoking. Brining provides the following advantages:

- Improves the flavor and looks of the fish.
- Improves texture by making flesh much stronger which is important when fish is hung.
- Prevents growth of bacteria.

Salt penetrates fish easier in places that are open or cut than through the skin. A medium size herring should remain in 80 degrees brine for about 4 hours. Fillets need to be submerged in the same brine for only 20-30 minutes.

Brine in degrees at 60° F	salt (gram/liter)	salt (lb/gallon)	% salt by weight
10	26.4	0.22	2.64
20	53.8	0.46	5.28
30	79.2	0.71	7.91
40	105.6	0.98	10.55
50	132.0	1.26	13.19
60	158.4	1.56	15.83
70	184.8	1.88	18.47
80	211.2	2.23	21.11
90	237.6	2.59	23.75
100	264.0	2.98	26.39

A typical 80 degrees brine:

    1 gallon water
    2.25 lbs. salt (4 cups)
    1 lb. brown sugar
    2 Tbs. Cure #1
    1/3 cup lemon juice
    1 Tbs. garlic powder
    1 Tbs. onion powder
    1 Tbs. allspice powder
    1 Tbs. white pepper

One gallon of brine is sufficient for 4 pounds of fish. Other ingredients like sugar and spices should be added to the solution after the correct brine strength has been established. Fish pieces should be completely immersed in brine and covered with a weight plate. The temperature of the brine should not exceed 60° F (15.5° C) at the start of the brining. If the brining time exceeds 4 hours, the solution must be placed in a refrigerator or ice should be added to the brine. Adding ice will change the strength of the brine and a better solution is to add re-usable blue ice packs. Keep in mind that brine loses its strength in time as the water leaves the fish and increases the volume of the original brine. At the same time salt penetrates the meat leaving behind a weaker brine. When brining times are long, the solution's strength should be periodically checked with a brine tester and readjusted accordingly.

Fish like any other meat is susceptible to food poisoning given the right conditions for the development of *C. Botulinum* spores into toxins. Those conditions (lack of oxygen, humidity, temperatures (40-140°F) always exist when smoking meats. Furthermore many times fish will be packed by the Reduced Oxygen Packaging Method that can create favorable conditions for *C.botulinum* to become toxin even after fish was hot smoked and cooked. To eliminate the possibility of such a danger Cure # 1 is added the same way it is used when smoking meats or sausages.

In order to eliminate nitrites (Cure #1) the salt concentration in the water should be high enough to inhibit the growth of *C. botulinum*, without making the product too salty to eat. A minimum concentration of 3% is considered to be effective for hot smoked fish. Also smoking and cooking temperatures should be kept above 180° F (82° C). People on a low salt diet who prefer low salt concentation are advised to include nitrites in the brine.

Brining Times

The brining time depends on the size of the fish and the salt concentration of the brine. Salt penetrates the flesh of the fish within minutes and brining times are much shorter than those for red meats. It is hard to derive time for fish fillets, fish with the skin on, and little fish or pieces of fish. The fish fillet will be oversalted if immersed for the same time in the same brine as a large fish. When brining many types of fish of different sizes use separate containers and classify fish according to its species and size. When using a single container, place small pieces on top so they can be removed earlier.

Brining times for **cold smoking:**

80 degrees brine

½" fillets	-	½ hr
1" fillets	-	1 hr
1 ½" fillets	-	2 hrs

Brining times for **hot smoking:**

80 degrees brine

½" fillets	-	15 min
1" fillets	-	30 min
1 ½" fillets	-	1 hr
whole fish	-	1-2 hours

Photo 26.5 The container may be outside, but notice the ice on top that keeps the brine ice cold.

Hanging/Drying Fish

The characteristic flavor of the fish is mainly due to salt and smoke, but its appearance is greatly influenced by drying. A fish that was properly dried would acquire color much faster and would also develop a better taste.

Photo 26.6 Fish may be patted dry with a paper towel, then left briefly to dry. If insects are present, the fish should be dried out in a pre-heated snokehouse (no smoke applied).

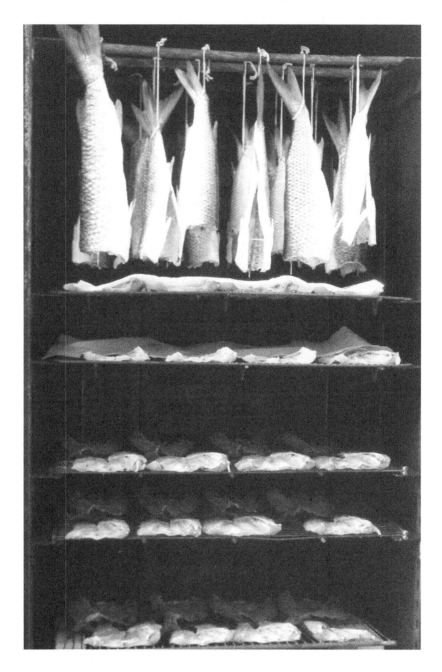

Photo 26.7 Fish drying.

After brining, the fish are carefully rinsed under cold running water to remove salt crystals and any traces of spices. The fish are then placed in a draughty area to develop a type of shiny secondary skin known as "pellicle". This gloss is due to the swelling of the protein caused by the salt in brine. Proteins dissolve in brine and create a sticky exudate on the surface. The longer the brined fish are permitted to hang, the better the gloss that develops. *The best gloss develops with 70-80% brine.* Weaker brines or not salting fish at all leaves smoked fish with a rather dull appearance. The longer hanging time, the better results and a 1 hour period may be considered minimum. For a large fish 12 hours hanging time is not unusual.

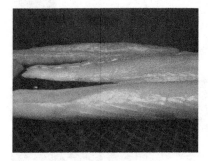
Photo 26.8 Drying fish and developing pellicle.

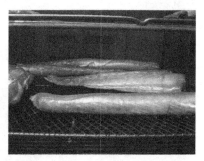
Photo 26.9 Smoked fish with well developed pellicle.

Brine vs. Dry Mix

A question arises as to which method is better; soaking fish in brine, sprinkling them with salt or with one of the commercially prepared seasonings. A better quality is obtained with brine. The fish looks much better and develops a glossy shine on the outside. This is why all commercial producers brine fish before smoking. Smaller establishments such as a fish restaurant or a take out store are very busy and often don't have enough storage space to keep fish in tanks filled with brine. They just sprinkle fish with a dry mix of their choice, and deliver them to a smokehouse. Only salt will penetrate the flesh of the fish, but the spices will remain on the surface. The salt will react with proteins and will produce the exudate which settles on the surface, becoming the pellicle in time. However, in the case of dry mix this exudate will mix with spices and will produce a kind of a paste that coats the surface affecting the shine. The flavor is fine, but the presentation suffers.

Smoking Fish

Cold smoking – fish is smoked below 80° F (26° C) from 1-5 days. If the temperature of the fish flesh exceeds 85° F (30° C) for longer than a few minutes the protein will be coagulated and parts of the fish will be cooked. Such fish will not have the elasticity and texture of the properly cold smoked product. Cold smoked fish is still considered raw meat as it was never submitted to high temperature. That is why it has to be heavily salted or brined at 16% salt (about 65 degrees brine) or higher to provide safety for the consumer.

The longer smoking period, the more moisture is removed (30-50%) and the drier the product becomes with of course a longer shelf life. Its color also changes from gold to brown. This method of smoking can last up to a few weeks and the fish will have excellent keeping qualities. It should be noted that the final product will taste much saltier and its texture will be much harder. After prolonged cold smoking the fish lose enough moisture not to be cooked at all. A typical fish done that way is salmon or sturgeon. Cold smoking requires heavy brine and longer brining times. Fish that were cold smoked hold well together and can be very finely sliced which can not be done if the fish were hot smoked. Because of the time and costs involved this method is rarely used today.

Hot smoking – fish are smoked and cooked at the same time. Hot smoking requires a lighter brine and a smokehouse temperature above 90° F (32° C). The fish are smoked/cooked from one to five hours. The fish can be smoked/baked in 30 minutes when the applied temperature is 300-350° F (150-180° C). Hot smoking is a commonly used method though the final product is tougher and more breakable than the fish that was smoked with cold smoke. Hot smoking is basically performed in three stages:

1. A preliminary smoking/drying period at 86° F (30° C) during which the skin is hardened to prevent breakage. The air dampers are fully open for maximum air flow and moisture removal. This period lasts from 30-60 minutes.

2. A heavy smoke is applied for about 30-45 minutes with the exit smoke damper left at ¼ open position. The temperature is gradually raised to 122° F (50° C).

3. The temperature is raised to 176° F (80° C) and the fish is cooked to 145° F (63° C) internal temperature for a minimum of 30 minutes. Depending on the size of the fish this stage may last from 30–60 minutes. A light smoke may be maintained. When the temperature is raised to 176-194° F (80-90°C) we are smoking/cooking fish until its flesh flakes out easily when pressed with a knife or a fork. Fish is considered done when cooked to 145° F (63° C) internal temperature.

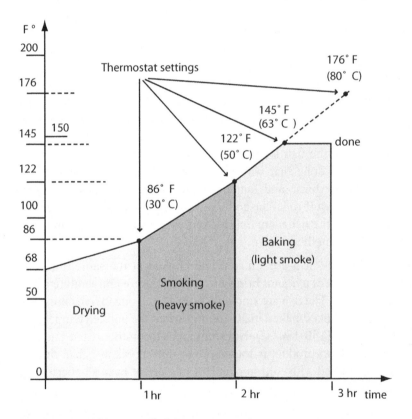

Fig. 26.5 Smoking small fish.

Typical fish fillets smoking times are 4-5 hours depending on the size. When smoking is finished, the fish should be cooled rapidly to the ambient 50° F (10° C), and then to lower temperatures 38° F (3° C) to prevent the growth of microorganisms. This cooling process should be accomplished within 12 hours. Smoking fish is a lot of trial and error and record keeping. Notes should be made for future reference.

Fig. 26.10 Smoking fish.

In the open fire smokehouse, the rear of the chamber is receiving most of the heat and re-arranging smoke sticks is a welcome idea. If the fish feels moist it is a sign that there is too much wet smoke inside and the draft must be open more. The back of the fish or the skin of the fillet should face the back of the smoker. That allows for the better judgment of the fish color and protects the flesh from higher temperatures that are normally found in the back of the smoker. When using a few levels of smokesticks insert the upper row first, then after 5-10 minutes the lower one, then the lowest one. If all three levels were placed in a smokehouse at the same time, the upper most row will get the least of the available heat during drying. On the other hand it will get the most moisture which it will gather from the smokesticks below. Like in any other meat, the proportion of salt in the flesh increases during smoking and cooking because of drying.

Storing

Fish can be eaten immediately after smoking though most people will say that it tastes better when cold. Fish should be wrapped up in wax paper or foil and placed in a refrigerator where it can remain for up to 10 days. To hold it longer we have to freeze it. Freezing fresh fish in a home freezer is not the best idea as it is a relatively slow process. As a result large ice crystals form inside and affect the texture of the flesh making it mushy. Fish that are commercially frozen at much faster times don't exhibit such symptoms.

Fish Flesh Color

Meat color is determined largely by the amount of *myoglobin* a particular animal carries. The more *myoglobin* the darker the meat. To some extent oxygen use can be related to the animal's general level of activity; muscles that are exercised frequently such as the legs need more oxygen. As a result they develop a darker color unlike the breast which is white due to little exercise. Fish float in water and need less muscle energy to support their skeletons.

Most fish meat is white, with some red meat around the fins, tail, and the more active parts of the fish which are used for swimming. Most fish don't have *myoglobin* at all. There are some antarctic cold water fish that have *myoglobin,* but it is confined to the hearts only (flesh of the fish remains white but the heart is of a rosy color). *The red color of some fish, such as salmon and trout, is due to astaxanthin, a naturally occurring pigment in the crustaceans they eat.*

Most salmon we buy is farm raised on a prepared commercial food that even includes antibiotics, its meat is anything but pink. The only reason that farmed raised salmon flesh is pink is that canthaxanthin (colorant) is added to the food the fish eats.

The pink color of smoked meat is due to the nitrite reaction with *myoglobin*. As most of the fish don't have *myoglobin* the meat is not going to be pink and that explains why very few fish recipes include cure. In addition, nitrites are not allowed in all species of fish used for smoking. The Food and Drug Administration currently allows nitrites to be used in salmon, sablefish, shad, chubs, and tuna. Why out of millions of species of fish swimming in the ocean, only five species can be cured with nitrite? What made those fish so special was a question that bothered me for a long time. The letter of inquiry was sent to the Food Safety and Inspection Service to clarify the matter and that was the answer:

"The reason nitrite is approved for use in those species is because someone submitted a petition for its use in those specific fish. Other species can be added through additional petitions."

Fish Sausages

Basic characteristics of fish when used for making sausages:

Cheap raw material. Easy to process. All varieties can be used, including de-boned meat.	Needs to be combined with pork or other meats. No *myoglobin* (white or grayish color). The final flavor is always fishy even when other meats were added.

Fish products and sausages are popular in countries such as the Philippines, Thailand, Malaysia, Japan, and China. The products are often made into fermented fish paste and fish sauce which are used for general cooking.

Rice is used as a filler and the source of carbohydrates for fermentation. Two known products are Balao Balao (fermented rice and shrimp) and Burong Isda (fermented rice and fish). There was research done on making fermented fish sausages and the customer acceptance in order of preference follows below:

- Fish-pork, the highest score.
- Fish-beef.
- Fish-chicken.

Making Fish Sausage

1. Grind skinless and boneless pieces of fish. Different species of fish can be mixed together. Adding pork fat will make a great sausage. Those who object to using pork, can add some vegetable oil (if needed). The flesh of the fish is very soft and it should be partly frozen for the clean cut.

2. Mix ground fish with all ingredients. Adding binders such as flour, cornstarch, bread crumbs or cooked rice, helps to develop a good texture. White of an egg is an excellent binder which is added to many sausages. Fish flesh is very light and white pepper will not be visible. Fish goes well with lemon so adding lemon salt or grated lemon zest is a good idea.

3. Stuff into casings. If you use binders (flour, bread crumbs etc) stuff casing loosely.

4. Smoke (optional).

5. Cook to 145° F (63° C) internal meat temperature. You can bake the sausage in a smokehouse or cook in water at 176-185° F (80-85° C).

6. Store in refrigerator.

Fish and Bacon Sausage

Meat	Metric	US
raw fish	750 g	1.65 lb.
pork belly	250 g	0.55 lb.

Ingredients per 1000 g (1 kg) of meat:

salt	18 g	3 tsp.
white pepper	3.0 g	1½ tsp.
ginger, ground	0.5 g	⅓ tsp.
nutmeg	1.0 g	⅓ tsp.
fresh parsley, chopped	10 g	1 bunch
onion powder	6 g	2 ½ tsp.
grated lemon peel	¼ lemon	¼ lemon
egg	1	1

Instructions:

1. Grind boneless, skinless chunks of fish through ¼" (6 mm) grinder plate. Fish should be partially frozen for easy grind. Grind bacon with the same plate.
2. Mix ground meat with all ingredients.
3. Stuff into 28-32 mm hog casings.
4. Smoke for 30 minutes with hot smoke. This is an optional step.
5. Cook in water at 176° F (80° C) for about 30 minutes.
6. Refrigerate.

Fish Links

Meat	Metric	US
raw fish	1000 g	2.20 lb.

Ingredients per 1000 g (1 kg) of meat:

	Metric	US
salt	18 g	3 tsp.
white pepper	4.0 g	2 tsp.
sugar	5.0 g	1 tsp.
onion, finely chopped	30 g	½ onion
bread crumbs	40 g	⅓ cup
egg white	1 egg	1 egg
grated lemon peel	½ lemon	½ lemon

Instructions:

1. Grind boneless, skinless chunks of fish through ¼" (6 mm) grinder plate. Fish should be partially frozen for easy grind.
2. Mix ground fish with all ingredients.
3. Stuff into 24-26 mm sheep casings.
4. Refrigerate and fully cook before serving.

Notes:

To make zest, lightly grate the outside of a lemon. Do not grate the bitter white under skin.

Fish Sausage with Oil (Kosher)

Kosher fish sausage made with olive oil.

Meat	Metric	US
raw fish	1000 g	2.20 lb.

Ingredients per 1000 g (1 kg) of meat:

salt	18 g	3 tsp.
pepper	4.0 g	2 tsp.
nutmeg	2.0 g	1 tsp.
coriander	2.0 g	1 tsp.
cumin	2.0 g	1 tsp.
turmeric	2.0 g	1 tsp.
red pepper, ground	0.5 g	⅓ tsp.
ginger, ground	0.5 g	½ tsp.
olive oil	100 g	0.22 lb.
flour	60 g	1/2 cup
bread crumbs	60 g	1/2 cup
water for bread crumbs	120 ml	4 oz fl.

Instructions:

1. Grind boneless, skinless chunks of fish through ¼" (6 mm) grinder plate. Fish should be partially frozen for easy grind.
2. Soak bread crumbs in water. Mix salt, flour, oil, bread crumbs, spices and fish together.
3. Stuff into 26-28 mm sheep of your choice. For bigger sausage use beef casings.
4. Refrigerate and *fully cook* before serving. This is a fresh sausage with a short shelf life.

Notes:

To make a ready-to-eat sausage place stuffed sausage into a pot and cook at 176° F (80° C) for 25 minutes or until the fish flesh reaches 150° F (66° C) internal temperature. Immerse in cold water for 5 minutes, cool in air to evaporate moisture and refrigerate. The sausage need only to be heated before serving.

Sausage should have a slight curry flavor as all above spices are used for making curry powder. Turmeric will add a yellowish color but it may be omitted from the recipe.

Cornstarch, flour or non-fat milk powder can be used.

Cooked rice can be used as a filler.

Smoked Eel

Smoked eel is a real delicacy.

Eel is a slimy fish and its skin has to be scraped with salt or sawdust to remove all traces of slime. Then it is rinsed with water. The eels are gutted, and the belly is slit beyond the vent in order to remove the kidney. All traces of blood are removed, and the eel is rinsed again. The head is left on.

The processing steps, eels about 1-2 lb weight:

1. Cleaned eels are brined in 80° brine for 2 hours or they may be lightly salted instead.

2. Eels are rinsed with water. The fish is impaled on a stick inserted from the stomach cavity up to behind the head.

3. The fish is dried for 1-2 hours.

4. Eels are hot smoked for 3 hours at 140° F (60° C) or higher. At the beginning they should be smoked at high temperature to prevent closing of the stomach cavity. After a while the fish hardens and the temperature can be lowered. To check whether the fish is cooked, press on its sides and the meat should separate from the backbone.

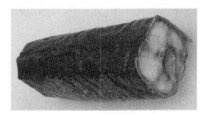

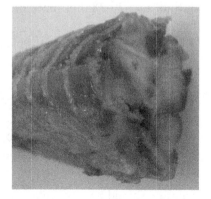

Photo 26.11 Smoked eel.

Photo 26.12 Smoked eel with the skin removed.

Smoked Fish

Hot Smoked Salmon

Place salmon fillets for 1 - 2 hours in 80 degrees brine. Remove the fish from the brine and rinse it quickly under cold running water. Place the fish on a rack and dry for two hours. Apply smoke gradually increasing the temperature and hold at 150° F (66° C) internal temperature for 30 minutes. To achieve this your smoker's temperature will have to be higher, around 170° F (76° C). Remove the fish from the smoker and cool it.

Cold Smoked Salmon

Place salmon fillets in 80 degrees brine for 6 – 12 hours, depending on the size of the fillets. Remove fish from the brine and rinse for 1 hour under cold running water. Place on smoking rack and dry the fish (3 hours). Place in a smoker and smoke below 70° F (22° C) for about 16 hours. Remove the fish from the smoker and cool it.

Smoked Trout

Gut and clean fish (1 lb. in weight) and place in 80 degrees brine for 2 hours. You may leave fish overnight in 30 degrees brine. Rinse and dry for 2 hours. Start applying smoke and hold at 90° F 32° C) for 15 minutes. Continue smoking increasing temperature and hold at 150° F (66° C) internal temperature for 30 minutes. Bigger fish will require longer smoking time. You can smoke/bake trout at 300–350° F (150–180° C) which will take only 20 minutes.

Smoked Fish Pâté

Smoked fish such as salmon, trout, and mackerel can be used for making wonderful pâtés and salads. Cream cheese, double cream, sour cream, mayonnaise, butter, eggs, and lemon juice are common ingredients. Pepper, cayenne, dill, parsley, curry, meat stock (consomme) and avocado are usually added.

Smoked Salmon and Cream Cheese

125 g (4.4 oz.) chopped or ground salmon trimmings
125 g (4.4 oz.) cream cheese
125 ml (½ cup) clear consomme
salt, pepper, lemon juice to taste.
Chopped parsley or dill for decoration.

1. Mix warm consomme with cream cheese.
2. Add seasonings, chopped salmon and mix everything together.
3. Place in refrigerator and when set, sprinkle with parsley or dill.

Smoked Salmon with Avocado

125 g (4.4 oz.) finely chopped or ground salmon trimmings
125 g (4.4 oz.) mashed avocado
125 g (4.4 oz.) mayonnaise
Lemon juice, salt, pepper.
Sour cream and croutons for decoration.

Mix all ingredients together and place in refrigerator. When set, garnish with sour cream and arrange croutons around it.

Smoked Salmon Pâté

125 g (4.4 oz.) finely chopped or ground salmon trimmings
75 ml (2 fl oz.) heavy cream
30 ml (1 oz.) single cream
15 ml (1 Tbs.) lemon juice
15 ml (1 Tbs.) vegetable oil
Salt, pepper, pinch of cayenne.

1. In a food processor blend single cream, lemon juice and oil.
2. Add other ingredients and chopped salmon and blend together.
3. Place in containers and refrigerate.

Chapter 27

Wild Game

The definition of wild game covers large animals such as dear, elk, moose, bear, mountain goat, and smaller animals such as squirrel, rabbit, opossum, and wild birds. Meat from wild animals is very lean, dark in color, and often has a gamey flavor which some people find objectionable. Fat is known to carry a lot of this flavor and *as much of the fat as possible should be cut away.* As the game meat contains very little fat to begin with, it is understood that smoking and cooking will produce a very dry product. The solution is to lace meat with pork back fat, add pork fat into sausages, cover smaller meat pieces with bacon strips or baste meat with marinade often.

Photo 27.1 Texas wild hog.

Photo courtesy Pat Jackson and Cory Mosby.

All meats will benefit from applying wet cure. The brine will not only tenderize the meat but will also remove any unpleasant gamey odors. If smoking meats at low temperatures, use sodium nitrite (Cure #1). You don't need nitrite when meats are smoked/cooked above 170° F (77° C).

Food Safety of Wild Game

Commercial meat is chilled rapidly but a game animal such as deer is often kept at higher than recommended temperatures which creates better conditions for the growth of bacteria. The safety of the meat can be affected by the wound location (spilling gut's content) and the processing skills of the hunter. If the animal is wounded or cut during slaughtering in such a way that the contents of its gut come in contact with the meat or hands of the operator, fecal bacteria can contaminate the meat.

Note that wild game such as wild boar or bear are often infected with the *trichinae* parasite which is destroyed at 137° F (58° C). If present in pork, this parasite may also be destroyed by keeping meat frozen for a certain time (explained in the chapter on food safety). Latest research has demonstrated that meat coming from wild animals living in cold climates is resilient to cold treatment for *trichinae* and the only way to be safe is to cook the meat to 160° F (71° C) internal meat temperature. The questions about game meat condition are hard to answer unless the hunter processes the meat himself. Meat processors engaged in commercial production of wild game will have the meat inspected by the meat inspector. Deer, being a herbivore is not susceptible to trichinae parasite.

The sooner the animal is dressed after shooting, the better quality of the meat will be. If the weather is hot, the skin removal will facilitate cooling. The deer will have to be inserted into cheese cloth and protected from flies. This can be accomplished with some black pepper. If the weather is cold, it is better to leave the skin on what will prevent meat from excessive drying and will keep the carcass clean.

"To age or not to age, that is the question" many hunters face. Aging of meat is the practice of holding carcasses at refrigerator temperatures 34-38° F (1-4° C) for 10 to 14 days.

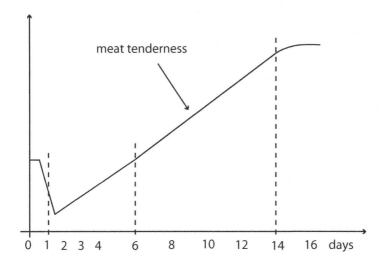

Fig. 27.1 Meat aging in time.

All animals generally follow the above curve, of course each one differently. Aging times for poultry are not in days but in hours only. After 14 days most large animals will heave perfectly aged meat. Young animals are tender by nature and a suckling pig or veal don't have to be aged. Operations like chopping or mechanically grinding tenderize meat and hunters who grind their meat don't have to worry about aging it. Game which is killed at 65° F (18° C) or above and held at this temperature over one day should be processes immediately. By the time this meat is brought back from the hunt, the aging is completed. The same meat will have to be aged for 2 weeks at 34° F (2° C). The best way to preserve wild game is by freezing. Freeze and store game meat at 0° F (-18° C) or lower. Such frozen meat will keep up to one year without loss of quality.

Big Game

Large animals will be butchered into smaller cuts, noble cuts such as loins will be barbecued. Tougher cuts from older animals may be stewed. Other cuts may be frozen for later use. If no freezer is available, they can be preserved by careful application of preservation methods. If large cuts are to be smoked with preservation in mind, use the dry cure method, rub salt, sugar and Cure #1 into the meat.

602   Home Production of Quality Meats and Sausages

Dry Cure Mix			
Salt	Sugar	Cure #1	Sodium Nitrite in PPM
6%	2%	1%	625

Example:
How much dry cure is needed for 1 kg (2.2 lbs) of meat?
Salt = 0.06 x 1000 g = 60 g
Sugar = 0.02 x 1000 g = 20 g
Cure #1 = 0.01 x 1000 g = 10 g

Processing of Game Meat

1. Rub dry mix over the entire meat piece and hold at refrigerator temperature for 2 days per pound of meat. Ten pounds leg will require 20 days curing time.

2. Dry mix should be applied at 3 separate stages:

1/3 of mix on first day
1/3 of mix on seventh day
1/3 of mix on fourteenth day

3. Soak for 60 minutes in tap water and scrub the surface with brush to remove any crystallized salt.

4. Hang to dry.

5. Smoke/Cook to 160° F (72° C).

6. Keep refrigerated or hang at 53° F (12° C). Meat will lose more moisture and will become more stable.

Small Game

Small game parts require about 6-10 hours of curing, whole squirrel about 24 hours, and rabbit 24-36 hours. After curing rinse meats with cold water, allow to dry and then smoke. Take note that rodents and rabbits can be infected with *tularemia* (rabbit fever) which can be transmitted by handling an infested animal or eating not fully cooked meat. Disease is rather rare and is easily treated with antibiotics. Game meat can be cured by stitch/dry curing method or brine (immersion) method. Follow curing and injection procedures explained in the Chapter on Ham.

Wild Fowl

The meat quality of wild birds is less predictable than farm raised chicken or turkey due to the different age of the birds that reside in different areas. They have fed on an unknown diet which affects the flavor of the meat. What is predictable is that these birds are very lean and will benefit from curing. Cure birds as you would domestic poultry. Wild birds require frequent basting during smoking and cooking. Place an aluminum pan under the bird to catch drippings which may be utilized for making gravy later. A good approach is to cover the whole bird with bacon strips and secure the strips with wooden toothpicks. Keep in mind that meat areas covered with bacon strips are not exposed to smoke and will develop a pale color. For uniform color bacon strips should be removed during the last 1-2 hours of smoking. During the cooking stage, the temperature will be raised to 170° F (77° C) or higher and the meat should be frequently basted to prevent drying.

Jerky

Quality jerky is made from lean meats with as much fatty tissue removed as possible. Fats become rancid in time and the jerky's flavor will deteriorate. Wild game meat is very lean by nature so it is not surprising that great jerky is made from venison.

Barbecuing Wild Game

If meat preservation plays a secondary role, wild game can be successfully smoked/cooked (barbecued) with fire. The traditional method of curing meat with salt and nitrite may be replaced with marinating. Marinade may include strong herbs or spices such as juniper or rosemary which can offset the gamey meat flavor. As smoking/cooking will be performed at 200-225° F (93-107° C) there is little to worry about *botulism* or *trichinae*. At these temperatures wild game lean meat will easily dry out and it should be frequently basted with oil rich basting marinade.

Marinades

Basic marinade includes water, vinegar, oil and flavorings. Often orange, lemon or pineapple juice are added. Don't add too much sugar as it tends to brown and caramelize the surface of the meat. Keep in mind that a basting marinade is thin, it is not a sauce. *The oil is always used in wild game marinades.*

Spices such as allspice, onion or garlic powder, ground celery, thyme, ginger, juniper, rosemary, sage, parsley, marjoram, and dry mustard are often added. Curry powder imparts a characteristic flavor to food and may be used with wild birds. In the wet smoking method marinade can be used instead of water when filling the pan. The pan should be placed under the meat to catch the meat juices dripping down. Then as the liquid evaporates, the marinade will baste meat with its own juices. If meat was marinated overnight, the marinade has picked up gamey odors and should not be used for basting purposes. Smaller parts may be marinated in wine marinade for about 6 hours. Then they are submitted to the smoking and cooking steps according to established rules.

Larding Meat

Larding is a technique used to add fat to very lean meat. It also helps to enhance the flavor of tougher cuts by internally basting and moisturizing them with fat. A strip of fat is cut from pork back fat or bacon and it should be chilled to harden it. All wild game, wild fowl included, will benefit greatly from this procedure. A larding needle is designed to push fat into meat.

Fat can be seasoned with herbs, or spices and the ingredients will fully penetrate the meat rather than remaining on the surface. A strip of fat or lard is forced into the larding needle, and then the needle is pushed through the cut of meat to be larded. As the needle passes through the meat, it leaves the strip of fat behind.

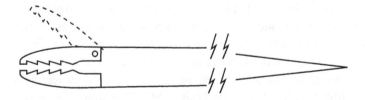

Fig. 27.2 A typical larding needle. The sharp point of the needle penetrates meat and exits on the other side. A serrated jaw swings outward to facilitate loading and releasing the fat strips.

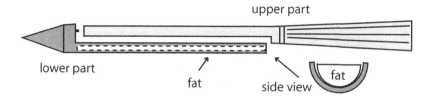

upper part

lower part   fat

fat   side view

Fig. 27.3 Adjustable depth larding needle. A two part design, consisting of two separate interlocking half tubes. A fat strip is loaded into the bottom half tube. Both parts are locked and the needle is inserted through the meat. The sharp part of the needle is removed on the exit side, the upper pushing part is removed at the insertion point and the fat strip remains inside.

Drawing adapted from U.S. Patent 2,124,700, March 9, 1935.

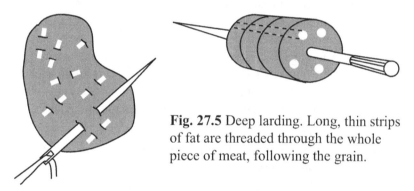

Fig. 27.5 Deep larding. Long, thin strips of fat are threaded through the whole piece of meat, following the grain.

Fig. 27.4 Surface larding. Thin strips of fat are threaded with the needle, just below the surface.

Barding Meat

Barding is a technique similar to larding that relies on the laying of fat over the meat rather than inserting it into the flesh. This method is more practical for fattening small pieces of meat and wild fowl. Commercially manufactured rendered lard (melted pork fat) can be spread on the surface of meat. A combination of larding and barding may be used as well.

twine

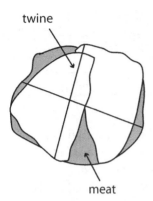

meat

Fig. 27.6 Barding. Cut thin but wide sheets of pork fat and cover the entire piece of meat, for example the breast of the goose. Secure with twine.

Wild Game Sausages

Wild game meat is lean and darker than other meats due to a lot of physical activity the animal is subjected to. This requires an increased supply of oxygen and as a result more myoglobin is developed. The more myoglobin is present the darker the color of the meat. Such a meat is often tougher but is good for sausages as meat for sausages must be ground first what is a tenderizing step. Even tough meat is easy to chew when it is ground through a small plate. Sausages made of venison are commercially made for sale in Canada and Alaska.

Venison is very lean meat so it should be mixed with pork back fat, fatty pork or a combination of pork and beef. A proportion of 50% venison to 50% other fatter meats is a good choice. It is recommended to add at least 30% of pork back fat or pork fat trimmings. Given that wild boar is fatter than deer 30% of pork fat should be added. Wild game sausages agree well with plenty of spices, rosemary and jupiter are often added.

Any type of sausage can be produced from game meat, the fermented types included. The manufacturing process for making wild game sausages remains the same as for other sausage types. Using starter cultures and good manufacturing processes as outlined in the book, a semi-dry fermented venison sausage can successfully be made at home.

| Venison | Good color, good price. Popular meat in Northwestern U.S. and Alaska. | Available during hunting season. May be infected with trichinae worms. Very lean, needs some pork fat. |

A typical procedure for smoking beef or wild game brisket

1. Making brine:

To make 40° brine (10° Baumé) add 333 g (0.73 lb) of salt to 1 gallon of water (3.8 liter). Add 120 g (4.2 oz) of Cure #1. This amount of brine will cure about 17 lbs. (7.3 kg) of meat.

Note: * the amount of salt in Cure #1 (112 g) has been accounted for when calculating brine strength.

To cure 1 kg meat about 500 ml (about 2 cups) brine is required.

Pump briskets with the amount of brine equal to 10% of the original meat weight. After meats are injected with brine, pack them tightly in a suitable container. Add sufficient brine of the same formula and strength used for pumping to cover the meat. Cover with a weighted lid. Cure 4-5 days at refrigerator temperatures (38-40° F).

2. Remove meats from brine, wash for 2 minutes with cold water and drain. Rub thoroughly with cracked black pepper and whole coriander. Be generous with your rub, it should be applied in a thick coating.

3. Hang pieces in a preheated to 140° F (60° C) smokehouse. With dampers fully open, hold at this temperature until meat surface is dry.

4. Readjust dampers to 1/4 open and apply light smoke for 2 hours. Close dampers, shut off smoke and raise temperature to 200 - 220° F.

5. Cook to 160° F (72° C) internal meat temperature.

Photo 27.2 Wild boar is delicious.

Corned Game

Wild game be it venison, moose, elk, antelope, bear can be corned the same way beef Pastrami is made. The advantage of corning wild game is that it removes the musky wild flavor and tenderizes the meat. The term "corn" in "corned game" refers to the "corns" or grains of coarse salts used to cure it. The slab of game is typically cured in a heavy, salty brine solution. After meat is removed from brine it drained and a combination of cracked black pepper and whole coriander is rubbed into it.

Meat	Metric	US
round, brisket or any cut of meat	1000 g	2.20 lb.

Instructions:
1. Making corning brine:

40° brine (10° Baumé)	
for **1 kg** (2.2 lb) of meat	for 7.3 kg (17 lb) of meat
water, 500 ml (2 cups)	water, 3.8 kg (1 gallon)
salt, 60 g (2.1 oz or 3.3 Tbs)	salt, 445 g (0.98 lb.)
cure #1, 16 g (1 Tbs)	cure #1, 120 g (4.2 oz)
sugar, 40 g (1.41 oz)	sugar, 295 g (0.65 lb)
1 bay leaf, ½ tsp. black pepper, ½ tsp, ground cloves, ½ tsp. dried juniper berries,	7 bay leaves, 1 Tbs. black pepper, 1 Tbsp. ground cloves, 1 Tbs. dried juniper berries,

Note: * the amount of salt in Cure #1 (112 g) has been accounted for when calculating brine strength.

2. Place meat in brine, cover with weight plate to keep meat below brine.
3. On the 5th and 10th day, reverse the order of meats (top piece on the bottom, and the bottom piece on top). Remove meat after 15 days.
4. Cook meat. Place in a pot with cover and add water to cover meat. Bring to a boil and simmer below the boiling point until tender. This may take 3-5 hours.
Notes:
Meat can be smoked as well. Follow instructions for smoking Pastrami.

Deer Sausage

Meat	Metric	US
deer meat	500 g	1.10 lb.
pork belly	500 g	1.10 lb.

Ingredients per 1000 g (1 kg) of meat:

salt	18 g	3 tsp.
Cure #1	2.5 g	½ tsp.
mustard, ground	2.0 g	1 tsp.
pepper	2.0 g	1 tsp.
marjoram, dry	3.0 g	2 tsp.
rosemary	1.0 g	1/2 tsp.
garlic	7.0 g	2 cloves
cold water	100 ml	⅜ cup

Instructions:

1. Grind all meats and fat through a 3/8" (10 mm) plate.
2. Mix ground meat with all ingredients adding water.
3. Stuff tightly into 32-36 mm hog casings. Make 6" long links.
4. Hold overnight in refrigerator or for 2 hours at room temperature.
5. Preheat smoker to 130° F (54° C) and when the casings feel dry apply hot smoke for 60 minutes. Continue smoking for additional 60 minutes slowly increasing temperature to about 170° F (77° C).
6. Stop baking when the meat reaches 160° F (72° C) internal temperature.
7. Cool the sausages in the air.
8. Store in refrigerator.

Notes:

If the sausage is not smoked, adding Cure #1 is optional. After stuffing, the sausage is cooked for 40 minutes in hot water at 176° F (80° C).

Rabbit Sausage

Meat	Metric	US
Rabbit	800 g	1.76 lb.
Pork back fat	200 g	0.44 lb.

Ingredients per 1000 g (1 kg) of meat:

salt	18 g	3 tsp.
Cure #1	2.5 g	½ tsp.
pepper	2.0 g	1 tsp.
allspice	2.0 g	1 tsp.
nutmeg	1.0 g	½ tsp.
sugar	2.0 g	½ tsp.
potato flour	4.0 g	1½ tsp.
cold water	100 ml	⅜ cup

Instructions:
1. Grind all meats and fat through a ¼" (6 mm) plate.
2. Mix ground meat with all ingredients adding water.
3. Stuff tightly into 32-36 mm hog casings.
4. Hang for 1 hour at room temperature.
5. Place sausage in a preheated to 130° F (54° C) smoker and when the casings feel dry apply smoke at 140° F (60° C) for 90 minutes.
6. Cook in hot water at 176° F (80° C). This will take about 30 minutes.
Stop cooking when the meat reaches 160° F (72° C) internal temperature.
7. Immerse for 5 minutes in cold water, then continue cooling in the air.
8. Store in refrigerator.

Venison Sausage

Venison is a naturally lean meat and to make a good sausage pork meat (70/30) or pork fat must be added.

Meat	Metric	US
venison	600 g	1.32 lbs.
pork butt or fat pork trimmings	400 g	0.88 lb.

Ingredients per 1000 g (1 kg) of meat:

salt	18 g	3 tsp.
pepper	2.0 g	1 tsp.
fennel seeds	3.0 g	2 tsp.
cumin	1.0 g	1/2 tsp
coriander	1.0 g	1/2 tsp
cold water	100 ml	⅜ cup

Instructions:

1. Grind all meats and fat through a 3/8" (10 mm) plate.
2. Mix ground meat with all ingredients adding water.
3. Stuff tightly into 32-36 mm hog casings. Make 6" long links.
4. Refrigerate. This is a fresh sausage that must be consumed within 1-2 days. Fully cook before serving by frying or grilling.

Ready-to-eat cooked sausage

Stuff the sausage then hold it for a few hours in refrigerator to let the spices release aroma.

Cook in water at 176° F (80° C) for 40 minutes.

Shower or immerse sausages for 5 minutes in cold water, then continue cooling them in the air.

Store in refrigerator.

Heat before serving.

Wild Boar Sausage

Wild boar is a naturally lean meat and to make a good sausage pork meat (70/30) or pork fat must be added.

Meat	Metric	US
Wild boar	600 g	1.32 lbs.
Pork butt or fat pork trimmings	400 g	0.88 lb.

Ingredients per 1000 g (1 kg) of meat:

salt	18 g	3 tsp.
Cure #1	2.5 g	½ tsp.
pepper	2.0 g	1 tsp.
dry juniper berries	2.0 g	1 tsp.
garlic	3.5 g	1 clove
cold water	100 ml	⅜ cup

Instructions:

1. Grind all meats and fat through a 3/8" (10 mm) plate.
2. Mix ground meat with all ingredients adding water.
3. Stuff tightly into 32-36 mm hog casings. Make 12" long links.
4. Hang for 1 hour or until casings feel dry.
5. Place sausage in a preheated to 130° F (54° C) smoker and when the casings feel dry apply smoke at 140° F (60° C) for 60 minutes. Continue smoking for additional 60 minutes slowly increasing temperature to about 170° F (77° C).
6. Stop baking when the meat reaches 160° F (72° C) internal temperature.
7. Cool the sausages in the air.
8. Store in refrigerator.

Notes:

If available - at the beginning and at the end of smoking add some juniper branches into the fire.

Wild Game Sausage

Meat	Metric	US
wild game meat	500 g	1.10 lb.
pork butt or fat pork trimmings	500 g	1.10 lb.

Ingredients per 1000 g (1 kg) of meat:

salt	18 g	3 tsp.
Cure #1	2.5 g	½ tsp.
pepper	4.0 g	2 tsp.
marjoram	2.0 g	1 tsp.
mustard seed	2.0 g	1 tsp.
garlic	3.5 g	1 clove

Instructions:

1. Grind all meats through a 3/8" (10 mm) plate.
2. Mix ground meat with all ingredients.
3. Stuff tightly into 32-36 mm hog casings.
4. Hang for 1 hour until casings feel dry.
5. Place sausage in a preheated to 130° F (54° C) smoker and when the casings feel dry apply smoke at 140° F (60° C) for 60 minutes. Continue smoking for additional 60 minutes slowly increasing temperature to about 170° F (77° C).
6. Stop baking when the meat reaches 160° F (72° C) internal temperature.
7. Cool the sausages in the air.
8. Store in refrigerator.

Chapter 28

Barbecuing

Smoking, Barbecuing, and Grilling

There is a significant difference between smoking, barbecuing, and grilling. When grilling, you quickly seal in the juices from the piece you are cooking. Grilling takes minutes. Smoking takes hours, sometimes even days. Don't be fooled by the common misconception that by throwing some wet wood chips over hot coals you can fully smoke your meat. At best you can only add some flavor on the outside because the moment the outside surface of the meat becomes dry and cooked, a significant barrier exists that prevents smoke penetration. A properly smoked piece of meat has to be thoroughly smoked, on the outside and everywhere inside. Only prolonged cold smoking will achieve that result. Smoking when grilling is no better than pumping liquid smoke into it and claiming that the product has been smoked. Let's unravel some of the mystery. All these methods are different from each other, especially smoking and grilling. The main factor separating them is temperature.

Smoking-very low heat	52° - 140° F (12° - 60° C)	1 hr to 2 weeks, depending on temperature
Barbecuing-low heat	190° - 300° F (93° - 150° C)	**low and slow,** few hours
Grilling-high heat	400° - 550° F (232° - 288° C)	**hot and fast,** minutes

The purpose of grilling is to char the surface of the meat and seal in the juices by creating a smoky caramelized crust. By the same token a barrier is erected which prevents smoke from flowing inside. The meat may have a somewhat smoky flavor on the outside but due to the short cooking time it was never really smoked.

Barbecuing is a long, slow, indirect, low-heat method that uses charcoal or wood pieces to smoke-cook the meat. Most backyard barbecuing is not barbecuing but grilling. *The best definition is that barbecuing is slow cooking with smoke.* It is ideally suited for large pieces of meat such as butts, ribs or whole pigs. The temperature range of 190–300° F (88-150° C) is still too high for smoking sausages as the fat will melt away through the casings making them greasy.

Barbecue is a social affair, people gather to gossip, drink, have fun and to eat the moment the meats are cooked. On the other hand, *traditionally smoked meats are usually eaten cold* at a later date. As barbecue brings people together, it is not surprising that everybody loves the event. Although barbecue is popular in many countries, nobody does it better than Americans. There, barbecue is a part of tradition like American jazz. It has become the art in itself with constant cookouts and championships all over the country. Although barbecued meats can be placed directly on the screen and cooked, in many cases they are first marinated. Marinades consist of many flavoring ingredients such as vinegar, lemon juice, and spices whereas traditional curing basically contains only water, salt and nitrite, sometimes sugar is added as well. To make great barbecued products the understanding of the following steps is required: controlling fire and temperature, moisture control, smoking with wood and the required time for barbecuing.

Choice of Fuel

1. Wood is the best but it is heavy and a lot of it is needed. It is difficult to control the combustion temperature especially in small units. For those reasons only a few restaurants use wood to generate heat. In large barbecue restaurants the system is designed in such a way that a product is kept a safe distance from a wood burning fire pit.

2. Charcoal briquettes are the choice fuel for backyard barbecue as they are light, burn slow, and are easy to control. They produce a hot, long-lasting, smokeless fire. When using charcoal briquettes it may seem that smoke is generated even without the addition of wood chips. This is due to fat dripping on hot coals which burst into flames but there is no smoke present. The resulting flavor is the flavor of burned fat. Charcoal is produced by burning wood in a low-oxygen atmosphere. This process removes the moisture, sap and volatile gases that were present in the original fuel. The final product is pure carbon.

Lump charcoal - irregularly shaped charred lump charcoal pieces. Very light, they burn hotter and faster than other charcoal types, producing sparks and crackling sounds. Lump charcoal gets hot in about 10 minutes.

Charcoal briquettes - lump ground charcoal mixed with natural starch and pressed into uniform size briquettes. Starch acts as a binder. They burn as fast and hot as lump charcoal. The advantage they offer is their uniformity which helps to create a smooth layer of coals.

Modified briquettes - lump ground charcoal mixed with natural starch, hard and soft coal powder (to raise and prolong heat) and limestone (to create a coating of white ash). They produce longer and more even heat than other types. This is the most common American charcoal briquette that should be pre-burned until covered with white ash. Adding black briquettes directly into the fire will create off flavors.

3. Gas is predominantly used for grilling and it can supply a lot of heat instantaneously. It is hard to obtain a smoky flavor when grilling due to a short cooking time. Adding a few wood chips will not cut it. A lot of heavy smoke must be generated and it is feasible to construct a small smoke generator from a little metal pan, about 5-6" (12-15 cm) in diameter, preferably made of stainless steel. The pan is filled with wood chips or sawdust and is placed on a hot plate to ignite the wood chips. Once they start producing smoke, the pan can be placed inside of the grill and the cooking process can be started. If there is an available burner inside of the unit the pan can be placed on it. Needless to say the pan should produce smoke before the meat is submitted to a cooking chamber. The charcoal should extend 3-4 inches beyond the piece of meat on the screen above. Otherwise the food will not cook properly. When adding wood chips to generate smoke, it must be kept in mind that smoke penetrates meat much faster at high temperatures. A traditionally smoked meat piece at 120° F (50° C) for 4 hours may acquire an over smoked bitter flavor if smoked at 250° F (120° C) for the same length of time.

How Hot Is It?

The best method is to check the reading of the built-in thermometer if the unit has one. When barbecuing on an open fire you can use the "palm method." Hold the palm of your hand about 1" above the cooking screen and start counting seconds until the heat forces your hand away.

Barbecue Guidelines

- Fire - allow briquettes to burn until they are covered with white ash. Only then place the meat above them. This means that for longer barbecuing, for example ribs, a steady supply of pre-burnt briquettes is needed. If the barbecue unit is big enough the briquettes can be pre-burnt in the area located away from the meat. In smaller units, they will have to be pre-burnt in a separate location and then transferred to the barbecue unit.
- Moisture - in order to prevent the premature drying of meat enough moisture should be present. That can be accomplished by using pre-soaked wood chips (when smoking) and placing a water pan inside of the unit. Another solution is to periodically moisten the meat with a basting marinade or beer.
- Wood - is needed to create a smoky flavor. Any hard wood such as oak, hickory, fruit trees or a combination of woods will do.
- Time - people that win barbecue contents have one thing in common: they are patient and they take their time. *Cook it low and cook it slow* is the rule.

Those elements combined with a good quality meat and a flavorful marinade will produce an outstanding product.

Indoor Barbecuing

Imitation barbecue can be successfully obtained at home by cooking meats in the oven. Of course, liquid smoke will have to be rubbed into meat or added into marinade as producing natural smoke in one's kitchen may not appeal to all members of the family.

There is a wonderful appliance called an electric crock pot that is inexpensive, easy to operate and will produce the highest quality meats, be it pulled pork, spare-ribs, chili or whatever else. A crock pot offers another great advantage for busy people of today: it is the most user friendly device there is. Switch it on when you go to sleep and the next morning the breakfast is hot and ready. Switch it on when going to work and when you return the dinner is ready to be served.

Dry Rubs, Marinades and Sauces

Instead of traditional curing techniques which rely on salt and nitrite, barbecuing employs dry rubs, liquid marinades and sauces. Rubs and marinades tenderize and flavor meats, sauces may be compared to salad dressings, it is the final culinary touch given to the process. Sauces which contain sugars and honey are usually applied in the last minutes of the barbecue to create a caramelized crust and shiny surface on the product.

Dry rub commonly consists of:

- Salt.
- Sugar, honey, maple syrup. Sugar burns easily on the surface of the food.
- Seasonings - pepper, lemon pepper, dry mustard, oregano, thyme, marjoram, sage.

The purpose of a marinade is not just to flavor the meat, but to tenderize it as well. There are three basic components of a marinade:

Acid	Oil	Seasonings
Vinegar, wine, lemon juice, orange juice, pineapple juice, Worcestershire sauce, tomatoes or ketchup.	Vegetable, olive or other oils. The leaner the food, the more oil it will need. Keep in mind that butter becomes solid in the refrigerator.	Spices, sugar, honey, flavorings

The degree of toughness of meat can be linked to the age of the animal and to a lesser degree the species. Often exercised parts of an animal will be tougher than inactive parts. Muscle cells and connective tissue can be significantly softened by placing them in an acidic solution containing wine and/or vinegar. When placed for 24 hours in such a solution collagen (connective tissue) starts to swell, taking up moisture and loosening its structure.

Look at the label of any commercially made product and you will see that the above ingredients are always present. Basting marinade is lighter and used on meats which are leaner. The amount of oil can be adjusted accordingly and will be higher in marinades used for lean wild game. Beer makes an excellent basting marinade.

Originally, they were two distinct barbecue sauces:

1. Vinegar based sauces (no ketchup or tomato paste added), which were popular in the Eastern parts of the Carolinas and Virginia.

2. Tomato ketchup based sauces more popular in the Western parts of the Carolinas, Virginia, Tennessee, Kansas, Kentucky and Texas. Texas sauces contained more hot peppers.

Today, there are dozens of marinades in every store. A typical dry rub and marinade:

Dry rub	Marinade
4 Tbsp. salt, 2 Tbsp. sugar, 2 Tbsp. powdered garlic, 2 Tbsp. paprika, 2 Tbsp. sugar, 2 Tbsp. ground celery seed, 1 Tbsp. black pepper, 1 tsp. cayenne.	1/2 cup oil, 1/2 cup lemon juice, 1 Tbsp. salt, 1 tsp. paprika, 1/2 tsp. garlic powder, 1/2 tsp. onion powder, 1 Tbsp. lemon peel (zest).

Most foods use 1/3 cup liquid marinade per pound of meat. Feel free to experiment! Adjust seasoning and liquid amounts to your preferences if you are making your own marinade. Fish and seafood usually require less seasoning, whereas wild game may require more.

Basic barbecue sauce

2 cups ketchup, 1/4 cup oil, 1/3 cup honey, 1/4 cup Worcestershire sauce, 1/2 cup soy sauce, 1/4 cup vinegar, 1 tsp granulated garlic, 1 tsp granulated onion, 1/2 tsp. liquid smoke, 1/2 tsp. Tabasco sauce.

Keep in mind that acidic foods react with most metals such as common steel, copper, aluminum and it is best to use containers made of glass, food grade plastic or stainless steel.

Barbecued meats are smoked/cooked at temperatures which kill bacteria and no sodium nitrite is needed. As a result they will not exhibit the pink color so typical of nitrite cured meats.

All purpose marinade	Basting marinade
1 cup oil, 1/2 cup vinegar, 1/4 cup lemon juice, 1/4 cup soy sauce, 1/2 cup Worcestershire sauce, 1 Tbsp. dry mustard, 1 Tbsp. black pepper, 1/2 tsp. cayenne.	1 cup olive or salad oil, 1 cup vinegar, 1/2 cup water (or red wine).

There are no recipes in this section as most people are familiar with barbecuing meats. This book is about making meat products for later use and barbecued meats are usually consumed the moment they are ready. When a large amount of meat is barbecued, for example the whole hog, any leftover meat can be frozen or canned.

Photo 28.1 Pouring beer over roasted pig is a common way of keeping the meat moist and flavorsome.

Electric Crock Pot

Electric crock pots, also known as slow cookers may be considered to be a modern version of a Dutch oven. They are easy to operate; apply a slight oil film to the bottom of the removable dish, add meat and all ingredients, then switch the timer on, and when you return from work, the dinner is ready.

Photo 28.2 Electric crock pot.

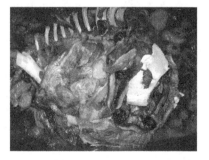

Photo 28.3 Wild boar cooked in a crock pot.

Dutch Oven

The Dutch oven is an extraordinary vessel for all purpose slow cooking. Certain meat dishes such as pulled pork will turn out great when cooked in a Dutch oven.

Although it does not have much in common with traditional meat smoking, nevertheless it a great way of cooking outdoors. A proper traditional oven is made of cast iron and is quite heavy, depending on its diameter. There are different sizes, starting from 8" diameter and up. A Dutch oven made of cast iron can handle heat up to 2,000° F (1093° C) and a fast burning open fire can sometimes reach 1,500° F (815° C). A good oven must have three strong legs, a hanging bail, rimmed lid and the cover handle. A good lid is concave shaped so it can be flipped over and used as a frying pan.

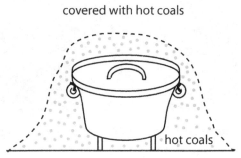

Photo 28.4 Dutch oven can stand on its legs or can hang on the hook.

Fig. 28.1 Dutch oven covered with hot coals. If kept clean and properly maintained, it is virtually indestructible.

A good lid must fit tight and must be thick enough to handle hot coals which are placed on it. The lid has a raised lip to confine coals inside. Dutch ovens can handle all cooking needs such as bread, stew, pulled pork, pies, turkey and other dishes.

Fig. 28.2 Oven hanging over camp fire.

Fig. 28.3 Ovens stacked up.

Chapter 29

Canning

After an animal's slaughter the biggest amount of meat has been traditionally preserved by canning. This preservation method will definitely appeal to people living on farms or in a cooler climate. This allows for keeping canned foods in kitchen pantries or basement cellars at about 50° F (10° C) or lower. Canning is popular everywhere although in Europe for many years it was a necessary survival skill. Many countries throughout history were involved in continuous wars which left buildings, stores and infrastructures destroyed. All that people could do was buy food at the farmer markets and preserve it by canning for later use. If items such as tomato paste, wine, sauerkraut, pickles, pickled mushrooms, canned meats, or lard were not processed in the summer, there would be famine in the winter time.

Canning meat offers many advantages:

- Meat can be preserved for a long time without any loss in quality. Fats or sausages become rancid in time even when kept in freezer. Canned meats don't face such problems.
- Larger meat cuts, with bone-in or without, can be processed by canning.
- Meats are immediately ready to serve and can be taken out on outdoor trips, contrary to frozen foods that have to be thawed out first.

Depending on canning temperature, there are two methods of canning:

1. Traditional hot bath method. At sea level water boils at 212° F (100° C), at higher elevations water boils at lower temperatures. Because *Clostridium botulinum* spores do not grow in the presence of acid, *high-acid foods* can be safely processed in a boiling water canner, however, the temperature of 100° C is not high enough to kill spores in *non-acidic* foods like meats or vegetables.

2. High pressure canning method. This is the recommended method for canning meats as it permits to obtain higher pressures inside of a sealed pot allowing water to boil at 240-250° F (115-122° C). This kills all bacteria and canned meat can be stored for a long time. The majority of cases of food poisoning (botulism) can be attributed to home canning and good canning practices must be always applied in order to produce a tasteful and safe product. The following information comes from the United Stated Department of Agriculture Complete Guide to Canning.

Ensuring Safe Canned Foods

Growth of the bacterium *Clostridium botulinum* in canned food may cause botulism-a deadly form of food poisoning. These bacteria exist either as spores or as vegetative cells. The spores, which are comparable to plant seeds, can survive harmlessly in soil and water for many years. When ideal conditions exist for growth, the spores produce vegetative cells which multiply rapidly and may produce a deadly toxin within 3 to 4 days of growth in an environment consisting of:

- A moist, low-acid food.
- A temperature between 40° and 120°F (4 - 49° C).
- Less than 2 percent oxygen.

Botulinum spores are on most fresh food surfaces. Because they grow only in the absence of air, they are harmless on fresh foods. Most bacteria, yeasts, and molds are difficult to remove from food surfaces. Washing fresh food reduces their numbers only slightly. Peeling root crops, underground stem crops, and tomatoes reduces their numbers greatly. Blanching also helps, but the vital controls are the method of canning and making sure the recommended research-based process times, found in these guides, are used.

The processing times in these guides ensure destruction of the largest expected number of heat-resistant microorganisms in home-canned foods. Properly sterilized canned food will be free of spoilage if lids seal and jars are stored below 95°F (35° C). Storing jars at 50° to 70°F (10 - 21° C) enhances retention of quality.

Food Acidity and Processing Methods

Whether food should be processed in a pressure canner or boiling-water canner to control botulinum bacteria depends on the acidity of the food. Acidity may be natural, as in most fruits, or added, as in pickled food. Low-acid canned foods are not acidic enough to prevent the growth of these bacteria. Acid foods contain enough acid to block their growth, or destroy them more rapidly when heated. The term "pH" is a measure of acidity; the lower its value, the more acid the food. The acidity level in foods can be increased by adding lemon juice, citric acid, or vinegar.

Low-acid foods have pH values higher than 4.6. They include **red meats, seafood, poultry,** milk, and all fresh vegetables except for most tomatoes. Most mixtures of low-acid and acid foods also have pH values above 4.6 unless their recipes include enough lemon juice, citric acid, or vinegar to make them acid foods. Acid foods have a pH of 4.6 or lower. They include fruits, pickles, sauerkraut, jams, jellies, marmalades, and fruit butters.

Although tomatoes usually are considered an acid food, some are now known to have pH values slightly above 4.6. Figs also have pH values slightly above 4.6. Therefore, if they are to be canned as acid foods, these products must be acidified to a pH of 4.6 or lower with lemon juice or citric acid. Properly acidified tomatoes and figs are acid foods and can be safely processed in a boiling-water canner.

Botulinum spores are very hard to destroy at boiling-water temperatures; the higher the canner temperature, the more easily they are destroyed. Therefore, *all low-acid foods should be sterilized at temperatures of 240° to 250°F (116 - 121° C),* attainable with pressure canners operated at 10 to 15 PSIG. PSIG means pounds per square inch of pressure as measured by gauge. The more familiar "PSI" designation is used hereafter in this publication.

At temperatures of 240° to 250°F (116 - 121° C), the time needed to destroy bacteria in low-acid canned food ranges from 20 to 100 minutes. The exact time depends on the kind of food being canned, the way it is packed into jars, and the size of jars. The time needed to safely process low-acid foods in a boiling-water canner ranges from 7 to 11 hours; the time needed to process acid foods in boiling water varies from 5 to 85 minutes.

Process Adjustments at High Altitudes

Using the process time for canning food at sea level may result in spoilage if you live at altitudes of 1,000 feet or more. Water boils at lower temperatures as altitude increases. Lower boiling temperatures are less effective for killing bacteria. Increasing the process time or canner pressure compensates for lower boiling temperatures.

Therefore, when you use the guides, select the proper processing time or canner pressure for the altitude where you live. If you do not know the altitude, contact your local county Extension agent. An alternative source of information would be the local district conservationist with the Soil Conservation Service.

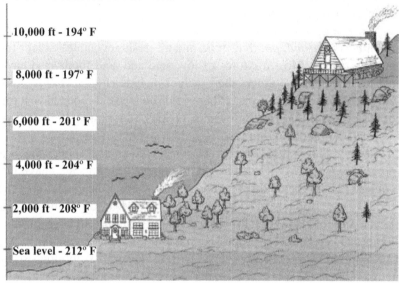

Fig. 29.1 Water boiling temperature at different altitudes.

Equipment and Methods not Recommended

Open-kettle canning and the processing of freshly filled jars in conventional ovens, microwave ovens, and dishwashers are not recommended, because these practices do not prevent all risks of spoilage. Steam canners are not recommended because processing times for use with current models have not been adequately researched. Because steam canners do not heat foods in the same manner as boiling-water canners, their use with boiling-water process times may result in spoilage. It is not recommended that pressure processes in excess of 15 PSI be applied when using new pressure canning equipment. So-called canning powders are useless as preservatives and do not replace the need for proper heat processing. Jars with wire bails and glass caps make attractive antiques or storage containers for dry food ingredients but are not recommended for use in canning. One-piece zinc porcelain-lined caps are also no longer recommended. Both glass and zinc caps use flat rubber rings for sealing jars, but too often fail to seal properly.

Ensuring High-Quality Canned Foods

Begin with good-quality fresh foods suitable for canning. Quality varies among varieties of fruits and vegetables. Many county Extension offices can recommend varieties best suited for canning. Examine food carefully for freshness and wholesomeness. Discard diseased and moldy food. Trim small diseased lesions or spots from food. Can fruits and vegetables picked from your garden or purchased from nearby producers when the products are at their peak of quality-within 6 to 12 hours after harvest for most vegetables. For best quality, apricots, nectarines, peaches, pears, and plums should be ripened 1 or more days between harvest and canning. If you must delay the canning of other fresh produce, keep it in a shady, cool place.

Fresh home-slaughtered red meats and poultry *should be chilled and canned without delay.* Do not can meat from sickly or diseased animals. Ice fish and seafoods after harvest, eviscerate immediately, and can them within 2 days.

Maintaining Color and Flavor in Canned Food

To maintain good natural color and flavor in stored canned food, you must:

- Remove oxygen from food tissues and jars,
- Quickly destroy the food enzymes,
- Obtain high jar vacuums and airtight jar seals.

Follow these guidelines to ensure that your canned foods retain optimum colors and flavors during processing and storage:

- Use only high-quality foods which are at the proper maturity and are free of diseases and bruises.

- Use the hot-pack method, especially with acid foods to be processed in boiling water.

- Don't unnecessarily expose prepared foods to air. Can them as soon as possible.

- While preparing a canner load of jars, keep peeled, halved, quartered, sliced, or diced apples, apricots, nectarines, peaches, and pears in a solution of 3 grams (3,000 milligrams) ascorbic acid to 1 gallon of cold water. This procedure is also useful in maintaining the natural color of mushrooms and potatoes, and for preventing stem-end discoloration in cherries and grapes.

You can get ascorbic acid in several forms:

- Pure powdered form - seasonally available among canners' supplies in supermarkets. One level teaspoon of pure powder weighs about 3 grams. Use 1 teaspoon per gallon of water as a treatment solution.

- Vitamin C tablets - economical and available year-round in many stores. Buy 500 - milligram tablets; crush and dissolve six tablets per gallon of water as a treatment solution.

- Commercially prepared mixes of ascorbic and citric acid - seasonally available among canners' supplies in supermarkets. Sometimes citric acid powder is sold in supermarkets, but it is less effective in controlling discoloration. If you choose to use these products, follow the manufacturer's directions.

- Fill hot foods into jars and adjust headspace as specified in recipes.

- Tighten screw bands securely, but if you are especially strong, not as tightly as possible.

- Process and cool jars.

- Store the jars in a relatively cool, dark place, preferably between 50° and 70°F (10 - 21° C).

- Can no more food than you will use within a year.

Advantages of Hot-Packing

Many fresh foods contain from 10 percent to more than 30 percent air. How long canned food retains high quality depends on how much air is removed from food before jars are sealed.

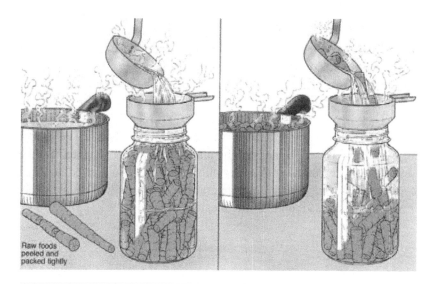

| Raw pack - add very hot canning liquid or water to cover raw food, but leave headspace. Raw foods peeled and packed tightly. | Hot pack - raw foods are boiled 3 - 5 minutes in a saucepan or blancher, then poured into jars. |

Fig. 29.2 Packing methods.

Raw-packing is the practice of filling jars tightly with freshly prepared, but unheated food. Such foods, especially fruit, will float in the jars. The entrapped air in and around the food may cause discoloration within 2 to 3 months of storage. Raw-packing is more suitable for vegetables processed in a pressure canner.

Hot-packing is the practice of heating freshly prepared food to boiling, simmering it 2 to 5 minutes, and promptly filling jars loosely with the boiled food. Whether food has been hot-packed or raw-packed, the juice, syrup, or water to be added to the foods should also be heated to boiling before adding it to the jars. This practice helps to remove air from food tissues, shrinks food, helps keep the food from floating in the jars, increases vacuum in sealed jars, and improves shelf life. Preshrinking food permits filling more food into each jar.

Hot-packing is the best way to remove air and is the preferred pack style for foods processed in a boiling-water canner. At first, the color of hot-packed foods may appear no better than that of raw-packed foods, but within a short storage period, both color and flavor of hot-packed foods will be superior.

Controlling Headspace

The unfilled space above the food in a jar and below its lid is termed headspace. Directions for canning specify leaving 1/4-inch for jams and jellies, 1/2-inch for fruits and tomatoes to be processed in boiling water, and from 1 to 1¼ inches in low acid foods to be processed in a pressure canner. This space is needed for expansion of food as jars are processed, and for forming vacuums in cooled jars. The extent of expansion is determined by the air content in the food and by the processing temperature. Air expands greatly when heated to high temperatures; the higher the temperature, the greater the expansion. Foods expand less than air when heated.

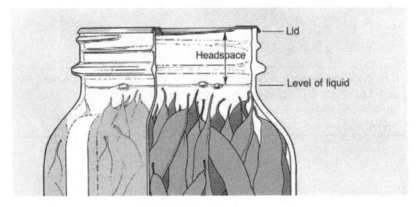

Fig. 29.3 Controlling headspace.

Jars and Lids

Food may be canned in glass jars or metal containers. Metal containers can be used only once. They require special sealing equipment and are much more costly than jars. Regular and wide-mouth Mason-type, threaded, home-canning jars with self-sealing lids are the best choice. They are available in ½ pint, pint, 1½ pint, quart, and ½ gallon sizes. The standard jar mouth opening is about 2⅜ inches. Wide-mouth jars have openings of about 3 inches, making them more easily filled and emptied. Half-gallon jars may be used for canning very acid juices. Regular-mouth decorator jelly jars are available in 8 and 12 ounce sizes. With careful use and handling, Mason jars may be reused many times, requiring only new lids each time. When jars and lids are used properly, jar seals and vacuums are excellent and jar breakage is rare.

Fig. 29.4 Jars and lids.

Most commercial pint and quart size mayonnaise or salad dressing jars may be used with new two piece lids for canning acid foods. However, you should expect more seal failures and jar breakage. These jars have a narrower sealing surface and are tempered less than Mason jars, and may be weakened by repeated contact with metal spoons or knives used in dispensing mayonnaise or salad dressing. Seemingly insignificant scratches in glass may cause cracking and breakage while processing jars in a canner. Mayonnaise-type jars are not recommended for use with foods to be processed in a pressure canner because of excessive jar breakage. Other commercial jars with mouths that cannot be sealed with two-piece canning lids are not recommended for use in canning any food at home.

Lid Selection, Preparation, and Use

The common self-sealing lid consists of a flat metal lid held in place by a metal screw band during processing. The flat lid is crimped around its bottom edge to form a trough, which is filled with a colored gasket compound. When jars are processed, the lid gasket softens and flows slightly to cover the jar-sealing surface, yet allows air to escape from the jar. The gasket then forms an airtight seal as the jar cools.

Gaskets in unused lids work well for at least 5 years from date of manufacture. The gasket compound in older unused lids may fail to seal on jars. Buy only the quantity of lids you will use in a year. To ensure a good seal, carefully follow the manufacturer's directions in preparing lids for use. Examine all metal lids carefully. Do not use old, dented, or deformed lids, or lids with gaps or other defects in the sealing gasket.

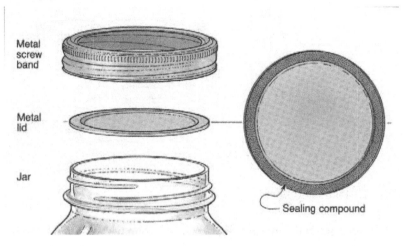

Fig. 29.5 Lid preparation.

Do not retighten lids after processing jars. As jars cool, the contents in the jar contract, pulling the self-sealing lid firmly against the jar to form a high vacuum.

- If rings are too loose, liquid may escape from jars during processing, and seals may fail.

- If rings are too tight, air cannot vent during processing, and food will discolor during storage. Over tightening also may cause lids to buckle and jars to break, especially with raw-packed, pressure-processed food.

Screw bands are not needed on stored jars. They can be removed easily after jars are cooled. When removed, washed, dried, and stored in a dry area, screw bands may be used many times. If left on stored jars, they become difficult to remove, often rust, and may not work properly again.

Recommended Canners

Equipment for heat-processing home-canned food is of two main types—boiling water canners and pressure canners. Most are designed to hold seven quart jars or eight to nine pints. Small pressure canners hold four-quart jars; some large pressure canners hold 18 pint jars in two layers, but hold only seven quart jars. Pressure saucepans with smaller volume capacities are not recommended for use in canning. Small capacity pressure canners are treated in a similar manner as standard larger canners, and should be vented using the typical venting procedures.

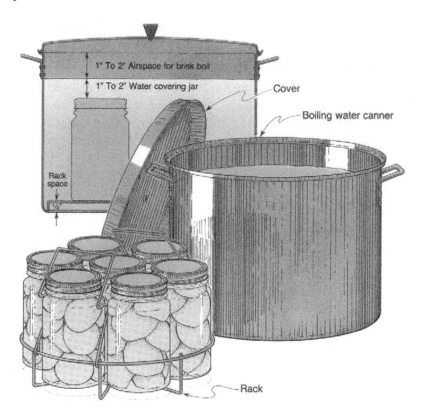

Fig. 29.6 Boiling water canner.

Low-acid foods must be processed in a pressure canner to be free of botulism risks. Although pressure canners may also be used for processing acid foods, boiling water canners are recommended for this purpose because they are faster. A pressure canner would require from 55 to 100 minutes to process a load of jars; while the total time for processing most acid foods in boiling water varies from 25 to 60 minutes. A boiling-water canner loaded with filled jars requires about 20 to 30 minutes of heating before its water begins to boil. A loaded pressure canner requires about 12 to 15 minutes of heating before it begins to vent; another 10 minutes to vent the canner; another 5 minutes to pressurize the canner; another 8 to 10 minutes to process the acid food; and, finally, another 20 to 60 minutes to cool the canner before removing jars.

Boiling-Water Canners

These canners are made of aluminum or porcelain-covered steel. They have removable perforated racks and fitted lids. The canner must be deep enough so that at least 1 inch of briskly boiling water will be over the tops of jars during processing. Some boiling-water canners do not have flat bottoms. A flat bottom must be used on an electric range. Either a flat or ridged bottom can be used on a gas burner. To ensure uniform processing of all jars with an electric range, the canner should be no more than 4 inches wider in diameter than the element on which it is heated.

Pressure Canners

Pressure canners for use in the home have been extensively redesigned in recent years. Models made before the 1970's were heavy-walled kettles with clamp-on or turn-on lids. They were fitted with a dial gauge, a vent port in the form of a petcock or counterweight, and a safety fuse. Modern pressure canners are lightweight, thin walled kettles; most have turn-on lids. They have a jar rack, gasket, dial or weighted gauge, an automatic vent/cover lock, a vent port (steam vent) to be closed with a counterweight or weighted gauge, and a safety fuse. Pressure does not destroy microorganisms, but high temperatures applied for an adequate period of time do kill microorganisms. The success of destroying all microorganisms capable of growing in canned food is based on the temperature obtained in pure steam, free of air, at sea level. At sea level, a canner operated at a gauge pressure of 10.5 lbs provides an internal temperature of 240°F (116° C).

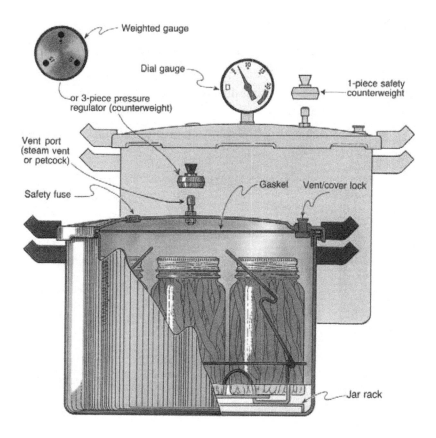

Fig. 29.7 Pressure canner.

Two serious errors in temperatures obtained in pressure canners occur because:

1. Internal canner temperatures are lower at higher altitudes. To correct this error, canners must be operated at the increased pressures specified in this publication for appropriate altitude ranges.

2. Air trapped in a canner lowers the temperature obtained at 5, 10, or 15 pounds of pressure and results in under processing. The highest volume of air trapped in a canner occurs in processing raw-packed foods in dial-gauge canners. These canners do not vent air during processing. To be safe, all types of pressure canners must be vented 10 minutes before they are pressurized.

Using Pressure Canners

To destroy microorganisms in low-acid foods processed with a pressure canner, you must:

- Process the jars using the correct time and pressure specified for your altitude.

- Allow canner to cool at room temperature until it is completely depressurized.

Fig. 29.8 Using pressure canner.

1. Put 2 to 3 inches of hot water in the canner. Some specific products in this Guide require that you start with even more water in the canner. Always follow the directions with USDA processes for specific foods if they require more water added to the canner. Place filled jars on the rack, using a jar lifter. When using a jar lifter, make sure it is securely positioned below the neck of the jar (below the screw band of the lid). Keep the jar upright at all times. Tilting the jar could cause food to spill into the sealing area of the lid. Fasten canner lid securely.

2. Leave weight off vent port or open petcock. Heat at the highest setting until steam flows freely from the open petcock or vent port.

3. While maintaining the high heat setting, let the steam flow (exhaust) continuously for 10 minutes, and then place the weight on the vent port or close the petcock. The canner will pressurize during the next 3 to 5 minutes.

4. Start timing the process when the pressure reading on the dial gauge indicates that the recommended pressure has been reached, or when the weighted gauge begins to jiggle or rock as the canner manufacturer describes.

5. Regulate heat under the canner to maintain a steady pressure at or slightly above the correct gauge pressure. Quick and large pressure variations during processing may cause unnecessary liquid losses from jars. Follow the canner manufacturer's directions for how a weighted gauge should indicate it is maintaining the desired pressure.

IMPORTANT: If at any time pressure goes below the recommended amount, bring the canner back to pressure and begin the timing of the process over, from the beginning (using the total original process time). This is important for the safety of the food.

6. When the timed process is completed, turn off the heat, remove the canner from heat if possible, and let the canner depressurize.

Do not force-cool the canner. Forced cooling may result in unsafe food or food spoilage. Cooling the canner with cold running water or opening the vent port before the canner is fully depressurized will cause loss of liquid from jars and seal failures. Force-cooling may also warp the canner lid of older model canners, causing steam leaks. Depressurization of older models without dial gauges should be timed. Standard-size heavy-walled canners require about 30 minutes when loaded with pints and 45 minutes with quarts. Newer thin-walled canners cool more rapidly and are equipped with vent locks.

These canners are depressurized when their vent lock piston drops to a normal position.

7. After the canner is depressurized, remove the weight from the vent port or open the petcock. Wait 10 minutes, unfasten the lid, and remove it carefully. Lift the lid away from you so that the steam does not burn your face.

8. Remove jars with a jar lifter, and place them on a towel, leaving at least 1-inch spaces between the jars during cooling. Let jars sit undisturbed to cool at room temperature for 12 to 24 hours.

To destroy microorganisms in low-acid foods processed with a pressure canner, you must:

- Process the jars using the correct time and pressure specified for your altitude.

- Allow canner to cool at room temperature until it is completely depressurized.

The food may spoil if you fail to select the proper process times for specific altitudes, fail to exhaust canners properly, process at lower pressure than specified, process for fewer minutes than specified, or cool the canner with water.

Using tables for determining proper process times

This following guides include processing times with altitude adjustments for each product. Process times for ½ pint and pint jars are the same, as are times for 1½ pint and quart jars. For some products, you have a choice of processing at 5, 10, or 15 PSI. In these cases, choose the canner pressure you wish to use and match it with your pack style (raw or hot) and jar size to find the correct process time.

Preparing and Canning Poultry, Red Meats, and Seafoods

Chicken or Rabbit

Procedure: Choose freshly killed and dressed, healthy animals. Large chickens are more flavorful than fryers. Dressed chicken should be chilled for 6 to 12 hours before canning. Dressed rabbits should be soaked 1 hour in water containing 1 tablespoon of salt per quart, and then rinsed. Remove excess fat. Cut the chicken or rabbit into suitable sizes for canning. Can with or without bones.

Hot pack-Boil, steam, or bake meat until about two-thirds done. Add 1 teaspoon salt per quart to the jar, if desired. Fill hot jars with pieces and hot broth, leaving 1¼ inch headspace. Remove air bubbles and adjust headspace if needed.

Raw pack - Add 1 teaspoon salt per quart, if desired. Fill hot jars loosely with raw meat pieces, leaving 1¼ inch headspace. Do not add liquid. Wipe rims of jars with a dampened clean paper towel. Adjust lids and process.

Process time for Chicken or Rabbit in a dial-gauge pressure canner						
Style of Pack	Jar Size	Process Time	Canner pressure (PSI) at Altitudes of			
			0-2,000 ft	2001-4000 ft	4001-6000 ft	6001-8000 ft
Without Bones:						
Hot and Raw	Pints	75 min	11 lb	12 lb	13 lb	14 lb
	Quarts	90	11	12	13	14
With Bones:						
Hot and Raw	Pints	65 min	11 lb	12 lb	13 lb	14 lb
	Quarts	75	11	12	13	14

Process time for Chicken or Rabbit in a weighted-gauge pressure canner				
Style of Pack	Jar Size	Process Time	Canner pressure (PSI) at Altitudes of	
			0-1,000 ft	Above 1000 ft
Without Bones:				
Hot and Raw	Pints	75 min	10 lb	15 lb
	Quarts	90	10	15
With Bones:				
Hot and Raw	Pints	65 min	10 lb	15 lb
	Quarts	75	10	15

GROUND OR CHOPPED MEAT

Bear, beef, lamb, pork, sausage, veal, venison

Procedure: Choose fresh, chilled meat. With venison, add one part high-quality pork fat to three or four parts venison before grinding. Use freshly made sausage, seasoned with salt and cayenne pepper (sage may cause a bitter off-flavor). Shape chopped meat into patties or balls or cut cased sausage into 3 to 4 inch links. Cook until lightly browned. Ground meat may be sauteed without shaping. Remove excess fat. Fill hot jars with pieces. Add boiling meat broth, tomato juice, or water, leaving 1 inch headspace. Remove air bubbles and adjust headspace if needed. Add 1 teaspoon of salt per quart to the jars, if desired. Wipe rims of jars with a dampened clean paper towel. Adjust lids and process.

Process time for Ground or Chopped Meat in a dial-gauge pressure canner						
Style of Pack	Jar Size	Process Time	Canner pressure (PSI) at Altitudes of			
			0-2,000 ft	2001-4000 ft	4001-6000 ft	6001-8000 ft
Hot	Pints	75 min	11 lb	12 lb	13 lb	14 lb
	Quarts	90	11	12	13	14

Process time for Ground or Chopped Meat in a weighted-gauge pressure canner				
Style of Pack	Jar Size	Process Time	Canner pressure (PSI) at Altitudes of	
			0-1,000 ft	Above 1000 ft
Hot	Pints	75 min	10 lb	15 lb
	Quarts	90	10	15

STRIPS, CUBES, OR CHUNKS OF MEAT

Bear, beef, lamb, pork, veal, venison

Procedure: Choose quality chilled meat. Remove excess fat. Soak strong-flavored wild meats for 1 hour in brine water containing 1 tablespoon of salt per quart. Rinse. Remove large bones.

Hot pack - Precook meat until rare by roasting, stewing, or browning in a small amount of fat. Add 1 teaspoon of salt per quart to the jar, if desired. Fill hot jars with pieces and add boiling broth, meat drippings, water, or tomato juice (especially with wild game), leaving 1 inch headspace. Remove air bubbles and adjust headspace if needed.

Raw pack - Add 1 teaspoon of salt per quart to the jar, if desired. Fill hot jars with raw meat pieces, leaving 1 inch headspace. Do not add liquid. Wipe rims of jars with a dampened clean paper towel. Adjust lids and process.

Process time for Strips, Cubes, or Chunks of Meat in a dial-gauge pressure canner						
Style of Pack	Jar Size	Process Time	Canner pressure (PSI) at Altitudes of			
			0-2,000 ft	2001-4000 ft	4001-6000 ft	6001-8000 ft
Hot and Raw	Pints	75 min	11 lb	12 lb	13 lb	14 lb
	Quarts	90	11	12	13	14

Process time for Strips, Cubes, or Chunks of Meat in a weighted-gauge pressure canner				
Style of Pack	Jar Size	Process Time	Canner pressure (PSI) at Altitudes of	
			0-1,000 ft	Above 1000 ft
Hot and Raw	Pints	75 min	10 lb	15 lb
	Quarts	90	10	15

MEAT STOCK (BROTH)

Beef: Saw or crack fresh trimmed beef bones to enhance extraction of flavor. Rinse bones and place in a large stockpot or kettle, cover bones with water, add pot cover, and simmer 3 to 4 hours. Remove bones, cool broth, and pick off meat. Skim off fat, add meat trimmings removed from bones to broth, and reheat to boiling. Fill hot jars, leaving 1 inch headspace. Wipe rims of jars with a dampened clean paper towel. Adjust lids and process.

Chicken or turkey: Place large carcass bones (with most of meat removed) in a large stockpot, add enough water to cover bones, cover pot, and simmer 30 to 45 minutes or until remaining attached meat can be easily stripped from bones. Remove bones and pieces, cool broth, strip meat, discard excess fat, and return meat trimmings to broth. Reheat to boiling and fill jars, leaving 1 inch headspace. Wipe rims of jars with a dampened clean paper towel. Adjust lids and process.

Process time for Meat Stock in a dial-gauge pressure canner						
Style of Pack	Jar Size	Process Time	Canner pressure (PSI) at Altitudes of			
			0-2,000 ft	2001-4000 ft	4001-6000 ft	6001-8000 ft
Hot	Pints	20 min	11 lb	12 lb	13 lb	14 lb
	Quarts	25	11	12	13	14

Process time for meat Stock in a weighted gauge pressure canner				
Style of Pack	Jar Size	Process Time	Canner pressure (PSI) at Altitudes of	
			0-1,000 ft	Above 1000 ft
Hot	Pints	20 min	10 lb	15 lb
	Quarts	25	10	15

CHILE CON CARNE

3 cups dried pinto or red kidney beans
5½ cups water
5 tsp salt (separated)
3 lbs ground beef
1½ cups chopped onions
1 cup chopped peppers of your choice (optional)
1 tsp black pepper
3 to 6 tbsp chili powder
2 quarts crushed or whole tomatoes
Yield: 9 pints

Procedure: Wash beans thoroughly and place them in a 2 qt. saucepan. Add cold water to a level of 2 to 3 inches above the beans and soak 12 to 18 hours. Drain and discard water. Combine beans with 5½ cups of fresh water and 2 teaspoons salt. Bring to a boil. Reduce heat and simmer 30 minutes. Drain and discard water. Brown ground beef, chopped onions, and peppers (if desired), in a skillet. Drain off fat and add 3 teaspoons salt, pepper, chili powder, tomatoes and drained cooked beans. Simmer 5 minutes. **Caution:** *Do not thicken.* Fill hot jars, leaving 1 inch headspace. Remove air bubbles and adjust headspace if needed. Wipe rims of jars with a dampened clean paper towel. Adjust lids and process.

Process time for Chile Con Carne in a dial-gauge pressure canner						
Style of Pack	Jar Size	Process Time	Canner pressure (PSI) at Altitudes of			
			0-2,000 ft	2001-4000 ft	4001-6000 ft	6001-8000 ft
Hot	Pints	75 min	11 lb	12 lb	13 lb	14 lb

Process time for Chile Con Carne in a weighted-gauge pressure canner				
Style of Pack	Jar Size	Process Time	Canner pressure (PSI) at Altitudes of	
			0-1,000 ft	Above 1000 ft
Hot	Pints	75 min	10 lb	15 lb

CLAMS

Whole or minced
Procedure: Keep clams live on ice until ready to can. Scrub shells thoroughly and rinse, steam 5 minutes, and open. Remove clam meat.

Collect and save clam juice. Wash clam meat in water containing 1 teaspoon of salt per quart. Rinse and cover clam meat with boiling water containing 2 tablespoons of lemon juice or ½ teaspoon of citric acid per gallon. Boil 2 minutes and drain. To make minced clams, grind clams with a meat grinder or food processor. Fill hot jars loosely with pieces and add hot clam juice and boiling water if needed, leaving 1 inch headspace. Remove air bubbles and adjust headspace if needed. Wipe rims of jars with a dampened clean paper towel. Adjust lids and process.

Process time for Clams in a dial-gauge pressure canner						
Style of Pack	Jar Size	Process Time	Canner pressure (PSI) at Altitudes of			
			0-2,000 ft	2001-4000 ft	4001-6000 ft	6001-8000 ft
Hot	Halfpints	60 min	11 lb	12 lb	13 lb	14 lb
	Pints	70	11	12	13	14

Process time for Clams in a weighted-gauge pressure canner				
Style of Pack	Jar Size	Process Time	Canner pressure (PSI) at Altitudes of	
			0-1,000 ft	Above 1000 ft
Hot	Half-pints	60 min	10 lb	15 lb
	Pints	70	10	15

KING AND DUNGENESS CRAB MEAT

It is recommended that blue crab meat be frozen instead of canned for best quality. Crab meat canned according to the following procedure may have a distinctly acidic flavor and freezing is the preferred method of preservation at this time.

Procedure: Keep live crabs on ice until ready to can. Wash crabs thoroughly, using several changes of cold water. Simmer crabs 20 minutes in water containing cup of lemon juice and 2 tablespoons of salt (or up to 1 cup of salt, if desired) per gallon. Cool in cold water, drain, remove back shell, then remove meat from body and claws. Soak meat 2 minutes in cold water containing 2 cups of lemon juice or 4 cups of white vinegar, and 2 tablespoons of salt (or up to 1 cup of salt, if desired) per gallon. Drain and squeeze crab meat to remove excess moisture.

Fill hot half-pint jars with 6 ounces of crab meat and pint jars with 12 ounces, leaving 1 inch headspace. Add ½ teaspoon of citric acid or 2 tablespoons of lemon juice to each half-pint jar, or 1 teaspoon of citric acid or 4 tablespoons of lemon juice per pint jar. Cover with fresh boiling water, leaving 1 inch headspace. Remove air bubbles and adjust headspace if needed. Wipe rims of jars with a dampened clean paper towel. Adjust lids and process.

Process time for King and Dungeness Crab Meat in a dial-gauge pressure canner						
Style of Pack	Jar Size	Process Time	Canner pressure (PSI) at Altitudes of			
			0-2,000 ft	2001-4000 ft	4001-6000 ft	6001-8000 ft
Hot	Half-pints	70 min	11 lb	12 lb	13 lb	14 lb
	Pints	80	11	12	13	14

Process time for King and Dungeness Crab Meat in a weighted-gauge pressure canner				
Style of Pack	Jar Size	Process Time	Canner pressure (PSI) at Altitudes of	
			0-1,000 ft	Above 1000 ft
Hot	Half-pints	70 min	10 lb	15 lb
	Pints	80	10	15

FISH in *Pint* Jars

Blue, mackerel, salmon, steelhead, trout, and other fatty fish except tuna

Caution: Bleed and eviscerate fish immediately after catching, never more than 2 hours after they are caught. Keep cleaned fish on ice until ready to can.

Note: Glass-like crystals of struvite, or magnesium ammonium phosphate, sometime form in canned salmon. There is no way for the home canner to prevent these crystals from forming, but they usually dissolve when heated and are safe to eat.

Procedure: If the fish is frozen, thaw it in the refrigerator before canning. Rinse the fish in cold water. You can add vinegar to the water (2 tablespoons per quart) to help remove slime. Remove head, tail, fins, and scales; it is not necessary to remove the skin. You can leave the bones in most fish because the bones become very soft and are a good source of calcium.

For halibut, remove the head, tail, fins, skin, and the bones. Wash and remove all blood. Refrigerate all fish until you are ready to pack in jars. Split fish lengthwise, if desired. Cut cleaned fish into 3½ inch lengths. If the skin has been left on the fish, pack the fish skin out, for a nicer appearance or skin in, for easier jar cleaning. Fill hot pint jars, leaving 1 inch headspace. Add 1 teaspoon of salt per pint, if desired. Do not add liquids. Carefully clean the jar rims with a clean, damp paper towel; wipe with a dry paper towel to remove any fish oil. Adjust lids and process. Fish in half-pint or 12 ounce jars would be processed for the same amount of time as pint jars.

Process time for Fish in Pint Jars in a dial-gauge pressure canner						
Style of Pack	Jar Size	Process Time	Canner pressure (PSI) at Altitudes of			
			0-2,000 ft	2001-4000 ft	4001-6000 ft	6001-8000 ft
Raw	Pints	100 min	11 lb	12 lb	13 lb	14 lb

Process time for Fish in Pint Jars in a weighted-gauge pressure canner				
Style of Pack	Jar Size	Process Time	Canner pressure (PSI) at Altitudes of	
			0-1,000 ft	Above 1000 ft
Raw	Pints	100 min	10 lb	15 lb

FISH in *Quart* Jars

Blue, mackerel, salmon, steelhead, trout, and other fatty fish except tuna

Note: Glass-like crystals of struvite, or magnesium ammonium phosphate, sometime form in canned salmon. There is no way for the home canner to prevent these crystals from forming, but they usually dissolve when heated and are safe to eat.

Caution: Bleed and eviscerate fish immediately after catching, never more than 2 hours after they are caught. Keep cleaned fish on ice until ready to can.

Procedure: If the fish is frozen, thaw it in the refrigerator before canning. Rinse the fish in cold water. You can add vinegar to the water (2 tablespoons per quart) to help remove slime. Remove head, tail, fins, and scales; it is not necessary to remove the skin.

You can leave the bones in most fish because the bones become very soft and are a good source of calcium. For halibut, remove the head, tail, fins, skin, and the bones. Wash and remove all blood. Refrigerate all fish until you are ready to pack in jars. Cut the fish into jar-length filets or chunks of any size. The one-quart straight-sided mason type jar is recommended. If the skin has been left on the fish, pack the fish skin out, for a nicer appearance or skin in, for easier jar cleaning. Pack solidly into hot quart jars, leaving 1 inch headspace. If desired, run a plastic knife around the inside of the jar to align the product;
this allows firm packing of fish. For most fish, no liquid, salt, or spices need to be added, although seasonings or salt may be added for flavor (1 to 2 teaspoons salt per quart, or amount desired). For halibut, add up to 4 tablespoons of vegetable or olive oil per quart jar if you wish. The canned product will seem moister. However, the oil will increase the caloric value of the fish. Carefully clean the jar rims with a clean, damp paper towel; wipe with a dry paper towel to remove any fish oil. Adjust lids and process.

Processing Change for Quart Jars: The directions for operating the pressure canner during processing of quart jars are different from those for processing pint jars, so please read the following carefully. It is critical to product safety that the processing directions are followed exactly. When you are ready to process your jars of fish, add 3 quarts of water to the pressure canner. Put the rack in the bottom of canner and place closed jars on the rack. Fasten the canner cover securely, but do not close the lid vent. Heat the canner on high for 20 minutes. If steam comes through the open vent in a steady stream at the end of 20 minutes, allow it to escape for an additional 10 minutes. If steam does not come through the open vent in a steady stream at the end of 20 minutes, keep heating the canner until it does. Then allow the steam to escape for an additional 10 minutes to vent the canner. This step removes air from inside the canner so the temperature is the same throughout the canner.

The total time it takes to heat and vent the canner should never be less than 30 minutes. The total time may be more than 30 minutes if you have tightly packed jars, cold fish, or larger sized canners. For safety's sake, you must have a complete, uninterrupted 160 minutes (2 hours and 40 minutes) at a minimum pressure required for your altitude. Write down the time at the beginning of the process and the time when the process will be finished.

Process time for Fish in Quart Jars in a dial-gauge pressure canner						
Style of Pack	Jar Size	Process Time	Canner pressure (PSI) at Altitudes of			
			0-2,000 ft	2001-4000 ft	4001-6000 ft	6001-8000 ft
Raw	Quarts	160 min	11 lb	12 lb	13 lb	14 lb

Process time for Fish in Quart Jars in a weighted-gauge pressure canner				
Style of Pack	Jar Size	Process Time	Canner pressure (PSI) at Altitudes of	
			0-1,000 ft	Above 1000 ft
Raw	Quarts	160 min	10 lb	15 lb

OYSTERS

Procedure: Keep live oysters on ice until ready to can. Wash shells. Heat 5 to 7 minutes in preheated oven at 400°F (204° C). Cool briefly in ice water. Drain, open shell, and remove meat. Wash meat in water containing ½ cup salt per gallon. Drain. Add ½ teaspoon salt to each pint, if desired. Fill hot half-pint or pint jars with drained oysters and cover with fresh boiling water, leaving 1 inch headspace. Remove air bubbles and adjust headspace if needed. Wipe rims of jars with a dampened clean paper towel. Adjust lids and process.

Process time for Oysters in a dial-gauge pressure canner						
Style of Pack	Jar Size	Process Time	Canner pressure (PSI) at Altitudes of			
			0-2,000 ft	2001-4000 ft	4001-6000 ft	6001-8000 ft
See above	Half-pints or pints	75 min	11 lb	12 lb	13 lb	14 lb

Process time for Oysters in a weighted-gauge pressure canner				
Style of Pack	Jar Size	Process Time	Canner pressure (PSI) at Altitudes of	
			0-1,000 ft	Above 1000 ft
See above	Half-pints or pints	75 min	10 lb	15 lb

SMOKED FISH

Salmon, rockfish and flatfish (sole, cod, flounder) and other fish

Caution: Safe processing times for other smoked seafoods have not been determined. Those products should be frozen. Smoking of fish should be done by tested methods. Lightly smoked fish is recommended for canning because the smoked flavor will become stronger and the flesh drier after processing. However, because it has not yet been cooked, do not taste lightly smoked fish before canning. Follow these recommended canning instructions carefully. Use a 16 to 22 quart pressure canner for this procedure; do not use smaller pressure saucepans. Safe processing times have not been determined. Do not use jars larger than one pint. Half-pints could be safely processed for the same length of time as pints, but the quality of the product may be less acceptable.

Procedure: If smoked fish has been frozen, thaw in the refrigerator until no ice crystals remain before canning. If not done prior to smoking, cut fish into pieces that will fit vertically into pint canning jars, leaving 1 inch headspace. Pack smoked fish vertically into hot jars, leaving 1 inch headspace between the pieces and the top rim of the jar. The fish may be packed either loosely or tightly. Do not add liquid to the jars. Clean jar rims with a clean, damp paper towel. Adjust lids and process.

Processing Change for Smoked Fish: The directions for filling the pressure canner for processing smoked fish are different than those for other pressure canning, so please read the following carefully. It is critical to product safety that the processing directions are followed exactly. When you are ready to process your jars of smoked fish, measure 4 quarts (16 cups) of cool tap water and pour into the pressure canner. (Note: The water level probably will reach the screw bands of pint jars.) Do not decrease the amount of water or heat the water before processing begins. Place prepared, closed jars on the rack in the bottom of the canner, and proceed as with usual pressure canning instructions.

Process time for Smoked Fish in a dial-gauge pressure canner						
Style of Pack	Jar Size	Process Time	Canner pressure (PSI) at Altitudes of			
			0-2,000 ft	2001-4000 ft	4001-6000 ft	6001-8000 ft
See above	Pints	110 min	11 lb	12 lb	13 lb	14 lb

Process time for Smoked Fish in a weighted-gauge pressure canner				
Style of Pack	Jar Size	Process Time	Canner pressure (PSI) at Altitudes of	
			0-1,000 ft	Above 1000 ft
See above	Pints	110 min	10 lb	15 lb

TUNA

Tuna may be canned either precooked or raw. Precooking removes most of the strong-flavored oils. The strong flavor of dark tuna flesh affects the delicate flavor of white flesh. Many people prefer not to can dark flesh. It may be used as pet food.

Note: Glass-like crystals of struvite, or magnesium ammonium phosphate, sometime form in canned tuna. There is no way for the home canner to prevent these crystals from forming, but they usually dissolve when heated and are safe to eat.

Procedure: Keep tuna on ice until ready to can. Remove viscera and wash fish well in cold water. Allow blood to drain from stomach cavity. Place fish belly down on a rack or metal tray in the bottom of a large baking pan. Cut tuna in half crosswise, if necessary. Precook fish by baking at 250°F (121° C) for 2½ to 4 hours (depending on size) or at 350°F (177° C) for 1 hour. The fish may also be cooked in a steamer for 2 to 4 hours. If a thermometer is used, cook to a 165° to 175°F (74 - 80° C) internal temperature. Refrigerate cooked fish overnight to firm the meat. Peel off the skin with a knife, removing blood vessels and any discolored flesh. Cut meat away from bones; cut out and discard all bones, fin bases, and dark flesh. Quarter. Cut quarters crosswise into lengths suitable for half-pint or pint jars. Fill into hot jars, pressing down gently to make a solid pack. Tuna may be packed in water or oil, whichever is preferred. Add water or oil to jars, leaving 1 inch headspace. Remove air bubbles and adjust headspace if needed. Add ½ teaspoon of salt per half-pint or 1 teaspoon of salt per pint, if desired. Carefully clean the jar rims with a clean, damp paper towel; wipe with a dry paper towel to remove any fish oil. Adjust lids and process.

Process time for Tuna in a dial-gauge pressure canner						
Style of Pack	Jar Size	Process Time	Canner pressure (PSI) at Altitudes of			
			0-2,000 ft	2001-4000 ft	4001-6000 ft	6001-8000 ft
See above	Half-pints or pints	100 min	11 lb	12 lb	13 lb	14 lb

Process time for Tuna in a weighted-gauge pressure canner				
Style of Pack	Jar Size	Process Time	Canner pressure (PSI) at Altitudes of	
			0-1,000 ft	Above 1000 ft
See above	Half-pints or pints	100 min	10 lb	15 lb

American pressure canners measure pressure in pounds per square inch (PSI). European pressure canners measure pressure in "bars" or in "kPa".

American PSI	European bar	European kPa
10	0.6890	68.94
11	0.7579	75.84
12	0.8268	82.73
13	0.8957	89.63
14	0.9646	96.52
15	1.0335	103.42

Photo 29.1 Well equipped kitchen pantry.

Photo: Andrzej Wawrzynek.

Recipe Index

#	Name	Type	Page
1	American Country Ham	hams	507
2	Andouille	fresh	231
3	Bacon, Cured & Smoked	other meats	531
4	Bacon Sausage	cold smoked	254
5	Biltong	air dried	559
6	Black Pudding	blood sausage, B	359
7	Bockwurst	fresh	232
8	Boerenmetworst	fermented	404
9	Bologna	emulsified	290
10	Boudin	fresh	233
11	Bresaola	other meats	532
12	Bratwurst	fresh	235
13	Braunschweiger	liver sausage	315
14	Breakfast Sausage	fresh	236
15	Cacciatore	fermented	405
16	Canadian Bacon	other meats	533
17	Cervelat	fermented	406
18	Chaurice	fresh	237
19	Chicken Curry	fresh	238
20	Chicken Meat Jelly	head cheese	338
21	Chicken Sausage	Kosher,	255
22	Chicken Smoked	smoked	569
23	Chinese Sausage	hot smoked	255
24	Coney Island Frank	emulsified	291
25	Chorizo	fermented	407
26	Chorizo - Argentinean	fresh	239
27	Chorizo - Mexican	fresh	240
28	Coppa	other meats	534

29	Corned Game	wild game	609
30	Deer Sausage	wild game	610
31	Drisheen	blood sausage	360
32	Duck Sausage	poultry	571
33	Finger Sausage	cooked	208
34	Fish and Bacon Sausage	fish	593
35	Fish Links	fish, Kosher	594
36	Fish Sausage	fish, Kosher	595
37	Frankfurter	emulsified	292
38	Fuet	fermented	408
39	Goose Sausage	poultry, Kosher	572
40	Goteborg	fermented	409
41	Gothaer	fermented	410
42	Grassland Sausage	cold smoked	411
43	Greek Sausage	fresh	241
44	Ham-Minced Butt	hams	508
45	Ham - Minced Picnic	hams	510
46	Ham-Minced Butt & Picnic	hams	509
47	Ham-Smoked & Cooked	hams	513
48	Ham-Smoked, Bone-in	hams	514
49	Ham-Molded	hams	511
50	Ham Sausage	cooked	257
51	Haggis	head cheese	340
52	Head Cheese - City	head cheese	341
53	Head Cheese - Farmer	head cheese	339
54	Head Cheese - Italian	head cheese	343
55	Head Cheese - Tongue	head cheese	344
56	Holsteiner	fermented	412
57	Hotdog	emulsified	293
58	Hurka	fresh	242
59	Hungarian Smoked Sausage	fermented	413
60	Italian Sausage	fresh	243
61	Jadgwurst	hot smoked	258

95	Mettwurst-Braunschweiger	fermented	426
96	Morcilla	blood sausage	362
97	Morcilla Blanca	blood sausage	363
98	Moscow Sausage	cooked	262
99	Mortadella di Bologna	emulsified	294
100	Mortadella Lyoner	emulsified	295
101	Mortadella - Polish	emulsified	296
102	Mysliwska	hot smoked	263
103	Navajo	blood sausage	364
104	Nham	fermented, K	427
105	Pancetta	other meats	538
106	Pastirma	jerky	560
107	Pastrami	other meats, K	539
108	Pemmican	jerky	561
109	Pennsylvania Scrapple	head cheese	346
110	Pepperoni - Dry	dry-fermented	429
111	Pepperoni - Semi-Dry	semi-dry fermented	430
112	Pickled Pigs Feet	head cheese	348
113	Podhalanska	hot smoked	265
114	Polish Smoked Sausage	cold smoked	431
115	Polish Smoked Sausage	hot smoked	267
116	Polish Sausage w/Oil Emulsion	hot smoked	458
117	Pork Loaf	other meats	541
118	Pork Curry Sausage	emulsified	297
119	Potato Sausage	fresh	249
120	Poultry Liver Sausage	poultry	574
121	Rabbit Sausage	wild game	611
122	Romanian Sausage	hot smoked	268
123	Russian Sausage	cold smoked	432
124	Russian Sausage	hot smoked	269
125	Salami - Genoa	fermented	433
126	Salami - Hungarian	fermented	434
127	Salami Krakowskie	hot smoked	270

161	Wild Boar Sausage	wild game	613
162	Wiener	emulsified	300
Pressure Canned Meats			
163	Chicken or Rabbit		638
164	Ground or Chopped Meat		639
165	Strips, Cubes, or Chunks of Meat		640
166	Meat Stock (Broth)		641
167	Chile Con Carne		642
168	Clams		642
169	King and Dungeness Crab Meat		643
170	Fish in Pint Jars		644
171	Fish in Quart Jars		645
172	Oysters		647
173	Smoked Fish		648
174	Tuna		649

Appendix A

Tables and Formulas

How To Calculate Cure # 1 in Comminuted Products (Sausages)

In case you are really curious and would like to know how to calculate ppm (parts per million) of nitrite when using Cure #1 here is the formula and an example:

How much Cure #1 is needed to cure 200 lbs of meat?

$$\textbf{ppm} = \frac{\textbf{cure mix x \% sodium nitrite in cure x 1,000,000}}{\textbf{weight of meat}}$$

Note that the weight of cure mix and the weight of meat must be in the same units (pounds, ounces, grams, kilograms)

Maximum allowed limit of sodium nitrite is **156 ppm**
Cure #1 contains 6.25% sodium nitrite = 0.0625
Solving equation for Cure #1:

cure mix = ppm x meat weight/% sodium nitrite in cure x 1,000,000
n = unknown amount of cure mix

156 = n x 0.0625 x 1,000,000 / 200
n = 156 x 200 / 0.0625 x 1,000,000
n = 0.4992 lb. of Cure #1, which equals 7.98 oz (226 g)

To cure 200 lbs of meat and stay within the prescribed 156 ppm nitrite limit we should use no more than 0.4992 lb. of Cure #1. This formula applies to the dry method of curing when the nitrite is directly applied to meat. The example will be meat that was ground and then will be mixed with spices and Cure #1 to make a sausage.

The same example using the metric system:
1 lb. = 0.453 kg, 200 lbs = 90.6 kg
n = 156 x 90.6 / 0.0625 x 1,000,000
n = 0.226 kg (226 g) of Cure #1

If 0.0625 is removed from the above formula, not Cure #1 but sodium nitrite will become a part of the equation:

ppm = sodium nitrite x 1,000,000 / weight of meat

sodium nitrite = ppm x meat weight/1,000,000
N = unknown amount of sodium nitrite
156 = N x 1,000,000 / 200
N = 156 x 200 / 1,000,000
N = 0.031 lb. of sodium nitrite, which equals 5 oz (14 g)
To find the amount of Cure #1 required, we have to divide the amount of sodium nitrite (14 g) by the percentage of sodium nitrite in the Cure #1 (6.25%)
14 / 0.0625 = 224 g of Cure #1

How to Calculate Cure #1 in Brined Products

Calculating cure in mixed products is more difficult when the traditional wet curing method is used. It is easy to calculate how many parts per million of sodium nitrite is in the brine, but it is harder to estimate how much sodium nitrite has made it into the meat. A meat piece can be immersed in brine for a day, a week or a month and a different amount of sodium nitrite will penetrate the meat. Brines with different salt concentrations will exhibit different speeds of salt and nitrite penetration. One will have to weigh the meat to estimate the amount of brine the meat has picked up.

All modern curing methods rely on injecting brine directly into the meat which eliminates this guessing game. We know exactly how much brine we inject and precise calculations can be performed. These figures are based on pump percentages and revolve around 10% average pump pick up. What it means is that a 10 lbs. meat piece will be injected with the amount of brine corresponding to 10% of its weight. In this case 1 lb. of brine will be injected into 10 lbs. of meat.

Maximum allowed limit of sodium nitrite in brined products is **200 ppm.** Cure #1 contains 6.25% sodium nitrite = 0.0625

Example:
Hams are to be pumped at 12% using Cure #1. How much cure can be added to 100 gallons of brine? Brine weight is 9.5 lb per gallon.

ppm = cure mix x % of sodium nitrite in cure x pump% x 1,000,000 / brine weight

One gallon of water weighs 8.33 lb but saturated brine (100 degree) contains 26.4% salt in it. One gallon of saturated brine contains 2.64 lb of salt and weighs 10.03 lb. Depending on the strength of your brine you can estimate its weight or use brine tables to arrive at more accurate values.

Example:

A meat piece is to be pumped at 10% using Cure #1. How much cure can be added to 1 gallon of brine? Brine weight is 9.5 lb. per gallon which corresponds to the brine strength of around 40°.

n = 200 x 9.5 / 0.10 x 0.0625 x 1,000,000

n = 0.30 lb. (4.8 oz, 136 g) of Cure #1.

If 0.0625 is removed from the above formula, not Cure #1 but sodium nitrite will become a part of the equation:

ppm = sodium nitrite x pump % x 1,000,000 / brine weight

sodium nitrite = ppm x brine weight / % pump x 1,000,000

N = 200 x 9.5 / 0.10 x 1,000,000

N = 0.019 lb. of sodium nitrite

To find the amount of Cure #1 required, we have to divide the amount of sodium nitrite (0.019 lb) by the percentage of sodium nitrite in the Cure #1 (6.25%).

0.019/0.0625 = 0.30 lb. of Cure # 1

Only established meat plants have access to sodium nitrite and they may formulate their own cures. A hobbyist will use Cure #1 which is pre-mixed and safer.

Brine Tables and How to Use Them

If you come across a recipe and you would like to determine what is the strength of the brine, just follow the two steps:

1. Find the percent of salt by weight in the solution: weight of salt/(weight of salt plus weight of water), then multiply the result by 100%.
2. Look up the tables and find the corresponding salometer degree.

For example let's find the strength of the brine that is mentioned in many recipes and calls for adding 1 pound of salt to 1 gallon of water (8.33 pounds).

% salt by weight = 1lb. of salt/1 lb of salt + 8.33 lbs. (1 gallon) of water = 0.1071

0.1071 x 100 % = 10.71 % of salt

Looking in the table at Column 2 (percent salt by weight) we can see that 10.71% corresponds to **40 ½ degrees.**

Another popular brine is made by adding 3/4 cup of salt (219 g) to 1 gallon (3.8 liters) of water

219 g / 219 + 3800 g = 0.05

0.05 x 100 = 5% of salt

Looking in the table at Column 2 (percent salt by weight) we can see that 5% corresponds to **19 degrees.**

Adding salt to water and checking the reading with a salinometer is a rather time consuming method and you can make brine much faster by using tables, the way professionals do. For example we want 22 degrees brine to cure chicken. If you follow the 22 degree row to the right you will see in Column 3 that 0.513 lb. of salt has to be added to 1 gallon of water to make 22 degree brine. To make 80 degree brine we need to mix 2.229 lbs. of salt with 1 gallon of water. Then check it with your salinometer and you can add a cup of water or a tablespoon of salt to get a perfect reading.

If you end up with not enough brine, make some more. If you think you may need just 1/2 gallon more of 80 degree brine, take 1/2 gallon of water and add 1/2 of salt that the table asks for. In this case looking at 80 degree brine (Column 1), going to the right you can see that in Column 3 the amount of the needed salt is 2.229 lbs. Yes, but this amount is added to 1 gallon of water to create 80 degree brine. Because we use only 1/2 gallon now, this amount of salt needs to be halved: 2.229 lbs./2 = 1.11 lbs. In other words if we add 1.11 lbs. of salt to 1/2 gallon of water we will also create 80 degree brine.

- Seawater contains approximately 3.695% of salt which corresponds to 14 degrees salometer.
- At 100 degrees brine is fully saturated and contains 26.395% of salt.
- 1 US gallon of water weighs 8.33 lbs.
- 1 US gallon = 3.8 liters = 3.8 kilograms.
- Bear in mind that when you add Cure #1 to your solution (it contains 93.75% salt) you will be changing the strength of the brine, especially at higher degrees. Simply subtract this amount from the salt given by the tables.
- There is another set of brine tables for UK Gallons (UK imperial gallon = 4.54 liters) and it can be looked up on the Internet.

Salinometer readings are calibrated to give a correct indication when the brine is at 60° F temperature. Each brine tester will have its own instructions for temperature compensation but the basic rule of thumb says that for every 10° F the brine is above 60° F, one degree should be added to the reading before using table. If the brine is below 60° F subtract 1 degree for each 10° F from the observed salinometer reading before using table.

For example, if a salinometer indicates 70 degrees brine and the brine's temperature is 40° F, the corrected salinometer reading would be 68 degrees (for each 10° F below 60° F, one salinometer degree is subtracted). If the brine temperature is 80° F and the salinometer indicates 40 degrees, the corrected reading would be 82 degrees SAL (for each 10° F above 60° F, one salinometer degree is added). These are very small differences which are of bigger importance for a meat plant curing huge amounts of meat at one time. Needless to say a thermometer is needed, too.

Sodium Chloride (Salt) Brine Tables For Brine at 60° F (15° C) in US Gallons

Salometer Degrees	% of Salt by Weight	Pounds of Salt per Gallon of Water
0	0.000	0.000
10	2.640	0.226
15	3.959	0.343
20	5.279	0.464
21	5.543	0.489
22	**5.807**	**0.513**
23	6.071	0.538
24	6.335	0.563
25	6.599	0.588
26	6.863	0.614
27	7.127	0.639
28	7.391	0.665
29	7.655	0.690
30	7.919	0.716
31	8.162	0.742
32	8.446	0.768
33	8.710	0.795
34	8.974	0.821
35	9.238	0.848
36	9.502	0.874
37	9.766	0.901
38	10.030	0.928
39	10.294	0.956
40	10.588	0.983
41	10.822	1.011
42	11.086	1.038
43	11.350	1.066
44	11.614	1.094
45	11.878	1.123
46	12.142	1.151
47	12.406	1.179
48	12.670	1.208
49	12.934	1.237

50	13.198	1.266
51	13.461	1.295
52	13.725	1.325
53	13.989	1.355
54	14.253	1.384
55	14.517	1.414
56	14.781	1.444
57	15.045	1.475
58	15.309	1.505
59	15.573	1.536
60	15.837	**1.567**
61	16.101	1.598
62	16.365	1.630
63	16.629	1.661
64	16.893	1.693
65	17.157	1.725
66	17.421	1.757
67	17.685	1.789
68	17.949	1.822
69	18.213	1.854
70	18.477	1.887
71	18.740	1.921
72	19.004	1.954
73	19.268	1.988
74	19.532	2.021
75	19.796	2.056
76	20.060	2.090
77	20.324	2.124
78	20.588	2.159
79	20.852	2.194
80	21.116	**2.229**
85	22.436	2.409
90	23.756	2.595
95	25.075	2.787
100	26.395	2.986

Baumé Scale

You may come across a scale in Baumé degrees that is based on the specific gravity of the brine measured with a hydrometer. It is a popular scale in metric countries and you can often find reference given in Baumé degrees. One can measure the gravity of the brine with a specially designed float (like a brine tester) and one can refer to the table and look up the % NaCl (salt) by weight. One Baumé degree corresponds to 10 g of salt in 1 liter of water. The table below compares brine strength degrees with Baumé scale.

Specific Gravity	% Salt by Weight	Baumé Degrees	Salometer Degrees
1.007	1	1.0	4
1.014	2	2.0	8
1.022	3	3.1	12
1.029	4	4.1	15
1.037	5	5.2	19
1.044	6	6.1	25
1.051	7	7.0	27
1.058	8	7.9	30
1.066	9	8.9	34
1.073	10	9.8	37
1.081	11	10.9	41
1.089	12	11.9	46
1.096	13	12.7	50
1.104	14	13.7	54
1.112	15	14.6	57
1.119	16	15.4	61
1.127	17	16.3	65
1.135	18	17.2	69
1.143	19	18.1	72
1.151	20	19.0	76
1.159	21	19.9	80
1.168	22	20.9	84
1.176	23	21.7	88
1.184	24	22.5	92
1.192	25	23.4	95
1.201	26	24.3	99

Humidity

Humidity or better said the "relative humidity" defines how much water (vapor) is present in the air at a particular temperature. The air almost always contains some water vapor and although we don't see it, it is there and it has a certain mass (weight).

The higher the temperature the more water can be held by air and vice versa. As the amount of moisture in the air is fixed for at least some time (the clouds can bring moisture and rain), raising the temperature lowers the relative humidity. There is a point for each temperature reading when air can hold the maximum possible amount of water and we call it a saturation or a dew point. At this point the relative humidity is 100%. If the dew point is below freezing, it is called the frost point and the water vapor will form the frost or the snow. Air with a temperature of 30° C (86° F), (can hold more than three times as much moisture as air at 10° C (50° F). In the same room at 100% relative humidity, if we suddenly lower the temperature, the air can now hold less moisture and the droplets of water will start condensing on smooth surfaces such as mirrors, knives, or even meat itself.

The humidity control in a meat plant is based on dew point control. *Dew point is the temperature at which condensation forms.* When air comes in contact with a surface (often metal or glass surfaces) that is at or below its Dew Point temperature, condensation will form on that surface. In a meat plant the item that is at risk is meat taken out from the cooler as its temperature will be about 2° C (35° F). In the processing room the temperatures are about 10-12° C (50-53° F), though they may reach even up to 16° C (60° F) if the meat will not remain there longer than one hour. By adjusting the room temperature and its humidity levels we can control the temperature of the dew point. In a well designed meat plant the temperature will stay more or less the same. If the facility is climate controlled, the amount of relative humidity should also remain at the same level. In the kind of "improvised" facility without automatic control, the relative humidity can be controlled by any of the following factors:

- Meat temperature - the worst solution as the meat's temperature will have to be increased which will lead to bacteria growth and shorter shelf life of the product.

- Room temperature - will have to be lowered which is acceptable.

- Room humidity - the best idea as it allows moisture removal (dehumidifier) or moisture introduction (humidifier) by separate devices. Those simple units will control the relative humidity without the need for room temperature adjustments or worrying about meat temperature. In the table below only a part of the table that contains temperatures that might be encountered in a meat processing facility is quoted.

• Tables that include all temperature and humidity readings can be obtained on the Internet. It is very unlikely that an average home sausage maker will ever bother with humidity control but those interested in making fermented sausages will need to know humidity control very well.

Dew Point Table in ° F

Air Temp. in ° F	% Relative Humidity								
	100	90	80	70	60	50	35	30	25
65	65	62	59	55	50	45	36	32	
60	60	57	53	50	45	**41**	**32**		
55	55	52	49	45	40	36			
53	53	50	46	43	39	35			
52	52	48	44	43	37	**33**			
50	50	46	44	39	35	32			
45	45	43	39	35	32				
40	40	37	34						
35	35	32							
32	32								

Example: if the temperature in the sausage factory is 60° F (16° C) and the relative humidity is 50%, the intersection of the two shows that the Dew Point is reached at the temperature of 41° F (5° C), or below. This means that the moisture that is present in the air at 60° F (16° C) will condense on any surface that is at or below the Dew Point temperature of 41° F (5° C). This also means that if the meat having a temperature of 35° F (2° C) was brought from the cooler into this room (60° F, 16° C) the moisture would condense on its surface. The meat's temperature of 35° F (2° C) is below the Dew Point limit of 41° F (5° C).

Until recently, measurements of humidity required knowledge of terms such as wet and dry bulb temperatures and a good command of relative humidity tables. Today, there are very accurate digital humidity meters, devices such as humidistats which measure humidity and will switch a humidifier on and off as needed. For typical meat smoking applications such humidity control is not needed unless one starts producing fermented products.

Title 9: Animals and Animal Products

PART 318 - ENTRY INTO OFFICIAL ESTABLISHMENTS;
REINSPECTION AND PREPARATION OF PRODUCTS

§ 318.10   Prescribed treatment of pork and products containing pork to destroy trichinae.

(a)(1) All forms of fresh pork, including fresh unsmoked sausage containing pork muscle tissue, and pork such as bacon and jowls, other than those covered by paragraph (b) of this section, are classed as products that are customarily well cooked in the home or elsewhere before being served to the consumer. Therefore, the treatment of such products for the destruction of trichinae is not required.

(2) Pork from carcasses or carcass parts that have been found free of trichinae as described under paragraph (e) or (f) of this section is not required to be treated for the destruction of trichinae.

(b) Products named in this paragraph, and products of the character hereof, containing pork muscle tissue (not including pork hearts, pork stomachs, and pork livers), or the pork muscle tissue which forms an ingredient of such products, shall be effectively heated, refrigerated, or cured to destroy any possible live trichinae, as prescribed in this section at the official establishment where such products are prepared: Bologna, frankfurter, vienna, and other cooked sausage; smoked sausage; knoblauch sausage; mortadella; all forms of summer or dried sausage, including mettwurst; flavored pork sausages such as those containing wine or similar flavoring materials; cured pork sausage; sausage containing cured and/or smoked pork; cooked loaves; roasted, baked, boiled, or cooked hams, pork shoulders, or pork shoulder picnics; Italian-style hams; Westphalia-style hams; smoked boneless pork shoulder butts; cured meat rolls; capocollo (capicola, capacola); coppa; fresh or cured boneless pork shoulder butts, hams, loins, shoulders, shoulder picnics, and similar pork cuts, in casings or other containers in which ready-to-eat delicatessen articles are customarily enclosed (excepting Scotch-style hams); breaded pork products; cured boneless pork loins; boneless back bacon; bacon used for wrapping around patties, steaks and similar products; and smoked pork cuts such as hams, shoulders, loins, and pork shoulder picnics (excepting smoked hams, and smoked pork shoulder picnics which are specially prepared for distribution in tropical climates or smoked hams delivered to the Armed Services); ground meat mixtures containing pork and beef, veal, lamb, mutton, or goat meat and other product consisting of mixtures of pork and other ingredients, which the Administrator determines at the time the labeling for the product is submitted for approval in accordance with part 317 of the regulations in this subchapter or upon subsequent reevaluation of the product, would be prepared in such a manner that the product might be eaten rare or without thorough cooking because of the appearance of the finished product or otherwise. Cured boneless pork loins shall be subjected to prescribed treatment for destruction of trichinae prior to being shipped from the establishment where cured.

(c) The treatment shall consist of heating, refrigerating, or curing, as follows:

(1) Heating. (i) All parts of the pork muscle tissue shall be heated according to one of the time and temperature combinations in the following table:

Minimum Internal Temperature		Minimum Time
° F	° C	
120	49.0	21 hours
122	50.0	9.5 hours
124	51.1	4.5 hours
126	52.2	2 hours
128	53.4	1 hour
130	54.5	30 minutes
132	55.6	15 minutes
134	56.7	6 minutes
136	57.8	3 minutes
138	58.9	2 minutes
140	60.0	1 minute
142	61.1	1 minute
144	62.2	Instant

(ii) Time and temperature shall be monitored by a calibrated recording instrument that meets the requirements of paragraph (d) of this section, except for paragraph (c)(1)(iv).

(iii) The time to raise product temperature from 60 °F. to 120 °F shall not exceed 2 hours unless the product is cured or fermented.

(iv) Time, in combination with temperatures of 138 °F to 143 °F, need not be monitored if the product's minimum thickness exceeds 2 inches (5.1 cm) and refrigeration of the product does not begin within 5 minutes of attaining 138 °F (58.9 °C).

(v) The establishment shall use procedures which insure the proper heating of all parts of the product. It is important that each piece of sausage, each ham, and other product treated by heating in water be kept entirely submerged throughout the heating period; and that the largest pieces in a lot, the innermost links of bunched sausage or other massed articles, and pieces placed in the coolest part of a heating cabinet or compartment or vat be included in the temperature tests.

(2) Refrigerating. At any stage of preparation and after preparatory chilling to a temperature of not above 40 °F. or preparatory freezing, all parts of the

muscle tissue of pork or product containing such tissue shall be subjected continuously to a temperature not higher than one of those specified in table 1, the duration of such refrigeration at the specified temperature being dependent on the thickness of the meat or inside dimensions of the container.

Table 1. Required Period of Freezing at Temperature Indicated			
° F	° C	Group 1 (Days)	Group 2 (Days)
5	- 15	20	30
- 10	- 23.3	10	20
- 20	- 28.9	6	12

(i) Group 1 comprises product in separate pieces not exceeding 6 inches in thickness, or arranged on separate racks with the layers not exceeding 6 inches in depth, or stored in crates or boxes not exceeding 6 inches in depth, or stored as solidly frozen blocks not exceeding 6 inches in thickness.

(ii) Group 2 comprises product in pieces, layers, or within containers, the thickness of which exceeds 6 inches but not 27 inches, and product in containers including tierces, barrels, kegs, and cartons having a thickness not exceeding 27 inches.

(iii) The product undergoing such refrigeration or the containers thereof shall be so spaced while in the freezer as will insure a free circulation of air between the pieces of meat, layers, blocks, boxes, barrels, and tierces in order that the temperature of the meat throughout will be promptly reduced to not higher than 5 °F., −10 °F., or −20 °F., as the case may be.

(iv) In lieu of the methods prescribed in Table 1, the treatment may consist of commercial freeze drying or controlled freezing, at the center of the meat pieces, in accordance with the times and temperatures specified in Table 2.

Table 2—Alternate Periods of Freezing at Temperatures Indicated		
Maximum Internal Temperature		Minimum Time
° F	° C	
0	- 17.8	106 hours
- 5	- 20.6	82 hours
- 10	- 23.3	63 hours
- 15	- 26.1	48 hours
- 20	- 28.9	35 hours
- 25	- 31.7	22 hours
- 30	- 34.5	8 hours
-35	- 37.2	1/2 hour

(v) During the period of refrigeration the product shall be kept separate from other products and in the custody of the Program in rooms or compartments equipped and made secure with an official Program lock or seal. The rooms or compartments containing product undergoing freezing shall be equipped with accurate thermometers placed at or above the highest level at which the product undergoing treatment is stored and away from refrigerating coils. After completion of the prescribed freezing of pork to be used in the preparation of product covered by paragraph (b) of this section the pork shall be kept under close supervision of an inspector until it is prepared in finished form as one of the products enumerated in paragraph (b) of this section or until it is transferred under Program control to another official establishment for preparation in such finished form.

(vi) Pork which has been refrigerated as specified in this subparagraph may be transferred in sealed railroad cars, sealed motortrucks, sealed trailers, or sealed closed containers to another official establishment at the same or another location, for use in the preparation of product covered by paragraph (b) of this section. Such vehicles and containers shall be sealed and transported between official establishments in accordance with §325.7 of this subchapter.

(3) Curing - (i) Sausage. The sausage may be stuffed in animal casings, hydrocellulose casings, or cloth bags. During any stage of treating the sausage for the destruction of live trichinae, except as provided in Method 5, these coverings shall not be coated with paraffin or like substance, nor shall any sausage be washed during any prescribed period of drying. In the preparation of sausage, one of the following methods may be used:

Method No. 1. The meat shall be ground or chopped into pieces not exceeding three-fourths of an inch in diameter. A dry-curing mixture containing not less than 3⅓ pounds of salt to each hundredweight of the unstuffed sausage shall be thoroughly mixed with the ground or chopped meat. After being stuffed, sausage having a diameter not exceeding 3½ inches, measured at the time of stuffing, shall be held in a drying room not less than 20 days at a temperature not lower than 45 °F., except that in sausage of the variety known as pepperoni, if in casings not exceeding 1⅜ inches in diameter measured at the time of stuffing, the period of drying may be reduced to 15 days. In no case, however, shall the sausage be released from the drying room in less than 25 days from the time the curing materials are added, except that sausage of the variety known as pepperoni, if in casings not exceeding the size specified, may be released at the expiration of 20 days from the time the curing materials are added. Sausage in casings exceeding 3½ inches, but not exceeding 4 inches, in diameter at the time of stuffing, shall be held in a drying room not less than 35 days at a temperature not lower than 45 °F., and in no case shall the sausage be released from the drying room in less than 40 days from the time the curing materials are added to the meat.

Method No. 2. The meat shall be ground or chopped into pieces not exceeding three-fourths of an inch in diameter. A dry-curing mixture containing not less than 3⅓ pounds of salt to each hundredweight of the unstuffed sausage shall be thoroughly mixed with the ground or chopped meat. After being stuffed, sausage having a diameter not exceeding 3½ inches, measured at the time of stuffing, shall be smoked not less than 40 hours at a temperature not lower than 80 °F., and finally held in a drying room not less than 10 days at a temperature not lower than 45 °F. In no case, however, shall the sausage be released from the drying room in less than 18 days from the time the curing materials are added to the meat. Sausage exceeding 3½ inches, but not exceeding 4 inches, in diameter at the time of stuffing, shall be held in a drying room, following smoking as above indicated, not less than 25 days at a temperature not lower than 45 °F., but in no case shall the sausage be released from the drying room in less than 33 days from the time the curing materials are added to the meat.

Method No. 3. The meat shall be ground or chopped into pieces not exceeding three-fourths of an inch in diameter. A dry-curing mixture containing not less than 3⅓ pounds of salt to each hundredweight of the unstuffed sausage shall be thoroughly mixed with the ground or chopped meat. After admixture with the salt and other curing materials and before stuffing, the ground or chopped meat shall be held at a temperature not lower than 34 °F. for not less than 36 hours. After being stuffed, the sausage shall be held at a temperature not lower than 34 °F. for an additional period of time sufficient to make a total of not less than 144 hours from the time the curing materials are added to the meat, or the sausage shall be held for the time specified in a pickle-curing medium of not less than 50° strength (salometer reading) at a temperature not lower than 44 °F. Finally, sausage having a diameter not exceeding 3½ inches, measured at the time of stuffing, shall be smoked for not less than 12 hours. The temperature of the smokehouse during this period at no time shall be lower than 90 °F.; and for 4 consecutive hours of this period the smokehouse shall be maintained at a temperature not lower than 128 °F. Sausage exceeding 3½ inches, but not exceeding 4 inches, in diameter at the time of stuffing shall be smoked, following the prescribed curing, for not less than 15 hours. The temperature of the smokehouse during the 15-hour period shall at no time be lower than 90 °F., and for 7 consecutive hours of this period the smokehouse shall be maintained at a temperature not lower than 128 °F. In regulating the temperature of the smokehouse for the treatment of sausage under this method, the temperature of 128 °F. shall be attained gradually during a period of not less than 4 hours.

Method No. 4. The meat shall be ground or chopped into pieces not exceeding one-fourth of an inch in diameter. A dry-curing mixture containing not less than 2½ pounds of salt to each hundredweight of the unstuffed sausage shall be thoroughly mixed with the ground or chopped meat.

After admixture with the salt and other curing materials and before stuffing, the ground or chopped sausage shall be held as a compact mass, not more than 6 inches in depth, at a temperature not lower than 36 °F. for not less than 10 days. At the termination of the holding period, the sausage shall be stuffed in casings or cloth bags not exceeding 3⅓ inches in diameter, measured at the time of stuffing. After being stuffed, the sausage shall be held in a drying room at a temperature not lower than 45 °F. for the remainder of a 35-day period, measured from the time the curing materials are added to the meat. At any time after stuffing, if the establishment operator deems it desirable, the product may be heated in a water bath for a period not to exceed 3 hours at a temperature not lower than 85 °F., or subjected to smoking at a temperature not lower than 80 °F., or the product may be both heated and smoked as specified. The time consumed in heating and smoking, however, shall be in addition to the 35-day holding period specified.

Method No. 5. The meat shall be ground or chopped into pieces not exceeding three-fourths of an inch in diameter. A dry-curing mixture containing not less than 3⅓ pounds of salt to each hundredweight of the unstuffed sausage shall be thoroughly mixed with the ground or chopped meat. After being stuffed, the sausage shall be held for not less than 65 days at a temperature not lower than 45 °F. The coverings for sausage prepared according to this method may be coated at any stage of the preparation before or during the holding period with paraffin or other substance approved by the Administrator.

Method No. 6. (A) Basic requirements. The meat shall be ground or chopped into pieces not exceeding three-fourths of an inch in diameter. A dry-curing mixture containing not less than 3.33 pounds of salt to each hundredweight of the unstuffed sausage, excluding the weight of dry ingredients, shall be thoroughly mixed with the ground or chopped meat. After the curing mixture has been added, the sausage shall be held for two time periods, a holding period and a drying period. The holding period will be for a minimum of 48 hours at a room temperature not lower than 35 °F. This holding period requirement may be fulfilled totally or in part before the drying period and then the remainder, if any, after the drying period or as an extension of the drying period. During the drying period, the sausage shall be held in a drying room at a temperature not lower than 50 (10.0 °F. (10.0 °C) for a period of time determined by Tables 3A, 3B, and 4. The length of the drying period, established in (c)(3)(i)(A), may be modified as provided in paragraphs (c)(3)(i)(B) and (c)(3)(i)(C) of this section.

Table 3A - **Sausage Drying Room Times** by Method No. 6	
Diameter of casing at time of stuffing[1]	Days in drying room[2]
1 inches	14
1½ inches	15
2 inches	16
2½ inches	18
3 inches	20
3½ inches	23
4 inches	25
4½ inches	30
5 inches	35
5½ inches	43
6 inches	50

[1]The drying room times for flattened or oval sausages shall use a diameter derived by measuring the circumference and dividing by 3.14 (pi).

[2]Drying room time may be modified as set forth in Tables 3B and 4.

(B) Reduction in Drying Room Time. During the holding period, the sausage may be smoked or fermented. If the temperature is increased to 70 °F. (21.1 °C) or higher, while the sausage is being held after adding curing materials but before the drying period, the subsequent drying room times prescribed for this method may be reduced according to the schedule in Table 3B. No interpolation of values is permissible.

Table 3B - **Percentage Reduction in Drying Room Time** (Table 3A) Permitted by Holding Times and Temperatures Prior to Drying[1]									
Min. Time in hours	Degree F								
	70°	75°	80°	85°	90°	95°	100°	105°	110	120
	Degree C								
	21.1°	23.9°	26.7°	29.5°	32.2°	35.0°	37.9°	40.6°	43.3	48.9
24	4%	5%	8%	10%	15%	23%	37%	57%	90%	[3]100
48	9%	12%	18%	25%	35%	49%	88%	[3]100	[3]100	[3]100
72	14%	19%	28%	39%	55%	74%	[3]100	[3]100	[3]100	[3]100
96	19%	26%	38%	53%	75%	98%	[3]100	[3]100	[3]100	[3]100
120	24%	33%	48%	67%	95%	[3]100	[3]100	[3]100	[3]100	[3]100

[1]In computing the days to be deducted, the number with any fraction shall be rounded to the next lower whole number and shall be deducted from the required total drying time. Example: Sausage stuffed in 3&inch; diameter casing requires 20 days in the drying room (from Drying Room Times, Table 3A). If allowed to ferment, after addition of curing materials, at 80 °F. for 48 hours, the 20 day drying time may be reduced 18% (from Table 3B). Eighteen percent of 20 day equals 3.6 days. Twenty days minus 3 days equals 17 days. The total drying time required in the drying room, therefore, will be 17 days.

[2]Either room temperature or internal product temperature shall be used for sausages that will be subsequently dried to a moisture-protein ratio of 2.3:1 or less. Internal product temperature shall be used for all other sausages.

[3]Trichinae will be destroyed during fermentation or smoking at the temperature and length of time indicated. Therefore, no drying room period is required for products so treated.

(C) Reduced Salt Content - Drying Room Times. Salt content of less than 3.33 pounds for each hundredweight of sausage formulation, excluding dry ingredients, (such as salts, sugars, and spices), may be permitted provided the drying time is increased according to the schedule contained in Table 4.

Trichina Treatment of Sausage by Method No. 6;

Table 4 - **Reduced Salt Content - Drying Room Times** [Required percentage increase in drying room time (table 3A) for added salt of less than 3.33 pounds per hundredweight of sausage]	
Minimum pounds of salt added to sausage[1]	Increase in drying room time[2]
3.3	1
3.2	4
3.1	7
3.0	10
2.9	13
2.8	16
2.7	19
2.6	22
2.5	25
2.4	28
2.3	31
2.2	34
2.1	37
2.0	40

[1]Calculate the salt content for column 1 as follows: Multiply the pounds of salt in the sausage formulation by 100. Then divide this number by the total weight of sausage formulation minus the weight of dry ingredients and round down to the next lowest 0.1%. Percents may be substituted for pounds.

Example: 120 lbs. pork, 3.56 lbs. salt, 2 lbs. spices, 0.5 lbs. wine, 1 lb. water and starter culture, 0.8 lbs. sugar, .012 lbs. sodium nitrite total weight is 127.872 lbs.

(3.56×100)/(127.872−3.56−2−.8−.012)=356/121.5=2.93

Therefore, the sausage drying time must be increased by 13 percent.

[2]In computing the days to be added to the required total drying time, fractions shall be rounded to the next higher whole number and added to the required total drying time. Example: Sausage stuffed in 3 1/2 inch diameter casing requires 23 days in the drying room (from Drying Room Times). If the quantity of salt added per hundredweight of sausage is 2 pounds instead of 3.33 pounds, the drying room time must be increased by 40 percent (from Reduced Salt Content-Drying Room Times), or 9.2 days. The 9.2 is rounded up to 10 days and is added to the 23 days to equal 33 days. The total drying time required in the drying room, therefore, will be 33 days.

Method No. 7, Dry Sausages. (A) General Requirements. The establishment shall use meat particles reduced in size to no more than 1/4 inch in diameter. The establishment shall add a curing mixture containing no less than 2.7 pounds of salt per hundred pounds of meat and mix it uniformly throughout the product. The establishment shall hold, heat, and dry the product according to paragraph (B) or (C) below.

(B) Holding, Heating, and Drying Treatment, Large Sausages. Except as permitted in (C) below, the establishment shall subject sausages in casings not exceeding 105 mm in diameter, at the time of stuffing, to all of the following minimum chamber temperatures and time periods.

Treatment Schedule for Sausages 105 Millimeters (4⅛ Inches) or Less in Diameter		
Minimum chamber temperature		Minimum time (hours)
°F	°C	
50	10	12
90	32.2	1
100	37.8	1
110	43.3	1
120	48.9	1
125	51.7	7

Following the preceding treatment, the establishment shall dry the sausages at a temperature not lower than 50 °F (10 °C) for not less than 7 days.

(C) Heating and Drying Treatment, Small Sausages. Alternatively, the establishment may subject sausages in casings not exceeding 55 mm in diameter, at the time of stuffing, to all of the following minimum chamber temperatures and time periods.

Treatment Schedule for Sausages 55 Millimeters (2 ⅛ Inches) or Less in Diameter		
Minimum chamber temperature		Minimum time (hours)
° F	° C	
50	10	12
100	37.8	1
125	51.7	6

Following the preceding heat treatment, the establishment shall dry the sausages at a temperature not lower than 50 °F (10 °C) for not less than 4 days.

(ii) Capocollo (capicola, capacola). Boneless pork butts for capocollo shall be cured in a dry-curing mixture containing not less than 4½ pounds of salt per hundredweight of meat for a period of not less than 25 days at a temperature not lower than 36 °F. If the curing materials are applied to the butts by the process known as churning, a small quantity of pickle may be added. During the curing period the butts may be overhauled according to any of the usual processes of overhauling, including the addition of pickle or dry salt if desired. The butts shall not be subjected during or after curing to any treatment designed to remove salt from the meat, except that superficial washing may be allowed. After being stuffed, the product shall be smoked for a period of not less than 30 hours at a temperature not lower than 80 °F., and shall finally be held in a drying room not less than 20 days at a temperature not lower than 45 °F.

(iii) Coppa. Boneless pork butts for coppa shall be cured in a dry-curing mixture containing not less than 4½ pounds of salt per hundredweight of meat for a period of not less than 18 days at a temperature not lower than 36 °F. If the curing mixture is applied to the butts by the process known as churning, a small quantity of pickle may be added. During the curing period the butts may be overhauled according to any of the usual processes of overhauling, including the addition of pickle or dry salt if desired. The butts shall not be subjected during or after curing to any treatment designed to remove salt from the meat, except that superficial washing may be allowed. After being stuffed, the product shall be held in a drying room not less than 35 days at a temperature not lower than 45 °F.

(iv) Hams and pork shoulder picnics. In the curing of hams and pork shoulder picnics, one of the methods below shall be used. For calculating days per pound, the establishment shall use the weight of the heaviest ham or picnic in the lot.

Method No. 1. The hams and pork shoulder picnics shall be cured by a dry-salt curing process not less than 40 days at a temperature no lower than 36 °F. The products shall be laid down in salt, not less than 4 pounds to each hundredweight of product, the salt being applied in a thorough manner to the lean meat of each item. When placed in cure, the products may be pumped with pickle if desired. At least once during the curing process, the products shall be overhauled (turned over for the application of additional cure) and additional salt applied, if necessary, so that the lean meat of each item is thoroughly covered. After removal from cure, the products may be soaked in water at a temperature not higher than 70 °F for not more than 15 hours, during which time the water may be changed once, but they shall not be subjected to any other treatment designed to remove salt from the meat except that superficial washing may be allowed. The products shall finally be dried or smoked at a time and temperature not less than a combination prescribed in Table 5 of Method No. 3.

Method No. 2. [Reserved]

Method No. 3. (A) Curing. (Other than bag curing): Establishments shall cure hams and shoulders by using a cure mixture containing not less than 70 percent salt by weight to cover all exposed muscle tissue and to pack the hock region. Total curing time consists of a mandatory cure contact time and an optional equalization time.

(B) Cure Contact Time. This is the cure contact period, during which the establishment shall keep exposed muscle tissue coated with the cure mixture at least 28 days but for no less than 1.5 days per pound of ham or shoulder. Overhaul is optional so long as the exposed muscle tissue remains coated with curing mixture.

(C) Equalization. The establishment may provide an equalization period after the minimum cure contact period in (B) above to permit the absorbed salt to permeate the product's inner tissues. Equalization is the time after the excess cure has been removed from the product at the end of the cure contact period until the product is placed in the drying room and the drying period begins. The total curing time (equalization plus cure contact) shall be at least 40 days and in no case less than 2 days per pound of an uncured ham or shoulder.

(D) Removing Excess Cure. After the required cure contact period, the establishment may remove excess cure mixture from the product's surface mechanically or by rinsing up to 1 minute with water, but not by soaking.

(E) Bag Curing. Bag curing is a traditional ham curing technique in which the manufacturer wraps the ham and all of the cure mixture together in kraft paper then hangs them individually. The paper keeps the extra cure mixture in close contact with the product making reapplication of salt unnecessary, and it protects the product from mites and insects. Establishments may employ the bag curing method as an alternative to (A) through (D) above. An establishment which elects to use the bag curing method shall apply a cure mixture containing at least 6 pounds of salt per 100 pounds of uncured product. The establishment shall rub the curing mixture into the exposed muscle tissue, pack the hock region with the curing mixture, and use uncoated wrapping paper to wrap the product together with any remaining curing mixture. The bag cured product shall remain wrapped throughout the curing period and may or may not remain wrapped during the drying period. In any case, the curing period shall be at least 40 days but not less than 2 days per pound of an uncured ham or shoulder. After curing, the cured product shall be exposed to a drying time and temperature prescribed in Table 5.

(F) Curing Temperature. During the curing period the establishment shall use one of the following procedures:

(1) The establishment shall control the room temperature at not less than 35 °F (1.7 °C) nor greater than 45 °F (7.2 °C) for the first 1.5 days per pound of an uncured ham or shoulder, and not less than 35 °F (1.7 °C) nor greater than 60 °F (15.6 °C) for the remainder of the curing period.

(2) The establishment shall monitor and record daily product temperature. The room temperature need not be controlled but days on which the product temperature drops below 35 °F (1.7 °C) shall not be counted as curing time. If the product temperature exceeds 45 °F (7.2 °C) within the first period of 1.5 days per pound of an uncured ham or shoulder or if it exceeds 60 °F (15.6 °C) for the remainder of the curing period, the establishment shall cool the product back to the 45 °F (7.2 °C) maximum during the first period or 55 °F (12.8 °C) maximum during the remainder of the period.

(3) The establishment shall begin curing product only between the dates of December 1 and February 13. The room temperature need not be controlled, but the establishment shall monitor and record daily room temperatures, and days in which the room temperature drops below 35 °F (1.7 °C) shall not be counted as curing time.

(G) Drying. After the curing period, establishments shall use one of three procedures for drying:

(1) The establishment shall subject the product to a controlled room temperature for a minimum time and minimum temperature combination prescribed in Table 5 or for a set of such combinations in which the total of the fractional periods (in column 4 of Table 5) exceeds 1.5.

(2) Establishments using uncontrolled room temperatures shall monitor and record the internal product temperature. The drying period shall be complete when, from the days which can be counted as curing time, one of the time/temperature combinations of Table 5 is satisfied or when the total of the fractional values for the combinations exceeds 1.5.

(3) Establishments using uncontrolled room temperatures shall dry the product for a minimum of 160 days including the entire months of June, July, and August. This procedure is obviously dependent on local climatic conditions and no problem exists with respect to current producers who use this procedure. Future applicants shall demonstrate that their local monthly average temperatures and the local monthly minimum temperatures are equal to or warmer than the normal average temperatures and normal minimum temperatures compiled by the National Oceanic and Atmospheric Administration for Boone, North Carolina, station 31–0977, 1951 through 1980.

Monthly Temperatures (°F) for Boone NC, 1951–1980								
Jan.	Feb.	Mar.	Apr.	May	June	July	Aug.	Sep.
Normal average temperatures								
32.2	34.1	41.3	51.2	59.1	65.1	68.3	67.5	61.6
Normal minimum temperatures								
22.8	24.2	30.8	39.6	48.1	54.7	58.5	57.6	51.6

Table 5. Drying Times and Temperatures for Trichina Inactivation in Hams and Shoulders *

Minimum Drying Temperature		Minimum days at drying temperature	Fractional period for one day of drying
°F	°C		
130	54.4	1.5	.67
125	51.7	2	.50
120	48.9	3	.33
115	46.1	4	.25
110	43.3	5	.20
105	40.6	6	.17
100	37.8	7	.14
95	35.0	9	.11
90	32.2	11	.091
85	29.4	18	.056
80	26.7	25	.040
75	23.9	35	.029

* Interpolation of these times or temperatures is not acceptable; establishments wishing to use temperatures or times not in this Table shall first validate their efficacy as provided by 318.10(c)(4) of this section.

Method No. 4. (A) Cure: Establishments shall cure hams and shoulders by using a cure mixture containing not less than 71.5 percent salt by weight to cover all exposed muscle tissue and to pack the hock region. Establishments may substitute potassium chloride (KCl) for up to half of the required salt on an equal weight basis.

(B) Curing. Establishments shall apply the cure at a rate not less than 5.72 pounds of salt and KCl per hundred pounds of fresh meat. The cure shall be applied in either three or four approximately equal amounts (two or three overhauls) at separate times during the first 14 days of curing.

(C) Cure Contact Time. Establishments shall keep the product in contact with the cure mixture for no less than 2 days per pound of an uncured ham or shoulder but for at least 30 days. Establishments shall maintain the curing temperature at no less than 35 °F (1.7 °C) during the cure contact time.

(D) Equalization. After the cure contact period, establishments shall provide an added equalization period of no less than 1 day per pound of an uncured ham or shoulder but at least 14 days. Equalization is the time after the excess cure has been removed from the product, the end of the cure contact period, and before the drying period begins. Establishments may substitute additional cure contact days for an equal number of equalization days.

(E) Removing Excess Cure. After the required cure contact period, the establishment may remove excess cure mixture from the product's surface mechanically or by rinsing up to 1 minute with water, but not by soaking.

(F) Drying. After the curing period, establishments shall use one of the controlled temperature methods for drying listed in Method No. 3 of this subparagraph.

Method No. 5 (A) Curing. The establishment shall cure the ham to a minimum brine concentration of 6 percent by the end of the drying period. Brine concentration is calculated as 100 times the salt concentration divided by the sum of the salt and water concentrations.

Percent brine = $100 \times$ [salt] / ([salt] + [water])

The Agency will accept the brine concentration in the biceps femoris as a reasonable estimate of the minimum brine concentration in the ham.

(B) Drying and Total Process Times. The establishment shall dry the cured ham at a minimum temperature of 55 °F (13 °C) for at least 150 days. The total time of drying plus curing shall be at least 206 days.

(C) Ensuring an Acceptable Internal Brine Concentration.

(1) To establish compliance, the establishment shall take product samples from the first 12 lots of production as follows: From each lot,

(i) One sample shall be taken from each of 5 or more hams;

(ii) Each sample shall be taken from the biceps femoris. As an alternative to the use of the biceps femoris, the Agency shall consider other method(s) of sampling the dry-cured hams to determine the minimum internal brine concentration, as long as the establishment proposes it and submits data and other information to establish its sufficiency to the Director of the Processed Products Inspection Division;

(iii) Each sample shall weigh no less than 100 grams;

(iv) The samples shall be combined as one composite sample and sealed in a water vapor proof container;

(v) The composite sample shall be submitted to a laboratory accredited under the provisions of §318.21 to be analyzed for salt and water content using methods from the "Official Methods of Analysis of the Association of Official Analytical Chemists (AOAC)," 15th Edition, 1990, Section 983.18 (page 931) and Section 971.19 (page 933) which are incorporated by reference. This incorporation by reference was approved by the Director of the Federal Register in accordance with 5 U.S.C. 552(a) and 1 CFR part 51. Copies may be obtained from the Association of Official Analytical Chemists, suite 400–BW, 2200 Wilson Boulevard, Arlington, VA 22201–3301. Copies may be inspected at the Office of the FSIS Hearing Clerk, room 3171, South Agriculture Building, Food Safety and Inspection Service, U.S. Department of Agriculture, Washington, DC 20250 or at the National Archives and Records Administration (NARA). For information on the availability of this material at NARA, call 202–741–6030, or go to: http://www.archives.gov/federal_register/code_of_federal_regulations/ibr_locations.html. If the time between sampling and submittal of the composite sample to the accredited laboratory will exceed 8 hours, then the establishment shall freeze the composite sample immediately after the samples are combined;

(vi) Once the laboratory results for the composite sample are received, the manufacturer shall calculate the internal brine concentration by multiplying the salt concentration by 100 and then dividing that figure by the sum of the salt and water concentrations;

(vii) Compliance is established when the samples from the first 12 lots of production have a minimum internal brine concentration of 6 percent. Lots being tested to establish compliance shall be held until the internal brine concentration has been determined and found to be at least 6 percent. If the minimum internal brine concentration is less than 6 percent, the lot being tested shall be held until the establishment brings the lot into compliance by further processing.

(2) To maintain compliance, the establishment shall take samples, have the samples analyzed, and perform the brine calculations as set forth above from one lot every 13 weeks. Lots being tested to maintain compliance shall not be held. If the minimum internal brine concentration is less than 6 percent in a lot being tested to maintain compliance, the establishment shall develop and propose steps acceptable to FSIS to ensure that the process is corrected.

(3) Accredited laboratory results and the brine calculations shall be placed on file at the establishment and available to Program employees for review.

Method No. 6 (A) Curing. The establishment shall cure the ham to a minimum brine concentration of 6 percent by the end of the drying period. Brine concentration is calculated as 100 times the salt concentration divided by the sum of the salt and water concentrations.

Percent brine = 100 × [salt] / ([salt] + [water])

The Agency will accept the brine concentration in the biceps femoris as a reasonable estimate of the minimum brine concentration.

(B) Drying and Total Process Times. The establishment shall dry the cured ham at a minimum temperature of 110 °F (43 °C) for at least 4 days. The total time of drying plus curing shall be at least 34 days.

(C) Ensuring an Acceptable Internal Brine Concentration.

(1) To establish compliance the establishment shall take product samples from the first 12 lots of production as follows: From each lot,

(i) One sample shall be taken from each of 5 or more hams;

(ii) Each sample shall be taken from the biceps femoris. As an alternative to the use of the biceps femoris, the Agency will consider other methods of sampling the dry-cured hams to determine internal brine concentration, as long as the establishment proposes it and submits data and other information to establish its sufficiency to the Director of the Processed Products Inspection Division;

(iii) Each sample shall weigh no less than 100 grams;

(iv) The samples shall be combined as one composite sample and sealed in a water vapor proof container;

(v) The composite sample shall be submitted to a laboratory accredited under the provisions of §318.21 to be analyzed for salt and water content using methods from the "Official Methods of Analysis of the Association of Official Analytical Chemists (AOAC)," 15th Edition, 1990, section 983.18 (page 931) and section 971.19 (page 933) which are incorporated by reference. This incorporation by reference was approved by the Director of the Federal Register in accordance with 5 U.S.C. 552(a) and 1 CFR part 51.

Copies may be obtained from the Association of Official Analytical Chemists, suite 400–BW, 2200 Wilson Boulevard, Arlington, VA 22201–3301. Copies may be inspected at the Office of the FSIS Hearing Clerk, room 3171, South Agriculture Building, Food Safety and Inspection Service, U.S. Department of Agriculture, Washington, DC 20250 or at the National Archives and Records Administration (NARA). For information on the availability of this material at NARA, call 202–741–6030, or go to: http://www.archives.gov/ federal_register/code_of_federal_regulations/ibr_locations.html. If the time between sampling and submittal of the composite sample to the accredited laboratory will exceed 8 hours, then the establishment shall freeze the composite sample immediately after the samples are combined;

(vi) Compliance is established when the samples from the first 12 lots of production have a minimum internal brine concentration of 6 percent. Lots being tested to establish compliance shall be held until the internal brine concentration has been determined and found to be at least 6 percent. If the minimum internal brine concentration is less than 6 percent, the lot being tested shall be held until the establishment brings the lot into compliance by further processing.

(2) To maintain compliance, the establishment shall take samples, have the samples analyzed, and perform the brine calculations as set forth above from one lot every 13 weeks. Lots being tested to maintain compliance shall not be held. If the minimum internal brine concentration is less than 6 percent in a lot being tested to maintain compliance, the establishment shall develop and propose steps acceptable to FSIS to ensure that the process is corrected.

(3) Accredited laboratory results and the brine calculations shall be placed on file in the establishment and available to Program employees for review.

(v) Boneless pork loins and loin ends. In lieu of heating or refrigerating to destroy possible live trichinae in boneless loins, the loins may be cured for a period of not less than 25 days at a temperature not lower than 36 °F. by the use of one of the following methods:

Method No. 1. Application of a dry-salt curing mixture containing not less than 5 pounds of salt to each hundredweight of meats.

Method No. 2. Application of a pickle solution of not less than 80° strength (salometer) on the basis of not less than 60 pounds of pickle to each hundredweight of meat.

Method No. 3. Application of a pickle solution added to the dry-salt cure prescribed as Method No. 1 in this subdivision (v) provided the pickle solution is not less than 80° strength (salometer).

After removal from cure, the loins may be soaked in water for not more than 1 hour at a temperature not higher than 70 °F. or washed under a spray but shall not be subjected, during or after the curing process, to any other treatment designed to remove salt. Following curing, the loins shall be smoked for not less than 12 hours. The minimum temperature of the smokehouse during this period at no time shall be lower than 100 °F., and for 4 consecutive hours of this period the smokehouse shall be maintained at a temperature not lower than 125 °F. Finally, the product shall be held in a drying room for a period of not less than 12 days at a temperature not lower than 45 °F.

(4) The Administrator shall consider additional processing methods upon petition by manufacturers, and shall approve any such method upon his/her determination that it can be properly monitored by an inspector and that the safety of such methods is adequately documented by data which has been developed by following an experimental protocol previously reviewed and accepted by the Department.

(d) General instructions: When necessary to comply with the requirements of this section, the smokehouses, drying rooms, and other compartments used in the treatment of pork to destroy possible live trichinae shall be suitably equipped, by the operator of the official establishment, with accurate automatic recording thermometers. Circuit supervisors are authorized to approve for use in sausage smokehouses, drying rooms, and other compartments, such automatic recording thermometers as are found to give satisfactory service and to disapprove and require discontinuance of use, for purposes of the regulations in this subchapter, any thermometers (including any automatic recording thermometers) of the establishment that are found to be inaccurate or unreliable.

(e) The requirements for using the pooled sample digestion technique to analyze pork for the presence of trichina cysts are:

(1) The establishment shall submit for the approval of the Regional Director its proposed procedure for identifying and pooling carcasses, collecting and pooling samples, testing samples (including the name and address of the laboratory), communicating test results, retesting individual carcasses, and maintaining positive identification and clear separation of pork found to be trichina-free from untested pork or trichina-positive pork.

(2) The establishment shall use the services of a laboratory approved by the Administrator for all required testing. Such approval shall be based on adequacy of facilities, reagents, and equipment, and on demonstration of continuing competency and reliability in performing the pooled sample digestion technique for trichinae.

(3) The establishment shall sample no less than 5 grams of diaphragm muscle or tongue tissue from each carcass or no less than 10 grams of other muscle tissue. Samples may be pooled but a pool shall not consist of more than 100 grams of sample. Sampling and sample preparation are subject to inspection supervision.

(4) Pork or products made from tested pork shall not be released as trichina free from the official establishment without treatment until the inspector in charge receives a laboratory report that the tested pork is free of trichina cysts.

(f) Approval of other tests for trichinosis in pork. The Administrator shall consider any additional analytical method for trichinosis upon petition by a manufacturer, and may approve that method upon the determination that it will detect at least 98 percent of swine bearing cysts present at a tissue density equal to or less than one cyst per gram of muscle from the diaphragm pillars at a 95 percent confidence level. Any such petitions shall be supported by any data and other information that the Administrator finds necessary. Notice of any approval shall be given in the Federal Register,and the approved method will be incorporated into this section.

[35 FR 15586, Oct. 3, 1970, as amended at 38 FR 31517; Nov. 15, 1973; 39 FR 40580, Nov. 19, 1974; 50 FR 5229, Feb. 7, 1985; 50 FR 48075, Nov. 21, 1985; 52 FR 12517, Apr. 17, 1987; 57 FR 27874, June 22, 1992; 57 FR 33633, July 30, 1992; 57 FR 56440, Nov. 30, 1992]

Information about the USA regulations about composition of sausages, hans, luncheon meats, loaves, jellied products and other meat specialties can be obtained from:

Code of Federal Regulations
Title 9: Animals and Animal Products
PART 319 - DEFINITIONS AND STANDARDS OF IDENTITY OR COMPOSITION

Useful Techniques

Smoking Poultry

If a chicken is placed down on a screen it will develop pale marks where the meat was in contact with the screen. This bears no influence on the taste of smoked meat but it looks unnatural. To avoid that poultry should be hung or inserted on a roasting rack. Another problem is that birds have a tendency to spread out their legs and wings and that shape is retained after smoking. When a whole bird is smoked it is a good idea to tie wings and legs in order to make the bird look more attractive. However, remember that any area which is not in direct contact with smoke will remain pale.

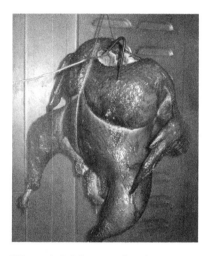

Photo A.1 A large turkey hung without tying its legs and wings.

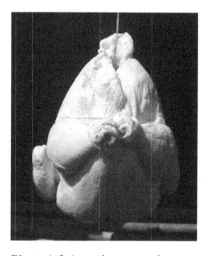

Photo A.2 A neatly prepared chicken.

Photo A.3 This is how a chicken usually looks. Fortunately, there is a simple fix for that.

Photo A.4 When tips of wings are flapped over their backs they usually stay that way.

Photo A.5 Tip of the right wing is tucked in and looks much neater than the one on the left. To bring legs together the technique known as trussing is usually employed. Trussing is securing a bird with either needles or butcher twine. There are many ways to truss a bird and they all work. Most cookbooks cover the technique in detail.

Simple trussing technique

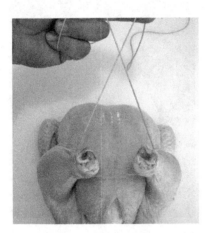

Photo A.6 Place chicken on its back. Take about three feet of twine and place it equally on both sides under leg ends. Pull on twine to bring legs together.

Photo A.7 Go around the legs, making a loop. Keep twine crossed.

Photo A.8 Pull twine under chicken thighs towards the neck.

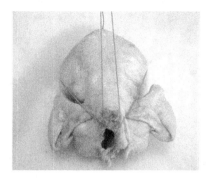

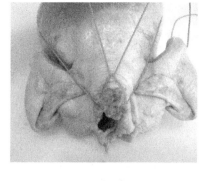

Photo A.9 Flip chicken over so its back is facing up.

Photo A.10 Cross twine around the neck making a loop.

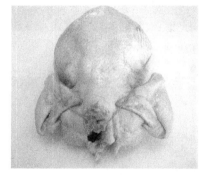

Photo A.11-left Make a secure knot around the neck.

Supporting Poultry for Smoking

A chicken roaster rack is a practical device that permits a vertical hold of the chicken. Chicken on the roaster can be placed on the screen or hung from the smokestick.

Photo A.12 Chicken roaster.

Photo A.13 Chicken on a roaster rack.

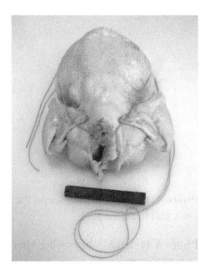

Photo A.14 The twine is threaded through the bird's cavity and attached to the smokestick.

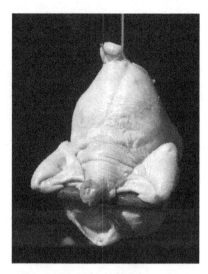

Fig. A.15 Stick and twine.

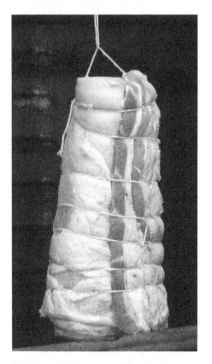

Photo A.16 Lacing offers strong support even to large pieces of meat.

Photo A.17 A large piece of meat can be supported with hangers, hooks or strong twine.

Photo A.18 Bicycle tire repair tool makes threading twine much easier. Pushing twine through thick meat is easy when a larding needle is used.

Photo A.19 There are many ways of supporting fish. A metal binder clip holder (fish on the left) does an excellent job.

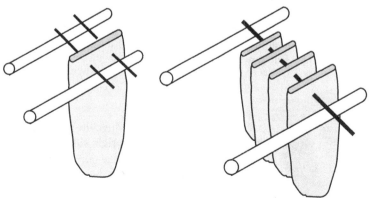

Fig. A.1 Jerky strips supported by toothpicks or a knitting needle.

A large size sausage, pork butt or rolled bacon (pancetta) may require reinforcement in order to hang it in the air. Once the technique is mastered, the lacing procedure can be applied to any product.

Photo A.20 Form a band around one end and secure it with a knot. Leave shorter end of twine about 6" long. If you lace pancetta (rolled bacon) make the second band on opposite side of rolled bacon. That will prevent bacon from unravelling. After bacon is laced, you can snip off this second band. You can tie the twine to the end of a stuffed sausage if there is enough casing sticking out. For the first half of the procedure you can leave twine on the spool.

Photo A.21 Use your hand as a guide and form a loop around it. The spool is on the right side now.

Photo A.22 Move the spool to the left in front of the standing line.

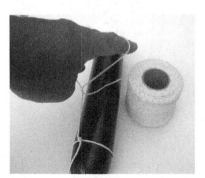

Photo A.23 Move the spool behind the line to the right side. The left hand remains the guide. You can already see that the loop will go on top of the sausage.

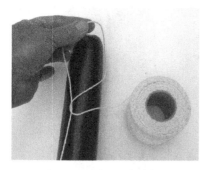

Photo A.24 The loop goes over the top and down to the bottom of the sausage.

Photo A.25 Pulling twine forms a snug band around the sausage.

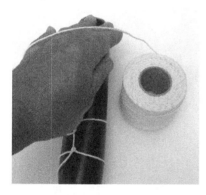

Photo A.26 The procedure starts again.

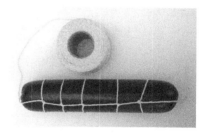

Photo A.27 The whole side is laced.

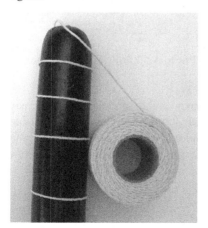

Photo A.28 The sausage is turned around.

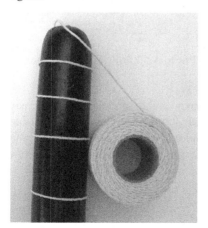

Photo A.29 About a foot of twine is cut off from the spool. The twine goes under the first top loop.

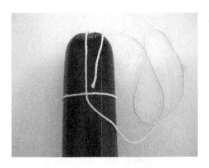

Photo A.30 And it goes behind the loop again.

Photo A.31 Forming a simple knot.

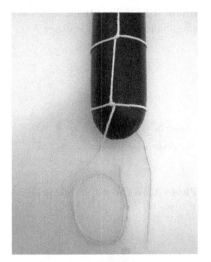

Photo A.32 After all bands are secured, the ends are tied and the hanging loop is formed.

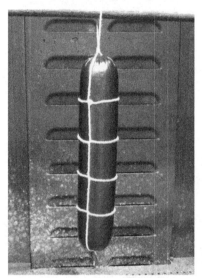

Photo A.33 Fully laced sausage.

Often different types of sausages are smoked at the same time and they may require different times. They may be stuffed in similar diameter casings and it is easy to mix them up. A simple solution is to place a band or two with butcher twine, the system that has been very effectively used in Russia. A few examples follow below:

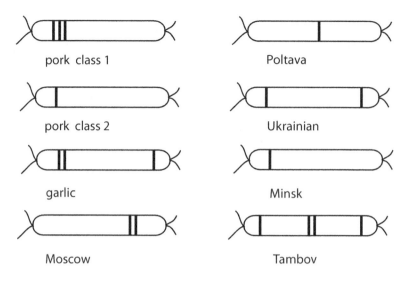

pork class 1

Poltava

pork class 2

Ukrainian

garlic

Minsk

Moscow

Tambov

Fig. A.2 An example of the Russian sausage marking system.

Photo A.34 Pick tying sausages method.

Wooden Pick Method of Tying Sausages

When the war ended in Poland in 1945 there was no butcher's twine available but people were making sausages all the same. A very simple and quite ingenious method of tying sausage casings was invented and people still use it today. The method had one big advantage over butcher's twine: all that was needed was a knife and a tree branch to make a few wooden picks. *The round wooden picks that are used for holding meats on sandwiches will be a perfect material.* This method is not suitable when poaching sausages in water as they move around and the picks might puncture the casings.

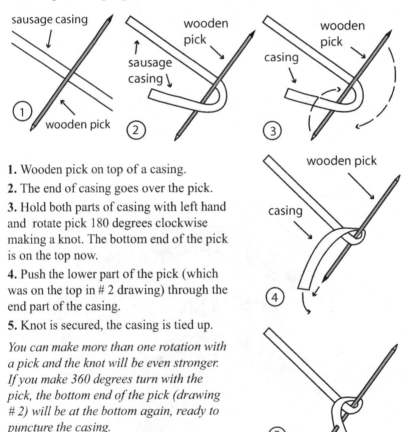

1. Wooden pick on top of a casing.

2. The end of casing goes over the pick.

3. Hold both parts of casing with left hand and rotate pick 180 degrees clockwise making a knot. The bottom end of the pick is on the top now.

4. Push the lower part of the pick (which was on the top in # 2 drawing) through the end part of the casing.

5. Knot is secured, the casing is tied up.

You can make more than one rotation with a pick and the knot will be even stronger. If you make 360 degrees turn with the pick, the bottom end of the pick (drawing # 2) will be at the bottom again, ready to puncture the casing.

Although the drawings might look confusing the method is very easy and fast. Practice with wooden toothpicks and a plastic bag for a minute and you will see how easy it is.

Useful Links and Resources

Sausage-Making Equipment and Supplies

The Sausage Maker Inc., 1500 Clinton St., Building 123
Buffalo, NY 14206, 888-490-8525; 716-824-5814
www.sausagemaker.com

Allied Kenco Sales, 26 Lyerly #1, Houston, TX 77022
713-691-2935; 800-356-5189
www.alliedkenco.com

UltraSource/Koch Equipment, 1414 West 29th Street, Kansas City,
MO 64108, 800-777-5624
www.ultrasourceusa.com

Specialized Equipment

Hanna Instruments USA, 584 Park East Drive, Woonsocket,
RI 02895, 800-426-6287, fax: 401-765-7575
www.hannainst.com/usa *Meat pH tester.*
Meter Group, 2365 NE Hopkins Court, Pullman,
WA 99163, *water activity meters*
www.metergroup.com/

Micro Essential Laboratory Inc., 4224 Avenue H, Brooklyn,
NY 11210, 718-338-3618, fax: 718-692-4491 *Meat pH testing strips.*
www.microessentiallab.com

Green Air Products Inc., PO BOX 1318, Gresham, OR 97030
(503) 663-2000 or (800) 669-2113, *Temperature and humidity controllers.*
www.greenair.com

The Ranco ETC Store, 330 Sunderland Road, Delphos, OH 45833
Ranco temperature controllers.
http://www.etcsupply.com

American Weigh Scales, Inc.,
2210 Ronald Reagan Blvd. Cumming, GA 30041
Highly Accurate Digital Scales.
http://www.awscales.com

Tejas Smokers,
8508 Rannie Rd., Houston, Texas 77080-2025
Smokers, grills, barbecues, burners.
www.tejassmokers.com

Zesco
www.zesco.com *Restaurant supplies.*

Spices and Supplies

Bulk Foods, http://www.bulkfoods.com *Grains, flours.*

Zamouri Spices, http://www.zamourispices.com Laos Powder, spices

Ta Tienda, http://www.latienda.com *Spanish pimentón.*

Government Sites

Electronic Code of Federal Regulations
TITLE 9--Animals and Animal Products
Part 319 - Definitions and Standards of Identity or Compositions
https://www.ecfr.gov/current/title-9/chapter-III/subchapter-A/part-319

United Stated Depertment of Agriculture - Food Safety and Inspection Service
https://www.fsis.usda.gov/

Sausages & Food Safety
https://www.fsis.usda.gov/food-safety/safe-food-handling-and-preparation/
meat/sausages-and-food-safety

Additives in Meat and Poultry Products
https://www.fsis.usda.gov/food-safety/safe-food-handling-and-preparation/
food-safety-basics/additives-meat-and-poultry

Ready to Eat and Shelf Stable Products - Process Familiarization
https://www.fsis.usda.gov/sites/default/files/media_file/2021-02/33_IM_
RTE_SS_Process.pdf

Principles of Preservation of Shelf-Stable Dried Meat Products
https://meathaccp.wisc.edu/validation/assets/Principles%20for%20
preservation.pdf

Jerky and Food Safety
https://www.fsis.usda.gov/food-safety/safe-food-handling-and-preparation/
meat/jerky

Cured Meat and Poultry Product Operations
https://www.fsis.usda.gov/sites/default/files/media_file/2021-03/fplic-5a-cured-meat-and-poultry-operations.pdf

Shelf-Stable Food Safety
https://www.fsis.usda.gov/food-safety/safe-food-handling-and-preparation/food-safety-basics/shelf-stable-food

Food Standards and Labeling Policy Book
https://www.fsis.usda.gov/sites/default/files/import/Labeling-Policy-Book.pdf

FoodData Central
Search for Nutritional Information of Different Foods
https://fdc.nal.usda.gov/

Food Code 2017 (latest)
https://www.fda.gov/food/fda-food-code/food-code-2017

Small Meat Plant Regulations

People often show interest in going into commercial meat production and they are faced with many obstacles. Meat plants are under jurisdiction of the USDA Food Safety and Inspection Service and there are many regulations. The following links provide valuable contacts for those who want to pursue the matter.

FAO
http://www.fao.org/DOCREP/004/T0279E/T0279E02.htm

FSIS, Sanitation Performance Standards Compliance Guide
https://www.fsis.usda.gov/inspection/compliance-guidance/sanitation-performance-standards-compliance-guide

Small & Very Small Plant Guidance
https://www.fsis.usda.gov/inspection/compliance-guidance/small-very-small-plant-guidance

Iowa Department of Agriculture: Guidelines for the Construction and Operation of an Official Red Meat Plant Establishment
https://iowaagriculture.gov/meat-poultry-inspection-bureau/construction-operation-guidelines

Southern Nevada Health Ddistrict Regulations Governing The Sanitation of Food Establishment
http://www.southernnevadahealthdistrict.org/download/eh/food-regs.pdf

Guidelines For the Design, Installation and Construction of Food Establishments In North Carolina
https://www.mecknc.gov/HealthDepartment/EnvironmentalHealth/PlanReview/Documents/FoodEstablishmentGuidelines-2002.pdf

Note: Every state has its own standards and regulations which can be accessed on the Internet.

As of this writing (March 1, 2022) all links are working. Government agencies occasionally change links structure what leads to a broken link. The best remedy is to look for the link title in a search engine.

Index

More books by Stanley and Adam Marianski

More information can be found at www.bookmagic.com

Meat Smoking and Smokehouse Design 978-09824267-0-8

Polish Sausages, Authentic Recipes and Instructions 978-09824267-2-2

The Art of Making Fermented Sausages 978-09824267-1-5

Home Production of Quality Meats and Sausages 978-02824267-3-9

Making Healthy Sausages 978-09836973-0-5

Sauerkraut, Kimchi, Pickles and Relishes 978-09836973-2-9

The Amazing Mullet 978-09824267-8-4

Curing and Smoking Fish 978-09836973-9-8

Home Production of Vodkas, Infusions and Liqueurs 978-09836973-4-3

Home Canning Meat, Poultry, Fish and Vegetables 978-09836973-7-4

The Art of Making Vegetarian Sausages 978-0-9904586-3-0

The Greatest Sausage Recipes 978-09904586-5-4

Spanish Sausages, Authentic Recipes & Instructions 978-0-9904586-6-1

German Sausages, Authentic Recipes and Instructions 978-0-9904586-7-8

Make Sausages Great Again 978-09904586-8-5